Lord Denning

Life, Law and Legacy

Lord Denning

Life, Law and Legacy

James Wilson

Wildy, Simmonds & Hill Publishing

© James Wilson, 2023

Contains Parliamentary information licensed under the Open Government Licence v3.0

ISBN: 9780854902941

British Library Cataloguing in Publication Data

A catalogue record for this book is available from the British Library

The right of James Wilson to be identified as the author of this Work has been asserted by him in accordance with sections 77 and 78 of the Copyright, Designs and Patents Act 1988.

All rights reserved. No part of this book may be reproduced, stored in a retrieval system, or transmitted, in any form or by any means, electronic, mechanical, photocopying, recording or otherwise, without the consent of the copyright owners, application for which should be addressed to the publisher. Such a written permission must also be obtained before any part of this publication is stored in a retrieval system of any nature.

First published in 2023 by

Wildy, Simmonds & Hill Publishing
Wildy & Sons Ltd
Lincoln's Inn Archway
Carey Street
London WC2A 2JD
www.wildy.com

Typeset by Heather Jones, North Petherton, Somerset.
Printed in Great Britain by CPI Group (UK) Ltd, Croydon CR0 4YY.

For Aran and Sam
and
to Helen

Lawyers on Lord Denning

Lord Denning is the best-known and best-loved judge in the whole of our history.

Lord Bingham of Cornhill

It is given to few men to become a legend in their lifetime. There would be few in this country who would deny that Lord Denning is one of these few.

Lord Hailsham of St Marylebone

Denning was a great master of the common law. He was one of the greatest and most influential judges ever to sit on the English bench.

Lord Goff of Chieveley

The name Denning was a byword for the law itself. His judgments were models of simple English which ordinary people understood.

He had huge intellect and reforming imagination in equal measures, and in court, he never failed to be an object lesson in judicial courtesy.

Lord Irvine of Lairg

[T]he greatest judge of our time.

Lord Scarman

In summation, although others disagree, Lord Denning was both a great man and a great judge.

Professor Claire Palley

Lord Denning: Life, Law and Legacy

During his lifetime, Lord Denning has articulated, shaped, and defined our system of law to reflect not only our humanity, but our spirituality as well.

David Kilgour MP

I certainly regard him as the most outstanding legal figure of this century. He was not only pre-eminent as a judge but was also a great man.

Roger Gray QC

[I]t was a mark of Denning's greatness that he had the scholarship, the courage and the sense of opportunity to restore the credit of the common law when the chance came his way.

Lord Justice Sedley

Whatever their views of his decisions and his approach to the law, common lawyers everywhere would say that the world would have been a poorer place had Lord Denning not graced it.

Sir Zelman Cowen

Denning was without doubt the most successful reformer of all in several centuries.

Ian Holloway, Dean of Law, Calgary University

[H]e has provided me, as a teacher of law, and the many other teachers of law in this country, with a tremendous amount of extraordinarily stimulating law over the last few years. His influence in a profession which tends to be rather conservative has been wholly admirable ...

Lord Chorley

However arid the topic or hung-over the lecturer, however unsocial the teaching hour, one has only to mention the name [Denning] to sense the quickening of interest; and the biros drive across the pages, desperate to ensure that not a syllable of wisdom is lost. And the lecturer, whether he endorses or dares to disown the opinions of the Master he is quoting, rides on a cloud, and briefly joins the immortals.

Professor Len Sealey

Denning's most abiding and probably least deserved reputation was as a liberal.

Lord Justice Sedley

I've given up teaching the law of contract because every time it gets to the Court of Appeal Lord Denning changes it.

Professor Bill (later Lord) Wedderburn

In my view, he fell considerably short of the stature of a great judge (or jurist).

Reuben Hasson, Osgoode Hall Law School of York University

In the eyes of some of today's lawyers he is rather a discredited figure.

Lord Justice Brooke

Lord Denning on Lord Denning

Each generation has its duty to keep the law in conformity with the needs of the time. Indeed, its function, as I would see it, is first to see that justice is done according to the law. The law should be such that it meets with the approval of the right-thinking members of the community, and only second to that would I put certainty.

The moral of it all is that a true balance must be kept between personal freedom on the one hand and social security on the other.

In all my career I've tried to stand up for the freedom of the individual against the power of the executive.

The law of England knows no colour bar, whether it be the colour of a man's skin or of his politics.

The avoidance of tax may be lawful, but it is not yet a virtue.

Denning's law is, I hope, good law.

Without religion there can be no morality: and without morality there can be no law.

To say that judges are remote from ordinary life is a complete misconception ... Some judges are imagined to be the sort of people who say 'Who is Mick Jagger?' As if only judges know nothing of ordinary life. But that's completely wrong nowadays ... any of us, I think, have been brought up amongst ordinary people, live amongst ordinary people and are just as much ordinary people as anybody else.

Lord Denning: Life, Law and Legacy

Lord Denning is the greatest living Englishman.
Litigant before Lord Denning MR

Tell that to the House of Lords.
Lord Denning MR in reply[1]

I am a common man and I speak for the common people of England and from the letters I receive, the great majority agree with me.

I'm on the liberal, or the progressive side. I believe in equal opportunity for everybody, and as an old grammar-school boy, I believe in independent schools. I believe in an elite of excellence, certainly not in an elite of the upper class. I would be against that.

Foreword

Alfred Thompson Denning was a truly remarkable, indeed a unique, judicial figure. He managed to combine legal scholarship with judicial creativity and personal humanity, and an excellent prose style – clear, engaging and persuasive. But perhaps his most remarkable quality was his uncanny ability, both in his judgments and in his other works, to communicate not only with lawyers and law students, but also with the wider public. And his influence was reinforced by a remarkable 38 years as a senior judge – a judicial longevity which would be almost impossible to match today.

In this excellent book, James Wilson has managed to capture both the man and the judge, and it may seem otiose to discuss his career, but a brief summary may be appropriate.

After seeing active service on the Western Front in 1918, Denning gained a First-Class degree in mathematics from Oxford. He then studied for the Bar, and was called to the Bar in 1923 by Lincoln's Inn, with which he enjoyed a close connection throughout his career, being elected a Bencher in 1944, and Treasurer in 1964. For many years, he had a flat in the Inn, although his home was in his beloved Whitchurch in Hampshire where he had been born and brought up.

As a barrister, he quickly developed an impressive practice, but he also had the ability and commitment to write impressive academic legal articles (the first was published in the *Law Quarterly Review* as early as 1925) and to edit *Smith's Leading Cases* and *Bullen & Leake's Precedents*. He became King's Counsel in 1938. When the Second World War broke out the following year, he soon volunteered for active service but was rejected on grounds of age. In 1944, he was appointed a High Court Judge, and became Mr Justice Denning, at the young age of forty-five.

He was Mr Justice Denning for only four and a half years, but in that period, he gave a number of significant decisions. They included what is probably the most famous twentieth-century first instance judgment, in the 1947 *High Trees* case, where he resurrected and developed the doctrine of promissory estoppel, characteristically combining legal erudition with a strong sense of morality, in crisp and clear prose. It is the only first instance judgment in the *ICLR 150 Years Anniversary Edition*, which contains what were thought by a panel of eminent lawyers to be the most important fifteen cases decided between 1865 and 2014 – all the rest were Court of Appeal or House of Lords' decisions.

Promotion to the Court of Appeal in 1948 enabled him, as Lord Justice Denning, to develop the law in a number of areas, including estoppel and negligence. He was characteristically ahead of his time in a noted dissenting judgment on the law of negligent misstatement (approved twelve years later by the House of Lords).

In 1957, he became a Lord of Appeal in Ordinary, a Law Lord, and from then on was, as he has since always been known, Lord Denning. He was equivocal about being a Law Lord, and in 1962, he made what was then the unusual move from Law Lord to Master of the Rolls. It was an elective demotion, as the Master of the Rolls sits in the Court of Appeal, but he is the senior civil judge in that Court and can select which appeals he tries. Lord Denning was also attracted by the fact that he would be the biggest fish in a three-judge pond than one of five big fishes in a five-judge pond, as the Court of Appeal normally sits in threes, whereas the House of Lords normally sits in fives.

What also must have appealed to Lord Denning was the greater volume of work and the greater variety which the Court of Appeal offered, and, equally attractive I suspect, was the greater human interest. While only very important cases got to the House of Lords, by no means all very important cases went there for all sorts of reasons – for example, the losing party gives up or runs out of money, the case involves insufficient money for a further appeal to be worth it, the parties settle, leave to appeal is refused – so the Court of Appeal often lays down the law in very important cases. And, given the relatively large volume of appeals which got to the Court of Appeal compared with the House of Lords, and the fact that the Master of the Rolls could select which appeals he wished to hear (and the fact that he could choose which two members of the Court he sat with), the attraction of being 'MR' was obvious.

And then, even more than now, there was more human life in the caseload of the Court of Appeal than in the House of Lords. There were no human

Preface

Lord Denning was the most famous English judge of the twentieth century. Arguably, he was the most famous of *any* century. He was – and remains – the most cited judge in the history of the law reports for England and Wales.[1] Outside the legal world, he was the only British judge of his era who truly resonated with the public; the only one in the pre-digital era to have a substantial media profile beyond reporting of the odd *cause célèbre*. More than twenty years after his death in 1999, aged 100, he remains the judge who most enchants law students and whose judgments remain longest in the memory beyond exam revision.

There are a number of reasons for Denning's legal immortality. First, and perhaps foremost, there is his inimitable prose, unrivalled in brevity and clarity, but also unrivalled in colour. 'It happened on April 19, 1964. It was bluebell time in Kent' began a judgment dealing with the aftermath of an horrific fatal road accident.[2] 'Mr Thornton was a freelance trumpeter of the highest quality' was the opening line of a case about a car park's terms and conditions.[3] At times he displayed an almost Dickensian touch as the chronicler of the life of the common man. One judgment started with the following:[4]

> In 1966 there was a Scripture Rally in Trafalgar Square. A widower, Mr. Honick, went to it. He was about 63. A widow, Mrs. Rawnsley, also went. She was about 60. He went up to her and introduced himself. He was not much to look at. 'He looked like a tramp' she said. 'He had been picking up fag ends'. They got on well enough, however, to exchange addresses.

In a similar vein, he began the tale of a merchant of Eccles thus:[5]

> Old Peter Beswick was a coal merchant in Eccles, Lancashire. He had no business premises. All he had was a lorry, scales, and weights. He used to take the lorry to the yard of the National Coal Board, where he bagged coal and took it round to his customers in the neighbourhood. His nephew, John Joseph Beswick, helped him in his business. In March 1962, old Peter Beswick and his wife were both over 70. He had had his leg amputated and was not in good health. The nephew was anxious to get hold of the business before the old man died. So they went to a solicitor, Mr. Ashcroft, who drew up an agreement for them, without giving any hint as to the cause of action.

Another well-known opening recalled the England of John Constable, AE Housman and, from more recent times, Julian Fellowes and Richard Curtis:[6]

> Broadchalke is one of the most pleasing villages in England. Old Herbert Bundy, the defendant, was a farmer there. His home was at Yew Tree Farm. It went back for three hundred years. His family had been there for generations. It was his only asset. But he did a very foolish thing. He mortgaged it to the bank. Up to the very hilt.

As can be discerned from that paragraph, Denning could effortlessly segue from his colourful openings into the question of law, as with another classic:[7]

> Mr. Deeble has a milk round. He sells milk to people at the doors of their houses. He runs his business from a dairy building where he keeps his equipment, refrigerator, spare milk bottles, and so forth, and a stable where he keeps his horse and float. His round is seven streets adjoining the premises. He does not actually have a shop as ordinarily understood. His lease of these premises is coming to an end, and he wants to stay on there. This depends on whether the premises come within the definition of a shop in the Leasehold Property Act.

The second reason for Denning's enduring fame is the sense of justice that pervades so many of his judicial opinions, reflected in his repeated championing of the underdog, the individual against the corporation or the state. 'To some this may appear to be a small matter', he once declaimed:[8]

> but to Mr. Harry Hook, it is very important. He is a street trader in the Barnsley Market. He has been trading there for some six years without any complaint being made against him; but, nevertheless, he

has now been banned from trading in the market for life. All because of a trifling incident.

Thirdly, hand in glove with his demotic yet effortlessly fluent writing style, Denning was also renowned for his benign manner in court and consequent ability to steady even the most nervous litigant. Part of his personal charm was that he retained (some say exaggerated[9]) his Hampshire burr all his life, even in the cloistered environs of the Court of Appeal, where anything other than received pronunciation was rare at the Bar in his time and almost unknown on the Bench in the appeal courts (in both respects, not much has changed).

Fourthly, there is the sheer number of important cases on which Denning sat over an almost unprecedented four decades as a senior judge, the best-known part of which was the twenty-year period (1962–82) in which he served as Master of the Rolls, the head of the Court of Appeal, Civil Division.

Denning's unique judicial style and outlook led to him being called a 'spokesman for the common people', or the champion of the men and women riding the Clapham Omnibus. Repeatedly, and often controversially, he would find a way of circumventing – or, if his more blunt critics were to be believed, ignoring – what he regarded as desiccated precedent standing in the way of justice. More controversially, he would do so not just in order to help the powerless or the oppressed, but also from time to time in cases involving arm's-length transactions between commercial entities of equivalent resources and standing.

Yet, for all his disdain of authority, reforming zeal and crusading for social justice, Denning could also be an arch-conservative, faithful to institutions and authority even to the extent of ignoring indisputable miscarriages of justice. He was in favour of wartime detention without trial. He played a role in the establishment obstinance that led to the creation of the Criminal Cases Review Commission. He was often (though not always) an implacable opponent of trade unions. His official report into the Profumo Affair was denounced by some critics as a government whitewash. (More entertainingly, it was also known as the 'raciest blue book ever', albeit, as I have written elsewhere, not against much competition.)

Towards the end of his judicial career, Denning came to the attention of book publishers, who had finally woken up to the fact that his unique writing style coupled with his public profile would appeal to a wider audience than the readers of his law reports and occasional published speeches and articles. He went on to write several best-selling non-fiction books about law and his life and family. It was one such work which led to his resignation in excruciating circumstances in 1982. Denning's words were dated, to put it politely, even by the standards of the day, and even his staunchest supporters could not avoid the conclusion that his time had now passed.

Almost a decade after his resignation, an interview with *The Spectator* magazine showed that Denning had fallen still further behind the *zeitgeist*. The interview was so damaging that Denning later said he had effectively libelled himself. Once again, he was a victim of time and the associated failings of old age, but there were others who were not so forgiving.

Despite all those latter-day controversies, Denning's popularity among lawyers and law students remained during his lifetime – as it remains today – largely undiminished. He inspired the naming of a law journal, a society at Lincoln's Inn, and many a law school appreciation society. Upon his death in 1999, the tributes were extensive both in the popular press and in the legal world.

More recently, in 2009, a three-volume work was published by the academic Charles Stephens, examining in detail Denning's jurisprudence and its legacy. In 2015, the Australian judge Justice James Douglas chose Denning as the subject of his Selden Society Lecture. In 2017, a nostalgic piece on Denning by the well-known legal journalist Joshua Rozenberg garnered much online attention from a young audience. The retired judge Sir Henry Brooke wrote a popular personal blog until not long before his death in 2018; his pieces on Denning gained the most hits and comments. In the late 2010s, the website *Legal Cheek* sold T-shirts with 'Denning is My Homeboy' printed on them. In 2017, a final year Cambridge University undergraduate launched a new legal search engine called 'DenninX', especially tailored for law students, reasoning that, like Denning, the search engine would 'not follow orthodoxy and tradition'.[10]

It should be emphasised, though, that Denning's legacy as a judge is much more than amusing quotations, or his name being appropriated for interesting articles or projects. The remorseless flow of judgments, statutes and statutory regulation over the years has inevitably made his law – and any of his contemporaries, much less predecessors – substantially less influential than during his career. Some have argued that Denning's own idiosyncrasies have led to the virtual unravelling of his work. For example, in 2017 Joshua Rozenberg wrote:[11]

> But Denning's judgments are rarely cited in court these days. The problem is not the way he wrote them, delightful though it was. It's that he tended to bend the law to fit what he saw as the justice of the case. Although Denning saw himself as champion of the underdog –

the ordinary citizen, the consumer, the deserted wife – he supported employers against trade unions, education authorities against students, and the Home Office against immigrants.

Of course, all judges try to achieve what they see as a fair outcome. But they have to be rather more subtle about it. They can no longer get away, as Denning did, with reading through a few old cases and manufacturing a precedent.

Pace Mr Rozenberg, as Appendix I to this book shows, Denning continues to be cited and discussed with frequency in cases even in the present day. Nor do his cases appear solely in the form of quotations of his famous storytelling, or in cautionary tales of his occasional infamous mis-judgements. Instead, as will be seen, he continues to be cited in quotidian cases turning upon black letter law.

There is accordingly no doubt that, more than forty years after he retired, and more than twenty years after his death, the name and work of Lord Denning MR lives on.

Denning's enduring fame and influence has not precluded some modern commentators from taking strongly against him both as a judge and as a person. Lord Justice Sedley wrote dismissively that 'Denning's most abiding and probably least deserved reputation was as a liberal'.[12] The historian Richard Davenport-Hines railed against Denning's Profumo report, claiming that he 'inflicted lasting harm on his country'.[13] The legal blogger David Allen Green told his Twitter audience of more than 200,000 followers in 2020 that Denning was 'the most over-rated judge in UK legal history', an 'old charlatan' who abused legal language and structure to obscure what he was really up to, and asserted that Denning's judgments were '[s]uperficially twee but often gruesome or disingenuous underneath'.[14]

Nevertheless, whatever one thinks of Denning's legal legacy, it cannot be disputed that, from a self-taught maths genius making his own way to Oxford to the teenage soldier on the Western Front, to the successful barrister, then the reforming judge, Denning's was a life very well and very fully lived. Moreover, the history of Lord Denning is in many ways the history of England in the twentieth century, a time period his life (1899–1999) almost exactly spanned.

The first question for any biographer of Denning is whether, and if so how, to separate his life from his law. Denning's personal life is a subject entire of itself, while his legal contribution has been enough to fill not just the volumes mentioned earlier, but also two dedicated scholarly compilations examining his effect across different areas of law. There have also been countless individual academic papers and theses over decades considering Denning's cases from a multitude of perspectives.

The approach I have taken has been to try to weave his important judgments into his life story, rather than to split the book into two halves consisting of life and law respectively. My reasoning is that placing cases in the context of his life and times better explains the decisions he reached. Further, the book is not intended to be a dry appraisal of now ageing law reports, but rather of Denning himself, and unlike overturned judgments and outdated statutes, stories of human interest never date.

The question arose as to how to refer to him. His eventual full legal title was Alfred Thompson Denning, Baron Denning of Whitchurch in the County of Southampton, OM, PC, DL. Outside the courtroom, to friends and acquaintances alike, he was simply 'Tom', reflecting the fact that as a great achiever from an unpretentious background he did not feel the need to put on airs. Nonetheless, it seemed rather overfamiliar for someone I had never met to use 'Tom', while to call him 'Lord Denning', or 'Lord Denning MR' as he was best known, would not be accurate for his life prior to his ennoblement in 1957 or outside his tenure as MR from 1962 to 1982. For simplicity and consistency, I have opted to refer to him throughout as 'Denning', the name by which he remains instantly recognisable, intending no disrespect thereby.

One other point of style was whether to change retrospectively the terminology in Denning's cases to the modern terms introduced by the Civil Procedure Rules 1998. I have decided to leave it as it was in his time. The most common examples are that I have retained 'plaintiff' rather than the CPR Newspeak 'claimant', and 'writ' rather than the distinctly less foreboding 'claim form'.

With the advantage of distance, in considering both Denning's life and law, I have tried to approach all the controversies in context, and as fairly as possible without withholding judgement where deserved, be it positive or negative – precisely the approach Denning himself took (or purported to take) to every case which came before him. If I have managed to give a fair account of who he was, then, as Denning himself might have put it, I will be able to say 'I did my bit'.

James Wilson
Beckenham
October 2022

Note on Currency

Throughout the book I have made passing reference to how much Denning was earning or spending at different points in his life. Until 1971, Britain did not operate a decimal currency and the amounts quoted are what was applicable at the time.[1] As well as pounds, shillings and pence, Denning also received money in his early days in 'guineas'. Even at the time, the 'guinea' was technically anachronistic since, from 1816, it had been replaced by the pound as the major unit of currency and in coinage by the sovereign. Nevertheless, it remained in use as a unit of account worth 21 shillings (£1.05 in decimalised currency) for 'upper class' items such as professional fees, land, horses, art, bespoke tailoring and expensive furniture. It fell out of use not long after decimalisation.

For most of the figures quoted I have added the sum in August 2022 according to the Bank of England online inflation calculator,[2] but it still does not provide a complete picture of Denning's standard of living at any given point in time, for three reasons. First, for most of the twentieth century there was nothing approaching the cheap imports and variety of choice of consumer goods familiar to modern readers. It was quite the opposite, since Denning lived through two world wars, the Great Depression and post-war rationing when even basic household essentials could be in short supply. Thus, when Denning stated with some pride that in 1930 he was a 'leading barrister' 'earning over £1,000 per year', the inflation calculation of about £50,000 in 2022 money gives little indication as to his comparative purchasing power. A 'leading barrister' in London in 2022 with a commercial practice would be expected to earn considerably more than £50,000, and would also be subject to a very different tax regime (VAT, for example, did not exist in 1930).

A different perspective is that in 1930 the average wage was £1 11s (shillings) 8d (pence) for a week of just over fifty hours, or roughly a shilling an hour, which equated to approximately £60 a year (working fifty-two weeks at fifty hours a week). That would make £1,000 some seventeen times the average annual income. The annual average income in the United Kingdom in 2022 was £31,447, so a wage of £1,000 in 1930 would be equivalent by that measure to £534,599. In fact, Denning's actual income in 1930 was just over £1,400 for the year – about twenty-three times the average wage, suggesting an income equivalent in modern times to £723,281. That would be more in the region of what a successful commercial barrister of Denning's experience might have earned in 2022, not £50,000 as suggested too crudely by the inflation calculator. Even so, Denning was not in the top bracket of practitioners as he did not have much work in the Chancery Division, which was generally the most lucrative of the time.

Secondly, the inflation calculator takes no account of house inflation. Denning purchased a detached property near Cuckfield in Sussex in 1940 for 'between £3,000 and £4,000'. According to the inflation calculator, that would translate to between about £130,000 and £173,000 in 2022 currency – insufficient to purchase even a one bedroom apartment in Cuckfield in 2022, while properties of similar size and location to Denning's were listed on property websites for sums exceeding £2 million.[3] Denning later purchased a number of properties in Whitchurch, including his home of The Lawn; again, they would in comparative terms to his income be far more expensive nowadays if one takes only the figure from the Bank of England inflation calculator – the result of various factors including much more limited borrowing possibilities in Denning's time, higher interest rates, fewer two-income households and a substantially different monetary policy. One should also note, though, that there was a severe housing shortage after the Second World War, due to bomb damage, general wartime depredations, a shortage of materials and a desire to form new households in peacetime.

Thirdly, and lastly, there is the question of the nature of the outgoings Denning would have been required to meet. The expectation for most of his life was for those of his socio-economic status to have domestic staff. Standard labour-saving home white goods were fewer, scarcer, less efficient and comparatively more expensive in his youth, and the patriarchal structure of the day proscribed 'gentlemen' from attempting domestic tasks anyway. Denning therefore had staff assisting his household as soon as he could afford it.

Note on Currency

Ultimately, to gain a full picture of Denning's earnings and his wealth would require a detailed economic analysis,[4] beyond the present scope, but it is hoped that the above will set his figures more in context than simply offering numbers without explanation.

List of Plates

Denning as a child, aged about three or four
The Denning shop, taken before the First World War
Denning in officer's uniform, 1918
Denning in an Officers' Ride, Aldershot, 1918, before his deployment to France
Denning as a barrister in the 1930s
Denning's marriage to Mary Harvey, 28 December 1932
Denning and Robert on his appointment as a High Court Judge, March 1944
Denning's wedding to Joan Stuart, 27 December 1945
Denning just after his appointment to the Court of Appeal, 1948
Denning as Master of the Rolls, 1968
Christine Keeler at the height of her Profumo fame
Denning on his way to delivering his report into the Profumo Affair
The crush at Her Majesty's Stationery Office as people try to buy copies of Denning's Profumo report
Denning arriving at Winchester Cathedral for Law Sunday, c 1970
Denning in Kenya on one of his frequent overseas visits
Denning and Joan on a bridge over the River Test on their beloved property, The Lawn, in Whitchurch, 1982
Denning in the grounds of The Lawn in 1989
The 'Great Tom' bell in All Hallows Church, Whitchurch, cast to commemorate Denning's 100th birthday

Contents

Lawyers on Lord Denning — vii
Lord Denning on Lord Denning — xi
Foreword — xiii
Preface — xvii
Note on Currency — xxiii
List of Plates — xxvii

Chapter I: Beginnings – From Whitchurch to Oxford — 1
Chapter II: The First World War — 13
Chapter III: 1920s – From Oxford to the Bar — 27
Chapter IV: 1930s – From First Marriage to the Second World War — 43
Chapter V: The Second World War — 55
Chapter VI: Judicial Beginnings – Wills, Wives and Wrecks — 67
Chapter VII: 1945–47 – Second Marriage; Second Judicial Role — 75
Chapter VIII: The Court of Appeal — 89
Chapter IX: The House of Lords — 113
Chapter X: Master of the Rolls – Appointment and Beginnings — 129
Chapter XI: Profumo — 147
Chapter XII: Master of the Rolls – Travel and Other Engagements — 173
Chapter XIII: Master of the Rolls – Pre-trial Remedies — 179
Chapter XIV: Master of the Rolls – Common Law — 185
Chapter XV: Master of the Rolls – Family Law — 201
Chapter XVI: Master of the Rolls – Employment Law — 207
Chapter XVII: Master of the Rolls – Public Law — 221
Chapter XVIII: Master of the Rolls – Security of the Realm — 235
Chapter XIX: Master of the Rolls – A Belated Author — 243
Chapter XX: Master of the Rolls – Resignation — 251
Chapter XXI: Later Years — 265
Chapter XXII: The End — 285
Chapter XXIII: A Final Judgment — 289

Appendix I: Denning in the Law Reports	313
Appendix II: Societies and Other Organisations	317
Appendix III: Select Bibliography	319
Acknowledgements	333
Notes	335
List of Cases	387
Index	393

CHAPTER I

Beginnings – From Whitchurch to Oxford

Denning the Viking

The name 'Denning' derives from Scandinavian languages and means 'son of the Dane'. That was the opening gambit of Denning's memoir *The Family Story*. With characteristic self-confidence, he used the etymology to claim descent from the Viking hordes.[1] That in turn allowed him to note with evident satisfaction the influence of the Scandinavians upon British maritime and legal traditions, including the observation that the word 'law' itself was Danish in origin and had outlived the respective Saxon and Latin equivalents '*doom*' and '*lex*'.

As for post-Viking ancestors, *The Family Story* contained a few sketches based on family lore. They included a ruinous schism during the English Civil War between eminent family members, and a later financial crisis prompted by what he called a family equivalent of Dickens' *Jarndyce v Jarndyce* in the Chancery Division.

The earliest ancestor of whom Denning had concrete knowledge through documentation and less-removed hearsay was his great-grandfather, Thomas Denning. Thomas was born in 1798 in Somerset. He grew up in Dursley, Gloucestershire, and became an organist and teacher of music, both solid middle-class occupations of the day. His third child was Denning's grandfather, William Denning, who carried on the same occupations.

As an adult William went on to head what all accounts related as a 'jolly happy family' consisting of himself, his wife Anne and seven children including Denning's father Charles (born 1859).[2] All the family were 'well-read and well-spoken – with a Gloucestershire accent'.[3] Denning recalled with evident pride that Charles was (unsurprisingly) especially literate, versed in the classical English canon including Shakespeare, Byron, Scott and Bunyan. He was also a poet – 'not very good' in Denning's opinion, though one effort composed before he was married was noteworthy. It was called 'The Dead Soldier', which Denning felt most poignant in retrospect given that Charles was to lose a son in wartime over thirty years later.[4]

In 1888 Charles married Clara Thompson, a schoolteacher and the daughter of a Lincolnshire coal merchant and church warden; a 'very respected' man according to Denning. Charles was twenty-nine and Clara twenty-three. They had met at a party for mutual friends held at Whitchurch. Evidently Clara developed an attraction to the town as well as to Charles, for after they were married her father purchased two seventeenth-century houses there for the couple, opposite the White Hart Hotel in the centre of Whitchurch. They converted one of the houses to a drapery business and the other for their accommodation. (The buildings survive in part and one has been renamed 'Denning House', while the other has a plaque commemorating Denning's life there.)

It was thus in Whitchurch where the story of Lord Denning himself properly began, and ended – since he was born Alfred Thompson Denning there on 23 January 1899 and died there a century later, on 5 March 1999, as Baron Denning of Whitchurch.

Whitchurch

Whitchurch was, and remains, Hampshire's smallest 'town'. It is situated on the River Test and surrounded by rolling countryside. Six miles to the north-north east lies the area known as 'Watership Down', made famous by the book of the same name by the Whitchurch resident and contemporary of Denning, Richard Adams. An earlier author who also wrote a paean to the area's natural beauty was William Cobbett, whose 1830 book *Rural Rides* was among Denning's favourite works. In 1888, around the time Charles and Clara moved there, the *Star* newspaper said of Whitchurch: 'People who live in it call it a town. People who live out of it call it a village. It is about as big as a good-sized pocket handkerchief'.[5]

Both Iron Age and Roman remains have been found around the town, though the earliest definite settlement dates from near the end of Roman Britain. The name 'Whitchurch' is usually presumed to derive from the Saxon for 'White Church', in reference to the church which has formed the centrepiece of the town for many centuries. The earliest record of a Christian church there dates from the ninth century, and one has existed on the same site ever since, the present manifestation being called All Hallows Church. The 'white' is usually assumed to refer to the original use of chalk (mined from the surrounding uplands) in the building's construction, or possibly the white-washing of its exterior. Denning, a devout Christian, became greatly attached to All Hallows: he attended services there for many years, first as a small child and later as the Master of the Rolls; his later house 'The Lawn' was situated directly opposite; he was involved in commissioning a commemorative bell for the men of the village who had died while serving during the First World War, and for years read out their names on Remembrance Sunday there; and near the end of his life a second bell named 'Great Tom' was made for the church to honour his 100th birthday.

The presence of the river enabled the construction of five water-powered mills over the centuries, used for grain, wool and paper production. From 1724 one of the mills supplied paper to the Bank of England for use as bank notes; the building survived until being destroyed by fire in 2018. (Cobbett, incidentally, a socialist who thought paper money would bring about the end of Western civilisation, did not care for any of the mills let alone the paper one, and ranted about how they spoilt the River Test. Denning dismissed his concerns as 'misplaced'.) In 1815 a silk mill was opened, which at the time of writing was Britain's only working silk mill, still operating from its original building. The website *Hampshire Life*[6] enjoyed making a connection between the mill and Denning's residence, since the gowns worn by QCs were made from its product. Denning also took pride in the connection in his book *The Closing Chapter*[7] and elsewhere,[8] and recalled how he had opened the mill following its restoration in 1982.

Rather less idyllic in the town's history was the fact that it was a rotten borough until the 1832 Reform Act. 'Rotten boroughs' were constituencies rigged to ensure one person's election, by drawing boundaries so as to include very few residents, whose co-operation could be secured by way of a bribe or threat because there was no secret ballot in those days.

That political blight aside, the continuity of the church and settlement from before time immemorial strongly appealed to Denning and formed one of the foundations of his own love of England and English history. His descriptions of his childhood there were not dissimilar to those of Flora Thompson's *Lark Rise* series of books recalling her upbringing a generation earlier in rural Oxfordshire. Both set out a way of life largely unchanged for centuries until the coming of the railway and then internal combustion. Both concerned mostly self-contained communities with focal points at the pub and the church and nearly all resident families engaged in a trade or working the land. Each knew their place, which dictated their occupations, broadly divided into labourers, tradesmen, middle class and the lord of the manor.[9] Even within those strata there were sub-classes, formally recognised or otherwise, as memorably described more than a century before Denning's time by an even more famous Hampshire resident, Jane Austen. Among the more prosperous in Whitchurch in Denning's youth were the owners of the paper mill and the local solicitor, the latter being sufficiently well-heeled that he owned more than one top hat.[10]

Until he ran into trouble in the First World War, Charles managed the business well enough to provide for his family, though Denning never thought it suited him,[11] perhaps unsurprisingly if Charles was inclined to be a man of letters rather than a man of affairs and trade. Charles's fundamental problem seems to have been a too-kind nature, since he never pressed indigent customers for payment while others paid in miniscule instalments. None of the nearby-printed notes ever passed through his till; instead it was exclusively coins – copper, silver or, on a good day, gold.[12] Denning doubted whether Charles ever visited London in his life, and only remembered him leaving the greater Whitchurch area to do jury service, much to his own cost as he had to fund the travel and leave the drapery for a week. (Denning himself did not go to London until he was sent there by the army aged eighteen.) Charles's tribulations included having his pony and cart overturned by runaway horses on one occasion,[13] though he fortunately escaped injury.

Clara assisted by doing the books for the business. Otherwise, her opportunities were limited by the general restrictions inflicted upon women of the day, so she poured her energy into ensuring her children had the best education and opportunities possible. There is no reason to doubt Denning's assessment of her as 'Very intelligent. Very hard-working. Determined to succeed in whatever she undertook. She was the driving force. Ambitious for her children'.[14]

The first of those children was Marjorie, born in 1891. She was followed by John (Jack) in 1892, Reginald (Reg) in 1894, Charles Gordon (Gordon) in 1897, Alfred Thompson (Tom) himself in 1899, and Norman (Norman or Ned) in 1904.

'Alfred' was chosen for Denning's first name as 1899 marked a thousand years since the death of Alfred the Great, King of Wessex and King of the Anglo Saxons,[15] while 'Thompson' as we saw was Clara's maiden name. He was always known to friends and family as Tom. He was baptised on 23 April.

It is worth pausing to note that Britain at the time of Denning's birth was an almost unimaginably different world to the post-war era in which he served as a judge, let alone the present day. Victoria was still on the throne.

Robert Gascoyne-Cecil, the 3rd Marquess of Salisbury, was Prime Minister. The wholly unelected House of Lords had the power to block the House of Commons. Only propertied men – and no women – had the right to vote. Overseas, the British Empire was at its apogee, with the Royal Navy the undisputed leading naval power and the British Army in continual action around the globe as a sort of colonial police force. The Mahdist War was still under way in Africa, but the Second Boer War was yet to begin. In technology, horses and steam railway were the usual form of transport, with petrol cars a novelty: on 25 February 1899 Edwin Sewell became the first driver of a petrol car to die in an accident, when he crashed in Harrow, London. Meanwhile, the Wright brothers in America were still experimenting with gliders. Telegrams were the most advanced form of communication. In March 1899, the world's first wireless distress signal was sent and Guglielmo Marconi successfully transmitted a radio signal across the English Channel for the first time. WG Grace, supposedly the most recognisable Victorian behind the monarch herself and Sir William Gladstone, was still captain of the England cricket team. The playwright Oscar Wilde was living out his last days in exile in France. More in the cultural ascendancy were the actors Ellen Terry and Herbert Beerbohm Tree, and authors including HG Wells, Rudyard Kipling and Bram Stoker. Notable births of 1899 include the famous actor, dancer and choreographer Fred Astaire in May and the acting, writing and composing legend Noël Coward in December. Significant works of literature published that year included Joseph Conrad's *Heart of Darkness* and Rhoda Broughton's *The Game and the Candle*.

An Edwardian home

All those affairs of life and state were far in the distance for the Denning family in Whitchurch. Instead, their energies were directed to the domestic tasks of earning money and educating their children as best they could in fairly basic circumstances. Denning described their house as 'totally unfit for human habitation'[16] by modern standards, with an outdoor toilet consisting of a deep pit covered by a seat, whose contents would be collected every three or four weeks by the night-cart – 'the presence of which was easily detected by anyone unfortunate to be in the vicinity' according to one of his contemporaries.[17] There was no running water, only a well just outside the property. There was no electric light and no gas save for a few flickering gas mantles in two of the downstairs rooms with a paraffin oil lamp as a stand-by. There was no daylight in the kitchen. There was no living room as such, only a makeshift affair in a long room with no windows, the only light coming from a skylight and a glass door. All in all, it was a rustic existence with many shortcomings even by the standards of the day, at least for the middle class as the Dennings would have considered themselves (bearing in mind that they were better off than families consigned to single rooms in the worst urban slums of the day, or those living essentially hand-to-mouth in agrarian communities).

Despite those apparent privations, Denning appreciated that his family was extremely fortunate in that all the children survived childhood, by no means the norm in late Victorian or early Edwardian times, even for the wealthiest or otherwise most advantaged families. Necessarily, survival entailed Clara suffering no difficulty during childbirth. At the time, any tear or cut suffered during childbirth was likely to result in septicaemia. Puerperal fever (also called childbed fever, or postpartum sepsis), a streptococcal infection introduced into the vagina by a mother's birth attendants, was also rife, while haemorrhages and eclampsia were often fatal. Clara, being in a rural location, was assisted by a neighbour, who would not have had the same risk of transferring puerperal fever because, unlike professional midwives or doctors, she would not have been regularly present at births in unsanitary houses.[18]

Much later in life, Denning retained the view that the process of birth was inherently dangerous and was extremely reluctant to assume it might be the fault of attending doctors if anything went wrong. He began his judgment in *Whitehouse v Jordan* [1980] 1 All ER 650 with the statement 'Being born is dangerous for the baby. So much so that an eminent professor in this case tells us that: "Throughout history, birth has been the most dangerous event in the life of an individual and medical science has not yet succeeded in eliminating that danger"'. He also parodied the psalmist by referring to 'the valley of the shadow of birth'.[19]

Following his own successful birth, though he does not seem to have realised it, the absence of many of the late Victorian and Edwardian innovations probably saved his life and those of his siblings on multiple occasions, just as the absence of a professional midwife at his birth had unknowingly removed one common source of deadly infection. Chief among the hidden dangers largely unknown, improperly understood and inadequately regulated at the time was adulterated food – the likes of alum in bread, strychnine, cocculus and copperas in rum and beer, sulphate of copper in preserves, and sulphate of iron and lead in beverages. In 1877 the Local Government Board found that approximately a quarter of the milk it examined contained excessive water, or chalk, and ten per cent of all the butter, over eight per cent of the bread, and fifty per cent of the gin had had copper added to enhance the colour.[20]

A second danger of the time was, ironically, the plethora of new cleaning products rushed onto the market in response to the new scientific understanding of germs. The problem was that such products were occasionally and fatally consumed, either by accident or by being added in what was wrongly thought harmless quantities to food and drink. An example of the former was carbolic acid, often stored in identical form to baking soda. As to the latter, tests on 20,000 milk samples in 1882 showed that a fifth had been adulterated by improper substances, largely by householders themselves rather than unscrupulous suppliers.[21] Boracic acid was thought to 'purify' milk, since it removed the sour taste and smell from milk that had gone off. Mrs Beeton advised the public that it was 'quite a harmless addition', when it was actually potentially lethal on two counts. First, boracic acid itself in the right (or, rather, wrong) quantity and concentration caused nausea, vomiting, abdominal pain and diarrhoea. Secondly, sour milk was likely to contain potentially fatal amounts of bovine tuberculosis.[22]

Largely atomised, rural communities such as Whitchurch would have been less exposed to risks from dangerous food additives since the supply chain would have been more local. Tragically for the Dennings, however, despite avoiding tuberculosis at home, they were later to lose adult family members to the disease.

The absence of electricity in the Denning household avoided another common hazard, since at the time there was a very limited understanding of insulation and earthing, and early electrical devices sometimes introduced other dangers.[23] The Dennings' minimal use of gas for lighting was yet another unintended safety measure, since the most common fuel for gaslights was coal gas, which was composed of hydrogen, sulphur, methane, and carbon monoxide – a dangerous concoction risking suffocation, carbon monoxide poisoning and fire.

The basic condition of the Denning house and their straitened financial circumstances would have meant little or no lead paint, another potentially harmful substance, especially to children who might have chewed furniture or toys covered with it. The Dennings would also have owned few (if any) of the common consumer items made of parkesine (better known as celluloid), a highly flammable material and thus wholly unsuited to most of the domestic uses to which it was put at the turn of the twentieth century. Further, their modest disposable income meant they would not have frittered away money on quack remedies, of which the Carbolic Smoke Ball might be the best remembered legally,[24] but was just one example of many in Victorian and Edwardian times. Thomas Holloway, for example, became a self-made millionaire selling largely ineffectual ointment and pills that were marketed as a 'universal cure'.[25]

Lastly – and probably of equal significance – the Denning family enjoyed the general benefits of living in the countryside that still apply today: better water and air quality, more outdoor activities and reduced exposure to communicable diseases.

Despite all those unintended advantages of rural poverty, survival was still a close-run thing in Denning's own case, since he was born two months premature and nearly died: a friend of Clara wrapped him in a blanket as a baby and gave him some brandy, and he slowly recovered. Clara evidently continued with the view that Denning was inherently physically infirm, as for a number of years she made him drink cod liver oil in a cup of milk before going to school. Brandy to modern readers would be a bizarre ingredient for children but at least in small doses it was nothing like as dangerous as boracic acid or any of the chemicals frequently endangering Victorian foodstuffs. Cod liver oil in milk would probably taste disgusting, but at least would not be poisonous.

As well as the inadvertent risk reduction, the lack of consumer comforts did not make for an unhappy childhood in Denning's recollection. Quite the contrary: he credited the stability and encouragement of his home life as the most important factor in his later success, as did his biographer Iris Freeman, who recorded: 'Throughout his life the simple principles learned by Tom Denning in his parents' home, in church and at school were to remain his guiding light; he would apply them, with little modification, to the problems of a changing world'.[26] When interviewed in his early eighties,[27] Denning affirmed those sentiments, emphasising the security of his home life and the certainty of the values he and his siblings were taught. Elsewhere he summed up his parents' respective characters as: 'Father kind and thoughtful, beloved by all. Mother strong and determined, standing no nonsense'.[28]

The values imparted by his family, school and village were those of a robustly traditional middle-class of the day: Anglican Christianity, patriotism, chivalry of men towards women (who, in return, owed duties to men), a taciturn sense of duty and a disdain of materialism or exhibitionism. In terms of patriotism, Cecil Rhodes famously said that to be born English was to win the greatest prize in the lottery of life, sentiments Denning controversially echoed much later in life. It was, incidentally, common at the time for 'English' and 'British' to be used interchangeably, as Denning himself would occasionally do – the distinction was thought more important after the rise of Scottish nationalism in the 1930s.

There is little evidence that the suffragette movement permeated the Denning household, though Whitchurch did not wholly escape the social movements of the time: the Salvation Army Band caused a riot when they played in the town square in Denning's childhood, principally because the local brewer (whose wife had been the one to assist Clara at Denning's birth), uncharitably described by Denning as a 'big, fat man', took exception to the temperance movement.[29]

The Denning children would not have been expected to pursue tertiary education (irrespective of their academic ability). Instead, the sons were supposed to follow their father into a trade and spend a life in honest and worthy toil, while their daughter might have been permitted to work in a suitable occupation before marrying someone of equivalent social status. To begin with all except Denning himself did just that: Marjorie worked at a local shop in Winchester and then Oxford before her marriage to a career soldier, John E Haynes, known as 'Johnny'. Jack found an apprenticeship as a draper in Southsea. Gordon joined the merchant navy. Reg worked at Gorringes, an upmarket department store in central London near Buckingham Palace. Norman, after the First World War, joined the Royal Navy. It was Jack who first broke the mould by becoming an officer in the armed forces, as did all the brothers after him.[30]

Education

One key component of Denning's later success was his education, though he always maintained it ran a poor second to his family life as a contributing factor. He was fortunate to have been born not long after significant educational reforms. Those began with the Elementary Education Act 1870, also known as Forster's Education Act, which set out a framework of education for children aged between five and thirteen,[31] although it was not until the twentieth century that free and compulsory education was provided for all.[32]

Marjorie, Jack, Reg, Gordon and Tom all initially attended the Whitchurch Grammar School, known as 'the Modern School', run by family friends. It charged only modest fees, but after Clara fell pregnant with Norman she and Charles reluctantly concluded they would not be able to sustain the expenditure. Their solution was for Gordon and Tom to move to the free equivalent, known as the 'National School', the name being a shortening of 'National Society for the Education of the Poor according to the Principles of the Church of England'. Denning's time there was a conventional school experience – he studied hard but also joined the games and japes of the schoolyard. Among other things, he played croquet, cricket and football, and learned music, the latter with more enthusiasm than talent by his own admission. As was standard at the time for those who were able, he learned to ride horses, writing fondly in his later letters of one called Molly.[33] It has been said of his time there that 'it may be that he felt that he was a cut socially above the other pupils and it may be that this accounts for the occasional glimpses of snobbery that one encounters in his later life and judicial career'.[34] No evidence survives to suggest such an inference, however, and given that he was the son of a struggling draper, it is difficult to imagine why Denning would have considered himself the social better of most of his peers.[35] In contrast, by attending Oxford, becoming an officer in the British Army, teaching at a leading public school and then becoming a barrister, Denning had many other opportunities in his life to imbibe some of the classic forms of English snobbery.

If anything, it was Denning's academic ability that made him stand out at school, as he managed to win a free place (scholarship) at Andover Grammar School.[36] Gordon did so as well, and both brothers began there in 1909. Attending involved a train journey and a substantial walk every day for children of their age, particularly for Denning as the younger child. The cost of the fares for the two boys stretched the family's finances tautly, even in the absence of school fees. Denning had no doubt, however, that it returned value for money: 'An Elizabethan grammar school. What could you have better?' he once remarked,[37] and he was strongly opposed to the government policy of closure of many of the grammar schools in the 1970s.

The syllabus of Denning's time included the classical English literature of Chaucer, Milton, Shakespeare, Byron and all the other familiar names which Charles Denning had learned with enthusiasm a generation earlier. Studies of them would have inculcated the standards and ethics of the time – robustly traditional Christian-based principles allied to unabashed British Empire patriotism and, it should not be downplayed, racial superiority – and Denning absorbed all of them. He would later make occasional literary references in his judgments and books, though he did not use many authors in doing so.[38] When added to the morals instilled in him at home and in his village, as described above, they constituted the basis of the values which informed what Denning decided was 'justice' in each case that would come before him throughout his forty-year judicial career.

Denning was aged fifteen and still attending Andover Grammar when, in August 1914, Britain entered the First World War. As he was too young to serve, he continued his studies as best he could, concentrating on his favourite subject of mathematics, for which he hoped to win a university scholarship. He faced the problem that many of the regular teachers left *en masse* for war service and their replacements did not have the same grasp of the subject matter. Denning therefore effectively had to teach himself. His natural ability and solid work ethic prevailed nonetheless, and he excelled at both English and mathematics. On the advice of the headmaster, he remained at school past the compulsory leaving age and strove to gain admission to Oxford or Cambridge. At just sixteen years old, he was offered a scholarship to study at Magdalen College, Oxford.

Oxford

Denning accepted the place – one can imagine the pride it would have given his family, his teachers and himself to have been accepted into the most elite of British educational institutions – but he faced an obstacle in that the scholarship he had been awarded (called an 'exhibition') was only £40 per year (about £2,681 in 2022 terms), on which he would struggle to get by.[39] Unlike many of his would-be Oxbridge peers his family was not in a position to help financially, even though the older children leaving home had lessened Charles and Clara's monetary commitments. Fortunately, not long after his arrival at Magdalen in October 1916, the President of the College, Sir Herbert Warren,[40] was clearly impressed by him and intervened on his behalf. First, Sir Herbert arranged for the exhibition to be increased to a 'demyship' of £80 per annum, and secondly, he managed to secure Denning an extra £30 from the Goldsmith's Company, making his total income £110 per year (£7,375.16 in 2022 terms). Denning recorded that Sir Herbert had a reputation as a snob, but denounced the epithet, pointing out how much Sir Herbert had helped him, someone from a comparatively disadvantaged background.

The money left Denning with little to spare, but he flourished academically, assisted by having proper tutors rather than the underqualified replacement teachers at Andover. In June 1917, he was awarded a First in Mathematical Moderations – at the age of just eighteen – but claimed with characteristic modesty that it was undeserved, thinking the examiner had to have made allowance.[41]

Although Denning did not struggle academically at Oxford, he initially felt something of an outsider, not having attended a public school or being from any sort of aristocratic background, at a time when class distinctions were much more rigid than in the present. Yet he soon overcame his fears and felt that all were welcoming.[42] He did not participate in debates, or regularly dine in hall, though he did enjoy some sporting activities. He neither smoked nor drank, partly because he could not afford to, though he never bothered with either later in life when he did have the means. One apparent luxury was having a 'scout' (manservant) assisting, but since the only duty Denning recorded the scout undertaking was bringing water to his room for a cold bath, there being no running water, 'luxury' would probably be an overstatement.

Due to the war, there were much reduced numbers at Oxford, with students of the usual age almost all away at the Front, leaving only the very young such as Denning, those considered infirm for military service, and a few Rhodes Scholars from the then-neutral United States. Regardless of external circumstances, Denning's academic achievements spurred him on. 'I am very ambitious, and I want to rise to the top and make a name' he wrote to Reg in November 1916.[43]

Perhaps reflecting to some extent being a stranger in a strange land (from a class perspective), but more his natural shyness and reticence, Denning had few if any dealings with women at Oxford. Although not permitted to matriculate at the time, women had been attending lectures and examinations there since the late 1870s, so it was not as though there were no women whom he might have met – indeed, of the seven others who sat the exams with him in June 1917, two were women, even if one should not underestimate the sexism within Oxbridge at the time. Yet, Denning seems to have been more or less completely unworldly in affairs of the heart in those days. Gordon wrote teasingly in December 1916 that he heard that Denning was 'transfixing all the girls in his OTC uniform', but the only woman in whom Denning showed a clear interest was a Whitchurch inhabitant and the future Mrs Denning, Mary Harvey. And it was not until he had fought in the war and built a successful career that he eventually had the courage to propose to her.

Throughout his time at Oxford, he practised military drilling. It was no mere square bashing: the army was clearly preparing them for battle. In November 1916, for example, as he recorded in a letter to Reg, his group went on a route march of twelve miles with rifles, followed the next day by bayonet training. In August 1917, upon reaching the age of eighteen-and-a-half, he duly received his call up papers. It was thus his fate to follow his elder brothers in serving his country in the bloodiest war in its history.

CHAPTER II

The First World War

It is to these men that we owe our freedom.

Lord Denning

The road to hell

On 28 June 1914, Archduke Franz Ferdinand of Austria and his wife Sophie, Duchess of Hohenberg, were assassinated in Sarajevo by Gavrilo Princip. The killings set in train events which would culminate in the largest conflict in European history to that point.

In the immediate aftermath of the Archduke's death, few in Britain had any idea of the significance of what had taken place. The *Manchester Guardian* on 30 June 1914, for example, began its analysis of the murder by stating 'It is not to be supposed that the death of the Archduke ... will have any immediate or salient effect on the politics of Europe'. Instead, life proceeded mostly as normal – certainly for the denizens of small towns such as Whitchurch – while the national press continued to focus upon more local concerns of the suffragettes, Irish nationalism and increasingly militant industrial disputes.[1]

By the end of July 1914, however, as Germany moved to threaten neutral Belgium, the likelihood of Britain joining the war rose substantially, due both to popular sentiment supporting the Belgians (by then the press had picked up the issue) and to the fear among British military and political leaders of the Germans obtaining control of the channel ports. On the eve of Britain's declaration of war, the country's best-known serving soldier, Lord Kitchener, was summoned to advise the cabinet. He told them bluntly that any conflict with Germany would last years, require the raising of a gigantic land army, incur casualties in the millions and cost billions of pounds.

Notwithstanding Kitchener's extremely prescient advice, the cabinet chose to join the conflict on 4 August 1914. Denning recalled the rapidly swelling national fervour:[2]

> On the outbreak of war all the young men flocked to the colours. None stopped to inquire the need for it. Everyone accepted that we were right to go to war. We were to defend Belgium – whose neutrality we had guaranteed. We had given our promise – on 'a scrap of paper' – and must honour it. The Germans made scorn of it. Their despatch to our Foreign Office said:
>
>> Just for a word – 'neutrality', a word which in wartime has so often been disregarded, just for a scrap of paper – Great Britain is going to make war.
>
> There was no conscription at the beginning. Volunteers came forward in thousands.

The 'scrap of paper' – the Treaty of London of 1839 guaranteeing Belgian neutrality – was not quite the full story of why Britain joined the conflict,[3] but Denning was correct that it was the official reason. He was also correct that there was no need for conscription at the outset given the number of volunteers, who in 1914 included his brothers Jack and Reg. Denning himself was too young at that stage.

It is worth pausing to reflect upon the support of the Denning family for the war. Modern readers might find their motivation and that of hundreds of thousands like them surprising, but one can proffer several reasons why. First, in a more homogenous, monocultural society, with much pressure to conform, the population was more likely to respond to a national crisis and call to arms in a unified fashion, though it would be wrong to suggest there was anything like complete unity in the population's response to the Great War.[4]

Secondly, modern media has left potential soldiers in no doubt about what they might expect to see during wartime, whereas there was a degree of ignorance in 1914. That factor might have applied to Jack and Reg, who enlisted as soon as war broke out, though not in Denning's own case, since by the time he was old enough to enlist he could not have been unaware of the perils.

Thirdly, the majority of the population in Britain in the twenty-first century are substantially better off materially than in 1914, when the promise of a regular square meal was a good inducement to patriotism for many living in the squalid industrial towns and cities of the day. That, however, did not apply to the large numbers of ex-public schoolboys who formed so many of the junior officers, the most dangerous occupation at the Front. Instead, their enthusiasm derived from the fact that they had been inculcated almost from birth with a sense of duty and responsibility to lead.[5] Neither factor applied in the case of the Denning family since, although not from a wealthy background, they did not live in abject poverty, nor had they attended a public school. Denning himself was at Oxford from 1916, where the same values would have held sway,[6] Jack and Reg were not at Oxford, yet were just as keen to enlist, as was Gordon when he was old enough.

Fourthly, patriotism and endorsement of the British Empire were concepts that were embraced, rather than disdained, 120 years ago. Denning's generation was brought up to be chivalrous to ladies, honour God and the King, salute the flag, revere the British Empire, and uphold the rule of law. Schoolboys were taught to keep a stiff upper lip, play the man, and observe the tradition of service. Those values were encapsulated in popular verses of the time such as Rudyard Kipling's *If* or Henry Newbolt's *Vitaï Lampada* ('play up, play up, and play the game'), along with long-discredited colonial notions represented by Kipling's phrase 'take up the white man's burden'.

Lastly, and perhaps most importantly, in 1914 the rights of individuals were accompanied by a very different concept of the rights and duties of nations. In particular, the notion of a country acting with 'honour' by not shirking from what was considered a just war was highly valued and formed 'a fundamental political and international currency in diplomatic affairs'.[7] Hence the Belgian nation stood firm against Germany, adhering to the Treaty of London, even though to do so was virtually an act of national suicide given the disparity in the two countries' respective military capabilities. Meanwhile, the British Foreign Secretary, Sir Edward Grey, told the House of Commons that he:[8]

> would like the House to approach this crisis in which we are now, from the point of view of British interests, British honour, and British obligations ... if, in a crisis like this, we run away from those obligations of honour and interest as regards the Belgian Treaty, I doubt whether, whatever material force we might have at the end, it would be of very much value in face of the respect that we should have lost.

'National honour' was also one of the reasons that all participating nations were prepared to accept the appalling casualties at the beginning of the war.

Arguably, it contributed to the seemingly reckless Allied strategy on the Western Front, in that the generals felt they had licence to mount attacks even if they knew in advance that they would be very costly, since the cause was just (albeit had they the means or imagination to pursue a more economical strategy they would have done). The historian Sir Michael Howard wrote that:

> the casualty lists that a later generation was to find so horrifying were considered by contemporaries not [as] an indication of military incompetence, but a measure of national resolve, of fitness to rank as a Great Power.[9]

One illustration was the effect of the 'Amiens Dispatch' of 1914, in which *The Times* wrote of a 'terrible defeat' conceded by the British on the retreat from Mons – contrary to the usual official line that all was proceeding to plan – and followed with three casualty lists in the following week, which totalled just over 15,000 killed, missing and wounded. Remarkably, through present eyes, recruitment numbers increased exponentially thereafter.

Denning himself signed off his letters[10] to his brothers during the conflict with Horace's phrase '*Dulce et decorum est pro patria mori*' ('it is sweet and fitting to die for one's country'), a sentiment which afterwards became almost exclusively associated with the anti-war poem by Wilfred Owen, who called it 'the old lie'. For Denning it was quite the contrary – a noble sentiment expressing the just cause in which his country was engaged.

The Dennings go to war

Johnny Haynes

Norman was too young to serve, but the four older Denning brothers each saw active service in the First World War. The family's eagerness to serve extended to Marjorie's future husband Johnny, who joined the nascent Royal Naval Air Service and fought in Belgium in the early days of the war. He returned to England and served in mechanical transport, with the vital role of sending supplies to the troops. According to Denning, Johnny's record during the conflict was 'in keeping with the rest of us'.[11] Johnny and Marjorie were married in September 1916. The timing meant what would normally have been an occasion for undiluted joy for both families took place instead in bleak wartime years. In 1917, Marjorie and Johnny, and their first child, Betty (born in September of that year), stayed for a time in Whitchurch with Charles and Clara.

After the war, Johnny remained in the forces and served in India for a number of years, including on the North West Frontier. He and Marjorie finally returned to Whitchurch after the Second World War, where Marjorie cared for the elderly Clara and Johnny served as a churchwarden at All Hallows. In that capacity he prepared the Roll of Honour of the fallen of Whitchurch and supervised the Remembrance Sunday commemoration.

Jack

Jack Denning had been a member of the territorials (a predecessor of today's Army Reserve) for almost a year by the time war broke out, and had trained as a gunner. He joined the 3rd Battalion, Lincolnshire Regiment (there being a family connection with the county, although it was not a 'pals' battalion' as such), a training unit, before being transferred to the 1st Lincolns and deployed to France. In *The Family Story*, Denning quoted a letter from Jack to his old schoolmaster in Whitchurch after gaining his commission, in which Jack said how easy the examinations were and that among the few who failed were some private school educated individuals. 'Of course they were absolute duffers'[12] Jack added, perhaps indicating satisfaction at his superior ability making nonsense of the class distinctions of the day. Evidently, Jack shared the sentiments of Burns' *A Man's A Man For A' That*:

> For a' that, an' a' that,
> His ribband, star, an' a' that:
> The man o' independent mind
> He looks an' laughs at a' that

In order not to prejudice his chances, Jack had written 'gentleman' as his father's occupation – or rather, as was stated on the form, his 'Position in Life' – on his application.

In spring and early summer 1916, the British Army prepared for what would become the largest battle in its history, near the Somme River in Northern France. Jack's unit was present near the Front whilst the artillery units undertook a vast preliminary bombardment. He was wounded by shrapnel from enemy counter-battery fire on 26 June. He refused to be returned to base or to England, and insisted on rejoining his unit at the Front. He was therefore in the line for the infamous 'first day' of 1 July, in which 57,470 British casualties were incurred, including 19,240 fatalities. Over the next few weeks he was rotated in and out of the line, as was standard practice in the British Army at the time.[13] On 24 September, while based at Fricourt, he wrote a letter home which was very typical of those on the

Western Front – telling his parents it might or might not be his last letter, but adding that 'you may rest assured that should I get pipped I shall have done my duty, and always remember it is far better to die with honour than to live in shame ... The main object is that to please me, do not worry if I do get pipped'.[14]

The next day, the 1st Lincolns went into action near Gueudecourt. The regimental history recorded:[15]

> The battalion moved from Fricourt Camp at 11am on the 24th to Pommiers Redoubt, arriving at 1pm. A hot meal was served and at 5pm the battalion moved again, and an hour later arrived at Switch Trench, where 64th Brigade Headquarters were established. Here, after rest, hot tea and rum were served just before 10pm, when the march to the assembly trenches began.
>
> By 11.30pm the battalion was disposed in the following positions: A and C Companies in Gap Trench (support); B and D Companies, the Battalion Bombers and Battalion Headquarters in Switch Trench (second support).
>
> Throughout the night the artillery bombardment, which began on the morning of the 24th, continued without abatement. As Gird Support Trench (part of the first objective) had been almost entirely demolished by our shell-fire, the first two waves of the attacking infantry received orders to dig in one hundred and fifty yards beyond it.
>
> Zero hour for the attack was fixed for 12.35pm on the 25th September. Two minutes before zero bayonets were fixed and the battalion 'stood to' ready to go over the parapet. Each man carried an extra bandolier and a Mills bomb in addition to the complement of bombs carried by the Battalion and Company Bombers.
>
> As the hands of the watches touched zero Captain J. Edes and Captain J.E.N.P. Denning, commanding A and C Companies respectively, followed by their men, sprang over the parapet of Gap Trench and advanced in quick time in two lines with a frontage of two platoons each company, fifty yards between the two lines. A Company was on the right, C on the left.
>
> Both companies had advanced about fifty yards when they came into the enemy's artillery barrage from the right and machine-gun fire from the right front. In spite of heavy casualties, there was no wavering until the brigade front line was reached. Instead, however, of finding the trench empty and the attacking troops of the 64th Brigade on their way to the first objective, the two units still occupied the trench. Apparently they had attacked the enemy but had fallen back to their original position.

> By this time Captain Denning and all the senior NCOs of C Company had been wounded, and it was found necessary to re-organize in the front line.

Jack had received a shrapnel wound to the stomach, from which he died the following day. He was twenty-three years old. He was buried in Heilly Station Cemetery, near Méricourt-l'Abbé. Initially, his grave was marked by a makeshift wooden cross, visited by Denning himself while he was serving in France in 1918. Denning instructed his sappers to make a new wooden cross, which was later replaced by the ubiquitous stone monument by the Commonwealth War Graves Commission.

In a letter to Reg of 15 November,[16] Denning wrote of Jack:

> He was born to be a soldier and had all the qualities to fit him for it, a splendid brain, a brilliant leader of men, great determination. Had he lived I feel confident England would never have produced a finer soldier.

Reg

Reginald Denning signed up at the beginning of the war. Initially, he was intent on serving as a private soldier, and to that end enlisted as a private with the 1/16th (County of London) Battalion (Queen's Westminster Rifles). With Jack's urging, however, he was later commissioned into the Bedfordshire Regiment. He went on to serve in several of the famous locations and battles of the Western Front. In 1914 and 1915, he was stationed near Ypres, in the mud and squalor as the mobile warfare of the opening months transmogrified into the bloody attrition of the trenches. Then, like Jack, he fought at the Somme in 1916. Reg's unit went over the top on 8 July, a week after the battle had begun. He morbidly recalled having to pick his way through lines of British dead. Another week later, on 15 July, he was wounded by a bullet in the head during the attack on Pozières. 'Give the blighters one for me' he reportedly said as he fell unconscious,[17] but despite the severity of his wounds he underwent a successful operation and, over the course of the next year, recovered sufficiently to return to duty.

In 1918, he again went to the Front, as a company commander for the 6th Bedfords. The effects of the bullet wound soon returned, though, and he was moved to a staff officer position behind the lines, in which capacity he served until the end of the war.

Following the Armistice, he remained in the army, and went on to a long and distinguished career in military administration, reaching the rank of lieutenant general and being awarded KCVO, KBE, CB and MC.

Gordon

While Jack and Reg fought at the Somme in the greatest land battle of the British Army in the First World War, Gordon Denning served in the greatest naval action of the war, the Battle of Jutland. Tragically, although he survived enemy action, the uncompromising conditions aboard ships of the day led to him contracting tuberculosis. The disease proved fatal and thus caused the second Denning family death during wartime.

Gordon had joined the merchant navy in 1913. Unlike the army, the Royal Navy allowed children to serve, and Gordon was appointed a midshipman in the Naval Reserve at the end of 1914, aged seventeen. His ambition was to become an officer, and in the usual Denning manner he excelled at training, particularly gunnery. In March 1915 he was appointed to HMS *Hampshire*, a ship which was to become famous when it was sunk by a German mine in June 1916 while carrying Lord Kitchener, with the loss of virtually all its crew and Kitchener himself. By then Gordon was no longer serving on her, but he knew many of those who were.

Gordon's new ship was the destroyer HMS *Morris*. Unlike capital ships, destroyers were engaged in almost-continual action, whether protecting larger vessels and troop transports from U-Boats,[18] or attacking armed trawlers and participating in raids along the enemy coast. In *The Family Story* Denning recorded a number of such actions in which Gordon participated. He then spent some time on Gordon's part in the great clash of dreadnoughts that was Jutland.

The Battle of Jutland came about because the German High Seas Fleet knew it could not survive a direct confrontation with the numerically superior British Grand Fleet. Instead, the Germans planned to draw out a portion of the Grand Fleet (comprising Vice-Admiral Sir David Beatty's battlecruiser squadron and the accompanying 5th Battle Squadron under Rear Admiral Hugh Evan-Thomas), which had been stationed south of the main base of Scapa Flow in response to raids by the Germans on the British coast. A smaller force of German ships was sent ahead to entice Beatty (known to be an aggressive commander) into the whole of the High Seas Fleet following some way behind. The flaw in the plan was that the British had intercepted their communications and set a counter-trap, in which Beatty was to find then lure the High Seas Fleet itself into the maw of the Grand Fleet under Admiral Sir John Jellicoe.

HMS *Morris* was involved in the action from the beginning, as she was attached to Beatty's squadron. Beatty followed the German bait, untroubled about engaging them directly even before his own force was properly positioned, until he met the entire High Seas Fleet. Beatty's keenness for action proved costly with the loss of two capital ships in that initial action (known as the 'Run to the South'), but once he encountered the full German force he correctly turned about and led them towards Jellicoe ('the Run to the North').

Thinking they were chasing a smaller and wounded enemy, the Germans suddenly discovered that they had run into almost an entire horizon consisting of British ships, crossing their 'T'.[19] They faced annihilation but, owing to the onset of darkness, poor British signalling, substandard British shells, Jellicoe's natural caution (principally fear of U-Boats, mines and superior German night gunnery) and a very well-executed initial retreat by the Germans, the bulk of their force managed to escape and thereby deny the British public the expected second Trafalgar.

Almost as soon as the engagement concluded, a debate began in British circles which has never been resolved: whether Jutland was a tactical victory, a strategic one, neither or both. The British had lost more ships and crew, but were at sea shortly afterwards enforcing the same blockade of shipping to Germany as before, while the Germans languished in harbour for many months and never attempted a reprise of the action. The *New York Times* offered a measured verdict: the prisoner (the Germans) had assaulted his gaoler but was still in gaol – referring to the fact that Jellicoe had managed to preserve the status quo, which was unquestionably to Britain's advantage.

Denning, on the other hand, with the benefit of many decades' hindsight, was critical of Jellicoe's reticence in battle:[20]

> Individual acts of gallantry do not win battles. They are won or lost by the dispositions made by the High Command. It has often been said that Jellicoe was the only man who could have lost the war in a single day. But I would put it differently. He was also the only man who could have won the war in a single day. If the German High Seas Fleet had been destroyed, the enemy would have capitulated at once. There would not have been the Battle of the Somme – with the loss of the flower of our English youth. There would not have been the sinking of our merchant fleet by U-boats. No wonder that the fleet and the nation suffered a great disappointment.

With due respect to Denning, his argument was pure conjecture. One might indeed devise plausible counter-factual scenarios in which the High

Seas Fleet could have been routed, but it would not have followed axiomatically that Germany would have surrendered on the Western Front. For all practical purposes the High Seas Fleet was out of the fight after Jutland anyway: it only took to sea on three inconsequential occasions thereafter, and when asked to make a futile last stand near the end of the war its sailors mutinied. It was unable to prevent the blockade which inflicted much deprivation on the German people and armed forces. Yet the German Army fought on until suffering irreversible defeats in the 1918 'Hundred Days' offensive of the Allies, in which Denning himself participated. Realistically, victory in the First World War could only ever come on the Western Front.

After Jutland, Gordon was promoted to sub-lieutenant, 'for the cool and skilful way in which he, as officer of the quarters, while continuously under heavy fire, controlled the foremost 4-inch guns, the primary control having broken down'.[21] He even managed to bring home a fragment of a shell he had retrieved from the deck of HMS *Morris*. By then, however, his health was in serious difficulty from the harsh conditions on board. In September 1916 he went on leave and, Denning recalled, looked distinctly unwell. He was admitted to hospital and in November 1916 came the terrible news that he had been diagnosed with tuberculosis. He was discharged from the navy but never recovered. His condition continued to deteriorate until June 1918, when he died at home, six days after his twenty-first birthday. Denning recalled many moving letters and other recollections of his last months: as one would expect, Gordon remained unbowed until the end.[22]

Tom

By 1918, the shattering cost of the war in blood and treasure had created greater cynicism across Europe about the notions of national honour, though not amongst the Denning clan. Jack had died, Gordon was in the late stages of tuberculosis and Reg had suffered his severe head wound, but Denning himself had an undiminished sense of duty and patriotism, and was spurred on rather than deterred by the family's suffering. 'We were not allowed to go to France until we were 19' he wrote. 'But we were all anxious to join as soon as we could. No hesitation – not even on my part in spite of the grievous loss the family had already borne. All the keener because of it'.[23]

For all Denning's enthusiasm, he was initially ruled unfit on the ground of a systolic heart murmur. He believed the doctor had invented the diagnosis because he was tired of sending young men off to die. Since at the time of being demobilised ('demobbed') in 1919 Denning was assessed as medical category A1, and he lived to the age of 100, his suspicion clearly had some credence. He appealed the decision successfully and enlisted as an officer cadet.

In February 1916, a new system of training for officers had been introduced, under which temporary commissions could only be granted if a candidate had been through an officer cadet unit. Entrants had to be aged over eighteen-and-a-half, and to have served in the ranks or to have been with an Officers' Training Corps (OTC). The training course lasted four-and-a-half months.[24] That was the system in place when Denning joined. He applied for the Royal Engineers, because he thought it the best use for his mathematical background.[25] He was sent to the OTC near Newark and was commissioned as a second lieutenant in November 1917. 'What I liked most was the horses'[26] he later mused.

Following years of the line shifting rarely if at all, in early 1918 the situation on the Western Front took a sharp turn for the worse for the Allies. Freed from the Eastern Front by the Russian Revolution of late 1917 but facing the prospect of the Allies now having virtually unlimited reinforcements from the United States, the Germans prepared for a final throw of the dice. They began with Operation Michael, a large-scale offensive launched in March 1918. Drawing upon all the lessons of the preceding three years, they made significant gains and threatened to break through the Allied lines. Within a week, three British divisions, each with losses of more than 7,000, had been almost wiped out. Soon even the prominent Allied commander General Pétain thought the war was lost.

Despite its initial gains, the German advance gradually began to stutter, running short of supplies and facing an unbroken enemy. Operation Michael itself ended on 5 April 1918. Four days later the Germans launched Operation Georgette to try to push the British First and Second Armies into the sea. Field Marshal Haig responded with his famous command of 11 April 1918:[27]

> There is no other course open to us but to fight it out. Every position must be held to the last man: there must be no retirement. With our backs to the wall and believing in the justice of our cause each one of us must fight on to the end. The safety of our homes and the Freedom of mankind alike depend upon the conduct of each one of us at this critical moment.

Denning's unit was rushed to France to try to hold the line. Before leaving, he crafted his first ever legal document – a short, hand-written standard-form will leaving all his estate to Clara. (Many years later he would be called upon to adjudicate on the same wording in respect of Second

World War servicemen.) He joined the 151st Field Company of the Royal Engineers, a unit of the 38th (Welsh) Division. They were placed on the front line on the Somme opposite the town of Albert, which was then in German hands.

Denning was under near-continuous shellfire for several months:[28]

> In trench and bivouacs. Never knowing where the next shell would fall. There was a cartoon by Bruce Bairnsfather which caught the mood exactly – the man looking over the top of a shell-hole, saying 'If you knows of a better 'ole, go to it'. Night after night we made a reconnaissance – creeping close up to the enemy. It was a dangerous task. The river Ancre was flooded to a width of 200 to 300 yards and there were no bridges. The enemy held the other side in force.

The tide of the war turned dramatically later in the year when the Allies began the 'Hundred Days' offensive that would lead to the Armistice. At an early stage in the Allied attack, in late August 1918, Denning's unit spent days building a bridge, only for the Germans to destroy it and force them to start again. At one stage they went forty-eight hours without sleep. Denning's work on the bridge was mentioned in the regimental history as having enabled an attack to be launched which resulted in the capture of Thiepval, with 634 prisoners and 143 machine guns being taken.[29]

As the advance continued, Denning was called upon to create access across the Canal du Nord. All the bridges had been destroyed and the valley was smothered in poisonous gas. Denning's unit therefore had to establish pontoons across the canal. They did so under shellfire, initially wearing gas masks but eventually without due to the discomfort.

Denning recalled 'heavy fighting all the way' over the Selle and Sambre rivers:[30]

> I can still see the line of infantry advancing under heavy fire – first one falling and then another – with us following close behind them. I can still see the battlefield strewn with hundreds of our best officers and men – lying dead – shot down as they went forward. I can still see the dead horses lying in piles beside the roads; and dead Germans black in the face. Such is war.

During much of 1918 and 1919, a malevolent phenomenon appeared across many parts of the globe in the form of an exceptionally deadly influenza pandemic. It became inaccurately known as the 'Spanish flu', and its history gained some considerable resonance a century later in the form of the Covid-19 pandemic. The 1918–19 flu was caused by a virus with genes of avian origin. Something in the order of 500 million people – one-third of the world's population – became infected, and the total number of deaths was estimated to be at least fifty million.[31] Denning caught the virus in November 1918 and was in hospital when the Armistice was signed. He recalled that illness meant he and his fellow patients felt little cheer, only relief that the war had ended.[32]

Aftermath

In spite of the suffering that the war had inflicted upon his family, Denning remained proud of his own service. In *The Family Story* he spent some time relating his experiences, and summed up his feelings by quoting from Shakespeare's *Henry V*, Act IV, Sc 3, in which the legendary phrase 'We few, we happy few, we band of brothers' appears.[33] He concluded with the melancholy observation that the survivors of both wars were dwindling in numbers each year, with fewer and fewer medals being worn at ceremonial occasions, but reasserted his belief that if it came to it, the next generation would fight for freedom, just as his had done.[34] For many years he read out the names of those lost in the conflict at the Remembrance Sunday commemoration in Whitchurch,[35] and admitted to a rare display of public emotion on each occasion, even after more than sixty years had passed.[36] In 1969, he became Patron of the Whitchurch Branch of the British Legion.

In his *Desert Island Discs* appearance in 1980,[37] he again recalled his service with evident pride. He mentioned Haig's order to fight to the last man, and chose as his first piece the *Colonel Bogey March*, which he said 'was the last march in our ears before we went up to the line'. He also chose *The Roses of Picardy*, which he said was one of the songs that appealed most to him and his colleagues whilst they were on active duty in 1918.

Although he was not the longest-lived First World War veteran, he was the last to sit in the House of Lords (in Parliament) and as Master of the Rolls in 1982 probably the last to hold any public office of significance. As much as he became a voice from another age, his experiences provided some counter to those who portrayed him later in life as an out of touch judge, living the cloistered life of Oxbridge and the Inns of Court. He had seen things in the trenches which no human should ever have to witness. It is also safe to assume that the life he saw behind the lines in France would not have been conducted exclusively on puritanical Victorian lines either,[38] although he recorded no amorous encounters of his own in France (or England) until he met Mary. If he was adamant later in life in trying to enforce by-then outdated and even quaint notions of morality in his work, his experience in the total breakdown of civilisation that was the First World War would undoubtedly have been a motivating factor. It is clear that the beliefs that had impelled him to sign up never faded. Nor did they in the case of Reg, who wrote movingly many decades after the war's end about the values that had led him to enlist, and which he still held.[39]

Denning's recollections read in a manner very familiar to those conversant with the First World War and the many memoirs that followed. More widespread public education in the years leading up to the conflict and the sheer number of those who fought at the Front created a mine of primary sources unequalled in size by any earlier conflict. There has been considerable discussion over the years as to how much weight to place even on near-contemporary records.[40] Yet there is no reason to cast doubt upon Denning or Reg's accounts. Unlike some other veterans, neither altered his views, exaggerated his service or gave contrary accounts, even into the great age to which both lived.

It was true that Denning was not enamoured with Jellicoe's command at Jutland. Ironically, his criticism was that Jellicoe had been too cautious, the opposite of the usual denigration of land commanders for being too aggressive and too ready to sacrifice their men. Iris Freeman went further and wrote that Denning became disillusioned with the Allied commanders of the First World War, who had presided over such horrendous losses from 1914 to 1918.[41] There was little in any of Denning's writing, at the time or later, to support Freeman's assertion, though he might have told her in person. Nor was there any indication he ever had any intellectual interest in scholarly debates about the strategy and tactics of the war.

Denning remained convinced of the righteousness of each of the major wars his country fought in his lifetime. More controversially, he retained an almost unbending trust in the security apparatus of the country. As will be seen, that trust caused some controversy with respect to his views on detention without trial in the Second World War, the actions of the ruling class in the Profumo Affair and, most notoriously, anyone suspected of Irish terrorism.

Ultimately, Denning was not broken by his experience, never relinquished his patriotism and always remained proud of his contribution. He was far from alone in those experiences and sentiments.[42]

CHAPTER III

1920s – From Oxford to the Bar

A land unfit for heroes

Following the Armistice on 11 November 1918, Denning remained in hospital for a few days before being sent to a convalescent home in Cap Martin, an idyllic location on the Mediterranean coast between Monaco and Menton. He returned to England on 5 February 1919, initially to an army camp near Salisbury, before being officially demobbed the following day. His final rank was temporary second lieutenant.

All returning soldiers were given a protection certificate, a railway ticket to get home, a pay advance, a fortnight's ration book and a voucher for the return of their coat (the famous 'trench' coat), with the option of a clothing allowance or a suit (of modest quality) which they would need for most occupations of the day. They – or, rather, the small percentage with the qualifications to apply for the available roles – received preferential treatment for civil service jobs for some years afterwards (of which there were far fewer than today, given the relative size of the state). Otherwise, returning servicemen were essentially left to fend for themselves in a depressed economy with a much thinner welfare system than in the present day. The declining economy following the war, the General Strike of 1926 and the onset of the Great Depression in 1929, meant that for the millions of ordinary people the phrase 'Roaring Twenties' would have struck a hollow note.

The Denning family themselves had actually suffered their worst economic reversal before the end of the war. Due to falling trade the drapery had failed, forcing Charles to petition for his own bankruptcy in July 1918. At the time, bankruptcy carried a crushing social stigma and imposed draconian restrictions upon future work prospects. Rather than simply an unfortunate but redeemable economic event, it was seen as a moral failure on the part of the bankrupt. For centuries, bankruptcy had also meant imprisonment. That had changed with the Debtors Act 1869, though imprisonment could still follow if the debtor failed to comply with severe procedural requirements.

If the punishment for bankruptcy had been slightly lessened by the 1869 reforms, the financial consequences and social opprobrium had not. In Charles's case, one result was that ownership of the two properties that had founded the basic but loving and sound Denning family home and business had passed to a rival draper. To add to his humiliation, his father-in-law had to sign the conveyance of the properties to the rival draper, as he held the deeds by way of security for a loan he had given to Charles years earlier to start the business.

Combined with the loss of Jack and Gordon, and the serious injury in combat to Reg, it had all been too much. Charles had suffered a nervous breakdown, with even the hitherto indefatigable Clara seemingly unable to help. The couple were, at least, able to remain as tenants above the shop, getting by on a meagre pension from Jack and Gordon's deaths.

Charles had wanted to spare his sons from the shame of his fall and so had not told them while they were away at the Front. The news would therefore have come as a grim shock for Denning upon his return to Britain. He tried to obtain an increase in their pension, but the civil servants with whom he dealt were unyielding. He also inquired into whether he could contest the bankruptcy, but it was too late.

Denning was incensed at what he saw as the pettiness of faceless bureaucrats obstructing the family's due. Many years later, his undiminished anger at what had happened to them informed how he would treat war pensions cases when they came before him as a judge. It seems probable too that his lingering sense of injustice about their fate formed a contributing factor to his general preference to side with the 'little man' against the state or large corporations.

On a happier note, Charles and Clara's circumstances were alleviated to some extent in 1922, when they moved to a cottage named 'The Hermitage' situated close to All Hallows Church. There remains some confusion about how exactly they financed the move. In *The Family Story*, Denning stated that Reg bought it for them. In the 1930s, however, Charles had written to Denning stating that the property had cost £500,[1] plus £25 paid for an unexpired lease, of which Reg had paid £265, Denning £160, and Charles and Clara themselves £100. The property was put in Reg's name as he had paid the most. Then, in a letter of 1941, Clara stated that Reg had paid £250 and Tom £150 towards the cost – which would be consistent with Charles's letter, assuming the missing £25 was the sum paid for the unexpired lease which she omitted to mention.

It seems unlikely that Charles would have been mistaken about how the purchase of his house had been funded, especially as his letter was written less than a decade later, while more than half a century had passed when Denning wrote *The Family Story*. Then again, it seems equally improbable that Denning in 1922 had a spare £150 or £160. One possibility[2] is that Reg might have purchased the property alone and told Charles and Clara a white lie that Denning had contributed, in order to help Denning's standing with them, or perhaps to save them worrying that they had taken too much from him. Alternatively, Denning might have promised Reg he would contribute the sum once he was able, and that detail was withheld from Charles and Clara. Or it is just about possible that Denning had saved the money from teaching, though given the short time he spent in the role that seems implausible, especially as by 1922 he was on a low income once more.

Whatever the explanation, if there was any internal tension over the purchase, it was at odds with all other evidence, which points to the family's trust, closeness, and determination to help each other. Norman was too young in 1922 to contribute meaningfully to the purchase of a house, but later, as the three brothers each gained disposable income, all of them sent money to help Charles and Clara.

Oxford and Mary

For himself, Denning had no doubt about what he wished to do after the war – return to Oxford to continue his study of mathematics – and he was fortunate to have the opportunity. He reached his lodgings in Oxford on 10 February 1919, less than a week after arriving back in England. On his first afternoon at Magdalen he was given a task for applied mathematics of tying a lead weight to a string of cotton. After it took him two hours to complete the apparently simple puzzle, he resolved to concentrate exclusively upon pure mathematics.

Once again, he lived an austere life in college, partly through a lack of means, partly through his naturally simple tastes – which never changed throughout his whole life – and partly through his innate shyness. As before, he attended the Oxford Union only infrequently, never spoke in any of the debates, did not join any of the clubs or societies, and by and large read only his studying materials. There was, however, one marked change: upon his return to Whitchurch for the 1919 summer vacation, he began seeing Mary

Harvey, the daughter of the local vicar. At the time it was only a platonic friendship, by Mary's choice. Denning had known her ever since her family had moved to Whitchurch in 1910, but they had not had much interaction beyond what he called his 'shy glances' from the time of their confirmation together at All Hallows in 1914. He recorded his later impression in *The Family Story*,³ a rare occasion on which the famous Denning prose attempted something like the genre of romantic novels:

> What was she like? I cannot put it into words. She was not pretty. She was not fair. But she was good by nature and good to look at. The first glance showed her bright dark brown eyes, sparkling with intelligence. Next, her well-shaped mouth and chin, ready to break into the most welcoming of smiles at the least provocation. Her nose was fine and straight; not broad and snubbed like mine. Her complexion was clear – not pale or blotchy – but glowing with good health – in those days. Overtopping all was her long black hair, falling a little over her wide open forehead. Never cut short. Always tied at the back of her head. In all –
>
> > A countenance in which did meet
> > Sweet records, promises as sweet.
>
> But there – you will see from the description how beautiful I thought her. I told her so – times out of number – but she would not have it so. 'You look at me through rose-coloured spectacles,' she said. 'Do not put me on a pedestal. I am not worth it.'

Unfortunately for Denning, Mary was interested in an older man at the time (fortunately for Denning, her parents did not approve),⁴ and so rebuffed his perhaps slightly fumbling proposal. He persisted nonetheless and managed at least to establish a friendship with her, seeing her during holidays and sending letters and gifts. She visited Oxford just the once, in company with a female friend, but the joy of the occasion lasted with Denning for the rest of his life, as he took time to recall the day in some detail in *The Family Story*, including his regret that the rain forced Mary to wear a practical coat rather than the fetching summer dress in which he had imagined she might arrive.

Fate seemed to intervene adversely in the early 1920s when Mary moved with her parents to Fawley, a village on the edge of the New Forest, but Denning never lost heart or hope, continuing their correspondence unabated.

A novice teacher

Happiness with Mary lay in the future as Denning worked towards the exams of 1920. Despite his difficulty with applied mathematics, he achieved a First. Not only had he far surpassed the usual academic expectations of the children of 'mere' tradesmen, but he had also exceeded those of Magdalen College. At the time, Magdalen was largely thought of as an intellectually idle repository for the sons of the wealthy, with no First having been awarded for years,[5] rather like Tom Sharpe's fictional Cambridge college in *Porterhouse Blue*.[6] Denning later recorded with evident satisfaction that Magdalen's reputation had increased substantially following his time there and that his son Robert had become Senior Dean of Arts.[7]

With an undergraduate degree under his belt, Denning now had to find an occupation. Unlike Reg or Norman, he did not consider returning to the forces. Nor did he have any interest in training for a scientifically-related career, despite his wartime service in the Royal Engineers. Doubtless that lack of interest stemmed from his dislike of applied mathematics. Instead, largely for want of any other ideas, Denning opted for teaching. There were, at least, many opportunities in that field, caused by the loss of so many of the First World War generation. Denning applied for vacancies at the well-known public schools of Charterhouse and Winchester. He was offered a role at the latter and accepted. He thought up a reserve plan to return to Oxford to study history and then attempt the Civil Service Exam should teaching not work out.

Winchester College, based in Hampshire, was founded in 1382, making it one of the oldest English public schools. In Denning's time, as now, it was an independent boarding school for boys, with the motto 'Manners makyth man'. Especially from the Victorian times to the end of the British Empire after the Second World War, public schools took upon themselves the task of preparing a cadre of boys to run the Empire – soldiers, civil servants, politicians and teachers. To do so it sought to inculcate its pupils with the idea that it was Britain's natural destiny to run the globe, or at least as much of it that could be secured. Despite the grand surroundings, life for the pupils could be harsh, in preparation for them enduring the privations of more remote postings. A joke of the time had it that the British kept their dogs at home and sent their sons to kennels. Stories of public school cruelty from the time abound, as any reader of Roald Dahl will know. Nonetheless, Denning was clearly not unenamoured with the school, since he later sent his son there.

Denning's first term at Winchester began in September 1920. As he had avoided public speaking at Oxford and had had no experience of it at school in Whitchurch or Andover, one can imagine the nerves he would have suffered at the beginning, facing the privileged children of the gentry and upper middle classes. Doubtless in time-honoured schoolboy fashion some would have sought a weakness and mocked his country accent and origins. With customary determination, though, Denning proved more than equal to the task. All evidence suggests he was broadly accepted by his fellow teachers as well as the students. The former especially would have been impressed by him having attended Oxford and holding a commission during the war.

Denning taught mathematics at all levels, as well as geography, reading up on the latter the night before each lesson since he had not studied it at university. His salary of £350 per year gave him a comfortable lifestyle,[8] and the location was within cycling distance of Whitchurch (about thirteen miles), a particular advantage while Mary still lived there. Denning admitted to feeling rather thrilled seeing his work in print after he set the examination questions – one can only wonder how much greater a thrill it would have given him to be told he would one day become the most widely cited lawyer in a thousand years of the common law.

Not long into his tenure, though, he resolved that he did not wish to remain teaching for the rest of his working life. He wrote to Mary:

> I feel restless again today. I feel that I don't want to settle down here doing the same thing day after day, a very mediocre schoolmaster with no ambition and no hope ... I have boundless ambition and today I want to cast myself free from here, go back to Oxford and once more throw myself with full force into that upward flight ...[9]

The question of what to do instead was answered on one fateful occasion, the date unrecorded, when to kill some time and curiosity Denning went over to the Great Hall at Winchester to watch the Assizes court. He was instantly captivated seeing the barristers, the judge and the law in action, and set his mind for good upon a legal career.

Oxford and Lincoln's Inn

Although at the time there were other routes into the legal profession besides studying law at university (indeed, only a minority of judges of the day had done so), Denning felt his best starting point would be to obtain an Oxford degree in the subject. He therefore reached out to his contacts at Magdalen.

He was welcomed by an unsurprised Sir Herbert Warren, who thought Denning had rather undersold himself by going into teaching. He offered to reactivate Denning's demyship and try to secure another scholarship.

Charles, somewhat recovered from his breakdown but still in a financially precarious position, was appalled that Denning was considering giving up a good salary and a secure job. But Denning was unwavering. With his demyship at Oxford, and the possibility – no more – of Sir Herbert securing another scholarship (which would not be known until the following academic year), he handed in his notice at Winchester and left at the end of the 1921 summer term. For once he allowed himself some recreation, undertaking a walking holiday with Reg in the French Alps before going up to Oxford again in October.

In his usual fashion, Denning started preparation of his own before the official beginning of his studies, by purchasing a copy of *Anson on Contract*. He was fascinated by the subject, which confirmed to him he was making the right career choice. Upon arrival at Magdalen, however, he was not impressed by his tutor, one Robert Segar. Denning dismissed him as a failed barrister who knew nothing about law save for the Statute of Frauds on which he once had a case. To make up the shortfall in Segar's tuition, Denning attended lectures of more learned dons, including two outstanding legal historians, Sir Paul Gavrilovitch Vinogradoff and Sir William Holdsworth.

On the financial front, Sir Herbert was as good as his word and managed to arrange for Denning another scholarship, valued at £100 per year.[10] Continuing to be impressed by Denning's abilities, he predicted that the young man would one day reach the House of Lords.

One of the requirements of the scholarship Sir Herbert had obtained was for Denning to join one of the Inns of Court, an essential step in any event towards becoming a barrister. Denning chose Lincoln's Inn, solely because the Under-Treasurer of the day was a Magdalen alumnus, a remarkable man by the name of Sir Reginald Rowe, who had been a stockbroker and a wartime military intelligence officer before becoming a barrister. On his application form for the Inn, Denning recorded his father's occupation as 'businessman' – not inaccurately, since the beleaguered Charles was attempting to make some money by offering his services to some of his old clients, though his career and lifestyle were sadly a long way short of how the term 'businessman' would have been understood by Denning's more privileged companions at Oxford. For his two referees he chose Sir Herbert and, with a knowing wink towards fate, his future father-in-law, Frank Harvey. The latter wrote that he had seen Denning daily during vacations and that 'I have had abundant opportunities of knowing him intimately'.

Denning's application was successful, taking effect from November 1921. It carried the requirement of dining in hall, something even more formal then than in the present day – attendees wore top hats for a start. In view of his ever-pressed finances, Denning stayed with a relative, his Aunt Min, in the South London suburb of Streatham on dining nights.

His admission to Lincoln's Inn roughly coincided with the early stages of a major social change, in the form of women entering the profession. Women had been permitted to join the Inns of Court following the passage of the Sex Disqualification (Removal) Act 1919, though the male stranglehold on senior posts in the profession remained, as it would throughout Denning's career.

Denning's great enjoyment in studying law meant he enthusiastically took part in moots, no doubt having gained some confidence in public speaking from teaching and from giving orders to his men in wartime. He still abstained from alcohol, ascribing his reticence to an early experience with port at Magdalen, which had left him somewhat 'dizzy', and largely concentrated on his work rather than extra-curricular activities and socialising. He did at least enjoy some sport, writing to Reg on 1 November 1921 that he thought it would be good to start playing football again.

As with his previous times at Oxford, Denning achieved outstanding grades. He was given a First in law having studied for less than a year – an extraordinarily short period of time. It has to be questioned whether even a student as assiduous and intellectually gifted as Denning really deserved that award. It would not be possible in the present day. Clearly, there was a more malleable and independent academic structure in the Oxford of the day, in which those recognised as truly outstanding could be rewarded in some exceptional fashion. There was also perhaps an inclination on the part of some of the old dons to assist the young men who had returned from the war.

There was one exception to Denning's apparently serene mastery of the law: he did not take to jurisprudence, the philosophy of law. It was, he later wrote:

> too abstract a subject for my liking, all about ideologies, legal norms and basic norms, 'ought' and 'is', realism and behaviouralism; and goodness knows what else. The jargon of the philosophers of law has always been beyond me. I like to get down to the practical problems which come up for decision. Contracts, torts, crime and the like.[11]

Denning's comments were slightly anachronistic, since jurisprudence in 1921–22 was a rather limited field, and some of the schools of thought he mentioned such as realism came later in the twentieth century.[12] There is, however, no reason to doubt that he was accurately recording how he felt both then and later on towards the subject. Iris Freeman thought his disparagement 'a strange remark from a judge who frequently propounded his own philosophy of law'.[13] With respect, Freeman was overstating the case: Denning never developed a sophisticated abstract theory which he then applied consistently to cases across his career. His judicial approach will be considered in later chapters, but for now it will suffice to note that he was never enamoured with legal philosophy. Instead, he was guided by his innate sense of right and wrong, imbued by all the experiences and influences already mentioned: chiefly, Clara, his schooling, the church and his experiences in the First World War.

Middle Temple and Failed All Souls

Once he had completed his degree, Denning's next step was to find a pupillage. It was no certainty then (as now) even for someone with excellent qualifications. Only junior barristers took on pupils, and the latter had to hope for a fortuitous introduction. Denning advised anyone following in his footsteps that a good degree helped, but a more important asset was 'good sense and a pleasing manner'.[14]

There was another factor of rather greater importance which he omitted: having the right contacts. At the time, nepotism and the need for connections in general were rife in pupillage applications. Fortunately for Denning, with his generation of the family now making their way, he was no longer just an outlier from the provinces. Reg had served with a King's Counsel during the war, who was able to facilitate an introduction to Henry O'Hagan, a junior barrister at 4 Brick Court, Middle Temple. Denning was offered a pupillage there, beginning in September 1922. He remained at the set until he was elevated to the Bench over twenty years later.

In October 1922, Denning went back to Oxford to attempt to reach the *ne plus ultra* of British intellectual status: admission to All Souls College. Rather like admission to the Bar, the criteria included social as well as academic factors, since candidates had to dine in halls with the fellows. He found it somewhat intimidating being surrounded by the likes of former Viceroys of India – doubtless an experience which contributed to him being famously charming and approachable when he attained high office later in life. He sat a series of exams covering not just law, but also philosophy and 'general' subjects (examples being 'What are the tests of a good prose style?' and 'Is the English character changing?' – questions simply expressed but, for All Souls, requiring answers of the highest erudition) as well as, inevitably, classics. It was the last of those that proved insurmountable for Denning, who thought that the snobbish dons did not like his Latin pronunciation. He therefore joined what he called 'the distinguished company of "Failed All Souls"'.[15]

It was rare for Denning to have failed at any goal, let alone an educational one. He was clearly embittered with the result, as he still complained about it seven decades later as a nonagenarian. Freeman reported that Denning, by then aged in his nineties, grumbled that his tutor told him the examiners thought his memory was good but that he lacked judgement.[16] He might have consoled himself that he was in good company: among the other unsuccessful candidates around the same time were Cyril Harvey,[17] with whom Denning would later co-operate on *Smith's Leading Cases*, and AP Herbert,[18] author of the *Uncommon Law* series of spoof legal cases which Denning immensely enjoyed. The only successful candidate from the same exams as Denning was Cyril Radcliffe, who would later become one of three barristers in the twentieth century appointed directly from the Bar to the Appellate Committee of the House of Lords, where he would serve for a time with Denning.[19] Infuriated but undeterred, Denning applied to All Souls again the following year, but in the event did not have time to sit the exams, his work in chambers having overtaken all else by then.[20]

Barristerial beginnings

The chambers at 4 Brick Court in Denning's time was unrelated to the modern 4 Brick Court, which is a large family law set.[21] When Denning joined, the address was occupied by a small commercial set founded in 1893 by the future law lord Richard Henn Collins. By the early 1920s the set consisted of O'Hagan and one other junior, Stephen Henn Collins, Richard's son. O'Hagan and Henn Collins each had a large room and private library to himself. The chambers also had a small, badly lit pupil room[22] housing two or three pupils, and an even smaller room shared by two clerks and a typist.

In his customary fashion, Denning had gone ahead of the usual route, by starting pupillage before he had taken the final Bar examination. He took the latter in June 1923 and won the Prize Studentship, worth 100 guineas a year for the next three years. The award was vital for his finances since, at the time, it was customary for juniors to remain 'briefless' for the first few years, working without pay (known as 'devilling') – something which drove many away from the profession and handed a weighty and no doubt intended advantage to those of independent means. Denning attributed his success in the exam not just to his Oxford education but also to the experience with the law he had been able to obtain by starting his pupillage at an earlier stage than the other candidates.

O'Hagan had a broad commercial practice with some libel, while Henn Collins specialised in railway work and copyright. Denning ploughed on devilling for them and other juniors of the day. He was entitled to see papers and follow his pupil master around court, but not normally to attend conferences with solicitors. He subsisted on his scholarship but also occasional welcome remuneration from a better-off and more beneficent leader, DN (Denis Nowell) Pritt QC. Pritt had begun as a specialist in worker's compensation cases, but later developed a colourful practice, among other things successfully defending Ho Chi Minh in the early 1930s against a French request for his extradition from Hong Kong. Denning usually assisted him on less historically memorable cases. The relationship was not all one way, since Denning was occasionally able to recommend Pritt as a leader. (Pritt also made an important if unintended contribution to Denning's career in that he encouraged his secretary, Mavis Hill, to read for the Bar and apply to the Middle Temple. She did both successfully, whereafter she became a law reporter with the Incorporated Council of Law Reporting. In that capacity she covered Denning's cases for very many years; upon her retirement in 1980 he called her 'Boswell to my Johnson'.[23])

Denning received no fee income for his devilling in 1923,[24] instead having to meet expenses of £69 10s (about £3,200 in 2022) for his robes, pupillage and clerk's fee out of his scholarship. In 1924, he was finally able to take on paid work, having made a good enough impression to be recommended to some solicitors. Even having passed that hurdle, it was necessary to make a name in order to attract work consistently. Over the course of 1924, Denning managed to bring in £94 10s while incurring lower practice expenses of £35 10s,[25] the latter reflecting the fact he did not have to buy new robes or other accoutrements.

Thereafter, his reputation and hence his income rose steadily throughout the decade. To begin with, a lot of his work was outside central London, necessitating higher travel expenses and usually lower brief fees. Denning often sailed close to the wind with bus and train timetables, and sometimes went too far – on one occasion he missed the train stop, pulled the communication cord to stop it, walked half a mile back along the track and still made it to court on time.[26] His work included some prosecution briefs (not for any serious crimes) obtained via Mary's uncle, who was serving as the Clerk of the Peace for the City of Winchester.[27]

That initially modest but soon burgeoning income enabled Denning to rent a room at 145 Beaufort Street, Chelsea – not as expensive a location then as it would be in the present day.²⁸ It was convenient to his chambers and to the Royal Courts of Justice on the Strand, being close to the District and Circle Line tube stations of South Kensington and Sloane Square, though the energetic Denning often walked home instead. He remained at the lodging until his first marriage. Nowadays the building is a single five-bedroom dwelling, though in Denning's time it was arranged into 'bachelor apartments'. The apartments were maintained by a landlady, one Mrs Cross, who prepared breakfast for the occupants at a time of their choosing, gentlemen of the day being presumed incapable of making their own (or it was thought inappropriate for them to do so, even if they were able to find their way around a kitchen).

Henn Collins lived in nearby Beaufort Gardens, and often walked home with Denning. He secured Denning an early break by recommending him to Southern Railway. Denning went on to receive many briefs from the company for prosecuting fare-dodging passengers. He was also commissioned to write a railway police manual and to redraft the railway byelaws. The increased opportunities led to him receiving brief fees of £315 in 1925 – more than twice his 1924 figure. He continued to seek to expand his profile in the profession, with the publication in 1925 of his first academic article, in the prestigious *Law Quarterly Review*.²⁹ Ironically, it was on the Statute of Frauds, the one subject of which he thought his original law tutor Robert Segar had any knowledge. 'Your article is a good one' wrote the editor in the letter accepting it for publication.³⁰

His income reached £360 in 1926, £470 in 1927, £860 in 1928 and £1,130 in 1929.³¹ The increasing sums reflected the fact that he was receiving briefs in the higher courts and instructions from more prestigious firms. The latter included Gosling & Wilkinson, Mayo, Elder & Co, Montagu's (and Cox & Cardale), Nicholson Graham and Jones (since incorporated into K&L Gates LLP), Soames, Edwards & Jones, Syrett & Sons (ultimately merged with Davenport Lyons) and Theodore Goddard & Co (since merged with Addleshaw Booth to form Addleshaw Goddard LLP).

Another leading firm of the day was Fladgate & Co (now Fladgate LLP), which could trace its origins to 1760. Denning was introduced to it in 1929 by a fellow lodger at Beaufort Street, Anthony Moir, who worked at the firm and later became a partner. The firm's clients included many of the landed aristocracy and their trustees.³² In those days, the aristocracy occupied a much more influential position in British society and had a substantially greater share of the nation's wealth. Later, the Parliament Act 1949 reduced the power of the House of Lords (already partly diminished by the earlier Parliament Act 1911), while tax reforms during and after the Second World

War forced the transfer of many great estates to the National Trust. Before the war, however, the aristocracy would have been exceptionally valuable clients for lawyers and other professionals.

Smith's Leading Cases

In 1927 Denning published another article in the *Law Quarterly Review*.[33] Then, towards the end of the decade, he was asked to contribute to a new edition of *Smith's Leading Cases*. The publication formed an important resource for barristers in that pre-digital age. At the time, judgments either found their way into the general or specialist law reports, or effectively vanished, leading a few judges over the years to bemoan the disproportionate influence editors of the law reports wielded over the development of the common law. The law reports also had indexes of varying quality and consistency, while the number of specialist textbooks was considerably fewer than in the present day. *Smith's*, begun in the nineteenth century, was therefore an important resource. The other contributors were Cyril Howard and Sir Thomas Willes Chitty.[34] A junior in Denning's chambers, Arthur Grattan-Bellew,[35] prepared the tables and index.[36]

The work on *Smith's* informed much of Denning's later work, not just as a barrister but also a judge. With his outstanding memory he was often able to cite authority and arguments which counsel had not mentioned, but which he recalled from *Smith's*. Most notably, he attributed his famous decision in *Central London Property Trust Ltd v High Trees House Ltd* [1947] KB 130 to his work on the publication.[37] Some time after he became a judge the publishers approached him to oversee a new edition, but he did not have the time and the work was discontinued.

A man about town

With his income expanding considerably, Denning also managed to enjoy the London *haute société* of the day, far removed from his early life.[38] In 1927, Reg had married Eileen Currie, the daughter of the wealthy shipping magnate Henry Currie. The Curries' family house was in Westbourne Terrace, a grand residence in what was then a salubrious address, with neighbours including Sir Herbert (later Viscount) Samuel, the Lord Chancellor Viscount Buckmaster and Field Marshal Sir William 'Wully' Robertson. Denning was best man at Reg's wedding, and through the Curries was able to attend functions in their more rarefied social strata. 'I was invited to dances in the large London houses' he later wrote, '[g]littering with youth and beauty and wealth. I went for weekends to country houses. I met the finest in the land'.[39]

Those familiar with Denning only through his later cases might find it surprising to imagine him as a dashing young bachelor thrust into the set of Evelyn Waugh's Sebastian Flyte and Basil Seal, or PG Wodehouse's Bertie Wooster: the world of Frazer Nash two seaters, Noël Coward plays, songs by Ivor Novello and Cole Porter, dancing the Charleston, dry martinis at the Drones Club and summer holidays in Le Touquet.

On the other hand, if he ever did become the subject of a Wodehousean maiden aunt's marital plot, nothing came of it, because he remained set on Mary. He wrote to her regularly for most of the 1920s. Her replies ranged from gentle teasing and hinting to a period when she did not reciprocate at all. In April 1928, for example, she wrote wondering if she might visit the Temple. He replied enthusiastically, suggesting dinner and dancing, only to receive the rather passionless response that she would prefer to attend with her mother and in those circumstances a visit to the theatre would be more appropriate. Mrs and Miss Harvey duly attended, and Mary's follow-up letter promised Denning he would be welcome to stay with her family at the Rectory in Fawley, though not for a romantic assignation. Later the same year Denning asked her reasonably directly (as if she could have been in any doubt about his intentions). Mary replied in July that she knew he had his hopes up, but:[40]

> Honestly, old man, you are the only person really to be consider[ing] – and it rests with you whether you think it wise or not. I was a bit troubled after meeting you in London to find that alas! things have remained in many ways unchanged for you and although I reverence (sic) your devotion and am surprised (and I would not be human and alas! I am *very* human if I was not *grateful*) this should be so after so many years and with no encouragement from me – For I think I have not given you encouragement. I know that in the memorable year 1919–20 I was unfair to you. I taxed you further than any woman ought to tax any man whom she has not *accepted* as a lover.

Mary there was obviously referring to their interactions while Denning was at Oxford, though what exactly took place in the form of her being 'unfair' or 'taxing' him was known only to the two of them. Although she kept a pocket diary for almost her entire adult life, the entries were necessarily short and often quite perfunctory, and do not contain many clues.[41]

Despite his near-complete lack of progress with Mary through the decade, Denning always maintained that he never had eyes for another. Even if that was not the whole truth, it was the effective truth since he was never engaged to anyone else, nor is there any record of him considering it. Yet, for the rest of 1928 and almost all of 1929, Mary barely acknowledged him at all. That all changed at the end of the year, as we will now see.

CHAPTER IV

1930s – From First Marriage to the Second World War

Mary

Just over ten years after his first admission of romantic feelings for Mary, Cupid's Arrow finally hit its mark for Denning in December 1929, when she wrote inviting him to a Spinsters' Ball in the New Forest. The event was scheduled for Saturday, 18 January 1930. Denning did not need a second invitation, and he travelled with giddy excitement to Fawley for the occasion. During the visit itself Mary rebuffed him as usual (despite saying of the dance in her diary 'I thoroughly enjoyed it'), but on the Monday, after he had returned to London, she wrote to him asking at long last:[1]

> Will you have me? I am almost ashamed to ask it of you, but since you went last night my life has been entirely revolutionised & I want you old man – & feel I must have you to make me happy.

Less than a week later, on 25 January 1930, they were engaged, Denning having returned to Fawley at the weekend to choose the ring with her ('Such a happy day', Mary wrote in her diary). Thereafter, their correspondence became more frequent, less one-sided and more unsubtle, with both introducing an unconcealed sexual element whilst agreeing to restrain themselves until marriage in accordance with the expectations of the age. The date was set for August 1930.

It had been a long wait, to put it mildly, though Denning consoled himself that even if Mary had shown interest in his advances a decade earlier, he would not have had the means to act on his hopes. The social mores of the day required marriage before cohabitation and for the husband to be able to afford a suitable family home. For most of the intervening years Denning had been an indigent student, then a pupil and then a briefless junior, and would therefore not have been able to meet that prosaic requirement. By 1930, though, his practice had built up a head of steam and he was able to support them both – his fee income that year was £1,410, a substantial sum for the time (indeed, a different league compared with the average wage of approximately £60 per year).[2] Also, although he (unsurprisingly) did not record the fact, marriage at the time also anticipated social equals, and in the small world of Whitchurch in his childhood the Dennings would have ranked below the Harveys in the unwritten social rankings. By becoming a successful barrister, Denning had moved up the scale socially as well as economically.

Coincidentally, Charles and Clara's financial position also improved in 1930, though from a sad source. Clara's father John Thompson died that year and she inherited £600 to add to an earlier sum of £300 he had given her.[3] Ever since they had moved to The Hermitage in 1922, life for Charles and Clara had been returning to happiness after the horrific loss of Jack and Gordon in the First World War coupled with Charles's emotional and financial breakdown. The Hermitage provided the hub of family life when any children or grandchildren were able to visit. Being in or married into the forces meant regular overseas postings for Marjorie, Reg and Norman, even though the first two had had children by then, complicating their arrangements.[4]

To prepare for his wedding and subsequent married life, Denning took on still more work. On a practical note he instructed Fladgate & Co to deal with his personal affairs, including the marriage settlement and insurance.[5] His instructions carried the unspoken hope that Fladgates' litigation team might send him something in return, which they duly did, including one interesting set of instructions during wartime, as will be seen in the next chapter.

Denning's personal and professional life both seemed to be in clover. In March 1930 he had his first appearance in the House of Lords. He won the case, with the only disappointment being that his name did not appear in the law report in *The Times* the following day. Later that year he received some non-remunerative but still welcome recognition when his regular leader, DN Pritt, was sufficiently impressed to give him a 'red bag' to replace the standard 'blue bag' carried by barristers at the time to store their papers.[6] Denning was delighted, as he wrote to Mary, with the slight regret that he could no longer use the blue bag upon which she had recently stitched his initials.

In June 1930, however, there came a hammer blow. Mary was diagnosed with tuberculosis, the deadly illness that had caused Gordon's death more than a decade earlier. Denning, staying with relatives in Exeter at the time for work, received the news by telephone and collapsed in shock. Marriage plans were necessarily put on hold while Mary was sent to Guy's Hospital.[7] Entirely in character, Denning was unswerving in his devotion, promising that they would get through it together[8] and being true to his word by standing by her throughout.

In August 1930 Mary was allowed to return home. Her parents had constructed a hut in the garden, isolating her from the rest of the family in accordance with medical advice, it being correctly realised that tuberculosis was transferred by close contact with infected people. Despite the improvement she was still weak and unable to think about wedding plans.

It is difficult from the perspective of developed countries in the twenty-first century, where tuberculosis has been much reduced if not wholly eradicated for generations,[9] to understand the cold terror in which it held people of the day, given the absence of a cure (eventually found in the form of antibiotics) and the agonising death it often inflicted. Recovery was usually extremely slow – in Mary's case it took fully two years. It was not until the end of August 1932 before she was well enough for her doctor to approve her marrying Denning at Christmas. The need for a doctor's approval seems antiquated; the reasoning would have been that Mary should not marry until she was physically robust enough to bear children, as was the societal expectation of the day for marriage of anyone in the appropriate age bracket.

In the meantime, Denning had provided unstinting support, quoting Cromwell's 'Trust in God and keep your powder dry' to her as Reg used to say to him when encountering any obstacles in life. He had also continued to throw himself into work. As well as his ever-expanding Bar practice, he was asked to supervise the ninth edition of the standard procedural manual *Bullen & Leake's Precedents*.[10] He received the substantial fee of £250 for the task, though most of the actual work was done by Grattan-Bellew, who had also assisted him with *Smith's Leading Cases*. Denning appropriately gave Grattan-Bellew most of the money (£180) accordingly.

When Mary finally had the all-clear from her doctor, Denning was spurred on to find accommodation for the two of them, his bachelor lodgings in Beaufort Street not being suitable for a married couple. In September 1932, he obtained the lease of a flat in Middle Temple, just opposite his chambers, as was common for barristers then and now.[11] Then, finally, he and Mary were married on 28 December 1932.

The ceremony took place at the church in Fawley. Mary's father jointly officiated with the Bishop of Southampton rather than giving her away. Instead, one of her brothers, Major F Barrington Harvey, took her down the aisle. According to the *Hampshire Advertiser*, Mary wore 'a dress of parchment satin with a shoulder train of old Indian embroidery and a veil of old Lyon lace',[12] carrying a bouquet of arum lilies. Grattan-Bellew was best man. Charles and Clara attended but Marjorie, Reg and Norman were all overseas on military postings. Mary recorded in her diary 'The most wonderful [day] of our lives!' and added that the Bishop had given 'a wonderful short address'.

No reception followed the service. Instead, the newlyweds travelled to Salisbury, where they stayed overnight before heading to their intended honeymoon destination in Torquay. In Torquay their accommodation was the Palace Hotel, one of the most glamorous establishments in the area.[13] They attended dances, including a fancy dress event on New Year's Eve, though they did not trouble staying up until midnight, preferring instead to turn in at around 10:30 (according to Mary's diary), and thus able in the traditional Denning manner to rise early in the morning for church. Otherwise, they enjoyed walks in the area and the other attractions of the English Riviera.

Following the honeymoon, back in London and happily married, Denning involved himself less in the world of bright young things and instead focused upon his home life. It seemed that, irrespective of all that he had achieved and endured in his life to that point, there remained a certain vulnerability, and he placed great dependence on his union with Mary.

Ever the workaholic, Denning often brought papers across the way from chambers and spent the evening reading and drafting. At least his work was by then more London-based, meaning fewer absences on circuit. He enjoyed being surrounded by legal panjandrums young and old in the Temple. The former included Jocelyn 'Jack' Simon, the future Lord Simon of Glaisdale, who also had chambers in Brick Court. Older luminaries included Denning's regular lunching companion Theobald Mathew, better known by the pseudonym 'O' under which he wrote the legal parody *Forensic Fables*. Denning subsequently laid claim to being the 'Double-First' in the fable of *The Double-First and the Old Hand,* though, if true, it was a story told against himself.[14]

Since Denning now both lived and worked in the Temple, he became an honorary member (or a member *ad eundem* in the Latin then still prevalent) of Middle Temple. He also took on pupils, who paid 100 guineas for the privilege, though he spent little time teaching them, instead leaving them to learn on the job as he himself had done.

Despite his successful career, life in London soon proved difficult. Although in her diary Mary described their flat as 'charming', it was very sparsely furnished, even by the standards of the time. It had no refrigerator and no lift, absence of the latter requiring a climb of sixty steps instead.

Worse, its heating was by coal, the use of which in domestic homes across London contributed to widespread air pollution. Another problem was that coal was also used for electricity generation, necessitating barges continually passing up and down the Thames serving Battersea and Southwark power stations. Contemporary photographs of well-known landmarks with blackened facades attest to the amount of soot in the air. There were far fewer motor vehicles than in the present, but, equally, they emitted much worse exhaust pollution.

The resultant abysmal air quality would have been oppressive enough even for the most robust individuals, but for those with weakened breathing and cardio-vascular systems such as Mary, it made London virtually uninhabitable. Her health started to deteriorate not long after the move. An attempted course of treatment in September 1933 caused her dermatological side effects while failing to cure her lung condition. In November, she was admitted to hospital for an operation on her lungs. In December, she required a second operation, and remained in hospital over the new year, leaving Denning to spend Christmas night in Streatham at his Aunt Min's.

In January 1934, Mary was at last able to leave hospital, but not to return home. Instead, she was sent to Mundesley Sanatorium in Norfolk to convalesce. Mundesley was a private facility, one of the first large centres in England built specifically for open-air treatment of tuberculosis. She stayed there until March 1934, when she moved to her parents' home, now located in a detached suburban house in Southampton, her father having retired from running the Fawley vicarage. Denning visited when he was able. He started to cut back on evening work, ostensibly because he thought it left him too drained the following day, but perhaps also with the realisation that it would not be in Mary's interests for him to continue being such a workaholic once they were able to resume married life.

L'Estrange v F Graucob Ltd – Denning and exemption clauses

Denning's first 'law student' case – an entry in the law reports which would be debated for decades after – came in February 1934, when he appeared before the Court of Appeal representing the defendant (appellant) in *L'Estrange v F Graucob Ltd* [1934] 2 KB 394. The subject matter concerned exemption clauses, something with which he would be closely associated throughout his career.

The facts were that in February 1933, the parties entered into an agreement for the delivery by the defendant of an automatic slot machine to the plaintiff. The plaintiff signed a written 'order form' containing the essentials of the contract in one font and a number of conditions in a smaller, though still legible, font. She gave the form to the defendant, and later received in writing an 'order confirmation'. After the machine was delivered the plaintiff brought an action contending that the machine was delivered in a condition unfit for purpose, in breach of warranty. The defendant pointed to the small print, which stated 'any express or implied condition, statement, or warranty, statutory or otherwise not stated herein is hereby excluded'. In response, the plaintiff argued that she had not read the fine print. The judge ruled in favour of the plaintiff, relying on *Richardson, Spence & Co v Rowntree* [1894] AC 217, and the defendant appealed.

The first judgment was given by Scrutton LJ, a distinguished commercial judge. He dealt with the point economically, stating that since the plaintiff had signed the document she could not avoid the consequences in the absence of fraud or misrepresentation. Maugham LJ regretted the small print but said the plaintiff could only avoid its effect if she established: (a) that the document had been signed in circumstances which made it not her act (*non est factum*); or (b) misrepresentation. Neither point was available on the facts and therefore the appeal succeeded.

The case was the first major step on a long journey for Denning through the law of exemption clauses. Many years later, when speaking in a debate in the House of Lords, he recalled:[15]

> To tell you the sequel, my Lords, that reporter in the courts did not report the case at once.[16] He did not think so much of it, but my company had it privately printed and I went round the county courts of England winning case after case, most unrighteously. That was the law as laid down in 1934 and it has remained so ever since.

Denning might indeed have won case after case in the county courts, but once on the Bench his approach turned to how he could dispense justice by avoiding the strict application of exemption clauses in similar cases. He fashioned (or attempted to fashion) many an exception to the rule, several of which we will see in later chapters. It should be stressed, however, that the broader principle of *L'Estrange v F Graucob Ltd* – that a written contract should be binding save for carefully defined exceptions – was not just the right result, but one fundamental to commercial dealings. In *Peekay Intermark Ltd and another v Australia and New Zealand Banking Group Ltd* [2006] EWCA Civ 386 at [43], Moore-Bick LJ made the point in ringing tones:

> It was accepted that a person who signs a document knowing that it is intended to have legal effect is generally bound by its terms, whether

he has actually read them or not. The classic example of this is to be found in *L'Estrange v Graucob* [1934] 2 KB 394. It is an important principle of English law which underpins the whole of commercial life; any erosion of it would have serious repercussions far beyond the business community. Nonetheless, it is a rule which is concerned with the content of the agreement rather than its validity. Accordingly, as both Scrutton LJ and Maugham LJ recognised in that case, the contract may be rescinded if one party has been induced to enter into it by fraud or misrepresentation.

It would not take much imagination to consider how chaotic business would be if any party to a signed contract could subsequently contest any provision with which they happened to disagree.

Sussex

With victory in *L'Estrange v F Graucob Ltd* leading to a steady stream of well-paid instructions, Denning set about improving his home situation with Mary. In November 1934, he left the Temple and moved back to his old rooms in Chelsea while he searched for a house in the countryside. Unfortunately, Mary had to go into hospital for yet another operation. She was released a few days before Christmas. Initially, she went back to her parents in Southampton, but then Denning managed to find a small house for them to rent in Tylers Green, Sussex, between Cuckfield and Haywards Heath. It was inside the London commuter belt, with direct trains to Waterloo Station, and thus convenient for Denning to travel to work. It had the added advantage of being not far from Reg, who lived with his wife and two children in Haywards Heath.

The Dennings soon built a happy life in the village. They attended church regularly and built a new social network with their fellow worshippers. They hired a fifteen-year-old Welsh girl, Rose Drummer, to assist in the house. She would serve them for many years and become, in Denning's words, 'a real friend' – another instance of Denning not adopting all facets of the snobbery of the upper classes of his generation, who would not usually refer in such terms to below-stairs staff.

For the next four years, life steadily improved for Denning in all respects. In 1936, his practising fees for the year exceeded £3,000 for the first time,[17] and they continued to rise steadily for the rest of the decade. Even so, that did not place him in the first rank of earners at the Bar – that was the preserve of the Chancery specialists, some of whom earned as much as ten times Denning's income – but it certainly meant money was never a worry for him as it had been for Charles and Clara. Despite his burgeoning wealth, Denning never developed any expensive tastes beyond buying comfortable houses. He disdained materialism, as ever following the ethos and values of the church of his time along with Clara's moral strictures, had virtually no interest in alcohol and only liked simple 'English' food. Nor did he have any interest in collecting expensive consumer items such as art, cars or wine, or any other common acquisitions of wealthy individuals of his era.

In 1937, he became Chancellor of the Diocese of Southwark. The Chancellor acted as the independent judge of the Consistory Court, overseeing legal issues across the Diocese, particularly those relating to the use of and alterations to church buildings and land.[18] Denning held the post until he became a High Court judge in 1944. From 1942 to 1944 he also served as Chancellor of the Diocese of London.

Among his cases of the mid to late-1930s, Denning singled out the sad story of Major Rowlandson as especially memorable. In 1925, the Major had taken out life insurance policies with the Royal Insurance Company, totalling the then-astronomical sum of £50,000. Each policy provided that if the assured died by his own hand, 'whether sane or insane', within a year from the commencement of the assurance, the policy would be void, irrespective of who was claiming under it. In 1934 the Major's business ventures failed. As it had been many years since the assurance began, he assumed that Royal would pay out even if he took his own life. He negotiated an extension of time to pay the premium to 3:00 pm on 3 August 1934, then committed suicide by shooting himself at 2:57 pm that day.

Since, at the time, suicide – *felo de se* – was still a crime under English law, Royal refused to pay. The Major's niece, as executrix, instructed Denning, who was later led by Sir William Jowitt in proceedings that went all the way to the House of Lords.[19] Even though there was some sympathy from Swift J at first instance, who told the jury rhetorically in his summing up that it was 'the act of a gallant English gentleman, killing himself for the sake of his creditors', the claim failed. No sympathy was forthcoming in the Court of Appeal or the House of Lords. Instead, they followed the religious and moral teachings of the day, which held suicide to be a heinous crime. Although they had no doubt that under the terms of the contract Royal was bound to pay, they held that the contract was unenforceable due to public policy, because of suicide being such a serious crime in the eyes of the law.

Denning told the story in rather breathless tones in *The Family Story*, recounting how the Major had engineered his own death in the back of a taxi just before the time to pay the premium expired, thus ensuring that the driver would be witness to that potentially crucial fact. None of his colourful narrative appeared in the law reports, however, and one suspects his more vivid account might have owed something to him having retold the story many times in the intervening years at after dinner speeches and similar occasions.

King's Counsel

The substantial income he was now earning, and the restoration of Mary's health, emboldened Denning to seek promotion to King's Counsel (KC),[20] the senior rank of the Bar. At the time, the procedure entailed writing to the Lord Chancellor. He (it was always a 'he' in those days) would then consider views of the candidate's peers, so it was necessary to canvass others before applying to ensure the necessary support would be forthcoming. In January 1938, therefore, Denning wrote to a number of his friends and contacts testing the water. A raft of letters came back wishing him all the best, thereby confirming his decision to apply.

Denning had been cautious about applying earlier, for two reasons. First, although it was a promotion in terms of seniority, often new KCs' incomes would dip for a time because they would have to decline a lot of the junior work which had formerly been a staple of their practice (KCs did not draft pleadings and would not go into court unaccompanied). Secondly, a failed application was considered something of a black mark.

In the event, the new silks were announced on 1 April 1938, and Denning was thrilled to find his name among them. He received effusive congratulations in the form of more than 100 cards and letters in support, much as one might nowadays receive 'likes' or comments on social media posts, albeit more effort was involved in pre-digital communications.[21] A few commented that the date of the announcement, being April Fool's Day, was unfortunate for the unsuccessful candidates. More than a few predicted it would not be their last letter of congratulations: 'I feel quite sure', wrote a fellow barrister, BA Harwood of 2 Mitre Court, 'that it will not be many years before we cease to appear with you, and appear before you'.

Denning's reputation among solicitors was evident. One partner wrote to him:[22]

> I feel that my firm's telegram, although very sincere, is not enough for me. I wish personally to congratulate you on the honour which has been conferred upon you and to offer you my best wishes for your

future, which I believe is assured. Your success up to date has been remarkable and I am convinced that you are one of those, whose abilities and devotion to a noble profession carry their owners to great heights.

No 4 Brick Court should be proud of its present and former occupants!

Apart from the legal profession, Denning received a letter from the editor of *The Drapers' Record*,[23] which called itself 'The world's most influential trade newspaper':

Dear Mr Denning
May I most respectfully tender my hearty congratulations on your promotion to the 'front row of the stalls', which I noted in last night's paper? I hope also that briefs will be as numerous as before!

Denning wrote in *The Family Story* that he was short of work initially, as feared, but it seems his memory was somewhat confused, since his fee books show that his income actually increased that year. Any shortfall in instructions had obviously been compensated quickly by him being able to charge higher rates in keeping with his elevated position.

Despite his evident success, the consensus seems to have been that Denning was not in the first rank of counsel for his day. He was not renowned as a legendary cross-examiner or courtroom impresario in the manner of his near-contemporaries Sir Patrick Hastings or Lord Birkett, and as noted the leading Chancery silks earned substantially more than him. He was, however, developing a good reputation for his knowledge of law, through both his appellate cases and his work on *Smith's* and *Bullen & Leake*.

Robert

The best news of all for Denning came slightly before the KC announcements: Mary was pregnant. Their son was born on 3 August 1938. He was christened Robert Gordon – the middle name obviously a reference to Denning's cherished older brother lost in the First World War. 'Caesarean section at 9:30' recorded Mary in her diary, as though writing a headnote for a law report, but she then added 'All went off admirably and we have a lovely little son. God bless him'. As was normal at the time for the upper middle classes, Mary had a maternity nurse who assisted her at home for a month after the birth before handing everything over to her and Rose Drummer.

1930s – From First Marriage to the Second World War

The gathering storm

The year 1938 had been the happiest of Denning's life, with the birth of Robert by far the first and foremost factor, allied with his continuing domestic bliss with Mary and his promotion and continued success at the Bar. About the only hiccup in his personal life was the pipes in his house bursting a few days before Christmas and flooding the hall, but he was wealthy enough and sufficiently contented in his domestic life that such incidents could be brushed aside as mere inconveniences.

In the world around him, things seemed to be improving as well. Most notably, at the end of September, Britain celebrated as the Prime Minister, Neville Chamberlain, returned from Munich with a piece of paper signed by Adolf Hitler, supposedly guaranteeing peace between Britain and Germany. Less than a year later, however, as no reader will need reminding, Chamberlain had to tell the House of Commons that 'no such undertaking' as sought had been received concerning the withdrawal of German troops from Poland and the country was therefore at war with Germany. It was a conflict which Denning would survive, but not without personal tragedy which, ironically, was unrelated to hostilities.[24]

CHAPTER V

The Second World War

Men of duty

Between the wars, there had been much public discussion in Britain about previously unquestioned notions of patriotism, duty and the justification for war, the ideas that led to the national rush to enlist in the First World War. After that disastrous conflict had ended – the 'war to end all wars' as it was forlornly hoped – the same values largely continued to hold sway officially, but competing ideas started to gain currency as well.

One diametrically opposed philosophy which rose in popularity in the inter-war period was pacifism. In 1933, the Oxford Union famously debated 'This House will under no circumstances fight for its King and country'.[1] The motion was passed 275 votes for versus 153 against, much to the disgust of the rebarbative backbencher Winston Churchill.[2]

A second counter to unquestioning patriotism was the simple point that few people, if any, wanted a reprise of the horrors of 1914–18. Amongst much of the general population, any glory associated with war rang hollow when one considered how many husbands, fathers, sons and brothers had been lost in those terrible years, reduced to little more than names on village walls and monuments.

There was a further disincentive: fascism as found in Italy, Germany and Spain provided a bulwark against communism. At least since 1917, the aristocracy and the privileged in general across Western Europe had been regarding the threat of Bolshevism with anxious eyes. One more malevolent factor was at play: various prominent public figures were less than critical of fascism's tenets, from the cricketer CB Fry to the former Prime Minister David Lloyd George.[3] Then again, fascism itself never became more than a small but noisome minority in British politics during Denning's lifetime, even when it dominated some other European countries: no British MP in the twentieth century was ever elected on a fascist platform. The ideology's most well-known British exponent, Oswald Mosley, was originally a Conservative and was elected as a Labour MP before leaving the Party and forming his own.[4]

It is therefore unsurprising that there was little popular or elite support in the early 1930s for confronting the triple threats composed of the rise of German expansionism, Mussolini's efforts to recreate the Roman Empire in the Mediterranean and Africa, and Japanese imperialism in the Far East. Instead, the official British government policy for most of the decade was appeasement: 'feeding the crocodile in the hope he will eat you last' to paraphrase Churchill, or 'peace at any price that others can be forced to pay'[5] as Lady Violet Bonham-Carter said when mocking Chamberlain. The change from Britain's stance towards European affairs in 1914 was clear. In 1914, Germany's threat to neutral Belgium had caused public outrage in Britain. In 1938, Chamberlain's blatant capitulation over Germany's threat to Czechoslovakia had the opposite reaction, receiving much (though not unanimous) popular support as it was thought to have averted war.

All that was reflected in the much more sombre national tone following the war's outbreak. Chamberlain himself said dejectedly 'You can imagine what a bitter blow it is to me that all my long struggle to win peace has failed'.[6] Outside, once again in contrast to the public mood when the First World War began, there were no bands playing, flags flying, lofty predictions of it all being over by Christmas, or white feathers for the refuseniks. Instead, 'Just the eternal questionnaire – name, age, address, married or single, educational qualifications, religion, any record of VD ...'.[7]

In stark contrast with that dilution in the overall public mood, the Denning family themselves had not changed at all from the stoic patriots who had served so willingly and unflinchingly in the First World War. Reg and Norman would each go on to perform vital roles in the army and navy respectively as senior officers working in military intelligence,[8] rather than the junior officers which all the older brothers had been in the First World War. Denning himself did not rejoin the forces but instead undertook a role suited to his position as a respected barrister, which would coincidentally place him as a bit-part player in one of the great legal controversies of the day.

'In any capacity'

In 1939 Denning himself was past the usual age of a combat soldier, but stepped forward once more to serve his country, offering himself 'in any capacity'. Part of Britain's long-standing preparation for war was a plan for the division of the country into administrative zones which could be self-governing in the event of any part of the country being successfully captured by the enemy. Each region had a Regional Commissioner with a staff including a legal adviser. The latter position was unpaid apart from expenses. Denning was appointed legal adviser to the North-East region. He graphically recalled the grimness of the time in *The Family Story*, writing of train journeys taking three times longer than usual, with bombs landing on London as he tried to travel from home to Leeds, the headquarters of his region.[9]

Regulation 18B

Along with the planned division of the country into self-governing regions, another contingent legal mechanism prepared between the wars was the Defence Regulations, intended to allow the detention of suspected traitors or spies in the event of another major war. Several drafts were prepared, and the final version was brought into force just before Britain's declaration of war in September 1939.[10] Regulation 18B was aimed at the detention of British nationals. It provided, *inter alia*:

> (1) If the Secretary of State has reasonable cause to believe any person to be of hostile origin or associations or to have been recently concerned in acts prejudicial to the public safety or the defence of the realm or in the preparation or instigation of such acts and that by reason thereof it is necessary to exercise control over him, he may make an order against that person directing that he be detained.

Much of Denning's work as the legal adviser to the North-East concerned authorising the detention of suspects under regulation 18B. He carried out the work in his usual diligent fashion, questioning suspects inquisitorially and recommending either detention or release. One suspect he rather tendentiously dubbed 'the Nazi Parson' was a local clergyman who had taken holidays in Germany. The man was suspected of preparing to assist expected German parachutists or otherwise trying to aid the enemy war effort.

Famously – or, rather, infamously – regulation 18B became the subject of one of the best-known British cases of the twentieth century, *Liversidge v Anderson* [1942] AC 206.[11] A majority of the House of Lords held that it was for the Secretary of State himself to decide what was 'reasonable' cause, not for a court. There was accordingly no legal recourse for anyone unfortunate enough to be detained under regulation 18B.[12] Lord Atkin dissented, and wrote himself into legal history with the following passage, quoted countless times since including by Denning himself:[13]

> In England, amidst the clash of arms, the laws are not silent. They may be changed, but they speak the same language in war as in peace. It has always been one of the pillars of freedom, one of the principles of liberty for which on recent authority we are now fighting, that the judges are no respecters of persons, and stand between the subject and any attempted encroachments on his liberty by the executive, alert to see that any coercive action is justified in law. ...
>
> I know of only one authority which might justify the suggested method of construction. 'When I use a word', Humpty Dumpty said, in rather a scornful tone, 'it means just what I choose it to mean, neither more nor less'. 'The question is', said Alice, 'whether you can make words mean so many different things'. 'The question is', said Humpty Dumpty, 'which is to be the master, that's all'. After all this long discussion the question is whether the words 'If a man has' can mean 'If a man thinks he has'. I have an opinion that they cannot and the case should be decided accordingly.

This brings us to another classic Denning contradiction. He enthusiastically participated in the detention of suspects in accordance with the decision of the House of Lords that they had no right of challenge. He recounted the work without a trace of regret in *The Family Story* and maintained in *The Closing Chapter* that *Liversidge* had been correctly decided. Yet, in the former book, after quoting Lord Atkin's dissent, he called it a judgment 'after my own heart'. Why did the legendary dissenter and defender of the meek against the powerful participate in an exercise of power by the state so in breach of the common law tradition represented (symbolically at least) by Magna Carta, that no one should be imprisoned without the lawful judgment of his or her peers?

It is true that Denning was not in any position to oppose regulation 18B. If he had tried, he would have been removed from his post and replaced by a more compliant barrister. That, however, seems a much weaker moral stance, and in any event he never made any such argument himself.

The correct explanation, which also applies to some of the other apparent Denning contradictions we will come to later in the book, is that the unshakeable patriot and former soldier considered that the interests of the nation's survival in wartime required temporary and limited suspension of the rule of law and basic liberties. Denning himself said as much on numerous occasions.[14] His reasoning was reminiscent of the theme of one of the great wartime films, *The Life and Death of Colonel Blimp*, in which the titular character was confronted by the reality that there was no point in maintaining the highest standards of civilised behaviour in the face of an unmitigated evil if it meant that evil would thereby triumph.

Ironically, by the time Denning wrote *The Family Story*, the weight of academic opinion had become firmly in favour of Lord Atkin's dissent[15] and, more importantly, the courts themselves had effectively buried the majority's decision.[16] He was therefore dissenting by supporting the majority.

From a safe distance in the twenty-first century, it seems clear there never was any realistic chance of the Germans crossing the Channel in numbers. But that information was not available in the desperate times of 1940–41. In those dark days, the British Empire and associated Dominions stood alone[17] and had been humiliated by the German Army in land battles on the Continent and in North Africa. At the time the *Liversidge* case was being argued before the Lords, the Germans seemed to have the upper hand in their invasion of the Soviet Union, while the United States was remaining ostensibly neutral (though providing assistance to the Allies by way of Lend-Lease). Ultimately, both the extraordinary blood sacrifice of the Soviets and the unparalleled industrial power of the United States were critical to the defeat of Nazi Germany (without in any way denigrating the contribution of the British Empire and Dominions); neither factor was evident at the time of *Liversidge*.

Similar arguments to those considered in *Liversidge* arose during the Irish Troubles in the 1970s. Internment in that later conflict has generally been regarded as a failure, partly because the IRA was never in a position to threaten the life of the British state in the way that Nazi Germany did, and partly because internment undermined the British claim for moral, legal and ethical superiority over the IRA. If anything, it served as an IRA recruiting tool.

The question of liberty versus security also arose in the early twenty-first century with the rise of fundamentalist Islamic terrorism, where some individuals were suspected of intending to commit mass murder on a scale hitherto not imagined in peacetime. At the time of writing, nothing approximating regulation 18B had been created,[18] though some saw some parallels between Lord Atkin's quote about the judges who 'show themselves more executive minded than the executive' and the Supreme Court's decision in R *(Begum) v Special Immigration Appeals Commission* [2021] UKSC 7.[19]

The assumption in most academic writing is that any future *Liversidge* case would follow Lord Atkin's approach and not that of the majority. That, however, assumes there will be no circumstances under which the life of the nation itself will be imperilled. If, for example, some terrorists (of whatever stripe) were known to possess some lethal biological weapon, it is not inconceivable that detention without trial might be authorised by Parliament as an emergency measure and supported by the courts until the danger was removed.

As a sidenote, the most severe restrictions on liberty in Britain's peacetime history were introduced while this chapter was first being drafted, with reams of Covid-19-related regulations confining the country to a near-complete lockdown. If nothing else, one thing could be said in favour of the Second World War Defence Regulations that did not apply in 2020: the state had tried to prepare properly for another war after 1918 by having draft regulations on the books ready to be implemented in case of emergency. That allowed much time for lawyers to debate and discuss how those regulations should be drafted and how they might work in practice. In 2020, on the other hand, despite the possibility of a pandemic having been known for many decades (or centuries for that matter), nothing like a comprehensive set of draft lockdown regulations existed. That lacuna was a straight indictment of politicians, their legal advisers, academics and public lawyers in general. At least their 1918–39 predecessors had tried to do the right thing by preparing for a known risk.

Life during wartime

As well as his work as the legal adviser to the North-East region, Denning maintained his barristerial practice throughout the war as and when he was able. The courts always remained open in some form, relocating to underground facilities and otherwise safer locations when air raids were threatened. At a particularly significant moment in the war, during the evacuation of British and French forces from Dunkirk in late May and early June 1940, Denning happened to be appearing before the House of Lords in *United Australia v Barclays Bank* [1941] AC 1. In his judgment in that case, Lord Atkin once again turned a memorable phrase: 'When these ghosts of the past stand in the path of justice clanking their mediaeval chains the proper course of the Judge is to pass through them undeterred' – a quote and a philosophy which Denning himself would adopt with vigour when he became a judge.

In both *United Australia* and another reported case during wartime, *Gold v Essex County Council* [1942] 2 KB 293, Denning acted *pro bono*, there being no legal aid at the time – indicating that money was not his prime concern and that, away from defending the country against suspected traitors, he was still bent on enforcing the rule of law and combatting injustice where he saw it.

Another of Denning's important wartime cases was acting as lead counsel for the respondent in *Hoani Te Heuheu Tukino v Aotea District Maori Land Board* [1941] AC 308, a Privy Council appeal from New Zealand. One issue in the case was whether an Act of the New Zealand Parliament was *ultra vires* because it was inconsistent with the rights conferred upon Maori by the Treaty of Waitangi 1840. The appeal was dismissed, the Board holding that a statute which had been duly enacted by Parliament could not be questioned by the courts.[20] The case was of constitutional significance for New Zealand, affirming the legal narrative that held sway in that country for more than a century, which held that the Treaty of Waitangi had no force in law save to the extent that it was incorporated by statute. That situation only began to change in the 1980s, leading to a succession of cases and legislation which contributed to the Treaty becoming part of the fabric of New Zealand society.[21]

Away from his legal work, an important event in Denning's life took place early in 1940 when he and Mary managed to find a suitable house for sale in Sussex. It was a five-bedroom detached house in Copyhold Lane, about halfway between Cuckfield and Haywards Heath. It had been built in the 1930s, so was comparatively modern. It was large enough for Denning to accommodate the family with ease and furnish himself a substantial private library. It came with two acres of land and Denning later purchased an adjoining twelve acres. The cost of the initial purchase was between £3,000 and £4,000 – a fraction of the house's present-day worth in comparative terms, indicating a radically different housing market at the time.[22] Denning was able to buy with no mortgage, as would be the case for all his subsequent property dealings.

The house was called 'Monandale', but the Dennings did not like the name. They changed it to 'Fair Close', recalling the mediaeval fairs which strongly appealed to Denning's sense of rural English history. That affection was evident in the case of *Wyld v Silver* [1962] 3 All ER 309, which Denning heard as Master of the Rolls and where, as will be seen in Chapter X, he rather allowed his love of the imagery of mediaeval rural England to blind him to the plight of a blameless litigant.

The Dennings lived through the Blitz of 1940 with the same terror of nightly bombing as so many others. Although Sussex itself was not on the German target list, it was on or near the flight path for the Luftwaffe attacking London. If the bombers could not find their target, or were disrupted by British defences, they would often drop their weapons wherever they happened to be, killing numerous unfortunate civilians. The Denning family sheltered under the stairs while raids were under way, harbouring few illusions about how much safety they were thereby afforded. Their house was never hit directly, though one blast was sufficiently close to knock the front door open, fortunately causing no further damage.

The year ended with Denning in hospital with meningitis. He was able to return home on New Year's Day 1941 but was compelled to rest for another ten days. He then received quite a memorable wartime brief from his old housemate Anthony Moir. The Prime Minister, Winston Churchill, was always one with a correctly high regard for his own literary and oratory skills (he would later receive the Nobel Prize for Literature) and an incorrectly low regard for living within his means.[23] Churchill wanted to know if he might retain the copyright in his parliamentary speeches, and instructed Fladgates who in turn retained Denning. Denning's advice is not recorded, though it would presumably have been in the negative, since Churchill did not earn royalties from his speeches and continued to have money worries intermittently as he had throughout most of his life. Denning later said wryly that he did not receive any royalties from his own best-seller, the Profumo report (it being subject to Crown copyright), though as someone with a steadier income, far less extravagant tastes, and much more disciplined home management, he never had anything resembling Churchill's financial troubles once his legal career was properly under way.

Those interesting instructions aside, 1941 would sadly prove to be the worst year of Denning's life. In February, Charles became ill. Denning rushed back to Whitchurch. Charles died shortly afterwards, aged eighty-one. Clara, according to Mary's diary, was 'splendid' at the funeral, but her stoicism was shaken. She wrote plaintively to the children expressing her wish that Marjorie might return and care for her, and despaired 'I feel so helpless and not much good to any of you only an expense, but I trust I will be able to leave something to help pay you back some of what you have done for me'.[24] Clara continued to receive financial support from all her children, and was able to stay with each of them for a time, but Marjorie and Johnny did not return to Whitchurch permanently until after the war.

Ominously, Mary's health started failing in May 1941. She seemed to recover but fell ill again in September, when she was admitted to hospital after being diagnosed with gallstones. By mid-October she had recovered sufficiently to return home, but it was a false dawn. She caught a cold in early November. One evening while Denning was working downstairs, he heard her fall to the floor. He rushed upstairs to find her coughing blood. Denning did all he could to assist. The doctor was called and oxygen cylinders were provided to aid Mary's breathing over the next few days. When they finally managed to take her to the hospital – no easy feat during wartime, with so much pressure on the emergency services – Denning accompanied her and remained by her side during the night. But nothing could be done. Mary died in the morning of 22 November 1941.[25]

Denning was utterly devastated. He maintained for the rest of his life that the strength of feeling had never left him. With Robert to provide for, though, he carried on working as hard as ever. The domestic help meant that he did not have to do it all on his own at home, though earlier in the year he had also lost the support of Rose Drummer, who had joined the Women's Royal Naval Service (known as the 'Wrens'). He and Mary had managed to find a replacement in the form of her old nanny, whilst they also had a gardener to assist them with their substantial plot.

Wartime was taking its toll in other respects since Denning's income from the Bar fell to its lowest level since 1936. In 1940 he had earned £3,230, but in 1941 that figure fell to £2,350. In fairness it still left him far better off than most in the country, even if the privations of wartime left little on which to spend it. A second positive development was his short but significant first judicial experience. He was temporarily appointed deputy recorder in Southampton after the incumbent had retired, until they managed to find a permanent replacement.

The strain which wartime placed on combatants and civilians alike could be observed in some of the cases in which Denning was instructed. In July 1942, he successfully defended a sailor on a charge of murdering his wife. The jury found the defendant guilty only of manslaughter, thus sparing him the death penalty. Denning had put the case for provocation to the jury, despite there being no evidence of it whatsoever. He inferred that the sailor might have suffered combat stress or shell-shock from having had a ship torpedoed under him three times. The judge was apoplectic, railing against the jury that they had disobeyed their oath, and pointing out that others whose ships had been torpedoed had not gone on to murder their spouses. Yet Denning felt wholly justified in *The Family Story*. It seems that, as a returned serviceman himself, Denning held a degree of sympathy for, and empathy with, other veterans and anyone else who had suffered during wartime.

Denning carried on through 1942, caring for Robert as best he could, tending Mary's grave and continuing to work as fully as he was able. In September 1943, he gave a speech on the BBC Home Service in which he explained the faith that not simply sustained him through difficulties but would later guide him on a daily basis as a judge:[26]

> My belief in God is due in part to my upbringing – to what I have been taught – and in part to what I have found out in going through life ... The aim of the law is to see that truth is observed and that justice is done between man and man ... But what is truth and what is justice? On those two cardinal questions religion and law meet. The spirit of truth and justice is not something you can see. It is not temporal but eternal. How does man know what is truth or justice? It is not the product of his intellect, but of his spirit ...
>
> How, then, is the right spirit created in man? ... Religion, or rather the Christian religion, is concerned with the creation of a spirit out of which right acts will naturally flow ... the law has been moulded for centuries by Judges who have been brought up in the Christian faith. The precepts of religion, consciously or unconsciously, have been their guide in the administration of justice.

The next significant event in his life and career came in December 1943, when he was made Commissioner of Assize in Manchester. It was usual at the time for the appointment to be an unofficial trial run for promotion to the High Court, and so it proved: Denning performed the role to the acclaim of all those he encountered[27] and, even though it had only been a three-week stint, the Lord Chancellor took note. In February 1944, Denning was appointed Recorder of Plymouth – a part time role – but there were bigger plans for him afoot.

To the Bench

By the start of 1944, Britain had been at war for more than four years. Hundreds of thousands of servicemen and women were away from home: all of the forces had been continuously deployed since the start of the war, and while the bulk of those in army uniform were still stationed in Britain, a number were either in the Far East or involved in the Mediterranean campaign, the latter being the only theatre where the British Army could engage the European Axis powers on the ground on any sort of scale before D-Day. In turn, hundreds of thousands of American servicemen were arriving in Britain in preparation for the invasion of German-occupied France. Tens of thousands of them would marry British women, while an uncountable number would have liaisons of a shorter nature. It was once said of American soldiers that they were 'overpaid, oversexed and over here', to which one wit responded that British soldiers were 'underpaid, undersexed and under Eisenhower'. In those circumstances, it was unsurprising that the courts in Britain were kept in business throughout the dark years of 1939–45 dealing with divorce and matrimonial property matters.

In early 1944, three positions became available on the Bench in the Probate, Divorce and Admiralty Division, known colloquially as 'wills, wives and wrecks'.[28] Although there were many divorce practitioners at the Bar, only one of the three vacant positions was filled by a specialist in the area, Harry Barnard. Of the other two appointments, Hubert Wallington had a civil practice in the King's Bench Division, while the third was Denning himself. Aged forty-five, he became the youngest judge in the High Court or above for 150 years. His salary was £5,000 per annum, another indication that he had not been in the first rank of earners among barristers, since the most successful KCs then as now earned much more than any judicial salary.

Perhaps owing to wartime exigencies, his appointment seems to have been of a rather hurried nature. He was appearing in an appeal before the House of Lords in early March. On 6 March, at the conclusion of his argument, the Lord Chancellor asked him to come to his chambers, where he offered him the post – an example of the then-customary 'tap on the shoulder' by which judicial appointments were made. The role was announced the next day and Denning was sworn in, all before the end of his case before the Lords.

No sooner had the modest swearing-in ceremony concluded than all three of the new judges started work, hastily reassigned from the backlog of the existing list. A week or so later, Denning went to Buckingham Palace to receive the customary knighthood granted to High Court judges. George VI was under some strain with wartime duties and thus, understandably, their conversation was brief and stilted.[29]

In spite of its apparently rushed nature, Denning's appointment was praised by the legal press. The *Law Times* predicted that 'his elevation to the High Court Bench at this unusually early age would seem to presage a long and outstanding career of public usefulness'.[30]

Denning also received more than 300 personal letters offering congratulations. Many mentioned his young age, whilst others showed the snobbery then prevalent in the profession towards less glamorous (and less remunerative) areas of law. Lord Greene MR, for example, wrote that he hoped Denning would soon be 'freed from divorce and put to work more worthy of you', while other correspondents referred to the appointment as a mere 'stepping stone'.[31] More positively, the barrister Guy Aldous wrote that 'pleasure is tempered with some awe at the thought that one day one might have to argue a bad point of law before you – with no chance of getting away with it. However, it can only be to the benefit of the law generally that the greatest lawyers be appointed to the bench'.[32]

Marjorie wrote from Whitchurch:[33]

> For the last 2 or 3 weeks Whitchurch has been ringing with your name & everyone is so proud of you.
> What would my dear old people have said, but they always thought something of the sort would happen to you.

Denning's increased happiness from his judicial appointment was tempered by the beginning of the 'Second Blitz', also in 1944, after some respite from German bombing in the mid-war years. The new threat came from 'doodle-bug' V1 flying bombs, and V2 rockets. Again, Denning's home in Sussex was not the intended target, but he still came under danger from any that fell short. He recalled nearby explosions of V1s and seeing the air defences try to counter them. (There was no defence to the V2, which was too fast for contemporary weapons to intercept it.)

As the tide of the war turned inexorably in favour of the Allies, Denning witnessed some of the massive weight of machinery being directed at Germany, including the bombers and airborne troop transports *en route* to the Continent. He mentioned in later writings being present at or witnessing various well-known events such as seeing aircraft on their way to Arnhem, the ill-fated Allied attempt to finish the war in 1944 later depicted in the film *A Bridge Too Far*. Whether he was accurate in matching his memories to the events is of no particular importance. There is no doubt he lived through and experienced the war on the Home Front, with the terror of bombing, the fears for family and friends in service, the material shortages and the overarching concern that a reversal at any point in the nation's fortunes could lead to the destruction of the country and the way of life he cherished. His garden afforded some mild respite from rationing, and he remained as phlegmatic as ever in adversity: 'We kept bees for honey. We kept chickens for eggs. We had no car. We went without. We won through'.[34] And that stoicism reinforced the strong sense of patriotism Denning had always displayed: later in life he would quote Churchill and Shakespeare in support of British wartime spirit.[35]

On the work front, Denning's time in the divorce courts lasted until after the conclusion of the war. We will now turn to consider his experience there in more detail.

CHAPTER VI

Judicial Beginnings – Wills, Wives and Wrecks

> The only basis for a sound family life is a Christian marriage.
> *Lord Denning, The Due Process of Law*

'Sordid in the extreme'

Denning started work on the Bench hearing divorce cases more or less immediately upon being appointed. Although his unceasing sense of duty meant he did his best in the role, his resolute Christian values led him to react with considerable distaste towards the work he found himself doing. Looking back in *The Due Process of Law*, he recalled:[1]

> I disliked the divorce work. It was sordid in the extreme. Everything depended on proof of a matrimonial offence – adultery, cruelty or desertion. Horrid details were the daily menu. In undefended cases the chambermaid would give evidence that, when she took up the early morning tea, the couple were there in bed. 'Was this the man?' asks counsel, showing a photograph of the husband. 'Yes, sir'. 'Was this the woman?', showing a photograph of the wife. 'No, sir'. In one contested case the husband said he had got infected with venereal disease from a lavatory seat. I did not believe him. In another, the wife denied there were stains on the sheet. I did not believe her. The sordidness was relieved when noble families were involved. Sir Patrick Hastings on one side, the most devastating cross-examiner ever. Gilbert Beyfus on the other – compelling by his choice of words and a strange twitch on his face.

One might find it curious why Denning felt 'the sordidness was relieved' when the nobility were involved, especially as he wrote that passage many years after professing great shock at the goings-on of the section of supposedly high society involved in the Profumo Affair. Presumably, he was referring to the fact that better counsel were involved, such as Hastings and Beyfus, whose brilliant advocacy made the lurid details easier on the ear. Or possibly there was an uncharacteristic (though not wholly unknown) touch of snobbery from Denning.

Still, whatever his personal feelings towards matrimonial litigants of any stripe, Denning tried to reform the law where he could in order to minimise the impact of divorce cases upon all concerned, especially children. Further, his Christian-based objections did not extend to a fundamental opposition to divorce, unlike his fellow judge Wallington, a devout Roman Catholic who Denning suspected allowed his faith to affect his judgments.[2]

As was common practice at the time, nearly all of Denning's judgments were delivered *ex tempore*,[3] that is, orally rather than in written form. During his first year he always gave judgment immediately following the conclusion of arguments rather than taking time to prepare (known as 'reserving judgment' and indicated in law reports by the Latin abbreviation '*cur ad vult*' – short for '*curia advisari vult*' or 'the court took time to consider'). 'But when I gained confidence I started to put principles into writing'[4] he later recorded.

Smith v Smith – future needs

His first reported judgment was *Smith v Smith* [1945] 61 TLR 331. As was typical for the time, it was particularly short compared with modern judgments. The parties had married in 1929 and later bought a house in their joint names. They lived in it as their home and brought up their three children there. In October 1943 the husband petitioned for divorce and in August 1944 he obtained a decree absolute. The wife remained in the house, against the husband's wishes. The issue was whether the husband was correct that the house was the subject of a 'post-nuptial settlement' within s 192 of the Supreme Court of Judicature (Consolidation) Act 1925. Denning stated:

> The conveyance expressly defined the interests of husband and wife in much the same way as would otherwise be imported by statute from the fact that it was taken in their joint names. The house was expressly conveyed to the husband and wife 'in fee simple as joint tenants,' and it was expressly stated that they were to stand possessed

of it 'upon trust to sell the same with power of discretion to postpone any sale' and to stand possessed 'of the net proceeds of sale' and 'of the net rents and profits until sale in trust for the husband and wife as joint tenants beneficially.' The result was that the husband and wife held a joint tenancy of the legal estate in the land (which could not be severed) and an equitable joint tenancy in the income of the land pending sale and of the proceeds eventually arising from the sale (which could be severed by taking appropriate steps). The presumption is that the interest of the wife was intended by the husband as an advancement by him. So long as husband and wife were living together in the house, they, of course, shared the occupation and acquiesced in a postponement of sale, and if they had continued in that way till one died, the survivor would take the whole legal and beneficial interest in it. If they together let or sold the house, either of them could sever the equitable joint tenancy in the income or proceeds whereupon each would be entitled to one-half. No letting or sale could, however, be effected by one without the consent of the other, except by order of the Court of Chancery, which would consider whether in the particular circumstances it was right and proper that such an order should be made. Neither party has yet applied for such an order.

Denning identified the relevant principle as:

> where a husband makes a continuing provision for the future needs of his wife in her character as a wife, which is still continuing when the marriage is dissolved, the provision is a 'settlement' which can be brought before the court to see whether the provision should continue now that she has ceased to be a wife. The same applies to a provision by a wife for her husband or by each or either for both.

He disposed of the case thus:

> ... the appropriate method, if the husband makes out a claim on the merits, would be to vary the deed by leaving the legal estate as it is, deleting the existing trust and substituting a trust for the husband absolutely and to order the wife to deliver possession to him. The wife has, however, not yet been heard on the merits, and the case must go back to the registrar for the purpose.

Denning subsequently drew upon the research involved in the case for an article in the *Law Quarterly Review*.[5] Upon receiving a draft of the article, the editor remarked that Denning should have referred to more authorities. Denning responded in customary fashion by adding the following paragraph:[6]

> The reader will have noticed that the illustrations in this article are all taken from familiar cases, but I have not given the references to many of them. This is because I am concerned here, not with particular branches of law, but with a new set of distinctions running through the whole law, in an attempt to remove the confusion produced by the old.

That paragraph contained an interesting insight into Denning's thinking – he was interested in broad principle, not technocratic interpretations of previous authority.

Churchman v Churchman – a love triangle

A few years later, some doubt was cast upon his decision in *Smith v Smith*,[7] but during the actual time he served in the divorce courts he was overturned on appeal only once, in *Churchman v Churchman* [1945] P 44.[8] The facts were redolent of a different age, involving rather complicated dealings in a love triangle. The husband and wife were married in December 1940, prior to which the wife had been the mistress of the co-respondent. In February 1941, the wife left the marriage and went to live with the co-respondent. The husband tried unsuccessfully to persuade her to return to him. He then set about negotiating with the co-respondent for damages, with a formal offer in May 1942 to divorce his wife upon payment of a sum of money. No bargain was ultimately concluded and so, in December 1943, the husband filed a petition against his wife and the co-respondent seeking £1,500 damages and a dissolution of the marriage on the ground of adultery.

Denning held that, in the circumstances, the presentation of the petition had not been tainted by collusion (a reference to the earlier negotiation between the two men). But he went on to hold that the husband had acquiesced in the continuance of the wife's adultery from February 1942 onwards, and that such connivance constituted a bar to the relief sought. In so holding, Denning did not deal expressly with the question whether he regarded the connivance at the continuance of the adultery as amounting by ratification to connivance of the earlier adultery. The husband appealed.

In allowing the appeal, the Court of Appeal held that the husband's attempt to make a collusive bargain for damages in respect of an admitted wrong could not be held to have effected a notional conversion of what was in fact strenuous objection on his part to the early stages of the adulterous association into connivance at any stage of the association, whether past or future.

One suspects that Denning's decision was motivated by his abhorrence of anything short of total commitment to Christian marriage, which was reflected in his implicit condemnation of the husband's attempt to strike a bargain with the adulterer. Nonetheless, the fact that the case was the only time in that period that Denning was overturned provided further evidence that his disdain for the subject matter did not preclude him from mastering it. It was true that the cost of proceedings would have militated against anyone attempting an appeal in a matrimonial property dispute whatever the merits of their case, which would have been less likely in large commercial cases. Equally, though, the lack of successful appeals against Denning could be read as an indication of how widely his views were shared amongst the judiciary of the time – something further evidenced by the fact that he sat in the Court of Appeal for six years before he dissented in a family case.[9]

Fletcher v Fletcher – sex and religion

The facts of *Fletcher v Fletcher* [1945] 1 All ER 582 were also somewhat unusual, for any time period. The husband became involved in a religious sect known as the 'Tramp Preachers', and at some point decided that the teachings of the sect compelled him not to engage in sexual intercourse with his wife, even though they were married. The wife tried to support his faith but ultimately decided that life in a closed and celibate religious sect was not for her. She petitioned for divorce on the ground of desertion.

Denning, with strong religious convictions of his own, had some sympathy for the husband's faith, and perhaps was relieved by the facts being the opposite of sordidness for once, but at the same time was realistic about how it would have affected the wife:

> This community is worthy of much admiration: but it is a community which lives, so to speak, continuously in retreat from the world; it is a community which lives a very special kind of life, a life of service of each to all, and although, no doubt, it is very satisfying to those who feel called to that kind of life, it is not the kind of life in which everybody can be expected to join. It needs a strong religious conviction on those particular lines, for it involves every aspect of the individual's life. It seems to me that for a husband to expect his wife to go and live in that community unless she feels called to do so, is

unreasonable. Even if she is only asked to live near the community and not actually inside it, that is, I think, still unreasonable because the husband himself is part and parcel of the community, where everything is in common; and the wife, if she went there not as a member of the community, would, I am satisfied, be living on her own altogether from all mental and psychological aspects.

He went on to find that the husband's conduct had indeed amounted to desertion, and granted the decree nisi accordingly.

Committee work

In October 1945, much to his relief, Denning was transferred from the Probate, Divorce and Admiralty Division to the King's Bench Division, which dealt with ordinary civil claims. He had plainly made a good impression with his divorce work, since in June 1946 he was asked by the Lord Chancellor to chair a committee on the administration of the law on divorce. It was the start of a period of time in which it was very common for senior judges to be asked to chair Royal Commissions and Departmental Committees.[10]

Denning and his colleagues on the committee[11] were all suffused with the tradition of service and did not seek any time away from their normal duties. Instead, they met after hours and approached their task with diligence, giving their first interim report in July 1946, only a month after their appointment. The report recommended reducing the period between decree nisi and decree absolute from six months to six weeks.

Their second interim report, delivered in November 1946, recommended that divorce cases should no longer be heard by High Court judges, but instead by county court judges sitting as commissioners, and suggested other reforms to bring down the cost of divorce.

Their third and final report was published in February 1947. It recommended a Marriage Welfare Service to provide help and guidance in preparation for marriage and in difficulties after marriages. It also recommended that welfare officers should be appointed to the courts, particularly to assist children.

All the recommendations in the three reports were accepted, which Denning later noted with satisfaction was not usual for reform committees, either at the time or since. The positive reception to the work also led to him being invited to become President of the Marriage Guidance Council, a charity which provided relationship support including counselling for couples, families, young people and individuals. Many years later it changed its name to Relate, by which it is still known today.[12]

More of Denning's work in family law will be seen later in the book. For now, we will return to the chronology by considering his tenure in the King's Bench Division and the other developments in his life which took place around the same time.

CHAPTER VII

1945–47 – Second Marriage; Second Judicial Role

Joan

Denning's new judicial role in the King's Bench Division was one of three significant developments for him in 1945. The second was the ending of the Second World War. The third was his marriage in December to Joan Stuart, a widow with two daughters and one son.

Marriage to Joan was the only way Denning could begin to lift himself from the personal depths into which he had sunk after Mary's death. The continuing pain of Mary's loss had rendered the VE Day celebrations rather mute for Denning: 'I had no heart for them',[1] he bleakly recorded.

Like Mary, Joan was born in 1900 and was the daughter of a clergyman, though in her life before meeting Denning she had been somewhat more worldly than him or Mary. In her late teens, following the First World War, she had been sent to France to learn the language, after which she attended the Guildhall School of Music and Drama to study elocution and voice production. She met her first husband, Jack Stuart, in 1922 in Rangoon. She had travelled there to escort her niece. Her sister and her husband, another clergyman, had already been posted there and had wanted to set up home before sending for their daughter.

Joan and Jack married in 1923 and had three surviving children: Pauline (born 1924), Hazel (born 1928) and John (born 1932); a fourth child, Patrick (born 1938), died in infancy. At some point after they were married, Jack left the army to pursue a career as a civil engineer. He and Joan set up a family home in Haywards Heath, Sussex, though Jack worked abroad in the Middle and Near East for a consultancy firm. He was not recalled to the forces during the war, but in 1942 he died suddenly from a heart attack.

Joan was left in a difficult financial position. She had enough to keep the home and to put food on the table, but to help make ends meet she took a job as an editor which required her to travel to London three times a week. It made for a demanding schedule when combined with her family duties. Pauline was about to start training as a teacher at the Royal Central School of Speech and Drama, then based in the Royal Albert Hall. Hazel was attending the famous Sussex girls' school, Roedean (temporarily based in the North due to wartime exigencies), while John was attending Parkfield School in Sussex with Denning's son Robert.

It was at Parkfield School where Joan and Denning met in September 1945, not long after VJ Day. Denning said of the occasion '[i]nstinctively we fell in love at first sight. Not in the headlong heedless way of youth. But in the deep sincere affection of maturity'.[2] They were engaged in under a month and intended to marry before the end of the year.

One might suspect from his fervent belief in the importance of a traditional home life, with housekeeping the exclusive preserve of women, that Denning would have been anxious to plug the gap in his own life left by Mary for practical as much as emotional reasons. Joan too stood to gain many practical benefits from the union, chiefly in the form of Denning's solid financial position and his status as a High Court judge. Decades later, Pauline opined that Denning had 'stampeded' Joan into an engagement within three to four weeks of their first meeting.[3] Yet there is no doubt the marriage was one of mutual love and affection, sustained until Joan's death almost half a century later. In the early 1980s, after Denning's retirement, Joan said in an interview, looking back on all the years they had spent together by then, 'We have been very happy. It has worked out very well for our respective families'.[4]

As with Clara and Mary, Joan was a woman of intelligence, energy and selfless duty. The latter point was reflected by her forthright and unsentimental practicalities, which even extended to her own wedding. As late as November 1945, the date had still not been settled, so she wrote to Denning with instructions:[5]

> If you could get down Friday [14 December], we could marry Sat after lunch, & Pauline could come home Sat, stay the night and you & I could leave Haywards Heath about 6pm and have a night in the flat & then you go back the next day. This would leave the 9th weekend

clear for Robert & by our leaving Sat evening 15th he would not miss you very much.

Denning had his orders, but as it turned out not even Joan was able to complete the arrangements as she had wished. Instead, the wedding took place on 27 December 1945, at Cuckfield Church followed by lunch at Fair Close.

Following the marriage, Joan sold her house and moved in with Denning at Fair Close. Denning's recovered happiness after the marriage was manifest. It restored his own personal situation to that which he desired above all else: a stable Christian marriage forming the basis of a happy family home.

Their respective children reported few difficulties with the integration of the two families. Although John called Denning 'Uncle Tom', and Pauline and Hazel called him by his first name, Robert soon referred to Joan as 'Mummy'. The difference reflected their ages: Pauline married in 1946, and was given away by Denning. Hazel, meanwhile, was boarding at Roedean for much of the year. Robert was thus the greatest beneficiary of the combined family: having been an only child, substantially cared for by a nanny, he now had siblings and an attentive stepmother. He went on to be educated at Denning's old employer of Winchester College followed by Denning's *alma mater* of Magdalen College, Oxford, where he chose chemistry rather than following his father into law.[6] Joan's children all went on to successful careers as well.[7]

Joan soon assumed responsibility for running the household, as Mary had before her and, indeed, as Clara had for Charles. Joan had a car which they nicknamed 'Dogpie' as a riff on its number plate of DGP 745. Denning had a near accident when driving it. At the end of 1945 he decided to give up driving altogether, having never enjoyed it to begin with.[8] Joan obligingly chauffeured him and the rest of the family thereafter. She was a skilled driver, still driving in her nineties.[9] The Dennings eventually replaced Dogpie with a more modern Humber, having to wait due to export sales being prioritised in the post-war years and production lines needing to be re-established. Petrol rationing ended in May 1950, which enabled them to drive much further afield, though it should be noted that private cars of the day were far slower, less comfortable and less reliable than at present, and although traffic volumes were much lower, there was no motorway network.

A less happy development at the end of the war was that, several years after the death of Charles, Clara, once a great force of nature, was struggling.

In 1946 she wrote a codicil to her will in which she noted that her sons had been paying her £8 a month. She expressed the thought, without giving any precise direction, 'Norman should have a share in The Hermitage', before adding what was less a testamentary bequest and more a lament wishing that Marjorie would return to live with and care for her:

> I thought Marjorie would have been here to help me before now. She has been very good to me and sent me a great deal. I have tried to help her with her children. I cannot see why they cannot come now. John [has] served all his time and the war is over. Everybody else I have heard or known about in India have come home.

Clara was referring to the tradition of the time that daughters were expected to care for parents in old age. Eventually, Marjorie and Johnny did move back, though they did not do so immediately upon the latter's retirement.

New judicial role

Denning soon settled into the King's Bench Division. He was supported by his extremely welcome new domestic arrangements following marriage. The one potential inconvenience was that he regularly had to go on circuit, though it was partly alleviated by the fact that he stayed not in hotels but in judges' lodgings. The lodgings consisted of grand private houses staffed by a butler, housekeeper and cook. Rationing was still in force at the time, however, which tempered the usual luxury somewhat, although it is possible the lodgings were somewhat less affected than other facilities.

The system of judges' lodgings, involving distinguished old houses with below-stairs staff, looks distinctly archaic to modern eyes,[10] particularly given that it would have been cheaper for the state simply to have housed judges in hotels and pay for extra security where the latter was thought necessary. From Denning's perspective, though, it appealed to his sense of ancient and modern and his new status as a judge. On one of the first occasions he went on circuit after they were married, Joan wrote to him jokingly 'I hope you won't be too grand for us all when you return! It will seem odd to come back to simplicity & domestic things'.[11] Denning enjoyed all the towns and cities on the Western Circuit, including Bodmin, Bristol, Dorchester, Salisbury, Wells and Winchester. The last of those afforded the chance to visit Clara at Whitchurch.

1945–47 – Second Marriage; Second Judicial Role

On the occasion of Denning's retirement, the Attorney General, Sir Michael Havers QC, recalled marshalling for him in the assize courts many years earlier:[12]

> My Lords, just over 36 years ago a young and nervous naval officer on demobilisation leave went to Carr Manor in Leeds as a marshal to three High Court judges, Mr Justice Henn-Collins, the distinguished criminal lawyer Mr Justice Byrne, and the third was Mr Justice Denning. The nerves were quickly calmed; the young marshal was welcomed and spoiled by his masters. One of the customs in those days was for the judges to lunch in the library at the assize court; and, inevitably, at lunch they discussed their cases. On these occasions Mr Justice Denning was likely to remark, for example, 'I think the case of *McManus v. Bowes* covers this problem', at which stage the marshal would get to his feet and walk over to the shelves where the library was kept. Then Mr Justice Denning would go on and say, 'I think you will find it in [1938] 1 King's Bench in the judgment of Lord Justice Slesser; I think at page 100.' And if I was fast enough I got the book open. Then he would go on and say, 'I think it is the paragraph which starts, "I would like to add a few words".' Your Lordship was always right. It was an attribute and an asset which I have no doubt has been of great value to you in your judicial life.

Denning was not always a stickler for convention since he took Joan on circuit wherever possible, even though it was not usual for spouses to accompany judges. In 1946, they managed to combine his duties with a family holiday by taking Hazel and Robert with them, the former before she went up to Oxford and the latter instead of being at school, there not being the general prohibition of the twenty-first century against taking children out of education for holidays.

Life was made considerably easier for Joan when Denning's former domestic servant Rose Drummer wrote wondering if she might return to work for them now her military career was over. The newly reconstituted Denning family was pleased to welcome her back.

Crime and punishment

Going on circuit meant Denning heard criminal cases, despite his relative lack of experience in criminal matters at the Bar. He had further criminal experience in London sitting in the Divisional Court and in the Court of

Appeal, Criminal Division. The latter was headed at the time by the formidable personality of Lord Goddard LCJ, then a towering figure in the law but one whose reputation would decline considerably after his death as the less edifying aspects of his personality became known.[13]

In two important respects the criminal law was much harsher in those days, in that the death penalty and the birch were still in force. Denning handed down sentences of both from time to time, doing so out of a detached sense of duty. Just as he had when at the Bar during wartime, he would contrive points of mitigation to ensure a lesser punishment where he thought it morally justified. In 1947, for example, when sitting at the Gloucester Assizes, he heard the case of an army captain charged with murdering his wife. The captain, who had been commissioned from the ranks, found his wife to be an incorrigible spendthrift, abusing the household finances. When he found she had passed a dud cheque for a third time, he lost control and shot her dead with his service revolver. He was charged with murder. Denning, applying the law properly, directed the jury towards a guilty verdict, but they found the captain guilty of the lesser charge of manslaughter. Denning then imposed a sentence of only two years' imprisonment. It seems likely the jury thought the death penalty would be disproportionate for a disturbed man such as the captain. They might also have shared some general empathy for those who had served in wartime. Denning, by passing the short sentence, ultimately concurred.

In 1949, Denning gave his thoughts on the death penalty to the Royal Commission on Capital Punishment. Initially, he said that 'in almost every case of a murder which is not premeditated the Home Secretary grants a reprieve', though he retracted the point when challenged. He went on, however, to argue that in cases of unpremeditated murder the death sentence was 'a useless anachronism'.[14] He further argued that the M'Naghten Rules should be discarded in favour of the recommendations of a committee which Lord Atkin had chaired some years earlier.[15]

There the reforming Denning stopped. He supported the death penalty for the most 'outrageous' cases such as the recently convicted 'acid bath murderer' John Haigh, one of the most notorious English murderers of the twentieth century. 'In such instances the community would demand the death penalty' he asserted, probably correctly adjudging majority public opinion at the time. He added that the black cap worn by judges on such occasions should also be retained, to give the proceedings the appropriate air of solemnity.

Much later in life, Denning would resile from those views and oppose the death penalty. At the time, though, there seems little doubt his views in favour of retaining it for the most serious murders were in accord with the majority of public opinion.

Pensions and Gunner James

A very different judicial assignment occurred in 1946, when Denning was appointed to hear wartime pension appeals. There was no right of appeal from his decisions, something with which he was very pleased, even if later in his judicial career he might himself have permitted a challenge to the decisions by way of judicial review. Instead, he had full rein to prevent any repeat of the injustices that he felt Charles and Clara had suffered with Jack and Gordon's pensions. He later described it as 'the most rewarding series of cases in my career ... Never before or since have I been entrusted with such absolute power'. [16]

One of the most notable of the cases he heard in that capacity was *James v Minister of Pensions* [1947] KB 867, arguably the first time that the famous Denning judgment-writing style properly appeared. He began:

> Gunner James joined the army on July 24, 1941, at the age of thirty-two. In January 1943, he had a swelling on the right side of his neck which gradually spread. He was sent to hospital, when a diagnosis of Hodgkin's disease was made. In April, 1943, he was discharged on account of it. He claimed a pension. It was rejected by the Minister. In February, 1946, he died on account of the disease. His widow claimed a pension. Her claim was also rejected by the Minister. She appealed to a tribunal who, on September 18, 1946, rejected her appeal. She did not apply to the tribunal for leave to appeal within the six weeks allowed by the rules of the tribunal. On November 21, 1946, the case of *Donovan v. Minister of Pensions*, which was also a case of Hodgkin's disease was decided in favour of the widow. When knowledge of this decision came to Mrs. James's advisers they sought from the tribunal leave to appeal out of time. The tribunal itself and the President of the Pensions Appeal Tribunals refused the application, refusing to extend the time or to grant leave. The widow now applies for leave to appeal.

A later Denning would probably have broken up the sentences even more and added a homily about the nature of Gunner James's military service. Nonetheless, the writing betrayed the author instantly. The Canadian academic Cameron Harvey undertook a detailed study of Denning's judgments and identified the case as the beginning of the famous style. He accordingly entitled his article 'It all started with Gunner James'.[17]

Denning went on to hold that where an application was made out of time to a pensions appeal tribunal for leave to appeal, and the tribunal refused to grant an extension of time, the judge had jurisdiction to give leave to appeal and to extend the time within which to appeal. In reaching that decision, some typical Denning reasoning could also be found:

> I am aware that the Court of Session in two early cases in 1945, Richardson's case and White's case, took a different view from that which I have taken in Phillips' case, and in the present case. I desire to state however, that in my opinion the doctrine of stare decisis does not apply in its full rigour to this branch of the law. It is inevitable that, in a field where the law has had to be declared and developed so rapidly, there should occasionally be errors. I do not, therefore, regard myself as absolutely bound by my previous decisions or by those of the Court of Session, but I follow them in absence of strong reason to the contrary.

It is true that the High Court was (and is) not bound by its own decisions, but few judges in the 1940s would have expressed a willingness to depart from earlier cases as openly and enthusiastically as Denning.[18] But the absence of the ability to appeal from the High Court in wartime pension cases meant that his decision could not be challenged in the Court of Appeal. And it was perhaps that judicial invincibility that empowered Denning to develop his own style of writing and reasoning, although some have argued that Denning was more conservative in the pension appeals than might have been expected given the absence of any right of appeal from his judgments.[19]

In another case from 1947, an ordinary decision in the King's Bench Division, Denning was to make his mark with a case of rare significance for a puisne judge.

Central London Property Trust Ltd v High Trees House Ltd – keeping promises

One of Denning's most famous decisions, *Central London Property Trust Ltd v High Trees House Ltd* [1947] KB 130, had fairly straightforward facts. By a lease of September 1937, a landlord let a new block of flats to the tenant for a term of ninety-nine years at a ground rent of £2,500 per year.[20] The intention was that the tenant would sub-let individual flats. The outbreak of war two years later caused the tenant to struggle to find sub-lets. It negotiated an agreement with the landlord, set out in a letter of January 1940, which stated 'we confirm the arrangement made between us by which the ground rent shall be reduced as from the commencement of the lease to £1,250 per annum'. The defendant paid the reduced sum from 1940 onwards. In 1941 the landlord went into receivership. By early 1945, war conditions having receded, the tenant had managed to sub-let all the flats. In September 1945, after VJ Day, the landlord's receiver wrote to the tenant demanding rent at the full rate and claiming the arrears. It then issued proceedings seeking the difference between the original and the reduced rent for the quarters ending September 1945 and December 1945.

Among the defences offered by the tenant was an argument that the landlord was estopped from claiming the original sum due to the promise contained in the 1940 letter. That defence failed because previous authority established that estoppel by representation had to be of an existing fact. Denning then went on to articulate his famous statement of principle:

> What, then, is the position in view of developments in the law in recent years? The law has not been standing still even since *Jorden v Money*. There has been a series of decisions over the last fifty years which, although said to be cases of estoppel, are not really such. They are cases of promises which were intended to create legal relations and which, in the knowledge of the person making the promise, were going to be acted on by the party to whom the promise was made, and have in fact been so acted on. In such cases the courts have said these promises must be honoured. There are certain cases to which I particularly refer: *Fenner v Blake* ([1900] 1 QB 426), *Re Wickham* (1917) (34 TLR 158), *Re William Porter & Co Ltd* ([1937] 2 All ER 361) and *Buttery v Pickard* (1946) (174 LT 144). Although said by the learned judges who decided them to be cases of estoppel, all these cases are not estoppel in the strict sense. They are cases of promises which were intended to be binding, which the parties making them knew would be acted on and which the parties to whom they were made did act on. *Jorden v Money* can be distinguished because there the promisor made it clear that she did not intend to be legally bound, whereas in the cases to which I refer the promisor did intend to be bound. In each case the court held the promise to be binding on the party making it, even though under the old common law it might be said to be difficult to find any consideration for it. The courts have not gone so far as to give a cause of action in damages for breach of such promises, but they have refused to allow the party making them act inconsistently with them. It is in that sense, and in that sense only, that such a promise gives rise to an estoppel. The cases are a natural result of the fusion of law and equity; for the cases of *Hughes v*

Metropolitan Ry Co (1877) 2 App Cas 439, *Birmingham & District Land Co v London & North Western Ry Co* (1888) (40 Ch D 268, and *Salisbury v Gilmore* [1942] 1 All ER 457, show that a party will not be allowed in equity to go back on such a promise. The time has now come for the validity of such a promise to be recognised. The logical consequence, no doubt, is that a promise to accept a smaller sum in discharge of a larger sum, if acted on, is binding, notwithstanding the absence of consideration, and if the fusion of law and equity leads to that result, so much the better. At this time of day it is not helpful to try to draw a distinction between law and equity. They have been joined together now for over seventy years, and the problems have to be approached in a combined sense.

Note the key qualification: 'the courts have not gone so far as to give a cause of action in damages for breach of such promises' – which Denning famously described in *Combe v Combe* [1951] 2 KB 215 as estoppel being 'a shield not a sword'. That much was reaffirmed fifty years later in English law by the Court of Appeal in *Baird Textile Holdings Ltd v Marks and Spencer plc* [2001] EWCA Civ 274, though it seems questionable why a principle might be relied upon to defeat a claim but not to found one, when in both situations the court would be asked simply to enforce a promise. Other jurisdictions did not all follow suit, notably the High Court of Australia in *Waltons Stores (Interstate) v Maher* (1988) 164 CLR 387.

As to the promise in the *High Trees* case itself, Denning held that it was understood by the parties only to apply under the conditions prevailing at the time it was made, namely when the flats were only partially let. It ceased to apply in early 1945 once the block was fully let. He therefore gave judgment for the landlord for the sum claimed – the quarter rents due for the quarters ending September 1945 and December 1945.

There were several odd features of the case. First, it was not clear why it was brought in the first place, since the tenant company was a subsidiary of the landlord, thus rendering the litigation 'friendly proceedings' as Denning noted. The money would presumably have ended up in the same shareholders' pockets whoever won the case. The answer might be that the landlord was insolvent and the action was brought by administrators of the insolvency to recover money for the landlord's creditors, to whom the tenant company would not be liable.

Secondly, Denning's principle of estoppel, for which the case became famous, only applied up until the point in 1945 when the flats became fully occupied. But the landlord did not seek to recover for that period – only for the later quarters. Thus, the principle for which the case became famous was, strictly, *obiter*.

Thirdly, Denning based his decision on 'a series of decisions over the last fifty years'. In fact none of the cases he mentioned really formulated any equivalent principle,[21] save for the decision of the House of Lords in *Hughes v Metropolitan Railway Co* [1877] 2 AC 439, as interpreted by Bowen LJ in *Birmingham & District Land Co v London & North Western Railway Co* (1888) 40 Ch D 268. Tellingly, neither of those two cases had been cited by counsel. Instead, Denning himself had relied upon them as counsel in a case a few years earlier, *Salisbury v Gilmore* [1942] 2 KB 38, and they had evidently remained in his mind as unfinished business. Ironically, Denning said more than once that a judge should 'act only on the evidence and arguments properly before him and not on any information which he receives from outside'.[22]

Both *Hughes* and *Birmingham* were cases in which a landowner sought to enforce a provision in a contract entitling him to take possession of land following the default by a person in occupation in the performance of an obligation owed to the landowner. They could accordingly have been disposed of as instances of equity's jurisdiction to relieve against forfeiture. In the *Birmingham* case, however, Bowen LJ had stated that the applicable principle in *Hughes* 'has nothing to do with forfeiture'. Instead:

> The truth is that the proposition is wider than cases of forfeiture. It seems to me to amount to this, that if persons who have contractual rights against others induce by their conduct those against whom they have such rights to believe that such rights will either not be enforced or will be kept in suspense or abeyance for some particular time, those persons will not be allowed by a Court of Equity to enforce the rights until such time has elapsed, without at all events placing the parties in the same position as they were before.

High Trees prompted a flurry of academic commentary at the time.[23] A much later review claimed 'Denning J's achievement in *High Trees*, and in the subsequent cases in which he applied and extended its principle, was to show how Bowen LJ's re-statement of the equitable principle applied in *Hughes v Metropolitan Railway Co* offered an elegant, simple and flexible alternative to the difficult common law rules concerning the variation of contractual obligations and alteration of the mode of their performance'.[24]

Whatever the flaws in Denning's decision, the doctrine of promissory estoppel was approved and developed in later cases, such as *Tool Metal*

Manufacturing Co Ltd v Tungsten Electric Co Ltd [1955] 1 WLR 761, where the House of Lords accepted in principle that *Hughes v Metropolitan Railway Co* could apply to a reduction by concession in payments due to a creditor and held that the concession could be terminated by giving reasonable notice. It should be noted, though, that the House of Lords never directly considered the decision in *High Trees* itself,[25] despite warnings in *Tool Metal* about overextending the relevant principle and the later caution expressed by Viscount Hailsham in *Woodhouse Ltd v Nigerian Produce Ltd* [1972] AC 741:

> I desire to add that the time may come soon when the whole sequence of cases based on promissory estoppel since the war, beginning with *Central London Property Trust Ltd v High Trees House Ltd* [1947] KB 130 may ned to be reviewed and reduced to a coherent body of doctrine by the courts. I do not mean to say that they are to be regarded with suspicion. But as is common with an expanding doctrine, they do raise problems of coherent exposition which have never been systematically explored.

More widely, Denning's achievement was to make a name for himself as a reforming judge, and in particular for his skill and perseverance in finding what he considered to be the just result by means of an appropriate remedy.

Many years later, in 2015, *High Trees* was selected for inclusion in a publication commemorating 150 years of the Incorporated Council of Law Reporting,[26] as one of the fifteen most significant cases in that period. In a speech to launch the publication, the then-President of the Supreme Court, Lord Neuberger, commented:[27]

> Not unpredictably, the one High Court Judge in the role of honour is Denning J, which may appear to confirm what many see as his star status. But the star dims somewhat once one sees that there is no other decision to which he was party.

R v West – A hint of prejudice?

A third case from 1947 was noteworthy for very different reasons. Denning presided over a widely publicised criminal trial, *R v West* [1948] 1 KB 709, which he thought of sufficient importance to recall in *The Family Story*. His description of the case was cursory, noting that six men had been charged with 'black market' offences during the war and the case, involving masses of documents, took six weeks to try, resulting in five convictions. All those convicted appealed. According to Denning,[28] none did so on the ground of any fault in his summing-up, only on the ground that the indictment was erroneous. Denning was dismayed with the result of the appeal, thinking that the jury had reached the right result.

Denning's description left out some important detail. The offences concerned a company which dealt in various goods, including what were then known as 'toilet preparations' – women's cosmetics to a modern audience. The allegation was that it had traded on the black market during wartime. Four of the defendants were brothers. The eldest was David Weitzman KC, a sitting Labour MP who had been Denning's junior some years earlier.

It was Weitzman's presence that attracted media attention to the case. Clara evidently read about it in the newspapers, as she wrote to Denning: 'I suppose you are on with your long uninteresting case, it should not be too bad with six important-sounding men been (sic) defrauding if they are proved guilty I expect they deserve severe punishment', and later 'I pray God will give you wisdom to judge it rightly'.[29]

There was one basic problem: the prosecution evidence was woefully short of that necessary to secure a conviction, especially in the case of Weitzman. The Court of Appeal allowed all the defendants' appeals and quashed all the convictions. It declared Weitzman's innocence before the others because there was simply nothing to connect him to any wrongdoing. Weitzman had merely lent some money in a conventional commercial transaction with the company – he had not participated in any of its allegedly wrongful transactions.

The question thus arose as to whether Denning had been incompetent in conducting the trial, in not dismissing the action at the conclusion of the prosecution's case, or in his summing-up, or whether there was something more sinister at play. No doubt the context of the alleged offending – illegal profiteering during wartime, when all should have had their shoulder to the common wheel of the war effort – would have struck at the heart of Denning's patriotism and his sense of right and wrong. Once again, the ardent patriot might have let the strength of his feelings get the better of his judicial impartiality. He would also have expected the highest standards from a member of the Bar and hence would have been inclined to be especially harsh on any barrister such as Weitzman appearing as a defendant before him.

An alternative explanation, raised by Iris Freeman, was that Denning's lapse was due to a tinge of anti-Semitism. The Weitzmans were Jewish, and classic anti-Semitic tropes had it that the Jews were always obsessed with money and were never quite full patriots of any country in which they found themselves.[30]

Any or all of those explanations might have formed the correct explanation for Denning's conduct of the trial, but Freeman quoted no independent evidence in support of them. It was true that anti-Semitism had been open in British society before the war and not wholly eradicated afterwards, even in the legal profession,[31] although it became steadily less acceptable in polite society. Denning would have fervently denied being infected by it: in a 1949 lecture he said of Jews: 'So also with all other races, it is a cardinal principle of our law, that they shall not suffer any disability or prejudice by reason of their race and shall have equal freedom under the law with ourselves'.[32]

It is therefore unsurprising that Freeman, who was Jewish herself (as recorded in the author profile in her book), did not pursue the allegation. If Denning had been charged with anti-Semitism, it would have been dismissed as unfounded. The better explanation is that advanced earlier: that Denning's patriotism and extreme moral censure of anyone suspected of profiteering in wartime had distorted his judgement. That, therefore, should remain our verdict on the rather sorry episode.

Clara Denning

In Denning's personal life the year 1947 ended in sadness. In December, Clara, matriarch of the Denning clan who had so successfully imbued all her children with formidable determination, industry, a sense of duty and an appreciation of right and wrong, died at the age of 83. She had had the satisfaction of seeing all her children who had survived the First World War survive the Second, with the bonus of Denning's marriage to Joan as well. Although her estate was of modest size, there was a complication in that Marjorie and Johnny wished to remain at The Hermitage. It fell to Denning as the legal expert of the family to work out a scheme to preserve the interests of all the siblings. He was able to do so to everyone's apparent satisfaction, in a way that permitted Marjorie and Johnny to remain in the house. Doubtless it was made easier by the fact that all the siblings were by that stage financially independent and not relying upon the sale of The Hermitage or their inheritance from Clara in general. If there was any dissatisfaction with the result, it remained within the family.

CHAPTER VIII

The Court of Appeal

A new role

Denning's greatest fear after the Court of Appeal had rubbished his work in *R v West* [1948] 1 KB 709 was that the case might jeopardise his career opportunities. Much to his relief, that fear proved unfounded. He had served in the High Court for less than five years in total when, on 14 October 1948, he was promoted to the Court of Appeal.

As with his earlier career milestones, Denning received a plethora of congratulatory letters and cards upon his appointment.[1] Representatives of both the Bar and academia praised the work he had done in the High Court. Professor Percy Winfield of Cambridge University, for example, wrote that Denning's judgments had 'given me the greatest pleasure and helpful instruction in all branches of the law'. Notably, Denning's old chambers colleague Henn Collins predicted Denning would be more at home as an appeal judge than on the King's Bench. Lord Simon, who had appointed Denning to the High Court back in 1944 while serving as Lord Chancellor, wrote that 'I am delighted that my choice is so soon a winner'.

His work in the Court of Appeal meant he would no longer be going on circuit. Denning missed the luxury, tradition and pageantry (not necessarily in that order) of the travels, though it made life logistically easier. In court his new role meant no more weighing of witnesses and managing trials. Instead, he was now dealing exclusively with law and procedure, which, as Henn Collins had noted, suited his interests more. It meant he was more regularly able to turn his mind to his abiding passion of law reform.

Significant cases

Denning heard too many cases to consider exhaustively, and therefore what follows is a representative selection, intended to show how his style and methods developed during his first stint in the Court of Appeal. As will be seen, his decisions ranged widely over different areas of law.

Re Wingham – Latin be damned

Denning's first case in the Court of Appeal was *Re Wingham* [1949] P 187. The subject matter involved another returned serviceman, a young pilot who was killed in a training exercise in Canada during the Second World War. He had made a will, but it did not comply with the formalities of the Wills Act 1837. The judge at first instance therefore declared it invalid. On appeal, the question was whether the will had been made by a serviceman in 'privileged circumstances'. That in turn depended on whether at the time the pilot had been *'in expeditione'*, which translated as 'on active service'. Denning was not going to let a Latin phrase get in the way of justice:

> ... the words of our statutes are plain English: 'in actual military service'. I found this easier to understand and to apply than the Latin: *in expeditione*. If I were to enquire into the Roman law, I could, perhaps, after some research say how Roman law would have dealt with its soldiers on Hadrian's Wall and the camp at Chester, but I cannot say how it would have dealt with an airman in Saskatchewan who was only a day's flying from the enemy. Nor can anyone else. This supposed throwback to Roman law has confused this branch of the law too long. It is time to get back to the statute.

Denning was criticised by one academic commentator for allowing his imagination, or perhaps his intention to do justice, to get the better of him, on the ground that the term was not Roman law at all but just another example of a Latin phrase like so many others in the common law.[2] That criticism, however, was unfair: in the earlier case of *Drummond v Parish* (1843) 3 Curt 522, 163 ER 812, Sir Herbert Jenner Fust had held that, because the idea of a soldier's privilege derived from Roman law, 'in order to ascertain the extent and meaning of the exception, the civil law may fairly be resorted to'. Later cases had followed suit by looking at civil law (in context, European law as distinct from the common law of England and Wales) concepts, until Denning and the rest of the Court of Appeal in *Re Wingham* put a stop to it. Instead, Denning and the others unanimously held that the question was what constituted military service, and that training during wartime immediately before being deployed to the front could indeed count as such. Denning added that 'military service' would include anyone on active duty in the forces – doctors, nurses, chaplains, Wrens, auxiliary transport workers and so on; essentially, everyone in uniform save officers on half pay or men in the reserves who had not been called up. Denning was therefore right to deal with the Latin origins of the phrase *in expeditione*.

Iris Freeman praised Denning's judgment rather floridly as a 'song of thanksgiving' for those who served in the war along with a promise to those who might serve in a future conflict.[3] It would certainly have taken a formidable obstacle to prevent Denning doing what he thought was right by serving members of the forces and their families, especially with wills or pensions from men who died in service for their country.

Seaford Court Estates Ltd v Asher – 'naked usurpation'

One common jurisprudential debate of the twentieth century concerned the proper method of interpreting statutes. Denning's own method was set out very early on in his career as an appellate judge. In *Seaford Court Estates Ltd v Asher* [1949] 2 All ER 155 he wrote:

> Whenever a statute comes up for consideration it must be remembered that it is not within human powers to foresee the manifold sets of facts which may arise, and, even if it were, it is not possible to provide for them in terms free from all ambiguity. The English language is not an instrument of mathematical precision. Our literature would be much the poorer if it were. This is where the draftsmen of Acts of Parliament have often been unfairly criticised. A judge, believing himself to be fettered by the supposed rule that he must look to the language and nothing else, laments that the draftsmen have not provided for this or that, or have been guilty of some or other ambiguity. It would certainly save the judges trouble if Acts of Parliament were drafted with divine prescience and perfect clarity. In the absence of it, when a defect appears a judge cannot simply fold his hands and blame the draftsman. He must set to work on the constructive task of finding the intention of Parliament, and he must do this not only from the language of the statute, but also from a consideration of the social conditions which gave rise to it and of the mischief which it was passed to remedy, and then he must supplement the written word so as to give 'force and life' to the intention of the legislature. ... Put into homely metaphor it is this: A judge should ask himself the question: If the makers of the Act had

themselves come across this ruck in the texture of it, how would they have straightened it out? He must then do as they would have done. A judge must not alter the material of which it is woven, but he can and should iron out the creases.

A short time after, in *Magor and St Mellons RDC v Newport Corporation* [1950] 2 All ER 1226, he said 'We sit here to find out the intention of Parliament and of Ministers and carry it out, and we do this better by filling in the gaps and making sense of the enactment than by opening up to destructive analysis'.

Denning's view was an example of what was known as the 'purposive interpretation'. On appeal in the *Magor* case ([1952] AC 189), Viscount Simonds was having none of it. As to divining Parliament's intention, he dispensed the following stricture:

> [T]he general proposition that it is the duty of the court to find out the intention of Parliament – and not only of Parliament but of ministers also – cannot by any means be supported. The duty of the court is to interpret the words that the legislature has used; those words may be ambiguous, but, even if they are, the power and duty of the court to travel outside them on a voyage of discovery are strictly limited.

In response to Denning's suggestion about filling in gaps, he stated:

> It appears to me a naked usurpation of the legislative function under the thin disguise of interpretation. And it is the less justifiable when it is guesswork with what material the legislature would, if it had discovered the gap, have filled it in. If a gap is disclosed, the remedy lies in an amending Act.

According to Lord Justice Sedley, the clash between Denning's purposive, or 'liberal', approach to statutory interpretation and Viscount Simonds' more literal approach constituted 'the single greatest judicial controversy of the post-war years'.[4]

Solle v Butcher – mistakes made

In many ways, the case of *Solle v Butcher* [1950] 1 KB 671 typified Denning's entire judicial career, or at least the popular perception thereof. He fashioned an inventive way of adapting a recent decision of the House of Lords, to do justice to the parties before him. His reasoning was soon relied upon as important new law. Eventually, he was reversed by a later appellate court which found his inventiveness had gone too far.

What is remarkable about the case is the length of time it took for that reversal – more than half a century. Nor did the overturning come from the House of Lords, but from Denning's successors in the Court of Appeal itself, as late as 2002.

As with *High Trees*, the background concerned property affected by the Second World War. In 1939 the house in question had been subdivided and let as flats subject to the Rent Restriction Acts, with the rent thus fixed at £140 per year. The house was damaged during the war. In 1947, it was acquired by the landlord. He carried out repairs and alterations to the house, during the course of which he re-constructed one of the flats. He then let the flat to the tenant on a lease for seven years at a rent of £250 per year, the parties not realising that the Rent Restriction Acts applied. In fact, the Acts did apply, so without going through statutory procedures for letting, the true rent should have been fixed at the first flat's previous rent of £140. When the tenant realised the mistake about rent regulation, he claimed the overpaid rent back (by way of restitution) from the landlord.

The landlord argued, *inter alia*, that the lease should be rescinded, as it had been entered into under a mutual mistake of fact. At the time, the leading case on the effect of mistake on contract was *Bell v Lever Brothers Ltd* [1932] AC 161. Applying *Bell*, the judge ruled there had been no common mistake of fact made by the parties, though possibly there had been one of law since both parties thought that the Rent Restriction Acts did not apply. The landlord appealed.

Denning, with Bucknell LJ agreeing and Jenkins LJ dissenting, allowed the appeal. They held that the lease should be rescinded on terms that the tenant be allowed to choose whether to have a lease at £250, or whether to leave the flat. Denning purported to identify an equitable jurisdiction which permitted the court to intervene where the parties had concluded an agreement that was binding in law under a common misapprehension of a fundamental nature as to the material facts or their respective rights:

> [A] contract will be set aside if the mistake of the one party has been induced by a material misrepresentation of the other, even though it was not fraudulent or fundamental; or if one party, knowing that the other is mistaken about the terms of an offer, or the identity of the person by whom it is made, lets him remain under his delusion and concludes a contract on the mistaken terms instead of pointing out the mistake ... A contract is also liable in equity to be set aside if the parties were under a common misapprehension either as to

facts or as to their relative and respective rights, provided that the misapprehension was fundamental and that the party seeking to set it aside was not himself at fault.

For the latter proposition Denning relied primarily on *Cooper v Phibbs* (1867) LR 2 HL 149. He went on to hold:

> the lease should be set aside because there had been 'a common misapprehension, which was fundamental'. The terms on which the lease was set aside were such as, in effect, to give the tenant the option of substituting the lease for one at the full rent which the law permitted.

For the next half century, judges and jurists considered how to reconcile *Solle* with *Bell*. Finally, in *Great Peace Shipping Ltd v Tsavliris Salvage (International) Ltd* [2003] QB 679, Lord Phillips MR (giving the judgment of the Court of Appeal) explained:

> In the court below Toulson J used this case as a vehicle to review this difficult area of jurisprudence. He reached the bold conclusion that the view of the jurisdiction of the court expressed by Denning LJ in *Solle v Butcher* was 'over-broad', by which he meant wrong. Equity neither gave a party a right to rescind a contract on grounds of common mistake nor conferred on the court a discretion to set aside a contract on such grounds.

Lord Phillips MR concluded:

> 153. A number of cases, albeit a small number, in the course of the last 50 years have purported to follow *Solle v Butcher* [1950] 1 KB 671, yet none of them defines the test of mistake that gives rise to the equitable jurisdiction to rescind in a manner that distinguishes this from the test of a mistake that renders a contract void in law, as identified in *Bell v Lever Bros Ltd* [1932] AC 161. This is, perhaps, not surprising, for Denning LJ, the author of the test in *Solle v Butcher*, set *Bell v Lever Bros Ltd* at nought. It is possible to reconcile *Solle v Butcher* and *Magee v Pennine Insurance Co Ltd* [1969] 2 QB 507 with *Bell v Lever Bros Ltd* only by postulating that there are two categories of mistake, one that renders a contract void at law and one that renders it voidable in equity. Although later cases have proceeded on this basis, it is not possible to identify that proposition in the judgment of any of the three Lords Justices, Denning, Bucknill and Fenton Atkinson, who participated in the majority decisions in the former two cases. Nor,

over 50 years, has it proved possible to define satisfactorily two different qualities of mistake, one operating in law and one in equity. 154. In *Solle v Butcher* Denning LJ identified the requirement of a common misapprehension that was 'fundamental', and that adjective has been used to describe the mistake in those cases which have followed *Solle v Butcher*. We do not find it possible to distinguish, by a process of definition, a mistake which is 'fundamental' from Lord Atkin's mistake as to quality which 'makes the thing [contracted for] essentially different from the thing [that] it was believed to be': [1932] AC 161, 218.

...

157. Our conclusion is that it is impossible to reconcile *Solle v Butcher* with *Bell v Lever Bros Ltd*. The jurisdiction asserted in the former case has not developed. It has been a fertile source of academic debate, but in practice it has given rise to a handful of cases that have merely emphasised the confusion of this area of our jurisprudence. In paras 110 to 121 of his judgment, Toulson J has demonstrated the extent of that confusion. If coherence is to be restored to this area of our law, it can only be by declaring that there is no jurisdiction to grant rescission of a contract on the ground of common mistake where that contract is valid and enforceable on ordinary principles of contract law. That is the conclusion of Toulson J.

Because *Solle* was inconsistent with a decision of the House of Lords, the Court of Appeal had jurisdiction not to follow it – in effect, to bury it.

Bater v Bater – burden of proof

During the course of *Bater v Bater* [1950] 2 All ER 458, Denning made some remarks about the burden of proof in civil cases later stated in the *Modern Law Review* to have had 'much influence'.[5] The background concerned a divorce petition brought by a wife on the ground of cruelty. In dismissing the petition, the commissioner said that she must 'prove her case beyond reasonable doubt'. On appeal, Bucknill LJ was as firmly old-fashioned about divorce as anything Denning ever came out with, confirming that the charge had to be proved beyond reasonable doubt.

Denning himself, though agreeing with the result, had some perceptive observations:

> The difference of opinion which has been evoked about the standard of proof in these cases may well turn out to be more a matter of words than anything else. It is true that by our law there is a higher standard of proof in criminal cases than in civil cases, but this is subject to the

qualification that there is no absolute standard in either case. In criminal cases the charge must be proved beyond reasonable doubt, but there may be degrees of proof within that standard. Many great judges have said that, in proportion as the crime is enormous, so ought the proof to be clear. So also in civil cases. The case may be proved by a preponderance of probability, but there may be degrees of probability within that standard. The degree depends on the subject-matter. A civil court, when considering a charge of fraud, will naturally require a higher degree of probability than that which it would require if considering whether negligence were established. It does not adopt so high a degree as a criminal court, even when it is considering a charge of a criminal nature, but still it does require a degree of probability which is commensurate with the occasion. Likewise, a divorce court should require a degree of probability which is proportionate to the subject-matter. I do not think the matter can be better put than Sir William Scott put it in *Loveden v Loveden* ((1810) 2 Hag Con 3):

> 'The only general rule that can be laid down upon the subject is that the circumstances must be such as would lead the guarded discretion of a reasonable and just man to the conclusion ...'

The degree of probability which a reasonable and just man would require to come to a conclusion – and likewise the degree of doubt which would prevent him from coming to it – depends on the conclusion to which he is required to come. It would depend on whether it was a criminal case or a civil case, what the charge was, and what the consequences might be, and if he was left in real and substantial doubt on the particular matter, he would hold the charge not to be established. He would not be satisfied about it.

What is a real and substantial doubt? It is only another way of saying a reasonable doubt, and a 'reasonable doubt' is simply that degree of doubt which would prevent a reasonable and just man from coming to a conclusion. So the phrase 'reasonable doubt' gets one no further. It does not say that the degree of probability must be as high as ninety-nine per cent or as low as fifty-one per cent The degree required must depend on the mind of the reasonable and just man who is considering the particular subject-matter. In some cases fifty-one per cent would be enough, but not in others. When this is realised, the phrase 'reasonable doubt' can be used just as aptly in a civil case or a divorce case as in a criminal case, and, indeed, it was so used by

Bucknill LJ in *Davis v Davis* and *Gower v Gower*. The only difference is that, because of our high regard for the liberty of the individual, a doubt may be regarded as reasonable in the criminal courts which would not be so in the civil courts. I agree, therefore, with my brothers that the use of the phrase 'reasonable doubt' by the commissioner was not a misdirection, any more than it was in *Briginshaw v Briginshaw*.

If the commissioner had, however, put the case higher and said that the case had to be proved with the same strictness as a crime is proved in a criminal court, then he would, I think, have misdirected himself because that would be the very error which this court corrected in *Davis v Davis*. It would be adopting too high a standard. The divorce court is a civil court, not a criminal court, and it should not adopt the rules and standards of a criminal court.

Howell v Falmouth Boat Construction Ltd – 'I know of no such principle'

The proceedings in *Howell v Falmouth Boat Construction Ltd* [1951] AC 837 concerned wartime regulations, bearing hallmarks of an era long vanished. By the Restriction of Repairs of Ships Order, 1940, art 1, the Admiralty, pursuant to regulation 55(1) of the Defence (General) Regulations 1939, ordered that no ship repairer was to carry out any repairs or alterations to ships 'except under the authority of a licence granted by the Admiralty'. In June 1942, as the Battle of the Atlantic raged, the Director of Merchant Shipbuilding and Repairs at the Admiralty sent a circular letter to all licensing officers stating:

> I understand that it has been made clear to you that where you are dealing with reliable ship repairers and owners with a good record you ought not to delay the putting in hand of obvious repairs, merely pending the actual issue of a licence.

The plaintiff carried out repairs on the defendant's ship. The issue was whether the work had been authorised by the Admiralty and whether the defendant was therefore liable to pay for it. At first instance, the judge found that certain work had been carried out without the written licence of the Admiralty and so was illegal, and, therefore, the plaintiff could not recover anything for it. The Court of Appeal including Denning reversed the decision, holding that an oral licence was sufficient, and the defendant appealed to the House of Lords.

The reason the case was noteworthy was the blunt rebuke issued by Viscount Simonds in the House of Lords to Denning:

[Denning] described the principle that he invoked as of particular importance in these days when the officers of government departments are given much authority by Orders and circulars which are not available to the public. I will state this principle in his own words: 'Whenever government officers, in their dealings with a subject, take on themselves to assume authority in a matter with which he is concerned, the subject is entitled to rely on their having the authority which they assume. He does not know and cannot be expected to know the limits of their authority, and he ought not to suffer if they exceed it. That was the principle which I applied in *Robertson v Minister of Pensions*, and it is applicable in this case also'. My Lords, I know of no such principle in our law nor was any authority for it cited.

That last sentence was as biting a criticism of a sitting judge as one could have expected to find in the usually dry law reports. Nonetheless, in the case itself, the House of Lords affirmed the actual result reached by the Court of Appeal, on different grounds.[6]

Candler v Crane, Christmas & Co – 'Timorous souls' and negligent misstatement

Denning's reforming spirit was in full flight when he sat on the case which became arguably his best-known dissent, and one which he himself occasionally called his most important judgment,[7] *Candler v Crane, Christmas & Co* [1951] 2 KB 164.

The proceedings concerned a professional negligence claim brought against an accountancy firm. The plaintiff had invested and lost money in a company whose accounts had been prepared by the defendant firm. At first instance, the judge held that no duty of care was owed by the accountants to the plaintiff. On appeal, the majority of the Court of Appeal (Cohen and Asquith LJJ) agreed, but Denning did not.

Denning set out what was to become the cause of action for negligent misstatement, relying on the neighbourhood principle as famously laid down by Lord Atkin in *Donoghue v Stevenson* [1932] AC 562 in the context of hypothetical snails and ginger beer. Lord Atkin had uttered his immortal words, drawing on the Biblical parable of the Good Samaritan:

> You must take reasonable care to avoid acts or omissions which you can reasonably foresee would be likely to injure your neighbour. Who then, in law is my neighbour? The answer seems to be persons

who are so closely and directly affected by my act that I ought reasonably to have them in contemplation as being so affected when I am directing my mind to the acts or omissions which are called into question.

To modern lawyers, Lord Atkin's speech remains one of the best-known in common law history, of equivalent fame yet of far wider relevance than his speech in *Liversidge v Anderson*. In the immediate aftermath of *Donoghue*, however, no such significance was attached to the case. Certainly the editor of the official law reports at the time missed the significance, the headnote effectively confining the *ratio* to manufacturers of food or similar, with no indication of the myriad of circumstances to which the case was subsequently applied.[8] Instead, it was Denning, like Lord Atkin a naturally reforming judge more concerned with justice than formality, who dusted off the case in *Candler* many years later and relied upon it when ruling in favour of the plaintiff.

In response to anticipated criticism, Denning wrote:

> This argument about the novelty of the action does not appeal to me in the least. It has been put forward in all the great cases which have been milestones of progress in our law, and it has always, or nearly always, been rejected. If you read the great cases of *Ashby v White*, *Pasley v Freeman* and *Donoghue v Stevenson* you will find that in each of them the judges were divided in opinion. On the one side there were the timorous souls who were fearful of allowing a new cause of action. On the other side there were the bold spirits who were ready to allow it if justice so required. It was fortunate for the common law that the progressive view prevailed. Whenever this argument of novelty is put forward I call to mind the emphatic answer given by Pratt CJ, nearly two hundred years ago in *Chapman v Pickersgill* when he said:
>
>> 'I wish never to hear this objection again. This action is for a tort: torts are infinitely various; not limited or confined, for there is nothing in nature but may be an instrument of mischief.'

The same answer was given by Lord Macmillan in *Donoghue v Stevenson* when he said:

> 'The criterion of judgment must adjust and adapt itself to the changing circumstances of life. The categories of negligence are never closed.'

I beg leave to quote those cases and those passages against those who would emphasize the paramount importance of certainty at the expense of justice. It needs only a little imagination to see how much the common law would have suffered if those decisions had gone the other way.

It was clear that although he was technically describing the judges in *Donoghue*, Denning was in effect calling himself a 'bold spirit' and the two judges sitting with him in the case, Asquith and Cohen LJJ, 'timorous souls'. Asquith LJ certainly thought so, and gave a memorable retort in his judgment:

I am not concerned with defending the existing state of the law or contending that it is strictly logical – it clearly is not. I am merely recording what I think it is. If this relegates me to the company of 'timorous souls', I must face that consequence with such fortitude as I can command.

Denning would be vindicated twelve years later when the not always bold spirits of the House of Lords did indeed approve the new cause of action, in *Hedley Byrne & Co v Heller & Partners Ltd* [1964] AC 465. Denning's judgment in *Candler* was described by Lord Bridge in *Caparo Industries plc v Dickman and others* [1990] 2 AC 605 as a 'masterly analysis'. It received similar praise from academic lawyers, Professor PS Atiyah, calling it what 'many will remember as Lord Denning's greatest single achievement in the common law',[9] and it was adopted in other jurisdictions such as Australia.[10] It was arguably the high point of Denning's career as a judge. It stands as proof that he was able to remain within the conventions of the common law whilst still advancing significant reform.

Karsales (Harrow) Ltd v Wallis – fundamental breach

Denning ultimately had less success with a different innovation, the concept of 'fundamental breach', which he developed in a line of cases beginning with *Karsales (Harrow) Ltd v Wallis* [1956] 2 All ER 866. The subject matter was, once again, exemption clauses, something with which Denning became synonymous, along with contract law in general.[11]

The defendant bought a car for £600 using a hire purchase scheme financed by the plaintiff company. When it was delivered, he discovered that it had been badly damaged since he had first inspected it, and the repairs would cost £150. He refused to pay instalments under the hire purchase scheme, and the plaintiff brought an action accordingly. In response to the defendant's complaint about the condition of the car, the plaintiff relied on cl 3(g) of the hire purchase agreement, which provided 'No condition or warranty that the vehicle is roadworthy or as to its age, condition or fitness for any purpose is given by the owner or implied herein'.

At first instance, the judge held that that clause meant that the plaintiff was not responsible in any way for the condition of the car when it was delivered, and that although it was in a deplorable condition and had been rejected by the defendant, the plaintiff could still recover the instalments due. On appeal, Denning held:

> In my opinion, under a hire purchase agreement of this kind, when the hirer has himself previously seen and examined the motor car and made application for hire purchase on the basis of his inspection of it, there is an obligation on the lender to deliver the car in substantially the same condition as when it was seen. It makes no difference that the lender is a finance company which has bought the car in the interval without seeing it. The lender must know, from the ordinary course of business, that the hirer applies on the faith of his inspection and on the understanding that the car will be delivered in substantially the same condition: and it is an implied term of the agreement that pending delivery the car will be kept in suitable order and repair for the purposes of the bailment.

He then turned to the concept of 'fundamental breach':

> Notwithstanding earlier cases which might suggest the contrary, it is now settled that exempting clauses of this kind, no matter how widely they are expressed, only avail the party when he is carrying out his contract in its essential respects. He is not allowed to use them as a cover for misconduct or indifference or to enable him to turn a blind eye to his obligations. They do not avail him when he is guilty of a breach which goes to the root of the contract. The thing to do is to look at the contract apart from the exempting clauses and see what are the terms, express or implied, which impose an obligation on the party. If he has been guilty of a breach of those obligations in a respect which goes to the very root of the contract, he cannot rely on the exempting clauses. I would refer in this regard to what was said by Mr. Justice Roche in the copra cake case (*Pinnock Bros v Lewis & Peat* [1923] 1 KB 690, at page 695) and the judgments of Mr. Justice Devlin in *Alexander v Railway Executive* ([1951] 2 KB 882) and *Smeaton Hanscomb & Company Limited v Sassoon I Setty, Son & Company* ([1953] 2 All ER 1471), and a recent case in this Court of *J. Spurling, Limited v Bradshaw* ([1956] 1 WLR 461), and the cases there mentioned. The

principle is sometimes said to be that the party cannot rely on an exempting clause when he delivers something 'different in kind' from that contracted for, or has broken a 'fundamental term' or a 'fundamental contractual obligation', but these are, I think, all comprehended by the general principle that a breach which goes to the root of the contract disentitles the party from relying on the exempting clause. In the present case the lender was in breach of the implied obligation that I have mentioned. When Mr. Wallis inspected the car prior to signing the application form, the car was in excellent condition and would go: whereas the car which was subsequently delivered to him was no doubt the same car but it was in a deplorable state and would not go. That breach went, I think, to the root of the contract and disentitles the lender from relying on the exempting clause.

There were numerous other cases of particular interest on exemption clauses heard by Denning during his first time in the Court of Appeal. In *J Spurling v Bradshaw* [1956] 1 WLR 461, he insisted on reading down a very widely drafted clause, though he then proceeded to uphold its application on the facts. In *Halbauer v Brighton Corporation* [1954] 1 WLR 1161, he concurred in the upholding of an exemption clause in a case where the plaintiff's caravan was stolen from the defendant's premises: according to Denning, the plaintiff should have insured the caravan. Notably, in that case and in *Williams v Linnett* [1951] 1 KB 565[12] the court was concerned not with an embattled consumer as such, but with the allocation of insurance losses, since the parties all were or could (or should, according to Denning) have been insured.

By contrast, in *Curtis v Chemical Cleaning Co* [1951] 1 KB 805, Denning held that a cleaning company could not rely upon an exemption clause where the customer had been misled as to the extent of the exemption. The decision seemed to grant relief for innocent misrepresentation of an executed contract – and thus contrary to settled authority – though Denning dismissed that notion, holding that executed contracts could be rescinded for innocent misrepresentation 'in a proper case'. In classic Denning style he was establishing himself for future cases since he could refer back to his own earlier decision as 'authority'.

Bendall v McWhirter – 'do us all a favour'

We have seen how Denning sought to reform divorce law by taking a more flexible approach than he or other judges would have taken to purely commercial transactions. His approach might have been laudable as between husbands and wives, but the situation was more complex when it came to the rights of third parties such as banks. Allowing one spouse rights over the other in terms of matrimonial property regardless of any written agreement might undermine a bank's rights to enforce its security. Famously, in *Bendall v McWhirter* [1952] 2 QB 466, Denning ruled that a deserted wife occupying the marital home had a personal licence to stay there. His reasoning began by identifying 'an irrevocable authority which the husband is presumed in law to have conferred on her ... This authority flows from the status of marriage, coupled with the fact of separation owing to the husband's misconduct'.

That was akin to a contractual licensee with an irrevocable authority, but Denning went on to describe the deserted wife as having an 'equity'. The other two judges hearing the appeal, Somervell and Romer LJJ, held that the case turned on the special position of a trustee in bankruptcy.

Not for the first or last time, Denning had found a development in the law was permissible not by extending common law analogies but by invoking the concept of equity: the distinctive concepts, doctrines, principles and remedies developed by the old Court of Chancery before it was fused with the common law by the late-nineteenth-century Judicature Acts.[13] The rights of the deserted wife established by the case became known as the 'deserted wife's equity',[14] later described as 'one of the boldest creations of the judiciary in this [the twentieth] century'.[15]

Bold it might have been, universally popular it was not. Denning famously received the following vituperative reproval from an aggrieved member of the public:[16]

> Dear Sir: You are a disgrace to all mankind. To let whores break up homes and expect us chaps to keep them. They rob us of what we have worked for and put us out on the street.
>
> I only hope you have the same trouble as us. So do us all a favour – take a Rolls and run off Beachy Head and don't come back.

It was not only exasperated husbands who objected: eminent lawyers including Sir Robert Megarry, Harman LJ and Upjohn J (later Lord Upjohn) all expressed contemporary criticisms.[17] Their primary concern was the potential complications of the wife having a right that could be upheld against a third party such as a mortgage lender. Upjohn J, for example, pointed out that a husband who knew he was facing bankruptcy would actually do his wife a financial favour by deserting her beforehand.

The House of Lords intervened in 1965 by holding that a wife had no right of property entitling her to remain in the property enforceable against a bank as mortgagee,[18] but they were in turn overruled by Parliament when it passed the Matrimonial Homes Act 1967.[19] Therein lay one of the important occasions on which Parliament confirmed and further developed a Denning-prompted reform.

R v Northumberland Compensation Appeal Tribunal, ex parte Shaw – administrative law beginnings

A case which Denning once called his 'second most important'[20] was *R v Northumberland Compensation Appeal Tribunal, ex parte Shaw* [1952] 1 KB 338. It was the first of many in which he made a significant contribution towards the development of modern administrative law.

It is important to note that when Denning began his legal career, administrative law was a small fraction of what it later became. The chief reason was that the British state itself was a small fraction of its current proportions. Although the country had had to commit itself to 'total war' from 1914 to 1918, the size of the peacetime state and the extent to which it sought to regulate affairs had not been substantially increased in the inter-war years, much of which were dogged by economic depression and industrial strife. The real increase in the size and role of the state began immediately after the Second World War, when the Attlee government attempted to meet its promise of a better society, as opposed to Lloyd George's unfulfilled 'Land fit for heroes' after the First World War.

There were two key features of Attlee's programme. The first was widespread nationalisation of strategic assets including railroads, coal mines, the Bank of England, road transport, docks and harbours, and electricity generation. The second, based partly upon the wartime Beveridge Report, was a greatly expanded social welfare system, including creation of the National Health Service.

An obvious question with the state now running those activities was how each might be regulated, including what rights citizens might have to go to the courts for redress for breaches of natural justice, or actions of government entities in excess of authority. That was the background to *ex parte Shaw*.

The case itself concerned the amount of compensation awarded to the plaintiff after he lost his job in a hospital board, following the passage of the National Health Service Act 1946. He appealed to the Compensation Appeal Tribunal, which upheld the award. He then moved for an order of certiorari (the old-fashioned term for judicial review of a lower court's decision) to remove into the King's Bench Division the decision of the tribunal, with a view to it being quashed. The ground of his application was that the tribunal had wrongly interpreted the regulations. The Divisional Court agreed and quashed the tribunal's decision. The tribunal appealed to the Court of Appeal. It conceded that its decision had been based on an error of law, but it argued nevertheless that certiorari could not be granted in respect of a decision of a tribunal on the ground of error on the face of the record. The Court of Appeal including Denning unanimously upheld the Divisional Court's decision that certiorari could indeed be granted for an error of law.

A year or so later, in *Barnard v National Dock Labour Board* [1953] 2 QB 18, the Court of Appeal, again containing Denning, extended the remedy so that it was available when a tribunal acted contrary to natural justice or made a mistake of law.

Those two cases formed the beginning of a line of authorities which emboldened Denning to proclaim in 1971 that 'It may truly now be said that we have a developed system of administrative law'.[21] Denning was clearly one of the key architects of that system.

Ladd v Marshall – fresh evidence

In *Ladd v Marshall* [1954] 1 WLR 1489, the issue on appeal was the admission of fresh evidence. The following passage from Denning's judgment became the standard test:

> In order to justify the reception of fresh evidence or a new trial, three conditions must be fulfilled: first, it must be shown that the evidence could not have been obtained with reasonable diligence for use at the trial: second, the evidence must be such that, if given, it would probably have an important influence on the result of the case, though it need not be decisive: thirdly, the evidence must be such as is presumably to be believed, or in other words, it must be apparently credible, though it need not be incontrovertible.

Note the entirely conventional judicial language in that paragraph; there was no identifiable uniquely Denning touch. According to the Lexis Library One Case Citation Database, the case had been cited in over 130 reported decisions by 2020. It thus provided another example of Denning's ability to master the common law.

Extra-curricular activities

In 1950, Denning took on two significant administrative roles aside from his legal duties. First, he became Chairman of Trustees of Cumberland Lodge, a charitable trust established three years earlier by George VI and Queen

Elizabeth at the eponymous building in Windsor Great Lodge. The trust was an educational charity run along Christian lines, something close to Denning's heart. His appointment was no mere lending of his name; he and Joan devoted much energy to the fund-raising and administration, and made a very good impression upon all with whom they dealt in the course of the work.[22]

The second role was President of the Lawyers' Christian Fellowship (UK),[23] a position Denning was to hold until 1987, whereupon he became its patron.

He had already been a member of the fellowship for many years. Somewhat surprisingly, he declined an invitation in September 1950 from the Archbishop of Canterbury to chair a commission to examine the work of the ecclesiastical courts. He cited pressure of work, though it was unusual for him to refuse any request for help from causes in which he believed, especially where it concerned the church.

Further evidence of Denning's commitment to Christian institutions was his presidential address given in 1950 to the fourth annual general meeting of the National Association of Parish Councils, on the constitutional position of parish councils.[24]

The following year, he took up still another significant new role, coming out of personal connections dating back to his Oxford days. For his unsuccessful All Souls application, his exams had been marked by Geoffrey Cheshire, an eminent legal scholar, and in the years that followed the two had become good friends. During the Second World War, Geoffrey's son Leonard served in the RAF with distinction. After the war, Leonard took a very keen interest in the welfare of returned servicemen and war widows. In 1948, he created The Cheshire Foundation Homes for the Sick, based in a large country house near Liss in Hampshire. In 1951, at Geoffrey's request, Denning helped draw up a trust deed to govern the foundation, then Denning became its chairman.

The trust appealed strongly to Denning's values. As with Cumberland Lodge, he and Joan devoted much energy and time to it, speaking at various events in support of fundraising, arranging an overdraft for it, and lending their intelligence and experience to the various problems it faced. Initially, Denning was opposed to the trust setting up overseas, thinking that Britain should have the first call upon its resources, but he subsequently gave the same support to its work in other countries when he was able. Over the new year period in 1958–59, for example, he and Joan were in India for some legal speaking engagements. They took the time to visit the local Cheshire homes, and Joan wrote a description for *The Cheshire Smile*, the project's quarterly magazine. She concluded:[25]

> We were very surprised and pleased to find how well the name Leonard Cheshire was known by everyone we met in India, and what a great interest there is in his work, particularly in the project 'Raphael' as an International centre. There is a tremendous feeling of goodwill towards everything that is being done for the relief of suffering under the name of Cheshire, and we felt very proud to be associated with it. Please do not think from this record of our happy visit that the Indian homes are self-sufficient. The need in India is great, much, much greater than ours – and the resources available pitifully small. Cannot we all help in some way?

Denning remained chair of the foundation until his appointment as Master of the Rolls in 1962.[26]

By 1949, Denning had written six articles for the *Law Quarterly Review*, as well as the work on *Smith's Leading Cases* and *Bullen & Leake's Precedents*. He was thus reasonably well-known as a legal author and commentator. He had not, however, made any speeches outside court when a barrister, and only one as a High Court Judge (on divorce laws, to King's College London[27]). He came to much wider attention when, as an appellate judge, he was invited to give the first ever Hamlyn Lectures.

The lectures were the result of a bequest from one Emma Hamlyn, who had died in 1941. As the daughter of a solicitor, she had wanted to promote the unique (as she saw it) features of the common law. After some delay, doubtless occasioned at least in part by wartime, a trust was established using her funds. Its objects were:[28]

> ... the furtherance by lectures or otherwise among the Common People of the United Kingdom of Great Britain and Northern Ireland of the knowledge of the Comparative Jurisprudence and Ethnology of the Chief European countries including the United Kingdom, and the circumstances of the growth of such jurisprudence to the Intent that the Common People of the United Kingdom may realise the privileges which in law and custom they enjoy in comparison with other European Peoples and realising and appreciating such privileges may recognise the responsibilities and obligations attaching to them.

The touches of patriotism and xenophobia in those objects might look dated through twenty-first century eyes, but not to Denning's generation, and thus he was pleased to accept the invitation. He took as his theme a phrase by which he would like to have defined his entire career, 'Freedom under Law'. In total he gave four separate lectures, respectively entitled: 'Personal

Freedom', 'Freedom of Mind and Conscience', 'Justice between Man and the State', and 'The Powers of the Executive'.

Throughout the lectures, Denning praised the protections of English law and its tradition of fairness and non-discrimination. He referred to one of the most famous historic cases, *Somerset v Stewart*.[29]

> So in 1771, when the coloured slave James Somerset was held in irons on board a ship lying in the Thames and bound for Jamaica, Lord Mansfield declared his detention to be unlawful. 'The air of England is too pure for any slave to breathe,' he said, 'Let the black go free,' and the slave went free.

The supposed quote of Lord Mansfield was widely reproduced, yet it did not appear in the report cited by Denning, (1772) 20 St Tr 1. When he came to give the 50th Hamlyn Lecture in 1998, Lord Justice Sedley was unable to find the Mansfield quote in any contemporary source, and concluded that it had to have been of Denning's own invention. In fact, Sedley LJ was only partially correct. The quote was actually from the speech of William Davy, representing Somerset (see (1772) 98 ER 499), so had not been made up by Denning. Nor was Denning the first to attribute it to Lord Mansfield.[30] It is however right to record that the case was not quite the definitive denunciation of slavery as is sometimes assumed.[31]

The accuracy of quotations aside, Denning's Hamlyn Lectures were very well received, both when delivered and when published in book form. The *Law Society Gazette*, endorsing Denning's parochialism, wrote that the book 'will be of interest and value to all, both lawyers and laymen alike, showing as it does so clearly the privileges which by law and custom they (the Common People of the United Kingdom) enjoy in comparison with other European Peoples'. *The Solicitor* magazine wrote that the book comprised 'lectures of such contemporary importance that no lawyer can properly regard himself as well informed unless he has read them' and that the lectures 'made a deep impression upon those who heard them, and in this volume their influence will be very wide'.

That critical and popular acclaim led to a multitude of further speaking engagements.[32] Invitations came from, among others, University College London, the Society of Public Teachers of Law, the AGM of the Magistrate's Association, the University of Birmingham, Birkbeck College London (of which Denning was elected President in 1953), the Law Society, Oxford University, Trinity College in Dublin, and Durham University. In 1953, he collected some of those lectures in a short book entitled *The Changing Law*.[33] The chapter titles once again revealed familiar Denning territory: 'The Spirit of the British Constitution'; 'The Rule of Law in the Welfare State'; 'The Changing Civil Law'; 'The Rights of Women'; and 'The Influence of Religion'. Denning was on his usual form explaining his more flexible approach to precedent and statutory interpretation. As with the Hamlyn Lectures the book was critically and commercially successful, *The Times* for example calling it 'important'.[34]

By way of an aside, Denning made a slightly misleading remark in respect of the Lord Chancellor. He said that the office had recently been reformed as Lord Haldane[35] had wanted many years earlier, when the Lord Chancellor was 'relieved of the daily duties of a judge who hears cases'.[36] Although the Lord Chancellor did not have the workload of a High Court judge, the holder of the post continued to hear cases in the House of Lords, and as we have seen the incumbent Gavin Simonds issued not infrequent admonishments to Denning when doing so.[37]

With his speaking and his books Denning was becoming very well known to all those interested in the law, including (especially) academics and students. The former Court of Appeal judge Sir Martin Nourse recalled an encounter of the time, when he was an undergraduate in awe of Denning's reputation:[38]

> Between 1953 and 1955 I was reading law at Cambridge. By that time the dons were up in arms at many of Lord Denning's judgments, especially his dissents. Not so the students. I remember us passing messages round at the back of the lectures saying such as: 'Have you read in the *Times* today and seen the latest judgment of hero Denning, LJ?' One Friday evening in February 1955 he came down to address the Law Society. I have his letter of acceptance still. I remember taking him into the largest room in the Old Schools, packed out to the limits, almost literally to the extent of people hanging on the rafters. I opened proceedings by saying that to introduce Lord Justice Denning to an audience such as that was rather like going onto the balcony at St Peters, Rome and introducing the Pope. Of course it was an outstanding piece of nerve, which only a student could have perpetrated. But the audience seemed to love it and the speaker himself did not demur.

A judicial ambassador; The Road to Justice

For all his patriotism and belief in the superiority of English common law, Denning had far from an inward perspective on the law. In June 1953, he became Chairman of the Society of Comparative Legislation and International

Law. The following year, he visited South Africa at the invitation of the Nuffield Foundation. It was the first of very many overseas trips. He always travelled with Joan, relying on her to make all the practical arrangements.

During the tour he spoke at every university in the country. The apartheid regime was in full force at the time, though the firm convention for visiting dignitaries was never to comment on the domestic affairs of other nations. There was also no sporting ban on South Africa and nothing in the way of economic sanctions. It is therefore not surprising that Denning agreed to visit in spite of the odiousness of the South African regime, though he could hardly have been unaware of it whilst there. It should also be noted that some other English visitors around the same time were not reticent about pointing out the injustices they observed, such as the cricket commentator John Arlott, or the entertainer George Formby,[39] while The Beatles refused to play in front of segregated audiences in the United States.[40] Yet, given the enthusiasm with which Denning visited other countries throughout Africa (his work on African legal education will appear in the next chapter) and his unambiguous statements against racial discrimination in his Hamlyn Lectures and elsewhere, it would be straightforwardly wrong to suggest that he had any sympathy with apartheid. It was simply that he would have regarded it as inappropriate to discuss the issue whilst in South Africa, just as with the iniquities of other regimes he visited, such as the communist regime in Poland. That said, in his old age he recalled his visits to South Africa with fondness, and did not comment on its internal affairs then either.[41]

In August 1955, he visited the United States and Canada. The lectures he gave there and in South Africa were published as *The Road to Justice*, a third short volume with the same publisher.[42] Once more the themes were familiar – fair trials, the need for the law to do justice, and structure and conduct of the legal profession. They also provided yet more examples of the importance Denning placed upon the Christian faith.

Of the work he was doing to modernise administrative law, Denning was open and unrepentant, stating that the old procedures for preventing abuse of power, such as *mandamus*, *certiorari* and actions on the case were outdated and insufficient. He called for them all to be replaced by newer legal machinery such as declarations, injunctions and actions for negligence.[43]

At times in his speeches, Denning could appear mildly naïve or myopic. One example of naïvety was when he wrote that in England it was unlikely any juror who had read a newspaper report of preliminary proceedings would remember enough to be influenced by it,[44] a statement frankly implausible in high profile cases such as the aforementioned acid bath murderer Haigh, whom Denning also discussed in the book.[45] The context of Denning's remarks was a subtle criticism of the 'yellow press' in America sensationalising trials.

An example of Denning's myopia was that, when writing of the legal profession in England, he focused almost exclusively on the Bar, virtually ignoring solicitors. His defence of the split profession was that keeping barristerial numbers low helped to uphold standards. That argument ignored the fact that, as Denning unquestionably knew, the Bar was structured to ensure that well-connected individuals had a distinct advantage in securing pupillage,[46] and in almost all cases only those with independent income could survive devilling for the first year or two of their working life. In both those respects the Bar was the opposite of a meritocracy and was therefore *less* likely to uphold standards. Economists would describe both features as deliberate barriers to entry of new competition, unjustifiably protecting the existing suppliers and almost creating a cartel.

More comments bordering on the naïve surfaced when Denning was writing about judges. He stated that there was 'no system of promotion of judges in England', which was odd coming from someone who had himself been promoted from the High Court to the Court of Appeal, and who would shortly join the House of Lords. Denning was presumably referring to the fact that his new job had had no increase in pay (something else which has since changed[47]), but anyone outside or inside the profession could see that the status of a Lord Justice was higher than that of a puisne judge and would regard elevation in the hierarchy as a 'promotion'.

Finally, Denning was being simplistic when declaring that lawyers 'must never suppress or distort the truth'.[48] Apart from anything else, he ignored the not-improper suppression of the clients' bottom lines when lawyers negotiated settlements.

Overall, though, his speeches contained many stimulating ideas, as well as reinforcing basic tenets of justice,[49] and as with his previous publications the book was well-received.[50]

One reviewer praised the book as 'a model of how to avoid either offending one's host by lecturing him on his deficiencies, or boring him by mouthing vapid platitudes'.[51] That natural diplomacy ensured a continuing stream of overseas invitations. In the remainder of the 1950s, as well as returning to the United States several times, Denning went to countries as diverse as Israel, Poland and India. Reflecting the Cold War then in progress and the austerity inevitable under communism, Denning found that not only were conditions grim in Poland, but also that his room was bugged.[52] He was pleased to be able to fly home from that trip, and thereafter took advantage of the burgeoning jet age by travelling exclusively by air when he went overseas.[53]

Promotion

Denning's next career opportunity came in early 1957, when Lord Oaksey made known his intention to retire from the Appellate Committee of the House of Lords. Denning was offered the role but did not accept immediately. One of his favourite quotes was that the House of Lords was like Heaven – 'you want to get there some day, but not while there's any life left in you'.[54] Instead, he had his eye on becoming either Lord Chief Justice or Master of the Rolls, which he knew would be more influential than the role of a single law lord. After mulling things over, however, he decided to accept the appointment. He would thus join the highest court in the land.

CHAPTER IX

The House of Lords

Pomp and circumstance

On 26 April 1957, the *London Gazette* recorded that Alfred Thompson Denning had become Baron Denning of Whitchurch in the County of Southampton.[1] The choice of Whitchurch was clear evidence that despite having spent many happy years in Sussex, Denning was still most emotionally connected with the small town of his youth. Rather mischievously, he wanted his coat of arms to show palm trees, in reference to the 'palm tree justice' of which he had been occasionally accused, but the College of Arms was deaf to his humour (as it usually was to anyone else's) and declined. Instead, his coat of arms incorporated references to two of his heroes, Sir Edward Coke and Lord Mansfield, both among the most famous judges in English history, as Denning himself was to become.

As before, the news of Denning's elevation prompted a flood of congratulatory cards and letters to his post box from across the profession – barristers, solicitors, academics and fellow judges.[2] Reflecting both his travels and his burgeoning reputation, they also included many messages from overseas, including Africa, where one correspondent expressed how much he looked forward to Denning sitting on Privy Council appeals from local courts. The Oxford University Law Society welcomed what they thought would be a more progressive voice in the Lords, as did the barrister Leonard O'Malley.

There was the odd note of caution: Denning was now a colleague of Viscount Simonds, and since neither had the remotest intention of changing his ways, some of his correspondents predicted further conflict, building on their earlier disagreements in cases such as *Seaford Court Estates*. Sir John Beaumont,[3] for example, wrote 'You will have, I suspect, some tussles with

Gavin behind the scenes'. In time, Denning and Viscount Simonds would enjoy good personal relations, with the latter and his wife occasionally staying with Denning at Whitchurch,[4] but things were more frosty when they actually worked together. Denning made friends more quickly with Lord Morris of Borth-y-Gest,[5] with whom he sometimes stayed in Wales, and Lord Reid,[6] the latter having one of the best reputations of all twentieth-century judges.

Denning was inducted into his new status by way of a colourful pageant in the Grand Chamber of the House of Lords, involving rituals dating back to 1620. He wore parliamentary robes supplied by the well-known outfitters Ede & Ravenscroft, but unlike some of his fellow peers, he did not purchase the robes for posterity. After leaving the ceremony, he assumed the business of a Lord of Appeal in Ordinary, or 'law lord' as per the usual shorthand.

His new role came with some incidental lifestyle opportunities, since the Appellate Committee only sat for four days a week at most, and always reserved judgment. Although he allowed himself the odd leisure pursuit, chiefly golf and tending to his substantial garden, Denning characteristically used the fifth day primarily for extra work. As well as spending more time preparing individual judgments, he continued planning more overseas trips, writing and delivering speeches, and working with the charities to whom he had lent his name. He also sat as Chairman of the Quarter Sessions for East Sussex for a few days each year while the Lords were on vacation. It would have been quite a contrasting experience going from the rarefied atmosphere of the highest court in the land to the sharp end of the criminal law, but Denning found it rewarding. It enabled him to see the criminal law in action as opposed to the law reports and journals, and to discuss things over lunch with magistrates at the judges' lodgings of the sort he had enjoyed a few years earlier when on circuit.

The other role which Denning now had was as a member of the House of Lords in Parliament (a function which was not transferred when the Appellate Committee of the House of Lords became the Supreme Court in 2009). His maiden speech concerned administrative law and how important he felt it was to keep government under law.[7] He would go on to participate in 328 debates in the Lords between 1957 and 1988 – more than any other law lord during his lifetime. Reflecting his catholic interests in law, he spoke on a range of subjects including charitable trusts, obscene publications, police, religious cults, suicide, the Law Commission, civil evidence, education, solicitors, public records and numerous issues of family and criminal law.[8] From a legal perspective, one of his more notable speeches concerned the Appellate Committee's then-inability to overturn its own decisions. Denning stated forthrightly:

> The law at the moment is illogical, inconsistent and absurd ... I am afraid one has to face the fact that it is the fault of the interpretation which has been put on it by this House sitting judicially, which is infallible, which never makes a mistake and which can never correct itself.[9]

Not long after his promotion, the Wolfenden Report[10] was published, which recommended decriminalisation of male homosexuality. Denning was appalled, stating that it was an unnatural and immoral practice,[11] sentiments he would repeat nearly thirty years later when speaking in support of what became the notorious s 28 of the Local Government Act 1988.[12] That was probably the least surprising of his old-fashioned views, for not only was he in company with much of his generation, as ever following the lead of the church,[13] but he was also in accord with the prevailing medical opinion of the day and the majority of the popular press.[14] The uncompromising public opinion which Denning shared made for much blatant hypocrisy amongst the establishment, though not Denning himself.[15]

We should add the qualification that even if other senior lawyers agreed at least outwardly with Denning's moral objection to homosexuality, they were not convinced it was the business of the law to prevent it amongst consenting adults in private, one of the chief reasons that the Wolfenden Report's recommendation for decriminalisation was eventually passed into law, albeit it took a decade after the 1957 report.

Outside the Lords, he continued to deliver lectures at home and abroad. In a 1960 lecture, he openly worried about the implications of equality for women.[16] As usual, he was not consistent on that front. He applauded successful career women, but still thought that any woman would find homemaking more rewarding than any more lucrative occupation. With respect to men, Denning could be equally anachronistic. He fretted that vasectomies were 'plainly injurious' to public welfare since they removed the potential burden of parental obligation for the recipient.[17] And he worried that if artificial insemination became widespread it would 'strike at the stability and security of family life, at the roots of our civilization'.[18] Equally predictably, he was revolted by pornography, which he claimed 'shocks and disgusts decent people ... They revolt from it and turn away from it'.[19] Again, he would have encountered no open dissenters on the Bench or virtually anywhere in public life at the time, however much society might have changed since.

Judgments

Following convention

In his time in the House of Lords and Privy Council, Denning participated in eighty judgments, of which sixty-three were reported in the *All England Law Reports*. With a few exceptions, not many remain of interest six decades later. His speeches (as individual House of Lords' judgments or opinions were referred to) contained less of the classic Denning style than found in his Court of Appeal judgments before and after. In *Brown v Rolls Royce Ltd* [1960] 1 All ER 577, for example, there was no idiosyncratic storytelling and few verb-less sentences. There was a mild Denning touch in his opening in *Wheat v E Lacon & Co Ltd* [1966] 1 All ER 582:

> My Lords, the 'Golfer's Arms' at Great Yarmouth is owned by the respondents, the brewery company, E Lacon & Co Ltd. The ground floor was run as a public house by Mr Richardson as manager for the respondents. The first floor was used by Mr and Mrs Richardson as their private dwelling. In the summer Mrs Richardson took in guests for her private profit. Mr and Mrs Wheat and their family were summer guests of Mrs Richardson. About 9 pm one evening, when it was getting dark, Mr Wheat fell down the back staircase in the private portion and was killed. Winn J held that there were two causes: (i) the handrail was too short because it did not stretch to the foot of the stairs; (ii) someone had taken the bulb out of the light at the top of the stairs.
>
> The case raises this point of law: did the respondents owe any duty to Mr Wheat to see that the handrail was safe to use or to see that the stairs were properly lighted? That depends on whether the respondents were 'an occupier' of the private portion of the 'Golfer's Arms', and Mr Wheat was their 'visitor' within the Occupiers' Liability Act, 1957: for, if so, the respondents owed him the 'common duty of care'.

As was the Denning way, the parties were identified by name, and some personal flavour was given by the name of the pub and the brewery which owned it, then the issue was clearly set out in the second paragraph. But the remainder of the judgment was composed of more usual-sounding judicial sentences, with no homilies or other Denning-esque features.

Similarly, in *Sykes v Director of Public Prosecutions* [1961] 3 All ER 33, a case involving the theft of weapons from an American air base with the apparent intention of selling them to the IRA, Denning's account of the facts had a touch of the thriller novel, but nothing like the hyperbole which would come back to haunt him in the 'Birmingham Six' judgment considered later in the book. Instead, for the rest of his speech, and most of the others which he delivered in the House of Lords, Denning used conventional judicial language, largely indistinguishable from his colleagues.

If the Denning style was mostly abandoned in favour of convention in the House, the same was not always true for the Denning reasoning, most notably when he had his predicted clashes with Viscount Simonds. The first of those judicial contretemps occurred soon after his appointment.

Rahimtoola v H E H The Nizam of Hyderabad and Others – a long story

Rahimtoola v H E H The Nizam of Hyderabad and Others [1958] AC 379 was a case arising out of the Partition of India upon the cessation of the British Raj, in the form of the refusal of the principality of Hyderabad to join either India or the new state of Pakistan. At the time of Partition in 1947, the princely states of India were largely self-governing, with agreements with Britain covering external relations. Those agreements ended when Britain withdrew, leaving the principalities with the option of independence or joining India or Pakistan. By 1948, nearly all had joined one of the two countries, with Hyderabad an important exception as the wealthiest principality. Hyderabad was still ruled by an absolute monarch, the seventh Nizam of Hyderabad. India sent its troops into the territory in what was euphemistically called a 'police action'. They met little organised opposition, but severe inter-communal violence took place nonetheless.

Substantial funds were held for the Nizam in a bank account in London. During the Indian invasion, money in the account was transferred into the name of the appellant, the High Commissioner of Pakistan in London, as agent of the government of Pakistan. The Nizam's government cabled the bank objecting to the transfer, contending that it was unauthorised. Subsequently, the Nizam brought an action seeking to recover the funds.

The appellant, who had since changed roles to become Pakistani ambassador to France, applied to set aside the proceedings against him and stay the proceedings against the bank on the ground that the action impleaded the state of Pakistan, which was entitled to sovereign immunity. That was despite the fact that Pakistan did not assert any beneficial interest in the funds. The judge agreed and stayed the action, holding that Pakistan's bare legal title in the funds, through the appellant as High Commissioner, was sufficient to establish sovereign immunity. The Court of Appeal disagreed and reinstated the action, leading to the appeal before the House of Lords.

The House of Lords unanimously allowed the appeal and stayed the action, but Denning still struck out on his own, even though he agreed with the result. He considered a number of authorities which had not been cited in the papers or in argument. He offered the following *apologia* at the end of his speech:

> My Lords, I acknowledge that, in the course of this opinion, I have considered some questions and authorities which were not mentioned by counsel. I am sure they gave all the help they could and I have only gone into it further because the law on this subject is of great consequence and, as applied at present, it is held by many to be unsatisfactory. I venture to think that, if there is one place where it should be re-considered on principle – without being tied to particular precedents of a period that is past – it is here in this House; and if there is one time for it to be done, it is now, when the opportunity offers, before the law gets any more enmeshed in its own net. This I have tried to do. Whatever the outcome, I hope I may say, as Holt CJ once did, after he had done much research on his own: 'I have stirred these points, which wiser heads in time may settle'.

Viscount Simonds was not amused:

> My Lords, I must add that, since writing this opinion, I have had the privilege of reading the opinion which my noble and learned friend, Lord Denning, is about to deliver. It is right that I should say that I must not be taken as assenting to his views upon a number of questions and authorities in regard to which the House has not had the benefit of the arguments of counsel or of the judgment of the courts below.

The remaining judges – Lord Reid, Lord Cohen and Lord Somervell – agreed with Viscount Simonds, making for a rather deflating experience for Denning. Not for the first or last time, though, Denning's view would eventually win out, since the State Immunity Act 1978 largely reflected his opinion rather than those of the other judges.

Somewhat surprisingly, the Nizam's money remained in the account and became subject to proceedings more than half a century after the House of Lords' decision.[20] It resulted in a confidential settlement in 2018 which allowed a part of the estate – approximately £400,000 – to be credited to the late Nizam's English estate. His son, the eighth Nizam, disowned the money, saying that after all that time he had had enough of the dispute.[21] Perhaps he regarded it as akin to Dickens' *Bleak House*, though at least unlike *Jarndyce v Jarndyce* the lawyers had not soaked up all the money on their fees before the case ended.

In Re Parliamentary Privilege Act 1770 – dissenting in the Privy Council

Relations between Denning and Viscount Simonds did not improve when both sat in the Privy Council to hear the case of *In Re Parliamentary Privilege Act 1770* [1958] AC 331.

The proceedings concerned a letter of February 1957 from George Strauss MP to the Paymaster General, Reginald Maudling. The letter alleged that the London Electricity Board was scandalously disposing of scrap cables at cut-price rates. The board responded by demanding the unqualified withdrawal of the allegations in the letter, or they would issue a libel writ. Strauss called the attention of the House of Commons to the correspondence, contending that the board's threat of a libel action was a breach of parliamentary privilege.

The Speaker of the House of Commons ruled that the threats constituted a *prima facie* case of breach of privilege. The House resolved to refer the matter to its Privileges Committee. The committee replied that in writing the letter Strauss had been engaged in a 'proceeding in Parliament' within the meaning of the Bill of Rights 1688, and that the libel threat from the board was threatening to impeach or question the freedom of Strauss in a court or place outside Parliament. Accordingly, the board and its solicitors had acted in breach of the privilege of Parliament.

The committee then sought the opinion of the Judicial Committee of the Privy Council on the question whether the House of Commons would be acting contrary to the Parliamentary Privilege Act 1770 if it treated the issue of a writ against a Member of Parliament in respect of a speech or proceeding by him in Parliament as a breach of its privileges.

In keeping with convention, the Privy Council gave only a single judgment (framed as 'advice' to Her Majesty), delivered by Viscount Simonds. It held that the House would not be acting contrary to the 1770 Act if it treated the issue of a writ against a Member of Parliament in respect of a speech or proceeding by him in Parliament as a breach of its privileges.

That was the end of it so far as the law reports were concerned. Behind the scenes, however, Denning had written a dissenting judgment. In classic Denning fashion, he thought that the decision of the majority obstructed 'the right of every Englishman to seek redress in the courts of law' and that therefore the House of Commons would indeed be acting contrary to the 1770 Act. The six other law lords were not amused. They refused to allow Denning's dissent to be appended to the judgment and made no mention of it in the single judgment that was issued.

By insisting on a single judgment with no published dissent, the other law lords were acting in accordance with convention, since the Privy Council had not published dissents since 1627. In 1911 there had been some complaints by the Dominions who had the Privy Council as their final appellate court, though no change was introduced until 1966, when at the behest of Australia dissenting opinions were allowed.

Despite the rule about dissenting judgments being clearly in place, the snubbing of his dissent clearly rankled with Denning, for he mentioned it in *The Family Story* decades later. In 1985, he provided a copy of his draft judgment to a legal academic, who published it as an appendix to an article in the journal *Public Law*.[22]

DPP v Smith – homicide and intent

DPP v Smith [1961] AC 290 was probably the best-known criminal appeal on which Denning sat while in the Lords. On that occasion he agreed with the other judges, so there was no intra-judicial controversy. But the decision of the House caused quite a stir amongst practitioners and academics of the day, leading Denning to take the unusual step of defending the judgment publicly.

The defendant was driving a car with sacks of stolen scaffolding clips in the back. A police constable, noticing the sacks, told him to pull over, but instead the respondent accelerated away. The constable clung on to the side of the car, which pursued an erratic course, but he was shaken off and fell in front of another car, receiving fatal injuries. The defendant drove on some 200 yards and dumped the stolen property. He was caught and charged with murder. The judge when summing-up told the jury:

> If you are satisfied that ... he must as a reasonable man have contemplated that grievous bodily harm was likely to result to that officer ... and that such harm did happen and the officer died in consequence, then the accused is guilty of capital murder. ... On the other hand, if you are not satisfied that he intended to inflict grievous bodily harm upon the officer – in other words, if you think he could not as a reasonable man have contemplated that grievous bodily harm would result to the officer in consequence of his actions – well, then, the verdict would be guilty of manslaughter.

The defendant was convicted of capital murder and appealed. The Court of Criminal Appeal allowed the appeal and substituted a verdict of manslaughter. The Attorney General certified that the case involved a point of law of exceptional public importance, and the Director of Public Prosecutions appealed to the House of Lords.

The only reasoned judgment was delivered by Lord Kilmuir. All the other law lords, Denning included, gave a one-line concurring speech. Lord Kilmuir stated (at 327):

> The jury must, of course, in such a case as the present make up their minds on the evidence whether the accused was unlawfully and voluntarily doing something to someone. The unlawful and voluntary act must clearly be aimed at someone in order to eliminate cases of negligence or of careless or dangerous driving. Once, however, the jury are satisfied as to that, it matters not what the accused in fact contemplated as the probable result or whether he ever contemplated at all, provided he was in law responsible and accountable for his actions, that is, was a man capable of forming an intent, not insane within the M'Naghten Rules and not suffering from diminished responsibility. On the assumption that he is so accountable for his actions, the sole question is whether the unlawful and voluntary act was of such a kind that grievous bodily harm was the natural and probable result. The only test available for this is what the ordinary responsible man would, in all the circumstances of the case, have contemplated as the natural and probable result.

He went on (at 330–31):

> My Lords, the law being as I have endeavoured to define it, there seems to be no ground upon which the approach by the trial judge in the present case can be criticised. Having excluded the suggestion of accident, he asked the jury to consider what were the exact circumstances at the time as known to the respondent, and what were the unlawful and voluntary acts which he did towards the police officer. The learned judge then prefaced the passages of which complaint is made by saying, in effect, that if in doing what he did he must as a reasonable man have contemplated that serious harm was likely to occur then he was guilty of murder.
>
> My only doubt concerns the use of the expression 'a reasonable man,' since this to lawyers connotes the man on the Clapham omnibus by reference to whom a standard of care in civil cases is ascertained. In judging of intent, however, it really denotes an ordinary man capable of reasoning who is responsible and accountable for his

actions, and this would be the sense in which it would be understood by a jury.

The appeal was therefore allowed and the conviction of capital murder restored.

The case attracted some criticism for what some saw as the importation of an objective test where it had always been subjective. The report in the *All England Law Reports* ([1960] 3 All ER 161) contained a note:[23]

> This decision restores the objective test of the mental element in murder as distinct from the subjective test, but the decision rests on the premise that there has been proof of an unlawful voluntary act 'aimed at' someone. The words 'aimed at' are used in order to exclude mere negligence ... but they may seem to predicate necessarily the existence of some initial purpose, if not of intention.

Denning never doubted the result in the case, though he was concerned that some had not fully understood the reasoning. He later gave a speech on 'Responsibility before the law',[24] in which he accepted that the defendant (Smith) had not intended to kill the constable. He argued:

> No doubt Smith had no *desire* to kill him: and it was not his *purpose* to kill him. But must he not have been aware that there was a very high probability that the policeman would suffer grievous bodily harm? And if so, was he not guilty of murder? ... The Lord Chancellor summarised the direction in this way: 'If in doing what he did, *he must* as a reasonable man have contemplated that serious harm was likely to occur, then he was guilty of murder'. Note the words '*he must*' – that is – *this particular man* must have contemplated. Thus it must be brought home to him subjectively.

Denning quoted the case and his subsequent speech in *The Family Story*,[25] indicating the significance he attached to it.

Scruttons Ltd v Midland Silicones Ltd – 'a judicial beheading'

One of the best-known Denning dissents during his time in the Lords occurred in *Scruttons Ltd v Midland Silicones Ltd* [1962] AC 446. The trial judge, then the Court of Appeal and finally the House of Lords all held that stevedores who had damaged cargo when unloading it were not entitled to rely upon exemptions contained in the bill of lading, because they were not party to it. Thus was the principle of privity of contract robustly affirmed.

Denning alone among all those judges disagreed.[26] It was ironic given that he was upholding an exemption clause, albeit the context of the case was allocation of insurance liability rather than an embattled consumer faced with impenetrable prose on the back of a receipt. For his lone act of defiance he earned another unsubtle reprimand from Viscount Simonds:

> [T]o me heterodoxy, or, as some might say, heresy, is not the more attractive because it is dignified by the name of reform. Nor will I easily be led by an undiscerning zeal for some abstract kind of justice to ignore our first duty, which is to administer justice according to law, the law which is established for us by Act of Parliament or the binding authority of precedent. The law is developed by the application of old principles to new circumstances. Therein lies its genius. Its reform by the abrogation of those principles is the task not of the courts of law but of Parliament.

Denning later called that a 'judicial beheading'.[27] And yet, he enjoyed a degree of subsequent vindication once more when, more than a decade later, the Privy Council reached the opposite result in *The Eurymedon* [1975] AC 154. Lord Wilberforce's decision in that later case read quite closely to Denning's dissent in *Midland Silicones*.

Later decisions of the House of Lords were also more aligned to Denning's thinking.[28] Finally, both had some eventual justification in the form of the Contracts (Rights of Third Parties) Act 1999, which watered down the privity rule by statute – Denning's preferred result by Lord Simonds' preferred means. During the second reading of the Bill which became the Act, it was said to be a 'birthday present to Lord Denning'[29] as it brought the law more into line with his thinking.

The Lawn

We saw how with his ennoblement Denning was still looking back to his origins in Whitchurch. In 1960, the chance to move back to the town permanently arose when he learned via Marjorie that a grand house named The Lawn, situated opposite his beloved All Hallows Church, had come onto the market.

Fair Close was now largely empty apart from him and Joan, since Joan's children had all married and were living independently while Robert, like his father before him, had gone up to Magdalen College, Oxford. Denning and Joan were struggling to find domestic help in the area and the house was also a long walk to the nearest village, something bound to be of greater concern in the coming years. They therefore carefully studied the opportunity to purchase The Lawn.

The Lawn had been advertised in 1868 as a desirable 'Family Residence' for a 'City Gentleman', being close to the railway and with hunting, shooting and fishing in its immediate vicinity (Denning was pleased to have a copy of that advertisement, a document crafted in finely wrought Victorian prose).[30] He remembered it as a grand house in his childhood. In the years since it had been purchased by the Bank of England to house staff evacuated during the Blitz and then used as an officers' mess by the army. Both the Bank of England employees and the soldiers had been less than sympathetic occupants, meaning the house was in poor condition by 1960.

It emerged that the Bank of England was prepared to sell the house and grounds for £7,000, subject to the tail-end of a lease to the War Department. More than any other monetary figure quoted thus far, the vastly different purchasing power of money at different times of Denning's life was illustrated by that figure. According to the Bank of England inflation calculator, £7,000 in 1960 translated to just £125,000 in 2022. In reality, the house would have fetched seven figures without question in 2022, even in poor condition as it was at the time of Denning's purchase.

Denning and Joan spent some time over the decision, and researched how the house might be restored. They decided to purchase it using a trust established for Robert. The trustees were Joan along with Anthony Moir, Denning's old housemate and long-standing man of affairs. Joan and Denning then set about extending the grounds by purchasing parcels of contiguous land, which enabled them to preserve the view from the main house. Denning also had his eye on the neighbouring cricket ground and pavilion owned by the St Cross Hospital, but the latter was unwilling to sell and so he took a lease of the ground instead.

In time he and Joan extended the house and refurbished it substantially, not all of which ran smoothly. Much of the building work was done without their direct supervision as they remained in Sussex or in their London flat while it was being undertaken. Various defects resulted, but eventually the works were completed to their satisfaction and they were to enjoy many happy decades living there – as Denning himself noted, in the style of leading judges of earlier eras, including those on his coat of arms, Mansfield and Coke. One room was furnished with Denning's private law library, while a new wing allowed visitors to stay without getting under his feet.

Denning and Joan tended the gardens assiduously and often used the substantial grounds to host village activities, while the cricket being played on the ground there brought Denning great joy.[31] Although Denning himself was not especially interested in fishing, he enjoyed hosting visitors who were and thus able to put the stretch of the River Test that ran through the property to use. He also became involved in local affairs, among other things becoming one of the trustees responsible for renovating the old town hall.[32]

The Dennings went on to sell Fair Close but kept about fifteen acres of land in Sussex, which they visited from time to time. Along with other properties Denning purchased in Whitchurch, including another large house called 'The Mount', which he converted into flats for the elderly, six small houses which he let to young married couples at a low rent,[33] and land contiguous to The Lawn, it amounted to an impressive property portfolio that would be well beyond any judge's income in the twenty-first century.

Africa

In 1957 the *African Law Journal* was founded by Professor Anthony Allott. Denning supplied the foreword to the first volume, in which he wrote:[34]

> In naming this Journal, the promoters imply that there is a body of law properly described as African law. I have heard of Roman law. I know something of English law. But what is this African law? It is at the moment a jumble of pieces much like a jig-saw. One group of pieces is founded on the customs of the African peoples, which vary from territory to territory and from tribe to tribe. Another group of pieces is founded on the law of Islam, with all its many schools and texts. Yet another group is founded on the English common law. Another on the Roman-Dutch law. Another on Indian Statutes. And so forth.

As well as the South African trip discussed in the previous chapter, Denning visited many other African countries during his career, where he made a universally positive impression. In 1960, he chaired a conference held in London on 'The Future of Law in Africa'. Denning said in his foreword to the record of the conference:

> Africa, like some great giant awaking out of centuries of slumber, stretches its limbs, stands up and looks at the dawn. It is the dawn of its own day it is looking at. We in the older civilisations have almost

forgotten what that kind of dawn can be. We no longer expect to see the dew on the grass. But Africa sees it now and will soon be on the march. Can we not help it gird on its coat for the journey – it is a coat of many colours – the coat of African law.

It was pointed out during the conference that there was inadequate training in the common law available in Africa, which had led many African lawyers to train in England: more than 3,000 were doing so at the time, most in one of the Inns of Court. Unfortunately, the Inns, seeking to be accommodating to the newly independent African states, had lowered admission standards to the point where many visiting students were struggling to pass the final examinations.[35] The conference recommended that a Committee on Legal Education for Students in Africa be established.

A committee was duly formed and Denning was appointed chair.[36] In that capacity he travelled extensively in Africa during the summer vacation, including Nigeria, Uganda, Kenya, Tanganyika and Zanzibar (the latter two joined in 1964 to form the modern state of Tanzania). As ever, his Protestant work ethic led to a detailed report in short order: it was finished by December 1960 and published the following month. It recommended that the Inns tighten requirements so that no students would be admitted without a sufficient background education to pass the Bar exams. It further recommended more training in England for the visiting students so they would be better prepared to practise upon their return to Africa. Most importantly, it stressed the importance for legal education to take place in Africa itself, stating 'in every territory there should be an Institute for Legal Training, call it a law school, if you will, where basic legal training can be given'.[37]

Denning's work heading the committee was well regarded and led to him developing a strong reputation across the continent. Among other things, Denning Societies appeared in the African law schools,[38] while back in England he received a standing ovation at one of the Inns from the African students then in attendance.[39] In January 1961, he delivered a lecture entitled 'Legal Education in Africa: Sharing our Heritage' to the Lawyers' Christian Fellowship, subsequently published in the *Law Society Gazette*.[40] A few years after Denning's retirement, the distinguished Nigerian jurist Taslim Olawale Elias[41] called Denning 'an indefatigable promoter of the development of the legal profession in the newer Commonwealth'.[42]

The House of Lords

A de-motional promotion

By 1962, the Master of the Rolls (MR), Lord Evershed, had decided that he could no longer manage the pressure of work heading the Court of Appeal, Civil Division, and wished to retire or at least move to a less demanding role. The Lord Chancellor, Lord Kilmuir, remembered Denning had expressed interest in the position of MR years before. He had a word in private with Denning following a lunch they both attended, the usual judicial recruitment technique of the day.

In theory, the role of MR would constitute a demotion in the judicial hierarchy, but Denning accepted the invitation with alacrity. He had not much enjoyed the Lords, writing years later that it had felt like going into retirement. Compared with the Court of Appeal, the House of Lords heard many fewer cases and Denning had many more colleagues whom he had to persuade to accept his point of view for his rulings to have any effect. It would have involved a long wait to become the senior law lord – in those days, the position, largely informal, fell to the longest-serving – and even then there would be no guarantee he would be able to persuade any other judges to his viewpoint. His dissenting judgments in the Lords had achieved little beyond providing intellectual gristle for academics. Admittedly, he had dissented in the Lords less often than one might have expected – Lord Diplock, for example, who was later to gain a reputation as the dominant figure in the House of Lords, dissented more often. It was instead the public nature of the reprimands from Viscount Simonds that set Denning apart, since it was rare then, as now, for judges in the appellate courts to bare their teeth at each other publicly.[43]

As it happened, Denning and Lord Evershed were the same age (62), both were Oxford alumni, and both had served in the Royal Engineers in the First World War. Lord Evershed, however, was in less good health than Denning. In effect the two swapped places, since Lord Evershed served for a time on the Appellate Committee of the House of Lords before his death in 1966.

For his part, Denning was stepping into the role which would secure him lasting fame.

CHAPTER X
Master of the Rolls – Appointment and Beginnings

Appointment

Denning's appointment as Master of the Rolls was announced in March 1962. Once more he received over a hundred letters and cards offering congratulations, this time from an even more diverse set of correspondents than his earlier appointments.[1] One letter came from the Friends of the Hebrew University of Jerusalem, while another was from the Vicarage of Colwyn Bay – showing how his fame had spread thanks to his judgments, his travels and his published lectures. The Bar Theatrical Society expressed their appreciation of his appointment and added that they hoped he had enjoyed their recent production of 'Dangerous Corner', though they regretted 'as usual the audience was not as large as we had hoped'. The well-known public intellectual Sir Julian Huxley[2] wrote 'I am afraid I know little about the legal world, but enough to be sure that this must be very gratifying'. The barrister BL Bathurst QC clearly knew Denning's character: 'You have certainly taken on a very full-time job – but then you're a tiger for work, and we need a tiger in that position'. James McCrudden of New South Wales wrote:[3]

> I warmly wish your Lordship a long tenure and extend the hope that it will be blessed with the absence of 'timid souls' and binding precedents for so long the 'Scylla and Charybdis' (or Tweedledee and Tweedledum?) of your judicial career.

The distinguished legal academic Professor HWR Wade wrote from Oxford University:[4]

> If I may say so, I feel that you will be moving back to the real centre of gravity of the law, where your creative powers can be of the greatest service. I have a presentiment that your escape from the House of Lords, if you will forgive my so putting it, will be a great event in the legal history of our time. The odds against enlightened decisions have now shortened once more!

Other well-wishes came from the Oxford University Law Society, the University of Manchester Faculty of Law, University College London, the University of Auckland,[5] the Association of the Bar of the City of New York, the University of the Witwatersrand, Johannesburg, the senior public administrator Sir Ivor Julian,[6] the publishers Sweet & Maxwell, the International Law Association, the British Institute for International and Comparative Law, the Dutch lawyer JCS Warendorf[7] and the American firm Simpson Thacher & Bartlett.

Most writers insisted that he did not reply, accurately predicting how many letters he would receive, thus avoiding a never-ending pendulum of thank-you letters or notes passing back and forth, but Denning did nevertheless respond to a handful. He wrote to the solicitor and amateur constitutional theorist Edward F Iwi: 'I am afraid it means a good deal more work but one of the most attractive things from my point of view is that it will bring me into association with the solicitors' side of the profession'.[8]

A letter from Judge Richard A Willes alluded to recent changes in procedure before the Court of Appeal:

> I am specially delighted to remember that this will mean that you of all people will preside over the early stages of the so called 'experiment' in Appeal Court procedure forecast by the MR a short while ago. I suppose the American and other jurists are right in advocating the reading in advance of the available documentary material including a more elaborate Notice of Appeal before an Appeal is opened in Court but I think this might be fraught with danger. If there is anyone left who appreciates draftsmanship in pleading he will enjoy drawing an argumentative Notice of Appeal. I am trying to visualize years ago opening an appeal in which the late LJ Scrutton and Slesser LJ having read in advance the available documentary material, arrived in Court each having formed diametrically opposite views as to the meaning and importance of a point raised in an elaborate Notice.

More than half a century later, it is next to impossible to imagine an appeal beginning with no pre-reading having been done by the court. It enables the judges to move expeditiously to the point in the case. Reducing court time saves not only public funds but those of litigants as well. Willes' objection that the pleadings might cause two judges to form opposite views was otiose since it would logically apply to oral argument as well.

The Master of the Rolls' role

The title 'Master of the Rolls' (MR) is one of the typical English titles that has evolved over the centuries to mean something quite removed from its origins, but has been retained for one reason or another, such as lending dignity to an office, lack of motivation for change, sufficient vestiges of the original function remaining, or because no satisfactory alternative has ever been proffered. Perhaps something of all of those reasons applied in the case of the MR. Denning for one certainly appreciated the historical origins and enjoyed explaining how the holder of the office was originally responsible for the safe-keeping of charters, patents and other public records written on parchment rolls. Often, he would begin with a joke about baking or expensive cars, before setting out the actual origins. In a radio interview he put it thus:[9]

> They're the old parchment rolls which many hundreds of years ago all the records were kept on. Of the courts and the government. They were all on parchment and not in books like we have now, but rolled up ... And the Master of the Rolls was in charge of them, and we have many now in the public record office. I'm in charge of the Rolls of the Realm.

Even in the present day, the MR retains a degree of formal responsibility for documents of national importance, being Chair of the Advisory Council on Public Records and Chairman of the Royal Commission on Historical Manuscripts.

A second important component of the role is officially authorising solicitors to practise. The MR deals with professional rules and regulations dealing with solicitors and appeals against rulings of the Solicitors' Disciplinary Tribunal.[10]

Denning's responsibility for public records and solicitors was reflected in many speeches he gave on both subjects to the House of Lords in Parliament after his appointment.

The central function of the MR, however, is as a judge of the Court of Appeal and the President of its Civil Division. He or she is responsible for the deployment and organisation of the work of the judges of the division as well as presiding in one of its courts.

Denning was not the first to become MR after first sitting as a law lord, nor indeed the last. Nor did he set the record, as is sometimes erroneously assumed, for the length of his service as a judge in general or the MR in particular. Instances of judges serving longer as MR can be found as far back as the seventeenth century, perhaps surprisingly given the shorter life expectancy of the time. The memorably named Sir Julius Caesar (also known as Julius Adelmare[11]) served for twenty-two years, while Sir Harbottle Grimston, who obtained the post by slipping the Lord Chancellor the then-astronomical sum of £6,000, held it for twenty-five years (1660–85). Both were outdone by Sir John Trevor, who served a total of twenty-seven years, consisting of two non-consecutive terms (1685–88; 1693–1717), the break coming due to him backing the wrong horse in the Glorious Revolution towards the end of the century. Trevor's successor was Sir Joseph Jekyll, who held the post for twenty-one years (1717–38). Denning enjoyed a remark of Alexander Pope about Jekyll:[12]

> An odd old whig,
> Who never changed his principles or his wig

Lastly, in the nineteenth century, Sir John Romilly served for twenty-two years (1851–73).

None of those records, nor even Denning's slightly shorter term of twenty years, seems likely to be beaten in the foreseeable future, given the compulsory judicial retirement age. The restriction was first introduced by s 2 of the Judicial Pensions Act 1959. It did not apply to Denning since he had already been appointed to the Bench by then, and thus he was able to serve until the age of 83. Again, he did not set any new records in that respect. His age at retirement was exceeded by Lord Cameron, who was eighty-five when he retired from the Court of Sessions in October 1985. The last serving senior judge who avoided the compulsory retirement age was Lord Diplock, who died in October 1985, just short of his seventy-eighth birthday. Diplock had been active until shortly before his death.[13]

Retirement aside, Denning had no intention of moving to any other judicial post once he became MR. Nor did his successor, Sir John Donaldson, although more recent holders of the office have not always stayed until their retirement, instead moving around other senior judicial posts.

Choosing the judges

In Denning's time, judicial appointments were made by the Lord Chancellor following a wholly opaque process, the 'tap on the shoulder' which he received with his original appointment to the Bench in 1944. There were many fewer judges in his time,[14] and they were all still housed in the main building of the Royal Courts of Justice on the Strand, the MR himself in Court 3. After Denning's time, the Court of Appeal, Civil Division, moved to the East Block, a fairly soulless addition to the same estate. The MR now makes do with Court 71, which lacks something of the grandeur of any of the rooms within George Street's creation. By contrast, the Lord Chief Justice, heading the Court of Appeal, Criminal Division, still sits in Court 4 in the main block, a distinctly more impressive room.

Another feature of judicial appointments in Denning's time was that the ranks of the senior judiciary were drawn from a very narrow pool. They were always barristers, rights of audience in the higher courts not then being granted to solicitors.[15] And, as seen earlier, the Bar in Denning's time was structured in such a way as to hand a substantial advantage to the children of existing, successful barristers.

As a result, Denning's contemporaries on the Bench were almost invariably white, male, late middle-age or elderly former barristers drawn from the upper middle classes. Another feature, certainly in the senior courts,[16] was the dominance of private schools and Oxbridge.[17] It meant that some senior judges could spend their childhood and adolescence in boarding schools followed by Oxbridge colleges, then their entire working life within the Inns of Court in London followed by the Royal Courts of Justice on the Strand; each one a cloistered environment alien in many respects to the majority of the population. The only break might be if they went on circuit as Denning had done when a barrister and a puisne judge, though in the latter capacity by staying in judges' lodgings they would hardly be experiencing much of life in the provinces.

In the late 1970s the academic JAG (John) Griffith wrote a critique of that narrow range of selection[18] as part of an overall thesis about the authoritarian nature of government and the close political, social and class links of the elites across all of the important public roles of the day. Griffith claimed that the elite composition of the judiciary rendered it incapable of responding adequately to the challenge of social justice that underpinned many of the disputes which came before it.

The establishment was not amused. A review in the *Times Literary Supplement* went as far as claiming that Griffith was essentially aligned with the Baader–Meinhof Gang in believing that every criminal trial was categorically unjust.[19] Denning, for his part, was apoplectic: 'The youngsters believe that we come from a narrow background – it's all nonsense – they get it from that man Griffith'.[20] Students in Toronto adapted the epithet and had T-shirts printed with the slogan 'that man Denning', which appealed to Denning's sense of humour. Denning could point to himself as not being from the traditional moneyed classes – and, indeed, he, Reg and Norman were a solid reply to anyone who suggested there was no social mobility in their time. Britain was also a tangibly less diverse country in terms of demographics at the time of Denning's appointment to the Bench than in the present day.

The admirable achievement of Denning (and his siblings) in ascending the class system aside, the bare statistics supported Griffith's general point about the composition of the Bench in the nineteenth and twentieth centuries.[21] During the First World War, the future Lord Buckmaster was told that before he was to be appointed as Lord Chancellor he ought to join the Athenaeum, one of the most elite of the traditional London gentleman's clubs, since all the other senior judges without exception were members.[22] Denning himself would go on to join the club.

It might be observed that the homogeneity of the judges throughout the twentieth century was an asset in achieving one aim of any justice system – certainty, or at least predictability, in the law. That, however, would not pass muster as a defence of an exclusive system which the majority of the population could never hope to join, yet which made decisions for the entire nation. For a start, one would ask why it had to be *that* narrow selection as opposed to any other. Or, indeed, whether it was the demographic homogeneity rather than appropriate education and experience, along with a shared commitment to the rule of law, that created that high level of certainty.[23]

Since the first edition of Griffith's book, a somewhat more transparent selection process for senior judicial roles has been developed.[24] Yet, even by 2020, according to government statistics, the holders of senior judicial posts were from backgrounds still not as diverse as the general population, even allowing for the fact that judges will invariably be of middle age and older due to the requirement for experience.[25] Further, the legal profession as a whole still disproportionately comprised children of lawyers and of the upper socio-economic demographic generally.[26]

Choosing the cases

As MR, one of Denning's tasks was to select the panel of judges to hear individual cases in the Court of Appeal. The English High Court was divided into different divisions – not always logically, as with Probate, Divorce and Admiralty – the intention being to ensure cases were heard by judges with specialist knowledge of the subject matter. The Court of Appeal, on the other hand, then as now had just two divisions: civil and criminal. In the civil division it was not always possible for all or even one of the judges hearing cases to have relevant subject-matter expertise, due to the small number of available judges compared with the diversity of potential appeal subjects. That would have been so even if the appointments had been drawn equally from all divisions of the High Court – which they were not, the Chancery Division usually being over-represented.

In American appellate courts of the day, a strict rota system was in place, rather like the barristerial 'cab rank' (though even under the cab rank system, lack of subject-matter knowledge was a permissible ground for a barrister to refuse instructions), obliging judges to sit on whichever case happened to come up. Denning, in contrast, felt that it was important that at least one of the three Court of Appeal judges on each case should have specialist knowledge:[27]

> The work of the Court of Appeal is so varied that it is important to see that the cases are heard by judges who are conversant with the subject matter. If it is a Chancery case, one or two should be experienced in chancery work. So with commercial cases, or cases on planning or family law. It is desirable as far as possible to arrange the work to suit the court and conversely man the court to suit the work.

One immediate qualification would be that some appeals concern only procedural issues – whether the trial below has been conducted fairly – and thus do not turn on any point of law. Any judge with experience at the Bar should be able to deal competently with questions of procedure.

That aside, Denning's approach seems more attractive than a strict rota system. In 2012, a well-known New Zealand barrister, Tony Molloy QC, argued that many local practitioners and judges were attempting cases well beyond their area of competence.[28] His attack was primarily directed at those who had as he saw it embarrassed themselves in his own specialisation of equity and trusts, but he added that it was an equal failure by the system to have judges without appropriate experience conducting criminal trials. He pointed out that in any other profession – engineering or medicine, for example – having specialists for any particular project would be not just desirable but essential. No electrical engineer would try to design a bridge, nor would a podiatrist attempt open-heart surgery. Any who did would be liable to be disciplined by his or her professional body as well as being sued for professional negligence.

Taking Molloy's medical analogy, however, the point is not quite so straightforward. For any legal system to be workable there would need to be general courts, just as there are general medical practitioners. Medical GPs deal with a myriad of cases and refer patients to specialists only when something is outside their knowledge. Equally, accident and emergency departments in hospitals deal with a wide range of injuries and complaints, and do not automatically call in specialists. It would be an obvious waste of resources (indeed, a practical impossibility) to try to have every possible medical complaint, however minor, considered only by a specialist. Similarly, the King's Bench Division in England and Wales deals with a wide range of general civil litigation, and transfers cases to the specialist courts such as Admiralty or Patents only when necessary. Often, judges sitting during the court vacation, or out of hours for emergency hearings, are presented with cases outside their speciality. If necessary, they apply injunctive relief pending the assignment of the case to the appropriate specialist court. Further, specialism at the Bar and amongst solicitors also fills in many gaps in judges' knowledge, and in cases where there is no particular issue of law in dispute, only factual or procedural arguments, any competent judge should be able to determine the disputes adequately. Lastly, judicial training might allow judges from, say, a civil law background to deal competently with the conduct of at least basic criminal trials, though the subject of judicial training is not uncontroversial.[29]

All those points are, however, only partial deviations from Denning's sound general principle that in appeal cases of any complexity it is preferable for at least one of the judges to have subject-matter expertise.

One other important aspect of the MR's role in matching judges to cases was that, in any case in which he himself was sitting, Denning would only need one of the other two judges to agree with him in order to form the majority. Denning's confidence grew to the point where he would joke that if the other two disagreed, they were both dissenting.[30]

Denning in the courtroom

In contrast with all the controversies over his judgments, Denning attracted near-universal praise for his stewardship of the courtroom. Lord Hoffmann, who frequently appeared before him as counsel, told an interviewer that Denning was:[31]

> wonderfully courteous. And very quick. He would get on to the point immediately, and because he knew so much more about the law than anybody else, he was sometimes a little intimidating to appear before. But only because you thought 'he probably knows I'm talking nonsense'. He was extremely good with litigants in person.

Lord Ackner recalled:[32]

> Whenever you appeared before Lord Denning – Tom as he was affectionately known – as an advocate, or sat with him as a judicial colleague – and I did both, he never made you feel inadequate. On the contrary, he created the impression, often with little foundation, that you had an important contribution to make. He brought out the best in you. He made you feel special.
>
> On that very first occasion in 1948, when I was waiting to come on in the Court of Appeal, there was in front of me an appeal against an order that the plaintiff give security for the costs of an impending appeal because it was considered that if he failed in the appeal he might well be unable to meet the costs. The appeal was being presented by a black advocate, unusual in those days. He was very young and very inexperienced. The President of the Court, a testy member of the judiciary, was giving him a very hard time, demanding to know upon which rule of the Annual Practice he was relying. Sadly, he had not a clue. Tom was not prepared to tolerate his humiliation and with a characteristic charming smile he intervened to say: 'I think you will find that it is Order 23. The relevant rule is set out in full on page 423 of the White Book.' This was my first of many experiences of the courtesy and kindness, indeed the helpfulness, which one could always expect when appearing before him.
>
> ...
>
> Tom's skill with litigants in person has known no equal. They almost queued up to have the opportunity of appearing before him, and those who did it on more than one occasion, he would recognise

with a cheerful 'Ah Mrs Brown! We haven't seen you for some time. What do you think we can do for you today?' The majority of the applications were hopeless, but those who failed went away entirely content that Tom had done the best he could for them. How different was the position after he left.

Lord Scarman wrote:[33]

> His way with that bête noire of lawyers, the litigant in person, can only be characterised as genius. He discovers by a series of unerring questions what, if any, is his case, upholds or dismisses it with all due speed – and sends him away with fond memories of the judge, even when he sorrows in defeat.

Lord Justice Brooke had similar thoughts:[34]

> His treatment of litigants in person – and there were fewer in those days – was a pleasure to watch. For a few minutes they walked tall, as he quietly and patiently let them develop their arguments, before bringing the hearing – and their appeals – to a dignified end.

Lord Justice Sedley wrote:[35]

> Denning's manner and image were part of his jurisprudence. The half-smile to be seen in every picture of him never left his face. People felt that they were in the presence of a benign judge with a ready ear for their problems. But while he could be readily influenced by the underlying agenda or the emotive side-issues of a case – 'I just want to get the feel of it', he would say as he probed to and beyond the margins of legal relevance – he would rarely display his hostility towards those cases which, in his court at least, did not stand a chance. Instead he would help the destined loser to articulate his or her argument: 'I expect you'd say ...', 'Yes, you'd put it this way, wouldn't you?' Losers, especially litigants in person, would go away feeling that they had gained something, and Denning's court got through a lot more work.

Not that Denning was under any illusions about the problems facing litigants in person or the difficulties they caused the court. In *Pett v Greyhound Racing Association* [1968] 2 All ER at 549 he stated:

> It is not every man who has the ability to defend himself on his own. He cannot bring out the points in his own favour or the weaknesses

on the other side. He may be tongue-tied or nervous, confused, or wanting in intelligence. He cannot examine or cross-examine witnesses. We see it every day. A Magistrate says to a man: 'You can ask any questions you like'; whereupon the man immediately starts to make a speech. If justice is to be done, he ought to have the help of someone to speak for him; and who better than a lawyer who has been trained for the task?

The same applied when Denning was acting in any other official category. After giving evidence to Denning's inquiry into the Profumo Affair, Mandy Rice-Davies remarked that Denning was 'quite the nicest judge I ever met'. It was not her most famous quip, but Denning would have accepted the compliment all the same.

It all mirrored Denning's persona outside the court, of which the academic Philip S James once wrote:[36]

> If anybody ever had the magic of 'charisma' it is Lord Denning. He seems in some strange way to dwell apart and, looking down on life, to see it 'steadily and see it whole'. Yet, in the world of everyday reality he by no means stands aloof: a friend of all the world if they will let him be he is easy of approach, likes to take people to himself and actually encourages them to call him 'Tom.'

A second commendable feature of Denning's stewardship of the court was that he was normally thoroughly prepared and thus able to cut to the nub of the case quickly. One of the more entertaining anecdotes on that point came from Lord Justice Brooke:[37]

> At one point in the 1970s, when the volume of paper was beginning to grow, Lord Denning announced that litigants in his court should expect that the judges had read all the papers before the appeal started. The following day Lord Justice Russell, who presided in the next most senior division of the court, announced that litigants in his court should expect no such thing.

Judgments

Re Rowland – 'preceding or coinciding'

Very early on in his tenure as MR, Denning endorsed a more flexible approach to the construction of legal documents than the literal approach which generally held sway at the time. The case of *Re Rowland* [1962] 2 All

ER 837 concerned a will made by a doctor, which included the provision 'In the event of the decease of [my wife] preceding or coinciding with my own decease' his residuary estate should be equally divided between his brother and his nephew. He and his wife had died when a ship they were travelling on sank. There was no evidence available about who had died first. The issue was whether the doctor had died first, in which case his estate would pass to his wife and thus form part of her estate, which would go to her niece, or whether their deaths were coincidental, in which case it would pass to the doctor's brother and nephew.

Section 184 of the Law of Property Act 1925 provided:

> In all cases where ... two or more persons have died in circumstances rendering it uncertain which of them survived the other or others, such deaths shall (subject to any order of the court), for all purposes affecting the title to property, be presumed to have occurred in order of seniority, and accordingly the younger shall be deemed to have survived the elder.

The judge held that the doctor had pre-deceased his wife and therefore his estate passed to hers.

On appeal, Denning held:

> ... in point of principle the whole object of construing a will is to find out the testator's intentions, so as to see that his property is disposed of in the way he wished. True it is that you must discover his intention from the words that he has used; but you must put on his words the meaning which they bore to him. If his words are capable of more than one meaning, or of a wide meaning and narrow meaning, as they often are, then you must put on them the meaning which he intended them to convey, and not the meaning which a philologist would put on them. In order to discover the meaning which he intended, you will not get much help from a dictionary. It is very unlikely that he used a dictionary, and even less likely that he used the same one as you. What you should do is to place yourself as far as possible in his position, taking note of the facts and circumstances known to him at the time, and then say what he meant by his words.

Denning felt it was preposterous to suggest that the doctor and his wife had not died coincidentally. The doctor had plainly intended to 'use the words "coinciding with", not in the narrow meaning of "simultaneous", but in the wider meaning of which they are equally capable, especially in this context, as denoting death on the same occasion by the same cause'.

Denning would therefore have allowed the appeal, but Harman and Russell LJJ disagreed. The latter asserted the more formalist approach in his judgment:

> the key to his expressed intention is the context of the words 'preceding or', which demonstrate that 'coinciding with' means 'coinciding in point of time with'. This cannot be equated with 'if we shall die together' in the sense in which people are referred to as *commorientes*. For these reasons I am clearly of the opinion that the testator's language does not fit the facts of the case, so far as they are known. To hold otherwise would not in my judgment be to construe the will at all: it would be the result of inserting in the will a phrase which the testator never used by guessing at what a man in his position would have wished had he directed his mind and pen to the facts as they now confront us. There is no jurisdiction in this court to achieve a sensible result by such means.

With respect, Denning's view was much more likely to have reflected the testator's intention. The will was home-made, drawn up before the couple set off on extensive travels which they knew involved danger from flights and voyages. Plainly, the testator would have intended 'coinciding with' to include an occasion such as that which occurred in fact, when he and his wife were killed in the same disaster. In all probability they died within minutes of each other; he would have been baffled if he had been told beforehand that such a happening would not be 'coincidental'.[38]

Wyld v Silver – 'and geese will still a common lack'

Soon after his common-sense decision in *Re Rowland*, Denning took the opposite approach in *Wyld v Silver* [1962] 3 All ER 309 by standing on a formality which produced a frankly ridiculous result even if legally correct. The other noteworthy feature of the case was Denning's reversion to his own idiosyncratic style of judgment writing. He began thus:

> In the eighteenth century the inhabitants of the village of Wraysbury in Buckinghamshire had a right by ancient usage to hold a fair or wake on the waste lands of the parish. It is so recorded in an Act of Parliament. This fair or wake was held on the Friday in Whitsun week in every year. It had its origin, no doubt, in the vigil which used to be held on the eve of a festival in the church. The fair was a gathering of buyers and sellers. The wake was the merry-making which went with it. There can be no doubt that this right of the inhabitants was a

customary right to which the courts would give effect, see *Hall v Nottingham*. It was part of the local law which could not be got rid of by abandonment or disuse, but only by Act of Parliament; see *Hammerton v Honey*.

In 1799 the parish of Wraysbury, like so many parishes in England, became the subject of an Inclosure Act (39 Geo 3 c 118) and in 1803 the Inclosure Commissioners made their award. Under it the waste lands of the parish were enclosed by fences and allotted to individual owners, but special provision was made by the Act and the award so as to preserve the right of the inhabitants to hold their fair or wake. The commissioners set out and appointed a piece of land specially for the purpose: and the Act itself enacted that on it the inhabitants 'shall for ever hereafter have the same right to hold such fair or wake annually'. This seems to me to confer a statutory right on the inhabitants: and the former right by custom became merged in the higher title conferred by Parliament; see *New Windsor Corpn v Taylor*. It, too, was part of the local law: and just as the customary rights could not be got rid of except by Act of Parliament, neither could this new statutory right. ...

During these last 160 years things have changed. There has not been a fair or wake on Whit Friday in the village during this century; and the Green has changed a good deal. The four and a half acres, which was allotted to Mr Adkins, are owned by the parish council, and cricket is played there. The three-quarters of an acre, which was allotted to Mr Mills, has been turned into tennis courts. The three-quarters of an acre, which was allotted to Mr Herbert, has stood derelict. Now, however, the defendant has bought this derelict piece and he wishes to build on it. He has got planning permission to put up five bungalows with garages on it, but the inhabitants, or at any rate some of them, have risen up in arms against him. They say that his piece of land is part of the land set out for their fair or wake and that no one must build on it so as to interfere with their holding it. True it is that no fair or wake has been held there within living memory: but no matter, they have a right, they say, to hold it on this piece of land if they wish to do so and no one shall gainsay them. And they come to the Queen's courts to enforce their right.

As Denning would have known, the Inclosure Acts were ostensibly a device for tidying up the legal ownership of real property, but in practice were often used by the aristocracy as a land grab.[39] A centuries-old poem (author unknown) protested:

> They hang the man and flog the woman
> Who steals the goose from off the common
> Yet let the greater villain loose
> That steals the common from the goose
> The law demands that we atone
> When we take things we do not own
> But leaves the lords and ladies fine
> Who take things that are yours and mine
> The poor and wretched don't escape
> If they conspire the law to break
> This must be so but they endure
> Those who conspire to make the law
> The law locks up the man or woman
> Who steals the goose from off the common
> And geese will still a common lack
> Till they go and steal it back

The defendant in *Wyld* did not steal the land back. Instead, he purchased a small section of it on the open market in good faith, only for the local 'Nimbys'[40] to bring a spiteful legal action to prevent him developing it as he intended. The defendant was not a faceless, wealthy corporation seeking to bulldoze the village. Rather, he was a private individual who hoped to build some bungalows and otherwise develop his own private property in much the same way that others in the village had already done – including on land subject to the same technical restriction. One might therefore have expected sympathy from Denning for his plight. Instead, Denning took a wholly formalist approach and bluntly upheld the plaintiffs' ancient but never-used rights.

Evidently, Denning the spokesman for the common people was more attracted by the village common, and was carried away by nostalgia for some imagined William Cobbett-style old village life. Yet no one in the case even pretended that it was really about that way of life, since no fête had been held for over a century, none was contemplated in the foreseeable future, and the right to hold one had not been used to stop anyone else's development on the same original land. Patently, the case was a local squabble in which someone had chanced upon a decisive litigation weapon.

With Denning adopting an intransigent stance, it was the more traditional judge Russell LJ who expressed sympathy with the defendant:

> When in those circumstances the defendant finds himself restrained from the use of his land for the purposes for which he paid the

particular purchase price, at the suit of four inhabitants whose leading purpose and motive is to prevent the building which the competent authority has approved in the interests of town planning, and with no hope of remedy under his ordinary qualified covenants for title, he has my unqualified sympathy, in no way lessened by the additional circumstance that the parish council has declined to take proceedings for the same purpose. If I could find a way to decide in his favour I should be happy to do so. Alas, – I cannot.

Denning was never repentant about the decision. Quite the contrary – he later linked the case with satisfaction to his earlier renaming of his Sussex house 'Fair Close'.[41]

Speeches and drama

Taking up the post of MR meant many more formal events, including evening speaking engagements at which he would be accompanied by Joan. To make life easier for them both, Denning found a flat in Lincoln's Inn, some thirty years after he had rented the flat in the Temple which had proved so unsuitable for Mary's health. Since that time, the Clean Air Act 1956 and other measures (notably, the shift from coal to gas for domestic heating) had led to somewhat improved air quality in London. He and Joan usually stayed in the flat during the week, returning at the weekend to Cuckfield and, once the renovations were finished, The Lawn.

Throughout his time as MR, Denning continued to speak in the debating chamber of the House of Lords. He took a particular interest in public records and the solicitors' profession, given that both fell directly under his authority as MR.

Outside his formal engagements, he continued to lend his name and time to worthy causes. One of the earliest came in 1962, the year of his appointment as MR. His step-daughter Pauline was teaching in the drama department of the Royal Academy of Music in London when she learned that the unit was to close. With the characteristic verve of the Stuart and Denning families, she and two colleagues decided to set up a new college to provide a replacement. They identified the legendary ballet dancer Anna Pavlova's former home in Hampstead as an appropriate location. For a solicitor they instructed Denning's one-time housemate Anthony Moir. He told them that he could raise finance for the project if they could find some well-known names as trustees. A week later they returned with Denning, Sir Ralph Richardson, Peter Sellers and Richard Dimbleby all having committed

CHAPTER XI

Profumo

I have come to realize that, by this deception, I have been guilty of a grave misdemeanour and despite the fact that there is no truth whatever in the other charges, I cannot remain a member of your Administration, nor of the House of Commons. I cannot tell you of my deep remorse for the embarrassment I have caused to you, to my colleagues in the Government, to my constituents, and to the Party which I have served for the past twenty-five years.

John Profumo, letter to Harold Macmillan, 5 June 1963

I have often been asked: Which of your cases was the most important? Beyond doubt, the Profumo Inquiry.

Lord Denning, Landmarks in the Law

In early 1963 the Leader of the House of Commons, Iain Macleod MP, met the Secretary of State for War, John 'Jack' Profumo MP. Macleod went straight to the point: 'Look Jack, the basic question is, "Did you fuck her?"'[1] 'No', Profumo lied, thereby repeating the falsehood which was to seal the fate of his own political career, while at the same time inadvertently securing political immortality for himself and the others involved in the scandal which has ever since been known by his name.

The Profumo Affair also brought Denning firmly into the wider public arena, after he was appointed to conduct an official inquiry into Profumo's extramarital assignations and any security implications arising from the louche circles in which he was moving. Denning's report still casts something of a shadow over his own reputation, primarily due to being seen by many as an establishment whitewash, but also because of some unsatisfactory procedural aspects for which he offered an unconvincing justification.

The background

The events of Profumo took place less than two decades after the end of the Second World War, when Britain was in a state of social, political and economic flux. Most of the ruling class, including Profumo himself, were veterans of one or both of the two World Wars. Outwardly, their 'establishment values' – essentially the Victorian and Edwardian stereotypes seen in relation to Denning's upbringing – clashed with the 'swinging Sixties' associated with The Beatles, The Rolling Stones, Mary Quant, Twiggy and the other classic names and imagery of the time. Officially, Roy Jenkins' campaign for a 'permissive society' had yet to be formally launched at the time of Profumo;[2] unofficially, the social transformations which formed the basis for his campaign were well under way.[3] The changing ethics and morals were summed up perhaps most famously by Philip Larkin's *Annus Mirabilis*, with its opening line about sexual intercourse beginning in 1963 – coincidentally, the year in which the Profumo Affair broke.

The truth was that, while many of the establishment of the time might have adhered to Victorian standards – Denning himself being one obvious example – many others did not. Instead, they preached one thing in public whilst carrying on affairs and various peccadillos in private. There was nothing new about such hypocrisy, as any biography of Edward VII, HH Asquith or David Lloyd George (to take a random selection of pre-Profumo senior public figures) would confirm. The journalist Malcolm Muggeridge raged at the time of Profumo: 'The Upper Classes have always been given to lying, fornication, corrupt practices and, doubtless as a result of the public school system, sodomy'.[4]

Leaving aside his implicit homophobia, Muggeridge's general point was supported by the fact that the upper classes had long established social conventions about what sort of conduct was acceptable, when and with whom.[5] The most important such convention was keeping it quiet, even (or especially) if something outré was involved. In 1959, a particularly notorious scandal erupted when the Duke of Argyll discovered pictures of his wife performing sex acts on a man whose head was not visible in the picture. The identity of the said 'headless man' became a celebrated tabloid question and would resurface during the Profumo Affair. In 1960, the barrister Mervyn Griffith-Jones famously asked the jury in the *Lady Chatterley's Lover* case rhetorically 'Is it a book that you would even wish your wife or your servants to read?'[6]

Griffith-Jones too would play a part in the Profumo Affair, as prosecutor in the trial of Stephen Ward. It was the *Lady Chatterley* trial which the historian

John Feather marked as the beginning of the permissive society,[7] since a phalanx of clergymen and others from the ranks of the establishment failed to persuade a jury that DH Lawrence's famous novel should be deemed criminally obscene. Instead, the defendant, Penguin Books Ltd, was allowed to publish the paperback and watch the sales rise exponentially thanks to the publicity from the trial.[8] It was, after all, an age long before the internet made pornography instantly accessible, and thus risqué prose caused much more of a stir than it would in the twenty-first century.

The other factor which added a considerable degree of *frisson* to the Profumo Affair was the cloak and dagger world of Cold War spies. In 1951, Britain had been rocked by the discovery of the 'Cambridge Spy Ring': several apparently respectable members of government and society were exposed as Soviet agents, having all converted to communism whilst at Cambridge together decades earlier. Their names – Burgess, Philby (not uncovered until less than a year before the Profumo Affair) and Maclean – became among the most notorious of all public figures of the era.[9] Added to them were the likes of George Blake and John Vassall. The latter was a low-level civil servant who had been caught in September 1962 sending military secrets to the Soviets. He had been blackmailed by the KGB over compromising photographs.[10] Much initial concern about the antics of Profumo derived from the possibility of British political and military figures being blackmailed as Vassall had been, or sharing paramours with Soviet spies – or, as a contemporary joke had it, whether the 'Reds' were now in the bed instead of under it.[11]

Dramatis personae

'Her' in Macleod's question to Profumo was Christine Keeler. Born in wartime Middlesex in 1942, Keeler had an impoverished and abusive childhood in Berkshire. She moved to London as a teenager and started working as a showgirl in Soho. It was there that she befriended a fellow worker by the name of Mandy Rice-Davies and a regular attendee called Stephen Ward.

Ward was an osteopath and part-time artist who numbered quite a few of Britain's celebrities and aristocrats among his clients. His legitimate income from his practice and his artwork was substantial, but his lifestyle was further enhanced by the fact he was as effective at manipulating personalities as he was lumbar muscles.

Keeler and Ward lived for a time outwardly as a couple, though she always denied there was a sexual relationship between them. Ward enjoyed setting up other couples for sex and was thus happy for Keeler to conduct affairs with several of his clients; indeed, that appears to have been the point of his relationship with her. Rice-Davies, like Keeler from a lower social strata than Ward, had a similar relationship with him. Although both women made the odd contribution to household expenses when they lived with him, and received occasional gifts from some of the men they slept with, neither was paid directly or via Ward for doing so – a material point in Ward's later troubles.

One member of Ward's informal set was the Soviet naval attaché and intelligence officer, Yevgeny Ivanov, whose presence introduced the spying element to the scandal. Ivanov enjoyed Western consumer goods and personal freedoms as much as most citizens of repressive regimes when given the chance. His taste for hedonism made him an obvious target for turning by MI5, who assigned a handler known as 'Woods' to deal with Ward.

Another of Ward's clients was Lord Astor, of the substantial newspaper and business dynasty. Astor allowed Ward the use of a cottage on one of the family's substantial estates, Cliveden in Buckinghamshire, for a nominal rent. Ward used the cottage at weekends to host parties whose guests came from across the social spectrum, the chief price of admission being a lack of inhibition. Occasionally, Ward's guests would interact with those visiting Astor in the main house. Astor himself enjoyed the company of some of Ward's women. Astor had previously clashed with another Fleet Street proprietor, Lord Beaverbrook. When the scandal broke, the latter saw a chance for revenge.

John Profumo himself was outwardly a quintessentially establishment figure. Born in 1915, a descendant of minor Italian royalty, he attended Harrow School before going up to Oxford, where he joined the bastion of privilege that was (and is) the Bullingdon Club. He had a distinguished war record as well as serving as an MP from 1940. By 1961 he was serving as Secretary of State for War. He was also married to a successful film actress, Valerie Hobson. In the euphemistic style of the day it was referred to as a 'modern marriage', or as the journalist Tom Mangold, an expert on the Profumo Affair, put it, 'He shagged everything in sight'.[12]

Profumo's Prime Minister was Harold Macmillan, like Denning a veteran of the First World War and thus of the older generation by the 1960s. Macmillan had been elected by a majority of more than 100 seats in 1959 and had gone on to tell the electorate 'you've never had it so good'. By 1963, his own political career had rarely had it so bad. In a disastrous by-election in Orpington in March 1962, a Conservative majority of almost 15,000 had turned into a Liberal majority of 7,800. In July of the same year, Macmillan had sacked a third of his cabinet in the rather melodramatically named 'Night of the Long Knives'. In his private life Macmillan was also a victim of establishment hypocrisy since his wife was conducting a long-term affair with the Conservative politician Robert Boothby.[13]

The beginning

Over the weekend of 8–9 July 1961, Profumo and Ivanov both attended a party at the main house at Cliveden as guests of Astor, while Keeler and Ward were staying at the cottage. Profumo saw Keeler swimming naked and was beguiled by her appearance, making some inquiries about seeing her again, although he did not do so that weekend. There has been some dispute about whether Ivanov had an affair with Keeler. Keeler claimed that they did so, beginning when Ivanov drove her home after the weekend, though she only made that allegation when trying to sell her story to newspapers about eighteen months after the event, while she had otherwise been open about her relationships.[14] Either way, on 12 July, Ward contacted MI5 to tell them of Ivanov meeting Profumo. He also said that Ivanov was seeking information about NATO plans to deploy nuclear weapons in West Germany. Woods, seeing the potential trouble, alerted MI5's director-general, Sir Roger Hollis.

Profumo's affair with Keeler began soon after.[15] He bought her the odd present and on one occasion gave her £20 as a 'gift for her mother'. On 9 August, he was informally approached by Sir Norman Brook, the Cabinet Secretary, who warned him that MI5 had concerns about Ward's reliability. Although Brook had not mentioned Keeler, Profumo quickly wrote to her in the following terms to cancel a planned liaison:[16]

> Darling, ... Alas something's blown up tomorrow night and I can't therefore make it ... I leave the next day for various trips and then a holiday so won't be able to see you again until some time in September. Blast it. Please take great care of yourself and don't run away.
> Love J

By sending that letter Profumo had handed Keeler written proof of their relationship, which would be fatal to his later denials.[17] His affair with her dwindled around the same time. In October 1961, Keeler began a new relationship with a Jamaican jazz singer called Aloysius 'Lucky' Gordon, who had a history of violence and petty crime. Gordon became aggressively possessive of her, becoming all the worse when she left Ward's house and started living in a flat in Pimlico.

One individual of whom both Keeler and Rice-Davies were mistresses at different times was a notorious 'slum landlord', Peter Rachman.[18] In 1962 Keeler also started seeing one of Rachman's former henchmen, the Antiguan Johnny Edgecombe. Keeler and Edgecombe lived together for a while in west London. Like Gordon, Edgecombe was highly jealous, leading to an altercation between the two men in October 1962, during which Edgecombe cut Gordon with a knife. Keeler then broke off relations with Edgecombe and returned to Ward's flat.

In December 1962, Edgecombe went to Ward's address. Upon being refused entry, he fired several shots at the door with a pistol. He was arrested and charged with attempted murder. As the story started to attract public interest, Keeler told various aspects to a former Labour MP, John Lewis, who detested Ward for personal reasons. Lewis passed the information to a serving Labour MP, George Wigg, who, sensing electoral advantage, began his own enquiries.

In January 1963, the Soviet government, alerted to a possible scandal, recalled Ivanov to Moscow. By that stage Keeler was actively touting her story to newspapers. Most stayed away through fear of libel, but she managed to secure an offer from the *Sunday Pictorial* of £1,000.[19] She gave them a copy of the 'Darling' letter. Profumo's lawyers tried to buy Keeler's silence. They failed, but they did manage to pressure the *Pictorial* into not running the story.

Things were still just about under control as far as Profumo was concerned. Thanks to Keeler the police knew of the affair, but since they did not consider security interests were engaged, they took no action. Rumours were all over the place linking a government minister to a woman who was also seeing a Soviet attaché, yet the Conservative Party (rather naïvely) accepted Profumo's denials and he retained the backing of Macmillan.[20]

Keeler poured petrol on the flames when she failed to attend Edgecombe's trial in March. The press speculated someone in power had spirited her away, but refrained from stating anything openly. Instead, they merely implied a connection between Keeler and Profumo by increasingly unsubtle juxtapositions of stories and pictures. Most notoriously, the Beaverbrook paper *Daily Express* ran a front-page headline on 15 March, 'War Minister Shock', with a story claiming that Profumo had offered his resignation, which had been rejected. Underneath, barely separated, was a picture of Keeler with the news about her not attending the Edgecombe trial. There was no express connection between the stories, but it was soon common currency that any vaguely informed person would have been able to draw their own conclusions.[21]

Edgecombe was found guilty of possessing a firearm with intent to endanger life. He was sentenced to seven years' imprisonment.

In mid-April, Keeler was staying with a friend, Paula Hamilton-Marshall, in London. She was attacked by Hamilton-Marshall's brother, leaving her bruised and with a black eye. Shortly after, Gordon lunged at her when she and friends were outside. The friends held him off so she could escape. She then accused Gordon of causing the earlier injuries. He was arrested and charged with assault. (Some later authors have alleged that Gordon was fitted up at the behest of the two police officers leading the investigation against Ward.[22])

Meanwhile, in the House of Commons, protected by parliamentary privilege, Wigg was on the offensive. He demanded that the Home Secretary, Henry Brooke,[23] answer rumours about 'a senior member of the government' being associated with Keeler, Rice-Davies and the Edgecombe crime. (Profumo was not named openly.) Brooke refused to comment, but the next day the Conservative Party compelled Profumo to make a personal statement to the House. He did so, in which he admitted knowing Keeler and Ward, and having met Ivanov twice, but insisted that there had been no impropriety with Keeler. He threatened libel actions against anyone who printed a story to the contrary.

At the time, by convention, ministerial statements of the type issued by Profumo were accepted as true by Parliament. His abuse – and thus destruction – of that convention was to become one of the most lasting effects of the scandal, since it shattered anyone's belief in an MP's uncorroborated word as a gentleman. Thirty years later, looking back on the affair after some of the papers had been declassified, Denning (by then aged ninety-five) was highly critical of the circumstances in which Profumo had made his statement: he had taken sleeping pills the night before, only to be effectively dragged out of bed and compelled to make a hurried statement, rather than having time to consider the implications more fully and under advisement.[24]

Keeler was soon found on holiday in Spain. She denied the affair with Profumo and dismissed her absence from Edgecombe's trial as a mix-up over dates. Ward appeared on television and also denied everything, but made a fatal error when he was later seen speaking to Wigg near Parliament. The Conservatives wrongly assumed Ward was supplying the Labour Party with ammunition (in fact, Ward was trying to persuade Wigg of Profumo's innocence). Either way, it seems clear that senior figures in government decided around that time that Ward would be the villain of the piece, his connections and previous loyalty counting for nothing.

Law and order was the responsibility of Henry Brooke as Home Secretary. He met with Sir Roger Hollis and the head of Scotland Yard, Sir Joseph Simpson. Hollis stated that there were only moral, not security considerations, and therefore no crime under the Official Secrets Act had been committed. Brooke asked Simpson if there was any police interest in Ward. Simpson said no, but took the hint and said they could probably find him guilty of a crime as long as they obtained the full story.[25] Afterwards, more than a hundred of Ward's associates were interviewed, his telephone was tapped and his home was put under surveillance.

One interpolates that the very fact of the government leaning on police to pursue anyone would constitute a flagrant breach of the rule of law, which requires complete independence of the police and prosecutorial process from political interference. Failure to observe that convention brought down the first Labour government,[26] and should at least have caused severe censure of the Conservatives once it became known they had asked the police to act against Ward.[27]

Keeler soon abandoned her defence of Profumo and publicly asserted the existence of their affair. Rice-Davies, meanwhile, was arrested on a minor driving offence and held in prison for nine days, then had her passport confiscated for some minor debt she had failed to pay, the pressure not letting up until she agreed to testify against Ward. Similarly, Keeler was interviewed by police no fewer than twenty-four times in an attempt to find something to pin on Ward.[28]

In desperation, Ward tried to contact Macmillan directly in early May, hoping that since he was at that point still protecting Profumo, the government might reciprocate by calling off the attack. After being rebuffed he wrote to the Labour leader Harold Wilson instead, stating that he was no longer prepared to suppress the truth.

The scandal breaks

At the end of May, Profumo and his wife went on holiday to Italy for the parliamentary Whitsun recess, but he could hold out no longer. Fearing imminent exposure, he confessed the affair to her. The two returned to Britain as soon as they could and, on 4 June, he admitted the affair publicly. 'A Shocking Admission' was the headline in *The Times*, which added sorrowfully that it was 'a great tragedy for the probity of public life in Britain'.[29] Profumo resigned, while Ward was arrested on charges of living off the earnings of prostitution and procuring a girl under the age of twenty-one. Ward did not know it, but a group of his friends were to meet in secret shortly afterwards at the Athenaeum Club in London, where they agreed to abandon him to his fate. He had asked them to give evidence in his defence; they all refused.[30]

On the same day that Profumo's admission became public, the trial of Gordon began for his alleged assault on Keeler. He maintained that his innocence would be established by two witnesses who, the police told the court, could not be found. He was convicted, with Keeler having been the lead witness for the prosecution (turning up to court each day in a Rolls-Royce hired by a newspaper).

Following Profumo's confession the threat of libel from him was spent, so the press started printing Keeler's stories, including the 'Darling' letter. The Labour Party was initially more muted, concentrating instead on the security implications, emphasising the supposed link between Keeler, Profumo and Ivanov.

By that time the press was throwing around salacious rumours with abandon. The Conservative Lord Hailsham, leader of the House of Lords, appeared on television and launched an extraordinary attack on Profumo.[31] In the House of Commons the Labour Party abandoned its earlier reserve and was veering to hyperbole instead ('There is clear evidence of a sordid underworld network, the extent of which cannot yet be measured', intoned Harold Wilson, having complained of 'disclosures which have shocked the moral conscience of the nation'[32]), while the press continued to run riot with speculation. The beleaguered Macmillan announced an independent inquiry to try to bring things under control, or at least establish who was doing what with whom, particularly with regard to any compromise of national security. Denning was appointed on 21 June to conduct that inquiry. His terms of reference were extremely wide:

> To examine, in the light of the circumstances leading to the resignation of the former Secretary of State for War, Mr. JD Profumo, the operation of the Security Service and the adequacy of their co-operation with the Police in matters of security, to investigate any information or material which may come to his attention in this connection and to consider any evidence there may be for believing that national security has been, or may be, endangered and to report thereon.

Ward's committal hearing began at the Old Bailey a week later, on 28 June. It resulted in him being committed for trial on charges of living off the earnings of Keeler, Rice-Davies and two other women working as prostitutes, and with procuring women under twenty-one to have sex with other persons – the latter a bizarre offence, given the age of consent was sixteen at the time.[33] The thrust of the prosecution's case related to Keeler and Rice-Davies. It turned on whether the small contributions to household expenses or loan repayments they had given to Ward[34] amounted to his living off their prostitution. During the committal hearing, when presented with Lord Astor's denial that he had had sex with her, Rice-Davies spoke herself into the *Oxford Dictionary of Quotations* with her legendary rejoinder 'He would, wouldn't he?' (often misquoted as 'he would say that, wouldn't he?').[35] Ironically, it is possible Astor was telling the truth.

Ward's trial itself began on 28 July. The prosecution was led by Mervyn Griffith-Jones, the same barrister who had been anxious about the possibility of his wife and servants reading the fiction of DH Lawrence. It is not difficult to imagine his indignation when he was confronted by the real-life activities of the Ward set. He raged that Ward's conduct was 'the very depths of lechery and depravity'. The witness evidence was less than satisfactory: among other things, two witnesses, Rice-Davies and an admitted prostitute, Margaret 'Ronna' Ricardo, claimed there had been police pressure on them to change their stories. The judge, Sir Archie Marshall, fell short of the expected standards of judicial impartiality in his conduct of the trial, frequently intervening tendentiously on the side of the prosecution. In his summing up he cruelly emphasised Ward's abandonment by his friends.

Worse than Marshall's conduct, however, was that of the Court of Appeal, Criminal Division. Shortly before Ward's trial concluded, Gordon's missing witnesses came forward and testified that Keeler had given false evidence at his trial. His conviction for assault was therefore overturned. Yet the Court of Appeal only stated that the conviction would be quashed, and added that '[i]t may well be that [Keeler's] evidence was completely truthful'. If the full account of the new evidence had been disclosed publicly by the Court of Appeal and relayed to the jury in Ward's trial, Keeler's credibility would have been damaged and, since she was also a key prosecution witness, it might have led to a collapse of the case against Ward. Instead, using the half-measured statement from the Court of Appeal, Marshall and Griffith-Jones were able to present the fact of Gordon's successful appeal to Ward's jury in a way which maintained Keeler's credibility.[36]

It was too much for Ward. He wrote a series of 'goodbye letters' to friends, took an overdose of sleeping tablets, fell into a coma, and was taken to hospital. The following day he was found guilty *in absentia* on the charges relating to Keeler and Rice-Davies, though he was acquitted on the other counts. Sentence was postponed until he was fit to appear, but he never regained consciousness and died soon after.

With any suicide, caution has to be exercised about speculating as to the victim's true motivation. It seems likely in Ward's case, given his situation and in light of the letters he wrote to friends just before taking the pills, that it was not the prospect of a short prison sentence that pushed him over the edge, but the realisation that he had never joined the establishment after all. He was simply a useful device who was discarded when he became a liability. His 'friends' turned out to be nothing of the sort, and he would have known he could never move in the same circles again. By way of grim confirmation, just as he had been abandoned in life, so he was abandoned in death: no one from his former life in high circles attended his cremation.[37]

Denning's report

Appointment

There has been occasional speculation as to why Denning was chosen ahead of any other senior judge, though there is not much on the point. Among other possible candidates, Lord Radcliffe might have been first choice, given his extensive experience in public inquiries, but he had already been engaged in 1963 conducting an inquiry into John Vassall. It is unlikely any of the other law lords, or another senior judge such as the Lord Chief Justice, would have been much less moralistic than Denning.[38] Whether any other judge would have been prepared to spare the government to the extent Denning did has to remain moot.

Some felt that making a judge inquire into febrile political matters posed a risk of politicising the judiciary,[39] though given that the inquiry was not being asked to inquire into party political matters, the task would have been no different – that is, no more 'political' – than any high-profile criminal trial of a politician or politicians. Moreover, given that the Profumo Affair concerned the actions of Members of Parliament, an independent voice was essential, as available among senior judges, especially Denning who, unlike many other judges of his time, had never stood for political office when at the Bar. On top of those advantages, a judge would also have the requisite skills to structure the inquiry, cross-examine witnesses and assess the evidence. Denning had experience both at the Bar and on the Bench in criminal matters (though he was not a criminal specialist), and when sitting in the divorce courts had dealt with many cases where factual inquiries into alleged adultery and related matters had been necessary. Nonetheless, he accepted the appointment with humility, writing to Macmillan that it was a great responsibility with which he had been entrusted, and 'I feel very apprehensive of my ability to carry it out. All I can say is that I will do my best faithfully'.[40]

Despite all of Denning's life and work experience to that point, the peccadillos of the supposed great and the good which he was to learn about still came as an evident shock to him. No one would have been under any illusion as to how he would regard the behaviour of the Ward set, since he had said publicly more than a decade earlier that 'infidelity should not be regarded, as it now is, as the private concern of the parties with which no one else has anything to do. It is the concern of everyone who has the welfare of the country at heart'.[41]

Preparation

Denning started work just three days after being appointed, clearing his desk of forthcoming appeals and setting aside the court summer vacation. He felt he had been asked to report not primarily because of Profumo himself, but to determine the truth behind the endless rumours now swirling around Fleet Street. 'The issue for me was in effect "Let justice be done"' as he later wrote,[42] also emphasising the security concerns deriving from any relationship between Keeler and Ivanov as well as Keeler and Profumo.

Denning clearly thought discretion was the best path to the truth, choosing to interview the witnesses in private in the rooms with which he had been provided at the Treasury.[43] At times he even sent the shorthand writers out of the room so that certain evidence went unrecorded.

In total, he sat for forty-nine days, hearing evidence from 160 witnesses. He was assisted by Thomas Critchley, a respected civil servant, as well as secretarial support. His report was signed on 16 September and published on 26 September. ('Denning is served' said the cover of *Private Eye*, under a cartoon by Gerald Scarfe of expectant ministers.) It ran to 70,000 words and represented remarkable industry given the time frame within which he had worked. Denning seemed rather to enjoy the spotlight: cameras followed him on his journey from Whitchurch to London to deliver the report (at the time of writing, short clips could be found on YouTube and many photographs of his journey could be seen on Google Images), showing him appearing confident and, as ever for his official duties, immaculately turned out.

Style

The report was written in the customary Denning style, if anything even more demotic than some of his better-known judgments. He used headings for his chapters that would normally be found in pulp fiction, such as: 'The slashing and the shooting'; 'Christine tells her story'; 'The police are told'; 'The lawyers are called in'; 'Ministers are concerned'; and 'The disappearance of Christine Keeler'.

His prose was typified by his description of a mysterious naked waiter:

> There is a great deal of evidence which satisfied me that there is a group of people who hold parties in private of a perverted nature. At some of these parties, the man who serves the dinner is nearly naked except for a small square lace apron round his waist such as a waitress might wear. He wears a black mask over his head with slits for eye-holes. He cannot therefore be recognised by any of the guests. Some reports stop there and say that nothing evil takes place. It is done as a comic turn and no more. This may well be so at some of the parties. But at others I am satisfied that it is followed by perverted sex orgies: that the man in the mask is a 'slave' who is whipped: that the guests undress and indulge in sexual intercourse one with the other: and indulge in other sexual activities of a vile and revolting nature. ...
>
> I have seen quite a number of those who were at these parties. Some of them were astonishingly frank about the goings-on. One of them in particular, a solicitor, impressed me with his truthfulness. He told me the names of many present. They did not include any Minister or any person prominent in public life. The host and hostess and the solicitor identified for me the man in the mask: and this man actually came and gave evidence before me. He is now grievously ashamed of what he did. He does not bear any resemblance whatever to the Minister who was the victim of rumour.

Findings

In answer to the central purpose of the inquiry, Denning declared that there had been no security threat, let alone breach, by Profumo's assignations with Keeler. He ridiculed the idea that Ivanov might have used Keeler as a go-between to obtain information about NATO. Profumo had been guilty of indiscretion, but not of disloyalty to the country. That being so, Profumo still had to take responsibility for his unwise association with Keeler, his lies to the party and, worst of all in Denning's view, his lie to the House of Commons.

Denning considered the primary culprit to be Ward. The fact that Ward was dead by then ensured Denning had a free hand,[44] evidently untroubled by any clichés about not speaking ill of the dead. He derided Ward as 'utterly immoral', calling him a seducer, a procurer, a drug fiend and a voyeur. He dismissed any suggestion that Ward had not had a fair trial and claimed that Ward was a communist sympathiser who had tried to help Ivanov when the latter asked him questions about British foreign policy.

As to Keeler, he considered her to be a vulnerable woman who was more a victim than anything else, but he still referred to her as a 'call girl', which was both damning and untrue. In reference to a series of pictures of Keeler in a bathing suit, he said that 'most people could readily infer her calling',[45] which appears ludicrous from a twenty-first century perspective and was already a dated opinion in 1963. As Denning knew, there was no evidence she was being paid for sex on any sort of formal basis, and Profumo's gifts to her were just that – random gifts from a wealthy man to his mistress. Denning's inaccurate description partly stemmed from the fact that his Victorian values judged her consensual relationships to be morally equivalent to prostitution, but also, one suspects, from the knowledge that Ward's conviction would have been wrongfully obtained if it was conceded Keeler and Rice-Davies were not prostitutes.

Denning declared that he intended to favour no one, still less shield the government from embarrassment, but at the same time was not interested in humiliating people where there was no public interest in disclosing their goings-on. He rounded on those who suggested the police should have tipped anyone off about Profumo's adultery (or anyone else's) in the absence of any security threat, stating, in classic Denning form, that Britain was not a police state: 'No one can understand the role of the Security Service in the Profumo affair unless he realises the cardinal principle that their operations are to be used for one purpose, and one purpose only, the Defence of the Realm'. On that basis he declined to name anyone else involved in rumours of extra-marital escapades which he had investigated:[46]

> I hope ... they will not feel that honour requires them to pursue these matters further. My findings will, I trust, be accepted by them as a full and sufficient vindication of their general good names. It is, I believe, better for the country that these rumours should be buried and that this unfortunate episode should be closed. Equally I trust that all others will now cease to repeat these rumours which have been proved so unfounded and untrue: and that newspapers and others will not seek to put names to those whom I have deliberately left

anonymous. For I fear that, if names are given, human nature being what it is, people will say 'there's no smoke without fire' – a proposition which in this instance is demonstrably untrue.

Those whom he excluded from his report probably included the transport minister Ernie Marples and the junior minister Denzil Freeth. Denning had been presented with cogent evidence that Marples had been engaged in various liaisons with prostitutes, and that Freeth had allegedly participated in a gay sex party. Both actions would have made them vulnerable to blackmail – more so than Profumo. Marples, unlike Profumo, was a senior member of the cabinet and a Privy Councillor. Further, since his actions were with a prostitute, they would under the mores of the time have incurred stronger moral disapprobation than random affairs. In Freeth's case, male homosexual acts were still illegal at the time and carried a much heavier social stigma than heterosexual adultery.

In later years it came to light that Denning had informed Macmillan about Marples and Freeth on the quiet, by what his assistant called a 'gentleman's agreement',[47] in which the two men would be excluded from the report – Macmillan wanted no annexes or secret codicils or anything else that would hint to the public that there was important material left unsaid – but Denning would write to him later on, in confidence, expressing concern about the private lives of some ministers. As a result, no public action ensued. Instead, Freeth was discreetly moved out of Parliament, standing down at the 1964 election. Marples remained in post but managed later in life to disgrace himself anyway with conflicts of interest and by committing tax fraud.

Another matter Denning investigated was the identity of the headless paramour of the Duchess of Argyll. The divorce case had been heard earlier in 1963 and the man (or men) in question was speculated to have been in the Ward set, but it was still a stretch to find that the issue fell within Denning's remit. Denning explained that his investigation had revealed the man not to be a minister, but declined to say which minister he had investigated or who he thought it actually was. In fact, the minister he investigated was Duncan Sandys,[48] who obtained medical evidence that his private parts did not match those of the man in the photograph – although Denning conveniently ignored the fact that the photographs were likely not always of the same man. With both the masked waiter and the 'headless man' Denning's approach was effectively to ridicule the story, with the intention that it would thereby fade from public attention and the natural order of things resume.[49] Otherwise, Macmillan and the cabinet received a smattering of criticism but no more.

Effectively, therefore, under Denning's findings the government was in the clear, at least as far as the behaviour of individual ministers apart from Profumo himself was concerned. So too were all the other public figures who had been anxiously waiting to see if their names would make it into the report, justifiably or otherwise. Denning explained their absence by stating that 'while the public interest demands that the facts should be ascertained as completely as possible there is a higher interest to be considered, namely the interest of justice to the individual which overrides all others'.

Regarding the reaction of Profumo's colleagues in the House, Denning stated that their mistake was to have asked themselves whether he *might* have been telling the truth (to which the answer would have been 'yes'), instead of asking whether reasonable people would have supposed him to be telling the truth on the basis of what they had already heard (to which the answer would have been 'no').

Reception

The report was an immediate best-seller, with over 100,000 copies being sold in the first few weeks after publication. Partly that was due to public interest in security matters, but mostly it was because of the interest in the scandalous actions which had attracted public and press interest in the first place. John Sparrow, the Warden of All Souls – the intellectual citadel that had spurned Denning decades earlier – called the report 'the raciest and most readable bluebook ever published',[50] though it was probably more accurate to call it the *only* racy or readable bluebook ever.

Initially, Denning was praised by both sides of the House, reflecting the esteem in which he personally and the judiciary in general was held. Macmillan paid tribute, though tried hard to dismiss security concerns and move on. Harold Wilson was not going to let him off the hook entirely:[51]

> I fully agree with the Prime Minister's tribute to Lord Denning, as we would all do, for his integrity, his thoroughness, his devotion to the task which was given him by the Government, and, not least – because everyone has noticed this; the Prime Minister paid tribute to it – for his superb gift of clarity in expressing his conclusions. But after the Prime Minister had paid that tribute to Lord Denning he then proceeded to try to demolish those parts of the Denning Report which were critical of the Government. So we have the situation that the Prime Minister is apparently prepared to accept the Report, apart from those parts which are critical.

George Wigg was less impressed, rubbishing the notion that Denning's report could be considered the last word on the affair.[52] Over the following months and indeed years, other criticisms started to emerge. Denning's flat assertion that there was no question of security having been breached, and his refusal to identify any minister (or any other significant public figure not already named in relation to the scandal) beyond Profumo himself as involved in anything questionable, was seen as a whitewash.[53] Certainly, the omission of Marples and Freeth from the report gave substance to that verdict, though their omission was not publicly known until much later.

Denning's detailed descriptions of some of the antics of the Ward set were seen as unnecessary for his findings.[54] His prescription about how ministers should have conducted themselves regarding the suspicion over Profumo was assailed as assuming the very 'no smoke without fire' he had elsewhere decried (Tory lawyers such as Viscount Dilhorne especially opposed the idea). His decision to hear all the evidence in secret and then criticise witnesses in the report without them having the chance to respond was criticised as a procedural error. Lastly, the fact that the transcripts of all the evidence to him were suppressed meant that no comprehensive review could be undertaken, nor definitive answers given.

In the twenty-first century an arch critic of Denning's work on Profumo, Richard Davenport-Hines, slated Denning as a 'lascivious old man', based partly on the way the report was written,[55] as with the chapter headings and paragraphs cited above. His attack contrasted with the unctuous praise for Denning's writing style by Alec Douglas-Home in the House of Commons shortly after publication, who said 'The clarity with which the story has been written has been widely acclaimed, and, by setting out what happened in the gripping style which Lord Denning has used, he has carried conviction as to its truth',[56] as well as the broader tributes of both Wilson and Macmillan.

In fairness, the subject matter meant that even the most anodyne author would have struggled to keep the prose completely bland, just as anyone would struggle to remain wholly unmoved by the evidence (Mavis Hill, Denning's long-standing law reporter, met him for lunch during the inquiry and said that Denning was 'really rather like a schoolboy with a secret'.[57]) As with some of his other controversial judgments, however, Denning's idiosyncratic style left him open to criticism in a way more conventional judicial prose would not have done. His admirably clear sentences and structure were certainly praiseworthy; the rather cheap chapter headings and cod-tabloid phrases were not. Macmillan himself thought the style owed something to the Victorian peddlers of scandal known as 'Penny Dreadfuls'.[58]

More substantively, Davenport-Hines charged that Denning upholding 'the primacy of cheap suspicions' led newspapers to publish rumours, harangue victims, and turn notoriety into an industry.[59] Elsewhere he added that the Profumo Affair was the first time the British press had destroyed a politician's career by aggressive and intrusive reporting, bribing witnesses and procuring falsities.[60]

It is true that misbehaviour by newspapers in Britain became steadily more notorious after the Profumo Affair, to the point where a much later Court of Appeal Judge, Leveson LJ, was instructed to investigate and report on press regulation. That, however, was not exactly Denning's fault: his report was critical of the press, stating 'the only thing that is clear is that something should be done to stop the trafficking in scandal for reward', although even the press were not the ultimate villains in Denning's view – that role was reserved exclusively for Ward. 'Chequebook journalism' pre-dated Denning's report, as indicated by the money swiftly offered to Keeler once there was a sniff of a scandal. 'Yellow journalism' had begun in earnest in the last quarter of the nineteenth century, led by the *News of the World*, so there was nothing really new about the Profumo Affair in that respect. The 'Crawford scandal' of 1885 which ended the career of the English politician Sir Charles Dilke, the case of *O'Shea v O'Shea* (1890) 15 PD 59 which ruined the career of the Irish politician Charles Stewart Parnell, and the divorce of John Russell in 1923 (the press reporting of which prompted Parliament to respond with the Judicial Proceedings (Regulation of Reports) Act 1926) were all fuelled by journalism at least as questionable as the worst regarding Profumo.

Further, whatever Denning had said or done, scandals would have continued unabated in public life. Davenport-Hines was right to draw attention to underhanded journalists, but it should also be acknowledged that the press has brought down more than a few public figures over the years, such as Jeffrey Archer or Jonathan Aitken – both of whom thought they could lie and expect the same deference as that upon which Profumo had relied.

Davenport-Hines also made a strong case for Denning's occasional acceptance of palpable nonsense: the *Daily Express* claimed that its juxtaposition of Profumo's offer of resignation with the picture of Keeler and the story about her missing from Edgecombe's trial had been 'entirely coincidental'. 'Accepting this to be so', wrote Denning, 'it had nevertheless unfortunate results'. The likelihood is that most of Fleet Street knew about Keeler's claims and was doing everything short of stating them outright.

Denning was certainly correct that the sole purpose of the security service was to defend the realm, though he should equally have held that the duty of the police was to investigate crimes proportionately and without the faintest influence of the government – factors which would have precluded any investigation of Ward in the absence of cogent evidence of criminal conduct.

From a legal perspective, the report lacked procedural fairness in: (a) not giving the witnesses a chance to respond to the adverse findings he intended to make; and (b) conducting all hearings in secret and without the publication of evidence (even suitably redacted). Both were straightforward breaches of natural justice. As with his regulation 18B detention during the Second World War, Denning seemed ready to tolerate procedural injustice where he thought the national interest required it.

Denning himself said in *The Due Process of Law*[61] about the form of inquiry which he undertook:

> It has the advantage that there can be no dissent, but it has two great disadvantages: first, being in secret, it has not the appearance of justice; second, in carrying out the inquiry, I have had to be detective, inquisitor, advocate and judge, and it has been difficult to combine them. But I have come to see that it has three considerable advantages. First, inasmuch as it has been held in private and in strict confidence, the witnesses were, I am sure, much more frank than they would otherwise have been. Secondly, I was able to check the evidence of one witness against that of another more freely. Thirdly, and most important, aspersions cast by witnesses against others (who are not able to defend themselves) do not achieve the publicity which is inevitable in a Court of Law or Tribunal of Inquiry.

It is not clear why Denning – the legendary dissenter – felt that an absence of dissent was necessarily an advantage. It is equally unclear why he felt the disadvantages he had identified were outweighed by his three 'considerable' advantages.

One classic justification for justice to be done behind closed doors is national security, though even where national security is indisputably engaged – as in trials of suspected terrorists, for example – the limits of secrecy are highly contested. But once Denning concluded – probably rightly, at least in the case of the interactions between Profumo, Keeler and Ivanov – that there had been no security breach of any significance, then the need for secrecy on those grounds fell away. In so far as he spared the government over Marples and Freeth, or anyone else, he was failing in the very duty imposed by his terms of reference. It was right not to want to publish idle tittle-tattle about individuals, but he had probative evidence about Marples and Freeth, and if their exposure would have embarrassed Macmillan into resigning and calling a general election, so be it.

In sending the shorthand writers out of the room, ostensibly to protect their sensibilities, he once again breached basic procedural justice because for justice to be seen to be done a full record of all proceedings should have been maintained. He also wrongly impugned the shorthand writers' professionalism: they might well have earlier covered murder trials, so it is unclear why he thought they would be too delicate to cope with the riotous acts of the Ward set.

Denning added to his own procedural errors by brushing aside the deficiencies in Ward's criminal trial. Had Ward lived he could almost certainly have appealed successfully on the ground that the trial had been unfair. It is impossible to imagine Denning on the Bench tolerating biased summings-up or other defects in an ordinary trial if, say, he had been sitting on the Court of Appeal, Criminal Division, and a conviction obtained the same way as Ward's had been appealed to him. Quite the reverse: it would have brought forth one of his classic paeans to the birthrights and freedoms of all Englishmen.

He was also plainly wrong about Ward being a communist sympathiser – he was in fact the opposite, who assisted MI5 – and about Ward living off the earnings of prostitution, since he did no such thing with Keeler and Rice-Davies. What was rarely pointed out at the time or since was that Ward had a comfortable lifestyle from his friends and connections as well as his legitimate work in osteopathy and art, so would not have needed to risk his own liberty and security by pimping prostitutes or selling secrets to Moscow.

Two central findings of Denning's report were thus incorrect, making it impossible to avoid the conclusion that Ward was the goat ritually burned to preserve not so much the Macmillan government as the very order of the establishment.

Denning's procedural steps were considered in a Royal Commission on Tribunals of Inquiry, headed by another law lord, Lord Salmon, in 1966. Lord Salmon wrote 'Lord Denning's report was generally accepted by the public. But that was only because of Lord Denning's rare qualities and high reputation. Even so, the public acceptance of the report may be regarded as a brilliant exception to what would normally occur when an inquiry is carried out under such conditions'.[62] Lord Salmon went on to recommend much stricter requirements for procedural fairness regarding witnesses to inquiries than had been permitted in the Denning inquiry.

Lord Nolan, who chaired an inquiry into standards in public life in the early 1990s, fondly compared his experiences with those of Denning, and was guarded in any criticism:[63]

> Such criticisms as have been made of the report are of two kinds. The first was the criticism which Denning himself had been at pains to acknowledge and forestall, namely that an inquisitorial procedure, rapidly carried out, ran the risk of causing injustice to those criticised. The second was of the more general nature that whenever the government of the day asks a judge to carry out an inquiry into a politically sensitive subject, it compromises the independence of the judiciary. I would not, for my part, accept this second ground of criticism as a general proposition, still less in relation to the Profumo inquiry. Plainly the situation demanded an independent inquiry, and who better to carry it out than a senior and respected judge, noted for his independence of mind? No doubt those looking for a stick with which to beat the government were disappointed by his conclusions, but no-one in his right mind could have suspected Denning of reaching them in order to lend a hand to a government in trouble.

Lord Nolan was evidently unaware of Denning's apparent collusion with Macmillan over Marples and Freeth.

Aftermath

Macmillan attempted to show defiance, but lasted less than a month after Denning's report was published. In October 1963 he was admitted for prostate surgery and resigned shortly afterwards, ostensibly on health grounds although his doctors had told him he was fit to continue. It soon became popular opinion that Profumo had caused Macmillan's resignation,[64] though Macmillan had been on borrowed time by the time of the scandal as it was. Further, the Conservatives still continued in office under Douglas-Home for another year, at which point the next general election was due anyway. They duly lost that election, but by then they had been in power for thirteen years, and the loss was by a slender margin.[65] Individual Conservative politicians who had accepted Profumo's initial denials were, however, undoubtedly personally affected.[66]

Upon Denning's retirement in 1982, Macmillan wrote to him thanking him for 'the kindness which you did to me nearly twenty years ago at a very difficult and delicate time in my life as Prime Minister'.[67] As Macmillan was aware, and as will be seen later in the book, 1982 was a very difficult and delicate year in Denning's own life, and he in turn was grateful for Macmillan's generous words.

Profumo withdrew from political life and resolved to seek redemption by dedicating the rest of his working life to Toynbee Hall, an old East End charity. He neither sought nor was granted vindication for any of his actions with Keeler or anyone else in the scandal. Nor did he ever comment on it publicly.[68] Hobson stood by him and joined him in his charity work. By the time of Profumo's death in 2001, his obituary writers were in near-unanimous agreement that he had atoned for his previous sins. Perhaps the most resounding illustration of his public redemption was the holding of a dinner at Lincoln's Inn to honour his outstanding contribution to Toynbee Hall, at which the guest speaker was none other than Lord Denning.[69] Then again, Profumo's own son did not think he felt any remorse over his behaviour beyond getting caught, and still conducted affairs albeit more discreetly.[70]

Keeler and Rice-Davies now had fame which they each sought to exploit as best they could, but it came at a price. Keeler found herself charged with perjury because of her evidence at Gordon's trial. She pleaded guilty in December 1963 and was sentenced to nine months' imprisonment, of which she served half. After being released, she went on to have two short marriages, with one child born in each. She soon spent all the money she had received from newspapers and thereafter struggled to find a career or even hold down a basic job due to her notoriety. She therefore tried to earn money from the scandal by giving interviews and participating in documentaries and ghost-written autobiographies. Inevitably, publishers and interviewers demanded 'new' revelations each time, meaning Keeler's successive accounts were flatly contradictory and increasingly imaginative – certainly of little probative value in the history of the scandal. She died in 2017, having lived her final years in relative poverty. In 2020, her son announced an attempt to have her conviction overturned posthumously.[71]

Rice-Davies made more of a success of her fame, running successful clubs and making a few acting appearances. Her friendship with Keeler did not survive the scandal. She later described her life as a 'slow descent into respectability'.[72] She died in 2014.

After Ivanov returned to Moscow in January 1963, he effectively vanished from international view. He served in the Black Sea Fleet for the next three decades. Following the breakup of the Soviet Union, he published his memoirs, in which he claimed that he had been able to obtain significant military intelligence from accessing British political circles, though he denied any of his superiors knew of his relationship with Keeler before the press broke the story.[73] As with Keeler, he had a book to sell and one should place little reliance upon it as an historical record. He died in 1994.

Astor's fate was one of the saddest of those involved. Caught up in the accusations by the Beaverbrook press, he maintained a dignified silence but died only three years later, in 1966. Cliveden was sold shortly afterwards.

Ward's reputation began to recover years after his death, albeit no thanks to Denning. In 1987, in response to publicity surrounding a new book on the scandal,[74] Denning dismissed the idea that Ward had been framed by the state,[75] adding that the charges against him were not 'bogus' and the 'conduct of the trial was beyond reproach'.[76] In contrast, the 1989 film *Scandal* portrayed Ward as the victim, not the villain, of the piece. Subsequently, the human rights lawyer Geoffrey Robertson QC wrote a book mounting a forthright defence of Ward.[77] He was extremely critical of Ward's trial, claiming to have found twelve grounds for challenging the fairness of the trial, and later alleged with some hyperbole that it was the 'worst miscarriage of justice in British history'.[78] He claimed that far from being a communist sympathiser, Ward was being used by the Foreign Office as a backchannel, through Ivanov, to the Kremlin.

In 2013, Robertson applied to the Criminal Cases Review Commission, hoping to have Ward's case heard by the Court of Appeal. The Commission held that the matter was of its time and that it was not in the public interest to rehear it. I would agree with its reasoning that, along with the resource implications:[79]

> ... no public interest would be served by referring a conviction from 1963 because, in the intervening 54 years there have been significant changes to the regulation and operation of the police, the security services, the legal system, the media, and the political system, which mean that any lessons from the case are unlikely to have practical relevance today.

Slightly bizarrely, however, the Commission also held there was no evidence that Ward's prosecution was 'politically motivated', or that the Court of Appeal had suppressed information which would have assisted Ward's trial. Either the Commission did not know of the meeting between Brooke, Hollis and Simpson where the clear message was communicated to stop Ward, or it did not believe the evidence of the meeting, or it somehow felt that independent of any political considerations the power of the state was justifiably aimed at Ward. The last of those seems improbable given the frankly feeble case which Ward faced.

The Commission did conclude that had Ward still been alive it would have been minded to refer the case to the Court of Appeal, on the grounds that: (a) Keeler's perjury conviction undermined her evidence against Ward; and (b) there was a possibility that contemporaneous media coverage of the case might have prejudiced Ward's trial.

Ultimately, a conclusive verdict on all aspects of the Profumo Affair, including Ward's trial and Denning's report, will only be possible with sight of the still-confidential Denning papers. In 1993, the question was raised as to whether they should be disclosed under the thirty-year rule, notwithstanding the promise Denning had made to witnesses that their evidence would never be released. Coincidentally, the Duchess of Argyll died that year. Denning was approached by the press and, although by then ninety-four years of age, was still able to produce a mischievous soundbite. He admitted being perhaps the only man of his generation who found the Duchess 'ordinary'. 'But then I'm an old veteran', he added. Denning went on to hint that the man in the pictures was, indeed, Douglas Fairbanks Jnr. Fairbanks Jnr was also still alive at the time, aged eighty-four, and effectively refused to comment. Prime Minister John Major, at the time faced with a series of sex scandals in his party, read the Denning papers in full and decided that they should be kept under seal until 2046.[80]

In 2014, Lord Wallace said in a written parliamentary answer to Professor Peter Hennessy, the peer and historian: 'I can confirm that the Denning Inquiry papers held by the Cabinet Office have been selected for permanent preservation'. He added that there were 'some sensational personal items' in the files, and that Denning had refused to allow the head of the Security Service access to them (though one struggles to believe Sir Roger Hollis never saw them).[81]

Given that almost sixty years have now passed since the Profumo Affair, and all those known to have been participants are now dead, the continuing suppression of the papers – especially the transcript of Ward's trial, which took place in open court[82] – seems difficult to justify. The applicable principle is open government: the onus is firmly on the state to justify withholding information. There was a plausible argument for allowing evidence to be suppressed during the lifetime of those who gave evidence, because Denning had assured them of complete confidence. Even in that case (assuming some are still alive – they would likely be nonagenarians or older), however, their names might be redacted but the papers otherwise released.[83] As shown by the abdication papers, the sealing of royal wills, the Mountbatten diaries,[84] or the aftermath of the Kennedy assassination in the United States, suppressing important information only fuels conspiracies, and embarrassment for individuals has to be weighed against the substantial public interest in open government – a concept which, away from Profumo, Denning was often associated.[85] Since it seems unlikely that questions of national security would be involved six decades after the end of the affair, it does the British government and the more nebulous concept of the 'establishment' no credit to continue to refuse to release the remaining Profumo files, at the very least in redacted form.

Coda

Back in 1963 the rank hypocrisy of the British ruling class did not go unnoticed elsewhere. One avid follower of Profumo's misadventures from over the Channel was the French President Charles De Gaulle, otherwise engaged in avoiding assassination attempts and in preventing Britain from joining the European Economic Community. After Profumo resigned, De Gaulle told an aide: 'That'll teach the English for trying to behave like Frenchmen'.[86]

CHAPTER XII

Master of the Rolls – Travel and Other Engagements

Having finished his labours on Profumo, Denning was able to resume his overseas travels in subsequent court holidays. As before, the destinations stretched across the globe. Over the Christmas break in 1963, for example, he visited Pakistan, and the following year he went to the American Bar Association in New York before going on to South America, the latter trip sponsored by the British Council.

Back in England, in 1964 Denning became President of the English Association, providing wider recognition of his inimitable prose style. His inaugural address was entitled 'Gems in Ermine', and in it he paid tribute to the 700 years of law reports, stating that '[w]hen great issues have been at stake the judgments are marked by eloquence, wisdom and authority. They have laid the foundations of freedom in our land'.[1]

In 1965 he played a central part in celebrations for the 750th anniversary of Magna Carta, including giving a presentation at Runnymede sponsored by the American Bar Association and writing an article for *The Times*. He described it as 'the greatest constitutional document of all times – the foundation of the freedom of the individual against the arbitrary authority of the despot', reflecting the standard view of Magna Carta of the day, however ahistorical it might have been.[2] Also in 1965 he was made an honorary Doctor of Civil Law at Oxford, while during the summer vacation he travelled to South America, where among other things he was welcomed by the Institute of Brazilian Lawyers.[3]

Denning regularly made speeches and attended formal dinners. Often such events took place in London, for which his Lincoln's Inn flat was invaluable, as well as sparing him a daily commute from Whitchurch.

Unfortunately, the flat was convenient in location but in no other respect. The problem was that it had previously been part of one flat, but on the death of the previous occupant the property had been inexpertly divided into two. Denning's had an inadequate kitchen, poor ventilation and insufficient room for entertaining more than one or two people at a time – the last of those a frustrating restriction given his popularity. It was also accessible only by a substantial number of stairs, which for the Dennings became a tiresome obstacle. Denning was less than amused, therefore, when the Inn proposed doubling the rent in 1968. He sent a rather terse démarche to the responsible officials warning that he might have to give up the flat and consequently 'be unable to fulfil many of the evening engagements which attend to my office'.[4] The said officials opted not to put up too much of a fight against the Master of the Rolls. They agreed to a smaller scale of increases over three years, thus enabling Denning to remain until after he had retired more than a decade later. One notes in passing that Denning had told them flatly that he could not afford the increase – yet another indication of a wholly different economic environment, given that he had been able to afford to purchase substantial detached properties mortgage-free outside London.

Having resolved his property issues, Denning was able to continue participating in an almost bewildering range of activities outside court. In 1969, he and Joan became founder members of the British Museum Society. He was also elected vice-president of two rather disparate organisations: the Supreme Court Sports Association, and the Society of Genealogists. A full list of the organisations upon which he served as president, vice-president or patron during his time as MR can be found in Appendix II.

In 1966 the Dennings travelled to New Zealand, where they inadvertently formed part of the background cast in a tragic murder case. The official reason for their trip was the Dominion Legal Conference, held in that year in the South Island city of Dunedin. Denning's address to the conference was later published in the *New Zealand Law Journal*.[5] Whilst there he was also elected Honorary President of the Law Students' Society of the University of Canterbury (he was re-elected in 1969 and 1974).

Sensibly, in view of the vast distances required to go to New Zealand, the Dennings took the opportunity to see some of the rest of the country.[6] They were invited by a Wellington lawyer, Lloyd Ellingham, and his wife Marjorie to stay over the Easter weekend at the Ellinghams' holiday home ('bach' in New Zealand parlance) in Taupo, a small town (in those days at least) in the middle of the North Island beside the eponymous lake.

Other guests for the weekend included the eminent Australian judge Sir WJV (Victor) Windeyer, and Hazen Hansard, the immediate past-President of the Canadian Bar Association, both of whom had also travelled to New Zealand for the conference. On Easter Sunday they were all joined for lunch by the future Chief Justice of New Zealand, Ron Davison, then an upcoming barrister, and his wife Jacqueline. The Davisons owned a neighbouring bach where they were staying for the weekend with their two young sons.

Although no one seems to have suspected (perhaps reflecting a less sympathetic age in that respect), Marjorie Ellingham suffered severe mental health problems. Her difficulties were exacerbated by the fact that she had been born and raised in England, moving to New Zealand only after meeting her husband, and had struggled to adjust to the new country. It reached the point where she was seriously contemplating suicide. At the time, suicide carried a crushing social stigma for the family of the deceased, so she set about devising a method which would make her death look like an accident. Her plan was to supply guests with a small dose of arsenic to induce symptoms that would seem like food poisoning, and to take a fatal dose herself. She experimented on several luckless dinner guests on different occasions to determine the right doses, before putting the scheme into action at the Easter Sunday lunch.

Initially, things went according to her gruesome plan. A number of guests developed mild discomfort, whilst Marjorie herself collapsed and was admitted to hospital. Unnoticed by anyone, however, before the guests had showed any symptoms, Jaqueline Davison had taken a slice of cake back to her bach for her younger son David. He soon became severely unwell. Tragically, while the adult guests recovered, David's much smaller frame could not cope with even the lesser dose, and he died a few days later. Confronted with that terrible news, Marjorie admitted responsibility for David's death, but did not admit having administered arsenic. She died just over a week later. The first time arsenic was associated with the case was when it was discovered during her own autopsy. By then, evidence such as food scraps had long disappeared.

An exhaustive investigation was held, during which very many witnesses were interviewed, including the Dennings. They gave hair samples which showed traces of arsenic. Eventually, the authorities had enough evidence to uncover Marjorie's appalling scheme.[7]

Fortunately, the Dennings' other overseas adventures proved somewhat less eventful. In 1967 they went to Australia, where among other things Denning participated in a radio discussion about recent changes in the law, and the relationship of law and morality.[8] In 1968 they went to India, and the next year to Canada and Pakistan. For the most part their trips involved the standard fare of attending conferences and making speeches to institutions.

In the summer of 1969, however, Denning received a different assignment when he was invited to Fiji to act as the arbitrator of a dispute over sugar, the major commodity of the country at the time. The parties were the sugar growers (primarily, though not exclusively, the descendants of labourers brought from India during the days of the British Empire) and the Australian-based sugar millers. Issues between the two had existed throughout the 1960s, the same decade in which steps were taken to make Fiji a fully independent, self-governing country (achieved in 1970). The parties had signed a contract in 1961 which was due to expire in 1970. Denning was appointed pursuant to an arbitration clause in the contract to determine how the money from sugar ought to be divided in future.

He arrived in Fiji in August and sat for twenty-one days, assisted by representatives of both sides and an accountant. Although both sides initially launched flanking attacks on his conduct of the arbitration, both were won round before the end of the hearing, partly because they accepted that he had allowed all voices to be aired fairly.

Denning's eventual award provided for the growers to have a considerably greater share of the proceeds from the sale of the sugar, which answered their complaint that the old arrangement had led to them being exploited.[9] The growers were overjoyed, their representative going as far as to call Denning 'a legend in his own lifetime'.[10] The millers, on the other hand, complained that the result would likely drive them out of business, which indeed proved the case as they withdrew from the arrangement shortly afterwards. The industry was then nationalised by the Fijian government.

Throughout the 1970s, Denning continued to receive well-wishing correspondence from Fiji. The sugar industry there further benefitted from a marketing agreement with the European Economic Community. Regrettably, though, hopes of long-term harmony and prosperity for the indigenous Fijians and the ethnic Indian community proved illusory.[11]

Denning's work on the Fijian arbitration was clearly well regarded, since in 1970 he was asked to mediate a dispute over the importation of bananas from Jamaica to Britain. The parties were the Jamaican Banana Board and a commercial entity known as the Fyffes Group. Fyffes were unhappy with the quality of bananas, whilst the Jamaican industry was struggling due to government interference. Denning met the parties, inspected premises and travelled to Jamaica, managing to fit in a lecture to the Bar and Law Society of Jamaica while he was about it.

For once, Denning was unable either to charm or reason the parties into agreement. Instead, he reported back to the government in a chastened tone that 'I must leave it to the Governments of the United Kingdom and Jamaica to bring peace and stability to the industry, if they can. It is nigh a hopeless task'.[12] The Foreign Secretary, Sir Alec Douglas-Home, expressed gratitude for Denning's efforts all the same.[13] In the opposite outcome to the Fijian arbitration, Denning might have failed but the parties eventually succeeded by themselves, reaching agreement in March 1971. Fyffes wrote to Denning afterwards crediting him with taking important steps towards the eventual resolution.

For the next six years, Denning continued to spend as much time travelling during vacations as he was able. He continued his interests in African law and legal education, visiting a wide array of countries on the continent and making a strongly positive impression each time.[14] There were far fewer long-haul flights at the time, but Denning used the number of stops his longer trips necessitated to his advantage, by finding places to see on the way. In the summer vacation of 1974, for example, he went to South Africa, Mauritius, Australia, New Zealand, Japan and Canada in less than two months,[15] a demanding itinerary under any circumstances – perhaps the reason why Joan had named the twenty-one uninterrupted days in Fiji for the arbitration as her favourite of all their trips.[16] In 1975 he went to Malaysia for the 4th Commonwealth Magistrates' Conference;[17] in 1976 to the American Bar Association conference at Atlanta, Georgia,[18] to Hong Kong to deliver lectures in 1977[19] and to Canada in 1979, where he sat in the Court of Appeal as a guest.[20] Denning wrote of his travels:[21]

> Much more could I tell of our visits to the universities, the judges and the lawyers, of the United States of America, of Canada and Australia, of India and Pakistan, of New Zealand and Hong Kong, of Jamaica and Trinidad, of Brazil and Guyana, of the Argentine (sic) and Chile, of Malaysia and Singapore, of Malta and South Africa, of Belgium and the Netherlands, of Israel, and even of Poland. In all of these countries we have friends with whom we correspond.

In *The Closing Chapter*, he looked back at some of the gifts he had received during his travels:[22]

> ... the large ceremonial bowl of Fiji, the cowboy's horse of Chile (made by the oldest prisoner in Santiago), the Eskimo of Northwest Canada, the ceramics of Hong Kong, the dolls of Japan, the wood carvings of Ghana, the pewter of Malaysia and the silver of India.

In 1977, Denning's travels came to a shuddering halt when Joan suffered angina and was advised not to travel abroad again. (At the time, he had outstanding invitations to visit Australia, America, Canada and India.[23]) There was no question of Denning going without her: he relied upon her completely for practicalities when travelling and, more importantly, would never have left her on her own with health problems. She recovered the following year to the extent that she was able to leave Whitchurch, though by then Denning had his own health issues in the form of arthritis in his hip. By 1979, one of his legs had shortened by an inch-and-a-half and he had to learn to walk again.

He therefore had to find ways to fill his spare time in England. He continued to accept a steady stream of speaking engagements. He had long belonged to the Athenaeum Club. In 1968 he had also joined the Savage Club, a rather more bohemian institution which had a more diverse membership than most London gentlemen's clubs of the day. Many of the 'Brother Savages' as they called themselves would have appealed to Denning as classic English eccentrics, but there is little evidence in the club records or elsewhere of Denning attending often if at all.[24] Not being a drinker, the occasionally infamous Savage bar would have held little attraction for him. Instead, when Joan's ability to travel abroad ended, he took up the more Denning-like pursuits of writing books to occupy himself during the vacation, as well as continuing speaking engagements within Britain.

Before considering his books, over the next six chapters we will look at some of Denning's more important cases. He heard so many as Master of the Rolls that it is not possible to begin to describe them all, even all those generally considered noteworthy. We will therefore confine ourselves to a potted survey of some of the more memorable. They are separated into loose categories of civil procedure, common law, family law, labour law, public law and security of the realm, more to impose a convenient narrative structure rather than for any sophisticated reason. No claim is made that the selection is exhaustive, and no attempt is made to offer a comprehensive review of his work in each field.[25] Rather, the intention is to show Denning's style, method, values and contradictions in action, and hence explain his judicial legacy.

CHAPTER XIII

Master of the Rolls – Pre-trial Remedies

In a world of instant communications, securing assets by means of injunction before trial is one of the most crucial weapons to ensure rights are not rendered illusory by unscrupulous defendants disposing of assets before any claim has been adjudicated. It is equally necessary on occasion to preserve evidence of wrongdoing which the culprits might destroy if warned of impending action. In 1975, Denning played a key role in the development of legal remedies to both of those problems, in what became two of his most famous cases. The names of the plaintiffs – 'Mareva' and 'Anton Piller' – soon became legal shorthand for the procedures they established. He was rightly acclaimed for those innovations (called by his successor Lord Donaldson MR the two 'nuclear weapons' of the law[1]), though he was not always successful in his reforming efforts – at least during his lifetime – as exemplified by the third case considered in this chapter, *The Siskina*.

In *Mareva Cia Naviera SA v International Bulkcarriers SA, The Mareva* [1975] 2 Lloyd's Rep 509,[2] Denning and the rest of the Court of Appeal created the injunctive relief by which a defendant's assets might be frozen if there was a danger of them being dissipated overseas prior to any judgment being obtained. Denning's approach not only endured, but also became codified by statute and universally accepted as a necessary, indeed vital, part of any functioning civil legal regime.

In many respects the case was classic Denning – a short judgment reaching the result necessary to do justice between the parties, contrary to existing precedent, and averting the disapproval of the House of Lords most probably because the losing litigant did not have the funds to appeal. The existing precedent was *Lister v Stubbs* (1890) 45 Ch D 1, in which Cotton LJ had said 'You cannot get an injunction to restrain a man who is alleged to be a debtor from parting with his property'. The result was that a rogue entity could dissipate its assets before anyone had the chance to bring proceedings, a risk present even in the less sophisticated world of the nineteenth century when *Lister* was decided. At that time, the risk was perhaps greatest in shipping law, where a foreign-owned ship might accrue debts in taking on supplies before departing English shores.

By the 1970s, with the advent of telexes and otherwise more efficient international banking, the risk had greatly increased in all fields of commerce, to the exasperation of the business community. The frustration was all the greater since appropriate remedies were available in some European jurisdictions.[3] Yet the House of Lords had never overturned *Lister*, which therefore remained binding on all the lower courts as a decision of the Court of Appeal.

Denning decided *Lister* could be ignored because of the wide discretion of s 45 of the Supreme Court of Judicature (Consolidation) Act 1925, which provided:

> A *mandamus* or an injunction may be granted or a receiver appointed by an interlocutory Order of the Court in all cases in which it shall appear to the Court to be just or convenient ...

Denning was being rather disingenuous there, since *Lister* had been decided under an identical provision in an earlier Act. It was true that the vast majority of lawyers and businesspeople alike agreed that the *Mareva* injunction was a worthy reform. But that was not how the system of precedent was supposed to work. It raised the question of just how much of a majority the proposed reform commanded or how desirable it was (from an abstract perspective) as a matter of principle. Therein lay the paradox of Denning – everyone would agree he dispensed justice, so long as they happened to agree with his concept thereof. Since there was effectively unanimous agreement that *Mareva* was the just result, it might be called the exception that proved the rule.[4]

The second Denning-led landmark reform of pre-trial remedies in the mid-1970s was created in *Anton Piller KG v Manufacturing Processes Limited* [1976] Ch 55.[5] The plaintiffs were West German manufacturers who owned the copyright in the design of a high frequency converter used in the burgeoning computer industry. They suspected that the defendants, their

English agents, were planning to supply rival manufacturers with their confidential information. They wished to bring proceedings to prevent the threatened abuse, but were concerned that the defendants, if notified of the threat of litigation, would take steps to destroy the documents or would send them out of the jurisdiction. The plaintiffs accordingly made an *ex parte* application for an order for permission to enter the defendants' premises in order to inspect, remove or make copies of documents belonging to them.

The Court of Appeal (Denning, Ormrod and Shaw LJJ) held that in exceptional circumstances, where the plaintiffs had a very strong *prima facie* case that they had incurred very serious actual or potential damage, and there was clear evidence that the defendants possessed vital material which they might destroy or dispose of so as to defeat the ends of justice before any application *inter partes* could be made, the court had inherent jurisdiction to order the defendants to 'permit' the plaintiffs' representatives to enter the defendants' premises to inspect and remove such material.

The order became widely used not long after, eventually being superseded by a statutory search order under the Civil Procedure Act 1997 – another example of Parliament subsequently codifying a Denning-led reform.

Denning's efforts at procedural reform did not always meet with success, one important failure occurring in *The Siskina* [1979] AC 210. The case involved the loss of the eponymous vessel, owned by a Panamanian company but managed by Greek shipowners, taking a valuable cargo from Italy to a port on the Red Sea. The cargo had been paid for in advance by the buyers, who also paid the freight for the voyage. Due to a dispute between the Greek shipping company and the Italian charterers, the ship was diverted to Cyprus, where she unloaded her cargo and then departed, sinking six weeks later in circumstances unknown at the time of the litigation.

The shipowners claimed on their insurance from London underwriters, and wished to bring proceedings against the charterers. They required leave to serve them out of the jurisdiction. They obtained it from Mocatta J in chambers, but it was overturned by the High Court on the application of the defendant charterers. Then, in the Court of Appeal, Denning and Lawton LJ (Bridge LJ dissenting) allowed the shipowners' appeal. They held that the court had jurisdiction to grant leave to issue a writ and notice of it in any case where an injunction was sought ordering a defendant to do or refrain from doing anything within the jurisdiction, and that the injunction did not have to be part of the substantive relief claimed or ancillary to a claim.

Knowing that he would be accused of going beyond what was permissible under the rules, Denning concluded with a flourish:

It was suggested that this course is not open to us because it would be legislation; and that we should leave the law to be amended by the Rule Committee. But see what this would mean: the shipowning company would be able to decamp with the insurance moneys and the cargo owners would have to whistle for any redress. To wait for the Rule Committee would be to shut the stable door after the steed had been stolen. And who knows that there will ever again be another horse in the stable? Or another ship sunk and insurance moneys here? I ask: why should the judges wait for the Rule Committee? The judges have an inherent jurisdiction to lay down the practice and procedure of the courts; and we can invoke it now to restrain the removal of these insurance moneys. To the timorous souls I would say in the words of William Cowper:

> 'Ye fearful saints fresh courage take,
> The clouds ye so much dread
> Are big with mercy, and shall break
> In blessings on your head.'

Instead of 'saints', read 'judges'. Instead of 'mercy', read 'justice'. And you will find a good way to law reform!

On appeal, the House of Lords was not amused. They ruled that a right to obtain an interlocutory injunction was not a cause of action. It depended on there being a pre-existing cause of action against the defendant arising out of an invasion, actual or threatened, by him of a legal or equitable right of the plaintiff.

As for the timorous souls, Lord Hailsham LC riposted:

> The second point on which I wish to comment is the argument of Lord Denning MR, fortified by the authority of a quotation from *Hymns Ancient and Modern*, that the judges need not wait for the authority of the rules committee in order to sanction a change in practice, indeed an extension of jurisdiction, in matters of this kind. The jurisdiction of the rules committee is statutory, and for judges of first instance or on appeal to pre-empt its functions is, at least in my opinion, for the courts to usurp the function of the legislature. Quite apart from this and from technical arguments of any kind, I should point out that the rules committee is a far more suitable vehicle for discharging the function than a panel of three judges, however eminent, deciding an individual case after hearing arguments from advocates representing the interests of opposing litigants, however ably.

Interestingly, despite chastising Denning for exceeding his authority in the case, the House took a more accepting line about the *Mareva* case, not just because the case was not directly under appeal, but also because of its obvious common sense and the welcome reception it had received from the commercial community. Had they been doctrinally consistent they would have acknowledged that Denning had acted outside the normal bounds of precedent by ignoring *Lister v Stubbs* when deciding *Mareva*.

The Siskina was yet another example of the approach Denning had long taken with injunctions or any other equitable remedy, which he had once described as: 'The remedy by interlocutory injunctions is so useful that it should be kept flexible and discretionary. It must not be made the subject of strict rules'.[6] One academic critic, having reviewed Denning's work in the field of pre-trial injunctions, concluded that he 'was too eager to develop the flexibility of judicial discretion and too ready to develop the law in great leaps and bounds when small steady steps are normally all that is required'.[7] Yet Denning's positive achievements were tangible and lasting. *Mareva* and *Anton Piller* were not small steps, and were most definitely 'required'. One wonders how long it would have taken for the law to reach the common-sense approach they introduced without Denning's foresight and boldness even if, as ever, he was apt to go too far at times.

Postscript

After the above had been drafted, the Privy Council in *Convoy Collateral Ltd v Broad Idea International Ltd* [2021] UKPC 24 rejected the House of Lords' decision in *The Siskina* [1979] AC 210, and rewrote the juridical basis for the grant of freezing orders and other interim injunctions in a manner more consistent with the decision of the Court of Appeal. Denning had triumphed after all. It would have especially pleased him given that in *The Due Process of Law* he had stated[8] that, although he was used to reversals by the House of Lords, *The Siskina* was the most disappointing, because he felt their lordships' decision was unjust to the buyers of the cargo.

CHAPTER XIV

Master of the Rolls – Common Law

The heading 'common law' encompasses the most diverse collection of Denning's cases, all concerning issues of tort or contract or both. Throughout, one can see the zeal with which he engaged the common law, frequently unencumbered by statute. It helped that usually – though not always – the cases involved subject matter that did not trouble him morally, unlike those involving criminality, matrimonial breakdown or challenges to the authority and stability of the state, where his rigid moral code sometimes prevented him either following the law or doing 'justice' as others might have viewed the individual cases.

One of his early decisions of note was *Letang v Cooper* [1965] 1 QB 232, when he refused to allow an action under the old form of trespass to the person, insisting it could be brought only under negligence.[1] Denning's reforming spirit came out strongly:

> I must decline, therefore, to go back to the old forms of action in order to construe this statute. I know that in the last century Maitland said 'the forms of action we have buried but they still rule us from their graves'. But we have in this century shaken off their trammels. These forms of action have served their day. They did at one time form a guide to substantive rights; but they do so no longer. Lord Atkin told us what to do about them:
>
>> 'When these ghosts of the past stand in the path of justice, clanking their mediaeval chains, the proper course for the judge is to pass through them undeterred': see *United Australia Ltd v Barclays Bank Ltd* [[1941] AC 1 at 29].

Just as he liked to do away with what he considered outdated restrictions, Denning was partial to creating new causes of action when needed to ensure justice could be done as he saw it. As noted earlier, his dissent in *Candler v Crane, Christmas & Co* [1951] 2 KB 164 was vindicated by the House of Lords in *Hedley Byrne & Co Ltd v Heller & Partners Ltd* [1964] AC 465, creating the cause of action of negligent misstatement. Elsewhere, in *Home Office v Dorset Yacht Club* [1970] AC 1004, Denning and the rest of the Court of Appeal allowed the Home Office to be sued for negligence in the exercise of statutory duties, notwithstanding the restrictions of the Crown Proceedings Act 1947.

He stopped himself short, however, in the case of *Rondel v Worsley* [1966] 3 All ER 657. The action arose out of rather squalid goings-on, incurring the inevitable Denning moral condemnation, but it nonetheless raised a fundamental point of legal principle with which he was avidly engaged.

The facts concerned a rent collector working for Peter Rachman, the slum landlord who had been a bit-part player in the Profumo saga. In April 1959, the rent collector went to a dance being held at a house owned by Rachman. He had an altercation with the doorman and was later convicted of causing grievous bodily harm with intent. A subsequent appeal, in which he argued that his counsel had been incompetent, was dismissed. He then attempted to sue the same counsel in negligence. The claim was struck out and he appealed to the Court of Appeal. The appeal was heard by Denning with Danckwerts and Salmon LJJ.

At the time, membership of a 'profession' carried greater implicit assumptions about duty, service and the outward manifestation of competence, if not infallibility, than in the present day. For one thing, the professions were precluded from advertising, because it was assumed the public should have confidence in any practitioner they might encounter.[2] But Denning had not wanted to stop professionals being sued in other contexts (indeed, he had expanded the possibility in *Candler v Crane, Christmas & Co*). He therefore had to distinguish the position of barristers. He did so on the basis that barristerial immunity was necessary so that counsel 'may do his duty fearlessly and independently as he ought, and to prevent him being harassed by vexatious actions such as this present one now before us'.

Not for the first or last time, Denning also begrudged the prospect of people making money out of what he regarded as spurious claims:

> If this action were to be permitted, it would open the door to every disgruntled client. You have only to read the applications made daily to the criminal division of this court. They are filled with complaints

against the judge, against the counsel, against the witnesses, against everyone who has had a hand in bringing the man to justice. If this action is to go for trial, it will lead to dozens of like cases.

He distinguished between solicitors and barristers by pointing out that, unlike barristers, a solicitor:

is not bound to act for anyone who asks him. He can pick and choose. He can sue for his fees. He can, and does, make a contract with every client who employs him. He is under a contractual duty to use care; and this extends to his conduct of a cause as well as an advocate as anything else. If he is negligent he can be sued.

The House of Lords upheld Denning's decision, though it later took a more restrictive view of barristerial immunity.[3]

If Denning was prone to being over-protective of the Bar, he was more sanguine and realistic when it came to criticism of judges than some of his contemporaries. In 1968, the former Lord Hailsham, Quintin Hogg, who had famously vented his spleen at John Profumo on television five years earlier (before renouncing his peerage with a view to becoming the Conservative Party leader), turned his sights on a decision of the Court of Appeal concerning gaming legislation. (Denning, incidentally, was predictably opposed to gambling, considering it a destructive vice.[4]) Hogg ridiculed the decision in an article for *Punch* magazine.

A publicly minded litigant in person, the former MP Raymond Blackburn, who would later call Denning the 'Greatest Living Englishman',[5] complained that Hogg's article amounted to contempt of court. Denning dismissed the claim, stating 'we will never use this jurisdiction as a means to uphold our own dignity. That must rest on surer foundations'.[6] Salmon and Edmund Davies LJJ concurred, the former ruling that '[t]he authority and reputation of our courts are not so frail that their judgments need to be shielded from criticism, even from the criticism of Mr Quintin Hogg'.

Similarly, in *Balogh v Crown Court at St Albans* [1974] 3 All ER 283 Denning reduced the sentence of an individual convicted of contempt of court after trying to release laughing gas into the courtroom ventilation system, from six months to fourteen days. In treating the matter thus, Denning was again being more realistic than some other judges of the era, some of whom could not take a joke or a cheap insult without coming across as insufferably pompous and self-important.[7]

Often, the famous Denning openings showed where his sympathies lay. In *D&C Builders v Rees* [1966] 2 QB 617 he began:

> The plaintiffs are a little company. 'D' stands for Donaldson, a decorator, 'C' for Casey, a plumber. They are jobbing builders. The defendant has a shop where he sells builders' materials.

'A little company' hinted that Denning would be inclined to be protective of its interests, and so it proved. The little company of builders performed work for the defendant in May and June 1964, for which they invoiced £482 13s. 1d. The defendant did not pay, leaving the builders in desperate financial trouble. Eventually, in November, the defendant offered £300 in final settlement,[8] which the builders felt compelled to accept due to their pressing circumstances. The defendant sent a cheque in exchange for a receipt stating that the sum was received 'in completion of the account'.

The builders brought an action seeking the balance of the account. The defendant argued *inter alia* that there had been a binding agreement for the lesser sum. The latter point was tried as a preliminary issue. The judge held that there was no consideration supporting the agreement for the lower sum, and thus decided in favour of the builders. The defendants appealed.

The Court of Appeal unanimously dismissed the appeal, holding that the builders had been under duress due to their financial position, which the defendant had exploited. An acceptance arising from a threat did not amount to a settlement. Denning stated:

> The creditor is barred from his legal rights only when it would be inequitable for him to insist upon them. Where there has been a true accord under which the creditor voluntarily agrees to accept a lesser sum in satisfaction and the debtor acts on that accord by paying the lesser sum and the creditor accepts it, then it is inequitable for the creditor afterwards to insist on the balance.

In the course of reaching his decision, Denning looked back with satisfaction at his by-then famous *High Trees* case, stating that '[t]he solution [in the case] was so obviously just that no one could well gainsay it'.

The case of *Broome v Cassell* [1972] AC 1027 was noteworthy for several reasons. It earned Denning one of his more stinging criticisms from the House of Lords for his disregard for precedent, even though they upheld his actual decision in the case. It concerned a notorious wartime event, and an even more notorious account written by a young historian who was later publicly discredited. Behind all those events lay the fact that all the trouble might have been averted had the Admiralty followed the advice of a different Denning, his younger brother Norman, given nearly thirty years earlier.

The background was the disastrous Convoy PQ 17 during the Second World War. The convoy was part of the British and American efforts to supply the Soviet Union with materials. The Admiralty received intelligence that the convoy was going to be attacked by the German battleship *Tirpitz* (sister ship of the better-known *Bismarck*). Lieutenant Commander Norman Denning, serving in the Operational Intelligence Centre,[9] advised that the warning was incorrect and that *Tirpitz* was returning to port. Norman was right, but his advice was not passed on and so the convoy's commander, JE Broome, ordered dispersal of the ships. Once the convoy scattered, the merchant vessels were much more vulnerable to attack from German U-Boats and aircraft. Had they stayed in convoy, the escort vessels would have seen off those smaller adversaries, but the entire convoy would have faced obliteration by the *Tirpitz*, hence the decision to take their chances by dispersal. Of the thirty-five merchant ships, twenty-four were sunk, with heavy loss of life and supplies.

At the time, no blame was placed on Broome, whose actions had been thought reasonable given the information he had. The fault lay with those who had given him that information.

In the mid-1960s, an aspiring historian by the name of David Irving wrote a book about PQ 17. Contrary to the official view, he lumped the blame for the disaster squarely on Broome. In response, Broome sued Irving and the publishers for libel. He won, which left the question of damages. Broome sought not simply compensatory damage but exemplary damages, in order to punish what he thought was outrageous behaviour by Irving.

At the time, the leading case on exemplary damages was that of the House of Lords in *Rookes v Barnard* [1964] AC 1129, in which Lord Devlin had severely restricted the circumstances under which exemplary damages could be awarded. Lord Devlin held that an award could only be made: (i) in cases of oppressive, arbitrary or unconstitutional acts by government servants; (ii) where the defendant's conduct had been calculated by him to make a profit for himself which might well exceed the compensation payable to the plaintiff; and (iii) where expressly authorised by statute.

In *Broome's* case Lawton J directed the jury that they could make an award under Lord Devlin's category (ii) if they found that Irving had knowingly lied for profit. The jury responded by awarding £15,000 in compensatory damages and £25,000 by way of exemplary damages.[10]

Despite being photographed outside court apparently shaking hands in a conciliatory fashion with Broome, Irving appealed against both awards. Cassell appealed only against the award of exemplary damages.

The Court of Appeal, consisting of Denning along with Salmon and Phillimore LJJ, dismissed the appeal. Extraordinarily, however, it went on to hold that the decision in *Rookes v Barnard* should not be followed, since it had been decided *per incuriam* in Latin, or 'wrongly' in English. The reasons, according to Denning, were that: (a) *Rookes v Barnard* was propounded in 1964 when the House of Lords was still bound by its own previous decisions[11] approving awards of exemplary damages on broad lines; (b) Lord Devlin's three designated categories of conduct were illogical, arbitrary and restrictive; and (c) Lord Devlin's judgment amounted to a change in the law without any prior discussion with counsel of the categories or the practical difficulties they would pose for judge and jury. Therefore, unless and until the House of Lords had had an opportunity to reconsider the subject, juries in cases where a plaintiff asked for exemplary damages should be directed according to the law as it was before *Rookes v Barnard* and need not assess compensatory and exemplary damages separately.

Predictably, the House of Lords was outraged. When the case was appealed, seven law lords instead of the usual five assembled. By majority they went on to dismiss the appeal, holding that the award had been justified under ground (ii) of *Rookes v Barnard*. They then set about pouring Denning back into his bottle. The harshest critic was Quintin Hogg, restored to the peerage by Prime Minister Ted Heath, who had made him Lord Chancellor. Lord Hailsham LC, as he had thereby become, delivered a rebuke every bit as openly critical of Denning as any by his predecessor Viscount Simonds:

> The fact is, and I hope it will never be necessary to say so again, that, in the hierarchical system of courts which exists in this country, it is necessary for each lower tier, including the Court of Appeal, to accept loyally the decisions of the higher tiers. Where decisions manifestly conflict, the decision in *Young v Bristol Aeroplane Co. Ltd* [1944] KB 718 offers guidance to each tier in matters affecting its own decisions. It does not entitle it to question considered decisions in the upper tiers with the same freedom. Even this House, since it has taken freedom to review its own decisions, will do so cautiously.

The criticism would not have come as a great surprise to Denning. It was a strikingly brave thing for him to have told the House of Lords that they had been plainly wrong at any time, let alone in so recent a decision. Perhaps more than any case to that point, it showed how Denning intended to carve his own path. It also showed how strong a personality and reputation he possessed, in that he was able to take colleagues in the Court of Appeal with him.[12]

Denning was on safer grounds in *Jarvis v Swan Tours* [1973] QB 233 when dealing with Mr James Jarvis, a solicitor who worked for a local authority in Barking, Essex. Jarvis normally took one overseas holiday a year, usually in the winter as he enjoyed skiing. In 1969, he was attracted by a brochure which promised 'a most wonderful little resort on a sunny plateau', but it turned out to be anything but wonderful. Instead, the resort was a drab affair with bad food, worse entertainment and almost no one speaking English.

Jarvis was not amused. He sued the tour company for breach of contract. The judge accepted that the holiday had not been what was promised, and awarded as damages half the cost of the holiday. Jarvis appealed the amount of damages, claiming it was insufficient.

In allowing the appeal, Denning pointed out:

> In a proper case damages for mental distress can be recovered in contract, just as damages for shock can be recovered in tort. One such case is a contract for a holiday, or any other contract to provide entertainment and enjoyment. If the contracting party breaks his contract, damages can be given for the disappointment, the distress, the upset and frustration caused by the breach. I know that it is difficult to assess in terms of money, but it is no more difficult than the assessment which the courts have to make every day in personal injury cases for loss of amenities.

On Denning's reasoning, failure to provide an enjoyable time deserved more than just the refund on the ticket. Instead, Jarvis was entitled to 'the sum required to compensate him for the loss of entertainment and enjoyment which he had been promised and did not get', his vexation and disappointment in the holiday being relevant considerations in arriving at that sum. Denning raised the damages due to £125, amounting to about £1,300 in 2022 terms, though the range and cost of holidays available by then (in the pre-Covid-19 world at least) bore little relation to Jarvis's time.[13] His decision was not free of controversy, one commentator expressing concern that Denning had not considered countervailing policy factors.[14]

Naturally some of Denning's best-known contract cases as Master of the Rolls involved exemption clauses. We saw earlier how, in cases such as *Karsales (Harrow) Ltd v Wallis* [1956] 1 WLR 936, he had attempted to develop the concept of 'fundamental breach' as part of his campaign against them. In *Suisse Atlantique Société D'armement Maritime SA v NV Rotterdamsche Kolen Centrale* [1967] 1 AC 361, the House of Lords was disapproving, Viscount Dilhorne stating:

In a number of cases there are judicial observations to the effect that exempting clauses, no matter how widely they are drawn, only avail a party when he is carrying out the contract in its essential respects. In my view, it is not right to say that the law prohibits and nullifies a clause exempting or limiting liability for a fundamental breach or breach of a fundamental term. Such a rule of law would involve a restriction on freedom of contract and in the older cases I can find no trace of it.

Lord Upjohn stated:

> The phrases 'fundamental breach' and 'breach of a fundamental term' have been used interchangeably in some of the cases; but in fact they are quite different. There is no magic in the words 'fundamental breach'; this expression is no more than a convenient shorthand expression for saying that a particular breach or breaches of contract by one party is or are such as to go to the root of the contract which entitles the other party to treat such breach or breaches as a repudiation of the whole contract. Whether such breach or breaches do constitute a fundamental breach depends on the construction of the contract and on all the facts and circumstances of the case.

That seemed a clear rejection of Denning's approach, but in *Harbutt's Plasticine Ltd v Wayne Tank and Pump Co Ltd* [1970] 1 QB 447, he took a rather optimistic interpretation of *Suisse Atlantique*, stating:

> I would just like to say what, in my opinion, is the result of the *Suisse Atlantique* case, It affirms the long line of cases in this court that when one party has been guilty of a fundamental breach of the contract, that is, a breach which goes to the very root of it, and the other side accepts it, so that the contract comes to an end – or if it comes to an end anyway by reason of the breach – then the guilty party cannot rely on an exception or limitation clause to escape from his liability for the breach.
>
> ... So, in the name of construction, we get back to the principle that, when a company inserts in printed conditions an exception clause purporting to exempt them from all and every breach, that is not readily to be construed or considered as exempting them from liability for a fundamental breach; for the good reason that it is only intended to avail them when they are carrying out the contract in substance; and not when they are breaking it in a manner which goes to the very root of the contract.

The House of Lords was not pleased. In *Photo Production Ltd v Securicor Transport Ltd* [1980] AC 827, Lord Wilberforce said of Denning's judgment in *Harbutt's* that 'it is clear to me that so far from following this House's decision in the *Suisse Atlantique* case it is directly opposed to it and that the whole purpose and tenor of the *Suisse Atlantique* case was to repudiate it'. The House went on to hold that there was no rule of law by which an exemption clause in a contract could be eliminated from a consideration of the parties' position when there was a breach of contract (whether fundamental or not) or by which an exemption clause could be deprived of effect regardless of the terms of the contract. The parties were free to agree to whatever exclusion or modification of their obligations they chose. Therefore, the question whether an exemption clause applied when there was a fundamental breach, breach of a fundamental term or any other breach, turned on the construction of the whole of the contract, including any exemption clauses. *Harbutt's* was overruled.

Fundamental breach aside, Denning's campaign to limit exemption clauses and to permit judges to read down onerous terms in contracts generally was not without long-term success. His best-known case in the field was probably *Thornton v Shoe Lane Parking* [1971] 2 QB 163. The plaintiff, memorably described by Denning as a 'freelance trumpeter of the highest quality', suffered an injury at the defendant's car park, and thereafter brought an action for damages. The defendant relied on the exclusions contained in the terms and conditions printed on the ticket which the plaintiff had received from a machine when he entered the car park. In Denning's words:

> They rely on the ticket which was issued to Mr. Thornton by the machine. They say that it was a contractual document and that it incorporated a condition which exempts them from liability to him. The ticket was headed 'Shoe Lane Parking.' Just below there was a 'box' in which was automatically recorded the time when the car went into the garage. There was a notice alongside: 'Please present this ticket to cashier to claim your car.' Just below the time, there was some small print in the left-hand corner which said: 'This ticket is issued subject to the conditions of issue as displayed on the premises.' That is all.
>
> Mr. Thornton says he looked at the ticket to see the time on it, and put it in his pocket. He could see there was printing on the ticket, but he did not read it. He only read the time. He did not read the words which said that the ticket was issued subject to the conditions as displayed on the premises.

> If Mr. Thornton had read those words on the ticket and had looked round the premises to see where the conditions were displayed, he would have had to have driven his car on into the garage and walked round. Then he would have found, on a pillar opposite the ticket machine, a set of printed conditions in a panel. He would also have found, in the paying office (to be visited where coming back for the car) two more panels containing the printed conditions.

Denning went on to rule in Thornton's favour, reiterating what was known as his 'red hand' defence:

> Mr. Machin admitted here that the company did not do what was reasonably sufficient to give Mr. Thornton notice of the exempting condition. That admission was properly made. I do not pause to inquire whether the exempting condition is void for unreasonableness. All I say is that it is so wide and so destructive of rights that the court should not hold any man bound by it unless it is drawn to his attention in the most explicit way. It is an instance of what I had in mind in *J Spurling Ltd v Bradshaw* [1956] 1 WLR 461, 466. In order to give sufficient notice, it would need to be printed in red ink with a red hand pointing to it – or something equally startling.
>
> But, although reasonable notice of it was not given, Mr. Machin said that this case came within the second question propounded by Mellish LJ, namely that Mr. Thornton 'knew or believed that the writing contained conditions.' There was no finding to that effect. The burden was on the company to prove it, and they did not do so. Certainly there was no evidence that Mr. Thornton knew of this exempting condition. He is not, therefore, bound by it.

Note the citation of his own *obiter dicta* from the earlier case of *J Spurling Ltd* – another example of Denning creating a precedent of his own which he later pulled up by its own bootstraps.

Ultimately, his battles with the House of Lords on exemption clauses were largely settled by Parliament. The Unfair Contract Terms Act 1977 gave statutory force to concepts Denning had long championed. A few years after his retirement, the case of *Interfoto Picture Library Ltd v Stiletto Visual Programmes Ltd* [1989] QB 433 held that the *Thornton v Shoe Lane* approach to unusual terms applied to contract terms in general, not just exclusion clauses. It further approved Denning's dicta in *J Spurling* – so that particular 'bootstraps' argument received independent affirmation.[15] A decade later, in 1999, the year of Denning's death, the Unfair Terms in Consumer Contracts

Left: Denning as a child, aged about 3 or 4.
Hampshire Archives 202M86/228a.

Below: The Denning shop, taken before the First World War.
Hampshire Archives TOP338/2/120.

Left: Denning in officer's uniform, 1918. Hampshire Archives 202M86/232.

Below: Denning (3rd from left) in an Officers' Ride, Aldershot, 1918, before his deployment to France. Both pictures are very typical of First World War imagery. Hampshire Archives 202M86/327.

Left: Denning as a barrister in the 1930s.
Hampshire Archives 202M86/236a.

Below: Denning's marriage to Mary Harvey, 28 December 1932. Denning's parents Charles and Clara are to his immediate right, and his best man, Arthur Grattan-Bellew is on his far right. Mary's parents are to her left.
Hampshire Archives 202M86/235.

Left: Denning and Robert on his appointment as a High Court Judge, March 1944.
Hampshire Archives 202M86/238.

Below: Denning's wedding to Joan Stuart, 27 December 1945. Note that as it was Joan's second wedding, the convention was for her not to wear white.
Hampshire Archives 202M86/239.

Left: Denning just after his appointment to the Court of Appeal, 1948.
Photoshot/TopFoto.

Left: Denning as Master of the Rolls, 1968.
Photoshot/TopFoto.

Above left: Christine Keeler at the height of her Profumo fame.
Hugo van Gelderen, National Archives of the Netherlands/Anefo.

Above right: Denning on his way to delivering his report into the Profumo Affair.
TopFoto.

Below: The crush at Her Majesty's Stationery Office as people try to buy copies of Denning's Profumo report.
TopFoto.

Above: Denning arriving at Winchester Cathedral for Law Sunday, c 1970.
Photo by EA Sollars, Hampshire Archives 202M86/373.

Below: Denning in Kenya on one of his frequent overseas visits. Official occasions and visits both home and abroad brought him much personal and professional satisfaction.
Hampshire Archives 202M86/542.

Above left: Denning and Joan on a bridge over the River Test on their beloved property, The Lawn, in Whitchurch 1982.
Photo by *Hampshire Chronicle*, Hampshire Archives 202M86/269.

Above right: Denning in the grounds of The Lawn in 1989. He and Joan added the wing forming the right of the house after they purchased the property.
Photoshot/TopFoto.

Below: The 'Great Tom' bell in All Hallows Church, Whitchurch, cast to commemorate Denning's 100th birthday.
Photo by Helen Sheridan 2022.

Regulations 1999 strengthened the consumer's hand along lines that Denning would doubtless have supported.

In tort, one of Denning's most important cases was *Spartan Steel and Alloys Ltd v Martin & Co Ltd* [1973] 1 QB 27, when he dismissed part of a claim for negligence on the ground that pure economic loss was unrecoverable. The definition of 'pure economic loss' and whether it should be recoverable in law formed one of the most fertile common law academic debates of the time.[16]

No book on Denning would be complete without mention of his opening paragraph in *Miller v Jackson* [1977] QB 966, when he heard the appeal of Lintz Cricket Club against the injunction obtained by their neighbours, Mr and Mrs Miller. When I wrote a book on cricket and law,[17] I spent some time looking at the case, primarily from the perspective of the cricketers. It feels rather self-indulgent quoting the opening paragraph yet again, but it is central to Denning's decision in the case as well as being one of his best-loved judgment beginnings:

> In summertime village cricket is the delight of everyone. Nearly every village has its own cricket field where the young men play and the old men watch. In the village of Lintz in County Durham they have their own ground, where they have played these last 70 years. They tend it well. The wicket area is well rolled and mown. The outfield is kept short. It has a good club house for the players and seats for the onlookers. The village team play there on Saturdays and Sundays. They belong to a league, competing with the neighbouring villages. On other evenings after work they practice while the light lasts. Yet now after these 70 years a judge of the High Court has ordered that they must not play there any more. He has issued an injunction to stop them. He has done it at the instance of a newcomer who is no lover of cricket. This newcomer has built, or has had built for him, a house on the edge of the cricket ground which four years ago was a field where cattle grazed. The animals did not mind the cricket. But now this adjoining field has been turned into a housing estate. The newcomer bought one of the houses on the edge of the cricket ground. No doubt the open space was a selling point. Now he complains that when a batsman hits a six the ball has been known to land in his garden or on or near his house. His wife has got so upset about it that they always go out at weekends. They do not go into the garden when cricket is being played. They say that this is intolerable. So they asked the judge to stop the cricket being played. And the judge, much against his will, has felt that he must order the cricket to

be stopped: with the consequence, I suppose, that the Lintz Cricket Club will disappear. The cricket ground will be turned to some other use. I expect for more houses or a factory. The young men will turn to other things instead of cricket. The whole village will be much the poorer. And all this because of a newcomer who has just bought a house there next to the cricket ground.

Once again, Denning's famous style was intended to direct the reader to what he considered to be the correct moral answer. He combined the imagery with hyperbole ('everyone' in the first sentence obviously did not include the Millers), and made clear that the case involved a thoroughly worthy activity being assailed by a local killjoy much to the public detriment.

The Millers' case was framed in negligence and in nuisance. They sought to curtail the cricket by way of an injunction. An impartial observer might have pointed out that they should not have moved next to a cricket ground if they did not want to risk balls coming into their back yard. Yet, a Victorian authority, *Sturges v Bridgman* (1879) 11 Ch D 852, held that 'coming to the nuisance' was no defence. Thus it did not assist the cricket club that the Millers had been the authors of their own misfortune. Denning was nonetheless able to reach the result he wanted because the remedy sought – an injunction – was equitable, giving him discretion as to whether to apply it. Equity, measured by Denning's foot if not that of the chancellor of old, was only ever going to side with the cricketers.[18]

Curiously, Denning's long-standing clerk,[19] Peter Post, told the *Daily Telegraph* that Denning was not a lover of cricket and that his only interests were 'rice pudding and the law'.[20] It is unclear who he thought might be fooled by that statement – no one could have written Denning's opening paragraph without being a true lover of cricket, and Post would have known Denning derived much pleasure from the village cricket in Whitchurch played on the ground next to The Lawn. At various times Denning served as president of both the Lincoln's Inn Cricket Club and the Whitchurch Cricket Club.[21]

Away from the isolated world of village cricket, Denning also occasionally dealt with the lives of the rich and famous. Three of the more successful pop stars of the 1970s had the stage names of Tom Jones, Engelbert Humperdinck and Gilbert O'Sullivan (real names: Thomas Woodward, Arnold Dorsey and Raymond O'Sullivan). A number of their respective songs were written by their manager Gordon Mills. Like many of their contemporaries, they sometimes found themselves in the news due to off-stage antics rather than their music. In early 1977, the three singers together with Mills went to court to try to protect their reputations against some lurid tabloid stories. The threat to their reputations had come about because they had fallen out with their former public relations manager, Christopher Hutchins. After they had ceased using Hutchins' services, he offered stories about their supposed hedonism to the *Mirror* newspaper group.

The plaintiffs applied for an injunction restraining publication on the ground of breach of confidence. They also sought damages for libel. The High Court granted the injunction and Hutchins appealed. The case was reported as *Woodward and others v Hutchins and others* [1977] 2 All ER 751. Denning explained the disputed material in language reminiscent of his Profumo report:

> The first article came out last Saturday, 16 April. It was headed: 'Why Mrs Tom Jones threw her jewellery from a car-window and Tom got high in a Jumbo jet'. It goes on to give a description of a very unsavoury incident in a jumbo jet. Mr Tom Jones is said to have become inebriated and to have behaved outrageously on the aircraft. Then on Monday, 18 April 1977, the *Daily Mirror* came out with the headline: 'Tom Jones and Marji [that is the name of a woman called Marjorie Wallace] The truth! Starts today: the most explosive show-business story of the decade. The Family by Chris Hutchins, the man on the inside. "I lived it. I'm telling it."' The article gives a long description of what is called 'The Marji Wallace Affair. Enter a Sexy Lady', with a photograph of them kissing one another. Now this morning, 19 April 1977, there is an article on the first page: 'Tom Jones's Superstud. More Startling Secrets of The Family by Chris Hutchins', together with an account of many more discreditable incidents in which members of the group were concerned.[22]

As one would expect, Denning was unimpressed by the application. He was particularly irritated by the hypocrisy of the plaintiffs wanting publicity but only on their own terms – in stark contrast to the lengths to which he went to shield politicians from their supposed antics in the Profumo Affair. The injunction was refused, Lawton and Bridge LJJ agreeing with him.

The immediate aftermath of the case was that Mills threatened to assault Hutchins,[23] whilst the *Daily Mirror* increased its circulation by 180,000, doubtless thanking the court proceedings for the additional publicity.

Many years later, the law on privacy changed, partly due to the Human Rights Act 1998, leading to memorable cases such as *Douglas v Hello! Ltd* [2008] 1 AC 1, as well as a period of time in which 'super-injunctions' were rather too liberally handed out by the court to protect the goings-on of public figures of perhaps dubious repute. Some of the judges in the latter cases might have remembered Denning's point about the hypocrisy of publicity seekers who avidly sought the attention of the press when it suited but tried to silence everyone when it did not.

As well as cases with memorable facts, Denning continued to make a substantial mark on the common law with decisions involving straightforward arm's-length commercial dealings. *Butler Machine Tool Co Ltd v Ex-Cell-O Corporation (England) Ltd* [1979] 1 All ER 965 showed him on form in a commercial dispute where there was no disparity in the parties, or any other factor which might have engaged his sense of morality or fairness.

On 23 May 1969, the plaintiff sellers offered to deliver a machine tool for the price of £75,535.[24] Delivery was to be in ten months' time and it was a condition that orders were accepted only on the terms set out in the quotation, which were to prevail over any terms in the buyers' order. The sellers' terms included a price variation clause whereby it was a condition of acceptance that goods would be charged at prices ruling at date of delivery. On 27 May the defendant buyers replied, giving an order with differences from the sellers' quotation and with their own terms and conditions which had no price variation clause. The order had a tear-off acknowledgement for signature and return which accepted the order 'on the terms and conditions thereon'. In June, the sellers acknowledged receipt of the order and returned the acknowledgement form duly completed with a covering letter stating that delivery was to be 'in accordance with our revised quotation of May 23 for delivery in ... March/April 1970'.

The machine was ready about September 1970, but the buyers could not accept delivery until November. The sellers invoked the price increase clause and claimed an extra £2,892.[25] The buyers refused to pay the extra and the sellers brought proceedings for breach of contract. The judge found for the sellers and awarded the sum claimed plus interest. The buyers appealed.

The Court of Appeal, comprising Denning along with Lawton and Bridge LJJ, unanimously allowed the appeal. The question, as Denning stated, came down to a 'battle of the forms', or as Lawton LJ put it, 'It is a battle more on classical 18th century lines when convention decided who had the right to open fire first rather than in accordance with the modern concept of attrition'.

Denning stated:

> If those documents are analysed in our traditional method, the result would seem to me to be this: the quotation of May 23, 1969, was an

offer by the sellers to the buyers containing the terms and conditions on the back. The order of May 27, 1969, purported to be an acceptance of that offer in that it was for the same machine at the same price, but it contained such additions as to cost of installation, date of delivery and so forth that it was in law a rejection of the offer and constituted a counter-offer. ... The letter of the sellers of June 5, 1969, was an acceptance of that counter-offer, as is shown by the acknowledgment which the sellers signed and returned to the buyers. The reference to the quotation of May 23 referred only to the price and identity of the machine. ...

In the present case the judge thought that the sellers in their original quotation got their blow in first: especially by the provision that 'these terms and conditions shall prevail over any terms and conditions in the buyer's order.' It was so emphatic that the price variation clause continued through all the subsequent dealings and that the buyers must be taken to have agreed to it. I can understand that point of view. But I think that the documents have to be considered as a whole. And, as a matter of construction, I think the acknowledgment of June 5, 1969, is the decisive document. It makes it clear that the contract was on the buyers' terms and not on the sellers' terms: and the buyers' terms did not include a price variation clause.

It is hard to see Denning's decision as other than a straightforward application of common sense, and the commercial community would have applauded it accordingly.

Common law legacy – 'ranging widely and freely'

Butler Machine Tool was a case that showed once more how Denning was quite capable of conventional judgments involving traditional reasoning and in line with the doctrine of precedent. It was the sort of case that led Professor PS (Patrick) Atiyah, one of the leading academic commercial lawyers of the twentieth century, to conclude that:

the absence of much statutory activity in contract and tort, combined with the intuitive appeal of the fundamental principles underlying these bodies of the law, enabled Lord Denning to range widely and freely over large bodies of law and theory. These have been fields of law which have lent themselves to development by broad statements of principle, which is the kind of thing Lord Denning always enjoyed doing, and often did supremely well.[26]

At the same time, commercial law requires certainty, and Denning's all-too-ready willingness to ignore it – even decisions of the House of Lords such as *Bell v Lever Bros*, *Rookes v Barnard* and *Suisse Atlantique* – was as damaging in the fields of contract and tort as any other area of law. The statutory codification of some of his decisions in exemption clauses and unfair terms show how far-sighted he could be in the sense of what the law *should* be, but that did not wholly offset the damage that his uncertainty caused to those who wanted to know what it *was* (allowing for the inevitable degree of uncertainty inherent in any area of law).

CHAPTER XV

Master of the Rolls – Family Law

We saw earlier in the book how family law showed Denning at his most contradictory: wanting to reform the law and achieve justice in the cases before him, but at the same time apt to show the morality of a bygone age. He continued in much the same vein as Master of the Rolls.

One of his more retrograde decisions was *Wachtel v Wachtel* [1973] Fam 72, in which he set out his thoughts about rights and responsibilities in marriage and divorce:

> When a marriage breaks up, there will thenceforward be two households instead of one. The husband will have to go out to work all day and must get some woman to look after the house – either a wife, if he remarries, or a housekeeper, if he does not. He will also have to provide maintenance for the children. The wife will not usually have so much expense. She may go out to work herself, but she will not usually employ a housekeeper. She will do most of the housework herself, perhaps with some help. Or she may remarry, in which case her new husband will provide for her. In any case, when there are two households, the greater expense will, in most cases, fall on the husband rather than the wife. As a start has to be made somewhere, it seems to us that in the past it was quite fair to start with one-third.

There was Denning out of touch with the public and inconsistent with himself. The idea that most men (then or now) could afford a housekeeper ('some woman') was as detached as when the Conservative grandee Nicholas

Ridley dismissed concerns about elderly people struggling to pay the poll tax by saying they could always sell a painting.[1] Modern readers would wonder why Denning thought men incapable of doing some or all of their housework but deemed women able to do so, and to do so for nothing, and getting only a third of the joint assets as a result (and at a time when the gender pay gap was more severe, although that was not something Denning would have considered).

One problem with Denning's view of the traditional family was that he seemed to believe that maintaining a household was not just 'women's work' but of no monetary value at all. In *Button v Button* [1968] 1 All ER 1064, the husband had purchased a property in his name only, but both spouses worked hard on the property, the wife assisting with painting, decorating and gardening. When they divorced and their dispute came before the Court of Appeal, Denning rejected the idea that the wife's efforts entitled her to any share of the property: 'A wife does not get a share in the house simply because she cleans the walls or works in the garden or helps her husband with the painting or decorating'. His reasoning was simply that 'Those are the sort of things which a wife does for the benefit of the family without altering the title to or interests in the property'. There was nothing unusual about Denning's attitude in that respect – in another case, the House of Lords agreed with him.[2]

Four years after *Button*, Denning was fractionally more generous in *Cooke v Head* [1972] 2 All ER 38, when he ruled that a woman was entitled to a share of the house in which she had done some work with a sledgehammer and wheelbarrow. 'Miss Cooke', he declaimed, 'did much more than most women would do'. In other words, she was entitled to some money because she had done a man's job. He reached a similar conclusion in *Eves v Eves* [1975] 1 WLR 1338.

When it came to children, Denning's paternalism of the sexist kind was equally apparent. In *Re L (Infants)* [1962] 3 All ER 1, he was concerned with the care of two young girls whose mother had committed adultery. He ordered that care and control of the girls should pass to the father, on the ground that there would be no chance of reconciliation of the marriage if they were given to the mother. That was effectively judicial blackmail – forcing the mother to return to the father if she wanted to see her children:

> It would be an exceeding bad example if it were thought that a mother could go off with another man and then claim as of right to say: 'Oh well, they are my two little girls and I am entitled to take them with

me. I can not only leave my home and break it up and leave their father, but I can take the children with me and the law will not say me nay.' It seems to me that a mother must realise that if she leaves and breaks up her home in this way she cannot as of right demand to take the children from the father.

Nowadays, rightly, the conduct of either parent would not be the decisive factor; the focus would be on the best interests of the children.

To be balanced against those regressive decisions were the instances of Denning the reformer. In *Hewer v Bryant* [1970] 1 QB 357, he took an important early step in developing the concept of the best interests of children and the concomitant reduction in parental control as children mature.[3] The plaintiff had been injured in a car accident when he was aged fifteen. He could not bring a claim himself as he was under twenty-one, the age of majority at the time. His father did not bring an action on his behalf, so when he turned twenty-one he sought to bring one himself. The defendant claimed the action was statute barred because, at the time the accident occurred, the plaintiff was in the custody of his father. Denning rejected that defence, since at the time of the accident the plaintiff was in fact living independently and working as an agricultural labourer. He was therefore in no sense within the 'custody' of his parents. In reaching that decision, Denning held that the concept of 'custody' within the Limitation Acts denoted a state of fact not law. He also firmly rejected the old Victorian notions of absolute parental authority over children, which had been reflected in the case of *In re Agar-Ellis* (1883) 24 Ch D 317:

> I would get rid of the rule in *In re Agar-Ellis*, 24 Ch D 317 and of the suggested exceptions to it. That case was decided in the year 1883. It reflects the attitude of a Victorian parent towards his children. He expected unquestioning obedience to his commands. If a son disobeyed, his father would cut him off with a shilling. If a daughter had an illegitimate child, he would turn her out of the house. His power only ceased when the child became 21. I decline to accept a view so much out of date. The common law can, and should, keep pace with the times. It should declare, in conformity with the recent Report of the Committee on the Age of Majority [Cmnd. 3342, 1967], that the legal right of a parent to the custody of a child ends at the 18th birthday: and even up till then, it is a dwindling right which the courts will hesitate to enforce against the wishes of the child, and the more so the older he is. It starts with a right of control and ends with little more than advice.

Many years later, in the famous case of *Gillick v West Norfolk and Wisbech Area Health Authority* [1986] AC 112, the majority of the House of Lords approved Denning's judgment in *Hewer*, Lord Fraser stating that he agreed with 'every word' of the above passage.[4]

In divorce cases, Denning continued to seek to protect the wife's interest in the matrimonial home, which in his time usually meant protecting housewives from third party creditors, given the disparity between men and women in the workplace.[5] Notably, in *Williams and Glyn's Bank v Boland* [1979] 2 WLR 550, he ruled that a lender who relied on the security of a matrimonial home should only have itself to blame for failing to consider that the wife might have an interest in the property which would be recognised by the courts. On that occasion, the House of Lords agreed with him.

Further, as much as Denning always despaired about divorce from a moral point of view, he continued to speak in praise of a modernised divorce law.[6] He took a purposive approach to concepts such as 'living with each other in the same household', recognising that couples might continue to do so after the marital breakdown even though they no longer had a 'relationship' as such.[7] Lawyers of his time thought his position on that point was 'liberal and most sensitive'.[8] Equally, Denning dissented in *Sydall v Castings Ltd* [1966] 3 All ER 770, a case in which he stated that an illegitimate child (using the parlance of the day) should have benefited from a group life assurance scheme of which her father had been a member. As to the majority's argument that only 'legitimate' children should be counted as legal 'descendants', Denning replied:

> I have no doubt that such an argument would have been acceptable in the nineteenth century. The judges in those days used to think that, if they allowed illegitimate children to take a benefit, they were encouraging immorality. They laid down narrow pedantic rules such as that stated by Lord Chelmsford in *Hill v Crook* [1874–80] All ER Rep 62 at p 66: 'No gift, however express, to unborn illegitimate persons is allowed by law ... '. In laying down such rules, they acted in accordance with the then contemporary morality. Even the Victorian fathers thought that they were doing right when they turned their erring daughters out of the house. They visited the sins of the fathers on the children – with a vengeance. I think that we should throw over those harsh rules of the past. They are not rules of law. They are only guides to the construction of documents. They are quite out of date. We no longer penalise the illegitimate child. We should replace those old rules by a more rational approach. If they are wide enough to include an illegitimate child, we should so interpret them.

In essence, Denning did not see why the child should suffer for the actions of her parents. He was true to that principle in his personal life too, on one occasion taking in a member of the family who had given birth out of wedlock.⁹

Another example of Denning being more progressive in respect of unmarried couples came in *Dyson Holdings v Fox* [1976] QB 503. The defendant was a woman aged seventy-four. She lived with her partner in a rented property from 1940, both paying rent from their joint incomes. He was a statutory tenant of the house and entitled to the protection of the Rent Acts. In 1961 he died. She remained in the property for another twelve years before the landlord discovered that, as she was unmarried, she could not rely on the statutory protection. Existing precedent would have allowed her to remain if she had had children,¹⁰ but she had not. Denning was unamused. That distinction, he declared, was 'ridiculous': 'So ridiculous that it should be rejected by this court'. As impatient as ever with the doctrine of precedent, he stated baldly:

> I prefer to say, as I have often said, that this court is not absolutely bound by a previous decision when it is seen that it can no longer be supported. At any rate, it is not so bound when, owing to the lapse of time, and the change in social conditions, the previous decision is not in accord with modern thinking.

A classic example of 'old Denning' and 'modernising Denning' appearing side by side in the same judgment was *Gurasz v Gurasz* [1969] 3 All ER 822, in which he spoke of a wife's right to remain in the family home (irrespective of formal legal title to the property), but 'so long as she behaves', a painfully condescending phrase.

Finally, it should be noted that Denning's family values would combine with his parochialism and his moralism to influence his decisions not just in divorce or child custody cases, but in other areas of law as well. In *Re Weston's Settlements* [1968] 3 All ER 338, a case concerning the variation of a trust (and resultant tax implications) where the settlor had moved to Jersey with his family, Denning said:

> [T]he court should not consider merely the financial benefit to the infants or unborn children, but also their educational and social benefit. There are many things in life more worth-while than money. One of these things is to be brought up in this our England, which is still 'the envy of less happier lands'. I do not believe it is for the benefit of children to be uprooted from England and transported to another

country simply to avoid tax. ... The only thing that Jersey can do for them is to give them an even greater fortune. Many a child has been ruined by being given too much. The avoidance of tax may be lawful, but it is not yet a virtue. The court of Chancery should not encourage or support – should not give its approval to it – if by so doing it would imperil the true welfare of the children, already born or yet to be born.

A man of contradiction

The verdict on Denning's family law work depends largely upon whether one thinks his modernising was outweighed by his occasionally outdated and (even by the standards of his age) offensive sentiments and rulings, and the wider implications of his judgments. His readiness to interfere with the terms of commercial bargains and with established precedent could not be ignored simply because he thought that family law should be determined on the basis of 'justice' rather than rigid black letter law. Commercial certainty benefits all the community since it forms part of the necessary conditions for economic activity. Couples who wish to arrange their own affairs (even if many do not give any thought to practicalities) would appreciate certainty or at least predictability in matrimonial property laws. And independent commercial entities should be entitled to deal with married people without having to give thought to the possibility that a judge in a subsequent divorce case might fail to enforce their contracts due to some notion of doing fairness between the spouses.[11]

Given that most judges, especially in the first half of his judicial career, were as conservative as Denning in traditional values (or at least would have claimed as much in public), one thing is certain: necessary reform of Britain's outdated children, divorce, matrimonial property and co-habitation laws would have taken much longer without Denning. If ever there was a field in which disregarding outdated precedent regardless of strict legal doctrine was justified, it was in the cases involving children where Denning brusquely dispensed with nineteenth-century authorities. Nor was Denning-led reform confined to his work as a judge – as noted earlier in the book, his sound work on the divorce law reform committee was well received. For all those efforts, he should receive due recognition, as much as one should also rightly point out the outdated views infecting some of his other family law judgments and the commercial uncertainty some of his decisions introduced.

CHAPTER XVI

Master of the Rolls – Employment Law

The field loosely described as 'employment law' might be separated into two distinct categories: (i) the contractual arrangements between individual workers and employers; and (ii) the relations between unions and employers. In this chapter we will consider each in turn. Beginning with individual workers, the two cases we consider under that heading follow logically on from Denning's time in family law, since his incorrigible sexism came to the fore in one, while he struck a blow for women in the workplace in the other.

Individual rights

Peake v Automotive Products Ltd [1977] IRLR 365 concerned the lawfulness of a factory's practice of allowing women to leave five minutes earlier than men each day. The practice was challenged by a male employee under the Sex Discrimination Act 1975, which precluded discrimination against either sex in the workplace.

The employee's case was unanswerable under the wording of the statute, according to the judge in the High Court, Phillips J. Yet Denning and the rest of the Court of Appeal (Goff and Shaw LJJ) allowed the employer's appeal. They reasoned that the factory's practice represented 'chivalry and administrative convenience'. That was a blatant invention of their own, since no such defence was mentioned in the Act.

Phillips J had said that instinctive feelings based on the 'women and children first' philosophy were 'likely to be the product of ingrained social attitudes, assumed to be permanent but rendered obsolete by changing values and current legislation'. Unfortunately, by overturning Phillips J's obviously correct decision, Denning and his colleagues had shown precisely those obsolete attitudes. Equally unfortunately, the House of Lords refused leave to appeal.

The reactionary nature of Denning's ruling rather contradicted Iris Freeman's statement that he had welcomed the 1975 Act and had 'interpreted this legislation liberally'.[1] To make the point, consider the following passage from his judgment:

> Although the Act applies equally to men as to women, I must say it would be very wrong to my mind if this statute were thought to obliterate the differences between men and women or to do away with the chivalry and courtesy which we expect mankind to give womankind. The natural differences of sex must be regarded even in the interpretation of an Act of Parliament. Applied to this case it seems to me that, when a working rule is made differentiating between men and women in the interests of safety, there is no discrimination contrary to section 1(1)(a) of the statute. Instances were put before us in the course of argument, such as a cruise liner which employs both men and women. Would it be wrong to have a regulation 'Women and children first'? Or in the case of a factory in case of fire? As soon as such instances are considered, the answer is clear. It is not discrimination for mankind to treat womankind with the courtesy and chivalry which we have been taught to believe is right conduct in our society.

Once more Denning's views were not unusual for a man of his age – Goff and Shaw LJJ agreed with him, for a start. What should be emphasised, however, is that the three judges were not wrong because of their outdated attitudes. They were wrong because they were directly contradicting the express words of the 1975 Act, as was subsequently confirmed by the drafter of the Act.[2]

Peake was fortunately overturned some years later by *Gill and another v El Vino Co Ltd* [1983] QB 425,[3] when a more progressive Court of Appeal swept aside the sexism of Denning and his colleagues by pointing out that the words of the 1975 Act were unambiguous in demanding equal treatment for men and women. Thus, in *El Vino*, it was not permissible for the eponymous wine bar to ban women journalists from being served at the bar (the work context being that the bar was somewhere journalists had to attend each day in order to horse-trade tips about cases over the road at the Royal Courts of Justice).

Justice had been belatedly done for women in the workplace, though there is no way of knowing how many other employers had been able to introduce discriminatory practices between *Peake* and *El Vino* by relying on the former.

In contrast with his backwardness in *Peake*, Denning had struck a blow for working women in the earlier case of *Nagle v Feilden* [1966] 2 QB 633. Ms Nagle had owned racehorses since the 1920s and bred them since the 1930s. She had been consistently refused a trainer's licence by the Jockey Club, solely on the ground that she was female. She brought proceedings challenging that refusal. She lost at first instance, but the Court of Appeal (Denning along with Danckwerts and Salmon LJJ) unanimously allowed the appeal. They did so not on the ground of unlawful discrimination, there being no sex discrimination legislation at the time, but on venerable common law authorities[4] that held that a person should not be prevented from carrying out employment without good cause.[5] Any person such as Nagle had a right to work, which the courts would enforce (though it should be noted that Denning also made some sexist remarks in his judgment about the suitability of women for certain occupations[6]).

The concept of a 'right to work' was something Denning spoke of in many other cases as well (and extra-judicially[7]), basing it upon concepts such as the right of freedom of association, natural justice, unreasonable restraint of trade or simple breach of contract. In a dissenting judgment during his first time in the Court of Appeal,[8] he had observed that horse racing authorities disqualifying a horse racing trainer constituted a much more serious step than an employer of any random business severing a contract of employment. His reasoning was that an employee of a normal business could look for work elsewhere. By contrast, a trainer excluded by the horse racing authorities could no longer ply his or her trade anywhere (at least within the jurisdiction of those authorities). Underlying Denning's thinking in that case was clearly the concept of a 'right to work'.

The same concept appeared in another Denning dissent from around the same time, *Abbott v Sullivan* [1952] 1 KB 189, where a corn porter (an archaic term for a dock worker who unloaded corn from ships) was removed from the register of the shop stewards' committee, and thus no longer able to work in his chosen trade. Denning said that the 'right of a man to work is just as important to him, if not more important, than his rights of property'. He warned against 'many powerful associations which exercise great powers over the rights of their members to work' and the danger posed by their monopoly power. That caution was one of the factors that informed Denning's approach to trade union disputes.[9]

Industrial relations

Industrial relations is the one area of law and society which has arguably moved on the most since Denning's time as MR. To understand the situation with which he was faced, it is necessary briefly to traverse some of the history of labour law in Britain.

Withholding of labour as a bargaining chip for better pay and conditions was a tactic employed from the early days of the Industrial Revolution, most famously with the Tolpuddle Martyrs. During the nineteenth century, however, unions were severely hampered by a series of court cases emasculating or virtually outlawing them altogether.[10] In response, they sought representation in and influence upon Parliament. They had a notable success when the Liberal government passed the Trade Union Act 1871, legalising unions, strikes and limited pickets. They then suffered a severe reverse at the start of the twentieth century, in the form of the notorious *Taff Vale Railway Company v Amalgamated Society of Railway Servants* [1901] AC 426.[11] In that case the House of Lords ruled that a union was liable for damages from a picket, which would have been another ruinous precedent for the union movement.[12] A new Liberal government responded with the Trade Disputes Act 1906, which prevented unions from being sued for damages incurred from a strike. The key wording was the exclusion of liability for unions for anything 'if done in contemplation or furtherance of a trade dispute'. That wording could still be found in UK legislation at the time of writing.[13]

Empowered by the protection of the 1906 Act, union actions soon became much more frequent and more militant. The tension between unions, employers and government was not abated even during the two World Wars.[14] Between the wars, the key industries of steel, coal, shipbuilding and textiles found demand falling off, causing employers to cut wages, lengthen working hours or lay off workers altogether – creating widespread poverty and discord thoroughly at odds with Lloyd George's promised 'Land fit for heroes'. The consequent resentment regularly manifested itself in industrial unrest: no fewer than eighty-five million working days were lost in 1921, for example. The nadir was arguably the General Strike of 1926.[15] As it happened, during that strike Denning served as a special constable, patrolling outside the power station in Lots Road, Chelsea, along with some other junior barristers who, like him, had served in the First World War. (Denning kept his truncheon as a memento and still had it in the 1980s.)

For the first half of the twentieth century, the 1906 Act ensured courts largely stayed out of the fray. In *DC Thomson & Co v Deakin and others* [1952]

2 All ER 361, for example, the Court of Appeal dismissed the appeal of an employer who had brought a claim against a trade union for procuring a breach of contract, holding that the action was barred by the Act. After the Second World War, however, three factors combined to draw the courts into conflicts between government, employers and unions. First, the nationalisation programme begun by the Attlee government meant that the state itself became a major employer and thus the direct opponent of a number of unions. Secondly, the steadily worsening economic situation led to Conservative administrations in the 1950s and 1960s trying to impose wage and price freezes, and otherwise to manage the economy directly in a way that previous governments had never contemplated. Thirdly, Parliament began to revise the legal position of trade unions, particularly the concept of a 'closed shop' which meant a worker could not be employed in a particular factory or production line unless he or she was a member of the relevant union.

Not long after Denning became MR, the House of Lords gave a landmark judgment in *Rookes v Barnard* [1964] AC 1129. It found that a union had been guilty of the tort of intimidation, by threatening to break contracts with their employer as a weapon to force the employer to end its contract with the plaintiff (an employee who had left the union in defiance of a 'closed shop' agreement). The Labour government responded quickly with the Trade Disputes Act 1965, which extended union immunity to threats to induce breaches of contract. Nevertheless, *Rookes* was taken as signifying a greater willingness by the judiciary to intervene in industrial disputes.[16]

It should be noted that Denning himself was not immediately or instinctively opposed to union action, as shown by two of his early cases as MR, *Stratford v Lindley* [1965] AC 269 and *Morgan v Fry* [1968] 2 QB 710, where he spoke in terms of the need to recognise the right to strike.[17]

By the end of the 1960s, industrial disputes formed a core party political issue at general elections. The Conservative government was elected in 1970 on a promise of curbing union power. Its chosen method was the Industrial Relations Act 1971, which introduced a register of trade unions, gave immunity to those upon it, and established a specialist National Industrial Relations Court (NIRC), which was empowered to grant injunctions as necessary to prevent injurious strikes and settle various forms of labour disputes.[18]

The unions mounted fierce opposition to the 1971 Act even before it came into force. The NIRC was headed by a High Court judge who was supposed to sit with two or more lay members, but the unions refused to nominate any members. Instead, they denounced the NIRC as a tool of the Conservative government.

In *Heatons Transport (St Helens) Ltd v TGWU* [1973] AC 15, Denning struck a blow in favour of the unions, when he held that 'a union, registered or unregistered, is not responsible for the conduct of its shop stewards when they call for industrial action, if in so doing those shop stewards are acting outside the scope of their authority'. He therefore set aside fines imposed upon a dock workers' union for the unauthorised action of their shop stewards in 'blacking' trucks carrying shipping containers. *The Times* called it a 'profoundly significant' defeat for the government. Although not sympathetic to the ruling itself, it nonetheless applauded the affirmation of judicial independence which the case represented[19] – a noteworthy accolade since, around the same time, Lord Hailsham as Lord Chancellor was trying to pressure Denning not to follow a different path from the NIRC.[20] Denning's decision was, however, overturned by the House of Lords ([1973] AC 15).

When the Secretary of State tried to impose a 'cooling off' order on the rail unions, compelling them to suspend a strike and hold a ballot for any further striking action, the unions responded by challenging the legality of the order. They lost in the NIRC and then again before Denning in the Court of Appeal (*Secretary of State for Employment v Associated Society of Locomotive Engineers and Fireman and others (No 2)* [1972] 2 All ER 949). Denning recorded gloomily in his judgment:

> On all the evidence, there is no possible doubt that the country is faced with an emergency such as Parliament envisaged when it passed the Industrial Relations Act 1971 and gave wide powers to the Secretary of State.

The continued industrial antagonism seemed to be leading towards another general strike. Denning was able to defuse the situation to some extent in *Churchman v Joint Shop Stewards Committee of the Workers of the Port of London* [1972] 3 All ER 603, when he overturned the conviction of three striking dock workers for contempt of court. They had been prosecuted because of their refusal to obey an order from the NIRC not to take industrial action.[21]

A general strike might have been averted, but the country's outlook in terms of labour relations was still bleak, with strikes continuing to cause power cuts and other shortages. By then the unions had effectively emasculated the 1971 Act, since they threatened a mass strike any time anyone was imprisoned under the Act. Without the sanction of imprisonment, there was no reason for anyone to obey the NIRC or otherwise comply with the legislation.

Things became still worse for the British economy following the 1973 'Oil Shock', whereby OPEC sought to exact punishment by way of an oil embargo on those who supported Israel in the Yom Kippur War of that year. Although Britain was less affected than some other nations, it still suffered from the inflation caused by rising world oil prices – worsened by the government pursuing a 'dash for growth' policy (at one stage in the 1970s inflation reached twenty-four per cent), causing panic-buying and stockpiling. As a sign of the desperate times, a series of coal and rail strikes led the government to tell the nation only to heat one room in their houses over the winter of 1973–74, and in early 1974 a three-day working week was imposed across industry to preserve power supplies.

The beleaguered Prime Minister, Edward Heath, felt compelled to call a general election later in 1974 under the slogan 'Who runs Britain?' By that he intended to ask whether it was the government or the unions. The answer he received was 'not the Conservatives', as they failed to retain their majority and Harold Wilson returned as Labour Prime Minister. Wilson's government swiftly repealed the 1971 Act and replaced it with the Trade Union and Labour Relations Act 1974, giving stronger immunity for unions than even the 1906 Act had done.[22] Denning remarked in a case of the time: 'Parliament has conferred more freedom from restraint on trade unions than has ever been known to the law before. All legal restraints have been lifted so that they can now do as they will'.[23]

Despite those concessions to the unions, Wilson had no more luck than Heath in stemming the tide of unrest and resigned in early 1976. His successor, Jim Callaghan, fared little better. The winter of 1978–79 became known as the 'winter of discontent', with waves of strikes leading to shortages and general misery, symbolised by uncollected refuse piling high in Leicester Square. Denning later recalled '[t]he dead were refused burial. Patients in hospital were denied treatment. Fire brigades would not put out fires. Trains did not run. The Government was under the thumb of the trade unions'.[24]

In 1979, the Conservatives returned to power under Margaret Thatcher. Against forthright opposition, they continued with the programme of closing coal mines (something which had begun under previous governments, though they had undertaken the programme of closures more slowly) and set out to end the power of unions. The result was some of the most severe peacetime civil strife in modern British history as police regularly clashed physically with striking workers.

The internecine tensions began to be reduced from the latter part of the 1980s onwards, some years after Denning had left office. Trade union power was eroded,[25] international competition brought down the price of consumer goods, and the Bank of England obtained an independent mandate to keep inflation under control. For the entirety of Denning's time as MR, however, industrial relations were a source of high-profile and politically incendiary litigation.

What is a trade dispute?

Due to the wording of the 1906 Act and its successors, the question of whether or not the courts would intervene in a union conflict with government or employers regularly turned on whether or not a particular action was a 'trade dispute'. So long as the actions could be classified as such, unions could not be sued. In a number of cases, Denning came down on one side and the House of Lords on the other. In *Star Sea Transport Corporation v Slater* [1979] 1 Lloyd's Rep 26, for example, a union 'blacked' a ship to try to force its owners to pay union wages, but Denning and the rest of the Court of Appeal held that that 'extraneous' action was not part of a trade dispute. Denning said that the statutory words had to be limited and 'the court can look at the motive for which the action was taken'. His decision was overruled in *NWL Ltd v Woods* [1979] 3 All ER 614.

In *Express Newspapers v McShane* [1980] AC 672, the House of Lords held that Denning had erred in granting an injunction restraining the defendants from instructing members of the National Union of Journalists employed on national newspapers to 'black' copy from the Press Association. Their Lordships ruled that the Court of Appeal had incorrectly concluded that the defendants were not likely to be held to have acted 'in furtherance' of the union's trade dispute with the provincial newspaper employers within the meaning of the 1974 Act.

Soon after, in *Duport Steels Ltd and others v Sirs and others* [1980] 1 WLR 142, Denning tried to evade that decision, only to be overturned once again by the House of Lords.[26] Lord Scarman assumed the role played by Viscount Simonds and Lord Hailsham in earlier cases by issuing a condemnation for what he thought was judicial indiscipline, though he admonished all three members of the Court of Appeal (including Lawton and Ackner LJJ), not simply Denning:[27]

> My basic criticism of all three judgments in the Court of Appeal is that in their desire to do justice the court failed to do justice according to law. When one is considering law in the hands of the judges, law means the body of rules and guidelines within which society requires

its judges to administer justice. Legal systems differ in the width of the discretionary power granted to judges: but in developed societies limits are invariably set, beyond which the judges may not go. Justice in such societies is not left to the unguided, even if experienced, sage sitting under the spreading oak tree.

Denning defiantly claimed to have received 'hundreds of letters in support' whereas, he believed, Lord Diplock in the House of Lords 'had only letters of abuse'. He concluded at the time: 'Surely at bottom the law must depend on the support of the majority of the people'.[28] The union leader Arthur Scargill, meanwhile, denounced Denning's decision as 'in line with Tory Party philosophy'.[29]

Pickets

Along with the question of when strikes were lawful, a regular issue before the courts concerned the conduct of workers during a strike, and in particular how far they could obstruct employers and the general public whilst picketing. Hence the case of *Hubbard v Pitt* [1975] 3 All ER 1, though not actually involving employment law, was keenly awaited by union, employer and government lawyers alike because it concerned the legality of picketing. Denning set out the background thus:

> Some years ago Islington was run down in the world. Its houses were in a dilapidated condition. They were tenanted by many poor families. In recent years Islington has become a desirable area. Property men have stepped in. They have bought up the houses and persuaded the tenants to leave. They have done them up and sold them at a profit. Now they are occupied by single families who are well-to-do. A group of social workers deplored this development. They have tried to stop it. They have conducted a campaign against it called the 'Islington Tenants Campaign'. They accuse the property men of 'harassing' the tenants, that is, of making the lives of the tenants so uncomfortable that they can stand it no longer and leave. Such 'harassment' is unlawful under s 30 of the Rent Act 1965. They also accuse the property men of 'winkling' out the tenants, that is, of offering the tenants sums of money to induce them to leave, or using other means of exerting pressure on them.

The social workers organised a campaign on behalf of tenants in the area. Their protest was focused particularly against the plaintiffs, a prominent firm of estate agents in the area. As part of their campaign a group including the future prime minister Tony Blair, then an unknown student, assembled outside the plaintiffs' offices for several weeks with placards and leaflets making various demands.

The plaintiffs brought an action seeking: (i) an injunction to restrain the campaigners from picketing the plaintiffs' premises and from conspiring to do so; and (ii) damages for nuisance and conspiracy.

The judge granted an injunction, holding that the use of the highway for picketing was not a lawful operation unless done in contemplation or furtherance of a trade dispute. Four of the defendants appealed.

Stamp and Orr LJJ dismissed the appeal, but Denning gave a rousing dissent:

> Finally, the real grievance of the plaintiffs is about the placards and leaflets. To restrain these by an interlocutory injunction would be contrary to the principle laid down by the court 85 years ago in *Bonnard v Perryman* and repeatedly applied ever since. That case spoke of the right of free speech. Here we have to consider the right to demonstrate and the right to protest on matters of public concern. These are rights which it is in the public interest that individuals should possess; and, indeed, that they should exercise without impediment so long as no wrongful act is done. It is often the only means by which grievances can be brought to the knowledge of those in authority – at any rate with such impact as to gain a remedy. Our history is full of warnings against suppression of these rights. Most notable was the demonstration at St Peter's Fields, Manchester, in 1819 in support of universal suffrage. The magistrates sought to stop it. Hundreds were killed and injured. Afterwards the Court of Common Council of London affirmed 'the undoubted right of Englishmen to assemble together for the purpose of deliberating upon public grievances'. Such is the right of assembly. So also is the right to meet together, to go in procession, to demonstrate and to protest on matters of public concern. As long as all is done peaceably and in good order without threats or incitement to violence or obstruction to traffic, it is not prohibited: see *Beatty v Gillbanks*. I stress the need for peace and good order. Only too often violence may break out: and then it should be firmly handled and severely punished. But, so long as good order is maintained, the right to demonstrate must be preserved.

The barrister and legal academic Louis Blom-Cooper QC wrote that Denning's dissent 'will go down in legal history as [his] finest hour in a remarkable judicial career'.[30] It was even praised by Denning's usual intellectual opponent Professor John Griffith, who called it 'the voice of freedom under law'.[31] Certainly, the case stood as evidence against the notion that Denning always sided against unions, though a cynic might wonder if Denning would have reached the same decision had it been framed as a case where a business was being choked by industrial action rather than one where an established way of English life was being elbowed aside by newcomers.

Trade disputes and moral campaigns

Disputes over labour relations during Denning's tenure as MR were not always concerned with pay and conditions, or picketing; they occasionally spilled over into moral and ethical disputes of the day. By the mid-1970s, the anti-Apartheid movement had been going for several years and was contesting contact with South Africa on various fronts.[32] In *BBC v Hearn* [1977] ICR 686, the BBC applied for an injunction to restrain the Association of Broadcasting Staff from stopping broadcast of the 1977 FA Cup Final. The Association objected to transmission unless the BBC agreed to not broadcast to South Africa. In the High Court, the judge ruled that the proposed action was in contemplation or furtherance of a trade dispute. On appeal, Denning thought otherwise, considering it 'coercive interference and nothing more'.

He applied similar reasoning in *Gouriet v Post Office* [1977] 1 All ER 696, another clash between those in favour of sanctions against South Africa and those who believed in free trade over government interference (to put it crudely). Into the latter camp fell John Gouriet, a businessman and former army officer. In 1975, he had founded the National Association For Freedom (later renamed the Freedom Association once its acronym 'NAFF' was thought risible). NAFF advanced a libertarian philosophy and was implacably opposed to the trade union movement.

In January 1977, the Union of Post Office Workers announced its intention to boycott all communications to and from South Africa, in protest against apartheid. Gouriet applied to the Attorney General, Sam Silkin, for his consent to act as plaintiff in a relator action for an injunction against the union, on the ground that the actions of the union's members in interfering with postal communications and the action of the union in soliciting or endeavouring to procure such interference would constitute criminal offences under the Post Office Act 1953. Silkin refused consent, so Gouriet applied in his own name.[33] Following some hurried interim hearings, the

Court of Appeal ruled in favour of Gouriet, restraining Post Office employees from acting on the union's instructions.

In his judgment, Denning wheeled out some constitutional big guns. After referring to James II, the trial of the Seven Bishops ((1688) 12 State Tr 183) and the Bill of Rights 1688, he concluded:

> If the Attorney General refuses to give his consent to the enforcement of the criminal law, then any citizen in the land can come to the courts and ask that the law be enforced. This is an essential safeguard; for were it not so, the Attorney General could, by his veto, saying 'I do not consent', make the criminal law of no effect. Confronted with a powerful subject whom he feared to offend, he could refuse his consent time and time again. Then that subject could disregard the law with impunity. It would indeed be above the law. This cannot be permitted. Now every subject in this land, no matter how powerful, I would use Thomas Fuller's words over 300 years ago: 'Be you never so high, the law is above you.'

The final line from Fuller, usually modernised as 'Be you ever so high, the law is above you', became one of the quotes most associated with Denning.[34] It was insufficient to sway the House of Lords, however, who overturned his decision ([1978] AC 435). Their Lordships held that, save for a limited statutory exception, only the Attorney General could sue on behalf of the public for the purpose of preventing public wrongs.

Industrial law legacy – 'The greatest threat to the rule of law'

The question of what amounted to a trade dispute went to the heart of party politics of the day. By being more restrictive in hearing cases than Denning, the House of Lords was trying to ensure that the judiciary did not become too obviously involved in politics. That was especially so in the run-up to the General Election of 1979. Yet Denning had no hesitation in publicly denouncing trade unions as 'the greatest threat to the rule of law'.[35]

He made that remark in April 1979 when accepting an honorary doctorate from the University of Western Ontario in Canada. Upon his return to England he was confronted by a mob of journalists who followed him to Whitchurch, while in the House of Commons he was heavily criticised by the Prime Minister, Jim Callaghan, and the leader of the House of Commons, Michael Foot. Denning always believed himself apolitical,[36] but still came out with statements asserting, for example, that the trade unions had become 'far too powerful for the nation's well-being' and that they 'take away the liberty of our individual', which for some cast him as the arch-enemy of the Labour Party.[37]

In February 1980, after the House of Lords had overturned him in the *McShane* case, he was interviewed on television and radio (in itself something likely to infuriate his fellow judges of the time, who would have considered themselves prohibited from appearing in the press[38]), though he again claimed to have received over a hundred letters in support from the public.

Denning's critics tended to dismiss his work in trade union cases as another example of his conservative side, inclined to defend the status quo and side with the state against more radical elements. The Scottish academic Kenneth Miller[39] concluded that Denning 'persistently attempted to place a particularly narrow construction' on legislation protecting unions, and had also 'create[d] a great deal of discretion in the courts for deciding when a particular type of action is unlawful'. Denning received similar criticisms from the unions themselves, one representative press letter complaining 'our legal system in general, and the Master of the Rolls in particular, are clearly out of touch with the realities of our society, if not positively anti-ordinary people and their organisations'.[40]

Denning's supporters countered[41] that his key concern throughout his career had been to uphold the rule of law and prevent abuses of power wherever he encountered them, including abuses committed by trade unions, and that he had played an important role in moderating the industrial conflicts of the early 1970s.[42] One might add that he never had a political agenda or economic theory of any sophistication. He despaired about the protection Parliament had given unions by means of the 'in contemplation of or furtherance of a trade dispute' exemption, and claimed his work had been to limit that protection, but that he had been frustrated by the House of Lords.[43]

The most comprehensive analysis of Denning's work in the field was by the academics Paul Davies and Mark Freedland.[44] They conceded that the cases did tend to show Denning as 'the leading protagonist of laissez-faire anti-collectivism towards trade unions', but added the sound qualification that Denning's judgments were too often viewed in isolation from those of his concurring colleagues. Also, when he received strictures from the House of Lords, it was often less because they held different values or beliefs, and more because of Denning's refusal to remain within the normal constraints of the judicial hierarchy.

Wherever one's sympathies lay, the various arms of government jointly or separately were unable during Denning's time as a judge to bring the industrial strife to an end. It seems improbable that the courts could ever have resolved the underlying industrial disputes whichever way they had decided the cases before Denning. The truth was that no terms and conditions would have equally satisfied all factions in most of Britain's industrial conflicts, and the chances of a consensus on pay and conditions being achieved by litigation over the meaning of 'trade dispute' were essentially non-existent. The disputes took place amidst other causes and effects of economic chaos which afflicted Britain for much of the time in which he served as MR. In those circumstances, blaming the courts for industrial strife was akin to blaming a surgeon for not fixing a patient with multiple injuries and ailments, rather than those who had injured or infected the patient in the first place.

It should also be said that Denning opposed social disruption nearly everywhere he found it.[45] Moreover, he was certainly not in favour of wholly unregulated labour relations which had prevailed for much of the nineteenth century and which had infamously enabled severe exploitation of workers. The better view is that he resented any group of any description either wielding what he considered to be excessive power, or irresponsibly using legitimate power, as he thought the unions had during his time as MR. The problem was that he all too frequently found unions to be the villains of the piece when a case could equally be made that intransigent employers and inept governments also made substantial contributions to causing the disputes.

CHAPTER XVII

Master of the Rolls – Public Law

Denning's work in public law was consistent with his work elsewhere. There were underlying tensions between his wish to uphold the rule of law and extend causes of action, on the one hand, and his iron-clad moral code and instinct to defend the state on the other. As ever, therefore, he supplied ammunition to both critics and supporters on a regular basis.

A good example of his moral code overriding legal principle was *Ward v Bradford Corporation* (1971) 70 LGR 27. The case concerned a female student who had been expelled from a teacher training college after she had been found to have had a male companion in her room at the hall of residence, in contravention of the rules of the college. She found alternative accommodation, and the principal of the college was prepared to let the matter rest, but the board of governors were not. Instead, they changed the rules of the college to allow themselves to overrule the principal's decision and refer the case to the disciplinary committee, and made the change retrospective. The committee went on to dismiss the trainee and, to no one's surprise, the governors approved that decision upon review.

The trainee applied by way of judicial review to quash the decision. Her counsel pointed out the blatant breaches of natural justice which the governors had committed by retrospectively re-engineering the rules, but Denning was unmoved. He thundered:

> [S]he had this man with her, night after night, in the hall of residence, where such a thing was absolutely forbidden. That is a fine example to set to others. And she a girl training to be a teacher. I expect the governors and the staff all thought that she was quite an unsuitable person for it.

That rather suggested Denning was not very forgiving about human nature. Despite his fondness for Shakespeare, he evidently did not share the attitude of Escalus in *Measure for Measure*:

> Well heaven forgive him, and forgive us all!
> Some rise by sin, and some by virtue fall.
> Some run from brakes of vice, and answer none;
> and some condemned for a fault alone.

Arguably, he was not actually being sexist as such, since he would have taken a similarly dim view of any male trainee teacher who had acted in the same way, although his language might have been less patronising or censorious. Instead, he was being the Victorian moralist, acting on the much more conservative attitudes of his generation. Ironically, in doing so he managed to offend the equally conservative landladies of the town in which the events had occurred. One wrote him an indignant missive stating that she would never have permitted any illicit late-night trysts on her watch and that it was a slur of Denning to infer any of her colleagues would have either.[1]

In the 1960s, two criminal gangs entered London folklore, gathering fame and notoriety in equal measure: the Kray twins north of the river and the Richardson clan in the south. One of the latter's best-known henchmen was 'Mad' Frankie Fraser, a wartime deserter, thief and black marketeer who once told a television interviewer that he had never forgiven Hitler for surrendering and thus curtailing good business opportunities. In later life Fraser became something of a minor celebrity, apparently charming those able to forgive the life of violence which had caused him to spend forty-two years in prison. Whilst he was still in jail he frequently committed acts of violence and disobedience. In 1969, he obtained damages in a settled claim against the Home Office following beatings by prison officers in the wake of a riot.[2] In 1975 he was charged with an offence against prison discipline. He instructed solicitors but was told that there was no right of representation. Fraser applied to challenge that decision to the High Court. His application was dismissed and he appealed.

Denning gave the appeal short shrift:[3]

> We all know that, when a man is brought up before his commanding officer for a breach of discipline, whether in the armed forces or in ships at sea, it never has been the practice to allow legal representation. It is of the first importance that the cases should be decided quickly. If legal representation were allowed, it would mean

considerable delay. So also with breaches of prison discipline. Those who hear the cases must, of course, act fairly. They must let the man know the charge and give him a proper opportunity of presenting his case. But that can be done and is done without the matter being held up for legal representation. I do not think we ought to alter the existing practice. We ought not to create a precedent such as to suggest that an individual is entitled to legal representation. There is no real arguable case in support of this application and I would reject it.

One can imagine Denning loathing the likes of Fraser gaining a public profile of any sort.

The case that showed Denning at his best in public law was probably *Congreve v Home Office* [1976] QB 629. He set out the facts thus:

> Every person who has a colour television set must get a licence for it. It is issued for 12 months, more or less. The fee up to 31 March 1975 was £12. As from 1 April 1975 it was increased to £18. This increase was announced beforehand by the Minister, but it did not become law until the very day itself, 1 April 1975. Up till that date the department could only charge £12 for a licence. On and after that date it was bound to charge £18. This gave many people, who already held a licence, a bright idea. Towards the end of March 1975 they took out new licences at the then existing fee of £12. These would overlap their old licences by a few days, but the new licences would last them for nearly the next 12 months. So they would save the extra £6 which they would have had to pay if they had waited after 1 April 1975. To my mind there was nothing unlawful whatever in their trying to save money in this way. But the Home Office were furious. They wrote letters to every one of the overlappers. They said, in effect: 'We are not going to let you get away with it in this way. You must pay up the extra £6 or we will revoke your new licence'.

Congreve lost at first instance and appealed to the Court of Appeal.

The appeal was unanimously allowed. Denning ruled that the Home Office demands 'were made contrary to the Bill of Rights. They were an attempt to levy money for the use of the Crown without the authority of Parliament; and that is quite enough to damn them'.

Before reaching that point, he left the Home Office in no doubt about what he thought of their behaviour:

> The conduct of the Minister, or the conduct of his department, has been found by the Parliamentary Commissioner to be maladministration. I go further. I say it was unlawful. His trump card was a snare and a delusion. He had no right whatever to refuse to issue an overlapping licence or, if issued, to revoke it.

The Times columnist Bernard Levin, ordinarily no friend of the legal profession, could not speak highly enough of Denning's judgment (as usual for the time, it had been delivered *ex tempore* in open court), praising Denning's oration as 'magnificent' and concluding that there was no judge alive, and few in history, as ready to stand up for the citizen against the executive.[4]

The case of *Smith v Inner London Education Authority* [1978] 1 All ER 411 showed that there were limits to how far Denning might bend existing authority even where he had a strong belief in the correct outcome. The plaintiff had obtained an interim injunction restraining the defendant local authority from ceasing to maintain a grammar school because of its policy of comprehensive education. Denning, with treasured memories of his childhood at Andover Grammar School, said regretfully:

> Search as I may, and it is not for want of trying, I cannot find any abuse or misuse of power by the education authority. So their proposals must take effect. It is sad to have to say so; after so much effort has been expended by so many in so good a cause. The fate of the grammar school is sealed ... Many will grieve 'when that which was great is passed away'.

As well as all the trade union disputes, Denning found himself deciding a different but equally politically combustible case when the legality of the Labour-controlled Greater London Council (GLC)'s 'fare's fair' policy came before him, in *Bromley London Borough Council v Greater London Council* [1982] 2 WLR 62. The policy involved a substantial public subsidy of London public transport. It had been set out in Labour's manifesto for the 1981 GLC elections. Due to the Conservative central government's objection, the subsidy did not apply to overland rail, only to buses and the London Underground. The Conservative Bromley Council opposed the subsidy *in toto*, claiming that because Bromley had no tube service, it would be subsidising those who did for nothing in return.

After Labour won the GLC election and set about implementing the policy, Bromley Council applied to challenge it by way of judicial review. The Court of Appeal, including Denning, held that the GLC had exceeded its powers under the Transport (London) Act 1969 and the policy was therefore *ultra vires*. Denning further held that the GLC had acted in breach of its fiduciary duty, in failing to hold the balance between the transport users and the ratepayers. He also remarked that the GLC had placed too much weight on its manifesto commitment, when it was unrealistic that all promises therein were or should have been treated as binding.

On appeal, the House of Lords upheld the Court of Appeal's decision. There was much public vitriol concerning the case – '[t]he hornets swarmed out and stung me with venom', Denning later recalled, '[t]hey accused me of being political. Whereas all I had done was to state what I believe is a principle of constitutional law'.[5] Protests on at least one occasion turned violent, though he escaped unharmed.[6] In Parliament, a Commons motion condemning the judgment was signed by almost 100 Labour MPs, calling Denning 'dangerously wrong to say that election policies and election mandates are to be disregarded'.[7] A correspondent to *The Guardian* and *The Times* suggested renaming London 'Denningrad' given what he saw as the overruling of a democratic mandate.[8]

Denning resented what his fame had brought him:[9]

> They treated me as if I alone was responsible and as if I had inflicted an injustice on the travellers by London buses and tubes. It was useless for me to say that it was not me but the House of Lords, and that they had decided it strictly on the interpretation of the statute. They blamed it all on me.

Not that it would have brought him much comfort, but he was wrong to say that he was the sole target of political anger. Ken Livingstone, the leader of the GLC, called Lord Scarman a 'two-faced old hypocrite',[10] while Professor John Griffith (correctly) concentrated almost wholly upon the decision of the House of Lords in his own critique of the case.[11]

Denning was quick to grasp the implications of Britain's accession to the European Economic Community. His words in *H P Bulmer Ltd and another v J Bollinger SA and others* [1974] 2 All ER 1226 about the impact on English law of the Treaty of Europe and the European Communities Act 1972 became among his most frequently quoted:

> The first and fundamental point is that the treaty concerns only those matters which have a European element, that is to say, matters which affect people or property in the nine countries of the Common Market besides ourselves. The treaty does not touch any of the matters which concern solely the mainland of England and the people in it. These are

> still governed by English law. They are not affected by the treaty. But when we come to matters with a European element, the treaty is like an incoming tide. It flows into the estuaries and up the rivers. It cannot be held back. Parliament has decreed that the treaty is henceforward to be part of our law. It is equal in force to any statute.

Despite his previously stated belief in the superiority of the common law, particularly in his early published speeches, Denning was rather taken by the more loose approach of European lawyers to statutory interpretation, feeling that the signing of the Treaty of Rome had given English courts the power to interpret statutes in the same purposive manner and otherwise in accordance with principles as he had always advocated himself.[12]

As ever, there were days when he veered in different directions. He was once told off by Lord Reid for encouraging forum shopping on the ground of England being a 'good place to shop in' because his judgment seemed reflective of a bygone era when 'inhabitants of this island felt an innate superiority over those unfortunate enough to belong to other races'.[13] Denning took the hint, for in *MacShannon v Rockware Glass Ltd* [1977] 2 All ER 449, a case with a Scottish legal element, he explicitly disowned his old parochialism:

> Previously we were disposed to think too much of our own legal system. It was so superior to all others that, if a plaintiff managed to secure a defendant while he was in this country, we nearly always let him continue with it. In so laying down the law, we were going back in mind to the days which Lord Reid described as 'the good old days', when inhabitants of this island felt an innate superiority over those unfortunate enough to belong to other races. Those good old days are gone. Our entry into the Common Market has brought many changes. One of them is recognition that the legal systems of other countries, have their merits too; and we must learn to live with them.

Although he had been seemingly relaxed about importing European law by means of the Treaty and the 1972 Act, Denning later became rather concerned about how far things were going:[14]

> The flowing tide of Community law is coming in fast. It has not stopped at the high-water mark. It has broken the dykes and the banks. It has submerged the surrounding land. So much so that we have to learn to become amphibious if we wish to keep our heads above water.

Writing many years later, the President of the Supreme Court (and former Master of the Rolls), Lord Neuberger, thought Denning had overreached himself with that refrain:[15]

> Despite the fact that Lord Denning was one of the three or four most influential common law judges of the 20th century, it seems to me that that notion, like his memorable image of the common law being submerged by an inexorable tide of European law, rests, I suggest, on a misunderstanding.

Lord Neuberger pointed out that the common law had always been the product of many different sources, such as Roman law and ecclesiastical law. Rather than dwelling upon the idea that English law was being drowned under the European tsunami, Lord Neuberger argued that 'Lord Denning would have been nearer the mark if he had focussed on how the common law might be invigorated by yet another external influence in a thousand years of external influences'.[16] One might add that in praising the more purposive approach to statutory interpretation that European judges followed, Denning had often in practice agreed with Lord Neuberger's suggestion, though Denning might not have admitted it.[17]

Human rights

For most of his time as a judge, Denning was not a supporter of the European Convention on Human Rights. Normally, his criticism was that the Convention was too broad and limited possible actions and arguments only to the imagination of counsel.[18] Conversely, at other times he worried that it might hem the judges in, by removing their discretion when protecting the liberty of the subject.[19]

Late in his career, reflecting on how often the House of Lords had reversed him in trade union cases, Denning wished that there had been power for the judges to override legislation. In a 1979 speech he said:[20]

> ... what has changed my mind is the tendency of some judges nowadays to forget that it is their duty to protect human rights. You will find that some of them go by the literal interpretation of Acts of Parliament and allow them to operate so as to make drastic inroads into our fundamental freedoms. It is time that there was some superior law by which the judges would be bound to give effect to human rights.

Denning said the reason for his *volte face* was that 'some of the judges are not strong enough ... In the old days the judges could and did protect our fundamental freedoms. The judges of today do not seem inclined to do it somehow'.

And yet, he was reluctant to see the expansion of the jurisdiction of the European Court of Human Rights or the European Court of Justice, despite their often more liberal interpretations being closer to his own approach than that of some of the more formalistic English judges.[21] In *What Next in the Law?*, he included a blunt chapter heading 'Do not incorporate the Convention.[22] He thought the situation which then obtained – where the English courts might be referred to the Convention, but not directly decide upon it – was 'just about right': 'Let the English courts have regard to the principles and exceptions set out in the Convention, but not so as to be bound by them'.[23] He himself had had regard to those principles on occasion, such as in *Associated Newspapers Group Ltd v Wade* [1979] 1 WLR 697, where he invoked the right of free speech under Article 10 of the Convention to allow a newspaper to express opinions without trade union influence.

Denning was not a fan of a British Bill of Rights performing an equivalent function either, arguing that the defence of human rights was not guaranteed by a constitutional document. Instead, he argued that what mattered above all was a country's political climate and traditions. Given the number of countries in history which have had impressive constitutional documents which their despotic rulers have ignored, Denning had a point. On the other hand, it might equally be said that accession to the European Convention on Human Rights has been a factor in improving the governance of states, particularly those from the former Soviet Bloc.

In England, Denning predictably thought that the independence of the judiciary was the key component of the political climate which had defended liberty.[24] He also placed importance on the jury system as a bulwark against state tyranny.[25] And he was always mindful of the balance between rights and responsibilities. In *The Due Process of Law*,[26] he wrote:

> Long have I associated myself with human rights ... But looking back over the cases of the intervening 30 years, I find that I have been concerned – not so much with freedom – as with keeping the balance between freedom and security. As I said in 1949 of personal freedom: 'It must be matched of course, with social security, by which I mean, the peace and good order of the community in which we live.'

In June 1980, however, Denning gave judgment in *Gaskin v Liverpool City Council* [1980] 1 WLR 1549, which showed how far his thinking could be from that of the European Court of Human Rights. It also showed how far he was falling behind popular sentiment. As a lifelong churchgoer dedicated to public service and the upholding of a moral code, he was occasionally partial to a nineteenth century conception of the 'deserving' and 'underserving poor'. As far as he was concerned the plaintiff, one Graham Gaskin, fell into the latter category. Denning's judgment began:

> Graham Gaskin, the prospective plaintiff, is now nearly 21. His mother died when he was six months old. He was taken into the care of the local authority – the Liverpool City Council – from the age of six months. He has a bad record. He was sent to various approved schools. He was sent to Borstal. He was afterwards arrested on a criminal charge, and was sent to prison for six months. Since he came out of prison, he has been unable to find work. He is living on social security. After this bad record, he blames it all on the Liverpool City Council. He has got legal aid and has consulted solicitors, Messrs. E. Rex Makin & Co. Through them, he seeks to bring an action against the Liverpool City Council. He says that they were guilty of negligence and breach of duty whilst he was in their care. He attributes all his misfortunes – and his present state of mind – to their want of care. He has not actually started an action. He has made an application under section 31 of the Administration of Justice Act 1970. That section enables the court, if it thinks proper, to order a potential defendant to disclose any documents which are relevant to the case which the applicant wants to bring. So here Graham Gaskin says: 'I cannot prove a case of want of care unless I can search through the records of the Liverpool City Council to see if I can find a case of negligence and breach of duty against them.'
>
> ... The history shows that this young man is a psychiatric case, mentally-disturbed, and quite useless to society. His solicitors now want to see all the reports so as to bolster up a claim for damages. Though what good damages would do him, I do not know.
>
> ... Let us face it. This application is just a preliminary to an action for damages. If it should be allowed, I wonder how many more actions might follow by children who have been in care up and down the country. How many of them would start blaming their misfortunes upon the local authority in whose care they had been? I regard this application as a 'fishing expedition.'
>
> ... The solicitors for the plaintiff ought not to be allowed to roam through the whole of this young man's file to see if in some way or another they can find a case to support his claim for damages for negligence. I think that the judge was right, and I would dismiss the appeal.

To most modern readers, Denning would probably come across as callous and unsympathetic. His words reflected his view that each person was responsible for his or her own fate.[27]

It took until almost the end of the decade, but Gaskin had success when he went to the European Court of Human Rights. By majority, the court held that persons in Gaskin's situation had a vital interest, protected by Article 8 of the Convention, in receiving the information necessary to know and to understand their childhood and early development. The failure to grant Gaskin access therefore constituted a failure to respect his private and family life as required by Article 8.[28]

Another litigant to lose in front of Denning but subsequently obtain vindication in Strasbourg was a young solicitor by the name of Harriet Harman, later a prominent Labour cabinet minister. In the early 1980s, Harman was working as a legal officer for the National Council of Civil Liberties (NCCL). She acted for Michael Williams, a long-term prisoner, in a claim for damages against the Home Office in respect of his detention in an experimental 'control unit' isolated from the rest of the prison system. In the course of the litigation, Harman obtained discovery of documents amounting to some 6,800 pages, many relating to the setting up of the control unit and the treatment of its inmates. At the request of the Home Office she gave an express undertaking that the documents obtained on discovery would 'not be used for any other purpose except for the case in hand'.

At the trial of the action, the material parts of some 800 documents were read out in open court by counsel for Williams. Some days after the trial, Harman allowed a journalist to have access to the 800 documents referred to in court. The journalist later wrote and published an article, based on the documents, which was highly critical of the Home Office and the setting up of the control unit. The Home Office applied for an order that Harman was in contempt of court.

At first instance, the judge held that Harman was guilty of a serious contempt. She appealed, contending: (i) that as part of the principle of justice being done in public a party to an action was released from any undertaking in regard to the other party's documents once they were quoted in open court: (ii) that the journalist could himself have obtained access to the contents of the documents if he had attended court when they were read out or if he obtained a transcript, and would not have been in contempt had he done so: and (iii) that to ensure the reports and comments on cases were accurate it was convenient for a litigant to be entitled to disclose to reporters and journalists all documents read out in open court.

The Court of Appeal including Denning unanimously dismissed the appeal. They held that the law requiring disclosure of documents on discovery in litigation was a restriction, in the interests of justice, on the right which the owner of any document had to keep the document and its contents private and confidential, and being limited to requiring disclosure in the public interest of doing justice it did not mean that further use could be made of documents so disclosed or that their contents could be disseminated elsewhere without the consent of the owner. Nor did it matter that the documents had been quoted in open court. In reaching its decision the court applied earlier dicta of Denning from *Riddick v Thames Board Mills Ltd* [1977] 3 All ER at 687.

It has to be said that the fact of documents being read in open court rather made a mockery of them supposedly remaining confidential. (Precisely the same point applied – and still applies – to the transcript of Stephen Ward's trial.) Templeman and Dunn LJJ held that if the accuracy of a document read out in court needed to be checked by a journalist or a reporter there was no reason why permission to see the document should not be sought from the party that owned the document rather than from the other side, but that hardly seems a complete answer. The only real point in the Home Office's favour was that Harman had made an undertaking not to use the documents for any other purpose. But that obligation was arguably rendered meaningless in the context of the documents read in open court (it would obviously still apply to the remainder).

The illiberal nature of the decision rather damaged Denning's reputation as a fighter against abuse of power.[29] Subsequently, the European Court of Human Rights vindicated Harman on free speech grounds (*Harman v United Kingdom*, App No 10038/82). In later speeches she cited the case as an example of the benefit of the Convention having force in English law.[30]

Public law legacy – bringing in the light

Those more dated or otherwise controversial Denning decisions should not detract from the important changes that he brought about in the field of administrative law, particularly during his first stint in the Court of Appeal. In *O'Reilly v Mackman* [1982] 3 WLR 604, towards the end of his career, Denning looked back on his legacy:[31]

> **The black-out**
> At one time there was a black-out of any development of administrative law. The curtains were drawn across to prevent the

light coming in. The remedy of certiorari was hedged about with all sorts of technical limitations. It did not give a remedy when inferior tribunals went wrong, but only when they went outside their jurisdiction altogether. The black-out started in 1841 with *Reg. v. Bolton* [1841] 1 QB 66 and became darkest in 1922, *Rex v Nat Bell Liquors Ltd* [1922] 2 AC 128. It was not relieved until 1952, *Rex v Northumberland Compensation Appeal Tribunal, Ex parte Shaw* [1952] 1 KB 338. Whilst the darkness still prevailed, we let in some light by means of a declaration. The most notable cases were *Barnard v National Dock Labour Board* [1953] 2 QB 18 and *Anisminic Ltd v Foreign Compensation Commission* [1969] 2 AC 147.[32] I sat in the preliminary hearings of both of them. We allowed each of those cases to go forward. It was because otherwise persons would be without a remedy for an injustice: see *Barnard v National Dock Labour Board* [1953] 2 QB 18, 43 and the *Anisminic* case [1969] 2 AC 147, 231B–C. In effect it was only by leave that the action for a declaration was allowed to proceed.

Judicial review
In 1977 the black-out was lifted. It was done by RSC, Ord. 53. The curtains were drawn back. The light was let in. Our administrative law became well-organised and comprehensive. It enabled the High Court to review the decisions of all inferior courts and tribunals and to quash them when they went wrong. And what is more, it enabled the High Court to award damages and grant declarations. No longer is it necessary to bring an ordinary action to obtain damages or declarations. It can all be done by judicial review. This new remedy (by judicial review) has made the old remedy (by action at law) superfluous.

Predictably, verdicts on Denning's work in public law were mixed. His intellectual *bête noire* Professor John Griffith was scathing, arguing that Denning's decisions constituted the opposite of a principled system of law.[33] Eric Young, a Scottish academic, returned an equally critical verdict:[34]

> In his readiness to intervene when intervention seems desirable, in his anxiety to achieve a just result, in his readiness to throw off the past, Lord Denning has, it is suggested, contributed to the creation of a body of law for which Tennyson's phrase 'a wilderness of single instances' is almost apt. In *The Discipline of Law* Lord Denning declares that the courts' actions to 'curb the abuse of power by the executive authorities' have been taken 'in support of the rule of law'. 'The rule of law' is, of course, a remarkably elastic concept, but it does imply

government conducted, in Wade's words, 'within a framework of recognised rules and principles'. Arbitrary exercises of judicial power do not provide an answer to arbitrary exercises of executive power. Whatever the inadequacies (and they would seem to be many) of present methods of political control over administrative bodies, the move, under the influence of Lord Denning, towards giving the judges an unfettered discretion to decide when and how to intervene in administrative action does not represent a satisfactory solution to the question of how to control the activities of public authorities.

One of Denning's successors as MR, Lord Woolf, wrote of the difficulty he had experienced as a barrister when Denning was rewriting the law reports and 'setting about government departments with an irrepressible enthusiasm'.[35]

In contrast, Sir Jeffrey Jowell was much more generous:[36]

Despite Lord Denning's own distrust of 'philosophy,'[37] his judgments in administrative law display a consistent approach to the role of the courts in a welfare state. At the outset of his judicial career this approach was not shared by his colleagues, who felt bound, by technical rules and constitutional role, to be deferential to the growth of strong state power.

Another academic, Christopher Forsyth, wrote in praise of Denning's considerable influence in the creation of modern English administrative law, but cautioned that it was not the work of Denning alone: other judges such as Lords Reid and Diplock, and scholars such as Sir William Wade and Professor De Smith, deserved equal recognition.[38]

It seems to me that Denning's key contribution to public law was a willingness to intervene in decisions of public authorities in order to enforce the rule of law. Unlike earlier judges, he did not simply absolve the courts from intervening when public authorities had failed to adhere to procedural fairness or some other aspect of natural justice. At the same time, he was concerned not to allow too wide a scope for challenging any and every decision of a public law nature, such as the claim by Frankie Fraser.

As with every other area of law, however, Denning's rulings tended to reflect his own values. His strong belief in natural justice might be sacrificed where someone had infringed his moral beliefs, as with *Ward* or *Gaskin*. His belief in open government did not extend to assisting Graham Gaskin or Harriet Harman's respective cases.[39] Perhaps most controversially, he would also abandon legal principle where national security was engaged, as we have already seen with regulation 18B in the Second World War and later with the Profumo report. He did so again with two infamous cases from the end of his time as MR, to which we will now turn.

CHAPTER XVIII

Master of the Rolls – Security of the Realm

Mark Hosenball was an American citizen working as a journalist in England in the mid-1970s. In 1976, he co-authored a story for *Time Out* magazine which mentioned the existence of Britain's Government Communications Headquarters (GCHQ). In November that year, he received a letter from the Home Office claiming that it had evidence that Hosenball was in possession of information harmful to the security of the United Kingdom. It proposed to deport him under the Immigration Act 1971. There was no right of appeal, but the decision to make such a deportation order was subject to a non-statutory advisory procedure whereby the proposed deportee could make representations and call witnesses before a panel of three advisers to the Secretary of State. The proposed deportee would also be given as much detail about the allegations against him or her as would not entail disclosure of sources of evidence.

Hosenball was given such a hearing, following which it was ordered that he be deported. He applied to challenge the decision by way of judicial review. The judge dismissed the application and Hosenball appealed. The case was reported as *R v Secretary of State for the Home Department, ex parte Hosenball* [1977] 3 All ER 452.

In the Court of Appeal, Denning acknowledged the procedural problems Hosenball had faced, but found that natural justice had to give way to security concerns:

> [T]his is no ordinary case. It is a case in which national security is involved, and our history shows that, when the state itself is endangered, our cherished freedoms may have to take second place.

Even natural justice itself may suffer a set-back. Time after time Parliament has so enacted and the courts have loyally followed. In the First World War, in *R v Halliday* ([1917] AC 260 at 270), Lord Finlay LC said: 'The danger of espionage and of damage by secret agents ... had to be guarded against.' In the Second World War in *Liversidge v Anderson* ([1942] AC 206 at 219) Viscount Maugham said:

> '... there may be certain persons against whom no offence is proved nor any charge formulated, but as regards whom it may be expedient to authorise the Secretary of State to make an order for detention.'

That was said in time of war. But times of peace hold their dangers too. Spies, subverters and saboteurs may be mingling amongst us, putting on a most innocent exterior. They may be endangering the lives of the men in our secret service, as Mr Hosenball is said to do. If they are British subjects, we must deal with them here. If they are foreigners, they can be deported. The rules of natural justice have to be modified in regard to foreigners here who prove themselves unwelcome and ought to be deported.

Denning went on to dismiss the appeal, and finished with the following:

> There is a conflict here between the interests of national security on the one hand and the freedom of the individual on the other. The balance between these two is not for a court of law. It is for the Home Secretary. He is the person entrusted by Parliament with the task. In some parts of the world national security has on occasions been used as an excuse for all sorts of infringements of individual liberty. But not in England. ... In this case we are assured that the Home Secretary himself gave it his personal consideration, and I have no reason whatever to doubt the care with which he considered the whole matter. He is answerable to Parliament as to the way in which he did it and not to the courts here.

In that passage Denning was being almost Panglossian in his belief in the unimpeachable probity of the security services. Before condemning him too harshly, however, it should be noted that he was joined by the other two judges hearing the appeal, Geoffrey Lane and Cumming-Bruce LJJ, and the House of Lords refused leave to appeal. Moreover, as Denning noted, the European Commission on Human Rights[1] did not object to the principle of being able to remove aliens (excusing the dated language) on security grounds.

Although Hosenball himself hardly seemed to pose a national threat, and the fact of the reading in open court made the decision essentially pointless, one might agree with Denning in the abstract that, in extreme circumstances, security concerns might require the suspension of some aspects of natural justice. On the other hand, Denning's blind faith in police incorruptibility was not so easily defended, as demonstrated by the case which came to represent the nadir of his judicial career, *McIlkenny v Chief Constable of West Midlands Police Force and another* [1980] QB 283.

The case concerned six individuals convicted of a terrorist attack in Birmingham in November 1974. Each confessed his role in the atrocity to police, but later, at trial, all contended that their confessions had been extracted by torture and should therefore be ruled inadmissible. There was no real evidence against them other than the confessions, so each would have been acquitted if that course had been followed. The judge rejected their defence and ruled the convictions admissible. The jury reached guilty verdicts in all six cases.

The 'Birmingham Six', as they became known, continued to maintain after their convictions that their confessions had resulted from torture at the hands of the police. They brought a civil action against the responsible chief constable, seeking damages for assault by the police. They relied upon fresh evidence in the form of: (i) statements by the prison officers; and (ii) expert evidence from a forensic specialist who stated that at least some of their injuries had been inflicted before they had left police custody.

The chief constable applied to strike out the action on the ground that it raised an issue identical to that which had been finally determined at the earlier criminal trial. The judge held that the new evidence was such that it was reasonably conceivable that another tribunal acting independently might accept at least part of the plaintiffs' case. The chief constable appealed. The case came before Denning, Reginald Goff LJ[2] and Sir George Baker.

Denning began his judgment thus:

> Thursday, 21 November 1974
> Eight minutes past eight in the evening. The telephone rang in a newspaper office in Birmingham. A young man picked it up. It was from a call-box. 'Is that *"The Birmingham Post"*?' asked a voice with an Irish accent. 'Yes'. The voice went on: 'There is a bomb planted at the Rotunda. There is another in New Street near the Tax Office.' That was all. At once the young man dialled the police. He repeated the message to them. The police were quick as lightning. Their cars rushed to those addresses – screeching their way. But they were too

late. The bombs went off before the police could get there. Each in a crowded public house. One in The Mulberry Bush. The other in The Tavern in the Town. Both were devastated. Dead and dying lay everywhere. Twenty-one people were killed and 161 injured.

Outside the police were going into action swiftly. To catch the terrorists. They sent out squads to every exit from Birmingham, by road, rail or air. They went to the railway station at New Street. It was quite close to the bombed premises. They found that a train had left New Street for Belfast. It had left at 7.55 pm, about 20 minutes before the bombs went off. It had many Irish passengers on it. It was due at Heysham, 200 miles away, a little before 11 o'clock at night. The passengers would then take the boat to Belfast. The police then did a fine piece of detective work. As a result they had reason to suspect five of the passengers on that train. They telephoned to the Lancashire police. They met the train. Four of the men came through the barrier at Heysham. They were arrested by the Lancashire police. The fifth was arrested on the boat. They were taken the four miles to the police station at Morecambe. The men told the Lancashire police that they were on their way to attend the funeral in Belfast of James McDade. He was a prominent member of the Irish Republican Army. He had made a mistake while setting a bomb in Coventry. It had exploded too soon and killed him. He was to be buried in Belfast.

He went on to hold that the plaintiffs were estopped from bringing the action (with which the other judges agreed). He stated:

> Just consider the course of events if this action were to proceed to trial. It will not be tried for 18 months or two years. It will take weeks and weeks. The evidence about violence and threats will be given all over again, but this time six or seven years after the event, instead of one year. If the six men fail, it will mean that much time and money and worry will have been expended by many people for no good purpose. If the six men win, it will mean that the police were guilty of perjury, that they were guilty of violence and threats, that the confessions were involuntary and were improperly admitted in evidence, and that the convictions were erroneous. That would mean that the Home Secretary would have either to recommend they be pardoned or he would have to remit the case to the Court of Appeal under s 17 of the Criminal Appeal Act 1968. This is such an appalling vista that every sensible person in the land would say: 'It cannot be right that these actions should go any further.' They should be struck out either on the ground that the six men are estopped from challenging the decision of Bridge J or alternatively that it is an abuse

of the process of the court. Whichever it is, the actions should be stopped.

He rounded off the judgment with some self-congratulatory patriotism:

> This case shows what a civilised country we are. Here are six men who have been proved guilty of the most wicked murder of 21 innocent people. They have no money. Yet the state lavished large sums on their defence. They were convicted of murder and sentenced to imprisonment for life. In their evidence they were guilty of gross perjury. Yet the state continued to lavish large sums on them – in their actions against the police. It is high time that it stopped.

In the event, during the 1980s, further and compelling evidence was obtained concerning police fabrication and subsequent suppression of evidence regarding the Six. Another appeal was brought in 1988 but dismissed by the Court of Appeal, presided over by the Lord Chief Justice, Lord Lane (who was supported from the side-lines by the then-retired Denning). Finally, in 1991 a further appeal was brought, which the Crown did not resist, meaning the Six were exonerated and set free. Denning's appalling vista had come true. In 2001, the Six were awarded compensation ranging from £840,000 to £1.2 million.[3]

In some respects, the fact that Denning was personally singled out for criticism over *McIlkenny* was unfair. He was not responsible for the actions of the police and Home Office in generating the false confessions and covering their trail, a course of events that was shocking even to those more cynical about the police and the state. Further, as had happened in the 'fare's fair' *Bromley London Borough Council v GLC* case, Denning was only one of five judges[4] who had all agreed on the same outcome. Given Denning's fame by that stage of his life, it was perhaps inevitable that any judgment from a court of which he was part would be labelled with his name and the other judges ignored. More importantly, though, Denning himself attracted much of his future criticism by the inappropriateness of his tone. It would have been possible to write an opening in his usual form without overdoing it. But, perhaps as a sign of an ageing belief in his infallibility, the old storyteller had adopted a hyperbolic style – 'quick as lightning', 'screeching their way' – which read like a novelisation of contemporary television crime dramas such as *The Sweeney* or *The Professionals*, not a judgment of the Court of Appeal. Denning quoted his opening passage with some satisfaction in *The Family Story*[5] as an example of his writing style. Had he written a wholly conventional judgment, as Goff LJ and Sir Gerald Baker had, the controversy would have been lessened, and he would have been not much more than a footnote in the story as another member of the British state who turned a blind eye to injustice. Instead, nearly forty years after the case, lawyers still spoke of 'the Denning culture' to mean unthinking acceptance of police probity in the face of contrary evidence.[6]

Plainly, Denning the old soldier would have loathed any entity which waged war on the British state and killed innocent civilians. We should add, however, that he was at a loss to understand hatred in Ireland between Catholics and Protestants. In *The Family Story*, he mentioned Reg's efforts to bring the two sides together while holding a senior post with the army in Northern Ireland, and quoted with approval Reg's thoughts:[7]

> I could not then understand, nor do I now understand why Churches who devoutly worship God should be so bitterly opposed – on what is, it seems to me, only a difference of ritual. Surely it is not ritual which appeals to God, but a heartfelt worship of His Being.

Security legacy – a different age

In the twenty-first century, several claims for compensation were made against the British government arising out of alleged mistreatment of foreign nationals at the hands of British soldiers in combat zones. In 2021, the human rights lawyer Conor Gearty surveyed a number of cases and noted, making a direct reference back to Denning:

> [t]he days were long gone when it was enough to declare litigation by convicted terrorists claiming to have been ill-treated by the authorities to be required to fail because of the 'appalling vista' such a case would open up were it successful.[8]

Gearty concluded that the landscape had changed substantially from the 1970s, especially in the context of British operations in Afghanistan and Iraq. The judiciary was now prepared to go much further, both as judges and heading inquiries, to entertain actions against the British state for abuses in the course of counter-terrorism work.

Yet the story was not one of undiluted success. One of the most active and, for a time, acclaimed lawyers in the field was struck off when it was found that he had been concocting or procuring false evidence of abuse by British soldiers.[9] The appalling vista had been reversed. Or perhaps, as ever with human nature, liars and the otherwise unscrupulous were everywhere to be found.

Overall, however, the picture of the legal system in 2021 was closer to one of justice – defined in a way with which Denning would normally have agreed – than in the 1970s, since it was at least recognised that there was a possibility of gross injustice being perpetrated by those in authority and that legal remedies ought to be available (although the application of the European Convention on Human Rights in a war zone and the liability in general of serving soldiers were disputed, there was no issue about the application of the law to the police in Britain). Denning's refusal to entertain such a possibility was not the most positive aspect of his legacy.

CHAPTER XIX

Master of the Rolls – A Belated Author

At the end of the 1970s, with Joan unable to travel overseas, coupled with his own reduced mobility, Denning had to find other ways of filling his spare time. Unsurprisingly, given the fame his judgments had achieved by then due to his unique writing style, he turned his hand to writing books. He chose not to attempt a practitioner text or any other form of monograph on a discrete area of law. Instead, he began with two books giving more general discussions of cases he had been involved in, aimed more at the law student rather than the specialist practitioner or academic. The books were much more readable accordingly, and probably of more enduring interest too, since Denning was concerned with justice and principle rather than legal formalism. He then wrote an autobiography, *The Family Story*, which was arguably his best work.[1] Unfortunately, he also wrote another general interest law book which had a much less happy reception, which we will come to in the next chapter.

The Discipline of Law

Denning's first book, *The Discipline of Law*, was published in early 1979 to coincide with his eightieth birthday.[2] The theme was law reform. It was presented in the form of a discussion of seven separate areas of law, with a liberal set of quotations in each from his own judgments. Characteristically, he phrased his aims for the work modestly, stating only that he hoped his proposals would be discussed in academia and might one day find favour elsewhere. He concluded on an even more modest (and not quite accurate) note, sighing that many of his judicial efforts had failed. He added that if he had had time, he would have mentioned three more of his innovations which the House of Lords had overturned, and a fourth which had survived for the while ('not up to now condemned by higher authority',[3] as he put it drolly). Perhaps his regrets were getting the better of him, since he omitted to mention that in two supposed failures his views were later restored by way of statute.[4]

Given his neo-Victorian or Edwardian morality, it was ironic that Denning should write in the introduction:[5]

> My theme is that the principles of law laid down by the judges in the nineteenth century – however suited to social conditions of that time – are not suited to the social necessities and social opinion of the twentieth century. They should be moulded and shaped to the needs and opinion of today.

The answer, as ever, was that he did in other instances try to advance the law, and at all times acted in accordance with what he thought was the 'right' morality, as given to him each week from the pulpit.

The book was generally well received (Professor John Griffith being a predictable exception[6]) and sold widely – going through several print runs – reflecting the accessible Denning style and the fame he had enjoyed ever since the Profumo Affair.

The Due Process of Law

The success of *The Discipline of Law* led Denning to follow up with *The Due Process of Law*, written in 1979 and published the following year. It was intended as a companion volume, looking at the practical working of the law rather than the more academic cases of the earlier book.

One section of interest contained a slightly more modern view of the place of women:[7]

> No matter how you may dispute and argue, you cannot alter the fact that women are different from men. The principal task in life of women is to bear and rear children: and it is a task which occupies the best years of their lives. The man's part in bringing up the children is no doubt as important as hers, but of necessity he cannot devote so much time to it. He is physically the stronger and she the weaker. He is temperamentally the more aggressive and she the more submissive.

> It is he who takes the initiative and she who responds. These diversities of function and temperament lead to differences of outlook which cannot be ignored. But they are, none of them, any reason for putting women under the subjection of men. A woman feels as keenly, thinks as clearly, as a man. She in her sphere does work as useful as a man does in his. She has as much right to her freedom – to develop her personality to the full – as a man. When she marries, she does not become the husband's servant but his equal partner. If his work is more important in the life of the community, hers is more important in the life of the family. Neither can do without the other. Neither is above the other or under the other. They are equals.
> Few will dispute the justice of women's claim to equality; but it is only in recent years that it has been realised. This is one of the most significant revolutions of our time. It has tremendous potentialities for our civilisation.
>
> ...
>
> The women of today are the companions of men. During the war they shared in its toils. They made munitions, they drove army cars, they decoded cypher messages, they plotted the course of aircraft. They were dropped for secret service behind the enemy lines. In peacetime they work alongside men in all tasks for which they are physically suitable. They work in the factories. They patrol the streets as police. They share in the cares of government. They serve in Parliament. A woman is now our Prime Minister. They become Ministers of the Crown and Mayors of cities. They are educated in the same way as men. The girls go to boys' schools: and the boys to girls' schools. Most of the colleges at Oxford and Cambridge have both men and women. They become doctors, lawyers, writers, directors of companies, and so forth. They become Queen's Counsel and Judges.

Compared with some of his earlier utterances, that passage read almost like a Damascene conversion.[8] Admittedly, the first paragraph still contained dated sentiment about temperament, initiative and diversities of function. Denning also seemed oblivious to the existence of mixed-sex schools. In stating that men's work was more important to the community but women's more important to the home, he was clinging on to his old notions about what really constituted 'women's work', or perhaps women's non-delegable duties. And it was not clear how he thought women would be able to achieve parity in the professions if they had unequal amounts of work at home. Perhaps he was happy with smaller numbers of unmarried or childless women enjoying careers while others performed their domestic duties. Yet he was still proffering a view of equality between the sexes which had come a long way from his earlier days.

As with *The Discipline of Law*, the book was a best-seller, clearly having an appeal much beyond the average legal memoir or monograph.

Desert Island Discs

In May 1980, as a reflection of his public profile, Denning was invited on to the long-running BBC radio programme *Desert Island Discs*.[9] The format involved the guest imagining being consigned to a desert island. They had to choose eight pieces of music, a book (not the complete works of Shakespeare or the Bible or equivalent) and a luxury item to take with them. Amidst the discussion about their musical selections, they would be asked a few biographical questions.

Over the years, the programme hosted a wide range of guests, reflected by those either side of Denning's appearance. Before him was the Hollywood actress Natalie Wood, who would die in tragic and controversial circumstances the following year, and after him was Earl Hines, the American jazz pianist. The choice of Denning was a clear indication of his status with the general public, well beyond any other judge of his time.

At the time of Denning's appearance, the programme was still being presented by its creator, Roy Plomley. Plomley was a genial interviewer, stopping short of being fawning but nonetheless imbued with the deference of his era and not one to pursue controversial subjects for their own sake. There were accordingly no surprises or traps lurking in his questions.

There were also no surprises in Denning's musical selections: his favourite track was *Fantasia on Greensleeves* by Ralph Vaughan Williams ('the most English tune'), his book was *The Golden Treasury* by Francis Palgrave, and his luxury item was the very English choice of Indian tea. No doubt only coincidentally, one of the popular songs he chose was a recording from *The King and I* by Valerie Hobson – the wife of John Profumo.

Denning answered all Plomley's inquiries in his genial Hampshire burr and affable, self-deprecating demeanour. 'I'm not at all musical. I like the lighter stuff' he conceded at the outset, and said he was the only one of his brothers not included in the school choir.

Plomley gently suggested Denning had been demoted from the House of Lords. He received a courteous but firm rebuke: 'Mark you, I'm in charge of the show', Denning told him, pointing out that the Court of Appeal heard many more cases than the House of Lords, most of which were not appealed.

Of those that were he added 'They may reverse us but that doesn't bother us ... it doesn't mean we're wrong'. Ever the spokesperson for passengers aboard the Clapham Omnibus, he added that he was gratified to have received many letters from the public in support of a decision on trade unions which the Lords had overturned.

The programme was far from the only media appearance Denning made around that time, notwithstanding he was in his ninth decade and still with a full-time job. In November 1980 he delivered the Dimbleby Lecture at the Royal Society of Arts, televised by the BBC. In response to questions, he dismissed the idea that the government might ever be able to pack the courts with lackeys for judges, and gave another of his favourite quotes 'Someone must be trusted. Let it be the judges'.[10]

The Family Story

In 1981, Denning's *The Family Story* was published. Of all the books he wrote, it remains the one of most lasting interest. I – along with all other biographers of Denning – have drawn upon it extensively. It remains the first port of call for anyone wanting more detail about his personal life and that of his family. His writing on his childhood and the First World War fitted very much into the respective canons – the former an affectionate yet honest portrayal of the hardships of life in Edwardian England, the latter an unsparing account of the latter days of the Western Front. There was much detail on the formidable achievements of Reg and Norman, and moving portraits of Jack, Gordon and Mary, whose early deaths caused so much sadness in his life.

The bulk of the book was predictably taken up with Denning's legal career. Of his general approach to the law he affirmed the pre-eminence of his Christian faith and his desire to do 'justice' as defined by that faith.

Once again, the book was a best-seller, and received praise in the general as well as legal press.[11]

Justice, Lord Denning and the Constitution

Another book published in 1981 was Robson and Watchman's collection of papers on Denning, entitled *Justice, Lord Denning and the Constitution*.[12] The contributors were all Scottish academics. The book was anything but an encomium. All the authors set themselves against Denning's judicial approach, claiming, in essence, that he was usurping the judicial role by his disregard of precedent and his loose approach to statutory interpretation.

Paul Watchman's introductory essay was entitled 'Palm Tree Justice and the Lord Chancellor's Foot'. He argued:[13]

> I have tried to demonstrate that we do not stand alone against Lord Denning's method. Other legal academics with widely differing interests and political viewpoints, share our fears and doubts about the correctness of Lord Denning's method of judicial decision-making and his views on law reform. The House of Lords too are unhappy with Lord Denning ... His fervour for lawmaking, his cavalier treatment of precedent and his apparent infidelity to that House have all provoked stern reactions from the Law Lords.

Denning was unmoved. The criticisms were not new and, certainly by that stage of his career, were unlikely to shift his beliefs.

As well as his academic critics, Denning went some way to losing the support of the popular press when, in *British Steel Corporation v Granada Television Ltd* [1981] AC 1096, he required a television company to reveal a source. Inevitably, that was a decision despised by investigative journalists and the press in general, though it was upheld by the House of Lords.

Time's winged chariot

On 20 January 1981 *The Times* published a letter from the former Parliamentary Draftsman Francis Bennion, headed 'Why Lord Denning Should Resign'. It included the following criticism:

> His Lordship presides over the civil division of the Court of Appeal. An index of the efficiency of that court is the extent to which its decisions are upheld on further appeal to the House of Lords. The normal ratio is about fifty-fifty. In 1980 the *All England Law Reports* contained 14 cases where decisions in which Lord Denning was in the majority were appealed to the House of Lords. All but two were reversed by that House. By contrast the sixteen cases where Lord Denning was not in the majority displayed the customary proportion. Eight were upheld by the Lords and eight reversed. This remarkable discrepancy gives cause for disquiet.

Bennion added that, despite disagreeing with Denning's legal methods for many years, he still held Denning in 'the highest esteem and affection', which was the reason for him urging him to hang up his robes.[14]

Either way, if he saw the letter, Denning did not take its advice. The following year was to prove that he had indeed tarried too long. One can but wonder how much greater a legacy he might have had if he had followed Bennion's advice and retired by the mid-1970s, or perhaps at the latest upon his eightieth birthday, in January 1979, an occasion on which he had been feted by the profession and the popular press.[15] Instead, he was eventually compelled to retire in circumstances which were, bluntly, humiliating. We now turn to that lamentable saga.

CHAPTER XX

Master of the Rolls – Resignation

> Chaos, umpire sits,
> And by decision more embroils the fray
> *John Milton, Paradise Lost, Book II, 907–8*

If there is one incident from Denning's life which showed how the sands of time had shifted beneath his feet, it is the sad tale of the end of his judicial career. Through ill-judged words he received enough public opprobrium to feel obliged to resign. Yet there was sufficient residual goodwill both to cushion the impact at the time and to preserve most – though not all – of his reputation.

Background

The end of the 1970s and early 1980s was a febrile time for Britain's community relations. Despite the passage of the Race Relations Acts from the 1960s onwards, different ethnic groups were represented in very different ways in social statistics. It would be invidious to try to rate the level of prejudice in Britain at the time compared with other countries, or Britain in the present day. What is beyond question is that there was much public discussion about the level of immigration from Commonwealth nations, which were composed of different ethnicities and cultures, and the implications for society's cohesion.

Denning tried to remain apolitical, at least in a party-political sense, but he could not wholly avoid those debates, given that a number of cases came before him concerning the rights of refugees and other immigrants. Throughout his time as MR a degree of disquiet about the level of immigration permeated his judgments.[1] In various cases under the Housing (Homeless Persons) Act 1977, for example, he went back to his old ways of the 'deserving' and 'undeserving' poor, frequently lumping any non-British claimants into the latter category. In *De Falco v Crawley District Council* [1980] QB 460 he began:

> Every day we see signs of the advancing tide. This time it is two young families from Italy. They had heard tell of the European Economic Community. Naturally enough, because it all stemmed from a Treaty made at Rome. They had heard that there was freedom of movement for workers within the Community. They could come to England without let or hindrance. They may have heard, too, that England is a good place for workers. In Italy the word may have got round that in England there are all sorts of benefits to be had whenever you are unemployed. And best of all they will look after you if you have nowhere to live. There is a special new statute there which imposes on the local authority a duty to house you. They must either find you a house or put you up in a guest house. 'So let's go to England,' they say. 'That's the place for us.'
> In that telling I have used a touch of irony, but there is a good deal of truth behind it. You will see it as I recount the story.

In the main body of the judgment Denning went on to distinguish the families in question from 'true born Englishmen', and concluded:

> The local council at Crawley are very concerned about these two cases. They have Gatwick Airport within their area. If any family from the Community can fly into Gatwick – stay a month or two with relatives – and then claim to be unintentionally homeless – it would be a most serious matter for their overcrowded borough. They should be able to do better than King Canute. He bade the rising tide at Southampton to come no further. It took no notice. He got his feet wet. I trust the councillors of Crawley will keep theirs dry – against this new advancing tide. I would dismiss this appeal.

It is important to stress that although such remarks would attract obloquy in the twenty-first century, they were at the time considerably less controversial. Such was evinced not only by the number of senior judges who agreed with Denning, but by the popular press as well – even the staunchly liberal newspaper *The Guardian* reported his comments[2] in moderate terms, while its more conservative counterpart *The Times* published opinion columns around the same time expressing views very similar to Denning's.[3]

In *Thakrar v Secretary of State for the Home Department* [1974] 2 All ER 261, Denning gave a refrain that summed up his view on immigration: that small numbers were not objectionable but large numbers were. Of the influx of people of Asian origin who were being expelled from East Africa, he said '[t]his country would not have room for them. It is not as if it was only one or two coming. They come not in single files, but in battalions'. He advised that the plaintiff would have been better off becoming a citizen of 'that great country', India, adding 'there may be more scope for him than here'.[4]

A year or so later, in *R v Home Secretary, ex parte Phansopkar* [1975] 4 All ER 497, he said of the Commonwealth Immigration Act 1971:

> It made a new man. It called him 'patrial'. Not a patriot, but a patrial. Parliament made him one of us: and made us one of them. We are all now patrials. We are no longer, in the eyes of the law, Englishmen, Scotsmen or Welshmen. We are just patrials. Parliament gave this new man a fine set of clothes. It invested him with a new right. It called it 'the right of abode in the United Kingdom'. It is the most precious right that anyone can have. At least I so regard it.

Denning again preached alarm at the increasing levels of immigration in *R v Hillingdon London Borough Council, ex parte Islam* [1981] 3 WLR 109. Further, as a general means to slow the tide of immigration, he said in *The Discipline of Law*, with the same faux-naïvety he had shown about the security services in *McIlkenny* and other cases, that '[i]t seems to me that the immigration officers do their work efficiently and honestly and fairly. I have never known a case where they have been unfair',[5] even though he himself had decided in some cases that they had failed to apply the rules correctly.[6]

As well as the bare fact of immigration, the question arose as to how Britain was accommodating all the communities which made up its increasingly diverse population. We saw earlier how Denning in his Hamlyn Lectures had spoken in a forthright manner about the law being colour blind and there being no place in English law for discrimination on racial grounds. He repeated those sentiments on numerous other occasions. In *Race Relations Board v Charter and others* [1972] 1 All ER 556, for example, he held that private clubs could not discriminate on ethnic grounds, stating 'Such clubs cannot, as I see it, reject a man solely because of his colour or race. Nor, I trust, would they wish to do so'.[7] In *Savjani v IRC* [1973] 1 QB 815, he stopped the

Inland Revenue from imposing higher obligations on taxpayers born in the Indian subcontinent than other United Kingdom taxpayers.[8]

Nonetheless, Denning could be chary about the extent to which the law should be used. In *R v Racial Equality Commission, ex parte Hillingdon London Borough Council* [1981] 3 WLR 520, for example, he prohibited the Commission for Racial Equality from investigating why a local authority had dealt differently with claims for accommodation by two families, one white Rhodesian and one East African Asian from Kenya. Denning stated dismissively that the difference was obvious in that the Rhodesian family were unintentionally homeless but the Asian family were not, and therefore there was nothing for the Commission to investigate. Cases such as that led Professor HWR Wade to remark that the courts had 'shown a marked reluctance to extend to aliens the same principles of procedural protection and fair play that apply to citizens of this country'.[9]

Denning's approach on all the above issues was broadly consistent with a speech he made as far back as 1966:[10]

> We have recently strengthened the law to deal with racial discrimination. It was at one time lawful for a hotel or restaurant, or for cafe proprietors or a dancehall, to refuse to admit or to supply coloured people. Not many did so. But it is now unlawful. Every place of public resort is open to every person, no matter what his colour, or race, or nationality. If the proprietor should seek to practise discrimination, the Courts can present an injunction to stop it.
>
> Previously, too, it was lawful to make speeches or to publish matter abusing groups of people for their race or nationality. Now all that is altered. It is now an offence for a person to publish written matter and make speeches in public with intent to step up hatred against any section of the public distinguished by colour, such as negroes, or race, such as the Jews, or nationality, such as the Germans. The punishment for so doing was to be as much as two years' imprisonment. Although we have thus ensured that every person is to be treated fairly and equally, whatever be his colour, race or nationality, nevertheless we have found it necessary to limit the entry of people from overseas into England. They seek to come to England because it is a place of liberty and equality, where they can earn high wages. But let there be no mistake about it. Many of them have a lot to learn. Their state of health, their standard of housing, their mode of living, their concepts of morality, are different from ours. We can teach a reasonable number of them, but we cannot assimilate millions of them. Else we might find our own standards brought down to

theirs. So we have had to limit the numbers, and this has been done by the common consent of both the main political parties with the approval of all those who have the well-being of the country at heart.

One sees therefore the clash between Denning's progressive support of racial equality with his outdated terminology and outdated assumption of English cultural superiority. It is a measure of post-war social change that some of the ideas he expressed were uncontroversial in 1966 but unacceptable by 1981.

Denning went on in his 1966 speech to express the hope that troubles such as the civil unrest which had occurred in Notting Hill in 1958 had been stamped out. He was in that respect painfully ignorant of the extent of discrimination that continued across society in spite of race relations legislation, and equally ignorant of the resultant tensions between some communities and the police. Doubtless his ignorance was partly due to the cloistered life he found in the Inns of Court and the semi-rural life he led in Whitchurch, both well away from any inner-city deprivation where many new immigrant communities had had to begin their lives in the United Kingdom.

At the end of the 1970s, those community tensions boiled over into riots in Brixton, Toxteth, Bristol and elsewhere. In response, the government commissioned Lord Scarman to head an inquiry into the causes of the riots and how the state ought to act to prevent any repetition. Denning's intervention in that debate was to be his undoing.

Mansion House speech

On 9 July 1981, a few months before Lord Scarman's report was due, Denning stood in for the Lord Chief Justice at a dinner at London's Mansion House. In attendance were a number of senior judges along with various figures from politics, business and elsewhere. Denning gave a speech entitled 'Our present discontents' in which he discussed the recent riots, with particular reference to the police and the jury system. He stated that:

> when it comes to dealing with mobs – with violence, with crime itself – the police are the first line of defence. All good citizens should and do support them. It is deplorable to see the way in which, on occasions, they are most unjustly attacked by vociferous groups and by the press and television.

He went on to say that trial by jury was under pressure, and one of the threats was the right of pre-emptory challenge – the right of the defence to object without reasons to any particular juror:[11]

> Let me tell you of the riots in Bristol. It was a coloured area. A few of the good Bristol police force went to inquire into some of the wrongful acts being committed there. They were set upon by coloured people living there. Much violence. Much damage. Twelve of them were arrested and charged with riot – a riot it certainly was. So they were tried by jury. There were 12 accused. Each had three challenges. That is 36 altogether. The accused challenged the white men, but not the coloured men, nor the women. Eight were acquitted. On four the jury could not agree. The prosecution proceeded no further. The cost was £500,000. This was, in my opinion, an abuse of the right of challenge, to get a jury of their own choice.

That passage contained a clear inference that black defendants had cynically used the right of pre-emptory challenge in order to secure a majority-black jury, which in turn was a guarantee of acquittal or at least a weighting of the odds in their favour, the assumption being that black people would close ranks against the police regardless of the evidence. It also contained yet another presumption of public authority infallibility ('the good Bristol police force').

The next day, page 2 of *The Times* carried a short report of his speech, in an edition which dedicated much space to discussing the riots. The report was headed 'Lord Denning criticizes jury vetting' and stated that Denning said the right of an accused to challenge jurors 'was being abused wholesale'. It quoted him adding that the Bristol defendants had been able:

> to get on the jury five coloured jurors. The jury so constituted acquitted eight of the accused defendants. Of the other four the jury could not agree, so they went free ... That was, in my opinion, an abuse of the right of challenge.

The Times placed the note of Denning's speech underneath a separate story reporting the views of Enoch Powell MP.[12] Powell was the most controversial post-war politician in Britain on the subject of immigration and race relations, and had been ever since a notorious speech he had given in 1968. According to *The Times*, Powell had been asked by the BBC in light of the riots whether he still advocated repatriation for 'coloured people', and had replied that that was the preferable option, and the majority of people would begin to support it if the alternative was civil war. Powell went on to dismiss deprivation, unemployment and other social factors as reasons behind the rioting, arguing that they had not caused riots in the past. Instead, he unsubtly inferred that the common factor was the ethnicity of those involved.

Perhaps because Denning's comments were mild in comparison with Powell's venom, they were not widely discussed, either in *The Times* or elsewhere.[13] There was one notable exception to the general indifference: Rudy Narayan, the Secretary of the Society of Black Lawyers, whom Denning had sponsored for the Bar, called for his resignation.[14] Assuming the message reached Denning, he either discounted it or considered it outweighed by the lack of criticism from anyone at the actual dinner or from most people afterwards. Thus, over the long vacation, he devoted himself to writing a new book in which he included a chapter expressing the same sentiments as his speech.

Lord Scarman delivered his report in November 1981.[15] He expressed the view that the riots had been a spontaneous outburst of built-up resentment sparked by particular incidents, with the background being 'complex political, social and economic factors'. He advised that 'urgent action' was needed to prevent racial disadvantages becoming an 'endemic, ineradicable disease threatening the very survival of our society'. He pointed to disproportionate and indiscriminate use of 'stop and search' powers by the police against black people, something which was to be repeated many times in the years that followed and was still a point of contention four decades later when this book was being written.

What Next in the Law?

By and large Lord Scarman's report was accepted by politicians, the police, the media and community leaders, but (assuming he read it) it did not cause Denning to rethink his position. When his book, entitled *What Next in the Law?*, was published in May 1982, it contained the following passages concerning the pre-emptory challenges in Bristol, essentially reprising his Mansion House remarks:[16]

> It was done so as to secure as many coloured people on the jury as possible – by objecting to whites. This meant that five of the jury were coloured and seven white. The evidence against two of the accused was so strong that you would think they would be found guilty. But there was a disagreement.

> The underlying assumption is that all citizens are sufficiently qualified to serve on a jury. I do not agree. The English are no longer a homogeneous race. They are white and black, coloured and brown. They no longer share the same standards of conduct. Some of them come from countries where bribery and graft are accepted as an integral part of life: and where stealing is a virtue so long as you are not found out ... They will never accept the word of a policeman against one of their own.

Denning did not go so far as to argue that black people should be precluded from serving on juries. Rather, he said that all potential jurors should be interviewed by magistrates and appointed only if they were 'sensible and responsible members of the community'.

Coming at any time since the late 1960s at least, such remarks would have likely been unacceptable from anyone in authority such as Denning. In the wake of the Scarman Report, and in the general atmosphere about race relations and inequality in Britain at the time, they caused outrage. Two days after the successful book launch at the publisher's premises, and one day after Denning had attended a signing at the publisher's bookshop in Bell Yard, the press reported the Society for Black Lawyers calling for Denning's resignation.[17] Later that afternoon, the journalist Ludovic Kennedy went to The Lawn and asked Denning whether he stood by the remarks. He confirmed that he did – evidently unaware of the scale of the storm that was brewing.

The impugned jurors indicated they intended to sue for libel. Another journalist who arrived at The Lawn seeking a comment reported that Joan answered the door and stated: 'My husband is seeking legal advice',[18] the irony being that no one in the land would have been thought to know more of the law than Denning. Joan also told *The Daily Mirror* 'He is very distressed. He had done more for the black people in this country than any other judge. He is very upset. He realises that he has made a mistake'.[19]

With help from the Vice-President of the Law Society, Max Williams, and the London firm Clifford Turner, Denning instructed two libel law experts, Andrew Leggatt QC and David Eady, both future High Court judges. Butterworths, the publisher, soon had no choice but to recall and pulp all unsold copies. The book was then reissued with the offending passages removed.[20] Denning conceded that his statements about the Bristol jury had been in error, and apologised to each of the jurors individually. As a result no writs were issued.[21]

Resignation

For all that his fortitude, drive and sense of duty remained undiminished, Denning knew his time had come. He announced that he would retire, and offered to step down immediately. At the wishes of the Lord Chancellor it was determined his resignation would take effect at the end of July, being the conclusion of the Summer term. The date was then extended to 29 September, the end of the long vacation, to enable Denning to finish all his reserved judgments. A touch of levity accompanied the announcement of his resignation in *Private Eye*, in the form of a cartoon of two barristers with one saying to the other 'I expect the House of Lords will overrule his decision'.[22]

Rudy Narayan was conciliatory in a letter to *The Times*, calling Denning 'one of the greatest judicial minds of this century' and stating that the publishers should take some of the blame. Narayan finished with an eloquent paragraph which has been quoted many times since:[23]

> A great judge has erred greatly in the intellectual loneliness of advanced years; while his remarks should be rejected and rebutted he is yet, in a personal way, entitled to draw on that reservoir of community regard which he has in many quarters and to seek understanding, if not forgiveness.

In *The Sunday Times*, the journalist Hugo Young wrote that once the story of his resignation had passed Denning's work would endure, and that Denning would remain a totem for those who believed that the law should be a force for liberation.[24]

Tributes appeared from around the world. A representative one came from the President of the Lord Denning Society in Queensland, who wrote of 'profound regret' amongst their members and added:[25]

> The controversy surrounding his latest book should not distract us from an appreciation of 'the Master's' contribution towards building a more modern and humane jurisprudence. Lord Denning is assured of an honoured place in our legal history, and his name will be remembered long after those of his contemporaries – the 'timorous souls' – have been forgotten.

The end of an era

Despite lingering controversy over his book, the actual occasion of Denning's retirement was a celebratory affair.[26] It was held on 30 July 1982, in the Lord Chief Justice's court (Court 4 in the main building of the Royal Courts of Justice) rather than Denning's usual Court 3, because of the extra space available. Even so, the court was still packed with well-wishers. Speeches were given, in order, by the Lord Chancellor Lord Hailsham, the Attorney General (as *ex officio* leader of the Bar) Sir Michael Havers QC, the Treasury Devil Simon Brown (later Lord Brown of Eaton-Under-Heywood, but at the time *ex officio* senior junior member of the Bar), the Chairman of the Bar, the senior silks of Denning's Inns of Court and of his old circuit, the leaders of the specialist Bars and, lastly, the President of the Law Society.

Lord Hailsham, who years before had upbraided Denning's approach to precedent and statute, stated that Denning 'has been, and is a golden legend'.[27] Sir Michael Havers announced the 'end of an era'. He added his appreciation of how Denning had protected the citizen against bureaucracy. Simon Brown paid tribute to Denning's concise judgment-writing style, and earned himself some fame with his quip 'We shall recall that short sentences are best, and verbs optional'.

Lord Hailsham concluded his speech with:

> Above all, we shall miss you and your gift of friendship, your sturdy independence, and your unflagging and effervescent enthusiasm. Now you belong to history. But here you see around you a company of admirers and friends. We wish you well, both you and Lady Denning. Come and see us often. Wherever lawyers are gathered together they will always rejoice to see you in their midst.

Denning himself recalled that he had first entered the Royal Courts of Justice sixty years before. He admitted to sharing with Oliver Cromwell 'many roughnesses, warts and pimples. I know them perfectly well – and so does the House of Lords'.

The Times itself ran a broadly though not wholly laudatory editorial, calling Denning one of the greatest judges of the century. It stated that only Lord Reid and Lord Devlin could compare in terms of legal intellectual brilliance, but neither had anything approaching Denning's influence over the development of the law.

That was not quite that for Denning, since he still had the four reserved judgments to deliver. Over the summer vacation he prepared them, but first spent some time in Plymouth as a guest of the Lord Mayor, who invited him and Joan to spend a few days in the house bequeathed to the city by Lady Astor.[28] Whilst there they observed ships returning from the Falklands War, a conflict in which Norman's son had served, having followed his father into the navy.[29] As ever, Denning the veteran watched with a mixture of pride and resolve, with his conviction about the British nation rising to the challenge of war affirmed.

Of his remaining judgments, the most controversial was *Mandla v Dowell-Lee* [1983] 1 All ER 1062. The plaintiff was a Sikh who enrolled his son in a private school. The male members of his family all wore turbans, but the school demanded its pupils wear the regulation school cap without exception. The plaintiff complained to the Commission for Racial Equality. The question was whether the school's demand constituted discrimination in breach of the Race Relations Act, which in turn depended on whether Sikhs were an ethnic group protected by the Act. The County Court and subsequently the Court of Appeal including Denning decided otherwise. Denning said that while he accepted Jews were a racial group (and added an explicit and emphatic denunciation of anti-Semitism), Sikhs were a religion only and thus not entitled to bring a claim alleging racial discrimination.[30] Denning's judgment was attacked by Sibghat Kadri, the chairman of the Society of Black Lawyers, who stated 'We say Lord Denning is a racist judge. The society says Denning has gone and the black people are rejoicing'.[31] One correspondent to *The Guardian* said that he wished Denning would spend his dotage 'trapped at a bus-stop every night in outer Ealing, without the money to pay for a taxi, in the stimulating company of blacks, gays, trade unionists and women'.[32]

The judgment was subsequently overturned by the House of Lords, who held that Sikhs were and should be considered at law an ethnic group, entitled to the protection of the Race Relations Act. Denning unhesitatingly accepted their decision as correct,[33] partly because he had taken note by then of proceedings in *Hansard* (from which it was clear Parliament had intended Sikhs to be covered by the Act), something which to his regret he had not been permitted to do in court.

The very last of Denning's judgments was *George Mitchell (Chesterhall) Ltd v Finney Lock Seeds Ltd* [1983] 2 AC 803. The subject matter was classic Denning: an exemption clause contained in a contract for the sale of goods to which the Supply of Goods (Implied Terms) Act 1973 applied. In reliance on the clause, the sellers sought to limit their liability to the buyers to a sum which represented only one-third of one per cent of the damage that the buyers had sustained from an undisputed breach of contract by the sellers.

The sellers failed before the trial judge, who held that the breach of contract in respect of which the buyers sued fell outside the clause.

In the Court of Appeal, both Oliver and Kerr LJJ held that the breach was not covered by the exemption clause. Denning was on his own in holding that the language of the exemption clause was plain and unambiguous; that it would be apparent to anyone who read it that it covered the breach in respect of which the buyers' action was brought; and that the passing of the Supply of Goods (Implied Terms) Act 1973 and its successor, the Unfair Contract Terms Act 1977, had removed from judges the temptation to resort to the device of ascribing to words appearing in exemption clauses a tortured meaning so as to avoid giving effect to an exclusion or limitation of liability when the judge thought that in the circumstances to do so would be unfair.

Denning agreed with the other members of the court that the appeal should be dismissed, but solely on the statutory ground under the 1973 Act that it would not be fair and reasonable to allow reliance upon the clause.

A few months after he had stepped down, the case reached the House of Lords, who gave fulsome praise of Denning and his career. Lord Diplock began:

> My Lords, I have had the advantage of reading in advance the speech to be delivered by my noble and learned friend, Lord Bridge of Harwich, in favour of dismissing this appeal upon grounds which reflect the reasoning although not the inimitable style of Lord Denning MR's judgment in the Court of Appeal. I agree entirely with Lord Bridge's speech and there is nothing that I could usefully add to it; but I cannot refrain from noting with regret, which is, I am sure, shared by all members of the Appellate Committee of this House, that Lord Denning MR's judgment in the instant case, which was delivered on September 29, 1982 is probably the last in which your Lordships will have the opportunity of enjoying his eminently readable style of exposition and his stimulating and percipient approach to the continuing development of the common law to which he has himself in his judicial lifetime made so outstanding a contribution.

It was Denning's final direct entry in the law reports, and constituted a much more positive last word than the circumstances that had compelled his retirement.

Denning's replacement as Master of the Rolls was Sir John Donaldson, a judge one generation younger. *The Times* suggested he would have felt like a cricketer coming to the wicket after some blistering Ian Botham heroics.[34] Donaldson later related how, when assuming Denning's office, he opened a cupboard and had a deluge of papers fall out – comprising all the interesting pending cases Denning had squirrelled away in case someone thought to list them before a different court.[35]

Donaldson went on to bring a reforming broom to the procedural aspects of the Court of Appeal's work.[36] His innovations included the requirement for skeleton arguments in appeal cases, a move to more written judgments ('handed down' in law reporting parlance) available to the parties, the press and law reporters, and a more professional, managerial approach to the administration of the court. The latter included employing a barrister in the civil appeals office to assist with case management and listing, and an annual review of the Court of Appeal's performance.[37] Donaldson was also more curt when in court than Denning, especially with counsel who were straying from the point or failing to keep their submissions concise.

The result was the near-elimination within six months of a backlog of over 600 cases.[38] It showed that the once-innovative Denning had allowed the Court of Appeal to slide into inefficiency over his last years.

Denning would no doubt have agreed with Donaldson's reforms, but had likely been too set in his ways and too locked in combat with the House of Lords to turn his mind to reform of procedure and judicial administration (though he would not have disputed the importance of both). He had always been primarily focused on matters of legal principle, and how to mould the common law to do justice. Now that he was retired, he could continue thinking – and speaking – more freely about both.

CHAPTER XXI

Later Years

Having done with all his court appearances, Denning now had to find other ways to fill his time. He maintained his enjoyment of publicity despite the circumstances of his retirement. To begin with, he was invited to many celebratory dinners, and kept his flat in Lincoln's Inn to make it easier to attend London events. In some of his after-dinner speeches he described the idealised lifestyle of the former judge as a leisurely round of gentleman farming, reading and enjoying a quiet snifter in the privacy of his own home, but insisted that would not be for him, for he would soon succumb to boredom. Instead, he maintained he did not intend to be idle, that he would now be free to engage in political controversy, and that he wished to continue to speak in the House of Lords, especially on social matters and law reform.[1]

Some time before stepping down, he was interviewed for a major newspaper by the barrister and author John Mortimer QC, best known as the creator of *Rumpole of the Bailey*.[2]

Mortimer's legendary cross-examination skills elicited an interesting admission. Denning stated that he had not been troubled by issuing the death penalty when a puisne judge, but conceded he had since changed his mind and was no longer in favour of capital punishment. Mortimer pointed out that Denning was a strong believer in natural justice – which Denning confirmed – then pointed out that if the death penalty was contrary to natural justice, it had always been so, 'but you didn't realize it at the time'. Denning readily accepted that proposition, leaving Mortimer rather stunned.

Denning was soon true to his word about speaking out. In October 1982, he told the Institute of Directors that the imposition of sanctions by the United States on Western European subsidiaries of companies which co-operated on a controversial Siberian pipeline would, or should, be illegal in

English law, though he added that there would be no remedy because the law 'tells judges to keep out of differences between sovereign states'.[3]

In November 1982, a dinner was held in his honour at the Inner Temple, attended by all thirty-six of the surviving members of the Court of Appeal who had sat with him. Lord Diplock gave a speech, as did Denning and, notably, Joan herself. She began in a self-effacing manner, 'Tom does all the speaking', but went on to recall a time when she had persuaded him to give the opposite decision to that he had initially preferred.[4] His fellow judges dissented but the House of Lords upheld the appeal and restored his outcome.

Not long afterwards, Denning spoke at a lunch at the Savoy Hotel to mark the thirty continuous years in which Agatha Christie's *The Mousetrap* had been performed in London's West End.[5] Over 1,000 guests were present. Denning called the play 'a better thriller than any other'.[6]

In February 1983, Denning inadvertently made a rod for his own back when he answered a query by Patrick Evershed, a cousin of his predecessor as MR, about a water strike then taking place. The strike had left Evershed's road without water for two days. Evershed asked Denning whether, since the water authority would not repair the pipes, the residents could do so themselves or by contractors and charge the cost to the authority. Denning gave a considered answer: the authority was under a statutory duty to provide a supply to homes and schools, and if their own workers happened to be on strike, they had to employ contractors. It would be an offence to dig up the public highway, but Evershed and his fellow residents could rely on the defence of necessity.

There was much press interest in Denning's advice, none of it to the amusement of an embattled government trying to deal with continuing industrial unrest.[7] The general public promptly flooded Denning's post box with requests for assistance with their own legal quandaries. He endeavoured to respond politely to each. His normal reply was that he did not give legal advice and they should consult solicitors. In a few instances, however, he did indeed involve himself in both public and private disputes and offered advice from time to time.[8]

Not long after his water controversy, he underwent a hip replacement and had a stair lift installed in The Lawn. Both his hearing and eyesight began to decline tangibly, but his failing health did not slow his intellectual output. He continued working studiously in his library. Later the same year, he published his book *The Closing Chapter*, recounting his version of the sad end to his judicial career (naming a critical editorial in *The Times* of 24 June 1982 as the prompt for his resignation) and adding a few thoughts on some of his more controversial decisions. 'A law student who has not read this book will not necessarily be failed in his examinations, but he should be' wrote the future Court of Appeal judge Christopher Staughton in a glowing review.[9]

As well as helping with the odd query from the public, Denning managed to create a dispute for himself when he erected a wall at a property he owned next to the Town Hall in Whitchurch to try to stop motorists using the yard. The local authority objected, though Denning said he would be willing to compromise.[10]

The Bar Association for Commerce, Finance and Industry had been founded in 1965 to promote the interests and professional status of barristers employed in commerce, finance and industry. In 1975 it inaugurated an annual lecture by an eminent lawyer, intended to be on a topic of general interest to the legal profession and the wider business community. In 1980 Denning served as patron and from 1981 the annual lecture became known as 'The Denning Lecture'. The reason for the name change was explained in that year's lecture by Lord Templeman, who referred to Denning as 'our most interesting and provocative Master of the Rolls' who had 'always been concerned about the state of the profession and is a supporter of the Association whose members help to ensure that the training, discipline and ethics of the Bar are fully maintained outside the narrow confines of advocacy and litigation'.[11]

Denning himself gave the lecture in March 1984,[12] entitled 'Trade Unions on Trial', in which he traversed the history of labour relations and some of his controversial cases in the field.

In July 1984 he was awarded an honorary degree from Nottingham University. Shortly after, showing how active he remained, his next book, *Landmarks in the Law*, was published. It was clearly a diverting work for him to have prepared, and perhaps more enjoyable than re-arguing his old battles as he had done in *The Closing Chapter*. The intention, as he explained in the introduction, was 'to tell of some of those great cases of the past which have gone on to make our constitution'. He went on to discuss classic historical trials such as those of Walter Raleigh, Roger Casement, William Joyce, Thomas Wolsey, and the Tolpuddle Martyrs, and the legal ramifications of Queen Caroline's matrimonial strife. He also included cases in which he had been involved himself, standing firm on his regulation 18B work during the Second World War and maintaining, against the tide of opinion, that *Liversidge v Anderson* had been rightly decided. At a launch party for the book in London, he gained some media attention when he said that those responsible for the 'Brighton bomb' at the recent Conservative Party conference could be charged with high treason – then still carrying the death penalty – before condemning striking miners as threatening the rule of law and undermining the trade unions.[13]

Another significant event in 1984 was the publication of a Denning *festschrift* of sorts, Jowell and McAuslan's book *Lord Denning: the Judge and the Law*. The work was substantial, totalling almost 500 pages. It comprised ten essays on Denning's work in discrete areas of the law, all written by legal academics with impressive credentials. It was broadly sympathetic to Denning, at times arguably too much. Some of the essays have since dated: RFV Heuston in a biographical sketch at the start of the book came out with a statement as backward as anything Denning himself ever said, when he wrote:[14]

> The change in social habits and beliefs since 1945 can also be seen if one mentions some of the terms and concepts which were then – happily – unknown: civil liberties, demonstrations, police harassment, racial and sexual discrimination, one-parent families, legal action groups, neighbourhood law centres.[15]

AWB Simpson wrote an essay on 'Lord Denning as Jurist' that barely mentioned Denning, thereby inadvertently confirming that Denning was never interested in legal philosophy. Those quibbles aside, the work stands as one of the more detailed and authoritative examinations of Denning's work. It remains essential reading for legal scholars wanting to know more of Denning's legal reputation as it was in his own time.[16]

In January 1985, Denning spoke to much acclaim at a lunch[17] hosted by the Reading Chamber of Commerce in Sindlesham, Berkshire, where he signed copies of *Landmarks in the Law*. The occasion was vintage Denning, starting with anecdotes about his days in the Quarter Sessions. Once, when summing up in the case of a man arrested bearing housebreaking implements, he told the jury that if they believed the defendant had presented himself on the doorstep at midnight in order to give him the tools as a gift, they should find him not guilty; they did. Denning then launched into something of a sermon, reminding guests that Magna Carta was signed nearby, but:[18]

> What do we see now? Mass pickets, with their hooliganism and violence, contrary to law ... people up and down the country breaking the law, including Sunday trading laws, in many smaller ways. We see increasing crime. ... What does it profit a man if he gaineth the world yet loseth his own soul?

He finished by demanding that patriotism should no longer be a dirty word: 'It is time we were proud of our country'. His beliefs in Christianity and patriotism were clearly as strong as ever.

In July 1985, Denning spoke at the Police Foundation lecture.[19] He complained that the pay of top lawyers was too high at the top and too low at the bottom. He also criticised the government's rises for top civil servants as 'impolitic and unwise': 'The problem is increased dramatically with the recent announcement of increased pay for judges. Their pay is often compared with that of the top earners of the Bar, but the comparison is false'. 'So far as I know', Denning went on, 'no top member of the Bar, however large his income, has refused appointment at the present level'. He qualified himself by stating that if the top members of the civil service had pay increases, then it was right for judges to have them as well.

A more forgettable incident also took place in 1985, when Denning appeared on a television programme called *Jim'll Fix It*. The format involved people (usually children) writing in each week asking for a wish to be granted, and the programme would then depict a lucky few having it made true in some form. In the episode in which Denning appeared, the child in question wished to become a barrister.[20] The programme filmed her appearing in a mock trial featuring Enid Blyton characters, presided over by Denning in full High Court regalia and affecting his usual genial yet authoritative courtroom persona. The script was by Clive Anderson, a barrister and well-known radio and television presenter. Lord Justice Sedley later wrote of the episode that Denning's performance was 'without a millimetre's deviation from his daily courtroom manner',[21] and that 'what impressed was not the incongruity but the homogeneity of it: the same benign moralism as the legal profession had known for 40 years, in language begotten by Samuel Smiles upon Enid Blyton'.[22]

The occasion would have been no more than a whimsical footnote, except that 'Jim' of the title and the presenter of the programme was Jimmy Savile, a popular entertainer and charity fundraiser for several decades who was exposed after his death as having been a serial rapist and paedophile. He had used his celebrity status and connections with police, politicians and others in positions of power to deflect suspicion and suppress any attempt to bring him to justice. As a result, it is safe to assume the programme will never be repeated on mainstream media, though a recording could be found on YouTube at the time of writing.

It should go without saying that Denning would have had no reason to suspect Savile, who would never have been so incautious as to misbehave in the presence of someone of the status of Denning. Moreover, Savile had no role in the production of the programme beyond appearing at the appointed time to read his lines, so his contact with the other participants would have been minimal. Nevertheless, some still chose to cast a negative comment about Denning's participation in the programme, after Savile's offending had come to light.[23]

A rather happier television appearance in 1986 took place on 9 May, when Denning appeared on *The Wogan Show*, a popular chat show hosted by the avuncular presenter Terry Wogan. Denning gave reminiscences and anecdotes of his life. Much like Roy Plomley's, Wogan's style was to be largely uncritical of his guests; the theme was entertainment, not interrogation.

Another positive event in 1986 was the publication of what Denning announced would be his final book, *Leaves from my Library*. It was an anthology of his favourite (non-legal) prose pieces from across the centuries. It began with extracts from Churchill, Nelson and Shakespeare – figures whose place at the forefront of English history and culture would have seemed unassailable to Denning, and indeed virtually anyone else at the time – and continued with pieces of classic literature from the likes of Lewis Carroll, Jane Austen and Geoffrey Chaucer. There were no surprises among either the selections or the short introductions and comments by Denning. He noted how central the class system was to *Pride and Prejudice*, and offered a few observations on how his family used to look up to lords of the manor. Understandably, though, given the tone he was trying to achieve with the book, he did not expound much further on how he thought the class system had changed during his lifetime. He clearly enjoyed the project, and although it did indeed turn out to be his last book, his work was far from done.

Perhaps most substantively for his legacy, in 1986 the University of Buckingham named its new legal journal after him, having previously named its law library after him as well. The *Denning Law Journal* was, and remains, a refereed journal, intended to 'provide a forum for the widest discussion of issues arising in the common law and to embrace the wider global and international issues of contemporary concern both of which Lord Denning would have approved'.[24] Denning provided the foreword to the first volume, adopting a self-effacing tone:

> My friends at the University of Buckingham have decided to launch a law journal. They are fortunate in that Lord Scarman has agreed to be Chairman of the Editorial Advisory Board. But I am most embarrassed that they should have called it the *Denning Law Journal*.

> I cannot think why, except that my judgments have often given rise to controversy and given the commentators something to write about.
>
> But I appreciate the compliment and would congratulate the University on its enterprise. It is of the first importance that there should be free and open discussion of the issues of the day. The members of this free and independent University – self-supporting as it is – are well placed to take the lead in these discussions. They will choose subjects of contemporary and practical importance. They will seek contributions from those in the law schools of other universities and also in the practising side of the legal profession. I trust it will be well supported.

He went on to identify *Candler v Crane, Christmas* as his most important judgment. In second place he named the administrative law cases of *R v Northumberland Compensation Appeal Tribunal, ex parte Shaw* and *Barnard v National Dock Labour Board*.

Denning continued to speak in the House of Lords. In 1986 he opined on the European Communities (Amendment) Bill. Initially, he sounded like the archetypal patriot, leading a revolt against the Bill on the ground that it would threaten British sovereignty and was inconsistent with the original purpose of the European Economic Community, which he believed had only been about free trade.[25] Yet, taking a pragmatic approach, he said in a later debate that the Bill should receive full support, and he exhorted others to embrace the change:[26]

> I am going to shed my wig and gown and I am going to adopt a politician's robe. Do not let us be isolationists any more. Let us go into Europe with vigour and enthusiasm. We must send our best people to Europe. When we send them there, it is inclined to be regarded as a backwater, and some people do not want to go because they feel they are losing out on opportunities here. This has got to change. ...
>
> Look, there is a ship coming in with the tide. She is called 'European Union'. But she is in difficulty. She is overloaded. Her gear and tackle are all adrift. She is in danger of stranding. Send out a good boat to help her. Here is one. It is called 'United Kingdom'. Put good men aboard the 'European Union'. Make good the rigging. Heave on the ropes. All together now. Get her clear. See that she can ride out any storm. She must be made equal to any ship that sails the oceans of the world. I have said all that – and everyone should believe this – so as to encourage us not to be isolationist any more. We must

recognise the importance of what we can contribute to European union. Let us help all we can to achieve that.

Denning had seemingly performed an ideological U-turn, but more likely it was another classic instance of him seeking the best of the situation in which he found himself. As with his work on divorce law, if he could not stop something with which he might have disagreed, he would attempt to reform it according to what he thought was in the parties' or the country's best interests.

In July 1987, Denning fired a broadside at his old opponent, the Appellate Committee of the House of Lords, in the context of the *Spycatcher* litigation. The case concerned the memoirs of a retired officer of the security service. Two national newspapers, *The Guardian* and *The Observer*, published stories based on the memoirs. The Attorney General tried to block publication in Australia and in the United Kingdom. The action was maintained even after sections of the book had been read in open court in Australia and the entire memoir had been published in the United States.

Because of the changed circumstances arising from the publication in the United States, the availability in the United Kingdom of the book and the disclosures in other newspapers, *The Guardian* and *The Observer* applied to have the interlocutory injunctions discharged. Meanwhile, the Attorney General applied to commit another paper, *The Sunday Times*, for contempt. The Vice-Chancellor ruled in favour of the newspapers, but the Court of Appeal reimposed the injunctions, and the House of Lords, by a majority of 3:2, dismissed the newspapers' appeal.[27]

Denning criticised the law lords' decision as contrary to freedom of speech and common sense. He assailed the ban which the Attorney General had obtained on reporting allegations or information emanating from Australian court proceedings over the book, stating that it was 'quite contrary to the general principle that everything said in open court is freely open to reports for the benefit of the public everywhere', adding that the horse had already bolted (taking a rather different position from that which he had in Harriet Harman's case).[28] He suggested to the BBC that the answer might lie in a short Act of Parliament to maintain freedom of the press.

With respect, Denning's position was preferable to that of the House of Lords. The situation was reminiscent of that in the 1930s when overseas papers were full of stories about Edward (Prince of Wales) and Mrs Simpson while the British papers refused to print any of them. Nothing could be gained from suppressing something already effectively in the public domain, other than drawing attention to what the government did not want people to know, rendering the litigation counter-productive (or 'the Streisand effect' to use a modern idiom).

Denning finished his commentary on the case with a criticism of the House for delivering judgment before preparing their reasoning, which had been promised in a few months' time. On that point he was unfair: the House of Lords never delivered unreserved judgments. No doubt their lordships thought it prudent to announce the decision prior to handing down judgment because of the exceptional public interest in the outcome.

One especially memorable occasion in Denning's 'retirement' came on 28 September 1987, when, at the age of eighty-eight, he once more donned his metaphorical advocate's hat (though not his actual barristerial wig and gown) and went into Andover Magistrates' Court to argue the case of villagers who wanted to maintain a footpath. It had been more than forty years since he had been at the Bar and some sixty years since he had last appeared in a Magistrates' Court. He was successful, his opponent remarking that 'Lord Denning is the most tenacious correspondent in these matters. He is very much like a terrier on every point'.[29] Denning clearly enjoyed the experience, for he repeated it a week later in a dispute over a different old footpath, and otherwise continued to busy himself in local affairs, including what was to become a protracted dispute with the trustees, the Vicars of Whitchurch and St Mary Bourne, over the fate of the old school building at Whitchurch.[30] He wrote about some of those concerns over 1988 and 1989 in *The Field* magazine. In total he had nine articles published in the magazine, comprising several panegyrics on traditional English country life as well as pieces describing the present-day disputes in which he was involved.[31]

Denning continued to enjoy media appearances here and there. In September 1988, he was interviewed by Radio Solent about his early days as a barrister.[32] In January 1989, not long before his ninetieth birthday, he was asked by the journalist Joshua Rozenberg 'how would you like to be remembered?' 'You want that for my obituary', Denning replied dryly, but then turned a classic Denning phrase: 'As a remembrance of me in good works. That is how I should like to be remembered'.[33]

To mark his ninetieth birthday he was also interviewed by the journalist Trevor Knight for Winchester Radio.[34] Knight elicited familiar stories from Denning about his childhood in Whitchurch and his devotion to the surrounding area. The interview also drew out his firm opposition to the loss of sovereignty to Europe, although Denning added the qualification that he thought that Britain should make the best of the situation and try to influence Europe for the better, just as he had argued in the House of Lords in 1986. In a way the interview foreshadowed some of the Anglo-centric and anti-European thoughts that would land Denning in difficulty the following year with *The Spectator*, though one difference was that Knight openly agreed with Denning's views and Denning did not say anything as offensive as he was later to do about any particular individual or group.

On the day of his ninetieth birthday itself, a dinner was held in his honour at Lincoln's Inn. It was attended by eighty-five benchers including Princess Margaret, the Royal Bencher. Denning told the press that he intended to carry on with his good works: 'I'm very well, apart from no end of weaknesses. My eyesight is bad, my hearing is bad, my walking is bad, I creep along very slowly with two sticks. But I hope my mind is alright still'.[35] He recalled his recent clashes with the local authority over footpaths and byways: 'They want to turn a lot of our country lanes into ways for motorists. I'm not having that'. But he conceded there would be no more appearances in court or in the House of Lords debating chamber, due to his failing health. 'For one thing, I can't hear and it isn't much good going into court if you can't hear. So what I do is I put it down. I write a lot of papers'. He had been told not to travel to London by train, and 'I find it such an awful business getting in and out by car. It tires me more than anything'. Looking back over how the world had changed during his lifetime, he expressed regret about the decline of marriage and religion, but relief in the emancipation of women and, reflecting on his experiences as a pioneering member of the jet set, the growth in the speed of transport.

At the time his works included resisting plans to close the village primary school at Upton Grey, Hampshire. He criticised the local authority as being motivated only by wishing to profit from the sale of the land. He also opposed plans to extract gravel from a site close to the River Test, contending that his own land should receive protected environmental status. Naturally, he combined the modern notion of environmentalism with a classical quote from Tennyson's *The Brook*: 'Men may come and men may go, but I go on forever', adding 'That's what our River Test says. We disappear, but the river goes on forever' – the same quote he had used when defiantly refusing to retire after his eightieth birthday.

If 1989 had contained instances of Denning on his best form, 1990 brought a series of increasingly unfortunate events. In March, he was reported as saying that ageing former Nazis should not face trial because no jury would convict them, and even if they did a judge would be bound not to impose a sentence of imprisonment.[36] Obviously, the war veteran Denning would have had no sympathy with Britain's former enemies, still less with the regime for which those enemies fought, but as an elderly man himself by then it seemed he felt so far removed from the events of his youth that he considered others of a similar age should no longer be held responsible for their actions in wartime nearly half a century earlier. That argument might pass muster for many crimes, but would be harder to justify in the case of Nazi atrocities – at least for anyone who had held a position of authority, rather than ordinary Wehrmacht soldiers or low-level Nazi Party functionaries. No one who has seen footage of witnesses at the trial of Adolph Eichmann could question the right of the victims of that regime to see justice done, however belatedly.

In May, Reg died at the age of ninety-five. Denning told a newspaper he felt 'desolate' but once more praised Reg's courage, as shown by his service during the First World War.[37] In the same month Denning appeared on the BBC interviewed by the journalist Bruce Parker, traversing much of his life and career.

Denning's third negative event in 1990 prompted greater controversy, which would foreshadow – and to some extent inform – the maelstrom he would shortly find himself in with *The Spectator* magazine. Three men had stood trial in 1988 for conspiracy to murder the Home Secretary, Tom King. All three exercised their right to silence. Towards the end of the trial, King said in Parliament that the government intended to change the law concerning that right. Denning was interviewed on television and said he supported the change. All defendants were found guilty, but in 1990 their convictions were quashed by the Court of Appeal. Their lordships held, *inter alia*:[38]

> The statements of Mr King and Lord Denning, which were powerfully made, were on the face of general application (sic), but had a particular relevance to the trial of the accused. Their Lordships were left with the definite impression that the impact which the statements made in the television interviews may well have had on the fairness of the trial could not be overcome by any direction to the jury and that the only way in which justice could have been done and have been seen to be done is by discharging the jury and ordering a retrial.

One wonders if a retired judge of lesser fame would have been held to have had the same influence. Denning was livid. He wrote to *The Times* railing that he had effectively been convicted of contempt of court with no opportunity of answering the charge.[39] Subsequently, however, he wrote again to *The Times* clarifying that he did not think the defendants were guilty, and thus the quashing of the verdict had in fact been appropriate.

On a more positive note, in 1990 the first biography of Denning appeared, written by Edmund Heward,[40] a former Chief Master of the

Chancery Division. The book was a concise account of Denning's life and career. Necessarily constrained by the length of a single volume, it sensibly did not attempt a comprehensive analysis of Denning's cases, but did offer some analysis and conclusions. In his preface, Heward wrote that Lord Denning was 'bold and innovative, wished to restate the law in accordance with established principles and hated the restrictions imposed by precedent'.

Predictably, Denning's inveterate critic Professor John Griffith was not impressed:[41]

> That is as fine a statement of contradictions as you are likely to meet in a summary of one man's endeavour. To be innovative and yet to restate, to restate and yet to rely on established principles, to rely on established principles and yet to find precedents restrictive, all this adds up to doing what you like and finding a label for every act, a subtitle for every position, a general proposition for every idiosyncrasy.

And yet, Heward had encapsulated the contradictions of Denning accurately – Denning was concerned to uphold the common law, but also to do justice, and if the latter required bending the stricter interpretations of the former, then, as far as Denning was concerned, so be it.

Heward had access to Denning himself, as well as many of Denning's legal contemporaries who have since died. That gave him the advantage of accessing many primary sources, with the concomitant disadvantage that on occasions he became arguably too close to his subject. Further, the sympathy which a personal relationship would have elicited was exacerbated by the difference in status between author and subject. It would have been unthinkable for a Chancery master to take the Master of the Rolls to task in court, and Heward's book suggested that it was not much easier in retirement. His treatment of the Profumo Affair, for example, was perfunctory and almost wholly exculpatory of Denning's procedural failings – in other words, a whitewash of Denning's establishment whitewash. He also omitted mention of Denning's offensive remarks about Irish prisoners, something that did not go unnoticed by Irish reviewers.[42]

Heward was more even-handed with Denning's resignation fiasco, stating that Denning 'had no colour prejudice'[43] – not quite the whole story, as we have seen – and attempted to downplay the affair by stating that it amounted to 'A couple of unguarded remarks, suggested by a member of the Western circuit'. That was simply wrong: the same remarks appeared on two occasions – the prepared Mansion House speech and later the book – and were therefore not unguarded or 'off the cuff'.

Nevertheless, the book was not uncritical. Perhaps the most cutting passage was: 'A serious criticism of him is that he lacked intellectual honesty; this certainly took second place to justice'.[44] Denning in response would have doubled down on the need for justice, but that would still have left him vulnerable to the clichéd point that everyone is in favour of justice until someone tries to define it. Or, as Griffith put it, 'Denning acquired a reputation as a protector of individual rights but the record is, to put it mildly, ambiguous. As usual, it depends whose rights you want to protect'.[45]

Denning continued to try to protect rights as and where he found a worthy cause, including helping the Upper Clatford Parish Council in a dispute with Hampshire County Council relating to the reclassification of a road as a byway open to all traffic.[46] On one occasion he had to withdraw a claim when it was made clear that it was without merit. After a discreet meeting in which Denning agreed to drop the action, Joan caught the attention of the defendants' solicitor: 'I do wish he would stop all this', she whispered.[47] He also kept writing letters, including one to the *Daily Telegraph* in which, referring back to his famous judgment at the dawn of Britain's entry into the European Economic Community as it then was, he stated 'No longer is European law an incoming tide flowing up the estuaries of England. It is now like a tidal wave, bringing down our sea-walls and flowing inland over our fields and houses – to the dismay of all'.[48]

The worst of Denning's misfortunes in 1990 took place in the summer, when a journalist from *The Spectator*, AN Wilson, conducted an interview with him which was to prove almost as damaging to his reputation as *What Next in the Law?*

The interview began with Denning talking about his childhood and time at Oxford, before some antediluvian chuntering in which he deplored the decline of marriage and said how he disapproved of homosexuality and non-traditional family structures, even if he did not think any should be illegal.[49] There was the man born in the nineteenth century, showing his age in both outmoded attitudes and a lack of discretion.

The interview continued with discussion about access to justice and some thoughts about miscarriages of justice. Denning said he thought the death penalty should be retained for murder most foul, and referred to campaigns for the release of the Birmingham Six. He admitted that there was always a danger of hanging the wrong person, and in reply Wilson referred specifically to the Guildford Four. Denning said they would 'probably' have hanged the right men, but 'Not proved against them, that's all'.

Denning went on to an attack on the European Union. It contained a flavouring of xenophobia, including an anti-Semitic slur against the politician and former barrister, Leon Brittan, whom Denning called a 'German Jew' as well as denigrating his ability as a barrister.

On the face of it, Denning had recanted his disapproval of the death penalty as expressed a few years earlier in his books and in the interview with John Mortimer mentioned earlier in this chapter. That showed the effects of ageing more than anything else, with Denning obviously more muddled and cantankerous than he had been a decade before.

More importantly, though, his comments about the Birmingham Six and Guildford Four were offensive and wrong. At the time of the interview, few still supported the Birmingham Six's convictions and they were formally acquitted the following year (a verdict which Denning accepted), while the Guildford Four had already been acquitted and released. Both cases came to be viewed rightly as shameful miscarriages of justice and a serious blow to the British government's claim for moral superiority over the IRA. Denning's views on Leon Brittan were as offensive as they were factually incorrect.

In the immediate aftermath of the interview, Denning started to have doubts about what he had said. He asked Wilson for the transcript of the interview. Wilson said it was not usual to provide one, but did send him three pages, crucially omitting a fourth which contained some of the more inflammatory remarks.

Once the interview was published, reaction in the press was swift and damning. The Guildford Four instructed lawyers to prepare for a libel action. *The Spectator* published a retraction and apology,[50] following which the threat of litigation was dropped. Denning and *The Spectator* agreed to pay the costs. The solicitor for one of the Guildford Four, Paul Hill, said: 'Paul Hill has been happy to accept the retraction and apology on the basis that *The Spectator* has been helpful to his case in the past and Lord Denning is now an old man who has made inconsistent statements about the case'.[51] *The Times*, somewhat more charitably, ascribed the affair to Denning's old age and provided some ironic mitigation for Denning by stating that he should no longer be taken as seriously as he wished.[52]

Denning maintained that his comments about Brittan had been 'chatty asides'.[53] Nonetheless, to try to limit the fallout, he appeared on a programme aimed at the Jewish community, broadcast on Spectrum Radio, a multi-ethnic radio network. He was told squarely by the interviewer, Harvey Kass, that his comments about Brittan could be interpreted as anti-Semitic. Denning replied:[54]

> I am most distressed that those words of mine should have been used by *The Spectator* magazine in that way. They were entirely out of

context. And I would like to take this opportunity through you to apologise to Sir Leon Brittan for any distress caused to him and certainly to all my many friends in the Jewish community in England.

I've been a friend of Israel. I have many friends there: I've visited it twice and think it one of the most delightful countries in the whole world.

Denning emphasised that he had only intended to assail the European Commission as an institution, rather than its individual members, but *The Spectator* had edited his remarks. He conceded his comments had been damaging nonetheless and added 'that is why I regret them wholeheartedly, that I should ever have said them'. He added that Jewish refugees from Hitler's Germany had contributed a great deal in the fields of science, culture, art, law and music: 'I'd like to express my gratitude to those of that origin who came and have done so much for England'.

That was an explicit confession that Denning recognised one of the old prejudices common in his youth was no longer acceptable. Clearly, in his dotage such views could properly be called unguarded in a way that the remarks in his Lord Mayor's speech and *What Next in the Law?* could not.

The journalist and author Edward Pearce thought Denning had become his own worst enemy, prone to vanity yet clearly out of touch and with dwindling intellectual powers. He added that he did not think poor remarks made in the twilight of Denning's life would undermine his reputation, concluding that Denning would still be remembered as one of the three great judges of the twentieth century along with Lord Greene and Lord Atkin.[55]

There was no doubt Denning's remarks about the Irish and the Jews were inexcusable, all the more so as they came from a highly intelligent, educated man who had held an important public office for so many years. The explanation was that he had descended into an ageing individual who had seen the world change beyond all recognition and lost some of his judgement. That was how the Guildford Four themselves chose to see it when they professed themselves satisfied with an apology. Denning nevertheless pursued *The Spectator* for a breach of copyright about the words on the tape. The Christmas issue contained an apology from Wilson for not sending him the fourth page of the transcript (which contained the remarks about the Guildford Four) and an expression of regret regarding the distress caused to him and Joan.[56] It was some mitigation for Denning, but the indisputable offence contained in his words would leave an indelible mark on his reputation.

If 1990 had caused him distress largely brought on by himself, 1992 saw Denning suffer a crueller blow from Father Time, when Joan died. Denning was naturally devastated. Nonetheless, the inextinguishable values of service and duty which he imbibed as the son of Clara Denning had never left him, and in time he resolved to carry on with his normal routine as best he could. He received many cards and letters of sympathy for his loss, and said in his reply to each that 'if I can carry on, I must do so for a while, as she would have me do, until I have finished my work as she has finished hers'.[57]

Denning relied greatly upon his staff not just for practicalities, but also for company. By then he had the full-time attention of a live-in nurse, as well as his gardener who had worked at The Lawn for decades. Denning also retained a maid and a cook, while his former clerk, Peter Post, still performed occasional secretarial duties such as typing up letters. Robert Denning was heavily engaged with his work at Oxford and thus only able to visit occasionally with his children, but such occasions always brought Denning much joy.

In 1993, the second full-length biography of Denning was published. It was written by the solicitor Iris Freeman, herself a noteworthy lawyer who, like Denning, possessed a powerful intellect and an equally powerful work ethic. Freeman's book contained much more detail on Denning's personal life than Heward's, or indeed even Denning's own work including *The Family Story*. It will remain the most exhaustive chronicle of his personal life.

Like Heward, Freeman had the advantages and disadvantages of knowing the subject – access to him and his family as a primary source, but at the same time familiarity occasionally skewed the necessary detachment when assessing some of his life's controversies. As with Heward, Freeman gave Denning virtually a free pass for his Profumo report. When it came to his later embarrassments, she had to deal not only with *What Next in the Law?* but also with *The Spectator* interview, which she wrote about in a measured fashion. Her obituary in *The Independent* subsequently recorded that she had developed a strong friendship with Denning, despite her clear disagreement with him about the impact of large-scale immigration on England.[58] Ultimately, she came to a conclusion not dissimilar to that offered here: that Denning was a man of his time, who suffered some of the vicissitudes of old age in losing a sense of discretion and proportion.

For all that he had lost – Joan, his health and, perhaps, some of his finer judgement – Denning's intellectual powers had not been extinguished. In 1995, he contributed a foreword to a book celebrating the Test Valley,[59] in the familiar Denning prose celebrating the longevity of the villages in the valley and their descent from the time of Alfred the Great.

In September 1995, the spokesman for the common people stepped forward once more when he argued in support of an embattled chemist, Allan Sharpe. Sharpe had been selling prescriptions privately for their actual cost where that was lower than the NHS standard charge of £5.25 (at the time, some drugs cost as little as 45p). He was fined by a disciplinary panel, but Denning exhorted him to appeal and, if necessary, apply for judicial review, calling him a 'Robin Hood' figure.[60]

In April 1996, aged ninety-seven, Denning came out with his own example of the classic English suburban argument known as 'nimbyism' (which, as noted in n 40 to Chapter X, stands for 'not in my backyard'), when he fought against a car park being built on land he owned in Whitchurch. He complained:[61]

> They say they want to take about half an acre, but I very much fear that is the thin edge of the wedge. They start with that and before long they will try and extend it. They also want to come in and make a public way and destroy my garden that way.

As to the threat of a compulsory purchase order, he said: 'I don't think they have in law any power to compulsory purchase. I have asked them for details but I have not received an answer'.

On 3 December 1996 came Denning's final contributions to the House of Lords in Parliament. He had submitted two written questions, deriving from his interest in English history and the original function of the Master of the Rolls. The first wondered whether Lord Nelson's will made before Trafalgar was kept among the public records. The Lord Chancellor, Lord Mackay, confirmed that it was, and could be viewed both on microfilm and, by special permission, in its original form. Denning's second question asked about the future of the old Public Records Office building in Chancery Lane. At the time no firm answer could be given, though it was later taken over by King's College London for their library, something of which Denning would have strongly approved.[62]

In 1997, Denning was awarded the Order of Merit.[63] He was too frail to travel to London and so a representative of the Queen, Sir Edward Ford, travelled to Whitchurch to present it to him. Sir Edward found Denning on fine form intellectually, speaking with charm and eloquence about his life and work.[64] In the same year, a 1989 lecture of Denning's entitled 'The Influence of Religion on Law' was published as a pamphlet by the Canadian Institute for Law, Theology & Public Policy.[65] The work reiterated much of what Denning had said over the years regarding concepts of truth, oath-taking and good faith, and their application to contracts, promises and criminal responsibility. As ever, he had an eye for history, saying of James I and the *Prohibitions del Roy* (1607) 77 ER 1342, 'Those words of Bracton, quoted by Coke, "The King is under God and the law", epitomise in one sentence the great contribution made by the common lawyers to the constitution of England'.

Centenary

On 23 January 1999 Denning turned 100. He received telegrams from both the Queen and the Queen Mother. A choir sang 'Happy Birthday' and All Hallows Church in Whitchurch, the fount of Denning's resolute Christian faith, had a new bell named 'Great Tom' cast in his honour. He received mentions in the daily news, the BBC giving a short biography which noted that he was struggling with daily life due to his age, being registered blind, reliant on a hearing aid and needing two residential nurses to assist him, but concluded that he could be assured his legacy in the law would last for many years.[66]

Visitors to The Lawn that day included Lord Goff of Chieveley. The incumbent Master of the Rolls, Lord Woolf, arranged for all members of the Court of Appeal to sign a birthday card and to contribute to a gift. Peter Post sent the following note by way of thanks to each of the judges:[67]

> When Lord Denning celebrated his 100th birthday recently, he received many cards, messages and letters which have all been read and described to him. He particularly treasured those from the Court of Appeal but regrettably, due to his virtual blindness and considerable frailty, he is unable to write personally to thank each for their remembrance of his very special occasion, and has asked me to do so for him. His son, Professor Denning, is writing separately to the Master of the Rolls to express his father's gratitude for the presentation made in Whitchurch on 30th January by Lord Woolf. Lord Denning was delighted that no less than 37 signatures were on his card, which evoked the spontaneous comment 'Far more than in my day!' Please accept his sincere thanks.

Denning was presented with a booklet by Hampshire County Council, entitled 'Lord Denning: A Hampshire Man', compiled by Rosemary Dunhill, the county archivist. It contained a short biographical sketch along with pictures and extracts from the council's archives, to which Denning had donated many of his papers and pictures.[68]

The University of Buckingham Law School held a symposium on the day to celebrate his life and work. Denning sent an apology explaining that he was 'too decrepit to travel now', though he offered his best wishes. The symposium had numerous experts reviewing Denning's legal legacy, including Lord Woolf MR. Several of the main contributors had earlier written chapters for Jowell and McAuslan's book. In the evening following the symposium the Law Students Society of Buckingham University held a dinner for the participants, with an address by Sir Richard Scott, Vice-Chancellor.[69] The papers presented were collected and published in a special edition of the *Denning Law Journal*.[70] One especially notable contribution was from the Australian judge Sir Michael Kirby. His Honour's appreciation showed the strength of Denning's name beyond the shores of England and Wales, and he explicitly endorsed Denning's reforming spirit:[71]

> We, his successors throughout the world, are not mechanics of the law. We are a profession sworn to justice. That is what gives the law its claim to moral nobility. This remains Denning's great instruction to us. ... But every judicial officer of the common law, high and low, is reminded by Denning's life and work that creativity is part of the genius of our vocation. We must explain this to each succeeding generation of lawyers, as Denning, by his example and ceaseless efforts, tried to do.

Another significant and lasting tribute in 1999 was the founding of Lincoln's Inn's Denning Society. As explained by the Society's website:[72]

> At Lord Denning's request, membership of the Society is restricted to members of Lincoln's Inn who hold scholarships or bursaries. The Society seeks to perpetuate his memory, by providing a forum for its members to meet and mix with all age groups on three major occasions each year; a summer reception, an autumn lecture, and a dinner in January to celebrate Lord Denning's birthday. A distinguished guest speaker is invited to the latter, to which members may bring guests.

The centenary evening and the founding of the Society showed that Denning still held legendary status in the profession. Neither the passage of time nor the bad publicity concerning his offensive public remarks had diminished the legacy of a uniquely recognisable voice in the common law over an almost unprecedented length of service. Denning, pleased to have made the landmark of 100, and reassured by the knowledge that he would indeed have a remembrance in good works, perhaps now felt that in due course his shade would rest content, for the end was not long in coming.

CHAPTER XXII

The End

On 5 March 1999, Denning fell ill. He was taken to the Royal Hampshire County Hospital, where he died shortly afterwards of an internal haemorrhage. He was buried in Whitchurch Cemetery, just around the corner from his beloved All Hallows Church.[1]

The news made the national press. The obituaries were mostly – though not wholly – positive in their assessments, with varying degrees of emphasis when it came to Denning's faults or some of his more discredited rulings and opinions. The BBC called him 'perhaps the greatest law-making judge of the century and the most controversial', adding that '[h]is achievement was to shape the common law according to his own highly individual vision of society'.[2] The *Telegraph* called him 'one of the outstanding judges of the century'.[3]

Lord Justice Sedley wrote in *The Guardian*[4] that Denning's judgments, more than those of any other, spoke directly and in a compelling fashion to the ordinary reader. He called Denning's approach to making law that of a 'radical conservative' and concluded that Denning's status not simply as a judge but as an important historic figure would endure.

The Times noted Denning's controversies and had some interesting anecdotes about his character, including that he once upbraided a fellow bencher for wearing shirt sleeves on a walk in the gardens of Lincoln's Inn one summer's evening.[5] With regard to Denning's controversial resignation, *The Times* wrote in mitigation that no judge had done more during Denning's lifetime to welcome students and lawyers from the new Commonwealth into the English legal community, and no judge was more highly regarded in the English-speaking countries of Asia, Africa and the Caribbean.

The *Independent*'s obituary was by Denning's first biographer Edmund Heward, who was by and large as uncritical as he had been in his book. Of the *What Next in the Law?* controversy, Heward wrote that 'In it were some unguarded remarks on picking a jury in a recent case. The passage was interpreted as if Denning was actuated by racial prejudice'. In fact, as we saw, the reason the passage was interpreted that way was because that was the obvious interpretation. Heward wrote of the notorious *Spectator* interview with AN Wilson almost euphemistically that 'some unwise remarks ... caused controversy ... He said later that he had been quoted out of context'. 'Out of context' was no defence since there was no context which would have justified Denning's comments. The failings of advanced age were the strongest plea in mitigation for Denning.

Responding to Heward's hagiography, AN Wilson in the same newspaper was less forgiving,[6] arguing that if he had died at seventy, Denning would have had 'an unblemished reputation as one of the great libertarians of English history', but that living to 100 inevitably meant his views had become painfully outdated.

Wilson also mentioned that Denning had advised some 'ordinary churchgoers' who had a 'Disgusted of Tunbridge Wells' issue troubling them to take a private action against the Archbishop of Canterbury (the plaintiffs objected to the ordination of persons who either were or were married to divorced persons whose former spouses were still living). They did so, lost the case and then found themselves bled dry by the costs awarded against them.[7] According to Wilson, Denning was unrepentant about his incorrect advice and only complained that the Archbishop's lawyers should not have sought costs – a naïve view from anyone with legal experience, never mind a former Master of the Rolls.

Wilson concluded that Denning's reputation had never been the same since his 1990 *Spectator* interview.

A more generous tone was found in the Irish newspaper *Sunday Independent*, which published an obituary by the British journalist Geoffrey Wheatcroft. He acknowledged Denning's offensive remarks to the Irish but did so in moderate terms, claiming that there was no reason to think Denning was motivated by anti-Irish prejudice.[8]

The *Irish Independent* slated Denning's 'appalling vista' remarks but noted that he was hardly alone in his beliefs and attitudes. It added that once the Birmingham Six convictions had been quashed, Denning admitted he had been wrong, apologised and condemned the West Midlands Police. It concluded that he was not 'anti-Irish' and added that he had been 'unfailingly courteous' with Irish journalists who asked about his controversies.[9]

In the legal press, a similar range of opinions could be found, one of the strongest endorsements of Denning's work coming from the New Zealand Court of Appeal judge Sir Edmund Thomas, a judge with a reputation not wholly dissimilar from Denning's, in that he was a reforming judge who disdained slavish adherence to precedent.[10]

A memorial service was held in June 1999 at Westminster Abbey. It was attended by:

> 67 fellow judges, 13 of the 25 law lords, 33 other peers, and so many QCs that the official attendance list did not bother to register the fact after their names. Among the 1,150 congregation, barristers jostled with solicitors, legal clerks and officials from provincial law societies in the side-pews.[11]

The address was given by the Lord Chief Justice, Lord Bingham of Cornhill. He began by saying that Denning was 'the best known and best loved judge in our history', and went on:[12]

> The peculiar genius of Lord Denning was perfectly matched to the need of the hour. 'When Tom and I were young', wrote Lord Devlin, 'the law was stagnant'. In Lord Hailsham's words, 'It seemed almost as if Our Lady of the Common Law had gone into a decline ...' The age of creation appeared to have gone. That of literalists, slavish adherents of precedent and quietist acceptors of the status quo appeared to have succeeded; and the glory of the common law appeared to have been extinguished forever. That the law was aroused from its torpor was not, of course, the work of one court or one judge. The credit must be much more widely shared. But in any roll of the great emancipators Lord Denning would be assured of an honoured place, probably at the head of the list. For he brought a new, adventurous and imaginative vision to bear. He was more concerned with the intention of a statute than with its precise terminology. He was not overly respectful of precedent. He was prepared to entertain unorthodox arguments if they appeared to lead to what he saw as justice. He did not shrink from novelty. ... The secret of his attraction to the legal profession and to the general public was (...) the belief that he opened the door to the law above the law. He had, to the end, an almost uncanny insight into the thoughts and values of his fellow countrymen.

The service showed once again that despite all his foibles, prejudices and idiosyncrasies, Denning remained a towering figure in the law.

CHAPTER XXIII

A Final Judgment

Denning the judge

> The post-war years I once described as the age of law reform, legal aid and Lord Denning. None of these would have been effective without the other two. They needed each other: and together they have established a memorable era in the long history of English law.
>
> *Lord Scarman*[1]

The style

> Lord Denning possessed star quality as a summarizer, an evoker of mood, a dispenser of analysis and judgement and wielder of a pen so potent that it has stimulated a degree of reaction almost as pungent as his own prose.
>
> *Peter Hennessey, Winds of Change: Britain in the Early Sixties*

Not many readers will have picked up this book without already being aware of Denning's unique, often homely writing style.[2] His prose would have ensured lasting fame for his judgments even if he had otherwise been wholly conventional in his legal methods and conclusions. As we saw, the style took some time to evolve, with the familiar combination of homily, story-telling and staccato simplicity only reaching its apogee after he was appointed Master of the Rolls.[3] One suspects that was no coincidence: before then he was either a junior judge or a junior member of an appellate division, necessarily more deferential to authority and convention. His sentences were always short, though in his early judicial days they almost always contained a verb and frequently included subclauses, two features regularly absent from his later judgments.

Once he became Master of the Rolls, he clearly felt he was in a position of almost unassailable authority, free to set his own course. The touches of storytelling that had appeared in earlier cases became routine. The most notable feature was the opening paragraph or paragraphs. The academic Cameron Harvey[4] identified nine sub-categories of the Denning 'opener': the intriguing opener ('It all started in a public house'); the historical opener ('Today we look back far in time to a town or village green'); the fatal and deadly opener ('A man's head got caught in a propeller. He was decapitated and killed'); the 'This is the case' opener ('This is the case of three smugglers'); the editorial opener ('Counsel for the vendor referred to this case as a comedy of errors. It is no comedy but a history of errors'); the non sequitur opener ('Many years ago Sir Edward Coke had a case about six carpenters. Now we have a case about six car-hire drivers'); the 'This is an interesting case' opener ('This is a short but fortunately a very rare point'); the whimsical opener ('A gigantic ship was used for a gigantic fraud') the picturesque opener ('In summertime village cricket is the delight of everyone. Nearly every village has its own cricket field where the young men play and the old men watch').

With due respect to Mr Harvey, separating the nine categories was probably overanalysing Denning. Denning was essentially doing the same thing each time – setting out a 'hook' in journalistic terms to draw the readers in, and to lead them to the same conclusion about the justice of the case that he himself had reached. Whether it was in the style of a cod-historical mystery, or intentionally shocking the reader, or making a play on words, the intention was the same – to catch the reader's attention and direct his or her sympathies.

Denning himself described his method as making the judgment 'live' so it could be understood, and somewhat immodestly likened his openings to Chorus in *Henry V*.[5] He stated that he tried to put the merits into the facts because that showed which way justice lay.

One might question whether describing parties by names as opposed to descriptors such as 'defendant' was advisable. Neutral descriptors give the appearance of impartiality and separate the summary of facts from the determination of the merits, whereas the Denning style was to present the facts deliberately in a manner which would lead readers to agree with him about the merits.

Memorable as they were, there were three more significant problems with Denning's 'classic openings'. First, by creating such a readily identifiable personal stamp, decisions tended almost invariably to be associated only with Denning himself, even when he was in the appeal courts and hence sitting with two or more other judges. It meant he was unfairly given sole credit for popular decisions and unfairly lumped with the sole blame for unpopular ones. The most painful example of the latter, as we saw, was his decision in the 'Birmingham Six' case of *McIlkenny*, but there were many others – his more controversial trade union cases, for example.

The second problem was that Denning's attempted manipulation of the reader's sympathy was inconsistent with the appearance of judicial impartiality. That was so whether or not one agreed with the result he reached. However famous his opening passage in *Miller v Jackson* became, it was not universally acclaimed.[6] By beginning 'In summertime village cricket is the delight of everyone' Denning was setting up the Millers pejoratively, as the villains of the piece. The majority of readers might have instinctively sided with the club for doing nothing more than the same activity it had been engaged in for decades. But he could have made the same point without unflatteringly painting the Millers as killjoys.

The third problem, which applied to all of his judgments, not simply the openings, was that his rhetorical style could become a distraction from the point at issue. In *HL Bolton (Engineering) Co Ltd v T J Graham & Sons Ltd (Matter No M 1678 OA 18)* [1957] 1 QB 159 at 172, for example, he described a company's controlling mind in the following terms:

> A company may in many ways be likened to a human body. It has a brain and nerve centre which controls what it does. It also has hands which hold the tools and act in accordance with the directions from the centre. Some of the people in the company are mere servants and agents who are nothing more than the hands to do the work and cannot be said to represent the mind or the will. Others are directors and managers who represent the mind and directing will of the company, and control what it does. The state of mind of these managers is the state of mind of the company and is treated by the law as such.

That approach found favour with the House of Lords in *Tesco Supermarkets v Nattress* [1972] AC 153. Much later, however, Lord Hoffmann, giving the judgment of the Privy Council in *Meridian Global Funds Management Asia Ltd v Securities Commission* [1995] 2 AC 500 at 509, stated 'this anthropomorphism, by the very power of the image, distracts attention from the purpose for which Viscount Haldane LC[7] said he was using the notion of directing mind and will'. A textbook on company law was harsher, calling Denning's description an 'indulgence in some medieval anthropomorphism'.[8]

As much as it contributed to his enduring popularity, and gained him many admirers[9] as well as critics,[10] on balance Denning's story-telling style was more harmful than helpful to his reputation. It made his name – but judges should not need names, at least not for idiosyncrasies of style rather than the substance of their judgments.

Those criticisms aside, Denning's writing style still had much to commend it, chiefly its brevity and clarity. Modern judgments are in general much longer than in his time, in part because of the cut-and-paste ease of citation (worse even than its predecessor of the 'photocopying disease'), and partly because modern legal research facilities enable ready access to far more authorities than in the pre-digital age. Longer skeleton arguments and more authorities cited to the court lead inevitably to longer judgments. If counsel cite reams of authority, judges will feel compelled to deal with them, especially those at first instance, fearing appeal.

Denning's judgments, on the other hand, were rarely too long, for three reasons. First, his career only coincided with the dawn of the photocopying age, and mostly pre-dated the digital age.[11] Secondly, he was never bothered by the prospect of an appeal. Thirdly, he was sufficiently confident not to be weighed down by a sea of authorities presented to him. His early work on *Smith's Leading Cases* would also have honed his ability to sift through judgments to find what was on point.

In terms of clarity, Denning's judgments remain a relief compared not just with many other judgments but also with some of the more turgid legal documents of different sorts one encounters from time to time. In *Oxonica Energy Ltd v Neuftec Ltd* [2008] EWHC 2127 (Pat), Peter Prescott QC said with some exasperation:

> The secret of drafting legal documents was best described by Nicolas Boileau, who was not only a literary critic but a qualified lawyer: '*Ce que l'on conçoit bien s'énonce clairement et les mots pour le dire arrivent aisément*'. What one conceives well can be stated with clarity and the words to say it come easily. We should all have that framed and displayed on our desks.

Denning might, indeed, have had that aphorism as a sign on his desk.

We should add one qualification: while one can certainly appreciate a well-written passage as opposed to poor grammar, needless complexity, or use of jargon where none is necessary, the point can be taken too far. Denning himself overstated things when he disdained reference to pleadings and orders as 'mere lawyer's stuff'.[12] He knew better than most that law was an expertise. Dismissive talk of 'mere lawyer's stuff' makes no more sense than dismissing technical terms in *Gray's Anatomy* as 'mere doctor's stuff'.[13] If one removed all technical terms from judgments then, to use another example from poetry, one might end up with the same paradox as the captain in Lewis Carroll's *The Hunting of the Snark*. He was acclaimed by his crew for finally producing a map they could all understand, without all the usual incomprehensible symbols – the only problem being the map was 'a perfect and absolute blank'.

Statutory interpretation

We saw when looking at Denning's first stint in the Court of Appeal how he clashed with Lord Simonds over his 'purposive' approach versus the latter's 'literal' approach to statutory interpretation.[14] Despite being told in *Magor and St Mellons RDC v Newport Corporation* [1952] AC 189 that he was attempting 'a naked usurpation of the legislative function', Denning was undeterred. If anything, his views hardened. Much later, in *Nothman v London Borough of Barnet* [1978] 1 All ER 1243, he wrote:

> The literal method is now completely out-of-date. It has been replaced by the approach which Lord Diplock described as the 'purposive' approach. He said so in *Kammins Ballrooms Co Ltd v Zenith Investments (Torquay) Ltd* ([1971] AC 850 at 881); and it was recommended by Sir David Renton and his colleagues in their valuable report entitled 'The Preparation of Legislation'. In all cases now in the interpretation of statutes we adopt such a construction as will 'promote the general legislative purpose underlying the provision'. It is no longer necessary for the judges to wring their hands and say: 'There is nothing we can do about it.' Whenever the strict interpretation of a statute gives rise to an absurd and unjust situation, the judges can and should use their good sense to remedy it – by reading words in, if necessary – so as to do what Parliament would have done had they had the situation in mind.

By and large posterity has adjudged Denning the victor, given that the leading text on statutory interpretation subsequently declared '[i]n the sense used in English law, purposive construction is an almost invariable requirement ... it is only where the literal (non-purposive) meaning is too strong to be overborne that the court will apply a non-purposive and literal construction'.[15]

Nevertheless, one thing Denning never achieved during his time on the Bench was the ability for counsel and the court openly to refer to *Hansard* as an aid to interpretation when arguing or considering an Act. Or at least he never achieved it as a general rule; in the usual Denning way he was minded to do so disarmingly openly when he felt it appropriate. Thus, in *R v Greater London Council, ex parte Blackburn* [1976] 3 All ER 184 at 189, he said:

> I propose to look at *Hansard* to find out. I know that we are not supposed to do this. But the Law Commission looked at *Hansard*. So did Lord Diplock in *Knuller (Publishing, Printing and Promotions) Ltd v Director of Public Prosecutions* [1973] AC at 480. So I have looked at *Hansard* to refresh my memory.[16]

Many years after he retired, Denning's wish came true in *Pepper v Hart* [1993] AC 593, where the House of Lords declared there were indeed circumstances under which *Hansard* might be consulted, although the decision was not universally acclaimed.[17]

Precedent

Lord Bingham once described the doctrine of precedent as 'a cornerstone of our legal system'.[18] That cornerstone caused Denning a certain amount of controversy throughout his judicial career.

Outwardly at least, Denning normally accepted the basic principle of the rule of precedent – that decisions of superior courts were binding on lower courts – but he would always try to avoid the binding effect of any decision which would compel him to produce what he saw as an unjust result. The most stark examples we saw earlier included *Scruttons Ltd v Midland Silicones Ltd* [1962] AC 446, when (in his own words) he was 'judicially beheaded' by Viscount Simonds for his heterodoxy, and *Cassell & Co Ltd v Broome* [1972] AC 1027, in which he decided that a recent decision of the House of Lords had been wrongly determined.

We also saw how Lord Hailsham LC in the latter case replied emphatically 'in the hierarchical system of courts which exists in this country, it is necessary for each lower tier, including the Court of Appeal, to accept loyally the decisions of the higher tiers'. Denning's subsequent rejoinder was 'What do you mean by the "decision" of the higher court?' (*Paal Wilson & Co A/S v Partenreederei Hannah Blumenthal, The Hannah Blumenthal* [1983] 1 AC 854 at 873).

Much later, Leggatt LJ in *R (Youngsam) v Parole Board* [2019] EWCA Civ 229 quoted the above exchange and expanded upon it with an orthodox description of the concept of precedent. His lordship gave a non-exhaustive list of the factors which might lead a court to reassess the ratio of an apparently binding earlier case:

[59] ... (1) the degree of unanimity or consensus among the judges (assuming there was more than one) who decided the precedent case; (2) the clarity or otherwise of the ruling and of the supporting reasoning; (3) whether or to what extent the point on which the court ruled was in dispute and/or the subject of argument; (4) whether or how clearly the court evinced an intention to establish a binding rule; (5) whether and to what extent prior relevant authorities were considered by the court; (6) whether the court would, or sensibly could, have reached the same result if it had not ruled as it did; (7) whether the court's ruling has been applied or approved in later cases; (8) whether the ruling or its underlying reasoning has been criticised by commentators or by judges in later cases; (9) whether the court considered or contemplated the factual situation that has arisen in the current case; and (10) the level in the court hierarchy of the court which decided the precedent case in comparison with the level of the court deciding the current case.

Yet Denning did not confine himself to declining to follow earlier cases when the factors identified by Leggatt LJ applied. We saw he was openly hostile to having to follow earlier decisions when, as he saw it, social conditions had changed. His problem (except when he was in the House of Lords) was that he was bound to follow earlier decisions of the Court of Appeal, mediaeval chains or not. The rule binding the Court of Appeal to itself was set out in *Young v Bristol Aeroplane Co Ltd* [1944] KB 718 at 729–30, where Lord Greene MR stated that the Court of Appeal was obliged to follow one of its previous decisions unless: (i) there are two conflicting decisions (in which case it was free to choose between them); (ii) the decision 'cannot ... stand' with a decision of the House of Lords; or (iii) the decision 'was given *per incuriam*' (in other words, decided without reference to a statutory provision or an applicable earlier judgment).[19] Towards the end of his judicial career, in *Davis v Johnson* [1979] AC 264, Denning took on the rule in *Young* squarely – and lost.

Denning still tried with varying degrees of success to evade authorities with which he disagreed. Sometimes he flat out ignored them, as in *Nippon Yusen Kaisha v Karageorgis* [1975] 1 WLR 1093 where he ignored *Lister v Stubbs* (1890) 45 Ch D 1. Then, when confronted with the *Lister* decision in the subsequent *Mareva* case itself, he evaded it by relying on a statutory discretion, even though *Lister* had been decided when identical statutory wording was in force. Other times Denning would simply dismiss an earlier judgment as wrongly decided and barely trouble with any counter-reasoning, as in *Dyson Holdings v Fox* [1976] QB 503. In *Solle v Butcher* [1950] 1 KB 671 he 'reinterpreted' a recent decision of the House of Lords in a way which was not overturned for more than fifty years. In *Verrall v Great Yarmouth BC* [1981] All ER 839 at 843 he brushed aside one authority as 'quite out of date'. And, in *London Transport v Betts* [1958] 2 All ER 636 at 655, he dismissed an earlier decision that involved an issue with a paint shop by stating that it 'may be binding ... if there is another such paint shop anywhere but it is not in my opinion binding for anything else'.

Outside court, Denning was usually frank about his approach and his priorities. Speaking in the House of Lords in support of the Bill which created the Law Commission, he stated: [20]

> Each generation has its duty to keep the law in conformity with the needs of the time. Indeed, its function, as I would see it, is first to see that justice is done according to the law. The law should be such that it meets with the approval of the right-thinking members of the community, and only second to that would I put certainty.

Denning would have thought the Law Commission might complement his own reforming efforts. We should note that one problem with relying on judges to develop the law (even if one agrees with Denning's concept of the reforming judge) is that they cannot do so unless an appropriate case is before them, which in turn depends on whether someone is prepared to fund litigation on the speculative basis that the judges will change the law to provide the desired outcome.

Denning especially felt that if there was no statutory obstacle, then he should not hold back in creating new rights and remedies where it was in the interests of justice to do so. Famously, in *Packer v Packer* [1954] P 15 at 22, he said:

> What is the argument on the other side? Only this, that no case has been found in which it has been done before. That argument does not appeal to me in the least. If we never do anything which has not been done before, we shall never get anywhere. The law will stand still whilst the rest of the world goes on: and that will be bad for both.

That was clearly the spirit which informed *High Trees* among many other cases. The question that always followed was what amounted to 'justice' in any particular case. In Denning's case, the answer was derived from the values taught to him at home, school and church. And of those three, it was the church that was the most important, given Denning's lifelong attendance and unwavering faith.

A Final Judgment

No religion, no morality, no law

> What was it that informed Lord Denning? It was his notion of Christian justice.
>
> *Andrea Minichiello Williams,*
> *founder and director of The Christian Legal Centre*[21]

Throughout his career Denning referred to the Christian faith as the foundation of the common law, just as it was the foundation of his home life. He famously said on numerous occasions 'Without religion there can be no morality: and without morality there can be no law'.[22] Three slight qualifications should be made. First, as we saw when discussing family law, Denning asserted that, unlike his fellow judge Wallington J, who was a devout Catholic, he did not make judgments according to his faith, but only the law. Secondly, Denning would have been aware of the famous case of *Bowman v Secular Society* [1917] AC 406, which made explicitly clear the separation of church and state for the purposes of the common law. Thirdly, Denning was predominately a believer in freedom of religion, though curiously he thought that principle was strengthened, not weakened, by the Church of England's establishment status,[23] and on one occasion, when concerned about the rise of religious cults, he proposed the most illiberal measure of requiring 'religions' to register with the state – an idea *The Times* justifiably called 'appalling'.[24]

Denning did not, therefore, attempt to transpose ecclesiastical law into the common law, or to substitute the Bible for the law reports. Further, in his Hamlyn lectures, he dismissed the law of blasphemy as a 'dead letter', on the ground that blasphemy assumed that 'a denial of Christianity was liable to shake the fabric of society, which was itself founded upon the Christian religion',[25] but that danger no longer existed.[26] Nevertheless, in his search for justice in every case before him, he was chiefly guided by Christian principles. He was always a regular churchgoer and his faith never wavered. He held several posts as a churchwarden and belonged to Christian organisations for many years. And, whether inside or outside the courtroom, he sought to apply the values and beliefs from the church in every situation he faced personally as well as professionally.

He applied those values and beliefs to family law, to the place of women in society in general, and to the law and morals of sex. His stuttering alterations of his views on the role of women mirrored the fits and starts of the Church of England through the twentieth century on that front. What would nowadays be called his homophobia was a direct result of the attitude of the Church of England. Christianity also underpinned Denning's loathing of pornography and his disapproval of sex outside marriage, unmarried and single parents, but it equally underpinned the more charitable stance he sometimes took, as we saw with *Sydall v Castings Ltd* [1966] 3 All ER 770.

Away from family law, Denning's faith created and maintained his sense of right and wrong. It led to the *High Trees* case where he held that promises should be made legally binding. It informed his decisions where he saw an individual being oppressed by the state, or conversely where he saw the individual as undeserving of state assistance because he or she had not conformed to the proper moral code, as in *Gaskin v Liverpool City Council* [1980] 1 WLR 1549. More broadly, it empowered him (as he saw it) not to be confined to strict, literal interpretations of legal documents of any form. In a 1953 lecture entitled 'The influence of religion on law',[27] he said 'I cannot help thinking that the literal interpretation of contracts and statutes is a departure from real truth. It makes words the master of men instead of the servant'.

In *The Road to Justice*,[28] Denning began with the stark proclamation: 'The legal profession, by its exponents in days past and present, must account for every injustice done in the name of the law'. He then repeated what he had said to the Lawyers' Christian Fellowship in 1954:[29]

> So I ask you to accept with me that law is concerned with justice and that religion is concerned with justice. And thence I asked the question - what is justice? That question has been asked by many men far wiser than you or I and no one has yet found a satisfactory answer. All I would suggest is that justice is not something you can see. It is not temporal but eternal. How does one know what is justice? It is not the product of his intellect but of his spirit. Religion concerns the spirit in man whereby he is able to recognise what is justice, whereas law is only the application, however imperfectly, of justice in our everyday affairs. If religion perishes in the land, truth and justice will also. We have already strayed too far from the faith of our fathers. Let us return to it, for it is the only thing that can save us.

That said, even for those who shared Denning's faith, there would have been ample room for dispute about its application from case to case. Denning's resistance to large scale Commonwealth immigration, for example, as shown by the hard line he took on immigration cases, might be said to have been at odds with the Biblical parable of the Good Samaritan. His changing views on the death penalty over the years showed that one could read the Bible either way on point – 'thou shall not kill' in the Ten

Commandments versus the substantial amount of killing that seemed authorised in the Old Testament along with the 'eye for an eye' philosophy. And, in the world of black letter law, his opposition to exemption clauses might be said to have been contrary to the church's teaching on personal responsibility and a man's word as his bond.

Such inconsistencies reflected the fact that the Church of England's views evolved considerably over Denning's lifetime (as before and since), and that the Bible was not drafted as a statutory code, but rather allowed for differing interpretations. A similarly shifting sand quality characterised the other important feature of Denning's identity, his sense of 'Englishness'.

For he is an Englishman

The standards, attitudes, and general culture with which Denning was imbued as he grew up were those of England of the late Victorian and the Edwardian periods. That much was well understood by his contemporaries. In 1984, the academic MDA Freeman undertook a comprehensive review of Denning in family law and argued that Denning's character, and in particular the contradictions in his attitudes and judgments, were down to his peculiar 'Englishness':[30]

> He has been both a harbinger of, and a catalyst for, reform. He has at times also been a bastion of reaction. It is unnecessary to resolve these conflicts: Lord Denning is, and will remain, a living paradox. And yet they can be resolved. The two sides of Lord Denning use two sides of his 'Englishness': an innate sense of justice coupled with a traditionalism that at times gives rise to moral fundamentalism. He may not be the 'greatest living Englishman'[31] but he is the very epitome of what being 'English' involves.

In Denning's childhood, as we saw, English superiority and the concept of 'Englishness' were taken for granted. Both popular and 'serious' literature of the time was full not simply of admirable notions of fair play, manners, chivalry and scientific inquiry, but also, less admirably, naked prejudice. The 'boys' stories' of Percival Gibbon, GA Henty and later WE Johns and HC 'Sapper' McNeile were derring-do tales of empire, conquest and dishing it out to Britain's enemies, while the famous 1911 edition of the *Encyclopaedia Britannica*, supposedly the apogee of scholarship of the time, contained blatant racism that would be shocking to modern readers. In light of the pervasiveness of such attitudes in his formative years, the surprise is not so much that Denning made unacceptable remarks later in his life, but that he did not make more.

Outdated attitudes aside, the values of the Victorian and Edwardian society in Britain were also responsible for Denning's more admirable traits including his adamantine sense of morality, duty and public service, along with his disdain for materialism and his commitment to the rule of law.

The qualities of diffidence, compromise and rejection of extremism that characterised the Anglican Church for much of the twentieth century were shared by Denning. Hence he was able to have the necessary cognitive dissonance to reach so apparently contrary decisions, especially in the matrimonial field where one day he would be carving out new rights for women, and the next day dismissing homemaking as worthless in monetary terms because it was what women were supposed to be doing anyway.

MDA Freeman and others might have called that the stereotypically English method of 'muddling through'. Whether England or the English had a monopoly on that approach, and whether it still describes the English (however so-defined) is another question.[32] By 1999, Freeman had disowned the idea of 'Englishness' as his own explanation of Denning. Instead, he repeated the paradox of Denning being a harbinger of reform and at the same time 'a bastion of reaction', and then quoted another writer ascribing those conflicts to Denning's 'Englishness' rather than his own earlier piece.[33]

Freeman's shift in his explanation reflected the fact that by the 1990s it had become controversial, at least in academic circles, to speak of 'Englishness', a concept that had become often associated with the far-right and outdated notions of colonialism and racial or cultural superiority. That retreat by academia from notions of 'Englishness' was examined in detail by Charles Stephens in his three-volume study of Denning. He entitled his second volume *The Last of England: Lord Denning's Englishry and the Law* and concluded that at some imprecise point between Denning's retirement and the writing of his book (published in 2009) 'Englishness' as understood by Denning had ceased to exist.[34]

One cannot ignore the fact that the ideas of England and Englishness were central to Denning's own identity and how he was perceived at the time. Denning had no doubt about his English origins and identity, and would have endorsed, not condemned, any notion that he was a patriotic and indeed stereotypical upper-middle class Englishman of his age. He would have cited in support his belief in fair play, chivalry, good manners and individual liberty – all mainstream values for his generation and social class.

A jurisprudential theory?

> A lot of judgment is a feel for what you think is right: I may consider previous rulings, but really I've just done the job as it comes along.
>
> Lord Denning[35]

Many who have reviewed Denning's judgments and other writing and speeches have searched for an overarching theory which could be said to have informed his decision-making at the time and which might be used to interpret and evaluate his judgments in retrospect. Ultimately, the search is futile: jurisprudence was never a subject which interested Denning either as a student, barrister, judge or legal author. That much was evident from his own writings. Denning did claim that during his time as a Lord Justice (1948–57) he had followed the following principles:[36]

— let justice be done;
— freedom under the law;
— put your trust in God.

But three broad principles do not a theory of law make – certainly nothing resembling HLA Hart's *Concept of Law*, Ronald Dworkin's *Law's Empire*, or Richard A Posner's *The Economic Analysis of Law*, to take three of the better-known jurisprudential works by scholars whose lives and careers had some overlap with Denning's.

To the extent one could identify an abstract approach governing Denning's judgments, it would involve defining his concept of 'justice' as above. Again, however, that would not involve a sophisticated theory, even if some commentators have loosely described Denning as a 'libertarian'[37] simply for supporting in principle the individual against the state.

Instead, justice according to Denning involved natural justice in procedure, which any judge from the common law or elsewhere would recognise and accept: the right to be heard in front of an independent tribunal, with representation as appropriate, for a decision within a reasonable time which the successful litigant could enforce with the mechanisms of the state, as nowadays encapsulated in Article 6 of the European Convention on Human Rights. In that respect we should repeat that Denning's successor as Master of the Rolls, Sir John Donaldson, did important work in improving efficiency within the court system, something central, not tangential, to justice. We therefore have to record a mark against the latter part of Denning's time in the role, for allowing a backlog of cases to form.

Beyond procedure, Denning believed in supporting the underdog, although his support rather depended upon who he decided was the underdog in any particular case. Denning's values included an underlying faith in institutions, the necessity of maintaining order in society, and, at the last, defending the British state from its enemies even if that required limited suspension of the rule of law.

Further, while he was able to see and oppose various forms of injustice against women, his religious faith stopped him seeking absolute sexual equality, for the sermons he received throughout his life told him that the Christian family was the bedrock of society and that a woman's first duties were raising children and running the household. It was all in contrast with his reforming spirit as a judge: that spirit seemed confined to the common law, and not to general morality.

Denning often performed the role of what later generations might call a 'disrupter', trying almost single-handedly to shake off some of the outmoded rules accepted unthinkingly by the other judges of his era. He was responsible for a substantial amount of modernisation of the law, from civil procedure to tort to contract to administrative law to matrimonial property. Even when his efforts were thwarted by the House of Lords, he occasionally prevailed in that Parliament subsequently legislated along the same lines as his decisions or later judges came around to his point of view. And there was no question that Denning was seeking to do the right thing for society as a whole in developing the common law. As Lord Bingham put it:[38]

> Not all his judgments, of course, will stand the test of time; some, indeed, were cut down in the pride of their youth; others were raked by academic grapeshot. But more, many more, left an indelible imprint on the living law of our country, and the spirit which inspired all these judgments will endure. He saw the law not as a code of rules, but as a collection of human stories, each with a moral; not as a fetter, but as a source of freedom; not as an unwelcome but inescapable response to the ills of society, but as a means of providing that justice upon which good government and social harmony fundamentally depend. He invested the art of the advocate and the role of the judge with a new nobility. He always looked forward, never back. He sought to build, not to pull down.

Yet, for all those times when one might have agreed with Denning's reforms, there remains the principled objection to his methods. There is no use agreeing with the Denning method when one happens to agree with the result and criticising his method when one does not. The reality was that Denning took his reforming zeal too far, too often, in pursuit of an agenda he did not have licence judicially to implement. While the good that he achieved should be acknowledged, and while one could always appreciate the clarity of his judgment-writing, it was and remains a relief that he did not represent the norm amongst judges. A cynical conclusion would be that Denning was a great judge but not a good one. Or, as Lord Devlin put it, 'Lord Denning is a specimen tree. You must not have a whole avenue of them'.[39]

Judicial legacy

Having criticised Denning for his judicial indiscipline, it is important not to lose sight of the fact that he delivered several thousand judgments that were largely conventional in their method and results. In turn, those cases were cited, and continue to be cited in the present day, in the same manner as those of any other judge. The table in Appendix I shows that Denning's name appears more than any other in the history of the *All England Law Reports*, and – crucially when assessing his legacy – continues to be cited with regularity in the highest courts today. While some of the more recent mentions have been quotations of a Denning soundbite,[40] or given as an example of his controversial jurisprudential approach,[41] many others have involved consideration of Denning's judgments on bland questions of black letter law. To take some examples, in reverse chronological order:

— As we have seen, in *Broad Idea International Ltd v Convoy Collateral Ltd (British Virgin Islands); Convoy Collateral Ltd v Cho Kwai Chee (also known as Cho Kwai Chee Roy) (British Virgin Islands)* [2021] UKPC 24, the Privy Council held that Denning had been right and the House of Lords wrong all those years ago in *The Siskina* [1979] AC 210. In the opposite outcome from *Solle v Butcher*, therefore, Denning's reforming spirit was reaffirmed, not reversed, years after his death.

— In the Supreme Court planning law case of *R (Wright) v Resilient Energy Severndale Ltd and Another* [2019] UKSC 53, Denning's judgments in *Pyx Granite Co Ltd v Ministry of Housing and Local Govt* [1958] 1 QB 554 and *Fawcett Properties Ltd v Buckingham CC* [1961] AC 636 were cited as proper authority – the latter applied as binding on the point at issue.

— In the property law case of *Sequent Nominees Ltd (formerly Rotrust Nominees Ltd) v Hautford Ltd* [2019] UKSC 47, the meaning of *dicta* of Denning in

Bickel v Duke of Westminster [1977] QB 517 at 524 was contested between the majority and Lady Arden, but its precedent value was not disputed.

— In the tax case of *Revenue and Customs Commissioners v Joint Administrators of Lehman Brothers International* [2019] UKSC 12, Denning's judgments in *Corinthian Securities Ltd v Cato* [1970] 1 QB 377 and *Jefford v Gee* [1970] 2 QB 130 both received careful consideration.

— In *R (Privacy International) v Investigatory Powers Tribunal* [2019] UKSC 22, the Supreme Court considered Denning's decision in *Pearlman v Keepers and Govrs of Harrow School* [1979] QB 56 at 69–70 as part of a relevant line of administrative law cases.

— In the motor insurance case of *UK Insurance Ltd v Holden and Another* [2019] UKSC 16, Denning's dissent in *Romford Ice & Cold Storage Co Ltd v Lister* [1956] 2 QB 180 was mentioned, but the Supreme Court reaffirmed the decision of the majority. We can imagine Denning as unsurprised and unrepentant as ever.

— In *Mazhar v Lord Chancellor* [2019] EWCA Civ 1558, the claimant sought a declaration that a judicial act was unlawful. The Court of Appeal dealt with two of Denning's earlier cases, *Sirros v Moore* [1974] 3 All ER 776 and *O'Reilly v Mackman* [1982] 3 All ER 680. Denning's ruling that he could see no difference between an action for damages and an action for declaration against a judge or similar body such as the Parole Board in that case was still good law.

— The case of *FSHC Group Holdings Ltd v GLAS Trust Corp Ltd* [2019] EWCA Civ 1361 concerned rectification of a contract due to common mistake. The Court of Appeal gave careful consideration to Denning's judgment in *Frederick E Rose (London) Ltd v William H Pim Junior & Co Ltd* [1953] 2 QB 450.

— In *M v P (Queen's Proctor Intervening)* [2019] EWFC 14, Sir James Munby considered an important point of procedure in family law, when a decree nisi had been granted though no one had noticed that the required continuous period of at least two years' separation immediately preceding the presentation of the petition had not elapsed. The issue arose as to whether the decrees were void or merely voidable. In holding that they were merely voidable, his lordship referred to Denning's judgment in *Wiseman v Wiseman* [1953] P 79.

A Final Judgment

— *Cameron v Liverpool Victoria Insurance Co Ltd* [2019] UKSC 6 was a decision of the Supreme Court in the case of an unidentified driver in a motor accident. Denning's judgment in *Gurtner v Circuit* [1968] 2 QB 587 was cited.

— In *R (Faqiri) v Upper Tribunal (Immigration and Asylum Chamber) (Secretary of State for the Home Department, Interested Party)* [2019] EWCA Civ 151, the Court of Appeal stated that the normal rule of judicial immunity was 'epitomised' by *Sirros v Moore* [1975] QB 118, a decision of the Court of Appeal, presided over by Denning, which held that as a matter of principle every judge was entitled to immunity from civil claims in respect of anything done by him acting in his capacity as a judge.

— *Devani v Wells* [2019] UKSC 4 concerned an estate agent's commission. The Supreme Court quoted Denning LJ in *Fowler v Bratt* [1950] 2 KB 96 at 104–5.

— The Court of Appeal decision in *Kaefer Aislamientos SA de CV v AMS Drilling Mexico SA de CV and Others* [2019] EWCA Civ 10 turned on a point of conflict of laws, though the court also had occasion to consider the law relating to undisclosed principals. It took the decision of Denning in *Teheran-Europe Co Ltd v ST Belton (Tractors) Ltd* [1968] 2 QB 545 at 552 as the starting point in the list of relevant authorities concerning the latter (i.e. the law of undisclosed principals).

— *Financial Reporting Council Ltd v Sports Direct International Plc* [2018] EWHC 2284 (Ch) was a case before the Chancery Division which turned on a question of legal privilege. Arnold J dealt carefully with Denning's decision in *Parry-Jones v The Law Society* [1969] 1 Ch 1 and the differently reasoned decision of Diplock LJ in the same case. He then cited *R (Morgan Grenfell & Co Ltd) v Special Comr of Income Tax* [2002] 3 All ER 1, in which Lord Hoffmann preferred Denning's reasoning.

— In dealing with a procedural point about costs of implementing injunctive relief, the Supreme Court in *Cartier International AG and others v British Telecommunications Plc and Another* [2018] UKSC 28 cited Denning in *Z Ltd v A* [1982] 1 All ER 556 at 564. *Z Ltd* was a case concerned with costs incurred in complying with freezing orders, and the practice established by Denning and Kerr LJ in that case was later embodied in the model wording in PD 25A of the Civil Procedure Rules.

— In *Deutsche Bank AG and Others v Unitech Global Ltd and Another; Deutsche Bank AG v Unitech Ltd* [2016] EWCA Civ 119, the Court of Appeal considered an application for summary judgment for a claim by a bank to enforce two loan or swap agreements. Longmore LJ gave the judgment of the court, in which he applied Denning's judgment in *Wilson, Smithett & Cope Ltd v Terruzzi* [1976] QB 683, a case later approved by the House of Lords in *United City Merchants (Investments) Ltd v Royal Bank of Canada* [1983] 1 AC 168. Thus, on a straightforward question of black letter law, Denning had been upheld by the House of Lords and his *dicta* were accordingly still valid.

— In *Trump International Golf Club Scotland Ltd and Another v Scottish Ministers* [2015] UKSC 74, the claimants challenged a consent given by the Scottish ministers for the development and operation of a wind farm off the coast of Aberdeenshire, pursuant to s 36 of the Electricity Act 1989. The challenge failed and they appealed to the Supreme Court. Denning's judgment in *Fawcett Properties Ltd v Buckingham County Council* [1961] AC 636, a House of Lords' case concerning a condition in planning permission, was given careful consideration both by Lord Hodge in the lead judgment and by Lord Carnwath in a concurring judgment. The latter also quoted an earlier decision of Denning, *Crisp from the Fens Ltd v Rutland County Council* [1950] 1 P&CR 48, where Denning had said characteristically '[i]t is a case where strict adherence to the letter would involve an error of substance'.

— In *Marks and Spencer Plc v BNP Paribas Securities Services Trust Co (Jersey) Ltd and Another* [2015] UKSC 72, the Supreme Court was concerned with the termination of a lease in a landlord and tenant case. The lead judgment was given by Lord Neuberger, who stated:

> [47] ... It is a very well established rule that a landlord who forfeits a lease under which the rent is payable in advance is entitled to payment of the whole of the rent which fell due on the quarter day preceding the forfeiture. The rule was well described by Lord Denning MR in *Canas Property Co Ltd v KL Television Services Ltd* [1970] 2 QB 433 at 442.

— In *Dixon and Another v Blindley Heath Investments Ltd and Others* [2015] EWCA Civ 1023, the Court of Appeal stated that the starting point for the modern development of the doctrine of estoppel by convention was *Amalgamated Investment and Property Co Ltd (In Liq) v Texas Commerce International Bank Ltd* [1982] QB 84, and gave careful consideration to Denning's judgment in that case.

— In *Dunbar Assets plc v Butler* [2015] EWHC 2546 (Ch), Jeremy Cousins QC, sitting as a deputy judge, mentioned Denning's decision in *Crabb v Arun District Council* [1976] Ch 179 and went on to apply *Central London Property Trust Ltd v High Trees House Ltd* [1956] 1 All ER 256 as settled law.

In those and other cases, Denning was appearing not as the greatest judge of the common law, nor as the worst – both of which he was called at various times. Nor was he being cited just to quote his famous prose, or to invoke (or condemn) the spirit of his radical approach to precedent. Few of the cases were instantly recognisable 'Denning classics' such as *Miller v Jackson*, or *Mareva*. Instead, Denning was being cited as a normal appellate judge in an unremarkable fashion concerning statutory interpretation and precedent.

We can conclude, therefore, with the mildly ironic observation that Denning was of the most lasting relevance in the common law when he was being the least 'Denning'.

Denning the person

One public debate while this book was being written concerned whether statues of public figures from years past should be torn down, on the grounds of their association with slavery or some other actions once accepted but which the present generation considers abhorrent.

In truth, there was not much new in the debate. The historian and polymath Eric Midwinter once mentioned to the author how from the 1970s onwards many schools who had houses, buildings and prizes named after heroes of empire were placed in an embarrassing position as it emerged that some of those heroes had feet of clay, or at least were not quite the men of legend (they were nearly all men) they were once thought to have been.[42]

The same process has long taken place in academic assessments of historical figures, as evinced by several of the public figures who have appeared in this book. In the first chapter we mentioned the author William Cobbett, whose depiction of the English countryside in his book *Rural Rides* Denning long admired. Cobbett clearly had literary and intellectual gifts, but through modern eyes he was also a racist and an anti-Semite.[43]

Even some of Britain's leading Second World War heroes, such as Sir Winston Churchill or Field Marshal Montgomery, have had their reputations subject to substantial revisions over the years, due in part to them expressing views that were offensive not just by today's standards but even in their own time. Churchill's views on racial supremacy have since caused much controversy, while in the late 1960s Montgomery, the hero of El Alamein, was wheeled out on television and radio on several occasions to sound like a clichéd clubland colonel, raging against the permissive society. They were hardly alone: Denning's near-contemporary student in the Bar exams, Mahatma Gandhi, who clashed with Churchill over Indian independence, made comments about race in South Africa that would appal modern readers.[44]

In the legal world, we saw how Denning often sat in his early judicial career with Lord Goddard LCJ. Lord Goddard's hardline views often caused controversy, though Denning and other judges stoutly defended him at the time.[45] Many years later, however, the views of Lord Goddard's critics began to gain currency as the less attractive side to his character emerged.[46]

One of Lord Goddard's predecessors as Lord Chief Justice, Lord Hewart, was ridiculed after his death for his incompetence,[47] while his treatise on unelected and unaccountable power[48] was highly controversial upon its release.[49] More recently, with a substantially expanded civil service, there have been thoughts that he might have been on to something with the latter.

Moreover, attitudes and values rarely develop in a linear fashion. There was not a seamless transition in liberal thought from the restrictiveness of Edwardian values of Denning's youth or the 1950s equivalent to whatever passes for a consensus today. Some of the self-styled 'progressives' of the 1960s advanced ideas that would be just as offensive to modern readers as the Victorian or Edwardian prejudices they sought to replace. For example, Vladmir Nabakov's *Lolita* was one of the best-selling books of the decade. Modern editions contain a warning about the paedophiliac content, but, as shown by the historian Peter Doggett,[50] at the time it was published the book was not only less controversial but inspired movements such as the Paedophile Information Exchange, which survived as late as the 1980s before being deemed completely beyond the pale. Other literature of the time might have featured more modern attitudes to sex, but often had distinctly un-modern attitudes to consent, as any reader of Ian Fleming's James Bond stories[51] or viewer of the early film adaptations would confirm.[52]

Further, even if Denning had moved with the times, the times would have continued to move after his death. It is not even as though there is a consensus in Britain today on all issues of sex, sexuality and identity. Thus, however progressive he might have become during his lifetime, at some point he would still have been exposed as having 'outdated' views.

Modern readers should not assume that they will be immune from similar revision to Denning. Future generations might be appalled that people once thought nothing of attending a sporting function in which two participants put on gloves and fought to inflict brain damage on each other, cheered on by the audience and reported afterwards by the media in intellectual and cultured tones.

The rather jejune conclusion is that we cannot expect from people in the past the values and language which society deems appropriate today, any more than we can expect to know what will be deemed correct in the future.

With that in mind, spending a great deal of time in Denning's virtual company often gave rise to contrasting feelings. There was always admiration for his intellect, determination, steadfast adherence to a moral code, and the way he and his siblings were able to rise from impoverished beginnings to the top of their respective professions. At the same time his stubbornness, and what could seem at times as almost absurd naïvety, regularly grated. I say 'absurd' naïvety because he would occasionally sound like a stereotypical Edwardian maiden aunt with his indignation about immoral behaviour. It seemed incongruous given that anyone who had had Denning's experiences serving on the Western Front, or presiding over divorce courts, should not have found anything especially shocking in the escapades of Stephen Ward's acquaintances or a trainee teacher living in halls. The answer is that Denning had an old-fashioned way of expressing his disapproval of any behaviour that would not have been endorsed by the pulpit from which he received his moral instruction. Moreover, exposure to the destruction of civilisation that the Western Front represented would likely have made him more, not less, determined to enforce what he thought were appropriate standards of civilised behaviour later in life.

If we have moved on from his moral code, and would consider ourselves justified in doing so, we should acknowledge that at least he did have a strong moral code, and there has never been a suspicion that Denning himself deviated from it in the same sort of hypocritical way as so many public figures before, during and after his time.[53] Richard Davenport-Hines' description of him as a 'lascivious old man' seems to me an overstatement. Denning relished the limelight, and enjoyed captivating his readers with his writing style, but if he had been seeking to maximise prurient interest in the Profumo Affair he would hardly have suppressed so many of the names and details.

Instead, considering how attached Denning was to both his marriages, and his almost naïf refusal to look for any other woman than Mary even when he was a single man in possession of a good fortune (or at least a good and rising income), it is clear he practised what he preached in terms of love, marriage and sex.

As well as strictly adhering to his own moral code, Denning rarely (or indeed never) attempted to deceive anyone about his views or his actions, another point that distinguished him from more than a few of his contemporaries such as Montgomery or Earl Mountbatten (the latter being an eminent public figure to whom Denning was once directly compared.[54]) Denning was generally unsparing and honest in his own memoirs and recollections, even if he usually – though not always[55] – stubbornly refused to admit that any of his judgments had been wrong. As with his other biographers, I have not uncovered anything like the naked self-promotion or distortion of the historical record as others have found with Montgomery or, especially, Mountbatten.[56] In *The Closing Chapter*, for example, Denning did not shirk from admitting the scale of the disaster he had brought upon himself with the ill-judged remarks that led to his resignation.

It is true that some of Denning's contemporaries managed to move beyond the regressive opinions of an earlier age to pass legislation relating to homosexual law reform, community relations and sex discrimination. One of the strongest reasons behind otherwise conservative thinkers coming around in each case was a belief in the limitation of state power and defending the rights of individuals.[57] Denning broadly shared those principles but sometimes failed to apply them. Had he done so he might also have reached the conclusion that the state did not have any business in the individual's bedroom where consenting adults were concerned. If we might offer mitigation in the form of Denning simply following the values of his youth, we can also criticise an otherwise radical and progressive thinker for a lack of imagination and inability to move on even when logic demanded it, especially given Denning's own arguments about individual liberty. He always denounced racial prejudice, but still referred to some minority communities as 'others'. He managed belatedly to (mostly) accept women's equality, after decades of making outdated chauvinistic judgments in the other direction. It was a matter of regret for those subjected to his outdated remarks and decisions that he did not undergo his conversion earlier in life. Instead, he always seemed to remain convinced on moral issues (or with the broader concept of 'justice') that the majority of the country (at least the 'right thinking' members thereof) supported him and that anyone who disagreed was plainly wrong.

In contrast with the fate of his views on morality, Denning would have been surprised and delighted about the eventual fate of Britain's membership of the European Union. During his lifetime, although he had been more welcoming than some to the influence of European law, and keen for Britain to be a leader within Europe, he was ultimately opposed to the idea of Parliament ceding sovereignty to Brussels.[58] He held no great hope for that situation to change, but as no reader will need reminding the United

Kingdom did indeed decide to withdraw from the European Union in 2016, even if the constitutional purity important to Denning was not the *casus belli* cited by most of those publicly campaigning for Brexit. (The economic consequences were not something Denning would have dwelt upon, economics being a subject in which he had no interest or expertise.[59]) On the subject of Europe and indeed generally, Denning became more cantankerous in retirement. No doubt the loss of the great influence and automatic deference he had enjoyed over forty years as a judge, particularly those spent as Master of the Rolls, had been a source of frustration for him in retirement, contributing to him sounding more intemperate than he would have done when younger.

We should finish by observing what was both consistent and admirable throughout Denning's life: his work ethic and his great devotion to public service, fuelled by his sense of duty, patriotism and Christian values. His contributions to charity, notably the Cumberland Lodge and the Leonard Cheshire Foundation (and there were countless others), were highly praised by those who knew nothing of his legal career and legacy. If in later years his battles with local authorities and others were occasionally quixotic (and did not always endear him to his fellow Whitchurch residents), his intentions were always to preserve the country for future generations as he had enjoyed it.

Denning once ended a speech with the words:[60]

> ... I would conclude by telling you of the Judge's oath, taken by every Judge in the land on his appointment. Every word of it is worth weighing.
>
> I do swear by Almighty God that ... I will do right to all manner of people after the laws and usages of this Realm without fear or favour, affection or ill-will.
>
> Take this oath word by word – 'I swear by Almighty God' – herein he affirms his belief in God and implicitly his belief in true religion. 'I will do right' – those are the guiding words which govern all the rest; I will do right, Which means 'I will do justice', not 'I will do law'. 'To all manner of people': rich or poor, Christian or pagan, capitalist or communist, black or white – to all manner of people he must do right; 'After the laws and usages of this Realm' – Yes, certainly, it must be according to law, but justice according to law, not injustice according to law: 'Without fear or favour, affection or ill-will' – Those are the words of the oath most frequently quoted, and highly important they are, enshrining the independence and impartiality of the Judge. Without fear of the powerful or favour of the wealthy. Without affection to one side or ill-will towards the other.

There can be no doubt Denning did his best to uphold every word of that oath and explanation, throughout his career. Sometimes he fell short of his own standards – but is there any one of us who hasn't?

APPENDIX I

Denning in the Law Reports

The following table shows that Denning's name appears more than that of any other judge in the history of the law reports.

To explain slightly further, during his career cases were almost exclusively available in the printed, recognised law reports (whether official reports of the Incorporated Council of Law Reporting (ICLR) or private series such as the *All England Law Reports* (All ER) or the *Lloyd's Reports*) or in newspapers such as *The Times*, whose reports were written by qualified barristers and were thus citable in court.[1] The editors of those law reports decided what to publish. There was no readily accessible repository of unreported judgments as found nowadays with the BAILII online service. Unless a solicitor, barrister, judge or legal author happened to know of an unreported case through personal involvement or connections, as Denning did for *L'Estrange v F Graucob Ltd*, the case would effectively vanish.

One or two judges over the years grumbled about the resultant power that editors of the law reports possessed to develop the law. Denning, on the other hand, occasionally used the inferior status of unreported judgments to his advantage, by dismissing them out of hand and thereby freeing himself to reach what he thought was the right result. In *Bremer Vulkan v South India Shipping* (1978) All ER 422, he stated 'I do not think we need pause on the unreported cases ... They should be left in the oblivion to which the reporters quite rightly consign them'. Elsewhere he was effusively grateful for the work of law reporters generally.[2]

During Denning's time, the All ER had the broadest general coverage of the traditional, citeable law reports. After their commercial success the ICLR responded with the *Weekly Law Reports* (WLR), a series reporting more widely and much more quickly than the official reports, aiming to be on a par with the All ER. Both the All ER and the WLR had (and have) equal status in terms of citation.

There are two columns of figures in the table. The first is a recent period. I chose 2015–20 rather than going to 2021, because, although the work of the courts was not halted completely by the Covid-19 outbreak, it was slowed in that time and I considered the period 2015–20 would be more representative overall. The second column constitutes the overall citations from each judge. It shows Denning well ahead of anyone before or since his time, with Lord Diplock in second place more than 500 cases behind. The numbers refer to all citations from each judge's career, not simply the higher offices that they held, such as Lord of Appeal in Ordinary or Master of the Rolls.

The figures do not show quite the full picture, since there would have been many occasions on which judges (including Denning) were cited in unreported cases, while other times their cases might have been mentioned in argument or in negotiations between parties but not referred to in judgments. Further, the mention of their name does not indicate the extent to which their judgments were considered, or whether they were followed, distinguished or overturned. Nonetheless, I believe the figures are sufficiently accurate to make confident conclusions about overall numbers and to demonstrate how ubiquitous each of the judges' names have been.

Judge	Number of citations June 2015 to June 2020	Total (no time restriction) as of June 2020
Denning (MR 1962–82)	90	3,500
MR predecessors		
Pollock (Baron Hanworth) (MR 1923–35)	6	309
Wright (MR 1935–37)	16	1,291
Greene (MR 1937–49)	10	1,312
Evershed (MR 1949–62)	6	685
MR successors		
Donaldson (MR 1982–92)	36	791
Bingham (MR 1992–96)	198	2,032
Woolf (MR 1996–2000)	60	1,127
Phillips (MR 2000–05)	61	571
Clarke (MR 2005–09)	126	577
Neuberger (MR 2009–12)	249	854
Dyson (MR 2012–16)	125	763
Etherton (MR 2016–21)	54	177
Notable contemporary Law Lords		
Diplock	102	2,959
Goff	72	1,363
Hobhouse	52	653
Keith	32	1,156
Templeman	34	1,035
Reid	60	1,987
Radcliffe	17	569
Dilhorne	11	680
Wilberforce	75	1,878
Simonds	15	529
Modern Law Lords/Ladies		
Browne-Wilkinson	67	1,140
Hale	300	1,099
Hoffmann	200	1,612
Millett	67	751
Steyn	111	1,093
Notable historic judges		
Atkin	22	1,018
Scrutton	15	1,038
Mansfield	23	371

APPENDIX II

Societies and Other Organisations

The following are the societies and other entities with which Denning was involved as patron, vice-president or president during his time as Master of the Rolls.

Drapers' Company: Presidency of Queen Elizabeth's College, Greenwich (ex officio, as MR)	1962–82
Denning Law Society, Dar-es-Salaam	1962–71
National Marriage Guidance Council	1966–82
Outpost Emmaus/Combined Action Now (holiday home for boys and the disabled)	1967–82
Birkbeck College	1953–82
Cumberland Lodge	1969–82
Hampshire Association of Parish Councils	1973–81
Knights of the Round Table (Winchester)	1975–76
British Legion, Whitchurch Branch	1969
British Museum Society	1969
Leeds University Union Law Society	1969–81
Canterbury University (NZ) Law Students' Society	1966–74
Queen's University Belfast Law Society	1969
Supreme Court Sports Association	1969
Legal Research Foundation, Auckland, NZ	1970
Friends of National Libraries	1971
United Law Clerks' Society	1971
Society of Genealogists	1972
Glasgow University Distributist Club	1972
Commonwealth Legal Education Association	1972
Victoria Institute	1974
Sea Cadet Corps, Andover Unit	1974

CPRE North Hampshire Branch	1974
Helwel Committee of Zululand Swaziland Association	1975
Holdsworth Club, University of Birmingham	1977
Friends of Devon Cottage	1978–80
University College Dublin Law Society	1978
Association of Queensland Institute of Technology Law Students	1978
Theatre Royal Winchester	1978
National Law Library Trust	1979
Hampshire Archives Trust	1979
Sir Robert Menzies Trust	1979
Jane Hodge Foundation	1980
Bar Association for Commerce, Finance and Industry	1980
Victorian Society	1981–82
International Students Trust	1981–82
City of London Polytechnic Society for Past Graduates	1982
Lincoln's Inn Cricket Club	1982
Denning Society, Queensland, Australia	1982
Denning Law Library, University College at Buckingham	1980s

Source: Hampshire Archives 202M86.

APPENDIX III

Select Bibliography

The works of Denning from which I have directly quoted or which I have referenced appear below. A full list of his publications before 1984 can be found in Jowell and McAuslan, p 477.

Speeches/pamphlets/articles

'Quantum Meruit and the Statute of Frauds' (1925) 41 LQR 79

'Re-entry for Forfeiture' (1927) 43 LQR 53

'Presumptions and Burdens' (1945) 61 LQR 379

'Freedom under Law', First Hamlyn Lectures (Stevens & Sons, 1949)

'Borrowing from Scotland' (Jackson, Son & Co, 1963)

'Gems in Ermine', Presidential Address to The English Association (The English Association, 1964)

'Recent Changes in the Law' [1966] NZLJ 167

'Let Justice Be Done' (1974) *Manitoba Law Journal*, Vol 6, No 2, 227

'The Incoming Tide', Inaugural Lord Fletcher Lecture, 10 December 1979

'Foreword' (1986) *Denning Law Journal*, Vol 1, No 1, 1

'This is My Life' (1986) *Denning Law Journal*, Vol 1, No 1, 17

Influence of Law on Religion (Canadian Institute for Law, Theology & Public Policy, 1997)

Official reports

Committee on Procedure in Matrimonial Cases and Two Interim Reports, Cmd 6881, 6945, 7024 (1946)

Committee on Legal Education for Students from Africa, Cmd 12, 55 (1961)

Lord Denning's Report, Cmnd 2152 (Profumo Affair)

Legal Records 1963–66, Cmnd 3084 (1900)

Report of the Secretary to the Commissioners 1969–76

Royal Commission on Historical Manuscripts (HMSO, 1969)

Books by Denning
(all published by Butterworths, except as otherwise indicated)

Smith's Leading Cases, 13th edn (Sweet & Maxwell, 1929)

Bullen & Leake's Precedents of Pleadings in Actions in the King's Bench Division of the High Court, 9th edn (Sweet & Maxwell, 1935)

The Changing Law (Stevens & Sons, 1953)

The Road to Justice (Stevens & Sons, 1955)

The Discipline of Law (1979)

The Due Process of Law (1980)

The Family Story (1981)

What Next in the Law? (1982)

The Closing Chapter (1983)

Landmarks in the Law (1984)

Leaves from my Library (1986)

Books about Denning

Curley, Sean (2016) *Lord Denning: Towards a theory of adjudication. An examination of the judicial decision making process of Lord Denning and his creation and use of the interstitial spaces within the law and legal process to assist in the exercise of his discretion and an examination of those factors which influenced that discretion*, Doctoral thesis, University of Huddersfield

Freeman, Iris, *Lord Denning: A Life* (Hutchinson, 1993) ('Freeman')

Select Bibliography

Heward, Edmund *Lord Denning: A Biography* (Weidenfeld & Nicolson, 1990; paperback edn, 1991) ('Heward')

Jowell, JL and McAuslan, JPWB (eds), *Lord Denning: the Judge and the Law* (Sweet & Maxwell, 1984) ('Jowell and McAuslan')

Robson, Peter and Watchman, Paul (eds), *Justice, Lord Denning and the Constitution* (Gower Publishing Company Ltd, 1981)

Stephens, Charles *The Jurisprudence of Lord Denning* (three volumes) (Cambridge Scholars Publishing, 2009) ('Stephens, Vol [I–III])'

Archives

Denning in his later years became friendly with the then head archivist in Hampshire, Rosemary Dunhill, and passed many of his papers to the archive from the mid-1980s onwards. He bequeathed a number of the books from his treasured library as well. Mrs Dunhill was responsible for the booklet produced for Denning's 100th birthday in 1999, 'Lord Denning: A Hampshire Man'.

Although Denning carefully preserved a number of personal and professional papers over his lifetime, he was not a professional archivist and thus the archive itself does not have each item listed in minute detail. The website of Hampshire Archives (https://calm.hants.gov.uk/default.aspx) can be searched for 'Lord Denning' and provides many references, though the full catalogue (which runs to some seventy pages) was not online at the time of writing. The archival reference for Denning is 202M86.

Otherwise, I obtained much material from The British Newspaper Archive (www.britishnewspaperarchive.co.uk/) and individual archives, including *The Times* (www.thetimes.co.uk/archive/) and *The Spectator* (http://archive.spectator.co.uk/).

General bibliography – books

Andrew, Susanna and Gracewood, Jolisa (eds), *Tell You What: Great New Zealand Nonfiction 2017* (Auckland University Press, 2017)

Arlidge, Anthony and Judge, Igor, *Magna Carta Uncovered* (Hart Publishing, 2014)

Barnett, Correlli, *The Collapse of British Power* (Pan Books, 1971; reprint, 2002)

Barnett, Correlli, *The Audit of War: The Illusion and Reality of Britain as a Great Nation* (Macmillan, 1986)

Barnett, Correlli, *The Lost Victory: British Dreams, British Realities, 1945–50* (Macmillan, 1995)

Barnett, Correlli, *The Verdict of Peace: Britain between her Yesterday and the Future* (Macmillan, 2001)

Bennion, Francis, *Bennion on Statutory Interpretation*, 5th edn (LexisNexis, 2008)

Bennion, Francis, *Professional Ethics: Consultant Professions and their Code* (Knight (Charles) & Co Ltd, 1969)

Bingham, Tom, *The Business of Judging: Selected Essays and Speeches* (Oxford University Press, 2000)

Bingham, Tom, *The Rule of Law* (Allen Lane, 2010)

Bingham, Tom, *Lives of the Law: Selected Essays and Speeches* (Oxford University Press, 2011)

Bix, Brian, *Law, Language and Legal Determinacy* (Clarendon Press, 1993)

Bresler, Fenton, *Lord Goddard* (Harrap, 1977)

Brown, Simon (Lord Brown of Eaton-under-Heywood), *Playing off the Roof & Other Stories: a patchwork of memories* (Marble Hill Publishers, 2020)

Bush, Julia, *Behind the Lines: East London Labour, 1914–1919* (Merlin Press, 1984)

Cannadine, David, *Class in Britain* (Penguin Books, 2000)

Chapman, Matthew, *The Snail and the Ginger Beer: The singular case of Donoghue v Stevenson* (Wildy, Simmonds & Hill, 2010)

Clark, Christopher, *The Sleepwalkers: How Europe Went to War in 1914* (HarperCollins, 2013)

Clegg, Hugh Armstrong (ed), *A History of British Trade Unions Since 1889, Vol 2, 1911–1933* (Clarendon Press, 1985)

Cohen, Robert, *When the Old Left Was Young: Student Radicals and America's First Mass Student Movement, 1929–41* (Oxford University Press, 1997)

Crafts, Nicholas, *Work and Pay in 20th Century Britain* (Oxford University Press, 2007)

Cronin, James, *Industrial Conflict in Modern Britain* (Croom Helm; Rowman and Littlefield, 1979)

Cronin, M (ed), *The Failure of British Fascism* (Palgrave Macmillan, 1996)

Darbyshire, Penny, *Sitting in Judgment: The Working Lives of Judges* (Hart Publishing, 2011)

Davenport-Hines, Richard, *An English Affair: Sex, Class and Power in the Age of Profumo* (William Collins, 2013)

Select Bibliography

De Smith, Woolf and Jeffrey Jowell, *Judicial Review of Administrative Action* (Sweet & Maxwell, 1995)

Deedes, WF, *Dear Bill: WF Deedes Reports* (Macmillan, 1997)

Devlin, Patrick, *The Enforcement of Morals* (Oxford University Press, 1965)

Devlin, Patrick, *The Judge* (Oxford University Press, 1979)

Doggett, Peter, *Growing Up: Sex in the Sixties* (Bodley Head, 2021)

Drewry, Gavin, Louis Blom-Cooper and Charles Blake, *The Court of Appeal* (Hart Publishing, 2007)

Dyson, John (Lord Dyson), *Justice: Continuity and Change*, Kindle edn (Bloomsbury, 2018)

Evans, Jim, *Statutory Interpretation: Problems of Communication* (Oxford University Press, 1988)

Ewing, KD (ed), *The Right to Strike: From the Trade Disputes Act 1906 to a Trade Union Freedom Bill 2006* (Institute of Employment Rights, 2006)

Feather, John, *A History of British Publishing* (Routledge, 2005)

Ferguson, Niall, *The Pity of War* (Penguin Books, revised edn, 2009)

Fox, Kate, *Watching the English* (Hodder Paperbacks, 2005)

French, Derek, Stephen Mayson and Christopher Ryan, *Mayson, French & Ryan on Company Law*, 26th edn (Oxford University Press, 2009)

Friedman, Sam and Daniel Laurison, *The Class Ceiling: Why it Pays to be Privileged* (Policy Press, 2020)

Gilbert, Martin, *Prophet of Truth. Winston S. Churchill. 1922–1939* (Minerva, 1990)

Goodman, Andrew, *How Judges Decide Cases*, 2nd edn (Wildy, Simmonds & Hill, 2018)

Griffith, JAG, *The Politics of the Judiciary*, 5th edn (Fontana, 1997)

Heffer, Simon, *High Minds: The Victorians and the Birth of Modern Britain* (Windmill Books, 2014)

Heffer, Simon, *Like the Roman: The Life of Enoch Powell* (Faber & Faber, 1998)

Hewart, Gordon, *The New Despotism* (Ernest Benn Ltd, 1929)

Hildred, Stafford and David Gritten, *Tom Jones: A Biography* (Sidgwick & Jackson, 1990)

Hill, Lamar, *Bench and Bureaucracy: The Public Career of Sir Julius Caesar, 1580–1636* (Stanford University Press, 1988)

Hill, Mark, and RH Helmholz (eds), *Great Christian Jurists in English History* (Cambridge University Press, 2017)

Hoggard, Richard, *A Measured Life: The Times and Places of an Orphaned Intellectual* (Routledge, 1994)

Holmes, Richard, *The Western Front* (BBC Worldwide, 1999)

Holmes, Richard, *Tommy: The British Soldier on the Western Front* (Harper Perennial, 2005)

Horne, Alistair, *Macmillan: The Official Biography, Vol 1, 1894–1956* (Macmillan, 1988)

Hostettler, John, *Lord Halsbury* (Barry Rose Law Publishers Ltd, 1998)

Ivanov, Yevgeny and Gennady Sokolov, *The Naked Spy* (Blake, 1992)

Jones, Thomas, *Lloyd George* (Harvard University Press, 1951)

Joseph, Philip *Joseph on Constitutional and Administrative Law*, 5th edn (Thomson Reuters, 2021)

Jowell, Jeffrey (ed), *The Growing Consensus in Favour of Independent Judicial Appointment Commissions in Judicial Appointments: Balancing Independence, Accountability and Legitimacy* (A collection of essays prepared under the auspices of the Judicial Appointments Commission) (2010)

Keegan, Sir John, *The First World War: An Illustrated History* (Hutchinson, 2001)

Kennedy, Ludovic, *The Trial of Stephen Ward* (V Gollancz, 1964; Penguin Books, reprint, 1965)

King, Anthony and Ivor Crewe, *The Blunders of our Governments*, Kindle edn (Oneworld Publications, 2013)

Knightley, Philip and Caroline Kennedy, *An Affair of State: The Profumo Case and the Framing of Stephen Ward* (Jonathan Cape Ltd, 1987)

Lamb, Richard, *The Macmillan Years 1957–1963: The Emerging Truth* (John Murray, 1995; Kindle edn, Lume Books, 2017)

Lane, Joan, *A Social History of Medicine: Health, Healing and Disease in England 1750–1950* (Routledge, 2001)

The Law Commission and The Scottish Law Commission, *Unfair Terms in Consumer Contracts: Advice to the Department for Business, Innovation and Skills* (March 2013)

Lee, Simon *Judging Judges* (Faber & Faber, 1988)

Levin, Bernard, *Taking Sides* (Jonathan Cape, 1979)

Select Bibliography

Levin, Bernard, *The Pendulum Years: Britain and the Sixties* (Jonathan Cape, 1970)

Lewis, Geoffrey, *Lord Atkin* (Butterworths, 1981)

Lewisohn, Mark, *The Beatles: All These Years* (Crown Archetype, 2013)

Linehan, Thomas, *British Fascism, 1918–39: Parties, Ideology and Culture* (Manchester University Press, 2000)

Lough, David, *No More Champagne: Churchill and his Money* (Head of Zeus, 2015)

Loughlin, Martin, *Sword and Scales: An Examination of the Relationship between Law and Politics* (Hart Publishing, 2000)

MacDougall, Ian (ed), *Cases that Changed Our Lives* (LexisNexis, 2010)

MacDougall, Ian with James Wilson (eds), *Cases that Changed Our Lives, Vol II* (LexisNexis, 2014)

Macintyre, Ben, *A Spy Among Friends: Philby and the Great Betrayal* (Bloomsbury Paperbacks, 2015)

Marr, Andrew, *A History of Modern Britain* (Macmillan, 2007)

Marsh, David Charles, *The Changing Social Structure of England and Wales, 1871–1961* (Routledge, 1958)

Marwick, Arthur, *British Society Since 1945* (Penguin Social History of Britain) (Penguin Books, 1996)

Massie, Robert K, *Castles of Steel* (Jonathan Cape, 2004)

Mathew, Theodore, *Forensic Fables by O* (Wildy, Simmonds & Hill, 2013)

McHugh, Paul, *The Maori Magna Carta* (Oxford University Press, 1991)

Mehrkens, Heidi and Frank Lorenz Müller (eds), *Sons and Heirs: Succession and Political Culture in Nineteenth-Century Europe* (Palgrave Macmillan, 2016)

Midwinter, Eric, *Yesterdays: Our Finest Hours 1939–1953* (Souvenir Press, 2001)

Miles, Andrew, *Social Mobility in Nineteenth- and Early Twentieth-Century England* (Palgrave Macmillan, 1999)

Morgan, Kenneth O (ed), *The Oxford Illustrated History of Britain* (Oxford University Press, 1984)

Mortimer, John, *In Character: Interviews with Some of the Most Influential and Remarkable Men and Women of Our Time* (Penguin Books, 1984)

Mount, Ferdinand, *The British Constitution Now* (William Heinemann, 1992)

Muggeridge, Malcolm, *Chronicles of Wasted Time* (Regent College Publishing, 2006)

Murray, Douglas, *Bosie: The Tragic Life of Lord Alfred Douglas*, reissue (Sceptre, 2020)

Oliphant, Ken (ed), *The Law of Tort* (LexisNexis, 2007)

Pannick, David, *The Judges* (Oxford University Press, 1987)

Parris, Matthew and Kevin MacGuire, *Great Parliamentary Scandals: Five Centuries of Calumny, Smear and Innuendo* (Robson Books, 2004)

Paterson, Alan, *The Law Lords* (Macmillan, 1982)

Paterson, Alan, *Final Judgment* (Hart Publishing, 2013)

Paxman, Jeremy, *The English: A Portrait of a People* (Penguin, 2007)

Profumo, David, *Bringing the House Down* (John Murray, 2006)

Radcliffe, Cyril, *Censors: The Rede Lecture* (Cambridge University Press, 1961)

Rawlinson, Peter, *A Price Too High* (Weidenfeld & Nicholson, 1989)

Roberts, Andrew, *Eminent Churchillians*, Kindle edn (Weidenfeld & Nicolson, 2010)

Robertson QC, Geoffrey, *Stephen Ward Was Innocent, OK: The Case for Overturning his Conviction*, Kindle edn (Biteback Publishing, 2013)

Sampson, Anthony, *The Changing Anatomy of Britain* (Hodder & Stoughton, 1982)

Sandbrook, Dominic, *Never Had it So Good: A History of Britain from Suez to the Beatles* (Little, Brown, 2005)

Scott, John, *Caught in Court* (Andre Deutsch, 1989)

Sedley, Stephen, *Law and the Whirligig of Time* (Hart Publishing, 2018)

Seldon, Anthony and David Walsh, *Public Schools and The Great War: The Generation Lost* (Pen & Sword Military, 2013)

Simpson, AWB, *In the Highest Degree Odious: Detention without Trial in Wartime Britain* (Clarendon Press, 1992)

Simpson, CR, *History of the Lincolnshire Regiment 1914–1918* (Naval and Military Press, 2009)

St John-Stevas, Norman, *Life, Death and the Law: Law and Christian Morals in England and the United States* (Beard Books, 1961; reprint 2002)

Stevens, Robert, *Law and Politics: The House of Lords as a Judicial Body 1800–1976* (Weidenfeld & Nicholson, 1979)

Stevens, Robert, *The English Judges: Their Role in the Changing Constitution* (Hart Publishing, 2005)

Summers, Anthony and Stephen Dorril, *Honeytrap* (Coronet Books, 1989)

Sumption, Jonathan, *Law in a Time of Crisis* (Profile Books, 2021)

Thomas, EW, *The Judicial Process: Realism, Pragmatism, Practical Reasoning and Principles* (Cambridge University Press, 2005)

Thorpe, DR, *Supermac: The Life of Harold Macmillan*, Kindle edn (Random House, 2010)

Wade, HWR, *Administrative Law*, 4th edn (Clarendon Press, 1977)

Williams QC, Graham, *A Short Book of Bad Judges* (Wildy, Simmonds & Hill, 2014)

Wilson, James, *Cases, Causes and Controversies: Fifty Tales from the Law* (Wildy, Simmonds & Hill, 2012)

Wilson, James, *Court and Bowled: Tales of Cricket and Law* (Wildy, Simmonds & Hill, 2014; revised 2017)

Wilson, James, *Noble Savages: The Savage Club and the Great War* (JH Productions, 2018; revised, 2020)

Wilson, James, *Trials and Tribulations: Uncommon Tales of the Common Law* (Wildy, Simmonds & Hill, 2015)

Wohl, AS, *Endangered Lives: Public Health in Victorian Britain* (Harvard University Press, 1983)

Woolf, Harry (Lord Woolf), *The Pursuit of Justice* (Oxford University Press, 2008)

General bibliography – articles

Note that all the *Denning Law Journal* issues are free to view online, at www.ubplj.org/index.php/dlj.

Atiyah, PS, 'Lord Denning's Contribution to Contract Law' (1999) *Denning Law Journal*, Vol 14, No 1, 1

Bainham, Andrew, 'Lord Denning as a Champion of Children's Rights: The Legacy of *Hewer v Bryant*' (1999) *Denning Law Journal*, Vol 14, No 1, 81

Bennion, Francis, 'Defending *Liversidge v Anderson*' (1988) *Denning Law Journal*, Vol 3, No 1

Bennion, Francis, 'If it ain't broke, don't fix it' (1994) 15 Stat LR 164

Bennion, Francis, 'How they all got it wrong in *Pepper v Hart*' (1995) *British Tax Review*, No 3, 325

Bennion, Francis, 'Is Law Still A Learned Profession?' (2008) 172 JPN 316

Bingham of Cornhill, Lord, 'Address to the Thanksgiving Service for Lord Denning OM' (2000) *Denning Law Journal*, Vol 15, No 1, 1

Blom-Cooper, Sir Louis, Margaret Howard Memorial Lecture of 2001

Bradley, AW, 'Judges and the media – the Kilmuir Rules' [1986] *Public Law* 383

Bradley, AW, 'Judicial Independence under Attack' [2003] *Public Law* 397

Burrows, Lord, 'Judgment-Writing: A Personal Perspective', Annual Conference of Judges of the Superior Courts in Ireland, 20 May 2021

Campbell, AIL, 'Lord Denning and EEC Law' (1988) *Denning Law Journal*, Vol 3, No 1, 1

Cardozo, Benjamin N, 'Law and Literature' (1925) 14 *Yale Review* 699

Chamberlain, Geoffrey, 'British maternal mortality in the 19th and early 20th centuries' (2006) 99(11) JR Soc Med 559

Cheshire, GC and HS Fifoot, '*Central London Property Trust Ltd v High Trees House Ltd*' (1947) 63 LQR 283

DPD, '*The Road to Justice* – Book Review' [1957] Res Jud 69

de Deney, Geoffrey, 'Denning: The Road to Justice', 54 Mich L Rev 1207 (1956)

Denning, Lady, 'Another English Visitor in India' (1959) *The Cheshire Smile*, Vol 5, No 1, Spring

Elias, TO, 'Organisation and Development of the Legal Profession in Africa, in particular the ability of the Bar and judiciary to uphold the rights of both the citizen and the state' (1986) *Denning Law Journal*, Vol 1, No 1, 49

Etherton, Sir Terence, 'Liberty, the archetype and diversity: a philosophy of judging' [2010] *Public Law* 727

Ewing, KD, 'A Theory of Democratic Adjudication: Towards a Representative Accountable and Independent Judiciary' (2000) 38 Alberta LR 708

Forsyth, Christopher, 'Lord Denning and Modern Administrative Law' (1999) *Denning Law Journal*, Vol 14, No 1, 57

Freeman, MDA, 'Family Justice and Family Values according to Lord Denning' (1999) *Denning Law Journal*, Vol 14, No 1, 93

Furmston, MP, 'Contract and Tort after Denning' (1987) *Denning Law Journal*, Vol 2, No 1, 65

Gargrave, A, 'Lord Denning of Whitchurch' (1974) *The Advocate*, Vol 32, 366

Gearty, Conor, 'British Torture, Then and Now: The Role of the Judges' (2021) 84(1) MLR 118

Gibson, Sir Peter, 'Law reform now: The Law Commission 25 years on', 1991 Denning Lecture

Gordon, DM, 'Creditors' promises to forgo rights' [1963] CLJ 222

Gower, LCB 'Review' (1956) 19(2) MLR 217

Griffith, JAG, 'The Political Constitution' (1979) 42 MLR 1

Griffith, JAG, 'Book Review (*The Discipline of the Law*)' (1979) 42 MLR 348

Griffith, JAG, 'That Man Griffith: review of *Lord Denning: A Biography*, by Edmund Heward' (1990) *London Review of Books*, Vol 12, No 20, 25 October

Griffith, JAG, 'The Law Lords and the GLC' (1982) *Marxism Today*, February, 29

Harrington, John A and Ambreena Manji, '"Mind with Mind and Spirit with Spirit": Lord Denning and African Legal Education' (2003) *Journal of Law and Society*, Vol 30, No 3, 376

Harrison, Mark, 'The British Army and the Problem of Venereal Disease in France and Egypt during the First World War' (1995) *Medical History*, Vol 39, Issue 2, 133

Harvey, Cameron, 'It all started with Gunner James' (1983) 17 Law Soc of UC Gazette 279, (1986) *Denning Law Journal*, Vol 1, No 1, 67

Heuston, RFV, '*Liversidge v Anderson* in Retrospect' (1970) 86 LQR 33

James, PS, 'Her Majesty's Judge' (2012) *Denning Law Journal*, Vol 14, No 1, 179

Kodilinye, Gilbert, 'Lord Denning in Perspective' (1986) *Denning Law Journal*, Vol 1, No 1, 127

Lee, Simon, 'Lord Denning and Margaret Thatcher, Law and Society' (2013) *Denning Law Journal*, Vol 25, No 1, 159

Lee, Simon, 'Lord Denning, Magna Carta and Magnanimity' (2015) *Denning Law Journal*, Vol 27, No 1, 106

Lord Lloyd of Berwick, 'The Judges and the Executive: Have the Goalposts Moved?' (2006) *Denning Law Journal*, Vol 18, No 1, 79

Lock, GF, 'Parliamentary privilege and the courts: the avoidance of conflict' [1985] *Public Law*, Spring, 64–92

MacMillan, Catharine, 'A Birthday Present for Lord Denning: The Contracts (Rights of Third Parties) Act 1999' (2000) 63(5) MLR 721

Malleson, K, 'Diversity in the Judiciary: The Case for Positive Action' (2009) *Journal of Law and Society*, Vol 36, No 3, 376

McAuslan, JPWB 'Review: *The Due Process of Law*' (1980) 44 MLR 244

Markesinis QC, Sir Basil, 'Two kinds of justice: human and divine, random thoughts à propos Milton's Paradise Lost' (2008) *Denning Law Journal*, Vol 20, No 1, 1

Molloy QC, Tony and Toby Graham, 'Editorial' (2012) *Trusts & Trustees*, Vol 18, No 3, 171

Munday, Roderick, 'Lawyers and Latin' (2004) 168 JPN 775

Nash, David 'Blasphemy on Trial' (2017) *History Today*, 15 November

Neuberger MR, Lord, 'Has Equity Had Its Day?', Hong Kong University Common Law Lecture, 2010, https://bit.ly/3ylPt8H

Neuberger, Lord, 'Magna Carta and the Holy Grail', Lincoln's Inn, 12 May 2015, www.supremecourt.uk/docs/speech-150512.pdf

Nolan, Lord 'The Role of the Judge in Judicial Inquiries' (1999) *Denning Law Journal*, Vol 14, No 1, 147

Nourse, Martin, 'Law and Literature: the legacy of Lord Denning' (2005) *Denning Law Journal*, Vol 17, No 1, 1

Oliver, Dawn, 'Lord Denning & the Public/Private Divide' (1999) *Denning Law Journal*, Vol 14, No 1, 71

Pearson, Megan, 'Empathy and Procedural Justice in Clash of Rights Cases' (2020) *Oxford Journal of Law and Religion*, Vol 9, No 2, 350

Polden, Patrick, 'The Uses of Power: Mr Justice Denning and the Pensions Appeal Tribunals' (1988) *Denning Law Journal*, Vol 3, No 1, 97

Robertshaw, Paul, 'The Review Roles of the Court of Appeal: *Grobbelaar v News International*' (2001) 64(6) MLR 923

Rodger of Earlsferry, Lord, 'The Form and Language of Judicial Opinions' (2002) 118 LQR 226

Sales, Philip, 'Judges and the Legislature: Values in Law' (2012) *Cambridge Law Journal*, Vol 71, No 2, July

Scarman, Leslie, 'Book Review' (1979) 95 LQR 445

Scarman, Leslie, 'Leslie Scarman writes in praise of a dynamic judge' (1980) *London Review of Books*, Vol 2, No 12, 19 June

Sealey, Len, 'Commercial law and Company law' (1999) *Denning Law Journal*, Vol 14, No 1, 13

Sedley, Stephen, 'This beats me' (1998) *London Review of Books*, Vol 20, No 7, 2 April

Sheridan, LA, 'Equitable Estoppel Today' (1952) 15 MLR 325

Stevens, John, 'Equity's Manhattan Project: The Creation and Evolution of the Mareva Injunction' (1999) *Denning Law Journal*, Vol 14, No 1, 25

Steyn, Johan, 'Democracy, the rule of law and the role of the judges' [2006] EHRLR 243

Stockmeyer Jnr, NO 'Beloved are the Storytellers' (2002) *Michigan Bar Journal*, Vol 81, No 1, 54

Thomas, EW, 'Lord Denning 1899–1999' [1999] NZLJ 92

Various authors, 'Valedictory speeches upon the impending retirement of the Master of the Rolls' (1986) *Denning Law Journal*, Vol 1, No 1, 7

Vos, Sir Geoffrey, 'Contractual Interpretation: Do Judges Sometimes Say One Thing and Do Another?' (2017) 23 *Canterbury Law Review* 1

Vos, Sir Geoffrey, 'Preserving the Integrity of the Common Law', Lecture to the Chancery Bar Association, 16 April 2018

Welstead, Mary, 'The deserted bank and the spousal equity' (1999) *Denning Law Journal*, Vol 14, No 1, 113

Williams, DGT, 'Lord Denning and Open Government' (1986) *Denning Law Journal*, Vol 1, No 1, 117

Wilson, JF, 'Recent Developments in Estoppel' (1951) 67 LQR 330

Woolf, Harry 'Public Law – Private Law: Why the Divide?' [1986] *Public Law* 220

Acknowledgements

The idea for this book came from Andrew Riddoch of Wildy, Simmonds & Hill. Andrew has given unstinting support throughout.

I am grateful to the Denning family for their assistance in answering questions and granting access to the Denning archive in Hampshire, permitting reproduction of extracts from Lord Denning's books and papers, and the reproduction of photographs. I would stress, however, that they never attempted to influence the content of the book, and all views expressed herein are my own.

I am also very grateful to Lord Neuberger for writing the Foreword.

The staff of Hampshire County Council Archives were unfailingly helpful and courteous, providing the bulk of the primary sources and being most assiduous in providing photographs and obtaining copyright permission. Especial thanks to Mr David Rymill, Chief Archivist.

I am also grateful to the following publishers for permission to quote from their publications: *Legal Cheek*, Sweet & Maxwell, Hart Publishing, Taylor & Francis Group, Legend Press Ltd and *London Review of Books*.

Every effort has been made to secure permission for photographs and to ensure that quotations fall within the guidelines of the Society of Authors (https://bit.ly/3Poy46J).

Allan Draycott freely offered me some diligent research into Profumo and earlier scandals, and into the history of labour relations in the United Kingdom, for which I am very grateful.

I should also acknowledge the labours of Denning's previous biographers, Edmund Heward and Iris Freeman, both of whom had the advantage of personal contact with Denning himself as well as family, friends and former colleagues who have since died.

From my immediate family, my mother Penny Wilson and my brother John Wilson proofread the entire book. Annette and Neil Harris were co-opted to read various chapters as well. Sam Wilson helped check figures, and he and Aran always gave support and encouragement.

As ever, the greatest support came from Helen, who provided every weapon in an experienced legal author and publisher's armoury in assisting with concepts, research, drafting, editing and artwork. In real life her assistance was much greater still.

All errors are my sole responsibility.

Notes

Lord Denning on Lord Denning

1. The exchange took place during the costs argument following *R v Police Commissioner, ex parte Blackburn*: see *The Times*, 7 March 1980.

Preface

1. See Appendix I, which shows the extent of Denning's citations in the Law Reports.
2. *Hinz v Berry* [1970] 2 QB 40.
3. *Thornton v Shoe Lane Parking* [1971] 2 QB 163.
4. *Burgess v Rawnsley* [1975] Ch 429.
5. *Beswick v Beswick* [1966] 3 WLR 396.
6. *Lloyd's Bank Ltd v Bundy* [1975] QB 326.
7. *Deeble v Robinson* [1954] 1 QB 77.
8. *R v Barnsley Metropolitan Borough Council, ex parte Hook* [1976] 3 All ER 452.
9. See for example Lord Nolan, 'The Role of the Judge in Judicial Inquiries' (1999) *Denning Law Journal*, Vol 14, No 1, 147 at 150; and Sir Henry Brooke, 'Lord Denning and I (2): 1962–1972', personal blog, 21 December 2016. https://bit.ly/3aBE8Vy. See also Freeman, pp 93 and 355.

   In terms of extant recordings of Denning, a panel discussion from Australian radio on 12 July 1967 betrays a definite Hampshire origin in his speech (see Hampshire Archives AV13/15/S1), but it is fair to say his accent was more pronounced in the later recordings such as his *Desert Island Discs* appearance in 1980 (see Hampshire Archives AV13/10/S1).
10. Alex Aldridge, 'Cambridge law student launches Lord Denning-inspired search engine', *Legal Cheek*, 26 April 2017. https://bit.ly/37urgjA. The search engine could not be accessed at the time of writing.
11. Rozenberg, 'Joshua Rozenberg on Lord Denning: Worthy of his law student favourite crown?', *Legal Cheek*, 23 January 2017. https://bit.ly/2P1tz82.
12. Sir Stephen Sedley, 'Lord Denning obituary', *The Guardian*, 6 March 1999.

13   Richard Davenport-Hines, *An English Affair: Sex, Class and Power in the Age of Profumo* (William Collins, 2013), p 332.
14   @davidallengreen, posts of 18 April and 27 May 2020.

Note on Currency

1   Monetary amounts were expressed as pounds (£), shillings (s.) and pence (d.), where £1 = 20s. = 240d.
2   www.bankofengland.co.uk/monetary-policy/inflation/inflation-calculator.
3   Websites I consulted included www.rightmove.co.uk and www.zoopla.co.uk.
4   A good starting point for those wanting more comparative figures is the website www.measuringworth.com. It allows for additional calculations of prices, wages and output.

Chapter I: Beginnings – From Whitchurch to Oxford

1   *The Family Story*, p 6. For his source Denning quoted GM Trevelyan, one of the most eminent English historians of the first half of the twentieth century.
2   Public records show Charles was born on 4 December 1859, in Norwood Terrace, Leckhampton, Gloucestershire.
3   *The Family Story*, p 11.
4   Denning reproduced the poem in *The Family Story*, p 12.
5   See Faith Eckersall, '10 things you might not know about Whitchurch', *Hampshire Life*, 2 August 2019. https://bit.ly/2G3dVEr.
6   Eckersell, *op cit*.
7   *The Closing Chapter*, p 29.
8   He referred to it with pride in an interview with Winchester Radio for his ninetieth birthday, January 1989, Hampshire Archives AV13/12/S1.
9   On the class system in Britain at the time, see for example David Cannadine, *Class in Britain* (Yale University Press, 1998; Penguin Books, 2000).
10 One finds in newspaper archives from the period many examples of how the community regarded its tradesfolk with affection and came together on regular occasions. The *Hampshire Chronicle* of 13 April 1907, for example, recorded the funeral for Mr R Hutchins, a 'tradesman of the old school', attended by 'a large number of professional and tradesmen of Whitchurch' including Charles Denning.
11 *The Family Story*, p 13.
12 *The Family Story*, p 18.
13 *Hampshire Chronicle*, 30 April 1904. The horses belonged to the 'Anglo American Oil Company'.
14 *The Family Story*, p 15.
15 Freeman, p 5.
16 *The Family Story*, p 17.
17 Freeman, p 10. The contents of the night cart were recycled as fertiliser. As grim as the 'facility' sounds to modern readers, it at least avoided some of the problems with Victorian sewerage: in cities, waste water found its way to rivers and became a source of cholera.

18 See Geoffrey Chamberlain, 'British maternal mortality in the 19th and early 20th centuries' (2006) 99(11) JR Soc Med 559.
19 The result in the case was upheld by the House of Lords: [1981] 1 All ER 267.
20 AS Wohl, *Endangered Lives: Public Health in Victorian Britain* (Harvard University Press, 1983), pp 52–53.
21 Wohl, *op cit*.
22 The danger of adding boracic acid to milk which had gone sour (in order to kill the taste and render it drinkable) derived from the absence of pasteurisation. TB was rife amongst cows. Milk that was not fresh had had ample time for the TB bacteria to multiply. Joan Lane, *A Social History of Medicine: Health, Healing and Disease in England 1750–1950* (Routledge, 2001), recorded (p 142) that by the mid-nineteenth century, TB accounted for as many as 60,000 children's deaths per year.
23 Domestic refrigerators, for example, were introduced in the Edwardian era, but early designs leaked harmful gases such as ammonia, methyl chloride and sulphur dioxide.
24 The smoke ball was advertised as a cure for influenza, released at a time when severe outbreaks had been occurring. It led to the famous unilateral contract case of *Carlill v Carbolic Smoke Ball Company* [1893] 1 QB 256.
25 Holloway outdid other snake oil salesmen by investing vast sums in advertising. Many advertisements appeared in the publications of the day which I sifted through while researching Denning's life, including the *Hampshire Chronicle* of 30 April 1904 containing the story of Charles Denning's unfortunate pony.
26 Freeman, p 15.
27 John Mortimer, 'Lord Denning: Long Life – Short Sentences' in John Mortimer, *In Character: Interviews with Some of the Most Influential and Remarkable Men and Women of Our Time* (Penguin Books, 1984), pp 9 and 12. As well as being a highly successful barrister (and Queen's Counsel), Mortimer was the creator of *Rumpole of the Bailey*.
28 *The Family Story*, p 21.
29 See Denning's unpublished lecture from 1990, entitled 'What happened 100 years ago: Salvation Army riots in Whitchurch'. Hampshire Archives 202M86/506.
30 On social mobility at the time generally, see Andrew Miles, *Social Mobility in Nineteenth- and Early Twentieth-Century England* (Palgrave Macmillan, 1999), and also David Charles Marsh, *The Changing Social Structure of England and Wales, 1871–1961* (Routledge, 1958).
31 In Denning's day, education was compulsory until the age of thirteen. For the early development which laid the basis for Denning's education, see Simon Heffer, *High Minds: The Victorians and the Birth of Modern Britain* (Windmill Books, 2014), Ch 12.
32 Marsh, *op cit*, p 207.
33 Letter to Reg, 25 April 1915. The family letters quoted herein are all from Hampshire Archives 202M86.
34 Curley, Sean (2016) *Lord Denning: Towards a theory of adjudication. An examination of the judicial decision making process of Lord Denning and his creation and use of the interstitial spaces within the law and legal process to assist in the exercise of his discretion and an examination of those factors which influenced that discretion*, Doctoral thesis, University of Huddersfield, p 216.
35 When interviewed in January 1989 for his ninetieth birthday by Winchester Radio (Hampshire Archives AV13/12/S1), Denning said that when he had met the 'higher ups' he found they were much like himself, 'very ordinary folk'. Although they tended to be 'first rate speakers', with outgoing personalities, 'they're just as simple and homely as you and me'.

36   Founded in 1570. By the time of the Dennings, it had been substantially expanded and took boarders as well as day pupils. The fact that Denning and Gordon started at the same time, despite being different ages, shows again how flexible (or inconsistent) the education system was at the time.
37   *The Family Story*, p vi.
38   The only authors found in his judgments were Shakespeare, Dickens, William Cowper, Wordsworth, Lord Tennyson, WS Gilbert, Lord Acton, Anthony Hope, Lewis Carroll and William Longfellow. See Stephens, Vol II, Ch 2.
39   In *The Family Story*, Denning stated that the exhibition was only £30 per year, but Freeman (p 38) discovered it was actually £40.
40   Sir Thomas Herbert Warren, KCVO (1853–1930), a lifelong academic, was president of Magdalen College from 1885 to 1928 and Vice-Chancellor of Oxford University from 1906 to 1910. In contrast with Denning's praise, the Duke of Windsor said of Warren: 'It was generally suspected that he was obsessed with the idea of filling Magdalen with titled undergraduates; hence, whenever he beamed upon me, I was never quite certain whether it was with a teacher's benevolence or from a collector's secret fascination with a coveted trophy'. See *A King's Story: The Memoirs of HRH The Duke of Windsor* (Cassell, 1951), p 94.
41   *The Family Story*, p 36.
42   *The Family Story*, p 37.
43   Hampshire Archives 202M86.

Chapter II: The First World War

1   See Christopher Clark, *The Sleepwalkers: How Europe Went to War in 1914* (HarperCollins, 2013). As we will see, women's rights, Irish independence and unification, and industrial strife continued to be significant issues throughout Denning's career and he would gain both fame and infamy in each of them.
2   *The Family Story*, p 43.
3   There has been much controversy among historians as to the true reasons Britain joined the conflict, irrespective of the ostensible reasons offered by the government of the day, but that is beyond our scope. See for example Niall Ferguson, *The Pity of War* (Penguin Books, revised edn, 2009) and Sir John Keegan, *The First World War: An Illustrated History* (Hutchinson, 2001) as well as Clark, *op cit*.
4   Modern scholars have challenged Denning's assumptions about the enthusiasm upon the outbreak of war: see for example Catriona Pennell, *A Kingdom United: Popular Responses to the Outbreak of the First World War in Britain and Ireland* (Oxford University Press, 2012).
5   See Anthony Seldon and David Walsh, *Public Schools and The Great War: The Generation Lost* (Pen & Sword Military, 2013).
6   Cambridge, on the other hand, was known for its pacifism, led by the academic Bertrand Russell, although many Cambridge students and alumni did enlist. See my earlier book *Noble Savages: The Savage Club and the Great War* (JH Productions, 2018; revised edn, 2020), p 378.
7   Heather Jones, 'A Prince in the Trenches? Edward VIII and the First World War' in Heidi Mehrkens and Frank Lorenz Müller (eds), *Sons and Heirs: Succession and Political Culture in Nineteenth-Century Europe* (Palgrave Macmillan, 2016), Ch 14, p 230.
8   Jones, *op cit*, p 229.

Notes

9   Quoted in Richard Holmes, *The Western Front* (BBC Worldwide, 1999), p 35. Though see also Clark, *op cit*, who argued that the European elites who vied to prove their virility in battle were suffering from a 'crisis of masculinity'.

10   The Denning family all wrote to each other with great frequency during the war, though only a few of the letters survive, preserved in Hampshire Archives 202M86. Bizarrely, to modern readers at least, as well as writing home throughout the conflict, the boys all sent washing through the post for Clara to attend to.

11   *The Family Story*, p 22.

12   *The Family Story*, p 44.

13   The rotation policy in and out of the line was introduced by the British in response to the increasing numbers of shell-shock victims that continuous trench warfare was producing. The numbers were still high – more than 80,000 diagnosed by the end of the war – though lower than some other armies, while the British Army was unique in serving in the war from the beginning without suffering a catastrophic loss of morale at any point.

14   Letter, 24 September 1916, Hampshire Archives 202M86, and also reproduced in *The Family Story*, p 46.

15   CR Simpson, *History of the Lincolnshire Regiment 1914–1918* (Naval and Military Press, 2009).

16   Hampshire Archives 202M86.

17   *The Family Story*, p 54.

18   Later in the war they would be a vital part of protecting convoys, though the convoy system to defend merchant ships against U-Boats had not been developed at the time of Gordon's service.

19   I have written about Jutland in *Noble Savages*, *op cit*, pp 113–25. For more detail on Jutland and the First World War at sea in general, a good starting point is Robert K Massie, *Castles of Steel* (Jonathan Cape, 2004).

20   *The Family Story* p 64.

21   According to his official citation. See the *London Gazette*, 15 September 1916, Supplement 29751, p 9079.
See also www.naval-history.net/WW1NavyBritishLGDecorations1916Jutland.htm.

22   *The Family Story*, pp 68–70.

23   *The Family Story*, p 71.

24   More than 73,000 men gained infantry commissions after being trained in an OTC, with increasing numbers coming from 'the ranks' as the war went on.

25   In a letter to Reg of 15 November 1916, he wrote that he had talked it over with Jack on the latter's last leave, and Jack had advised 'whatever you do, don't go into the poor old infantry; go into the artillery or engineers'.

26   *The Family Story*, p 72.

27   The order was handwritten. It was reproduced verbatim in many newspapers, often without commentary (see for example *The Western Daily Press*, 13 April 1918). After the war it was passed to Haig's private secretary and later to the British Library, where it remains.

28   *The Family Story*, p 73.

29   History of the 38th (Welsh) Division, quoted in *The Family Story*, p 74. Thiepval is now the site of one of the great British war memorials, by Sir Edwin Lutyens.

30   *The Family Story*, p 75.

31 See '1918 Pandemic (H1N1 virus)', Centers for Disease Control and Prevention, https://bit.ly/2YjhlIW.
32 *The Family Story*, p 75.
33 *The Family Story*, p 75.
34 *The Family Story*, p 252.
35 The memorial within the Church has the names of all residents who died in service during the Great War. The presence of Gordon Denning confirms that the tuberculosis from which he died was attributed to his war service (as does the fact his grave in the nearby cemetery has a Commonwealth War Graves Commission headstone). Interestingly, very few apart from Jack and Gordon were officers, another example of how the Dennings were exceptional in their ability to rise above the social strata of the day.
36 A recording of him doing so on one occasion is available at Hampshire Archives AV13/20/S1. The emotion and power in his voice was uncharacteristically strong, clearly betraying the depth of his feelings.
37 23 May 1980. Available at the time of writing at www.bbc.co.uk/programmes/p009mw7n.
38 The rate of venereal infections, for example, was consistent with men not troubling with social norms given they faced death on a daily basis when in the frontline trenches. See Mark Harrison, 'The British Army and the Problem of Venereal Disease in France and Egypt during the First World War' (1995) *Medical History*, Vol 39, No 2, 133.
39 *The Family Story*, p 51.
40 See *Noble Savages, op cit*, pp 68–69.
41 Freeman, p 79. On the controversy about the generals of the First World War, see *Noble Savages, op cit*, Ch 4.
42 See *Noble Savages, op cit*, p 329.

Chapter III: 1920s – From Oxford to the Bar

1 £500 in 1922 equated to £21,899.76 in 2022, according to the Bank of England inflation calculator. In October 2022 the property website rightmove.co.uk was advertising three-bedroom properties in Whitchurch ranging from about £300,000 to more than £600,000.
2 Freeman, p 117. It was suggested to the author while researching this book that the exact arrangements over The Hermitage had caused some difficulty between the brothers, but in the absence of primary source documents I can draw no definitive conclusion.
3 *The Family Story*, pp 81–82.
4 Freeman seemed to think it odd that Mary never said the name of her other suitor and nor did Denning ever ask. There seems no reason, however, why she would have written his name down, since nothing ever came of their relationship.
5 See Heward, p 13.
6 Which, it should be stressed, is not to suggest that Magdalen went so far as to facilitate bribery arrangements in which ungifted sons of the rich would pay more capable scholars to write papers and sit exams for them.
7 In *The Family Story*. See Magdalen's website (www.magd.ox.ac.uk/news/professor-robert-denning/, accessed 4 October 2020).
8 About £12,000 in 2022, according to the Bank of England inflation calculator, but on the other hand many times what a labourer might have earned in 1920.

9 Letter, 26 November 1920. Hampshire Archives 202M86. It might have been that his sense of restlessness had been in some way prompted or increased by his war service.
10 According to the Bank of England inflation calculator, £100 in 1922 was equivalent to about £4,380 in 2022, not riches at Oxford even allowing for the minimal lodging costs Denning would have incurred.
11 *The Family Story*, p 38.
12 RFV Heuston, 'Lord Denning: The Man and his Times' in Jowell and McAuslan noted that the language Denning used in that passage was redolent of Hans Kelsen, which would not have reached Oxford when Denning was a student.
13 Freeman, p 77.
14 *The Family Story*, p 92.
15 *The Family Story*, p 39.
16 Freeman, p 80. I have had independent corroboration of Denning's continued disgruntlement with his All Souls' rejection into his dotage.
17 Cyril Harvey (1900–1968), who obtained Firsts in Jurisprudence (1922) and BCL (1923), winning the Vinerian Scholarship in 1923 as well. He became a KC in 1950 and was elected a Bencher of the Inner Temple in 1958.
18 Alan Patrick (AP) Herbert (1890–1971), author and MP. He read for the Bar but never practised. See my book, *Noble Savages: The Savage Club and the Great War* (JH Productions, 2018; revised edn, 2020), pp 325–33. Denning quoted one of the *Uncommon Law* spoofs in *The Family Story*, pp 95–96.
19 The others were Lord (Edward) Carson, like Radcliffe better known among the general public for his part in a contentious boundary dispute – in his case the creation of Northern Ireland – and Lord Reid, who had been a Tory Attorney General but received near-universal praise for his work as a law lord. After the Supreme Court was created in the twenty-first century, some controversy ensued when Jonathan Sumption QC was appointed directly from the Bar. Initially, he withdrew his candidature in the face of opposition from existing judges, but later reapplied and accepted the post. Upon his retirement he revealed that Denning had advised him to stay working as a professional historian, rather than retraining as a barrister: see Thomas Connelley, 'Lord Denning once told Lord Sumption becoming a barrister would be a "big mistake"', *Legal Cheek*, 12 December 2018. https://bit.ly/3ghxCXy.
20 Cyril Radcliffe, *Censors: The Rede Lecture* (Cambridge University Press, 1961), pp 26–27.
21 See https://4bc.co.uk/about-us/.
The 4 Brick Court of Denning's time later merged with 3 Pump Court and, in 1967, was absorbed into 7 King's Bench Walk, which continues in the present day. See https://7kbw.co.uk/about-us/history/.
22 *The Family Story*, p 93.
23 *The Times*, 31 July 1980, reporting Denning's speech upon Ms Hill's retirement. Note that here and elsewhere in the book I am distinguishing between press reporters and 'law reporters'; the latter refers to what Lord Neuberger accurately called 'scholarly law reporters' who write expert headnotes and digests for a legal audience (see Lord Neuberger, President of The Supreme Court, First annual BAILII Lecture, 'No Judgment – No Justice', 20 November 2012).
24 Denning's fee books are preserved in Hampshire Archives 202M86.
25 The sum of £94 10s was worth about £4,400 in 2022 money and £35 10s about £1,600.

26 Heward, p 21.
27 'Clerk of the Peace' was an office in England and Wales responsible for the records of the quarter sessions and the framing of presentments and indictments. Officeholders were legally trained and advised justices of the peace.
28 The property sold as a five-bedroom terraced house in November 2011 for £3,000,000 and, having been substantially renovated, for £4,990,000 in March 2016 according to the Land Registry.
29 'Quantum Meruit and the Statute of Frauds' (1925) 41 LQR 79.
30 See Hampshire Archives 202M86/602.
31 Respectively, the equivalents in 2022 according to the Bank of England inflation calculator: £360 in 1926 was £16,961.06; £470 in 1927 was £22,758.71; £860 in 1928 was £41,643.60; and £1,130 in 1929 was £55,332.56. Again, they were many times the average wage and, in that context, placed Denning in a very high income bracket for the time, the final amount being in the region of twenty times the average wage.
32 See www.fladgate.com/about-us/our-history/.
33 'Re-entry for Forfeiture' (1927) 43 LQR 53.
34 Sir Thomas Willes Chitty, 1st Baronet (1855–1930), judge and legal scholar. From 1901 to 1920, he was a Master of the King's Bench Division. From 1920 to 1926, he served as the King's Remembrancer; the oldest judicial position in continual existence.
35 Sir Arthur John Grattan-Bellew QC (1903–85). Irish in origin, Grattan-Bellew attended Downside School, Bath followed by Christ's College, Cambridge. In 1935, he left the Bar and joined the Civil Service. During the Second World War, he was an officer in the 3rd/7th Dogra Regiment of the Indian Army, and was a POW from 1942 to 1945. Afterwards, he returned to Whitehall and was sent to various senior empire postings, including Attorney General of Tanganyika and, from 1956 to 1959, Chief Secretary of Tanganyika.
36 Denning also contributed a few entries to a similar publication, *The English and Empire Digests* (published by Butterworths), but he soon gave up as the pay was too low.
37 See *The Discipline of Law*, p 202.
38 See Freeman, pp 75–77.
39 *The Family Story*, p 84.
40 Hampshire Archives 202M86, also reproduced in Freeman, p 98.
41 The diaries are preserved in Hampshire Archives 202N86/41/17–18. Almost every entry began with Mary noting the weather and then recording briefly any outings or visitors.

Chapter IV: 1930s – From First Marriage to the Second World War

1 Hampshire Archives 202M86, also reproduced in Freeman, p 99. 'I wrote and accepted Tom ... So happy!' she recorded in her diary. The following day she wrote 'Tom rang me up in the evening. All too wonderful for words!'
2 According to the Bank of England inflation calculator, £1,410 would be £71,038.76 in 2022 money. In 1930 the average wage for a timework labourer in the engineering field was just under a shilling per hour. See Nicholas Crafts, *Work and Pay in 20th Century Britain* (Oxford University Press, 2007).
3 According to the Bank of England inflation calculator, £900 in 1930 equated to £45,343.89 in 2022.

Notes

4   Norman, like Denning, was unmarried at that point. Norman went on to marry Iris Curtis, the daughter of a master mariner, in May 1933.

5   Mindful of the fact they were self-employed, married barristers of the day often insured themselves against loss of income. Henn Collins recommended seeking insurance of £4,000, requiring an annual premium of £100. The respective 2022 figures were £201,528.38 and £5,038.21, as per the Bank of England inflation calculator.

6   Pritt's covering letter with the gift (dated 23 October 1930) predicted that Denning would become 'one of the most noted judges of the day'. Pritt clearly knew Denning well by that stage. Hampshire Archives 202M86/63/10.

7   On 18 June, Mary recorded in her diary that she had been diagnosed with TB ('Sickening', she wrote). The next day she wrote that she had been to a doctor in London, and that 'Encouraging – says I shall be cured. Says I am not to marry for 2 years. Boo-hoo!' Hampshire Archives 202N86/41/17–18.

8   *The Family Story*, p 86.

9   According to the British Lung Foundation, 381 deaths from tuberculosis occurred in the United Kingdom in 2008 and 282 in 2012: see https://statistics.blf.org.uk/tb.

10   Since renamed *Bullen & Leake & Jacob's Precedents of Pleadings*, and up to the 19th edition at the time of writing, published by Sweet & Maxwell. It remains one of the standard works on procedural law.

11   The lease was £187 10s per annum, approximately £10,000 in 2022 figures.

12   In that pre-digital age, local newspapers often performed a function not dissimilar to modern social media, recording both formal and informal social events and the minutiae thereof such as bridal outfits.

13   The Palace Hotel was originally a stately home built in 1841 by Henry Philpotts, Bishop of Exeter, financed by compensation he received from freeing slaves from a plantation in the Caribbean. It was converted into a hotel in 1921. During the Second World War, while being used as an RAF hospital, it suffered damage during an air raid which caused thirty-seven casualties. It reopened as a hotel in 1948, closed in 2017 and was demolished in 2020.

14   Theodore Mathew, *Forensic Fables by O* (Wildy, Simmonds & Hill, 2013), pp 15–16. The fable concerned an arrogant Double-First defending a railway company (here giving credence to the Denning claim, given his experience of the same) against an inflated claim for personal damages brought by an Old Hand at the Bar. The Double-First 'misunderestimated' his opponent, to borrow a phrase from George W Bush, and the Old Hand successfully played the jury and won the case. The day ended in disaster for the Double-First, with the moral of the story being 'Despise not your enemy'.

15   *Hansard*, HL Deb, 23 May 1977, vol 383, col 1119.

16   Denning's assertion of disinterest on the part of the law reporters was not entirely fair, given that the case was reported in the official reports at [1934] 2 KB 394. Those reports usually took months to appear after the judgment was given, however, because the reporters had to summarise the arguments in court as well as the judgment, and their draft report had to be checked by the responsible judge or judges. The case predated the *Weekly Law Reports* and the *All England Law Reports* so there was no quicker means by which a citeable report might have been obtained. (The All ER later published it as part of its reprint series of notable historic cases at [1934] All ER Rep 16.)

17   Some £163,426.92 in 2022 terms just by the measure of inflation.

18 See www.london.anglican.org/kb/care-of-churches-glossary/.
19 Reported as *Beresford v Royal Insurance Co Ltd* [1938] AC 586.
20 Otherwise known as 'taking silk', in reference to the fact that KCs used to wear silk gowns instead of those made of more plebian material. If a female sovereign was on the throne the rank would change to QC, just as the King's Bench Division of the High Court would become the Queen's Bench Division.
21 The letters are preserved in Hampshire Archives 202M86. Most were written by hand with the stylish calligraphy of the day; unfortunately, many of the signatures have since faded to illegibility. One remaining identifiable was Gilbert Beyfus (1885–1960). His clients included Liberace, whose famous libel case I wrote about in *Trials and Tribulations* (Wildy, Simmonds & Hill, 2015), p 139.

In amongst Denning's letters of congratulation was one dated 7 April from BL Pavey of Annesley, 10 Minehead Road, Streatham Common, thanking him for the support for his old regiment, which was celebrating its 250th anniversary, and hoping that Denning might put in a word for him should he find a solicitors' firm in need of a clerk.
22 Letter from Montagu's and Cox & Cardale, 1 April 1938.
23 Letter signed BA Cooper, 9 April 1938.
24 Many years later, Denning gave an interview looking back on 1938, in which he quoted from Mary's diary and opined on various events of the year including the Major's suicide. He thought that the Major's case would have succeeded in later times. He defended Chamberlain on the ground that appeasement had bought Britain time to rearm – a controversial opinion, to put it mildly. Overall, he felt, 'we lived a quiet family life, like so many people do. Not worrying overmuch about the war or threats of war, just carrying on'. See Hampshire Archives AV13/13/S1. (The date of the interview is unclear: it is stated in the Archives as 1938, but it was obviously made many years after.)

Chapter V: The Second World War

1 See Robert Cohen, *When the Old Left Was Young: Student Radicals and America's First Mass Student Movement, 1929–41* (Oxford University Press, 1997).
2 Martin Gilbert, *Prophet of Truth. Winston S. Churchill. 1922–1939* (Minerva, 1990), p 456.
3 See for example Thomas Jones, *Lloyd George* (Harvard University Press, 1951) and Thomas Linehan, *British Fascism, 1918–39: Parties, Ideology and Culture* (Manchester University Press, 2000). Andrew Roberts, *Eminent Churchillians*, Kindle edn (Weidenfeld & Nicolson, 2010), Ch 1, contains an excoriating attack on the royal family and appeasement in the 1930s.
4 See for example M Cronin (ed), *The Failure of British Fascism* (Palgrave Macmillan, 1996).
5 Mark Pottle, 'Carter, (Helen) Violet Bonham, Baroness Asquith of Yarnbury (1887–1969)', *Oxford Dictionary of National Biography*, online edn (Oxford University Press, 2007). Lady Violet's father, HH Asquith, had been Prime Minister at the time Britain entered the First World War.
6 Chamberlain's radio broadcast, 3 September 1939, 11:00 am.
7 Malcolm Muggeridge, *Chronicles of Wasted Time* (Regent College Publishing, 2006).
8 Denning set out Reg and Norman's service in some detail in *The Family Story*. Both received great praise from Lord Mountbatten: Reg served on Mountbatten's staff in the Far East, while after the war Norman was selected by Mountbatten for high-ranking intelligence roles in the Royal Navy.

I should note at this point that I was critical of Mountbatten in various respects in my book *Noble Savages: The Savage Club and the Great War* (JH Productions, 2020). It is right to record, however, that Mountbatten was an exceptional motivator of those under his command and skilled at choosing the right men for his staff. Accordingly, his praise of Norman and Reg should not be diluted by any of his own personal shortcomings.

9   *The Family Story*, pp 129–30.
10 In late August 1939, as Germany and the Soviet Union concluded the Nazi–Soviet Pact which opened the way for the German invasion of Poland, Parliament passed the Emergency Powers (Defence) Act 1939. It gave authority to implement the Defence Regulations. Code A was brought into effect that day and Code B followed on 1 September.
11 Note that counsel for Liversidge was DN Pritt KC, Denning's old leader and mentor.
12 Apart from Liversidge himself, those detained under regulation 18B included Oswald Mosley and the author Henry Williamson.
13 In *The Family Story*, pp 130–31. The story of Lord Atkin's speech is told more fully in his biography, Geoffrey Lewis, *Lord Atkin* (Butterworths, 1981).
14 See for example Denning, 'Freedom under the Law', First Hamlyn Lectures (Stevens & Sons, 1949). He was still making the same point four decades after the Second World War: see for example 'Harrods bombing shows peril still present', *The Times*, 24 February 1984, p 4.
15 See AWB Simpson, *In the Highest Degree Odious: Detention without Trial in Wartime Britain* (Clarendon Press, 1992); RFV Heuston, '*Liversidge v Anderson* in Retrospect' (1970) 86 LQR 33. The opinion has not been universal: see Francis Bennion, 'Defending *Liversidge v Anderson*' (1988) *Denning Law Journal*, Vol 3, No 1.
16 The Privy Council in *Nakkuda Ali v Jayaratne* [1951] AC 66 at 76–7 restricted *Liversidge* to an interpretation of regulation 18B itself. In 1980 Lord Diplock in *R v IRC, ex parte Rossminster Ltd* [1980] AC 952 at 1011 stated that the time had come 'to acknowledge openly that the majority of this House in *Liversidge v Anderson* were expediently and, at that time, perhaps, excusably, wrong and the dissenting speech of Lord Atkin was right'.
17 I use the phrase 'British Empire and associated Dominions' advisedly. It was not Britain herself alone, but in conjunction with Australia, Canada, India, New Zealand and others, all of whom made substantial contributions to defending Britain and British interests in the Second World War.
18 See Alexander Horne, 'The Courts and Counter-Terrorism – Asserting the Rule of Law? *A v Secretary of State for the Home Department*' in Ian MacDougall (ed), *Cases that Changed Our Lives* (LexisNexis, 2010), p 195.
19 *Begum* concerned a woman born in the United Kingdom who at the age of fifteen travelled to Syria to join the Islamic State of Iraq and the Levant (ISIS). In 2019 she expressed a wish to return to Britain, which the British Government opposed. A series of proceedings resulted in the Supreme Court upholding the Home Secretary's decision not to grant Begum leave to enter the United Kingdom. The comparison with *Liversidge* was made by, among others, the legal commentator David Allen Green. See his blog *The Law and Policy Blog*, 27 February 2021, https://bit.ly/3uXkkq0.

20 After he became a judge, Denning sat on the Privy Council in another case relating to Maori land, see *Maori Trustee v Ministry of Works* [1958] 3 All ER 336. That case did not raise issues of constitutional principle, however, instead turning on the interpretation of the Public Works Act 1928.
21 See for example Paul McHugh, *The Maori Magna Carta* (Oxford University Press, 1991) and Philip Joseph, *Joseph on Constitutional and Administrative Law*, 5th edn (Thomson Reuters, 2021).
22 By the Bank of England inflation calculator, £4,000 in 1940 would be £172,596.09 in 2022. A comparable house in Copyhold Lane (recently refurbished, six bedroom detached with two acres) sold in 2015 for £2,675,000.
23 See David Lough, *No More Champagne: Churchill and his Money* (Head of Zeus, 2015).
24 Hampshire Archives 202M86.
25 Mary's final diary entry was on 17 November 1941. It recorded a visit from a friend who brought a rabbit and some eggs, but added ominously 'I had a strange haemorrhage about 8:30pm!' and that the doctor had come and given her an injection. Hampshire Archives 202N86/41/17–18.
26 AT Denning, 'Why I Believe In God', Transcript of a talk delivered on the BBC Home Service, 14 September 1943. Quoted in Andrew Phang, 'A Passion for Justice: Lord Denning, Christianity and the Law' in Mark Hill and RH Helmholz (eds), *Great Christian Jurists in English History* (Cambridge University Press, 2017), Ch 15.
27 The Lord Chancellor would solicit the views of the leader of the Bar on the circuit, which in Denning's case was George Lynskey KC, himself later a well-respected High Court judge. Lynskey told Denning he had won 'golden opinions': see *The Family Story*, p 133.
28 The Probate, Divorce and Admiralty Division was one of the not entirely logical ways in which the High Court was divided in those days. Nowadays, the Chancery Division hears probate matters (except non-contentious ones, with which the Family Division still deals) and the Family Division hears divorce, while the Admiralty Court is administratively joined with the Commercial Court.
29 Freeman, p 149.
30 MDA Freeman, 'Family Matters' in Jowell and McAuslan, pp 109 and 147. MDA Freeman was not related to Iris Freeman and their works should not be confused.
31 Again, the letters are preserved in Hampshire Archives 202M86. Regrettably, many of the signatures are no longer legible.
32 Letter from 6 Pump Court, 15 March 1944. Incidentally, Aldous was the father of Sir William Aldous, a much later judge of the Court of Appeal.
33 Letter, 20 March 1944. Hampshire Archives 202M86. Note that Marjorie had not returned to live permanently at Whitchurch at that stage, much to Clara's frustration. In 1941 Clara had written to Denning about the finances concerning The Hermitage, stating that she thought Johnny should repay the money Reg and Tom had contributed to the purchase of the house, the assumption being that Johnny and Marjorie would then live there and care for her. See Freeman, p 136.
34 *The Family Story*, p 134.
35 On a speech marking his eightieth birthday he looked back over his life, quoting Churchill's 'fight on the beaches' speech and Shakespeare's *King John* (Act 5, Scene 7), which begins 'This England never did, nor never shall, Lie at the proud foot of a conqueror ... Nought shall make us rue, If England to itself do rest but true'. See Denning, 'This is My Life' (1986) *Denning Law Journal*, Vol 1, No 1, 17 at 22.

Notes

Chapter VI: Judicial Beginnings – Wills, Wives and Wrecks

1 *The Due Process of Law*, p 189.
2 *The Due Process of Law*, p 188. The Catholic Church of the day was implacably opposed to divorce, a fact which Denning felt influenced Wallington.
3 In the context of law reporting, '*ex tempore*' can mean one or both of two things: a judgment delivered immediately at the conclusion of the hearing, rather than reserved, or delivered orally rather than in writing. In Denning's time, before computers shortened the time required for judgment preparation, oral judgments were the norm even for reserved judgments. The House of Lords' judgments were referred to as 'speeches', from the archaic times before the formation of the Appellate Committee of the House of Lords. With reference to Denning's time in the divorce courts, his judgments were normally *ex tempore* in both senses: delivered orally immediately following the end of the hearing.
4 *The Due Process of Law*, p 190.
5 'Presumptions and Burdens' (1945) 61 LQR 379.
6 *The Due Process of Law*, p 190.
7 See *Prescott v Fellowes* [1958] P 260.
8 Denning's claim that he had been overturned only once in that time has been repeated by others (see for example MDA Freeman, 'Family Justice and Family Values according to Lord Denning' (1999) *Denning Law Journal*, Vol 14, No 1, 93), though since law reporting in those days was not comprehensive I have been unable to verify his claim through primary sources.
9 Freeman, p 97.
10 Between 1945 and 1969 judges (usually law lords) chaired seven of twenty-four Royal Commissions and 118 of the 358 Departmental Committees. See Robert Stevens, *The English Judges: Their Role in the Changing Constitution* (Hart Publishing, 2005), p 29.
11 Terence Donovan, the future Lord Donovan, Sir Edwin Herbert, later Lord Tangley and John Foster, later Sir John Foster.
12 See www.relate.org.uk. Denning became President in 1949.

Chapter VII: 1945–47 – Second Marriage; Second Judicial Role

1 *The Family Story*, p 140.
2 *The Family Story*, p 140.
3 Freeman, p 157.
4 Interview with the *Mail on Sunday*, 24 October 1982.
5 Letter quoted in Freeman, p 164.
6 On leaving Winchester Robert did National Service, where he reached the rank of lieutenant in the King's Royal Rifle Corps and served in Libya, before going up to Oxford and beginning a distinguished academic and scientific career. During his studies at Oxford he also met his future wife Elizabeth Chilton, who was operating an infrared spectrometer in the laboratory. They had two children, Mark (born 1974) and Paul (born 1977). See Robert's obituary in *The Times*, 28 June 2013.

7   Pauline taught at the Royal Academy of Music until setting up the New College, where she taught full time as well as being an examiner for London University and the Institute of Education. She continued training students at the Royal Academy of Music and produced operas there. She later directed operas at Trinity College of Music, London, where she was made a fellow in 1976. She married the BBC producer Derick Simond. She died in 2017.

Hazel became a highly successful barrister, taking silk as well as teaching at Oxford part time. She married Michael Fox, who later became a Lord Justice of Appeal.

John studied physics and had a successful career with the ICI chemicals company. He died in 2020.

8   Freeman, p 108.

9   Heward, p 41, who noted also that Joan's father had held the first driving licence issued in London.

10 In 1995 an internal review into the lodgings recommended stringent cost controls. The cost of the lodgings then was £3.9m a year. The cost had risen to £4.785m by 2000. As late as 2014 the Ministry of Justice announced it was reviewing the system of lodging 'to ensure better value for hardworking taxpayers' money', and Labour proposed reform of the system in its 2015 manifesto.

11 Hampshire Archives 202M86.

12 'Valedictory Speeches upon the Impending Retirement of the Master of the Rolls', 30 July 1982, Hampshire Archives 202M86/760. A recording is in Hampshire Archives AV13/16/S1.

13 See for example David Pannick QC, 'Why Levin merits an honourable mention in our legal history', *The Times*, 7 September 2004.

14 *Report of Royal Commission on Capital Punishment, 1949–1953*, Cmd 8932, 53, p 18. See, further, HLA Hart, *Punishment and Responsibility: Essays in the Philosophy of Law* (Oxford University Press, 1968), pp 2 and 36. Denning's remarks were quoted in a United States' case: *Furman v Georgia* (1972) 408 US 238 at 453.

15 In the 1920s, Lord Atkin had chaired a committee to consider whether any changes should be made to the law of insanity. See Geoffrey Lewis, *Lord Atkin* (Butterworths, 1981), pp 158–65.

16 *The Family Story*, p 165.

17 Cameron Harvey, 'It all started with Gunner James' (1983) 17 Law Soc of UC Gazette 279, (1986) *Denning Law Journal*, Vol 1, No 1, 67.

18 Patrick Polden, 'The Uses of Power: Mr Justice Denning and the Pensions Appeal Tribunals' (1988) *Denning Law Journal*, Vol 3, No 1, 97.

19 Polden concluded that 'Denning's achievement in pensions cases, therefore, was principally to impose on an informal, expert tribunal, the traditional model of due process developed by the courts of law, and to ensure by unprecedently close supervision that the claimants received the "justice" to which they were entitled. What he did not do was stretch and bend the law so as to favour the claimants in their fight for pensions. There is an impressive coherence and consistency in his pensions decisions which shines out in the poverty of English administrative law in the 1940s and deserves recognition'. Patrick Polden, 'The Uses of Power: Mr Justice Denning and the Pensions Appeal Tribunals' (1988) *Denning Law Journal*, Vol 3, No 1, 97 at 122. Legend Press Limited. Reproduced with permission of the Licensor through PLSclear.

20   High Trees House itself was – and is – an Art Deco block on the south side of Clapham Common. The building was designed by RWH Jones, best known as architect of the Saltdean Lido.
21   See DM Gordon QC, 'Creditors' promises to forgo rights' [1963] CLJ 222.
22   See for example *The Road to Justice*, p 25 and *Goold v Evans* [1951] 2 TLR 119.
23   See for example GC Cheshire and HS Fifoot, '*Central London Property Trust Ltd v High Trees House Ltd*' (1947) 63 LQR 283; JF Wilson, 'Recent Developments in Estoppel' (1951) 67 LQR 330; and LA Sheridan, 'Equitable Estoppel Today' (1952) 15 MLR 325. Denning's later thoughts on the case were set out in *The Discipline of Law*, Part Five (pp 197 *et seq*). He thought there had been no appeal because the decision could be supported on other grounds.
24   Robert Pearce QC, 'A promise is a promise: *Central London Property Trust Ltd v High Trees House Ltd*' in Ian McDougall (ed), *Cases that Changed Our Lives* (LexisNexis, 2010), pp 91 and 95. Among the later cases was Denning's decision in *Charles Rickards Ltd v Oppenhaim* [1950] 1 KB 616, in which he extended promissory estoppel from an actual promise or assurance to circumstances where there had been neither, only conduct.
25   In the *Tool Metal Manufacturing* case, the House of Lords only mentioned *High Trees* in passing. According to the LexisNexis 'case overview' (www.lexisnexis.com), *High Trees* had been considered or applied in sixteen cases up until June 2021, though never by the House of Lords or Supreme Court. The most recent consideration was by the Court of Appeal in *Collier v P & M J Wright (Holdings) Ltd* [2007] EWCA Civ 1329, [2008] 1 WLR 643.
26   *ICLR 150 Years: creating case history* (ICLR, 2015).
27   Lord Neuberger, 'Reflections on the ICLR Top Fifteen Cases: A talk to commemorate the ICLR's 150th Anniversary', 6 October 2015. The 150 years were divided into five separate periods, with three cases chosen from each.
28   *The Family Story*, p 163. The Court of Appeal's decision was reported as *R v West* [1948] 1 KB 709.
29   Hampshire Archives 202M86/781/2.
30   Note that Denning's earlier biographer, Edmund Heward, accepted without question Denning's explanation that the appeal had succeeded because the indictment was incorrectly framed, which had precluded a fair trial. He exculpated Denning on that point by suggesting that he was concerned with the merits of the case over and above the procedural question of a fair trial. Heward made no mention of the way in which the Court of Appeal had rubbished the charge against David Weitzman KC, and also made no mention of any suggestion of anti-Semitism. See Heward, p 45.
31   According to Robert Stevens, *The English Judges: Their Role in the Changing Constitution* (Hart Publishing, 2005), p 39, anti-Semitism had driven HLA (Herbert) Hart away from the Chancery Bar, but it subsequently disappeared from legal appointments, at least after 1944 when Lord Schuster (1869–1956) ceased his long tenure as Permanent Secretary to the Lord Chancellor. Ironically, Lord Schuster was of Jewish origin himself.
32   Denning, 'Freedom under the Law', First Hamlyn Lectures (Stevens & Sons, 1949). A modern reader would question Denning's contradistinction between 'Jews' and 'ourselves', but the principle of non-discrimination that he was urging was clear.

Chapter VIII: The Court of Appeal

1. As before, the letters and cards are preserved in Hampshire Archives 202M86.
2. See Curley, Sean (2016) *Lord Denning: Towards a theory of adjudication. An examination of the judicial decision making process of Lord Denning and his creation and use of the interstitial spaces within the law and legal process to assist in the exercise of his discretion and an examination of those factors which influenced that discretion*, Doctoral thesis, University of Huddersfield.
3. Freeman, p 195.
4. Stephen Sedley, 'This beats me' (1998) *London Review of Books*, Vol 20, No 7, 2 April.
5. Paul Robertshaw, 'The Review Roles of the Court of Appeal: *Grobbelaar v News International*' (2001) 64(6) MLR 923 at 932.
6. See [1951] 2 All ER 278.
7. In his foreword to the first edition of the *Denning Law Journal*: (1986) Vol 1, No 1, 1. He discussed the case at some length in *The Discipline of Law*, pp 229 *et seq*.
8. Others considered that Lord Atkin's judgment did not reflect the opinion of the majority anyway, because the other two judges did not use the same terminology and their speeches seemed less far-reaching. The full history of the case is set out by Matthew Chapman in *The Snail and the Ginger Beer: The singular case of Donoghue v Stevenson* (Wildy, Simmonds & Hill, 2010).
9. PS Atiyah, 'Contract and Tort' in Jowell and McAuslan, p 56. As early as 1951, long before it was approved by the House of Lords, Denning's judgment was praised in the *Law Quarterly Review* by Professor Goodhart and by the American academic Warren A Seavey: see Freeman, p 210.
10. See *Mutual Life and Citizens Assurance Co v Evatt* [1971] AC 793.
11. Other well-known contract cases Denning decided in his first Court of Appeal stint included *Hain Steamship Co Ltd v Minister of Food* [1949] 1 KB 492, on payment of freight in carriage by sea; *Olley v Marlborough Court Hotel* [1949] 1 KB 532, on exclusion clauses in contract law; *Leaf v International Galleries* [1950] 2 KB 86, on the right to rescind; *Hoenig v Isaacs* [1952] 2 All ER 176, on substantive performance of an entire obligation; *Frederick E Rose (London) Ltd v William H Pim Junior & Co Ltd* [1953] 2 QB 450, on interpretation and rectification; and *Entores Ltd v Miles Far East Corporation* [1955] 2 All ER 493, on offer and acceptance.
12. In that case Denning applied the same principle – that the owner should insure – and therefore dissented where the majority of the Court of Appeal used old authority to uphold the publican's liability for a car stolen from his premises.
13. Other examples of Denning invoking equity to reach his preferred result abound; one from around the same time was *Errington v Wood* [1952] 1 KB 290, concerning agreement and the right to specific performance of an assurance upon which reliance had been placed. He was occasionally critical of the Chancery judges of old, however: see *The Discipline of Law*, p 23.
14. See Mary Welstead, 'The deserted bank and the spousal equity' (1999) *Denning Law Journal*, Vol 14, No 1, 113.
15. MDA Freeman, 'Family Matters' in Jowell and McAuslan, p 109 at 146.

16 Denning mentioned the letter in a lecture delivered to the Inns of Court School of Law on 1 March 1979, marking his eightieth birthday, reproduced in (1986) *Denning Law Journal*, Vol 1, No 1, 17. Heward also featured it but in a sanitised version in which he did not use the word 'whores', though like Denning himself I have assumed my readers to have more robust sensitivities.

17 MDA Freeman, 'Family Matters' in Jowell and McAuslan, p 109 at 146–47.

18 *National Provincial Bank v Ainsworth* [1965] AC 1175.

19 Denning was relieved that Parliament had restored a measure of protection to the deserted wife, but expressed concern in *The Due Process of Law* that the Act required a wife to register a charge to secure her rights. Years later one of his successors as MR, Lord Neuberger, wrote that Denning's efforts to create a deserted wife's equity was a 'wonderful example of his judicial advocacy': see Lord Neuberger MR, 'Has Equity Had Its Day?', Hong Kong University Common Law Lecture, 2010, p 4.

20 In his introduction to the first volume of the *Denning Law Journal*, *op cit*.

21 *Breen v Amalgamated Engineering Union* [1971] 2 QB 175. Denning in that case was characteristically dissenting. The plaintiff had been accused but cleared of misappropriating union funds. He was voted in as shop steward at his oil refinery in Fawley – the village Mary Harvey lived in at the time of her engagement to Denning – but the district secretary in Southampton who had been party to the dispute rejected his election. The plaintiff argued that the district secretary had acted contrary to natural justice. The High Court and subsequently the majority of the Court of Appeal held that rules of natural justice did not apply, and the committee had unfettered discretion under the rules. Only bad faith would suffice. Denning, by contrast, stated that administrative law applied to statutory and also to domestic bodies, and that it required fair hearings.

22 See Freeman, p 215.

23 Founded in 1852 as the Lawyers' Prayer Union in London, it was subsequently renamed the Lawyers' Christian Fellowship. It is still active today, see: https://lawcf.org/.

24 Hampshire Archives 29A05/PX13. Denning expressed the same view of the inextricable link between religion and morality, and the importance of Christian marriage many times. In 1952, for example, he gave a well-received and widely distributed centennial address to the Lawyers' Christian Fellowship.

25 Lady Denning, 'Another English Visitor in India' (1959) *The Cheshire Smile*, Vol 5, No 1, Spring.

26 In 1976 the foundation was renamed the Leonard Cheshire Foundation. In 2007 it changed names again to Leonard Cheshire Disability. Finally, in 2018 it shortened the name simply to 'Leonard Cheshire'.

27 Hampshire Archives 202M86/101.

28 Written by John Murray, Chairman of the Trustees, in November 1949 and reproduced in the foreword to Denning's Hamlyn Lectures, *op cit*.

29 Hamlyn Lectures, *op cit*, p 7.

30 The great American judge Benjamin Cardozo (who had other similarities with Denning, in particular his somewhat populist style of judgment-writing) had done so in a famous article, 'Law and Literature' (1925) 14 *Yale Review* 699.

31 For a start, the case only applied to people within the United Kingdom itself; British subjects continued to own slaves in the Empire and elsewhere. It would be decades before the practice was definitively outlawed by Britain, and then only made possible by compensating the slave owners rather than the slaves themselves. That said, it is also true that Britain was ahead of any other major slave trading entity of the time in voluntarily ending the practice, and the Royal Navy undertook anti-slavery patrols at its own expense and risk for many years after abolition.

32 There are over 100 Denning speeches in the Hampshire Archives, roughly half published and half unpublished, dating from 1947 to 1990. See the Denning Papers catalogue, pp 35–42.

33 Denning, *The Changing Law* (Stevens & Stevens, 1953).

34 'Judges as Lawmakers: The law on Trial', *The Times*, 17 June 1953. It added that Denning had laid bare the fiction that judges did not make law, only interpret it.

35 Viscount Haldane held the post from 1912 to 1915, having previously been a major reformer of the British Army as a member of the cabinet before the Great War.

36 Denning, *The Changing Law* (Stevens & Stevens, 1953), p 43.

37 The Lord Chancellor by then had evolved over many centuries into one of the strange hybrid roles that the British Constitution was apt to create: a judge, leader of the profession, a member of the House of Lords and a member of the cabinet. In the twenty-first century the position was downgraded to just another cabinet post, with no judicial function at all. The post was largely ignored since the holder was always the Secretary of State for Justice as well, a more public-facing role.

In my view another important protection of the rule of law was thereby lost, since the holder of the old post of Lord Chancellor, unlike normal MPs, was not beholden to the executive for their future career prospects. Instead, being a senior KC, the holder would always have independent means and thus have no fear about standing up for the rule of law and giving advice the government might not want to hear.

38 Sir Martin Nourse, 'Law and Literature: the legacy of Lord Denning' (2005) *Denning Law Journal*, Vol 17, No 1, 1 at 12. Legend Press Limited. Reproduced with permission of the Licensor through PLSclear.

39 Arlott (like Denning, famous for speaking with a Hampshire burr) toured South Africa in 1948–49 with the England cricket team and was appalled by apartheid (see his *Wisden Cricketers' Almanack* obituary, available online at https://es.pn/37nL2kk). Formby had toured the country in 1946. See Martin Chilton, 'The dark side of George Formby, a "dirty little Northern would-be Casanova"', *The Daily Telegraph*, 4 March 2021.

40 'The Beatles banned segregated audiences, contract shows', *BBC News*, 18 September 2011. https://bit.ly/3giyo71.

41 Interview with Winchester Radio for his ninetieth birthday, January 1989, Hampshire Archives AV13/12/S1.

42 Denning, *The Road to Justice* (Stevens & Sons, 1955).

43 *The Road to Justice*, p 126.

44 *The Road to Justice*, p 67.

45 *The Road to Justice*, pp 70–71.

46 Note that Freeman said disarmingly of Denning's stepdaughter Hazel, after she passed her Bar exams, 'He arranged a pupillage for her' (Freeman, p 236). No doubt Hazel's formidable intellectual powers – she had ranked second in the country in her exams – would have stood her in good stead to win one on her merits, and she went on to a highly distinguished legal career, so was not in need of Denning's intervention, but he clearly saw nothing wrong with using his influence in that respect.

47 According to the Ministry of Justice website in 2019, Heads of the High Court divisions received £226,193, Lord Justices of Appeal received £215,094 and High Court judges received £188,901.

48 *The Road to Justice*, p 89.

49 For example, in *The Road to Justice* at p 73 Denning wrote of open justice that 'the importance of having all judicial proceedings in public outweighs ... all the suggested disadvantages', for the press was 'the watchdog of justice'. There he overstated the case, for it is generally accepted that some aspects of family cases are best heard in private due to the personal nature of the evidence and the need to protect children. Similarly, in some national security cases justice might properly take place behind closed doors. In both cases the limits are highly contested – and, indeed, Denning himself made contentious decisions regarding open justice with regard in his Profumo report, discussed in Chapter XI, and later in cases involving national security, as we will see in Chapter XVIII.

50 See for example DPD, '*The Road to Justice* – Book Review' [1957] Res Jud 69.

51 LCB Gower, 'Review' (1956) 19(2) MLR 217.

52 Heward, p 173.

53 Much later in life, when interviewed by Winchester Radio for his ninetieth birthday (Hampshire Archives AV13/12/S1), he mentioned how he had suffered jet lag and thought there was 'a lot to be said' for the older, more sedate forms of transport.

54 He made the joke more than once; among other places it was noted in his *Times* obituary, 6 March 1999. www.thetimes.co.uk/article/lord-denning-9f2fpmghmth.

Chapter IX: The House of Lords

1 *The London Gazette*, 26 April 1957, No 41055, p 2519.

2 Preserved in Hampshire Archives 202M86.

3 Sir John Beaumont (1877–1974) was a servant of empire. He was appointed Chief Justice of the Bombay High Court in 1930 and served there until 1943.

4 Lord Nolan, 'The Role of the Judge in Judicial Inquiries' (1999) *Denning Law Journal*, Vol 14, No 1, 147 at 151.

5 John William Morris, Baron Morris of Borth-y-Gest (1896–1979) was a law lord from 1960 to 1975.

6 James Reid, Baron Reid (1890–1975) who, as noted earlier, was a politician before being (exceptionally) promoted directly to the House of Lords.

7 *Hansard*, HL Deb, 27 November 1957, vol 206, cols 522–92.

8 See https://api.parliament.uk/historic-hansard/people/mr-alfred-denning/ index.html.

9 *Hansard*, HL Deb, 25 April 1963, vol 248, col 1333.

10 Its formal title was the *Report of the Committee on Homosexual Offences and Prostitution*. The chair was Sir John Wolfenden.

11 *Hansard*, HL Deb, 4 December 1957, vol 206, cols 753–832. Denning in that speech set out all manner of things he thought morally reprehensible, including adultery, under-age sex, bestiality, attempted suicide, sadism, lesbianism and male sterilisation.
12 *Hansard*, HL Deb, 18 December 1986, vol 483, cols 310–38.
13 Notable among his fellow judges in that context was the future Lord Devlin, whose homophobic views led him to engage in a famous public debate with HLA Hart about law and morality. See Patrick Devlin, *The Enforcement of Morals* (Oxford University Press, 1965).
14 The British Medical Association provided what in modern terms would be seen as a strongly homophobic brief to the Wolfenden Committee. In terms of popular culture, the *Sunday Mirror* in 1963 printed a two-page guide on 'How to Spot a Homo'. Readers were advised to watch out for 'shifty glances', 'dropped eyes' and 'a fondness for the theatre'. See Richard Davenport-Hines, *An English Affair: Sex, Class and Power in the Age of Profumo* (William Collins, 2013).
15 Lord Alfred 'Bosie' Douglas, some-time *inamorato* of Oscar Wilde, claimed that homosexuality had been rife at Winchester when he attended. See Douglas Murray, *Bosie: The Tragic Life of Lord Alfred Douglas*, reissue (Sceptre, 2020).
16 Lord Denning, 'The Equality of Women', Eleanor Rathbone Memorial Lecture, 1960.
17 MDA Freeman, 'Family Matters' in Jowell and McAuslan, p 109 at 163. As ever, Denning's objection was based on religion, a curious stance since he was not Roman Catholic and had expressly distinguished himself from his fellow judge Hubert Wallington by stating that his religious beliefs did not interfere with his judgments.
18 Norman St John-Stevas, *Life, Death and the Law: Law and Christian Morals in England and the United States* (Beard Books, 1961; reprint 2002), p 142. See also some of Denning's speeches in the House of Lords in Parliament, such as *Hansard*, HL Deb, 26 February 1958, vol 207, col 943.
19 *R v Greater London Council, ex parte Blackburn* [1976] 3 All ER 184.
20 *High Commissioner for Pakistan in the United Kingdom v Prince Mukarram Jah, His Exalted Highness The 8th Nizam of Hyderabad and others* [2019] EWHC 2551 (Ch).
21 See '8th Nizam of Hyderabad wants "clean break" from funds battle in UK', *The Indian Express*, 24 July 2020.
22 GF Lock, 'Parliamentary privilege and the courts: the avoidance of conflict' [1985] *Public Law*, Spring, 64–92.
23 A customary practice in the All ER at the time, which has long since been discontinued.
24 'Responsibility before the law', Lionel Cohen Lecture Series 7, 1971, Hebrew University of Jerusalem.
25 *The Family Story*, pp 195–97.
26 See also Denning's judgments in *Smith and Snipes Hall Farm LD v River Douglas Catchment Board* [1949] 2 KB 100 at 514; *Drive Yourself Hire Co v Strutt* [1954] 1 QB 250 at 272; *Adler v Dickson* [1955] 1 QB 158; and *Beswick v Beswick* [1966] Ch 538 at 557.
27 See *The Family Story*, p 202 and *The Discipline of Law*, pp 288–89.
28 See *Norwich City Council v Hervey* [1989] 1 All ER 1180 and *Marc Rich & Co AG and others v Bishop Rock Marine Co Ltd and others* [1996] AC 211. According to Professor PS Atiyah in his article 'Lord Denning's Contribution to Contract Law' (1999) *Denning Law Journal*, Vol 14, No 1, 1 at 8, those cases provided 'almost total vindication' for Denning's analysis in *Midland Silicones*. See also *The Mahkutai* [1996] AC 650 at 665.

Notes

29 See Catharine MacMillan, 'A Birthday Present for Lord Denning: The Contracts (Rights of Third Parties) Act 1999' (2000) 63(5) MLR 721–38. In Professor MacMillan's opinion, 'While the birthday present is not quite the right size (the Act does not abolish the privity rule but merely reforms it in certain circumstances) it would have suited Lord Denning's purposes in a number of contract cases'.

30 See *The Family Story*, pp 153–58. The 1868 document is in Hampshire Archives 202M86/554.

31 Freeman, p 270.

32 A Gargrave, 'Lord Denning of Whitchurch' (1974) *The Advocate*, Vol 32, 366.

33 Before modern discrimination law, it was common for certain properties to be let only to married couples.

34 AT Denning, 'Foreword' (1957) 1 JAL 1. See also 'Introduction to the 50th Volume' (2006) *Journal of African Law*, Vol 50, No 2, 91–93 and Heward, pp 173–75.

35 In those days the solicitors' exams were considered more difficult, meaning visiting students usually opted for the Bar, which entitled them to practise in most African jurisdictions.

36 Other members included Lord Diplock, Sir Seymour Karminski (1902–1974), who was a High Court judge at the time and was promoted to the Court of Appeal in 1969, and Professor JND (Norman) Anderson (1908–1994), a legal academic who at the time was head of the Department of Law at the School of Oriental and African Studies in London.

37 *Report of the Committee on Legal Education for Students from Africa*, Cmnd 1255 (1961), chairman Lord Denning.

38 Including at Dar-es-Salaam: see Freeman, p 282. Denning's work on African legal education was discussed at length by John A Harrington and Ambreena Manji, '"Mind with Mind and Spirit with Spirit": Lord Denning and African Legal Education' (2003) *Journal of Law and Society* Vol 30, No 3, 376–99.

39 Heward, p 175.

40 (1961) 56 LS Gaz 147.

41 Elias was at various times Attorney General and Chief Justice of Nigeria, and a judge and president of the International Court of Justice.

42 TO Elias, 'Organisation and Development of the Legal Profession in Africa, in particular the ability of the Bar and judiciary to uphold the rights of both the citizen and the state' (1986) *Denning Law Journal*, Vol 1, No 1, 49. Legend Press Limited. Reproduced with permission of the Licensor through PLSclear.

43 In *Fitzwilliam v IRC* [1993] 3 All ER 184 at 215, for example, Lord Templeman bluntly stated: 'I have read a draft of the speech of my noble and learned friend Lord Keith. I am unable to follow his reasoning or to agree with his conclusions'. More recently, in *R (McDonald) v Royal Borough of Kensington and Chelsea* [2011] UKSC 33, a case from the Supreme Court's infancy, Lord Brown and Lord Walker were extraordinarily (for senior judges) open in their criticism of Lady Hale's judgment in the same case.

We might also note that Viscount Simonds did not always avoid the sort of criticism he directed at Denning. In the somewhat notorious *Shaw v DPP* [1962] AC 220 he received a severe rebuke from Lord Reid for rushing in to create an offence of 'conspiracy to corrupt public morals' where Parliament had chosen not to tread.

Chapter X: Master of the Rolls – Appointment and Beginnings

1. As before, preserved in Hampshire Archives 202M86.
2. Sir Julian Huxley FRS (1887–1975), evolutionary biologist, eugenicist and internationalist.
3. Letter, 7 September 1962. The address was given as 73 Frances Street, Lidcombe NSW, but I have not been able to unearth any other details about the author.
4. Letter, 27 March 1962. Sir Henry William Rawson Wade QC (1918–2004) was one of the best-known English academic lawyers of the twentieth century in the fields of real property and administrative law.
5. The letter was from Professor AG Davis, one of the pioneers of New Zealand legal education, after whom the law library at Auckland was subsequently named.
6. Sir Kenneth Ivor Julian, CBE (1895–1971), known by his middle name of Ivor. He served for many years in senior hospital administration posts.
7. JCS Warendorf was one of the founders of *Het Parool*, the newspaper of the Dutch resistance during the Second World War, and practised law after the conflict.
8. Letter, 12 April 1962.
9. *Desert Island Discs*, 23 May 1980.
10. 'Judicial Profiles – Master of the Rolls', Judiciary of England and Wales website, https://bit.ly/3oJAiTf.
11. Sir Julius Caesar (1557/58–18 April 1636). His rather memorable name derived from being the son of Cesare Adelmare, a doctor originally from Treviso, Italy. See Lamar Hill, *Bench and Bureaucracy: The Public Career of Sir Julius Caesar, 1580–1636* (Stanford University Press, 1988). Other memorably-named Masters of the Rolls included Sir Dudley Digges and Cuthbert Tunstall.
12. Quoted in *The Family Story*, p 201.
13. The compulsory retirement age for England and Wales was originally seventy-five, later lowered to seventy. In 2021, following a consultation, the government announced that the age would be raised once again to seventy-five, reflecting a longer life expectancy compared with previous generations.
    See www.gov.uk/government/consultations/consultation-on-judicial-mandatory-retirement-age.
14. Prior to 1947, there were only six Court of Appeal judges. That year the number was raised to nine, and by Denning's retirement in 1981 the number had reached eighteen. At the time of writing the number had reached thirty-nine.
15. The first solicitor appointed to the High Court Bench was Michael Sachs in 1993.
16. In technical terms, I refer to courts of record – the High Court and above – whose decisions have precedent value.
17. The point should be qualified by the fact that private schools and Oxbridge did not have a total monopoly, but they certainly produced a disproportionate share of senior judges in Denning's time. The grammar school system of the day did facilitate others who, like Denning, were not from a wealthy background, including Lords Diplock, Atkin and Templeman (though all three went to Oxbridge afterwards).
18. JAG Griffith, *The Politics of the Judiciary*, 5th edn (Fontana, 1997).
19. Martin Loughlin, 'John Griffith obituary', *The Guardian*, 25 May 2010. Loughlin noted that the publicity from the *Times Literary Supplement* review did not harm sales of the book.
20. Anthony Sampson, *The Changing Anatomy of Britain* (Hodder & Stoughton, 1982), p 159.

21. One survey analysed the social class of the Bench from 1820 to 1968. Defining class by father's occupation, it recorded that only 2.8 per cent of appointments to the Bench from 1820 to 1875 were from the working class, and for the rest of the period under consideration it was only ever between 1 per cent and 1.3 per cent. The landed upper class, by contrast, was as high as 17.9 per cent in the early period and overall 12.7 per cent. The largest entry was from 'upper middle class'. See Griffith, *op cit*, p 19.

22. Griffith, *op cit*, p 1.

23. See also K Malleson 'Diversity in the Judiciary: The Case for Positive Action' (2009) *Journal of Law and Society*, Vol 36, No 3, 376–402. For an alternative view, see Lord Sumption, 'Home Truths About Judicial Diversity', in his book *Law in a Time of Crisis* (Profile Books, 2021), p 101.

24. The Constitutional Reform Act 2005 introduced the Judicial Appointments Commission, a non-departmental public body which recommended appointments to the Lord Chancellor. The latter could still reject a recommendation, or ask the Commission to reconsider it, but no longer wielded unfettered power. As noted, in the twenty-first century the post of Lord Chancellor was reduced to a simple cabinet position. For further discussion, see Jeffrey Jowell (ed), *The Growing Consensus in Favour of Independent Judicial Appointment Commissions in Judicial Appointments: Balancing Independence, Accountability and Legitimacy* (A collection of essays prepared under the auspices of the Judicial Appointments Commission) (2010), and Dawn Oliver, 'Constitutionalism and the abolition of the office of Lord Chancellor' (2004) 57 *Parliamentary Affairs* 754.

25. See www.gov.uk/government/statistics/diversity-of-the-judiciary-2020-statistics. See, further, www.judiciary.uk/diversity/ and Penny Darbyshire, *Sitting in Judgment: The Working Lives of Judges* (Hart Publishing, 2011), Ch 3.

26. According to Sam Friedman and Daniel Laurison, *The Class Ceiling: Why it Pays to be Privileged* (Policy Press, 2020), children of lawyers were seventeen times more likely than other children to become lawyers. According to the Bridge Group study 'Admissions to selective UK law schools' (July 2020), '[t]he legal profession remains dominated by people from higher socio-economic backgrounds, especially within leading law firms and in the judiciary'. See https://bit.ly/2X1QX9g.

27. Interview with Hugo Young, *The Sunday Times*, 17 June 1973. See also *What Next in the Law?*, p 174, when Denning criticised a decision of the House of Lords on libel law (*Hulton v Jones* [1910] AC 20) and pointed out not one of the law lords in the case had any experience of English libel law.

28. Tony Molloy QC and Toby Graham, 'Editorial' (2012) *Trusts & Trustees*, Vol 18, No 3, 171–82. The then Chief Justice of New Zealand, Sian Elias, was reported to have been opposed to judicial specialisation and to have favoured a 'broad general competence' instead: see Phil Taylor, 'Justice in the Firing Line', *New Zealand Herald*, 4 May 2012.

29. See Darbyshire, *op cit*, Ch 6.

30. Freeman, p 358.

31. Interview with Bryan A Garner, available on YouTube at the time of writing. See www.youtube.com/watch?v=iolf0XUVPqg.

32. *New Law Journal*, 14 April 1995, p 527.

33. Scarman, Leslie 'Book Review' (1979) 95 LQR 445.

34. Sir Henry Brooke, 'Lord Denning and I (2): 1962–1972', personal blog, 21 December 2016. https://bit.ly/37Wc2F0.

35. © Stephen Sedley, (2018), *Law and the Whirligig of Time*, Hart Publishing, an imprint of Bloomsbury Publishing Plc, p 243.

36 PS James, 'Her Majesty's Judge' (2012) *Denning Law Journal*, Vol 14, No 1, 179 at 179. Legend Press Limited. Reproduced with permission of the Licensor through PLSclear.
37 Sir Henry Brooke, 'Lord Denning and I (2): 1962–1972', personal blog, 21 December 2016, https://sirhenrybrooke.me/2016/12/21/lord-denning-and-i-2-1962-1972/.
38 Years later, Denning took an even more blunt approach to a will in *Re Tuck's Settlement Trusts* [1978] 1 All ER 1054. See also *The Discipline of Law*, pp 23 *et seq* for Denning's later thoughts on *Re Rowland*.
39 The Inclosure Acts were active from 1604 to 1914. See 'Enclosing the Land' on the Parliament website: https://bit.ly/389A2mG.
40 'Nimby' is an English idiom standing for 'Not In My Backyard' usually applied to a hypocritical stance where someone supports an activity but only if done elsewhere.
41 *The Family Story*, p 142.
42 See Pauline Stuart obituary, *The Guardian*, 15 October 2017, written by Pauline's daughter Kate.
43 Published by Jackson, Son & Co, 1963.

Chapter XI: Profumo

1 Martin Kettle, 'Profumo: a scandal that keeps giving, even after 50 years', *The Guardian*, 4 June 2020.
2 Roy Jenkins, Baron Jenkins of Hillhead, OM, PC (1920–2003). Jenkins became Labour Home Secretary in 1965. His 'permissive society' referred to his efforts which included abolishing capital punishment, decriminalising homosexuality, abolishing theatre censorship, easing divorce laws and liberalising abortion.
3 There are many social histories of the period, for example Eric Midwinter, *Yesterdays: Our Finest Hours 1939–1953* (Souvenir Press, 2001); Mark Lewisohn, *The Beatles: All These Years* (Crown Archetype, 2013); Dominic Sandbrook, *Never Had it So Good: A History of Britain from Suez to the Beatles* (Little, Brown, 2005).
4 Malcolm Muggeridge, 'The Slow, Sure Death of the Upper Classes', *Sunday Mirror*, 23 June 1963, p 7.
5 See DR Thorpe, *Supermac: The Life of Harold Macmillan*, Kindle edn (Random House, 2010), who observed that divorce carried a heavy stigma as late as the 1950s, hence affairs were kept quiet as much as possible even if all affected parties were aware of them.
6 Although Griffith-Jones' comment was thought ridiculous both at the time and since, it was actually not uncommon among the better-off of that generation to speak of servants as an almost non-human class. Denning himself once wrote of a hypothetical immoral husband 'who commits adultery within a few weeks of marriage, or who commits adultery promiscuously with more than one woman or with his wife's sister, or with a servant in the house, may probably be labelled as exceptionally depraved' (*Bowman v Bowman* [1949] 2 All ER 127 at 129). The implication of the remarks by Griffith-Jones and Denning was that anyone listening to them would employ servants, or at least not be one of them. Numerous other examples of servants being described in terms that rendered them mere chattels can be found in pre-war law reports, such as *Re Patten* [1929] All ER Rep 416. In Denning's case, it was in contrast with him elsewhere describing his domestic servant Rose Drummer as a 'true friend'.

Notes

7   John Feather, *A History of British Publishing* (Routledge, 2005), p 205. The academic Richard Hoggard, an expert witness in the trial, took a more measured view in his autobiography of the impact of the trial on the formation of the 'permissive society' (*A Measured Life: The Times and Places of an Orphaned Intellectual* (Routledge, 1994), p 52).

8   See *R v Penguin Books Ltd* [1961] Crim LR 176. The reason the case was brought so many years after the book was written was that earlier versions published in England had been expurgated. Penguin decided to publish the full text in 1960 and faced prosecution under the recently enacted Obscene Publications Act 1959, but it won the case.

9   See for example Ben Macintyre, *A Spy Among Friends: Philby and the Great Betrayal* (Bloomsbury Paperbacks, 2015). Philby disappeared in January 1963 on the eve of being arrested, though MI5 did not officially confirm he had fled to Russia until July – just as the Profumo Affair was reaching its apogee, which rather suggests they thought it was a good time to bury bad news.

10 See for example Vassall's obituary in *The Times*, 6 December 1996.

11 John Banville, 'A family affair', *The Irish Times*, 14 October 2006.

12 Helen Rumbelow, 'How accurate is The Trial of Christine Keeler? The truth about the Profumo affair', *The Times*, 1 January 2020.

13 Alistair Horne, *Macmillan: The Official Biography, Vol 1, 1894–1956* (Macmillan, 1988), pp 85–90.

14 See Philip Knightley and Caroline Kennedy, *An Affair of State: The Profumo Case and the Framing of Stephen Ward* (Jonathan Cape Ltd, 1987), pp 86–87; and Richard Davenport-Hines, *An English Affair: Sex, Class and Power in the Age of Profumo* (William Collins, 2013), pp 248–50.

15 It was later described by her as 'a screw of convenience'. Anthony Summers and Stephen Dorril, *Honeytrap* (Coronet Books, 1989), p 139.

16 Knightley and Kennedy, *op cit*, pp 86–89.

17 Ward claimed that Profumo had written five notes to Keeler, of which he had destroyed two and another boyfriend of Keeler had destroyed one. See Davenport-Hines, *op cit*, p 251.

18 Perec 'Peter' Rachman (1919–1962) was a Polish-born landlord who operated in Notting Hill, London, England in the 1950s and early 1960s. His infamous exploitation of tenants led to the word 'Rachmanism' entering the *Oxford English Dictionary* as a synonym for abusive behaviour by landlords. He died of a heart attack in 1962, whereafter the Profumo Affair brought him posthumous notoriety.

19 About £16,300 in 2022 terms, according to the Bank of England inflation calculator. Keeler was paid £200 up front with the promise of the balance upon publication.

20 See WF Deedes, *Dear Bill: WF Deedes Reports* (Macmillan, 1997), pp 163–75. Deedes was Minister without Portfolio at the time of the Profumo Affair. See also Richard Lamb, *The Macmillan Years 1957–1963: The Emerging Truth* (John Murray, 1995; Kindle edn, Lume Books, 2017).

21 Clive Irving, Ron Hall and Jeremy Wallington, *Scandal '63* (Heinemann, 1963), p 90 and Wayland Young, *The Profumo Affair: Aspects of Conservatism* (Penguin Books, 1963), pp 14–15.

22 Knightley and Kennedy, *op cit*, p 170. Davenport-Hines, *op cit*, p 284, supported that thesis.

23 Henry Brooke, Baron Brooke of Cumnor CH PC (1903–1984). He was a career politician who served as Chief Secretary to the Treasury and Paymaster-General from 1961 to 1962 and Home Secretary from 1962 to 1964. He was the father of the Court of Appeal judge Sir Henry Brooke, who was a great admirer of Denning.

24 Lamb, *op cit*, Kindle edn, ref 663.
25 Minutes were taken of the meeting but never released. See Tom Mangold, 'How the official report into the Christine Keeler affair covered up a FAR more sensational sex scandal... and Tory Minister Ernest Marples' kinky antics made Profumo look like a choirboy!', *Mail on Sunday*, 25 January 2020.
26 The Labour government led by Ramsay MacDonald had meddled in the 'Campbell case' to prevent a prosecution of a communist newspaper editor, JR Campbell. The Liberal leader, HH Asquith, demanded a committee of inquiry. MacDonald said that if MPs voted in favour of the inquiry, then the government would resign. They went on to vote for the inquiry by a large majority, so MacDonald made good his promise and the government ended after just nine months in office.
27 'Arguably disgraceful' was the understated verdict of the authors Matthew Parris and Kevin MacGuire, who correctly observed the police should investigate crimes, not individuals. See their book *Great Parliamentary Scandals: Five Centuries of Calumny, Smear and Innuendo* (Robson Books, 2004), p 167.
28 See Geoffrey Robertson QC, *Stephen Ward Was Innocent, OK: The Case for Overturning his Conviction*, Kindle edn (Biteback Publishing, 2013).
29 *The Times*, 6 June 1963, p 13. Five days later *The Times* groaned 'Eleven years of Conservative rule have brought the nation psychologically and spiritually to a low ebb'.
30 Mangold, *op cit*, and Davenport-Hines, *op cit*, pp 311–12. The latter added that one of them related twenty years later 'I can't tell you of the moral awfulness of abandoning a friend when he needs you most, and a friend ... completely innocent of the charges against him'.
31 Quintin Hogg, Lord Hailsham (1907–2001). He told the BBC that there were security implications from a minister and a Russian spy sharing the same woman's favours, and railed that blackmail implications necessitated resignation. It amounted to stabbing Profumo not in the back but in the front. The Labour MP Reginald Paget called his attack on Profumo 'a virtuoso performance of the art of kicking a friend in the guts', adding 'When self-indulgence has reduced a man to the shape of Lord Hailsham, sexual continence involves no more than a sense of the ridiculous'. See Parris and MacGuire, *op cit*, p 175.
32 *Hansard*, HC Deb, 17 June 1963, vol 679, col 34.
33 Under s 23 of the Sexual Offences Act 1956, if someone introduced a male to a female who was over the age of 16 but under 21, and the pair subsequently had sex, then the introducer had committed the offence of procuration. In practice, that meant more than a few young people were technically criminals.
34 One example given was that in early 1961, Keeler then living with Rice-Davies, gave their landlord a cheque from Lord Astor for £100 for rent.
35 Her aphorism was often shortened thereafter to MDRA – 'Mandy Rice-Davies Applies'. It is often wrongly assumed Rice-Davies made the quotation during the actual trial, but it was at the committal hearing earlier, as recorded by *The Guardian* on 1 July 1963. See also Chris Elliott, 'The readers' editor on why that cheeky Mandy Rice-Davies quote needs no correction', *The Guardian*, 27 January 2013.
36 Robertson QC, *op cit*.
37 Only six mourners were present, including his brothers and his sisters. There was however a card placed with a wreath on his grave, signed by Kenneth Tynan, which stated succinctly 'To Stephen Ward, victim of hypocrisy'. See Robertson QC, *op cit*.

Notes

38 For example, the judge who heard the Duchess of Argyll's divorce case around the same time as Profumo was Baron Wheatley. He was a Catholic judge who, if anything, was even more moralistic than Denning, and was notorious for passing harsh sentences when anything sexual was involved.
39 Lord Nolan, 'The Role of the Judge in Judicial Inquiries' (1999) *Denning Law Journal*, Vol 14, No 1, 147.
40 Letter, Denning to Macmillan, 24 June 1963. Hampshire Archives 202M86/656.
41 *The Changing Law*, p 121. Six years after Jenkins had been appointed as Home Secretary, Denning's views were unchanged: 'It is time for all good folk to take a stand, else the permissive society will soon become the decadent society', *The Times*, 1 October 1971.
42 *Landmarks in the Law*, p 351.
43 'The Profumo affair – sex, power and a Russian spy', *The Daily Telegraph*, 25 September 2016.
44 It has been suggested (see Spencer, Vol II, p 63, fn 178) that had he lived Ward might have sued Denning for libel, since the latter would not have been able to rely on the protection of judicial privilege for anything said in his report.
45 See Denning, *op cit*, Kindle edn, ref 994; Ludovic Kennedy, *The Trial of Stephen Ward* (V Gollancz, 1964; Penguin Books, reprint, 1965), p 234.
46 Denning, *op cit*, Kindle edn, ref 2113.
47 The existence of the Denning letter to Macmillan was discovered by Richard Lamb (*op cit*, Kindle edn, ref 689–90), though he did not name Marples or Freeth, because he and the publisher felt it would betray Denning's promises of confidentiality to witnesses (especially since Freeth was still alive at the time). He did, however, mention Marples' reputation for consorting with prostitutes. Both Marples and Freeth have since been named a number of times as the subjects of the Denning letter: see for example Jack Malvern, 'Profumo report hid lurid details of a bigger scandal', *The Times*, 27 January 2020; Anthony Howard, 'Lord Hutton's report is unlikely to rival Lord Denning's of 40 years ago as a bestseller. But at least we've heard the evidence on which it will be based', *The Times*, 9 September 2003; Tom Mangold's BBC documentary *Keeler, Profumo, Ward and Me*, broadcast 11 February 2020 and Mangold's article 'How the official report into the Christine Keeler affair covered up a FAR more sensational sex scandal... and Tory Minister Ernest Marples' kinky antics made Profumo look like a choirboy!', *Mail on Sunday*, 25 January 2020. Mangold based his revelations on the diaries of Thomas Critchley. He alleged that Denning had to have authorised a substantial payoff for the prostitute who gave evidence about Marples, or she would have sold her story to the papers.
48 Baron Duncan-Sandys (1908–1987). He was an MP from 1935 to 1974. In 1935 he married Winston Churchill's daughter Diana; they divorced in 1960. In 1962, he married Marie-Claire (née Schmitt). The marriage lasted until Sandys' death. Sandys was linked to the Duchess partly because the photographs were taken on a then very new Polaroid camera which printed them instantly instead of having to have the film developed elsewhere. Sandys, as Minister of Defence, had access to one. He once cryptically referred to possible involvement with the Duchess as 'safety in numbers'. See Hugh Davies, 'Duchess's "headless man" was Fairbanks Jnr', *Daily Telegraph*, 10 August 2000.
49 The Duke and Duchess's divorce case had taken place in 1963, just before Denning's inquiry, but the Duchess had declined to identify the man (or men) in the pictures.
50 John Sparrow, *Controversial Essays* (Chilmark Press, 1966), p 33.

51 *Hansard*, HC Deb, 16 December 1963, vol 686, cols 853–983. https://bit.ly/32gcYQx.
52 See Freeman, p 296.
53 There are many examples: the author John Kampfner went one further than most by calling the Profumo report not just a whitewash, but 'a masterpiece of whitewash'. Kampfner, 'An English Affair: Sex, Class and Power in the age of Profumo by Richard Davenport-Hines – review', *The Observer*, 14 January 2013. Mangold (*op cit*) called it 'an ageing establishment's answer [to a question] which it believed was consuming the nation' and 'seared with the old man's prejudices'.
54 See for example Kennedy, *op cit*, p 233.
55 *An English Affair: Sex, Class and Power in the Age of Profumo*, *op cit*.
56 *Hansard*, HC Deb, 16 December 1963, vol 686, cols 853–983. https://bit.ly/3cuG0kx. WF Deedes (*op cit*, p 174) also called Lord Denning's report 'a model of clarity' and indicated his disagreement that the report was a whitewash, thinking that that abusive epithet derived from a politically-motivated verdict by Labour politicians.
57 Freeman, p 293.
58 Freeman, p 294.
59 Freeman, p 294.
60 Richard Davenport-Hines, 'Stephen Ward and the Profumo Affair: Historian Richard Davenport-Hines on the truth behind Andrew Lloyd Webber's new musical', *Evening Standard*, 3 December 2013.
61 *The Due Process of Law*, p 69.
62 See *Report of the Royal Commission on Tribunals of Inquiry*, Cmnd 3121.
63 Lord Nolan, *op cit*.
64 *The Times* said as much upon Christine Keeler's death, see the 6 December 2017 edition. Andrew Marr in *A History of Modern Britain* (Macmillan, 2007), p 219 wrote '[t]he Profumo Affair caused such national interest that it might well have tipped the balance against the Tories'. See also Parris and Maguire, *op cit*, p 157.
65 The Conservatives lost by 0.7 per cent of the vote, and Labour gained an overall majority of just four seats. If a mere 900 voters in eight constituencies had switched their votes, the Conservatives would have stayed in power. See 'Obituary: Lord Nolan', *The Guardian*, 26 January 2007. Having said that, Macmillan's biographer Alistair Horne, *op cit*, felt he never recovered from the scandal and it sank an already fading individual.
66 Deedes (*op cit*, p 174) thought the Attorney General John Hobson and the Solicitor-General Peter Rawlinson were both 'deeply affected' and their careers were never the same afterwards.
67 As recorded by Denning in *Landmarks in the Law*, p 365. See also Freeman, p 298.
68 Parris and Maguire recorded (*op cit*, p 180) that they had sent their draft chapter on the affair to him, and received a courteous response declining to comment.
69 Lord Bingham, 'Address to the Thanksgiving Service for Lord Denning OM', delivered at Westminster Abbey on 17 June 1999, (2000) *Denning Law Journal*, Vol 15, No 1, 1. A similar confirmation of Profumo's rehabilitation was that, at a party at Claridges in 1995 celebrating Margaret Thatcher's seventieth birthday, he sat at the Queen's right hand: see Deedes, *op cit*, p 175.
70 David Profumo, *Bringing the House Down* (John Murray, 2006). Davenport-Hines (*op cit*, p 344) reported Profumo still playing the old rake in his seventies, trying to seduce a seventeen-year-old at a formal dinner.

71 www.christine-keeler.co.uk/ (accessed 19 May 2021).
72 Rowan Pelling, 'Mandy Rice-Davies' wise words for those caught in flagrante', *The Daily Telegraph*, 1 October 2013.
73 Yevgeny Ivanov and Gennady Sokolov, *The Naked Spy* (Blake, 1992).
74 Philip Knightley and Caroline Kennedy, *op cit*. It was the basis for the 1989 film *Scandal*.
75 'MI5 frame-up denied', *Reading Evening Post*, 5 May 1987.
76 Davenport-Hines, *op cit*.
77 Robertson QC, *op cit*. Andrew Lloyd Webber also created a musical, *Stephen Ward was Innocent*, based on Robertson's research, though it did not enjoy an especially long run in the West End. Lord Astor's son William enjoyed the musical, though noted that Ward had a darker side to his character, given his manipulation of often vulnerable young girls. See William Astor, 'My father, his swimming pool and the Profumo scandal', *The Spectator*, 11 January 2014.
78 When interviewed by Tom Mangold for *Keeler, Profumo, Ward and Me*, *op cit*.
79 See the Criminal Cases Review Commission, 'Commission statement on its review of the 1963 conviction of Dr Stephen Ward (deceased)', 8 September 2017. https://bit.ly/3ceNeKg.
80 Fairbanks Jnr was again supposedly identified in 2000, after an investigation by Channel 4, based on the handwriting on the photographs. See Hugh Davies, 'Duchess's "headless man" was Fairbanks Jnr', *The Daily Telegraph*, 10 August 2000. The programme further claimed that the photographs actually showed different men at different times, one of whom was, indeed, Duncan Sandys. Others alleged at different times to have been the man included John Cohane, an American businessman, Peter Combe, a former press officer at the Savoy Hotel, and Sigismund von Braun, brother of the German rocket scientist Werner.
Incidentally, Mandy Rice-Davies had claimed in Ward's trial to have slept with Fairbanks Jnr, which he denied. See Ludovic Kennedy, *op cit*, p 59.
81 Sam Marsden, '"Sensational" secret Profumo scandal papers will be preserved, Government says', *Daily Telegraph*, 1 January 2014. See also *Hansard*, HL Deb, 16 January 2014, cols 341 *et seq*.
82 In late 1963, Ludovic Kennedy tried to obtain a transcript for his book on the trial, and pressed for reasons when he was rebuffed. He was eventually told the decision was made by the Lord Chief Justice, Lord Parker, but was given no indication why. Given that Kennedy had already sat through the trial itself, and only wanted the transcript to double-check his own accuracy, and had access to the Press Association's own record of the trial, the decision was in legal terms unsupportable and in lay terms ridiculous.
83 Davenport-Hines thought that the papers probably contained rumours about the Royal Family, which was the reason they were not being released. See James Hanning, 'Is this why the Profumo file is still secret? Author believes desire not to upset royals is reason documents are still under wraps', *The Independent*, 5 January 2014.
84 At the time of writing, the historian Andrew Lownie was trying to raise money for a case to compel Southampton University to release the Mountbatten archive to the public. See www.crowdjustice.com/case/andrew-lownies-case/.
85 See for example DGT Williams, 'Lord Denning and Open Government' (1986) *Denning Law Journal*, Vol 1, No 1, 117.
86 Martin Kettle, 'Profumo: a scandal that keeps giving, even after 50 years', *The Guardian*, 4 January 2020.

Chapter XII: Master of the Rolls – Travel and Other Engagements

1. Lord Denning MR, 'Gems in Ermine', Presidential Address to The English Association, 1964.
2. The reality of Magna Carta's history and status is somewhat more controversial than Denning's encomium implied. For contrasting views, see Lord Sumption, *Law in a Time of Crisis* (Profile Books, 2021), pp 44 *et seq* and Anthony Arlidge and Igor Judge, *Magna Carta Uncovered* (Hart Publishing, 2014). For an entertaining comparison of Magna Carta with the Holy Grail, see Lord Neuberger, 'Magna Carta and the Holy Grail', Lincoln's Inn, 12 May 2015, www.supremecourt.uk/docs/speech-150512.pdf. See also the essays in the dedicated volume of the *Denning Law Journal*: (2016) Vol 27.
   Although Denning enjoyed the symbolism and other myths about the Charter in his speeches and books, he was more reserved as a judge, only referring to it on three occasions in his judgments. See Stephens, Vol II, pp 87 *et seq*. Yet on one of those – *R v Home Secretary, ex parte Phansopkar* [1976] 1 QB 606 – an academic argued that Magna Carta had played an important role in the Court of Appeal's decision (Simon Lee, 'Lord Denning, Magna Carta and Magnanimity' (2015) *Denning Law Journal*, Vol 27, No 1, 106 at 117; cf Adam Tomkins, 'Magna Carta, Crown and Colonies' [2001] PL 571, who described the judges' references to Magna Carta in the case as *obiter*).
3. Newspaper cuttings relating to the visit are preserved in Hampshire Archives 202M86/626.
4. Freeman, p 357.
5. 'Recent Changes in the Law', Address to 13th Dominion Legal Conference, Dunedin, 13 April 1966, [1966] NZLJ 167. The word 'Dominion' was later replaced by 'Commonwealth'.
6. Nowadays, the journey can be made in about twenty-four hours, but in 1963 there were no direct flights, requiring multiple stops and taking much longer as a result.
7. For more detail, see Jane Phare 'The poisoning at the lake: The death of 11-year-old David Davison' in Susanna Andrew and Jolisa Gracewood (eds), *Tell You What: Great New Zealand Nonfiction 2017* (Auckland University Press, 2017).
8. The recording is preserved in Hampshire Archives AV13/15/S1. Newspaper cuttings relating to the trip are stored in Hampshire Archives 202M86/478.
9. The award is in Hampshire Archives 202M86/673.
10. Heward, p 178.
11. Internecine tensions ultimately led to two military coups d'état by the Fijian-dominated army against the first Indo-Fijian-led government in 1987, followed by years of discriminatory laws and practices against the Indian community. In 2013 a new, democratic constitution was introduced, which was still in force at the time of writing.
12. Heward, p 179.
13. See his letter to Denning of 6 November 1970, preserved in Hampshire Archives 202M86/678.
14. In 1973 he visited Nairobi and Dar-es-Salaam, following which he was made an Honorary Life Member of the Commonwealth Magistrates' Association (Hampshire Archives 202M86/628), and in 1975 he went on a lecture tour to Ghana and Nigeria (Hampshire Archives 202M86/631).
15. See Hampshire Archives 202M86/630.
16. Freeman, p 328.

17 See Hampshire Archives 202M86/633. Earlier the same year he went to Ghent, Belgium, where he gave a lecture on the role of the judge in the English trial: Hampshire Archives 202M86/632, which includes the text of the lecture.
18 See Hampshire Archives 202M86/634.
19 See Hampshire Archives 202M86/636. In the same year he also went to Tiburg, Holland, to receive an honorary degree (Hampshire Archives 202M86/635; there is also a photograph album of the visit: Hampshire Archives 202M86/490).
20 See Hampshire Archives 202M86/637.
21 *The Family Story*, p 245.
22 *The Closing Chapter*, p 277.
23 Noted in the Hampshire Archives catalogue, p 17. He had also declined an invitation from Trinidad in 1977, though it is unclear whether the invitation was before Lady Denning fell ill, as the papers have not been retained.
24 See my book *Noble Savages: The Savage Club and the Great War 1914–18* (JH Productions, 2018; revised edn, 2020), which includes a short biography of Denning himself. There was little in the Club records pertaining to Denning, other than his name appearing in some lists of members. I suspect he was given honorary membership, which the Club did quite frequently in the twentieth century for notable individuals.
25 The latter has already been done in dedicated works, most importantly Jowell and McAulsan, and Stephens, as well as Denning's own books.

Chapter XIII: Master of the Rolls – Pre-trial Remedies

1 In *Bank Mellat v Nikpour* [1985] FSR 87 at 92.
2 See also the earlier case of *Nippon Yusen Kaisha v Karageorgis* [1975] 1 WLR 1093, when Denning and the Court of Appeal reached the same result as *Mareva*, but it was soon noted that the court had not been referred to *Lister*, hence the later case of *Mareva*.
3 It has been argued that Denning's enthusiasm to bring in the *Mareva* remedy was spurred on by his appreciation of European law being brought into the common law by Britain joining the EEC. The *Mareva* remedy was similar to the civil law doctrine of *saisie conservatoire*. See Stephens, Vol II, p 181, n 38.
4 *Mareva* also exposed something of a flaw in the system of case reporting at the time, as set out further in Appendix I. Law reporters at that time habitually attended court – necessary since so many cases were delivered *ex tempore*. They would not necessarily have bothered for all *ex parte* applications, most of which were vanishingly unlikely to include any new point of law. Thus it is likely that they did not do so for *Mareva*. Either way, the chief private general series of the time, the *All England Law Reports*, missed the case – or misunderstood its significance – and was thus compelled to report it very belatedly in 1980 ([1980] 1 All ER 213), by which time the case had been cited countless times.
5 Note that although Denning was much to the fore in the development of what became known as the *Anton Piller* order, Templeman J (as he then was) had an important antecedent decision at first instance, in *EMI v Pandit* [1975] 1 WLR 302.
6 *Hubbard v Vosper* [1972] 2 QB 84 at 96.
7 DJ Hayton, 'Equity and Trusts' in Jowell and McAuslan, pp 79 and 107. See also John Stevens, 'Equity's Manhattan Project: The Creation and Evolution of the Mareva Injunction' (1999) *Denning Law Journal*, Vol 14, No 1, 25.
8 *The Due Process of Law*, p 141.

Chapter XIV: Master of the Rolls – Common Law

1. See also *Morris v CW Martin & Sons Ltd* [1966] 1 QB 716, where Denning endeavoured to modernise the law of bailment, and *Abbott v Sullivan* [1952] 1 KB 189 at 200, in which he wrote 'I should be sorry to think that, if a wrong has been done, the plaintiff is to go without a remedy simply because no one can find a peg to hang it on. We should then be going back to the days when a man's rights depended on whether he could fit them into a prescribed form of action; whereas in these days the principle to be applied is that where there is a right there should be a remedy'.
2. See Francis Bennion, *Professional Ethics: Consultant Professions and their Code* (Knight (Charles) & Co Ltd, 1969).
3. See *Saif Ali v Sidney Mitchell* [1978] 3 WLR 849.
4. See *JM Allan [Merchandising] Ltd v Cloke* [1963] 2 All ER 258; *J and C Moores Ltd v Commissioners of Customs and Excise* [1963] 2 All ER 714; *Fisher v CHT Ltd* [1966] 1 All ER 88; and *Avais v Hartford Shankhouse and District Workingmen's Social Club and Institute Ltd* [1967] 3 All ER 987.
5. *The Times*, 7 March 1980. The case which Hogg was writing about was *R v Commissioner of Police of the Metropolis, ex parte Blackburn* [1968] 2 QB 118 (mandamus sought to require the Commissioner to enforce the law on gaming; Blackburn lost). Blackburn also appeared in front of Denning in *Blackburn v AG* [1971] 1 WLR 1037 (seeking a declaration that the UK government had had no right to sign the Treaty of Rome; he lost again); *R v Commissioner of Police of the Metropolis, ex parte Blackburn* [1973] QB 241 (seeking to require the Commissioner to enforce the law on obscene publications; Blackburn lost yet again); and *R v Greater London Council, ex parte Blackburn* [1976] 1 WLR 550 (Blackburn gained a win, when the GLC was prevented from using the test of 'obscenity' rather than 'gross indecency' in licensing a film). See *The Discipline of Law*, pp 118 et seq.
6. *R v Metropolitan Police Commissioner, ex parte Blackburn (No 2)* [1968] 2 All ER 319.
7. See Bernard Levin, *Taking Sides* (Jonathan Cape, 1979), p 14, who recounted the story of a man imprisoned for giving the 'V sign' to two minor judges whom he had mistaken for local authority potentates.
8. £482 13s. 1d in 1964 translates to approximately £7,600 in August 2022 figures, and £300 to £4,736, according to the Bank of England inflation calculator.
9. Norman had established the centre in 1939 to co-ordinate efforts between decryption units such as the Government Code and Cypher School and the staff and command officers planning operations. It was based in the Admiralty Citadel in London.
10. The total of £40,000 in 1972 would have equated to approximately £422,000 in 2022, according to the Bank of England inflation calculator.
11. The House of Lords being bound by its own earlier rulings was established in *London Tramway Co v London County Council* [1898] AC 375, and modified by the Practice Statement (Judicial Precedent) [1966] 1 WLR 1234, which held that, while treating former decisions of the House as normally binding, the House of Lords would depart from a previous decision 'when it appears right to do so'.
12. To complete the story, Irving continued publishing books but eventually lost all credibility as an historian with a series of apologias for Nazi Germany. See my earlier book, *Cases, Causes and Controversies: Fifty Tales from the Law* (Wildy, Simmonds & Hill, 2012), Ch 13.

Notes

13 Jarvis was not the last person to sue over a disappointing holiday. Denning delivered a similar judgment in *Jackson v Horizon Holidays* [1975] 3 All ER 92, in which he said straightforwardly 'People look forward to a holiday. They expect the promises to be fulfilled. When it fails, they are greatly disappointed and upset. It is difficult to assess in terms of money; but it is the task of the judges to do the best they can'. More recently, the Court of Appeal in *Milner and another v Carnival plc (trading as Cunard)* [2010] 3 All ER 701 set out comprehensive guidance on damages awards in 'bad holiday' cases.

14 See PS Atiyah, 'Contract and Tort' in Jowell and McAuslan, p 51.

15 See The Law Commission and The Scottish Law Commission, *Unfair Terms in Consumer Contracts: Advice to the Department for Business, Innovation and Skills* (March 2013), paras 4.30 and 4.45.

16 See for example Ken Oliphant (ed), *The Law of Tort* (LexisNexis, 2007), pp 707 *et seq*.

17 James Wilson, *Court and Bowled: Tales of Cricket and Law* (Wildy, Simmonds & Hill, 2014; revised 2017).

18 Geoffrey Lane LJ dissented on the point. The club was ordered to pay £400 for past and future damages. See, further, Wilson, *Court and Bowled*, *op cit*. On 'coming to the nuisance', see the later case of *Lawrence and Another v Fen Tigers Ltd and Others* [2014] UKSC 13, [2014] AC 822.

19 Judges' clerks in England in Denning's time did not bear much relation to those in America. The English clerks' role then was administrative, rather than that of a legal researcher. See Nina Holvast, 'The Power of the Judicial Assistant/Law Clerk: Looking Behind the Scenes at Courts in the United States, England and Wales, and the Netherlands' (2016) 7 *International Journal for Court Administration* 10 at 19. It was not until 1997 that the function of 'Judicial Assistant' (the UK version of American law clerks) was created for the Court of Appeal of England and Wales, and not before 2001 that it was extended to the House of Lords. (It continued when the latter became the Supreme Court in 2009.) See, further, John Smillie, 'Who Wants Juristocracy?' (2006) 11 *Otago Law Review* 183 at 191–92.

20 See John Scott, *Caught in Court* (Andre Deutsch, 1989), p 237.

21 *The Closing Chapter*, p 23.

22 *Private Eye* also made a connection between the case and the Profumo Affair by depicting Denning on its front cover shortly after the judgment in Woodward. With its characteristic humour, it showed him whispering in a speech bubble to a passer-by 'Psst! Want to buy the dirty old Profumo report, Guv'nor?' See Issue 401, 29 April 1977.

23 Stafford Hildred and David Gritten, *Tom Jones: A Biography* (Sidgwick & Jackson, 1990).

24 £978,450.12 in August 2022 according to the Bank of England inflation calculator.

25 £35,362.47 in August 2022 according to the Bank of England inflation calculator.

26 PS Atiyah, 'Contract and Tort' in Jowell and McAuslan, p 77. See also PS Atiyah, 'Lord Denning's Contribution to Contract Law' (1999) *Denning Law Journal*, Vol 14, No 1, 1; MP Furmston, 'Contract and Tort after Denning' (1987) *Denning Law Journal*, Vol 2, No 1, 65; and Len Sealey, 'Commercial law and Company law' (1999) *Denning Law Journal*, Vol 14, No 1, 13.

Chapter XV: Master of the Rolls – Family Law

1. Anthony King and Ivor Crewe, *The Blunders of our Governments*, Kindle edn (Oneworld Publications, 2013).
2. *Pettitt v Pettitt* [1970] AC 777.
3. Andrew Bainham, 'Lord Denning as a Champion of Children's Rights: The Legacy of *Hewer v Bryant*' (1999) *Denning Law Journal*, Vol 14, No 1, 81.
4. Not only was Denning's decision a breakthrough at the time, but some commentators considered it more enlightened than many decisions which followed. Bainham, *op cit*, p 91 wrote that Denning's decision in *Hewer* was much more enlightened than 'much of the clumsiness' which had followed in the decades after.

   Incidentally, *Gillick* concerned a child's ability to consent to medical treatment (contraception) without the knowledge of her parents. On that point Denning had said in *B (BR) v B (J)* [1968] P 466 at 473 that a judge of the High Court had the power to order a blood test of an infant to be taken whenever it was in the best interests of the child; while an older child should be consulted, her view would not be decisive. In the same case he also said '[t]he object of the court always is to find out the truth. When scientific advances give us fresh means of ascertaining it, we should not hesitate to use those means whenever the occasion requires it'.
5. For a fuller consideration of the relevant cases, see MDA Freeman, 'Family Matters' in Jowell and McAuslan, p 109.
6. In *The Times*, 1 October 1971, for example, he praised the new Divorce Reform Act 1969.
7. See *Fuller v Fuller* [1973] 2 All ER 650 and *Bradley v Bradley* [1973] 3 All ER 750.
8. MDA Freeman, 'Family Matters' in Jowell and McAuslan, p 109 at 129.
9. Freeman p 348, who does not identify who the individual was beyond saying 'a young member of Tom's family'.
10. *Hawes v Evenden* [1953] 1 WLR 1169.
11. Long after Denning's time, in *Prest v Petrodel Resources Limited* (subsequently appealed to the Supreme Court, see [2013] UKSC 34), the Court of Appeal issued a strong reprimand to the Family Division for ignoring settled company law principles developed by the Chancery Division to try to fashion justice between parties in individual matrimonial property cases.

Chapter XVI: Master of the Rolls – Employment Law

1. Freeman, p 372. See also *Ministry of Defence v Jeremiah* [1980] QB 87.
2. The drafter was Francis Bennion, who wrote to *The Times* on 15 July 1977 and again on 1 June 1978 complaining of 'elderly judges [who] insist on upholding those obsolete attitudes and rejecting the principle of equal treatment clearly laid down by the Act'. Bennion singled out Judge Ruttle in *Peake* (b 1906) and Denning himself (b 1899). He received a reply on 7 June 1978 from one Nicholas Thorowgood (b 1945) stating that Bennion (b 1923) should defer to the judge's interpretation of the intention of Parliament (b circa 1265). Fortunately, in the *El Vino* case the right result was reached by Everleigh LJ (b 1917), Griffiths LJ (b 1923) and Sir Roger Ormrod (b 1911).

3   See my earlier book, *Cases, Causes and Controversies: Fifty Tales from the Law* (Wildy, Simmonds & Hill, 2012), Ch 31. El Vino, incidentally, was one of the inspirations behind the fictional Pommeroy's Wine Bar in John Mortimer's *Rumpole of the Bailey*.
4   Including one from the seventeenth century, *Ipswich Tailors' Case* (1614), 11 Co Rep 53a, 77 ER 1218.
5   The case bore some similarity to that brought during the Second World War by the famous West Indian cricketer Learie Constantine. See my earlier book, *Trials and Tribulations: Uncommon Tales of the Common Law* (Wildy, Simmonds & Hill, 2015).
6   Denning added 'It is not as if the training of horses could be regarded as an unsuitable occupation for a woman, like that of a jockey or speedway-rider. It is an occupation in which women can and do engage most successfully'.
7   For example, during his trip to Canada and the United States during the long vacation of 1955, in which he received an honorary degree from the University of Ottawa, he wrote an article 'A British View of Right to Work Laws'. See Hampshire Archives 202M86/623.
8   *Russell v Duke of Norfolk* [1949] 1 All ER 109. See also *Abbott v Sullivan* [1952] 1 KB 189 (Denning's dissent subsequently became the law); *Lee v Showmen's Guild* [1952] 2 QB 329; *Bonsor v Musician's Union* [1954] Ch 479 (again, Denning dissented but his view later became accepted); and *Dickson v Phamaceutical Society of Great Britain* [1967] Ch 708.
9   See also *Faramus v Film Artistes Association* [1964] AC 925, decided shortly after Denning became MR, when he alone among the Court of Appeal and House of Lords ruled in favour of the plaintiff who had been excluded from membership of his union – and therefore from any chance of working in the film industry – because of a criminal offence. Denning felt that the rule should be discretionary, not mandatory, and that it would also be an unlawful restraint of trade. The other judges were still intent on keeping the courts out of union disputes. See, further, Denning's lecture 'The Rule of Law in the Welfare State' in his book *The Changing Law*, pp 35–37 and *The Road to Justice*, pp 99–103.
10 See *R v Rowlands* (1851) 17 QB 671, 169 ER 540; *R v Druitt* (1867) Cox CC 592; and *J Lyons v Wilkins* [1896] 1 Ch 811.
11 See also *Quinn v Leathem* [1901] AC 495 where an employer was awarded damages for conspiracy after the union tried to operate a 'closed shop'.
12 Prior to the case, it had been assumed that a union could not be sued in its registered name. By overturning that assumption, the House of Lords ensured that a union could be sued for the acts of its agents, whether authorised or not, and would be liable to pay damages to successful plaintiffs in civil actions against it. The decision only stopped short of making strikes unlawful again. The resultant anger in the labour movement led to the Liberals gaining 377 seats in the next general election and no fewer than fifty-three Labour supporters as opposed to the previous Parliament's two (Keir Hardie and Richard Bell). See, further, HGC Matthew, 'The Liberal Age' in Kenneth O Morgan (ed), *The Oxford Illustrated History of Britain* (Oxford University Press, 1984), Ch 9.
13 In s 219(2) of the Trade Union and Labour Relations (Consolidation) Act 1992.
14 See Julia Bush, *Behind the Lines. East London Labour, 1914–1919* (Merlin Press, 1984); Hugh Armstrong Clegg (ed), *A history of British Trade Unions Since 1889, 1911–1933, Vol 2* (Clarendon Press, 1985) and James Cronin, *Industrial Conflict in Modern Britain* (Croom Helm; Rowman and Littlefield, 1979) on the Great War; and Correlli Barnett, *The Audit of War: The Illusion and Reality of Britain as a Great Nation* (Macmillan, 1986; republished by Pan, 2001), pp 154–57 for the Second World War.

15 The strike was called by the General Council of the Trades Union Congress in response to wage reductions and worsening conditions for locked-out coal miners. It lasted nine days with about 1.7 million workers involved, but the government countered with volunteers and others who maintained enough essential services for the strike to end in defeat for the unions.
16 The principle of *Rookes* was also applied shortly after in *Stratford v Lindley* [1965] AC 269. See Roger Welch, 'Judicial Mystification of the Law: *Rookes v Barnard* and the Return to Judicial intervention' in KD Ewing (ed), *The Right to Strike: From the Trade Disputes Act 1906 to a Trade Union Freedom Bill 2006* (Institute of Employment Rights, 2006), pp 195–218.
17 See also *Hill v CA Parsons Ltd* [1972] Ch 305 for another important early Denning labour relations case.
18 Before the Act came into force, in the case of *Keys v Boulter* [1971] 1 All ER 289, Denning noted that a union was a legal entity 'which can sue and be sued and make contracts in the same way as any other legal entity'.
19 *The Times*, 14 June 1972.
20 Robert Stevens, *The English Judges: Their Role in the Changing Constitution* (Hart Publishing, 2005), p 42.
21 The workers themselves did not challenge the convictions, preferring instead to take a stance as martyrs, but the Official Solicitor intervened, using the same jurisdiction normally engaged for minors or others incapable of managing their affairs.
22 Labour also renamed the Conciliation and Advisory Service 'the Conciliation and Arbitration Service' and separated it from government control. It was given an independent Council to direct it. 'Advisory' was added to its name in 1975 (usually shortened to 'ACAS'). The Employment Protection Act 1975 turned ACAS into a statutory body.
23 *BBC v Hearn* [1977] ICR 686.
24 Lord Denning, 'Trade Unions on Trial', lecture to the Bar Association for Commerce, Finance and Industry, 20 March 1984.
25 Significant measures included the end of compulsory union membership, making workplace secret ballots before strike action mandatory, along with secret ballots for union elections. The changes reflected the fact that, for Thatcher's supporters at least, unions had effectively ceased being a form of protection for workers and had become a special interest group needing to be curbed instead. When Labour regained power in 1997, it generally left the labour laws alone, save notably for bringing in a minimum wage.
26 The background was a major steel strike. At the time, British Steel was a state-owned steel company, but there were private operators in the same industry. The public sector employees declared a strike, but the private sector employees refused to join them. The steel union nonetheless 'called out' the private sector workers, as a form of secondary strike. Denning granted an injunction against the union precluding its action, but the House of Lords reasserted the union's immunity.
27 Scarman also attacked Denning's approach to judicial law-making in *Lim Poh Choo v Camden and Islington Area Health Authority* [1979] QB 196.
28 Denning's thoughts were set down in a letter he wrote to PS Atiyah, quoted by the latter in his 'Lord Denning's Contribution to Contract Law' (1999) *Denning Law Journal*, Vol 14, No 1, 1 at 3–4.
29 See *The Closing Chapter*, p 190. Scargill had earlier slated Denning's decision in *Duport Steels*.

30. Writing in *The Observer*, 18 May 1975.
31. JAG Griffith, *The Politics of the Judiciary*, 5th edn (Fontana, 1997), p 271.
32. See Wilson, *Court and Bowled*, op cit, pp 151 *et seq*.
33. There was a very last-minute interim hearing before Denning sitting alone. See Sir George Newman obituary, *The Daily Telegraph*, 24 June 2019.
34. See for example *Gulati v MGN Ltd and other cases* [2016] 3 All ER 799 at [107], where Denning's quote was repeated by Arden LJ.
35. See also JAG Griffith, 'That Man Griffith: review of *Lord Denning: A Biography*, by Edmund Heward' (1990) *London Review of Books*, Vol 12, No 20, 25 October.
36. For example, *The Sunday Telegraph* of 13 November 1977 reported Denning as claiming not only had he not voted in any parliamentary election since becoming a judge, but that he could not remember who he voted for before then, and that he had 'no political views at all'.
37. Kenneth Miller, 'The Labours of Lord Denning' in Peter Robson and Paul Watchman (eds), *Justice, Lord Denning and the Constitution*, © 1981 by Gower Publishing Company Ltd, p 126 at 129. Reproduced by permission of Taylor & Francis Group.
38. Until Lord Mackay of Clashfern became Lord Chancellor in 1987, the so-called 'Kilmuir rules' proscribed radio or television interviews for judges, and deprecated press interviews generally, on the slightly odd reasoning that 'so long as a judge keeps silent his reputation for wisdom and impartiality remains unassailable'. Lord Widgery LCJ said in 1972 that the best judge was the one 'least known to the readers of the *Daily Mail*', while Lord Hailsham thought it inadvisable for judges to speak or they would make fools of themselves. Characteristically, Denning evidently dissented from all those senior judges. See Lord Pannick QC, 'An amazing amount has changed over a lifetime of covering law', *The Times*, 7 February 2019.
39. Kenneth Miller, 'The Labours of Lord Denning' in Peter Robson and Paul Watchman (eds), *Justice, Lord Denning and the Constitution*, © 1981 by Gower Publishing Company Ltd, p 126 at 146. Reproduced by permission of Taylor & Francis Group.
40. *The Spectator*, 5 May 1979. The letter was in response to Denning's decision in *MacGregor Wallcoverings Ltd v Turton* [1979] 1 WLR 754.
41. See for example Freeman, p 311, and Denning himself in *The Discipline of Law*, Part Four (pp 147 *et seq*).
42. Stephens, Vol III, p 179.
43. *What Next in the Law?*, p 321. In retirement he was asked whether he thought that the legal process would help or hinder the resolution of the miners' strike. He replied that he had no opinion one way or the other, adding '[a]ll I know is that the law ought to be obeyed, and that is all the courts are doing'. 'Pathetically simplistic' replied the Labour politician Roy Hattersley (*The Times*, 3 December 1984, p 1).
44. 'Labour Law' in Jowell and McAuslan, p 367. See also Denning's own account, in *The Closing Chapter*, Section Six.
45. Allowing freedom to protest such as in *Hubbard v Pitt* did not threaten social order in the same way that more aggressive pickets did.

Chapter XVII: Master of the Rolls – Public Law

1. Freeman, p 349.
2. See James Morton, '"Mad" Frank the litigator', *Law Society Gazette*, 5 December 2014.
3. The case was reported as *Fraser v Mudge and others* [1975] 3 All ER 78. Generally, prisoners before Denning received little or no sympathy: see for example *O'Reilly v Mackman* [1982] 3 WLR 604, and Professor Claire Palley, 'Lord Denning and Human Rights – Reassertion of the Right to Justice' in Jowell and McAuslan, p 251 at 307.
4. Bernard Levin, 'The Victory of Us over Them' in his book *Taking Sides* (Jonathan Cape, 1979), pp 201 and 202.
5. *The Closing Chapter*, p 143.
6. *The Closing Chapter*, p 143.
7. *The Times*, 11 November 1981.
8. George Stern, letters to *The Guardian* and *The Times* published on 13 November 1981. He also wondered if a future voting slip might have the sole name 'Denning' upon it.
9. *The Closing Chapter*, p 183.
10. Lord Scarman obituary, *The Daily Telegraph*, 10 December 2004.
11. JAG Griffith, 'The Law Lords and the GLC', *Marxism Today*, February 1982, p 29.
12. Stephens, Vol II, p 173.
13. *The Atlantic Star* [1973] 2 WLR 795 at 800.
14. *Shields v E Coomes (Holdings) Ltd* [1979] 1 All ER 456.
15. Lord Neuberger, 'Has the identity of the English Common Law been eroded by EU Laws and the European Convention on Human Rights?', Speech to the Faculty of Law, National University of Singapore, 18 August 2016.
16. Neuberger, *op cit*.
17. For a thorough review (if now somewhat dated through no fault of the author) of Denning's work on European Law see AIL Campbell, 'Lord Denning and EEC Law' (1988) *Denning Law Journal*, Vol 3, No 1, 1.
18. Claire Palley, 'Lord Denning and Human Rights – Reassertion of the Right to Justice' in Jowell and McAuslan, pp 265 *et seq*.
19. *Ibid*, pp 265 *et seq*.
20. Lord Denning, 'The Incoming Tide', Inaugural Lord Fletcher Lecture, 10 December 1979.
21. See *What Next in the Law?* Part 7, Sections 5 and 6.
22. *What Next in the Law?* Part 7, Section 5.
23. *What Next in the Law?* Part 7, Section 5, p 291.
24. *What Next in the Law?* Part 7, Section 7.
25. See for example 'Recent Changes in the Law', Address to 13th Dominion Legal Conference, Dunedin, 13 April 1966.
26. *The Due Process of Law*, p 101.
27. A similar lack of sensitivity and fear of 'floodgates' being opened underlay his decision in the well-known case of *Liverpool City Council v Irwin* [1976] QB 319, in which the plaintiff was unable to recover damages from a local authority for the abysmal condition of his social housing. Denning said that the tenants were 'all in a sense responsible for the deplorable state of affairs'.
28. *Gaskin v United Kingdom* (Application no 10454/83), 7 July 1989.

13 Peter Robson and Paul Watchman (eds), *Justice, Lord Denning and the Constitution*, © 1981 by Gower Publishing Company Ltd, pp 1 and 33. Reproduced by permission of Taylor & Francis Group.
14 On 22 January 1981, *The Times* published two letters defending Denning in reply to Mr Bennion, one of which (from a Martin Weston) called him 'possibly the most distinguished living Englishman'. A week or so later, Parliament debated retirement ages for judges, in which Denning was both assailed (by the Labour MP Michael Meacher) and defended (by the Conservative Attorney General, Sir Michael Havers, among others). See *The Times*, 10 February 1981.
15 Denning had been made an Honorary Bencher of Gray's Inn to coincide with his birthday. He received much praise from the legal profession (among other things, being presented with a copy of *Paradisi in Sole* by the solicitors of England and Wales) and an all-party greeting from the House of Commons. There was comment from all the major newspapers, while the BBC called him 'a legend in his own lifetime'. He even appeared on stage at the Theatre Royal, Winchester (a few years later, he rallied some well-known thespians to save the theatre from closure: see *The Times*, 15 February 1983, p 12). Hampshire Archives AV/13/17/S1 contains a recording of events for Denning's eightieth birthday. He also gave the Child & Co Lecture in the Inns of Court School of Law, reproduced as 'This is My Life' (1986) *Denning Law Journal*, Vol 1, No 1, 17.

Chapter XX: Master of the Rolls – Resignation

1 Peter Robson and Paul Watchman (eds), *Justice, Lord Denning and the Constitution*, © 1981 by Gower Publishing Company Ltd, pp 7–11 and 168–70.
2 *The Guardian*, 13 December 1979.
3 See for example Ronald Butt, 'Rebirth of a Nation', *The Times*, 19 February 1981.
4 Denning held that the admission by Britain of Ugandan Asians expelled by the government of Idi Amin was not required by international law, and even if it was, the rule of international law was excluded by the Immigration Act constituting a code. In fact, Article 12(4) of the Civil Rights Covenant, together with international practice, would have required the admission of those expelled by Amin. In time the East African Asians (not just from Uganda) became recognised as a great immigration success story for Britain, given their high standing in most social statistics such as employment and education.
5 *The Discipline of Law*, p 176.
6 See for example *R v Chief Immigration Officer, Gatwick Airport, ex parte Kharrazi* [1980] 1 WLR 1396.
7 His decision was reversed by the House of Lords at [1973] AC 868. It should be noted that all judges in the case approached it as purely one of statutory construction of the Race Relations Act 1968, and whether members and visitors to a local political club constituted a 'section of the public' under s 2(1) of the Act.
8 Affirmed by the House of Lords, see [1975] AC 259. The Revenue had been requiring them to supply full birth certificates for children, even those born in the United Kingdom, rather than the shorter form which other taxpayers had to provide. See also *R v Race Relations Board, ex parte Selvarajan* [1975] 1 WLR 1686 and *Commission for Racial Equality v Amari Plastics Ltd* [1982] 2 WLR 972.
9 HWR Wade, *Administrative Law*, 4th edn (Clarendon Press, 1977), p 483.

10   'Recent Changes in the Law', Address to 13th Dominion Legal Conference, Dunedin, 13 April 1966, [1966] NZLJ 167.
     Note that Denning also stated '[t]he way in which the Maori people have been integrated into the community is a model for all'. That view reflected official thinking in New Zealand at the time – Denning would have been assured that there were no racial problems in New Zealand and that all were treated equally – but would be dismissed in the present age as an arrogant assumption of assimilation and an ignorance of the social statistics which showed Maori did not enjoy parity in many areas of life at the time.
11   Heward, p 195.
12   John Enoch Powell (1912–1998). Powell's 1968 speech is normally referred to as the 'Rivers of Blood' speech, though he did not actually use those words. See Simon Heffer, *Like the Roman: The Life of Enoch Powell* (Faber & Faber, 1998).
13   *The Times* also recorded the dinner in its Court Circular but did not mention Denning's remarks in its opinion pages.
14   As recalled in Narayan's later letter to *The Times*, 28 May 1982.
15   Lord Scarman, *The Brixton Disorders, 10–12 April 1981* (Penguin Books, 1982).
16   Joshua Rozenberg, 'Joshua Rozenberg on Lord Denning: Worthy of his law student favourite crown?', *Legal Cheek*, 23 January 2017. https://bit.ly/2P1tz82.
17   *The Times*, 24 June 1982. Its editorial of that day held Denning responsible for his own misfortune.
18   Joshua Rozenberg, *op cit*.
19   *The Closing Chapter*, p 11.
20   Inevitably, a few copies were retained by purchasers, including one by the journalist Joshua Rozenberg, who inveigled Denning into signing it. See Rozenberg, *op cit*. See also Freeman pp 390–400 on the resignation events.
21   The saga meant that the bulk of *What Next in the Law?* was largely ignored. In it, Denning had repeated the themes of many of his previous judgments and published writings, chief among them his belief that 'the law itself should provide adequate and efficient remedies for abuse or misuse of power from whatever quarter it may come. No matter who it is – who is guilty of the abuse or misuse. Be it government, national or local. Be it trade unions. Be it the press. Be it management. Be it labour. Whoever it be, no matter how powerful, the law should provide a remedy for the abuse or misuse of the power, else the oppressed will get to the point when they will stand it no longer. They will find their own remedy. There will be anarchy' (pp 309–10). Earlier he quoted an unnamed 'great historian' saying that the jury system was 'the strongest of all the forces making for the nation's peaceful continuity' (p 33). Throughout, the book was liberally sprinkled with historical references to the likes of Magna Carta, Lord Mansfield and other familiar constitutional and common law icons. Not for the first time, however, Denning could be somewhat naïve. His statement that '[English Judges] are not, as some suggest, drawn from the upper classes of society. They are – in their birth and upbringing – as mixed a group as you could find' (p 334) was wide of the mark, as we saw earlier, and somewhat ironic given that elsewhere in the book he dismissed the law lords as living in an ivory tower (p 202).
22   *The Closing Chapter*, p 12.
23   *The Times*, 28 May 1982.
24   *The Sunday Times*, 30 May 1982.
25   *The Times*, 28 May 1982. Denning quoted from the article in *The Closing Chapter*, p 12.

26 Among other events around the same time, on 5 July 1982 the Speaker of the House of Commons, George Thomas (later Viscount Tonypandy), held a dinner in Denning's honour at the Speaker's House. Attendees included the Prime Minister Margaret Thatcher.
27 'Valedictory Speeches upon the Impending Retirement of the Master of the Rolls', 30 July 1982, Hampshire Archives 202M86/760. See also 'Lord Denning: a "golden legend" retires', *Belfast Telegraph*, 31 July 1982.
28 Nancy Astor, Viscountess Astor, CH (1879–1964), the first woman to sit as an MP, and mother of William Astor, who as we saw was the owner of Cliveden at the time of the Profumo Affair.
29 Norman had two sons and a daughter. His eldest son, John, served in the Royal Fleet Auxiliary, but died in 1975 after a fall.
30 The solicitor for the Commission, Geoffrey Bindman, later said he had been so offended by Denning's remarks about Jews that he walked out of the court (Sir Geoffrey Bindman QC (Hon), 'A Rare Judge', 5 October 2018. https://bit.ly/3arUwta). Yet, in his judgment, as mentioned, Denning was utterly opposed to anti-Semitism. The problem was that he was still using the language of his youth, such as 'the Wandering Jew'.
31 'Lord Denning: a "golden legend" retires', *Belfast Telegraph*, 31 July 1982.
32 Freeman, p 396.
33 In his book *The Closing Chapter*, pp 76–87.
34 *The Times* editorial, 30 July 1982. At the time Ian Botham (later Lord Botham) was at the height of his powers as a cricketer, and one of the best-known sportsmen in England after his swashbuckling efforts had helped England to win the Ashes in 1981.
35 Simon Brown, *Playing off the Roof & Other Stories: a patchwork of memories* (Marble Hill Publishers, 2020), p 81.
36 'Until Lord Denning retired there was no serious pressure on the courts or the machinery of the administration of justice to modernise the workings of the appellate system', Gavin Drewry, Louis Blom-Cooper and Charles Blake, *The Court of Appeal* (Hart Publishing, 2007), p 38.
37 Lord Donaldson of Lymington obituary, *Daily Telegraph*, 2 September 2005. See also Lord Roskill, 'Does the Law Stand Still?', Denning Lecture to the Bar Association for Commerce, Finance and Industry, 29 March 1983. His lordship reviewed developments to the court structure and legal administration in general such as the introduction of the Divisional Court and two-judge Court of Appeal hearings, which enabled much more efficient disposal of cases.
38 Lord Donaldson of Lymington obituary, *ibid*.

Chapter XXI: Later Years

1 Interview with the editor of the *Financial Times*, quoted in Heward, p 203.
2 John Mortimer, 'Lord Denning: Long life – Short Sentences' in his book, *In Character: Interviews with Some of the Most Influential and Remarkable Men and Women of Our Time* (Penguin Books, 1984), Ch 1, pp 10–11. In July 1983, Denning gave an interview to ITN, in which he repeated that he had changed his mind about the death penalty, having concluded that it was not morally right for society to order something (the execution of a man) that no individual would be prepared to do.
3 'Denning says US sanctions are illegal', *The Times*, 20 October 1982, p 7.

4. *The Closing Chapter*, pp 37–38.
5. *The Closing Chapter*, pp 39–40.
6. He would no doubt have been both surprised and delighted to learn that the play was not even half way through its run – performances only ceased in March 2020, due to the Covid-19 lockdown, and they resumed in May 2021 once the West End was permitted to reopen. See Mark Lawson, 'The case of the Covid-compliant murder: how The Mousetrap is snapping back to life', *The Guardian*, 5 May 2021.
7. The Junior Minister for the Environment told the House of Commons in a slightly aggrieved tone 'With all respect to the former Master of the Rolls, I must warn householders that they cannot go on digging up highways at will'. *The Closing Chapter*, p 73. Denning recalled the water authority stating curtly that 'Lord Denning is retired and should stay that way'. He also observed that contractors were reluctant to undertake work lest they be 'blacked' by unions, and bemoaned the consequent reflection of union power.
8. Denning's correspondence with members of the public is preserved in Hampshire Archives 202M86.
9. *The Times*, 31 December 1983, p 35.
10. *The Times*, 5 August 1983, p 3.
11. Lord Templeman, 'The State of the Legal Profession', The Denning Lecture, 26 March 1981. www.bacfi.org/files/Denning%20Lecture%201981.pdf.
12. See www.bacfi.org/history.htm. Denning's lecture is reproduced at www.bacfi.org/files/Denning%20Lecture%201984.pdf.
13. *The Times*, 18 October 1984, p 2. *The Times* had earlier reported Denning's statement in the book that trade unions 'faced extinction' if they continued to defy the law: see *The Times*, 15 October 1984, p 4.
14. RFV Heuston, 'Lord Denning: The Man and his Times' in Jowell and McAuslan, p 9.
15. Heuston ignored the fact that civil liberties had developed in England over many centuries (symbolically if not actually beginning in 1215); that demonstrations since the Chartists had compelled much welcome social change; that police responses since at least the Peterloo Massacre had sometimes been worse than harassment; that anti-Irish, and anti-Semitic abuse was woven throughout centuries of the country's history; that women had been restricted in rights for much of the same time and that single parents had been treated as 'undeserving poor'. It was also unclear why he would think neighbourhood charities informing indigent citizens of their rights was a bad thing.
16. See also the review, Gilbert Kodilinye, 'Lord Denning in Perspective' (1986) *Denning Law Journal*, Vol 1, No 1, 127.
17. *Reading Evening Post*, 11 January 1985.
18. *Reading Evening Post*, 11 January 1985.
19. *The Times*, 26 July 1985.
20. See Judge John Hack, 'Throwback Thursday: Lord Denning and Noddy on "Jim'll Fix It"', *Legal Cheek*, 24 July 2014.
21. Sir Stephen Sedley, 'New corn from old fields: ministerial government, history and the law', The Denning Lecture, 2012.
22. © Stephen Sedley, (2018), *Law and the Whirligig of Time*, Hart Publishing, an imprint of Bloomsbury Publishing Plc, p 242.

Notes

23 Justice James Douglas of the Queensland Supreme Court called it 'One of the saddest episodes of [Denning's] later life'. See Douglas, 'Lord Denning: His judicial philosophy', lecture delivered on 19 November 2015 for the Selden Society, Australian Chapter, at the Banco Court, Supreme Court of Queensland.

24 See www.buckingham.ac.uk/research/denning. See also 'Editorial' (1986) *Denning Law Journal*, Vol 1, No 1, 5; and 'Introduction to the 2019 General Edition' (2019) *Denning Law Journal*, Vol 31, No 1, 1. Legend Press Limited. Reproduced with permission of the Licensor through PLSclear.

25 *Hansard*, HL Deb, 31 July 1986, vol 479, cols 1046–88.

26 *Hansard*, HL Deb, 3 November 1986, vol 481, cols 913–39. See also 'Denning backs Euro Bill', *Dundee Courier*, 4 November 1986.

27 *Attorney General v Guardian Newspapers Ltd and others* [1987] 3 All ER 316. See also the later *Attorney General v Observer Ltd, Attorney General v Times Newspapers Ltd, sub nom Attorney General v Guardian Newspapers Ltd (No 2)* [1990] 1 AC 109.

28 'Obituary: Lord Oliver of Aylmerton', *The Daily Telegraph*, 23 October 2007.

29 'Master of the Courts', *Illustrated London News*, 1 November 1987.

30 See Hampshire Archives 96M82/PW55. The dispute rumbled on until the mid-1990s. Also in 1987, Denning entered into a dispute over a wrought iron bench in Whitchurch: see Hampshire Archives 84M94/94/4.

31 Hampshire Archives 202M86/164.

32 Hampshire Archives AV74/OR608/S1.

33 Rozenberg, 'Joshua Rozenberg on Lord Denning: Worthy of his law student favourite crown?', *Legal Cheek*, 23 January 2017. https://bit.ly/2P1tz82.

34 Interview with Winchester Radio for his ninetieth birthday, January 1989, Hampshire Archives AV13/12/S1.
The archive title is 'Lord Denning: Interview with Lord Denning on his 90th Birthday by Trevor Knight of Winchester Hospitals Radio', though the recording does not mention 'hospitals' at all.

35 'Lord Denning (90) still fighting for the causes he believes in', *Aberdeen Press and Journal*, 23 January 1989. In the Winchester Radio interview (*op cit*) Denning admitted that there were arguments in favour of the collection of gravel from the area – essentially, the need for progress – but continued his opposition all the same.

36 'It's pure poppycock, your Lordship', *Newcastle Evening Chronicle*, 31 March 1990.

37 Norman died in 1979, from a reaction to a tetanus shot after separating two dogs fighting. Marjorie died in 1982.

38 *R v Cullen* (1990) 92 Cr App Rep 239.

39 *The Times*, 30 April 1990. It will be recalled that in *The Road to Justice* Denning had stated that he did not believe juries would be influenced by media coverage.

40 Edmund Heward (1912–2006). Heward was a solicitor before becoming a Chancery master in 1959. For the full citation of his book, see Appendix III.

41 JAG Griffith, 'That Man Griffith' (1990) *London Review of Books*, Vol 12, No 20, 25 October.

42 See for example Simon Lee, 'Lord Denning: not the last judgment', *Sunday Tribune*, 28 October 1990. At the time, Lee was Professor of Jurisprudence at The Queen's University of Belfast. Heward did put in a reference to the event in later editions of the book.

43 Heward, p 199.

44 Heward, p 218.
45 Griffith, *op cit*.
46 The Parish Council decided to drop the case in 1991. See Hampshire Archives 125M94/PX21.
47 David Higham, 'When Lord Denning got it wrong', *The Oldie*, 26 March, 2020. Higham wrote that the incident occurred 'in the mid-90s' though given that Lady Denning died in 1992 it would obviously have to have been some time earlier. *The Oldie* also published another anecdote about seeing Denning on the train and mistaking him for a gentleman of the road or an impoverished aristocrat trying to recover the family fortune, thanks to his slightly dishevelled appearance and briefcase full of papers: see Roger Houghton, 'Lord Denning's lost banana', *The Oldie*, 21 May 2019.
48 Stephens, Vol III, p 9, n 7.
49 AN Wilson, 'England, his England', *The Spectator*, 18 August 1990, p 8.
50 *The Spectator*, 25 August 1990, p 9. The retraction and apology was given in the names of 'Lord Denning, *The Spectator*, Dominic Lawson (the editor) and AN Wilson'.
51 'Apology from Lord Denning and Magazine', *Dundee Courier*, 23 August 1990.
52 *The Times*, 18 August 1990.
53 'Denning's anger at interview', *Dundee Courier*, 17 August 1990.
54 Rozenberg, 'Joshua Rozenberg on Lord Denning: Worthy of his law student favourite crown?', *Legal Cheek*, 23 January 2017. https://bit.ly/2P1tz82.
55 Edward Pearce, 'Vain old bird', *Sunday Tribune*, 26 August 1990. Pearce (1939–2018) was an English political journalist and author. He was a leader writer for both *The Daily Telegraph* and *The Guardian*, and the author of a number of political biographies.
56 Letter from AN Wilson, *The Spectator*, 22 December 1990, p 54. On the copyright issue, see Hector L MacQueen, '"My tongue is mine ain": Copyright, the Spoken Word and Privacy' (2005) 68(3) MLR 349.
57 Hampshire Archives 202M86. The full note was reproduced by Freeman, p 416.
58 Michael Sherrard, 'Obituary: Iris Freeman', *The Independent*, 23 October 2011, https://bit.ly/3bjAjFc.
59 Denning, 'Foreword' in Cyril Pigott, *The Test Valley Tapestry* (Test Valley Borough Council, 1995), p viii.
60 Patrick Wilkins, 'Lord Denning backs rebel', *Sunday Mirror*, 17 September 1995. Sharpe did appeal, and had the fine overturned on procedural grounds, though the NHS did not change its stance on the principle of selling privately. See Glenda Cooper, 'Chemist wins fight for cheap medicine', *The Independent*, 8 January 1997.
61 'Lord Denning, 97, resists car park plan', *Aberdeen Press and Journal*, 29 April 1996.
62 See https://api.parliament.uk/historic-hansard/people/mr-alfred-denning/1996. Denning had made several contributions earlier in the year about the move.
63 *The London Gazette,* 28 November 1997, Issue no 54962, p 13399.
64 Despite his greatly reduced mobility Denning had insisted on dressing appropriately for the occasion in his morning coat, grey waistcoat and black striped trousers. See Lord Lloyd of Berwick, 'The Judges and the Executive: Have the Goalposts Moved?' (2006) *Denning Law Journal*, Vol 18, No 1, 79 at 80. Lord Lloyd had been given the letter sent by Sir Edward to the Queen relating the occasion.
65 It could be found online at the time of writing: https://archive.org/details/denning-religion-law/page/n3/mode/2up.

Notes

66 'Lord's century: Denning at 100', BBC News, 23 January 1999. http://news.bbc.co.uk/1/hi/uk/260718.stm.
67 Sir Henry Brooke, 'Lord Denning and I: (3) The Final Years', personal blog, 27 December 2016. https://bit.ly/343D9vR.
68 Denning had also been involved in setting up the Hampshire Archives Trust in the mid-1980s, turning up to the first meeting with a facsimile of Magna Carta, and causing quite a stir when he brandished it about without telling anyone it was a copy. See Barry Shurlock, 'Hampshire Archives Trust is celebrating its 35th anniversary', *Hampshire Chronicle*, 7 February 2021.
69 'Vice-Chancellor' was the then-title for the head of the Chancery Division, now renamed simply 'Chancellor', I suspect because it was always shortened to V-C, which led people to assume only military heroes held the post. Sir Richard later became Lord Scott of Foscote.
70 *Denning Law Journal* (1999) Vol 14, No 1.
71 Michael J Kirby, 'Lord Denning: An Appreciation' (1999) *Denning Law Journal*, Vol 14, No 1, 127 at 146. Legend Press Limited. Reproduced with permission of the Licensor through PLSclear.
72 See www.lincolnsinn.org.uk/members/our-professional-community/groups-societies/denning-society/.

Chapter XXII: The End

1 The reference for Denning and Joan's grave is S2RTG04 (section 2, row T, grave 04). Charles and Clara's shared grave is very close by in the cemetery, as is Gordon's.
2 BBC News, 5 March 1999. On the same day, the lead notice of his death on the BBC (https://bbc.in/3470hIG) reported that 'Lord Denning was known for his sense of morality and campaigning fervour, as well as his outspoken views on many issues', and repeated the claim that the Profumo Affair had brought down the Macmillan government.
3 Obituary, *Telegraph*, 6 March 1999.
4 Obituary, *The Guardian*, 6 March 1999.
5 Obituary, *The Times*, 6 March 1999. Conversely, Denning had said during a 1967 panel discussion that he did not object to the long hair increasingly found on (presumably male) barristers (albeit adding 'I shouldn't say anything but I think a lot'), 'as long as they don't start throwing things at me'. See Hampshire Archives AV13/15/S1. The quip about throwing things no doubt referred to an occasion on 6 June 1964, when a disgruntled litigant called Vera Stone threw books at him after her plea for a review of taxation of costs in a recent action had been refused. She was removed from the court, unrepentantly threatening to return and hurl some more. Clearly, she was one litigant who had not been charmed by Denning's famously genial courtroom demeanour.
6 AN Wilson, 'If only Lord Denning had died at seventy…', *The Independent*, 7 March 1999.
7 The case was *Brown and others v Runcie and others* (unreported, Hoffmann J, Chancery Division, 20 June 1990), and on appeal was heard by Dillon, Leggatt and Nolan LJJ (unreported, Court of Appeal, Civil Division, 13 February 1991). The claim and appeal failed and both times costs were awarded against the plaintiffs. Denning had said during *The Spectator* interview that it was most un-Christian for the Archbishop to have sought costs. Some years before, Denning had advised a body called Marriage Solidarity that to permit remarriage in church would constitute a change in Anglican doctrine (*The Times*, 4 January 1984, p 3).

8   7 March 1999.
9   Bernard Purcell, '"Appalling vista" judge dies at 100', *Irish Independent*, 6 March 1999. He added '[i]t should be remembered that until a number of England's "establishment" figures took up the cases of the Maguire Seven, Guildford Four, and Birmingham Six, their guilt was also the settled belief of most Irish ministers and TDs'.
10 The Rt Hon Justice EW Thomas, 'Lord Denning 1899–1999' [1999] NZLJ 92. See also his *The Judicial Process: Realism, Pragmatism, Practical Reasoning and Principles* (Cambridge University Press, 2005).
11 John Ezard, 'Law bids farewell to Lord Denning', *The Guardian*, 18 June 1999.
12 Lord Bingham of Cornhill, 'Address to the Thanksgiving Service for Lord Denning OM', delivered at Westminster Abbey on 17 June 1999, (2000) *Denning Law Journal*, Vol 15, No 1, 1.

Chapter XXIII: A Final Judgment

1   Leslie Scarman (Lord Scarman), 'Leslie Scarman writes in praise of a dynamic judge' (1980) *London Review of Books*, Vol 2, No 12, 19 June.
2   Some clue about how Denning drafted his judgments can be found in the surviving parts of his notebooks which contain handwritten draft judgments, such as his notes on *Secretary of State for Employment v Associated Society of Locomotive Engineers and Fireman and others (No 2)* [1972] 2 All ER 949, preserved in Hampshire Archives 202M86/683.
3   See also Sir Martin Nourse, 'Law and Literature: the legacy of Lord Denning' (2005) *Denning Law Journal*, Vol 17, No 1, 1.
4   Cameron Harvey, 'It all started with Gunner James' (1983) 17 Law Soc of UC Gazette 279, (1986) *Denning Law Journal*, Vol 1, No 1, 67.
5   See *The Family Story*, pp 207–8.
6   See for example Megan Pearson, 'Empathy and Procedural Justice in Clash of Rights Cases' (2020) *Oxford Journal of Law and Religion*, Vol 9, No 2, 350 at 359–60.
7   In *Lennard's Carrying Co Ltd v Asiatic Petroleum Co Ltd* [1915] AC 705 at 713.
8   Derek French, Stephen Mayson and Christopher Ryan, *Mayson, French & Ryan on Company Law*, 26th edn (Oxford University Press, 2009), p 634.
9   See for example NO Stockmeyer Jnr, 'Beloved are the Storytellers' (2002) *Michigan Bar Journal*, Vol 81, No 1, 54–55; Sir Basil Markesinis QC, 'Two kinds of justice: human and divine, random thoughts à propos Milton's Paradise Lost' (2008) *Denning Law Journal*, Vol 20, No 1, 1 at 16–19; and more recently the Supreme Court judge Lord Burrows, 'Judgment-Writing: A Personal Perspective', Annual Conference of Judges of the Superior Courts in Ireland, 20 May 2021. https://bit.ly/3wuaKf8. Lord Burrows wrote 'How much easier it was to read and understand Lord Denning and Lord Wilberforce than it was to absorb dry sub-clause after sub-clause of a Lord Diplock judgment'.
10 Prominent among whom were Sir Louis Blom-Cooper in his Margaret Howard Memorial Lecture of 2001, and the Supreme Court judge Lord Rodger of Earlsferry in 'The Form and Language of Judicial Opinions' (2002) 118 LQR 226.
11 The Lexis computer-based retrieval system began in the 1970s but was rarely used by English barristers in those days. It was not really comparable to modern repositories of England and Wales case-law as provided by the major publishers such as Sweet & Maxwell and LexisNexis, nor to the free source of BAILII.

Notes

12   *The Family Story*, p 208.
13   See also Roderick Munday, 'Lawyers and Latin' (2004) 168 JPN 775; Francis Bennion, 'If it ain't broke, don't fix it' (1994) 15 Stat LR 164; and Francis Bennion 'Is Law Still A Learned Profession?' (2008) 172 JPN 316. Richard Harrison, 'Linguistics and litigation' (1999) 149 NLJ 1491.
14   A contemporary study of Denning's early judicial approach to statutory interpretation is JL Montrose, 'The Treatment of Statutes by Lord Denning' (1959) *University of Malaya Law Review*, Vol 1, No 1 (July), 87–110.
15   Francis Bennion, *Bennion on Statutory Interpretation*, 5th edn (LexisNexis, 2008), pp 954–55. The cases where Denning made controversial remarks about the liberties he intended to take with statutory interpretation are legion: see for example *R v Sheffield Crown Court, ex parte Brownlow* [1980] QB 530 at 539, which even earned him a reproach in the popular press: see *The Times*, 3 March 1980. See also the Renton Committee's report *The Preparation of Legislation* (Cmnd 6053, 1975), which endorsed Denning's purposive approach.
16   See also Denning's words in *Hadmor Productions Ltd v Hamilton* [1983] 1 AC 191 at 201 and Lord Diplock's response at 232–33. Also see Denning's judgment in *R v Secretary of State for the Environment, ex parte Norwich City Council* [1982] QB 808 at 824.
17   See for example Lord Steyn, '*Pepper v Hart*: A Re-Examination' (2001) 1 *Oxford Journal of Legal Studies* 59–72, Francis Bennion, *Statutory Interpretation*, 4th edn (Butterworths, 2002), p 53, also Francis Bennion, 'How they all got it wrong in *Pepper v Hart*' (1995) *British Tax Review*, No 3, 325, and Lord Dyson, *Justice: Continuity and Change*, Kindle edn (Bloomsbury, 2018). For a fuller discussion of the concept of 'literal' versus 'purposive' statutory construction, see for example Bennion, *Statutory Interpretation, op cit*, pp 516 *et seq*.
18   *Kay v Lambeth London Borough Council* [2006] UKHL 10, [2006] 2 AC 465 at [42].
19   His observation was approved on appeal at [1946] AC 163. '*Per incuriam*' means literally 'through lack of care'.
20   *Hansard*, HL Deb, 1 April 1965, vol 264, col 1210. See also Sir Peter Gibson, 'Law reform now: The Law Commission 25 years on', 1991 Denning Lecture. https://bit.ly/3DUmfjF.
21   Andrea Minichiello Williams, 'Modern legal thought eliminates Christian morality', *Law Society Gazette*, 28 April 2011.
22   See for example *The Changing Law*, p 99. See also Andrew Phang, 'A Passion for Justice: Lord Denning, Christianity and the Law' in Mark Hill and RH Helmholz (eds), *Great Christian Jurists in English History* (Cambridge University Press, 2017), Ch 15.
23   Stephens, Vol III, p 23. Denning contrasted the English position with the Soviet Union, which demanded 'undivided loyalty' to the state and hence sidelined all religion. He might instead have contrasted the position with that of the United States. Most if not all of the founding fathers were religious, and would have been happy to write protection of their own faith into the Constitution, but they recognised that their own faith (different sects of Christianity) might not be the one protected by the state, so it was better to ensure no religion was and therefore no one would be better (or worse) off under the law – rather like the 'prisoner's dilemma' philosophical puzzle.
24   14 August 1984, p 13. *The Times* sarcastically observed that at least the provision Denning had in mind would be easy to draft, since one could simply transpose some Soviet law. It added that cults might do some absurd things, but a free society had to tolerate them, since the alternative would be worse.

Denning also spoke about religious cults on BBC Radio's *Woman's Hour* in 1986 and corresponded with some members of the public on the issue: see Hampshire Archives 202M86/715/1–5.

25 *Freedom under Law*, First Hamlyn Lectures (Stevens & Sons, 1949), p 49.
26 Denning was not quite correct despite his confidence: the morals campaigner Mary Whitehouse instigated a prosecution for the common law offence of blasphemy in the 1970s. See David Nash, 'Blasphemy on Trial', *History Today*, 15 November 2017. www.historytoday.com/miscellanies/blasphemy-trial.
Blasphemy was not formally ended in England and Wales until 2008.
27 Delivered as the 33rd Earl Grey Lecture, Newcastle, 27 May 1953.
28 Denning, *The Road to Justice* (Stevens & Sons, 1955).
29 He often made essentially the same exhortation: see, for example, *The Changing Law*, p 122.
30 MDA Freeman, 'Family Matters' in Jowell and McAuslan, p 109, pp 159–60, and 'Family Justice and Family Values according to Lord Denning' (1999) *Denning Law Journal*, Vol 14, No 1, 93.
31 MDA Freeman was quoting Raymond Blackburn in *The Times*, 7 March 1980.
32 See Kate Fox, *Watching the English* (Hodder Paperbacks, 2005) and Jeremy Paxman, *The English: A Portrait of a People* (Penguin, 2007) for some thoughtful recent musings on the subject.
33 MDA Freeman, 'Family Justice and Family Values according to Lord Denning' (1999) *Denning Law Journal*, Vol 14, No 1, 93 at 111.
34 See also his Vol III, Ch 2.
35 Anthony Sampson, *The Changing Anatomy of Britain* (Hodder & Stoughton, 1982), p 160.
36 Patrick Devlin, *The Judge* (Oxford University Press, 1979), p 172.
37 AN Wilson, 'If only Lord Denning had died at seventy ...', *The Independent*, 7 March 1999. In fairness, the remark was made in a journalistic context and hence more informally.
38 Lord Bingham of Cornhill, 'Address to the Thanksgiving Service for Lord Denning OM', delivered at Westminster Abbey on 17 June 1999, (2000) *Denning Law Journal*, Vol 15, No 1, 1.
39 Interview with Robin Day. See https://sirhenrybrooke.me/2016/12/27/lord-denning-and-i-3-the-final-years/.
40 See for example *Tillman v Egon Zehnder Ltd* [2019] UKSC 32; *R v Sarker and Another* [2018] EWCA Crim 1341; or *Gulati v MGN Ltd and Other Cases* [2015] EWCA Civ 1291.
41 Such as in *R (Youngsam) v Parole Board* [2019] EWCA Civ 229.
42 Something he repeated in his review of my book *Noble Savages*, which appeared in *Drumbeat* (the quarterly journal of the Savage Club), No 144, Winter 2019.
43 This led to the cancellation of a planned celebration to mark the 200th anniversary of *Rural Rides* in Hampshire: see 'Organisers scrap celebrations for author William Cobbett because of his anti-Semitism', *Hampshire Chronicle*, 4 March 2021. https://bit.ly/39iMipq.
44 See Ashwin Desai and Goolem Vahed, *The South African Gandhi: Stretcher-Bearer of Empire* (Stanford University Press, 2015).
45 Upon Goddard's death in 1971, Denning, in a tribute delivered in court, called him a Lord Chief Justice of 'incomparable distinction ... respected as no other judge of our time', and that he was sure to 'go down in our annals as one of the greatest of Chief Justices'.

Notes

46 David Pannick QC, 'Why Levin merits an honourable mention in our legal history', *The Times*, 7 September 2004 and Marcel Berlins, 'A Chief Justice got away with murder', *The Independent*, 22 October 2011.

47 See Graeme Williams QC, *A Short Book of Bad Judges* (Wildy, Simmonds & Hill, 2014), Ch 4.

48 Gordon Hewart, *The New Despotism* (Ernest Benn Ltd, 1929). By way of random coincidence, Lord Hewart like Denning was the son of a draper, who was able to attend a grammar school and then Oxford. He worked as a journalist after graduating and only became a barrister in his thirties.

49 See Caroline Morris and Ryan Malone, 'Regulations Review in the New Zealand Parliament' (2004) 4 *Macquarie Law Journal* 7.

50 Peter Doggett, *Growing Up: Sex in the Sixties* (Bodley Head, 2021).

51 Doggett, *op cit*, points out other highly disturbing passages in literature from John Updike, Leslie Thomas, Ian Fleming and Norman Mailer, all of which involved men forcing themselves on women.

52 See Tatiana Siegel, 'No Time to Lose: Hollywood Pins Its Hopes on Bond Director Cary Fukunaga', *The Hollywood Reporter*, 22 September 2021. One might add that, in popular music, Flanders & Swann's 1959 song 'Have Some Madeira, M'Dear' contained brilliantly crafted syllepsis, but would be interpreted by modern listeners as an atrociously bad taste song about date rape.

53 As well as various members of the Profumo set, I would also note that as this book was being written, Lord Devlin's daughter Clare revealed to a newspaper that she had been sexually abused by her father. See Beatrix Campbell, '"Our silence permits perpetrators to continue": one woman's fight to expose a father's abuse', *The Observer*, 25 July 2021.

54 See JPWB McAuslan, 'Review: *The Due Process of Law*' (1980) 44 MLR 244 at 246, who wrote 'What Lord Mountbatten was to the Royals, Lord Denning is to the judiciary: unorthodox, larger than life, a great performer, eager to emphasise his own considerable contributions to public life'.

55 As we saw, he was quick to concede that his decision in *Mandla v Dowell-Lee* regarding the Sikh schoolboy had been incorrect, and he admitted to John Mortimer that his support of the death penalty had been wrong. In *What Next in the Law?* he conceded his earlier opposition to majority jury verdicts had been misplaced.

56 See for example Andrew Roberts, *Eminent Churchillians*, Kindle edn (Weidenfeld & Nicolson, 2010). With respect to Montgomery, see my book, *Noble Savages: The Savage Club and the Great War* (JH Productions, 2018; revised edn, 2020), pp 409 *et seq*.

57 A number of prominent figures signed a letter to *The Times*, published on 11 May 1965, which called for the implementation of the Wolfenden Report (decriminalising male homosexuality). The letter stated that the law as it stood 'did more harm than good' and was out of step with both liberal and Christian opinion.

58 In his infamous *Spectator* interview of 18 August 1990, for example, he had finished with a lament that England had become 'a tenement of Europe', referring to the recent *Factortame* litigation, though he did not mention it specifically (only the subject matter of fisheries). For an introduction to the series of cases which constituted that litigation, see Jo Hunt, 'The Factortame Litigation' in Ian McDougall (ed), *Cases That Changed Our Lives* (LexisNexis, 2010), p 27.

59 This is not a criticism as such: see for example Richard Epstein, 'Do Judges Need to Know any Economics?' [1996] NZLJ 235, who argued that judges attempting economic analysis would likely produce worse outcomes than those who applied rules in the fashion of nineteenth-century commercial judges who simply sought to apply the letter of contracts before them in the way the drafters would have intended.

60 'Recent Changes in the Law', Address to 13th Dominion Legal Conference, Dunedin, 13 April 1966, [1966] NZLJ 167. He made similar sentiments in his speech 'Gems in Ermine', Presidential Address to The English Association in July 1964 (The English Association, 1964).

Appendix I: Denning in the Law Reports

1 For the hierarchy of authorities as it now is, see Practice Direction (Citation of Authorities (2012)) [2012] 2 All ER 255.

2 See *The Family Story*, p 221, and his tribute to Mavis Hill at *The Times*, 31 July 1980, mentioned in Chapter III, where he said 'Law reporting is a profession of its own. It demands much skill and hard work. It is an essential part of our legal system.'

List of Cases

Abbott v Sullivan [1952] 1 KB 189	209
Agar-Ellis, Re (1883) 24 Ch D 317	203
Amalgamated Investment and Property Co Ltd (In Liq) v Texas Commerce International Bank Ltd [1982] QB 84	306
Anton Piller KG v Manufacturing Processes Limited [1976] Ch 55	180–1, 183
Associated Newspapers Group Ltd v Wade [1979] 1 WLR 697	228
Attorney General v Guardian Newspapers Ltd and others ('Spycatcher' litigation) [1987] 3 All ER 316	272
Baird Textile Holdings Ltd v Marks and Spencer plc [2001] EWCA Civ 274	84
Balogh v Crown Court at St Albans [1974] 3 All ER 283	187
Barnard v National Dock Labour Board [1953] 2 QB 18 (CA)	105, 271
Bater v Bater [1950] 2 All ER 458	95–6
BBC v Hearn [1977] ICR 686	217
Bell v Lever Brothers Ltd [1932] AC 161	93, 94, 200
Bendall v McWhirter [1952] 2 QB 466	102–3
Bickel v Duke of Westminster [1977] QB 517	304
Birmingham & District Land Co v London & North Western Railway Co (1888) 40 Ch D 268	85
'Birmingham Six' judgment. *See* McIlkenny v Chief Constable of West Midlands Police Force and another	
Bowman v Secular Society [1917] AC 406	297
British Steel Corporation v Granada Television Ltd [1981] AC 1096	248
Broad Idea International Ltd v Convoy Collateral Ltd (British Virgin Islands); Convoy Collateral Ltd v Cho Kwai Chee (also known as Cho Kwai Chee Roy) (British Virgin Islands). *See* Convoy Collateral Ltd v Broad Idea International Ltd	
Bromley London Borough Council v Greater London Council [1982] 2 WLR 62	224–5, 239
Broome v Cassell [1972] AC 1027	188–90
Brown v Rolls Royce Ltd [1960] 1 All ER 577 (HL)	116

Butler Machine Tool Co Ltd v Ex-Cell-O Corporation (England) Ltd
 [1979] 1 All ER 965 — 198–9
Button v Button [1968] 1 All ER 1064 — 202

Cameron v Liverpool Victoria Insurance Co Ltd [2019] UKSC 6 — 305
Candler v Crane, Christmas & Co [1951] 2 KB 164 (CA) — 98–100, 186, 271
Caparo Industries plc v Dickman and others [1990] 2 AC 605 — 100
Cartier International AG and others v British Telecommunications Plc and
 Another [2018] UKSC 28 — 305
Cassell & Co Ltd v Broome [1972] AC 1027 — 294
Central London Property Trust Ltd v High Trees House Ltd
 [1947] KB 130, [1946] 1 All ER 256 — xiv, 39, 82–5, 86, 93, 188, 296, 298, 307
Churchman v Churchman [1945] P 44 — 70–1
Churchman v Joint Shop Stewards Committee of the Workers of the Port of
 London [1972] 3 All ER 603 — 212
Combe v Combe [1951] 2 KB 215 — 84
Congreve v Home Office [1976] QB 629 — 223–4
Convoy Collateral Ltd v Broad Idea International Ltd [2021] UKPC 24 — 183, 303
Cooke v Head [1972] 2 All ER 38 — 202
Cooper v Phibbs (1867) LR 2 HL 149 — 94
Corinthian Securities Ltd v Cato [1970] 1 QB 377 — 304
Crabb v Arun District Council [1976] Ch 179 — 307
Crisp from the Fens Ltd v Rutland County Council [1950] 1 P&CR 48 — 306
Curtis v Chemical Cleaning Co [1951] 1 KB 805 — 102

D&C Builders v Rees [1966] 2 QB 617 — 187–8
Davis v Johnson [1979] AC 264 — 295
DC Thomson & Co v Deakin and others [1952] 2 All ER 361 (CA) — 210–11
De Falco v Crawley District Council [1980] QB 460 — 252
Deutsche Bank AG and Others v Unitech Global Ltd and Another; Deutsche
 Bank AG v Unitech Ltd [2016] EWCA Civ 119 — 306
Devani v Wells [2019] UKSC 4 — 305
Dixon and Another v Blindley Heath Investments Ltd and Others
 [2015] EWCA Civ 1023 — 306
Donoghue v Stevenson [1932] AC 562 — 98–9, 100, 145
Douglas v Hello! Ltd [2008] 1 AC 1 — 197
DPP v Smith [1961] AC 290 — 120–2
Drummond v Parish (1843) 3 Curt 522, 163 ER 812 — 90
Dunbar Assets plc v Butler [2015] EWHC 2546 (Ch) — 307
Duport Steels Ltd and others v Sirs and others [1980] 1 WLR 142 — 214–5
Dyson Holdings v Fox [1976] QB 503 — 205, 295

Eurymedon, The [1975] AC 154 — 123
Eves v Eves [1975] 1 WLR 1338 — 202
Express Newspapers v McShane [1980] AC 672 (HL) — 214, 219

Fawcett Properties Ltd v Buckingham County Council [1961] AC 636 — 303, 306

List of Cases

Financial Reporting Council Ltd v Sports Direct International Plc [2018] EWHC 2284 (Ch)	305
Fletcher v Fletcher [1945] 1 All ER 582	71–2
Fowler v Bratt [1950] 2 KB 96	305
Frederick E Rose (London) Ltd v William H Pim Junior & Co Ltd [1953] 2 QB 450	304
FSHC Group Holdings Ltd v GLAS Trust Corp Ltd [2019] EWCA Civ 1361	304
Gaskin v Liverpool City Council [1980] 1 WLR 1549	228–30, 233, 298
George Mitchell (Chesterhall) Ltd v Finney Lock Seeds Ltd [1983] 2 AC 803	261–2
Gill and another v El Vino Co Ltd [1983] QB 425 (CA)	208–9
Gillick v West Norfolk and Wisbech Area Health Authority [1986] AC 112	204
Gold v Essex County Council [1942] 2 KB 293	60
Gouriet v Post Office [1977] 1 All ER 696	217–8
Gouriet v Post Office [1978] AC 435 (HL)	218
Great Peace Shipping Ltd v Tsavliris Salvage (International) Ltd [2003] QB 679 (CA)	94–5
Gurasz v Gurasz [1969] 3 All ER 822	205
Gurtner v Circuit [1968] 2 QB 587	305
Halbauer v Brighton Corporation [1954] 1 WLR 1161	102
Harbutt's Plasticine Ltd v Wayne Tank and Pump Co Ltd [1970] 1 QB 447	192, 193
Harman v United Kingdom, App No 10038/82 (ECtHR)	231
Heatons Transport (St Helens) Ltd v TGWU [1973] AC 15	212
Hedley Byrne & Co v Heller & Partners Ltd [1964] AC 465	100, 186
Hewer v Bryant [1970] 1 QB 357	203, 204
HL Bolton (Engineering) Co Ltd v TJ Graham & Sons Ltd (Matter No M 1678 OA 18) [1957] 1 QB 159	291
Hoani Te Heuheu Tukino v Aotea District Maori Land Board [1941] AC 308 (PC (NZ))	61
Home Office v Dorset Yacht Club [1970] AC 1004	186
Howell v Falmouth Boat Construction Ltd [1951] AC 837	97–8
HP Bulmer Ltd and another v J Bollinger SA and others [1974] 2 All ER 1226	225–6
Hubbard v Pitt [1975] 3 All ER 1	215–7
Hughes v Metropolitan Railway Co [1877] 2 AC 439	85, 86
Interfoto Picture Library Ltd v Stiletto Visual Programmes Ltd [1989] QB 433	194
J Spurling v Bradshaw [1956] 1 WLR 461	102, 194
James v Minister of Pensions [1947] KB 867	81–2
Jarvis v Swan Tours [1973] QB 233	191
Jefford v Gee [1970] 2 QB 130	304
Kaefer Aislamientos SA de CV v AMS Drilling Mexico SA de CV and Others [2019] EWCA Civ 10	305
Karsales (Harrow) Ltd v Wallis [1956] 2 All ER 866	100–2, 191

L (Infants), Re [1962] 3 All ER 1	202–3
Ladd v Marshall [1954] 1 WLR 1489	105
L'Estrange v F Graucob Ltd [1934] 2 KB 394 (CA)	47–8, 49
Letang v Cooper [1965] 1 QB 232	185
Lister v Stubbs (1890) 45 Ch D 1 (CA)	180, 183, 295
Liversidge v Anderson [1942] AC 206 (HL)	57–8, 59, 99, 267
London Transport v Betts [1958] 2 All ER 636	296
M v P (Queen's Proctor Intervening) [2019] EWFC 14	304
MacShannon v Rockware Glass Ltd [1977] 2 All ER 449	226
Magor and St Mellons RDC v Newport Corporation [1950] 2 All ER 1226; on appeal [1952] AC 189	92, 293
Mandla v Dowell-Lee [1983] 1 All ER 1062	261
Mareva Cia Naviera SA v International Bulkcarriers SA, The Mareva [1975] 2 Lloyd's Rep 509 (CA)	179, 180, 183, 295, 307
Marks and Spencer Plc v BNP Paribas Securities Services Trust Co (Jersey) Ltd and Another [2015] UKSC 72	306
Mazhar v Lord Chancellor [2019] EWCA Civ 1558	304
McIlkenny v Chief Constable of West Midlands Police Force and another ('Birmingham Six' judgment) [1980] QB 283	117, 237–40, 253, 291
Meridian Global Funds Management Asia Ltd v Securities Commission [1995] 2 AC 500	291
Miller v Jackson [1977] QB 966	195–6, 291, 307
Morgan v Fry [1968] 2 QB 710	211
Nagle v Feilden [1966] 2 QB 633	209
Nippon Yusen Kaisha v Karageorgis [1975] 1 WLR 1093	295
Nothman v London Borough of Barnet [1978] 1 All ER 1243	293
NWL Ltd v Woods [1979] 3 All ER 614	214
O'Reilly v Mackman [1982] 3 WLR 604	231–2, 304
O'Shea v O'Shea (1890) 15 PD 59 (CA)	164
Oxonica Energy Ltd v Neuftec Ltd [2008] EWHC 2127 (Pat)	292
Paal Wilson & Co A/S v Partenreederei Hannah Blumenthal, The Hannah Blumenthal [1983] 1 AC 854	294
Packer v Packer [1954] P 15	296
Parliamentary Privilege Act 1770, Re [1958] AC 331 (PC)	119–20
Parry-Jones v The Law Society [1969] 1 Ch 1	305
Peake v Automotive Products Ltd [1977] IRLR 365	207–8, 209
Pearlman v Keepers and Govrs of Harrow School [1979] QB 56	304
Peekay Intermark Ltd and another v Australia and New Zealand Banking Group Ltd [2006] EWCA Civ 386	48–9
Pepper v Hart [1993] AC 593	294
Pett v Greyhound Racing Association [1968] 2 All ER 545	138–9
Photo Production Ltd v Securicor Transport Ltd [1980] AC 827	193
Prohibitions del Roy (1607) 77 ER 1342	282

List of Cases

Pyx Granite Co Ltd v Ministry of Housing and Local Govt [1958] 1 QB 554	303
R v Greater London Council, ex parte Blackburn [1976] 3 All ER 184	294
R v Hillingdon London Borough Council, ex parte Islam [1981] 3 WLR 109	253
R v Home Secretary, ex parte Phansopkar [1975] 4 All ER 497	253
R v Northumberland Compensation Appeal Tribunal, ex parte Shaw [1952] 1 KB 338	104–5, 271
R v Racial Equality Commission, ex parte Hillingdon London Borough Council [1981] 3 WLR 520	254
R v Secretary of State for the Home Department, ex parte Hosenball [1977] 3 All ER 452	235–7
R v West [1948] 1 KB 709 (CA)	86–8, 89
R (Begum) v Special Immigration Appeals Commission [2021] UKSC 7	59
R (Faqiri) v Upper Tribunal (Immigration and Asylum Chamber) (Secretary of State for the Home Department, Interested Party) [2019] EWCA Civ 151	305
R (Morgan Grenfell & Co Ltd) v Special Comr of Income Tax [2002] 3 All ER 1	305
R (Privacy International) v Investigatory Powers Tribunal [2019] UKSC 22	304
R (Wright) v Resilient Energy Severndale Ltd and Another [2019] UKSC 53	303
R (Youngsam) v Parole Board [2019] EWCA Civ 229	294
Race Relations Board v Charter and others [1972] 1 All ER 556	253
Rahimtoola v H E H The Nizam of Hyderabad and Others [1958] AC 379	117–9
Revenue and Customs Commissioners v Joint Administrators of Lehman Brothers International [2019] UKSC 12	304
Richardson, Spence & Co v Rowntree [1894] AC 217	48
Riddick v Thames Board Mills Ltd [1977] 3 All ER 677	231
Romford Ice & Cold Storage Co Ltd v Lister [1956] 2 QB 180	304
Rondel v Worsley [1966] 3 All ER 657	186–7
Rookes v Barnard [1964] AC 1129 (HL)	189, 190, 200, 211
Rowland, Re [1962] 2 All ER 837	139–41
Salisbury v Gilmore [1942] 2 KB 38	85
Savjani v IRC [1973] 1 QB 815	253–4
Scruttons Ltd v Midland Silicones Ltd [1962] AC 446 (HL)	122–3, 294
Seaford Court Estates Ltd v Asher [1949] 2 All ER 155	91–2, 113
Secretary of State for Employment v Associated Society of Locomotive Engineers and Fireman and others (No 2) [1972] 2 All ER 949	212
Sequent Nominees Ltd (formerly Rotrust Nominees Ltd) v Hautford Ltd [2019] UKSC 47	303
Seven Bishops (Trial of the) (1688) 12 State Tr 183	218
Sirros v Moore [1975] QB 118, [1974] 3 All ER 776	304, 305
Siskina, The [1979] AC 210	179, 181–2, 183, 303
Six Carpenters' Case (1610) 8 Co Rep 146	290
Smith v Inner London Education Authority [1978] 1 All ER 411	224
Smith v Smith [1945] 61 TLR 331	68–9, 70
Solle v Butcher [1950] 1 KB 671	92–4, 95, 295–6, 303
Somerset v Stewart (1772) 20 St Tr 1, (1772) 98 ER 499	108
Spartan Steel and Alloys Ltd v Martin & Co Ltd [1973] 1 QB 27	195

'Spycatcher' litigation. *See* Attorney General v Guardian Newspapers Ltd
    and others
Star Sea Transport Corporation v Slater [1979] 1 Lloyd's Rep 26   214
Stratford v Lindley [1965] AC 269   211
Sturges v Bridgman (1879) 11 Ch D 852   196
Suisse Atlantique Société D'armement Maritime SA v NV Rotterdamsche
    Kolen Centrale [1967] 1 AC 361 (HL)   191–2, 193, 200
Sydall v Castings Ltd [1966] 3 All ER 770   204–5, 298
Sykes v Director of Public Prosecutions [1961] 3 All ER 33 (HL)   117

Taff Vale Railway Company v Amalgamated Society of Railway Servants
    [1901] AC 426 (HL)   210
Teheran-Europe Co Ltd v ST Belton (Tractors) Ltd [1968] 2 QB 545   305
Tesco Supermarkets v Nattress [1972] AC 153 (HL)   291
Thakrar v Secretary of State for the Home Department [1974] 2 All ER 261   253
Thornton v Shoe Lane Parking [1971] 2 QB 163   193–4
Tool Manufacturing Co Ltd v Tungsten Electric Co Ltd [1955] 1 WLR 761   85–6
Trump International Golf Club Scotland Ltd and Another v Scottish Ministers
    [2015] UKSC 74   306

UK Insurance Ltd v Holden and Another [2019] UKSC 16   304
United Australia v Barclays Bank [1941] AC 1 (HL)   60
United City Merchants (Investments) Ltd v Royal Bank of Canada
    [1983] 1 AC 168   306

Verrall v Great Yarmouth BC [1981] All ER 839   296

Wachtel v Wachtel [1973] Fam 72   201–2
Waltons Stores (Interstate) v Maher (1988) 164 CLR 387 (HCA)   84
Ward v Bradford Corporation (1971) 70 LGR 27   221–2, 233
Weston's Settlements, Re [1968] 3 All ER 338   205–6
Wheat v E Lacon & Co Ltd [1966] 1 All ER 582 (HL)   116
Whitehouse v Jordan [1980] 1 All ER 650   6
Williams v Linnett [1951] 1 KB 565   102
Williams and Glyn's Bank v Boland [1979] 2 WLR 550   204
Wilson, Smithett & Cope Ltd v Terruzzi [1976] QB 683   306
Wingham, Re [1949] P 187 (CA)   90–1
Wiseman v Wiseman [1953] P 79   304
Woodhouse Ltd v Nigerian Produce Ltd [1972] AC 741   86
Woodward and others v Hutchins and others [1977] 2 All ER 751   197
Wyld v Silver [1962] 3 All ER 309   61, 141–2, 143–4

Young v Bristol Aeroplane Co Ltd [1944] KB 718   295

Z Ltd v A [1982] 1 All ER 556   305

Index

Administrative law
  certiorari, grant for error of law   105
  contribution to development   104–5, 110
  criticism of old procedures   110
  mistake by tribunal   105
  post-Second World War developments, relevance   104
  tribunal acting contrary to natural justice   105
Africa
  Committee on Legal Education for Students in Africa
    chair   126
    report and recommendations   126
  Denning Societies in   126
  'Legal Education in Africa: Sharing our Heritage' lecture   126
  praise for promotion of legal profession in   126
  reputation in   126
  'The Future of Law in Africa', London conference   125–6
  visits to   110, 125, 126
African Law Journal, foreword to   125
Allan Sharpe, support for, over private sale of prescriptions   281
Andover Magistrates' Court, personal appearances in   273
Anecdote about accused housebreaker   268
Anti-Semitism
  apology for remarks   279
  Israel, fondness and support for   279
  Leon Brittan, remarks about   278
  unfounded allegations   87–8
Anton Piller order, role in development   180–1
Arthritis   178
Artificial insemination, views on   115
Athenaeum, membership   134, 178
Authorship *see also* Lectures
  Closing Chapter, The   3, 58, 177, 266, 267, 310
  Discipline of Law, The   243–4, 246, 253
  Due Process of Law, The   67, 165, 183, 228, 244–6
  Family Story, The   1, 17, 20, 25, 28, 29, 30, 50, 52, 57, 58, 59, 63, 86, 120, 122, 239, 240, 243, 247
  Field, The, articles in   273
  Landmarks in the Law   267, 268
  Leaves from my Library   270
  What Next in the Law?   228, 257, 279, 280, 286

Bar Association for Commerce, Finance and Industry
  annual Denning lecture   267
  patron   267
Birmingham Six case   237–40, 278
Borrowing From Scotland   145
Brighton bomb, whether perpetrators guilty of high treason   267

British Legion, Patron of Whitchurch
    Branch 25
British Museum Society, founder member
    with Joan 174
Bullen & Leake's Precedents, work on 45,
    107

Centenary
    Australian judiciary, praise from 283
    booklet to commemorate 282
    celebrations 282
    generally 282–4
    'Great Tom' bell, casting 282
    Lincoln's Inn Denning Society,
        foundation 283
    University of Buckingham symposium
        283
Chancellor of Diocese of London, as 50
Chancellor of Diocese of Southwark, as
    50
Changing Law, The
    contents 108–9
    misleading remark about Lord
        Chancellor in 109
    Times', The, praise for 109
Changing world, reflections on 274
Charisma and courteousness 137–9
Cheshire, Geoffrey
    examiner for unsuccessful All Souls
        application 106
    friendship 106
Cheshire Foundation Homes for the Sick
    chairman 106
    India, visit to local homes in 106–7
    opposition to overseas trust 106
    trust deed, work on 106
    work with Joan for 106, 311
Christian faith
    death penalty, and 298–9
    exemption clauses, and 299
    foundation of common law, as 297
    immigration concerns, and 299
    importance 64 247, 269, 297
    informing his values and views 297–8
    morality and law following on from
        religion 297
    regular church attendance 297

search for justice, and 297
sense of right and wrong, informing
    298
Christian institutions, commitment to
    address to National Association of
        Parish Councils 106
    Cheshire Foundation Homes for the
        Sick, work with 106
    Cumberland Lodge *see* Cumberland
        Lodge
    generally 106
    Lawyers' Christian Fellowship *see*
        Lawyers' Christian Fellowship (UK)
Closing Chapter, The 3, 58, 177, 266, 310
Court of Appeal
    American system contrasted 135
    authority, using own cases as 102
    cases heard, subject matter
        administrative law *see* Administrative
            law
        admission of fresh evidence, test
            105
        banks, involving 103
        burden of proof, approach to 95–7
        deserted wife's equity *see under* Equity
        error of law, certiorari 105
        exemption clauses *see* Exemption
            clauses, law as to
        fundamental breach 100–2
        hire purchase scheme 100–2
        innocent misrepresentation 102
        Latin expressions, approach to 90, 91
        mistake on contract 92–5
        negligent misstatement 98–100
        oral licence to repair ship, whether
            sufficient 97–8
        personal licence to occupy marital
            home 103
        privileged will 90–1
        Rent Restriction Acts 93
        statutory interpretation, approach to
            91–2
    civil and criminal divisions, problems
        inherent in 135
    congratulatory response to promotion
        89
    final case in 261–2

first case in   90–1
inefficiency in Denning's last years   263
justice over formality, search for   99
law reform, opportunities for   89
Master of the Rolls *see* Master of the Rolls
promotion to   89
specialist knowledge, Denning's belief in need for   135
Courteousness, reputation for   137
Cricket, fondness for   125, 195, 196
Cumberland Lodge
Chairman of Trustees, election   105
Christian nature   106
establishment   105
work for, with Joan   106, 311

David Murray Foundation lecture   145
Death and burial   2, 285
Death penalty
Christian faith, and   298–9
opposition to   80, 265
passing sentence   80
Royal Commission, evidence to   80
support for   80, 277
views on, in John Mortimer interview   265
Denning, Alfred Thompson (Lord)
baptism   4
Baron Denning of Whitchurch *see* Denning of Whitchurch, Baron
birth   2, 6
Britain into which born   4–5
death   2, 285
education
early   9–11
Oxford, time at   11–12
scholarship to Grammar School   10
family home, dilapidated state   5–7
inherent risks in early life   6–8
military service *see* Military service
parents, assessment of strengths   8
person, as   307–12
reason for first name   4
siblings
birth   4
early work experiences   9

values ingrained in at early age   8–9, 10
Denning, Charles (father)
bankruptcy of firm   27–8
birth   1
business shortcomings   4
death   62
improved financial position   44
marriage   2
'The Hermitage', move to   28–9
Whitchurch, move to   2
Denning (née Thompson), Clara (mother)
children   4
death   88
Denning's assessment   4
family business, role in   4
later years   77–8
marriage   2
'The Hermitage', move to   28–9
Denning, Reginald (brother)
death   273
war service   19–20
Denning, Robert Gordon (son)
birth   52
education   77
Magdalen College, at   123
occasional visits to The Lawn   280
Senior Dean of Arts, Magdalen   31
Denning, William (grandfather)   1–2
Denning House   2
Denning Law Journal   270–1, 283
Denning of Whitchurch, Baron
coat of arms   113
congratulatory response to elevation   113
elevation   113
Desert Island Discs, appearance on   25, 246–7
Detention without trial
circumstances warranting   59, 60
Irish Troubles   59
Second World War, during *see under* Second World War
Dimbleby Lecture   247
Discipline of Law, The   243–4, 246, 253
Divorce work
attempts to reform law   68, 102

395

Divorce work *(continued)*
　dislike for 67
Donaldson, Sir John
　anecdote about cupboard full of
　　interesting pending cases 262–3
　backlog of cases, rapid elimination 263
　Master of the Rolls, Denning's successor
　　as 132, 262
　reform of procedures, responsible for
　　263, 301–2
Driving, decision to stop 77
Drummer, Rose
　employment in Sussex household 49, 52
　return to Denning household 79
　Women's Royal Naval Service, joining
　　63
Due Process of Law, The 67, 165, 183, 228,
　244–6

Earliest ancestor 1
Early legal career
　aristocratic clients 38–9
　Bar examination 36
　Beaufort Street, renting rooms at 37–8
　Brick Court chambers 36
　Bullen & Leake's Precedents, work on 45
　decision to follow 32
　devilling work 36–7
　firms, briefs from 38
　first 'law student' case 47
　House of Lords, first appearance in 44
　income in early years 37, 38, 44
　jurisprudence, dislike 34–5
　legal panjandrums, association with 46
　Lincoln's Inn, admission 33–4
　Middle Temple
　　honorary member 46
　　pupillage 35
　outstanding grades 34
　paid work for the first time 37
　Prize Studentship 36
　pupils, taking on 46
　'red bag', first 44
　scholarship, reliance on 37
　Smith's Leading Cases, contribution to
　　39, 45
　social life 39–41

Southern Railway, briefs from 38
Ecclesiastical courts, declining invitation to
　chair investigatory commission 106
English Association
　inaugural address to 173
　President 173
Englishness, sense of *see also* Patriotism
　Charles Stephen's analysis 300
　MDA Freeman's analysis 299–300
　values informing his character 299–
　　300
Equality for women, concerns over 115
Equity
　deserted wife's equity in home
　　criticism 103
　　development of concept 103
　　House of Lords overruling concept
　　　105
　　Parliament supporting 103–4
　use, to develop law 103
Estoppel as a shield not a sword 84
Europe
　concerns over legal implications 226
　criticism of European law 277
　European Convention, opposition to
　　227, 228
　House of Lords speeches on 271–4
　implications, grasp 225–6
　Lord Neuberger's observations 227
　need to influence Europe for the better
　　273
　opposition to loss of sovereignty 273,
　　310
　Spectator, The, interview 277
Evidence, test for admission of fresh 105
Exemption clauses, law as to
　attempts to refashion 48
　Christian faith, and 299
　cleaning company 102
　Court of Appeal cases 100–2
　dissenting judgment upholding clause
　　123
　final case 261–2
　first case 47–9
　fundamental breach 100–2
　hire purchase scheme, involving 100–2
　innocent misrepresentation 102

396

insurance losses, allocation 102
Master of the Rolls, cases heard before 191–5
parliamentary vindication of approach 194–5
sale of goods, statutory protection for buyer 262
stolen caravan 102
widely drafted clause 102

Faith, importance *see* Christian faith
Family life
  birth of son 52
  marriage *see* Marriage
  Sussex, life in *see* Sussex, life in
Family Story, The 1, 17, 20, 25, 28, 29, 30, 50, 52, 57, 58, 59, 63, 86, 120, 122, 239, 240, 243, 247, 280
Field, The, articles in 273
First World War
  aftermath 25–6
  Amiens Dispatch 16
  background 13
  demob 27
  effect on later approach to life 25–6
  family involvement
    Battle of Jutland 20–2
    Gordon Denning 20–2
    Jack Denning 17–19
    Johnny Haynes 16–17
    Reginald Denning 19–20
    Somme, at 17–19
  outbreak 14
  personal involvement
    bridge-building work 24
    enlistment as officer cadet 23
    generally 22–5
    initially ruled unfit for 22
    Royal Engineers 23, 24
    second lieutenant, commission as 23
    Somme 24
    'Spanish flu', infected with 25
  prevailing values, importance 15–16
  public support for 14–15
  Treaty of London 14, 15
Free speech, *Spycatcher* ligation 272–3
Freedom of religion, belief in 297

Freedom of the press, support for 272
Freeman, Iris, biography by *see Lord Denning: A Life*
Fundamental breach, examination of concept 101–2
General Strike, special constable during 210
'Greatest Living Englishman', Raymond Blackburn's view 187
Guildford Four, comments on 277, 278, 279

Hamlyn Lecture
  accuracy of quotations used, doubts as to 108
  blasphemy as a dead letter 297
  book form, publication of lectures in
    Law Society Gazette review 108
    The Solicitor review 108
  'Freedom of Mind and Conscience' 108
  'Justice between Man and the State' 108
  origins and purpose 107
  'Personal Freedom' 107–8
  positive reception 108
  racial discrimination, criticism 110, 253
  'The Powers of the Executive' 108
Harvey, Mary (first wife)
  correspondence with, in 1920s 40
  death 63
  deterioration in health 47, 49, 62
  early meetings with 29–30
  engagement 43
  Fawley, move to 30
  honeymoon 46
  marriage 45–6
  Spinster's Ball, invitation to 43
  tuberculosis, diagnosis and recovery 44–5
  unsatisfactory nature of first marital home 46–7
Health
  centenary, by 282
  failing, acknowledgment 274
  final illness and death 285
  hearing and eyesight, deterioration 266

Health *(continued)*
  hip replacement   266
Heward, Edmund
  biography by *see Lord Denning: A Biography*
  obituary in *The Independent*   186
High Court
  appeal, only decision overturned on   70–1
  appointment to   50, 65
  committee work, recommendations
    county court judges to hear divorce cases   72
    decree timetables   72
    generally   72–3
    Marriage Welfare Service   72
  congratulatory letters following appointment   65–6
  divorce work   67–8
  ex tempore judgments   68
  first reported judgments
    collusion case   70–1
    desertion case   71–2
    post-nuptial settlement, approach to   68–70
  King's Bench Division, transfer to *see* King's Bench Division
  knighthood following   65
  praise for appointment   65
  Probate, Divorce and Admiralty Division, appointment to   65
Hill, Mavis (law reporter)
  Boswell to Denning's Johnson   37
  Profumo report, lunch with, during inquiry   163
Hip replacement   266
Homes
  dispute over wall erected at The Lawn   267
  Fair Close   61, 123, 125
  stair lift installed at The Lawn   266
  Sussex in, *see* Sussex, life in
  The Lawn *see under* Whitchurch
Homosexuality
  Christian faith informing views on   297
  Local Government Act 1988, s 28, support for   115

views on   115, 277
House of Lords (court)
  Baron Denning of Whitchurch *see* Denning of Whitchurch, Baron
  departure from   127
  disenchantment with   127
  elevation to
    acceptance   112
    favourite quote   112
    refusal   112
  first appearance in   44
  friendships with other Lords   114
  incidental lifestyle opportunities   114
  judgments
    capital murder   122
    classic Denning style, absence   116
    conventional judicial language, use   117
    dissenting judgment later vindicated   118, 123
    dissenting judgment not published   120
    examples of mild Denning touch   116–17
    exemption clause, upholding   123
    homicide and intent   120–2
    number   116
    parliamentary privilege, as to   119–20
    Partition of India, case arising out of   117–19
    privity of contract   123
    public defence   120
    reported cases   116
    Viscount Simonds, in conflict with   118, 119, 123, 127
  Master of the Rolls, leaving to become *see* Master of the Rolls
  pageant to induct   114
  Privy Council
    dissenting judgment not published   120
    parliamentary privilege case   119–20
    praise from, following resignation   262
    Viscount Simonds, anticipated conflict with   113–14
House of Lords (Parliament)
  final contributions   281

homosexuality, views on 115
Local Government Act 1988, s 28,
    support for 115
maiden speech 114
participation in debates 114
topics debated 114–15
Immigration, concerns over
  case law, voiced in 252
  community tensions, etc, lack of
      awareness 255
  generally 254–5
  large numbers, as to 253
  naïve view of immigration officers 253
  press support 252–3
  whether at odds with Christian faith
      298
Important judgments, Denning listing 271
Infidelity, views on 158
Injunctions
  Mareva, role in development 183
  views on importance 183
Institute of Directors, speech on legality of
    US sanctions 265–6
Internment *see* Detention without trial
Ireland
  'appalling vista' remarks 238, 286
  Birmingham Six case 237–40, 278
  difficulty in understanding hatred
      between Catholics and Protestants
      240
  Guildford Four, comments on 277,
      278, 279
  obituaries in Irish newspapers 286

Jim'll Fix It, appearance on 269–70
Judge's oath, analysis and adherence to
    311–12
Judges, criticism of lack of promotional
    structure 111
Judicial appointments
  academic criticism
    Denning's response 133
    establishment response to criticism
        134
    Griffith (JAG) by 133
  dominance of private schools and
      Oxbridge 133

improvements in process 134
manner 133
narrow pool, from
  benefits 134
  Denning's rebuttal 134
  generally 133, 134
  restricted lifestyle and experience 133
  social justice, whether limiting response
      to 133
Judicial approach, criticism 247–8
Judicial legacy 303–7
Judicial system, lack of specialists
  academic criticism 135–6
  Denning's views 135, 136
Jurisprudence
  dislike 34–5
  no real interest in 301
Jury system
  advocating new vetting approach
      258
  Bristol jury, criticisms, threats of libel
      and apology 256, 257–8
  concerns as to threats to 256
  Ludovic Kennedy's interview 258
  Mansion House speech *see* Mansion
      House speech
  views on 258
Justice
  approach to achieving 86, 99
  common law, attempts to develop
      302
  disregard for precedent in search for
      294, 296
  inefficiency of court system under
      Denning 301–2
  natural justice, importance 301
  successes in search for 302
  underdog, support for 302
  whether approach always acceptable
      302–3
  whether values and faith sometimes in
      conflict with search for 302
Justice, Lord Denning and the Constitution
    247–8

King's Bench Division
  birching, passing sentence 80

King's Bench Division *(continued)*
   circuit work
      assize courts, Sir Michael Havers'
         memories 79
      criminal cases 79–81
      family outings, combined with 79
      judges' lodgings 78
   criminal cases 79–81
   death penalty, passing sentence 80
   just result, approach to achieving 86
   promissory estoppel, ruling on 82–6
   reforming judge, reputation as 86
   transfer to 72
   wartime pensions *see* Wartime pension appeals
   whether personal beliefs affecting judgment 88
King's Counsel, promotion to
   application 51
   increase in income following 52
   response of others to promotion 51–2
Knighthood 65

Landmarks in the Law 267
'lascivious old man', Davenport-Hines labelling Denning as 163, 309
'law', Danish origin of word 1
Law Quarterly Review, articles for 107
Law reports
   entries in 313–15
   final direct entry in 262
   'Gems in Ermine' lecture 173
   Mavis Hill's role 37
Law Society Gazette, 'Legal Education in Africa: Sharing our Heritage' 126
Law Students' Society of the University of Canterbury, Honorary President 174
Lawyers' Christian Fellowship (UK)
   address to, on truth and justice 298
   membership 106
   patron 106
   President, appointment 106
Lectures *see also* Speaking engagements
   artificial insemination, views on 115
   David Murray Foundation, at 145
   Dimbleby Lecture 247
   equality for women, concerns 115
   Hamlyn Lecture *see* Hamlyn Lecture
   Lawyers' Christian Fellowship, to 126, 298
   'Legal Education in Africa: Sharing our Heritage' 126
   Police Foundation 269
   pornography, views on 115
   'Responsibility before the law' 122
   The Changing Law 108–9
   'The Influence of Religion on the Law' 281–2, 298
   The Road to Justice 110, 298
   'Trade Unions on Trial' 267
   vasectomies, views on 115
Leisure pursuits 114
Legal philosophy, no interest in 268
Legal profession, lack of diversity, etc 134
Libertarianism 301
Lincoln's Inn Cricket Club, president 196
Lincoln's Inn Denning Society, foundation 283
Lincoln's Inn flat
   inadequacies 174
   refusal to pay increased rent 174
   use 144, 173–4
Lord Denning Society, praise on resignation 259
Lord Denning: A Biography
   author's preface summarising Denning 276
   criticisms 276, 277
   primary sources, author's access to 276
   publication 275
'Lord Denning: A Hampshire Man', booklet to celebrate centenary 282
Lord Denning: A Life
   Denning as a man of his time 280
   primary sources, author's access to 280
   publication 280
   values instilled in early life 8
Lord Denning: the Judge and the Law
   essays in 268
   'Lord Denning as Jurist' 268
   RFV Heuston's biographical sketch 268

Index

Magna Carta
  celebrations, role in   173
  Reading Chamber of Commerce, remarks in speech to   268
Mansion House speech
  call for resignation following   257
  Lord Scarman's report following   257
  support for police   255
  Times, The, coverage   256–7
  trial by jury, threats to   256
  What Next in the Law?, reprising remarks in   257–8
Mareva injunction, role in development   179–80, 183
Marriage
  first *see* Harvey, Mary (first wife)
  regrets as to decline in   277
  second *see* Stuart, Joan (second wife)
Marriage Welfare Service
  President, appointment as   72
  recommendation to set up   72
  Relate, change of name to   73
Master of the Rolls
  administrative law *see* public law *below*
  age at retirement   132
  All England Law Reports, cases in   145, 303
  appointment
    changes in procedure at time of   130–1
    congratulatory response to   129–30
    date   129
    Lord Evershed, prior discussion with   127
  authorship *see* Authorship
  backlog of cases on resignation   263
  'Be you never so high, the law is above you'   218
  Birmingham Six case   237–40
  books *see* Authorship
  central function   131–2
  common law
    allowing Home Office to be sued for negligence   186
    arm's length commercial transaction, common sense approach   198–9
    barristers' immunity, upholding   186
    breach of contract, holiday resort   191
    contempt of court for practical joke, reducing sentence   187
    conventional judgment, traditional reasoning   198–9
    criticism of judges, allowing   187
    Denning's legacy   199–200
    disregard for precedent, House of Lords criticising   188, 190
    equitable injunction to protect cricket club   195–6
    exemplary damages, award   189–90
    exemption clauses   191–5, 261–2
    House of Lords' criticism   188, 190, 193
    Lord Neuberger's observations   227
    negligence over trespass to the person   185
    negligent misstatement as cause of action   186
    new causes of action, creation   186
    pop stars, law on privacy   196–8
    pros and cons of Denning's approach   199–200
    prose style indicating sympathies   187–8
    pure economic loss, unrecoverable   195
    spurious claims, opposing   186–7
    tort   195
    zeal for   185
  courtroom, in
    courteousness and kindness   137–9
    grasp of facts and law   137, 139
    litigants in person, skill with   137–9
    Lord Ackner's observations   137–8
    Lord Justice Brooke's observations   138, 139
    Lord Justice Sedley's observations   138
    Lord Hoffmann's observations   137
    Lord Scarman's observations   138
    praise for stewardship   137
    see also Court of Appeal
  EEC membership, effect
    concerns over legal implications   226

Master of the Rolls *(continued)*
  EEC membership, effect *(continued)*
    grasp of implications 225–6
    Lord Neuberger's observations 227
  employment law
    Attorney General's right to sue on public's behalf 218
    bleak economic background, at time of 213
    categories 207
    chivalrous attitude towards women 208
    individual rights 207–9
    Jockey Club, sex discrimination 209
    outdated views on women 207–9
    right to strike, recognition 211
    right to work 209
    sex discrimination favouring women 207–8
    statutory concessions to unions, Denning's response 213
    trade union disputes *see* trade disputes *below*
  family law
    best interests of child, advancing concept 203
    children, paternalistic approach 202–3
    household work of no monetary value 202
    illegitimate child, rights 204–5
    importance of reforms championed by Denning 206
    modernised divorce law, support for 204
    out of touch with changing times 201–2, 205, 206
    parental authority, rejection of outdated notions 203–4
    precedent, disregard for 205, 206
    Rent Acts protection 205
    rights and responsibilities in marriage and divorce 201
    variation of trust 205–6
    wife entitled to share of house, where 202
    wife's interest in matrimonial home, protection 204
  historical background of post 131
  human rights
    balance between rights and responsibilities, importance 228
    British Bill of Rights, opposition to 228
    changing views 227–8
    European Convention, opposition to 227, 228
    free speech, invoking right 228
    generally 227–31
    Harriet Harman, disclosure of documents, contempt 230–1
    judicial independence, importance 228
    jury system, importance 228
    moral code in conflict with popular sentiment 228–30
    political climate and traditions, importance 228
    respect for private and family life, Denning at odds with concept 230
  What Next in the Law? 228
  judgments
    All England Law Reports, publication in 145
    ancient rights over progress, upholding 141–4
    Attorney General's right to sue on public's behalf 218
    common law *see* common law *above*
    construction of legal documents, flexible approach to 139–40
    employment law *see* employment law *above*
    example of writing style 141–2
    family law *see* family law *above*
    Fijian arbitration, sugar industry 176
    formalist approach 143
    inclosures 142–3
    Jamaican Banana Board arbitration 176–7
    Sikhs, whether racial group 261
    will, doubt over order of deaths 139–41

Index

judicial system at the time *see* Judicial appointments
Lincoln's Inn flat   144, 173–4
matching judges to cases   135–6
New College of Speech and Drama, support for foundation   144–5
panels of judges, selection   135
predecessor   127
pre-trial remedies
   role in development   179–82
   generally   179–82
   injunction   179
previous holders of position   132
procedural reform
   Anton Piller order   180–1
   failed attempt, interlocutory injunction   181–2, 183
   generally   179–83
   Mareva injunction   179–80, 183
   vindicated after death   183
public law
   Bill of Rights, citing   223
   criticism of Denning's approach   232–3
   Denning's legacy   231–4
   EEC membership, effect *see* EEC membership, effect *above*
   executive, praise for supporting citizens against   224
   forum shopping, criticised for encouraging   226
   generally   221–7
   GLC's 'fare's fair' policy   224–5
   grammar school case   224
   human rights *see* human rights *above*
   moral code sometimes overriding legal principle   221–3, 233
   national security over legal principle   234
   open government, moral code in conflict with belief in   233
   support for citizens over Home Office   223–4
   support for Denning's approach   233
resignation
   announcement   259
   background   251–5

Bristol jury, criticisms, threats of libel and apology   256, 257–8
   calls for   257, 258
   celebratory party   260
   Francis Bennion's letter advising   248–9
   House of Lords, praise from   262
   humiliating circumstances   249
   immigration, concerns over *see* Immigration, concerns over
   Mansion House speech *see* Mansion House speech
   praise for Denning   259, 262
   Private Eye cartoon   259
   reserved judgments following   260–2
   tributes   259, 260
   visit to Plymouth following   261
role   131–2
security of the realm
   Birmingham Six case   237–40
   changing nature of legal system in twenty-first century   240–1
   European Commission's support for deportation on security grounds   236
   freedom of the individual, in conflict with   236
   GCHQ case, newspaper article   235–7
   natural justice giving way to   235–7
   police incorruptibility, Denning's blind faith in   237
speaking engagements   144
specialist knowledge, Denning's belief in need for   135, 136
successor   132, 262
trade disputes
   academic analysis of Denning's work on   219
   anti-apartheid campaigns, and   217–18
   Arthur Scargill denouncing decision   215
   cooling off order on strike action   212
   contempt of court conviction, overturning   212
   criticisms of Denning's approach to   219

Master of the Rolls *(continued)*
  trade disputes *(continued)*
    economic background, at time of 213, 220
    generally 214–15, 217–18, 219–20
    history of labour law, background 210–11
    House of Lords overruling decisions 214–15
    industrial relations 210–14
    interviewed on TV and radio about 219
    moral campaigns, and 217–18
    pickets, support for 215–17
    political background 213–14
    right to strike, recognition 211
    shop stewards, union not responsible for 212
    social disruption, whether views on affecting approach 220
    support for Denning's approach to 219
    unions as a threat to rule of law 218
    winter of discontent, and 213
    worthy causes, support for 144
Memorial service 287
Military service
  drilling at Oxford 12
  First World War *see* First World War
Miners' strike, condemning 268
Modern world, disenchantment with 268
Moral approach
  acting in accordance with personal moral code 244
  human rights, moral code in conflict with popular sentiment 228–30
  legal principle, sometimes overriding 221–3, 233
  moral censure in wartime, whether affecting judgment 88
  open government, in conflict with belief in 233
Murder, justification of reasoning for mental element test 122
Myopia, example 111

Naïvety, examples 110, 111

Name, origins,
Natural justice, belief in 265
Nazis, opposed to holding trials 274
Negligent misstatement, attempt to set out new cause of action 98–100
New College of Speech and Drama, support for foundation 144–5
New Zealand
  arsenic murder case, inadvertent involvement in 175
  obituary from judiciary 287
Nottingham University, honorary degree 267
Nuffield Foundation, visit to South Africa at invitation of 110

Obituaries
  newspapers 280, 285–6
  New Zealand judiciary, praise from 287
Order of Merit 281
Overseas trips
  Africa 110, 125, 126, 177
  Australia 175, 177
  Brazil 173
  Canada 110, 175, 177, 218
  Fiji 176
  gifts received during 177
  Hong Kong 177
  India 106–7, 111, 175
  Israel 111
  Jamaica 176
  Japan 177
  Malaysia 177
  Mauritius 177
  New Zealand 174, 177
  Pakistan 173, 175
  Poland 110, 111
  South Africa 110, 177
  South America 173
  United States 110, 111, 173, 177
Oxford
  after the war 29–30
  All Souls College, failure to win admission to 35–6
  before the war 11–12
  graduation from 31

Index

honorary Doctor of Civil Law   173
legal scholarship   33
Magdalen College   11, 29, 31, 32
return to, to pursue law   33
Sir Herbert Warren's assistance   11, 33

Patriotism
   importance   269
   whether affecting judgment   88
Pearce, Edward, observations on Denning   279
Pornography, views on   115, 297–8
Post, Peter (Denning's clerk)   196, 280, 282
Precedent
   disregard for
      attempts to justify   295–6
      Christian faith, importance   296
      family law cases, in   205, 206
      generally   294–6
      House of Lords criticising   188, 190
      just result, in search for   294, 296
      no statutory obstacle, where   296
      social conditions changing, where   295
   factors relevant to possible reassessment   294–5
   importance, Lord Bingham's view   294
Principles followed while Lord Justice   301
Profumo Affair
   Astor, Lord
      client of Stephen Ward   150
      cottage, allowing use of   150
      Mandy Rice-Davies, and   156
      sexual liaisons   150
   background
      blackmail fears   149
      Cambridge Spy Ring   149
      changing standards   148
      Cold War spy era   149
      generally   148–9
      'headless man' scandal   148
      Lady Chatterley's Lover case   148
      permissive society, beginning   149
      upper class conventions   148
   Daily Express, 'War Minister Shock' headline   152

dangers inherent in   145
Edgecombe, Johnny
   affair with Keeler   152
   Aloysius Gordon, attacking   152
   arrest for attempted murder   152
   imprisonment   153
Gordon, Aloysius 'Lucky'
   affair with Keeler   151–2
   arrested and falsely charged for assaulting Keeler   153
   attacked by Johnny Edgecombe   152
   trial and conviction   155
government asking police to act, whether breach of rule of law   154
Hollis, Sir Roger, alerted to possible risks   151
importance   147
Ivanov, Yevgeny
   Christine Keeler, possible affair with   151
   hedonistic tastes   150
   MI5 handler   150
   NATO plans, attempt to uncover   151
   Profumo, meeting   151
   recalled to Moscow   152
   Stephen Ward, and   150
Keeler, Christine
   admitting to affair with Profumo   154
   affair with Profumo   151
   Aloysius 'Lucky' Gordon, affair with   151–2
   attacked and injured   153
   background   149
   denial of affair with Profumo   153
   failure to attend Edgecombe's trial, press speculation   152
   interviewed by police   154
   John Lewis, passing information to   152
   Johnny Edgecombe, affair with   152
   Mandy Rice-Davies, meeting   149
   newspapers, touting story to   152
   Peter Rachman, affair with   152
   Stephen Ward, meeting   149
   Sunday Pictorial pressured into not running story   152

405

Profumo Affair *(continued)*
  Labour Party's response 155
  letter of resignation from Profumo 147
  Macmillan, Harold
    backing for Profumo 152
    political fortunes, rise and fall 150–1
    wife's affair with Robert Boothby 151
  origins 147
  parliamentary questions 153
  press coverage and speculation 155
  Profumo, John
    abuse of parliamentary convention 153
    admission of affair 154
    background 150
    beginning of affair with Keeler 151
    Denning's criticism of Profumo's treatment 153
    end of affair with Keeler 151
    letter to Keeler cancelling get-together 151, 155
    libel threats by 153
    Lord Hailsham's attack, on TV 155
    Macmillan's backing 152
    personal statement to House 153
    resignation 155
    war record 150
    warnings about Ward's reliability 151
    Yevgeny Ivanov, meeting 151
  Rachman, Peter, affairs with Keeler and Rice-Davies 152
  report *see* Profumo report
  Rice-Davies, Mandy
    Christine Keeler, meeting 149
    Lord Astor, and 156
    Peter Rachman, affair with 152
    Stephen Ward, relationship with 150
    view of Denning 139
  Sunday Pictorial pressured into not running story 152
  The Times, news report 154–5
  Ward, Stephen
    abandonment by friends and others 157
    acquittal on some charges 157
    affairs, encouraging 149–50
    arrest 155
    associates interviewed, etc 154
    Christine Keeler, meeting and living with 149
    committal for trial 156
    Court of Appeal's conduct, effect on trial 156
    denial of involvement 153
    government asking police to act against 154
    guilty *in absentia*, judgment 157
    Harold Wilson, writing to 154
    judicial impartiality at trial 156
    lifestyle 149
    Lord Astor, and 150
    suicide 156–7
    surveillance on home 154
    telephone tapped 154
    trial 156
    unsatisfactory witness evidence at trial 156
    Yevgeny Ivanov, and 150
Profumo report
  aftermath
    Charles De Gaulle's observation 171
    continued suppression of papers, whether justifiable 170–1
    decision to keep Denning papers under seal 170
    failed attempt to rehear Ward's case 169–70
    'headless man's' possible identity 170
    Ivanov's subsequent life 168–9
    Keeler and Rice-Davies' subsequent lives 168
    Lord Astor's subsequent life 169
    Macmillan's resignation 167
    political consequences 167
    Profumo's ultimate public redemption 168
    Profumo's withdrawal from political life 168
    Stephen Ward's reputation, recovery 169
  appointment of Denning 145, 155, 157–8

Index

Due Process of Law, The, observations in 165
duration of sitting 158
failure to discomfit government 165–6
fears of politicising the judiciary 157
findings
   Britain not a police state 160
   chequebook journalism, criticism 164
   effectively clearing government 162
   errors in 166
   'headless man' 161
   House of Commons lied to 159
   inaccurately labelling Keeler a 'call girl' 160
   Keeler a vulnerable woman 160
   Macmillan told of unpublished findings in private 161
   mistake of colleagues in House, observations 162
   no security threat 159
   persons excluded from report 160–1, 162
   police, lack of criticism 165
   press, criticism 164
   Profumo indiscreet but not disloyal 159
   reasons for not naming certain people 160–1, 162
   security service's purpose, as to 165
   unwise association with Keeler 159
   Ward the primary culprit 160
form of inquiry, advantages and disadvantages 165
headings, use 159
help with preparation 158
independent voice, Denning as 157
infidelity, Denning's views on 158
judges rejected in favour of Denning 157
'lascivious old man', Davenport-Hines labelling Denning as 163, 309
length 158
Macmillan, Denning's collusion with over certain ministers 167
mysterious naked waiter, description 159
preparation 158–9
Private Eye's response 158
procedural fairness, lacking 165, 166
reception
   Alex Douglas-Home, praise from 163
   best-seller status 162
   criticisms 163
   elements argued to be unnecessary 163
   George Wigg's response 163
   Harold Wilson's response 162
   initial praise 162
   Macmillan's response 162
   procedural errors, suggestions of 163
   Richard Davenport-Hines' criticism 163, 164
   style, criticisms 163
   suppressed transcripts, drawbacks 163
   Warden of All Souls' comment 162
   whitewash, accusation 163
repercussions for Denning's reputation 147
Royal Commission on Tribunals of Inquiry, later observations 166–7
skills required to prepare 157–8
style 159, 163
terms of reference 155
TV coverage 158
witnesses heard
   interviewed in private 158
   numbers 158
Promissory estoppel, King's Bench ruling on 82–6
Property portfolio
   flats for the elderly 125
   land in Sussex 125
   low-rent houses for young married couples 125
   The Lawn 123–5
   The Mount 125
Protection of sources, press response to judgment against 248
Public Law, dissenting judgment published in 120
Public service, devotion to 311

Quarter Sessions for East Sussex, Chairman   114

Racial discrimination, criticism   110, 253–4, 310
Racism, accusation   261
Radio Solent interview   273
Reduced mobility   243
Reforming judge, reputation as   86
Religion *see also* Christian faith
   blasphemy as a dead letter   297
   freedom of, belief in   297
   state registration of religions, proposal for   297
Remuneration for judges, views on   269
Right to silence, views on proposed change   275
Retirement
   advice in public and private disputes, offering   266, 267
   BBC interview on life and career   275
   car park in Whitchurch, opposition to   281
   centenary   282–4
   changing world, reflections on   274
   chemist privately selling prescriptions, support for   281
   Closing Chapter, The
      glowing review   267
      publication   266
   controversial comments   274
   forays into local magistrates' court   273
   foreword to book celebrating Test Valley   280
   hip replacement   266
   Inner Temple, dinner with surviving Court of Appeal judges   266
   Institute of Directors, speech to, on US sanctions   265–6
   interview by John Mortimer   265
   Jim'll Fix It, appearance on   269–70
   Joshua Rozenberg interview on being remembered   273
   Landmarks in the Law, publication   267
   Leaves from my Library, publication   270
   letter writing to the press   277
   local affairs, involvement in   273, 274, 277
   Lord Denning: the Judge and the Law   268
   ninetieth birthday celebrations   274
   no wish to be idle   265
   Nottingham University, honorary degree   267
   Order of Merit   281
   Radio Solent interview   273
   Savoy Hotel, lunch to celebrate *The Mousetrap*'s longevity   266
   Spectator, The, interview see *Spectator, The*, interview
   talks and lectures   265, 266, 267, 268–9
   'Trade Unions on Trial', lecture   267
   water strike controversy after request for advice   266
   Winchester Radio interview for ninetieth birthday   273
   Wogan Show, The, appearance on   270
Road to Justice, The
   publication   110
   review   111
Rowlandson, Major, unenforceable life insurance policy due to suicide   50–1

Savage Club, membership   178
Scarman, Lord, on Denning's legacy   289
Second World War
   Blitz   61
   Denning family's response   56
   detention without trial
      background to   59
      Defence Regulations   57–60
      Denning's wartime work on   57
      'Nazi Parson'   57
      views on   26, 58–9
   High Court, appointment to   65
   inter-war period, public attitudes during   55–6
   legal adviser to North-East region   57
   life during
      BBC Home Service, speech on   63
      Blitz   61
      faith, importance   64
      father's death   62
      generally   60–4

Index

Mary's death 63
Mary's health, deterioration in 62
meningitis, contracting 62
Second Blitz 66
Sussex, move to new house in 61
outbreak 53
practice during
   Churchill, acting for 62
   Commissioner of Assize in
     Manchester 64
   continuation 60
   deputy recorder in Southampton 63
   High Court, appointment to 65
   income, falling 63
   murder case, returned serviceman 63
   Privy Council appeal from New Zealand 61
   pro bono cases 60–1
   Recorder of Plymouth 64
Second Blitz 66
self-governing regions, division of country into 57
wartime memories 66
Security apparatus, faith in 26
Servicemen
   approach to cases involving 91
   wartime pensions *see* Wartime pension appeals
Sex outside marriage, views on 298
Sikhs, whether racial or ethnic group 261
Simple lifestyle, preference for 50
Smith's Leading Cases, contributions to 39, 45, 107, 292
Social disruption, opposition to 220
Societies and organisations, involvement with 317–18
Society of Comparative Legislation and International Law, Chairman 109
Society of Genealogists, vice-president 174
'Someone must be trusted. Let it be the judges' 247
Speaking engagements *see also* Lectures
   Borrowing from Scotland, speeches in 145
   examples 108
   'Gems in Ermine' 173
   Hamlyn Lecture *see* Hamlyn Lecture
   myopia, example 111
   naïvety, example 110, 111
   Sir Martin Nourse's recollection 109
   The Changing Law, lectures collected in 108–9
Spectator, The, interview
   apology to Denning 279
   Birmingham Six 277, 278
   breach of copyright action by Denning 279
   damaging nature of 277
   death penalty, support for 277
   Denning's apology 278–9
   European Union 277
   Guildford Four, comments on 277, 278
   Leon Brittan, anti-Semitic remark 278
   marriage, homosexuality, family structures 277
   retraction and apology by magazine 278
   xenophobia, suggestions of 278
Split profession, defence of 111
Spycatcher litigation, Denning's criticism of House of Lords' decision 272–3
Statutory interpretation, approach to 91–2, 293–4
Stuart, Joan (second wife)
   angina 177
   background and previous marriage 75–6
   birth 75
   children 75, 77
   Cumberland Lodge, work for 106
   death 280
   family life 77
   first meeting with Denning 76
   forthright and practical nature 76–7
   marriage 77
   running of the household 77
Style
   brevity and clarity 292
   Cameron Harvey's analysis 290
   Chorus in *Henry V*, comparison with 290
   credit or blame for decision, leading to 291

Style *(continued)*
   detailed study 81
   development, reasons for 82
   drawbacks 292–3
   early days 289
   evolving nature 289
   homely writing style 289
   'hook', use 290
   making the judgment 'live', purpose 290
   Master of the Rolls, following appointment 290
   merits into the facts, putting 290
   opening paragraphs 290
   origins 81
   Peter Hennessey's analysis 289
   problems with 'classic' openings 290–1
   reader's sympathy, attempt to manipulate 291
   rhetorical style as distraction from point at issue 291
   story-telling nature 289, 291
   sub-categories of 'opener' 290
Supreme Court Sports Association, vice-president 174
Sussex, life in
   Blitz 61
   Fair Close 61, 123
   move to new house in Second World War 61
   rented marital home 49
   Second Blitz 66
   village life 39
   Whitchurch, decision to move back to 123

Teaching career
   decision to leave 32
   salary 32
   subjects 32
   Winchester College 31–2
Trade unions as a threat to rule of law 218
Travel *see* Overseas trips

Values
   changing nature of world, and 308–9
   Christian faith informing 297–8
   Englishness, sense of 299–300
   honesty 309–10
   ingrained in at early age 8–9, 10
   justice, whether sometimes in conflict with search for 302
   moral code, strength 309
Vasectomies, views on 115

War pension appeals
   appointment to hear 81
   attitude towards 28, 81
   willingness to depart from earlier decisions 82
What Next in the Law? 228, 257, 279, 280, 286
Whitchurch
   All Hallows Church 3
   car park in, opposition to 281
   Christian church, earliest record 2
   cricket
      fondness for 124, 196
      president of Whitchurch Cricket Club 196
   generally 2–5
   'Great Tom' bell 282
   history 2–3
   influence on Denning 3–4
   return to 123–5
   rotten borough 3
   Saxon derivation of name 2–3
   Star newspaper's description 2
   suffragette movement 9
   The Lawn
      advertisement for, from Victorian era 124
      Bank of England, purchase from 124
      cricket and fishing 124
      history 124
      move to 123–5
      private law library 124
      purchase 124
      restoration 124
      staff 280
      trust to purchase 124
      village activities at, hosting 125
      visitors' wing 124

Index

The Mount   125
town hall, role in renovating   125
Wilson, AN
   observations following Denning's death   286
   Spectator, The, interview in *see Spectator, The*, interview
Winter of discontent, observations   213
Wogan Show, The, appearance on   270
Women
   chivalry and courtesy, importance   208

   differences between the sexes, views on   244–5
Due Process of Law, The   244–5
equality
   belief in   245, 246
   concerns as to implications   115
   old-fashioned views   115, 208, 245
Work ethic   311
Writing style *see* Style

Xenophobia, suggestion of   277

CARDIOLOGY RESEARCH AND CLINICAL DEVELOPMENTS

A CLOSER LOOK AT HEART RATE

CARDIOLOGY RESEARCH AND CLINICAL DEVELOPMENTS

A CLOSER LOOK AT HEART RATE

ANDRÉ ALVES PEREIRA
EDITOR

Copyright © 2020 by Nova Science Publishers, Inc.

All rights reserved. No part of this book may be reproduced, stored in a retrieval system or transmitted in any form or by any means: electronic, electrostatic, magnetic, tape, mechanical photocopying, recording or otherwise without the written permission of the Publisher.

We have partnered with Copyright Clearance Center to make it easy for you to obtain permissions to reuse content from this publication. Simply navigate to this publication's page on Nova's website and locate the "Get Permission" button below the title description. This button is linked directly to the title's permission page on copyright.com. Alternatively, you can visit copyright.com and search by title, ISBN, or ISSN.

For further questions about using the service on copyright.com, please contact:
Copyright Clearance Center
Phone: +1-(978) 750-8400   Fax: +1-(978) 750-4470   E-mail: info@copyright.com.

NOTICE TO THE READER

The Publisher has taken reasonable care in the preparation of this book, but makes no expressed or implied warranty of any kind and assumes no responsibility for any errors or omissions. No liability is assumed for incidental or consequential damages in connection with or arising out of information contained in this book. The Publisher shall not be liable for any special, consequential, or exemplary damages resulting, in whole or in part, from the readers' use of, or reliance upon, this material. Any parts of this book based on government reports are so indicated and copyright is claimed for those parts to the extent applicable to compilations of such works.

Independent verification should be sought for any data, advice or recommendations contained in this book. In addition, no responsibility is assumed by the Publisher for any injury and/or damage to persons or property arising from any methods, products, instructions, ideas or otherwise contained in this publication.

This publication is designed to provide accurate and authoritative information with regard to the subject matter covered herein. It is sold with the clear understanding that the Publisher is not engaged in rendering legal or any other professional services. If legal or any other expert assistance is required, the services of a competent person should be sought. FROM A DECLARATION OF PARTICIPANTS JOINTLY ADOPTED BY A COMMITTEE OF THE AMERICAN BAR ASSOCIATION AND A COMMITTEE OF PUBLISHERS.

Additional color graphics may be available in the e-book version of this book.

Library of Congress Cataloging-in-Publication Data

Names: Alves Pereira, André, editor.
Title: A closer look at heart rate / [edited by] André Alves Pereira.
Description: Hauppauge : Nova Science Publishers, [2020] | Series:
   Cardiology research and clinical developments | Includes bibliographical
   references and index. |
Identifiers: LCCN 2019058245 (print) | LCCN 2019058246 (ebook) | ISBN
   9781536169799 (paperback) | ISBN 9781536170344 (adobe pdf)
Subjects: LCSH: Heart beat. | Heart beat--Measurement. | Heart
   beat--Physiological aspects. | Electrocardiography.
Classification: LCC QP113 .C57 2020 (print) | LCC QP113 (ebook) | DDC
   612.1/7--dc23
LC record available at https://lccn.loc.gov/2019058245
LC ebook record available at https://lccn.loc.gov/2019058246

Published by Nova Science Publishers, Inc. † New York

CONTENTS

Preface		vii
Chapter 1	Short-Term Resting-State Heart Rate Variability *Siddharth Nayak, Arthur C. Tsai, Lydia Chen, Jiun Wei Liou and Michelle Liou*	1
Chapter 2	Estimating and Correcting the Regression to the Mean in Heart Rate Variability Studies *Dimitriy A. Dimitriev, Elena V. Saperova, Olga S. Indeykina and Aleksey D. Dimitriev*	41
Chapter 3	Previously Unrecognized Fetal Behavior with Pre- and Postnatal Cardiorespiratory Implications *Patrick A. Zemb, Tarik El Aarbaoui, Jean-Yves Bellec, Pauline Lelièvre, Marie-Laure Mille and Fabrice Joulia*	71
Chapter 4	Meditation: A Simple Inexpensive Technique for Voluntary Control of Heart Rate *Satish G. Patil, Ishwar V. Basavaraddi and Mallanagoud S. Biradar*	115
Index		133
Related Nova Publications		141

PREFACE

A Closer Look at Heart Rate opens with an examination of the latent structures underlying short-term heart rate variability indices in a sample of 96 young adults under 4-min eyes-closed followed by 4-min eyes-open resting-state conditions. Electrocardiograms recorded during the two resting-state conditions were then analyzed using a variety of heart rate variability indices in which latent structures were identified using principal component analysis.

Additionally, the authors test the hypothesis that the statistical artefact regression to the mean explains part of the baseline effect. To do this, the regression to the mean effect is illustrated through heart rate recording carried out on 1233 volunteers, from which 137 were randomly selected to obtain an estimate of the stress response.

Next, 14,000 antepartum fetal heart rate tracings obtained during 2,000 pregnancies are analyzed. After 30 weeks, fetal behavior progressively changes and differentiates into three main states: active sleep, quiet sleep, and active wakefulness. The fetal heart rate pattern during quiet sleep is usually homogeneous. It appears that a heterogeneous pattern reflecting a specific quiet sleep variant has been unrecognized.

In the closing chapter, the role of meditation in cardiovascular risk reduction through beneficial modulation in heart rate, and heart-rate variability is reviewed and discussed. Meditative practices are aimed at training the mind to achieve a state of increased consciousness.

Chapter 1 - Resting-state heart rate variability (HRV) has been proposed as a predictor of behavioral and cognitive responses in various experimental tasks. Specifically, high resting-state HRV has been associated with enhanced cognitive control in tasks requiring working memory, voluntary attention, and inhibitory control. HRV can be analyzed in the time-domain as well as frequency-domain using linear or non-linear indices. The resting-state condition has been operationally defined as relaxing quietly with eyes-closed or eyes-open. Differences among HRV indices and the definition of resting states tend to undermine efforts to link resting-state HRV and performance in cognitive control tasks in terms of predictive ability and consistency. In the current study, the authors examined the latent structures underlying short-term HRV indices in a sample of 96 young adults (43 women; average age 25.69 ± 4.32) under 4-min eyes-closed followed by 4-min eyes-open resting-state conditions. Electrocardiograms (ECGs) recorded during the two resting-state conditions were then analyzed using a variety of HRV indices, of which latent structures were identified using principal component analysis. The authors' results revealed that time-domain indices were robust to resting-state conditions and provided clear measurements within a single dimension, whereas frequency-domain and non-linear indices measured different dimensions according to whether the participant was relaxing with eyes-closed or eyes-open. Participants also completed questionnaires pertaining to state-trait anxiety, self-referential thoughts, and behavioral inhibition/activation before/after obtaining the resting-state ECG recordings. The HRV dimensions differed in the way they related to scores obtained on these psychological scales. The latent dimensions that were strongly associated with non-linear HRV indices were better predictors of scale scores, compared to dimensions that were more strongly associated with indices in the time-domain and frequency-domain. The authors' results have suggested that short-term resting-state HRV indices measure different aspects of physiological and psychological states in human participants. It appears that latent dimensions of short-term resting-state

HRV indices may be used as regressors to predict cognitive, affective, and behavioral responses in experimental tasks.

Chapter 2 - Background. There is now a substantial body of evidence linking the baseline level of heart rate variability (HRV) with the magnitude of stress-induced changes in autonomic control of heart rate. However, the extent to which these interindividual differences in stress responses can be attributed to the statistical phenomenon of regression to the mean (RTM) remains unproven. The authors sought to test the hypothesis that the statistical artefact RTM explains part of the baseline effect.

Methods. The authors illustrate the RTM effect using heart rate recording was carried out on 1233 volunteers, from which 137 were randomly selected to obtain an estimate of the stress response. Participants were monitored on a rest day and just before an academic examination for state anxiety and HRV. Participants were monitored on a rest day and just before an academic examination to establish their state of anxiety and HRV. Participants were divided into quartiles according to baseline HRV levels, and their response to academic stress was compared. In addition, the authors re-analyzed the dataset of orthostatic tests following strength training (ST) and high-intensity interval training (HIIT) overload and subsequent recovery.

Results. The authors observed a significant academic stress-induced reduction in HRV in subjects with a high-baseline HRV (>75th percentile), while a significant increase was found in the group with a low-baseline HRV. Univariate regression analysis demonstrated that the value of baseline HRV correlated with the magnitude of stress reaction consistent with the RTM model. A baseline-adjusted analysis of covariance did not reveal any significant intergroup differences in the changes in heart rate (HR) and HRV from rest to the examination. RTM-adjusted estimates confirmed an examination effect for HR, the standard deviation of the normal-to-normal interval series, and the high-frequency power of HRV, and they also revealed a significant decrease of low-frequency component of HRV spectrum. SIT and HIIT data analysis revealed that baseline heart rate was negatively associated with orthostatic reactivity that reflects the

RTM. In conclusion, the authors' findings underline the importance of controlling for RTM when examining the effect of baseline HRV on HRV reactivity.

New & noteworthy. Studies of autonomic flexibility have demonstrated that high-baseline HRV is associated with a decline in HRV and subjects with a low-baseline HRV have an inverse reaction to stress. This suggests that baseline HRV is a marker of stress-adaptive capacity. The results of the authors' study strongly support an alternative view: RTM is the major source of variability of stress-related changes in HRV.

Chapter 3 - After 30 weeks, fetal behavior progressively changes and differentiates into three main states: active sleep, quiet sleep, and active wakefulness. Each state is associated with a characteristic fetal heart rate (FHR) pattern, mainly in a physiological context. Quiet sleep has been linked with parasympathetic dominance and gives rise to a specific heart-rate pattern named "Pattern A" (PA), defined by the seven following diagnostic criteria: ± 20-minute duration, reduced episodic accelerations, reduced maternal perception of fetal mobility, lower long- and short-term variability (STV) than in adjacent sequences, narrow oscillation bandwidth, and homogeneous aspect. Two homogeneous PA variants have already been identified: the "High-STV" variant and the "Oscillatory baseline" variant. Each differs in its own way from PA with respect to criteria 5 and 6.

The authors analyzed 14,000 antepartum FHR tracings obtained during 2,000 pregnancies (>30 weeks; high-risk cases included). This analysis led us to identify a heterogeneous PA variant called "Meta-Pattern A" (Meta-PA) in which criterion 7 differed from conventional quiet-sleep patterns. The Meta-PA was characterized by a "saltatory variability and baseline" pattern (SVBP), defined by a saltatory succession of short FHR sequences presenting with high- and low-STV (saltation> 50 centiles identified by computerized analysis over one-minute windows), and with saltatory FHR baseline (> 4 beats/minute). Typically, Meta-PA covers 4 to 6 saltatory sequences, lasting 2 to 10 minutes each. In the authors' database, the Meta-PA/typical PA ratio is around 1/20 and 1/10 for the attenuated Meta-PA (smaller saltations).

Meta-PA could reflect a specific fetal oxygen-conserving mechanism during quiet sleep. This mechanism could trigger a major conflict between the parasympathetic inhibition required by the oxygen-conserving mechanism and the physiologically high parasympathetic activation during quiet sleep, specifically when the underlying cortisol level is high. The two high- and low-STV components of Meta-PA could be respectively related to an alternate sympathovagal antagonism and sympathovagal inhibition.

The authors have named "Meta-quiet sleep" (Meta-QS) the specific fetal behavior linked with Meta-PA. Recognizing Meta-QS could help assess fetal and placental status. Moreover, an inappropriate postnatal resurgence of Meta-QS could well be the cause of sudden infant death syndrome. This article reviews the place of Meta-PA among other quiet-sleep patterns and describes the main fetal pathways interfering with the authors' understanding of Meta-QS.

Chapter 4 - High resting heart rate (HR) is an independent cardiovascular risk factor and predictor of all-cause mortality in individuals with or without cardiovascular disease. Studies have demonstrated that drugs that increase the heart rate worsen the prognosis, while those that reduce the heart rate such as beta-blockers have a beneficial effect after acute myocardial infarction and in chronic cardiac failure. Available data suggest that a strategy which reduces the heart rate and improves heart-rate variability prevents cardiovascular morbidity, increase longevity and also has a favorable effect on the prognosis of cardiovascular disease. Meditation is a practice where an individual focuses their mind on a particular object, thought or activity for self-realization and inner awareness. Meditative practices are aimed at training the mind for an achievement of a state of increased consciousness. It allows the mind to calm down and relax mentally, increases attention and concentration, reduces stress and anxiety, and enhances inner peace and happiness. In this chapter, the role of meditation in cardiovascular risk reduction through beneficial modulation in heart rate and heart-rate variability will be reviewed and discussed.

In: A Closer Look at Heart Rate
Editor: André Alves Pereira

ISBN: 978-1-53616-979-9
© 2020 Nova Science Publishers, Inc.

Chapter 1

SHORT-TERM RESTING-STATE HEART RATE VARIABILITY

Siddharth Nayak[1,2], Arthur C. Tsai[2], Lydia Chen[3], Jiun Wei Liou[2] and Michelle Liou[2,]**

[1]Taiwan International Graduate Program in Interdisciplinary Neuroscience, National Cheng Kung University and Academia Sinica, Taipei, Taiwan
[2]Institute of Statistical Science, Academia Sinica, Taipei, Taiwan
[3]Institute of Biomedical Engineering, National Chiao-Tung University, Hsinchu, Taiwan

ABSTRACT

Resting-state heart rate variability (HRV) has been proposed as a predictor of behavioral and cognitive responses in various experimental tasks. Specifically, high resting-state HRV has been associated with enhanced cognitive control in tasks requiring working memory, voluntary attention, and inhibitory control. HRV can be analyzed in the time-

---

* Corresponding Author Email: mliou@stat.sinica.edu.tw.

domain as well as frequency-domain using linear or non-linear indices. The resting-state condition has been operationally defined as relaxing quietly with eyes-closed or eyes-open. Differences among HRV indices and the definition of resting states tend to undermine efforts to link resting-state HRV and performance in cognitive control tasks in terms of predictive ability and consistency. In the current study, we examined the latent structures underlying short-term HRV indices in a sample of 96 young adults (43 women; average age 25.69 $\pm$ 4.32) under 4-min eyes-closed followed by 4-min eyes-open resting-state conditions. Electrocardiograms (ECGs) recorded during the two resting-state conditions were then analyzed using a variety of HRV indices, of which latent structures were identified using principal component analysis. Our results revealed that time-domain indices were robust to resting-state conditions and provided clear measurements within a single dimension, whereas frequency-domain and non-linear indices measured different dimensions according to whether the participant was relaxing with eyes-closed or eyes-open. Participants also completed questionnaires pertaining to state-trait anxiety, self-referential thoughts, and behavioral inhibition/activation before/after obtaining the resting-state ECG recordings. The HRV dimensions differed in the way they related to scores obtained on these psychological scales. The latent dimensions that were strongly associated with non-linear HRV indices were better predictors of scale scores, compared to dimensions that were more strongly associated with indices in the time-domain and frequency-domain. Our results have suggested that short-term resting-state HRV indices measure different aspects of physiological and psychological states in human participants. It appears that latent dimensions of short-term resting-state HRV indices may be used as regressors to predict cognitive, affective, and behavioral responses in experimental tasks.

Keywords: behavioral inhibition system, heart rate variability, resting-state conditions, self-referential thoughts

INTRODUCTION

Heart rate variability (HRV) refers to the variations in successive inter-beat intervals within electrocardiogram (ECG) time series, which can be considered as a physiological index for monitoring autonomic activity (Camm et al. 1996; Acharya et al. 2006). HRV indices have been used as markers for cardiac vagal activity in human participants under various psychological conditions such as social engagement (Kemp et al. 2012), the perception of affective stimuli (Park, Van Bavel, et al. 2013; Park and Thayer 2014), and emotion regulations (Williams et al. 2015). These indices can also be used to predict affective instability in daily life (Koval et al. 2013). Previous studies have treated resting-state HRV as a psychophysiological phenomenon characterizing the degree of vagal activity prevailing over sympathetic activity (Thayer et al. 2012; Thayer et al. 2009). High resting-state HRV is accompanied by enhanced cognitive control over tasks requiring working memory, selective attention, or inhibitory control (Hansen et al. 2004; Hovland et al. 2012; Park, Vasey, et al. 2013; Colzato et al. 2018). Research has shown that chronic reductions in vagal activity are associated with poor physiological, emotional, cognitive, and behavioral regulations, which can result in low self-rated health (Alvares et al. 2013; Jarczok et al. 2015; Thayer et al. 2012; Thayer et al. 2009) and a high risk of psychopathology (Beauchaine and Thayer 2015; Kemp et al. 2010; Koenig, Kemp, Feeling, et al. 2016; Koenig, Kemp, Beauchaine, et al. 2016; Clamor et al. 2016). Overall, HRV is associated with a wide range of psychophysiological functions related to general well-being in humans.

HRV analysis has been recommended for long-term (24-hr) as well as short-term (5-min) recording procedures (Camm et al. 1996). While 24-hr HRV analysis is helpful for increasing resolution in the frequency-domain and particularly in the low frequency range, it is difficult to be implemented in typical volunteers. The short-term ECG recording procedure is more practical than the long-term procedure, offering a number of notable advantages: (i) relative ease in recording, (ii) convenience in controlling confounding factors, such as variations in the physical or mental states of experimental participants and in the recording environments, (iii) computational efficiency in data processing, and (iv) flexibility in visualizing dynamic changes in HRV within a short period of time (Li, Rüdiger, and Ziemssen 2019). Short-term and long-term HRV recordings have both been widely used in clinical settings. One factor that is commonly overlooked is the "set point" (or resting baseline) of normal HRV, which is itself regulated by the body's negative feedback mechanism to maintain homeostasis (Zhang 2007). Crucially, the set point is not changed by short-term fluctuations in the heart rate other than trauma (Antelmi et al. 2004; Tuomainen et al. 2005). In this chapter, we focus on short-term HRV indices which are independent of the influence of day-to-day activity, a factor that may crucially affect the validity of long-term recordings.

Few ECG studies have clearly specified eyes-closed or eyes-open conditions as the resting-state baseline in HRV measurements. One previous study reported that the high-frequency (HF) power was higher under the eyes-closed resting state than under the eyes-open resting state (Amin et al. 2013). That study also reported that the low-frequency (LF) power and LF/HF ratio were higher under eyes-open than under eyes-closed conditions. We reported similar findings in terms of HF, LF, and LF/HF ratio expressed in normalized units (Liou et al. 2018). The HF power has conventionally been used as an index for parasympathetic (i.e., vagal) dominance, whereas the LF power and LF/HF ratio are used as indices for sympathetic dominance (Camm et al. 1996; Acharya et al. 2006). Another study compared the effect of eyes-closed and eyes-open resting states on mental fatigue by obtaining ECG readings before and after assigned tasks (Mizuno et al. 2014). The authors reported no variations in sympathetic or parasympathetic sinus modulation during the pre-task rest period under eyes-open or eyes-closed conditions. Nonetheless, the authors reported that during the post-task rest period, sympathetic nerve activity was higher and parasympathetic nerve activity was lower under eyes-open than under eyes-closed conditions. This difference was attributed to variability in attentional levels associated with the two conditions, wherein sympathetic nerve activity was thought to be higher under the eyes-open condition than under the eyes-closed condition (Hori et al. 2005). Thus, it is possible that the eyes-closed resting-state (baseline) condition could be used as a proxy for parasympathetic activity, whereas the eyes-open resting-state (baseline) condition could be used as a proxy for sympathetic activity. Those studies have provided preliminary evidence that results obtained under eyes-open and eyes-closed conditions should be analyzed separately; that is, they should not be combined for resting-state analysis.

According to a recent report, cardiovascular diseases (CVDs) are among the leading causes of death worldwide for men and women (Mozaffarian et al. 2015). However, the onset of CVDs affects the health of men and women differently, with the result that the prevalence of CVD-related mortality and morbidity is higher and tends to occur earlier in men (Berry et al. 2012; Mikkola et al. 2013). One recent meta-analysis on gender differences (Koenig and Thayer 2016) in HRV among healthy controls (10-74 years) revealed several interesting findings. In time-domain HRV indices, the mean RR interval and standard deviation of RR intervals (SDNN) were significantly lower among women on the average. The spectral power density of HRV was characterized, on the average, by a significantly lower total power, a significantly higher HF power and a significantly lower LF power. These effects were also manifested as the lower LF/HF ratio. Overall, women showed greater vagal activity, as indexed by higher HF powers in HRV readings. The authors concluded that the autonomic control of female hearts is dominated by parasympathetic activity (in spite of the higher mean heart rate), whereas male hearts are dominated by sympathetic activity (in spite of the lower mean heart rate). The heart rates (HRs) of women are generally higher than those of men; however, their risk of CVDs is not higher (Cordero and Alegria 2006). Thus, it appears that the HR does not have the same predictive power for mortality and morbidity in women as it does in men (Sacha 2014). This paradoxical situation warrants additional research involving the analysis of gender differences in the autonomic control of the heart, as indexed by HRV.

In the past three decades, there have been a number of independent reports on the age influence on short-term HRV recordings (Migliaro et al. 2001; Schwartz, Gibb, and Tran 1991; Zhang 2007; Antelmi et al. 2004). It appears that time-domain HRV indices, such as SDNN, root mean square of successive RR differences (RMSSD), and the proportion of successive RR intervals that differ by more than 50-ms (pNN50), consistently decrease with age, whereas the mean RR interval increases with age.

Among the frequency-domain indices, it appears that HF, LF, and very-low-frequency (VLF) powers consistently decrease with age. The LF/HF ratio does not present this age decline effect, however. Some studies have demonstrated age-related and gender-related variability in short-term HRV, both of which have significant effects on most linear and non-linear HRV indices (Voss et al. 2015; Voss et al. 2012). For example, research reported significant increases in detrended fluctuation analysis (DFA) indices (i.e., α_1 and α_2) across five age groups ranging from 25 – 74 years (10-year intervals). Poincare plot analysis indices (SD_1 and SD_2) presented similar decreases across age groups. Significant gender differences were observed in DFA_α_1 results among participants ranging in age from 25 – 64 years. Gender differences were not observed with SD_1, SD_2, or DFA_α_2 indices. These results have highlighted the degree to which gender and age can affect short-term HRV indices, and have also underlined the importance of considering these factors in any study based on HRV. In this chapter, we focus on young adults (19-39 years), due to the fact that this age group presents the highest HRV on all of the time-domain, frequency-domain, and non-linear indices (Voss et al. 2012; Voss et al. 2015).

Self-referential processes are those associated with stimuli that are experienced as strongly as that of real-life experiences. For example, the way we perceive pictures of ourselves with close friends versus pictures of a random people on the street, or pictures of a home where we spent most of our childhood versus random houses on the street. Meta-analysis of fMRI studies has revealed considerable overlap between the neural correlates of self-referential processing and those associated with the default mode network (Gusnard and Raichle 2001; Raichle et al. 2001), including brain regions that are functionally active even under the resting-state conditions.

There is also considerable overlap between the EEG correlates of self-referential processing and the anterior hub of the default-mode network, particularly in the medial prefrontal cortex (Knyazev 2013; Knyazev et al. 2012).

In the time-domain, distinguishing between self- and others-related information is associated primarily with the P300 ERP component. In the frequency-domain, spontaneous self-referential processing is associated primarily with lower spectral powers in the theta and alpha frequency bands (Bocharov et al. 2019; Knyazev et al. 2012). Previous research reported minor differences in brain regions in the default mode network (Bluhm et al. 2008) across ages and genders. It is important to examine the role of self-referential processing in HRV dimensions.

Anxiety is a feeling of apprehensive uneasiness triggered by stressful events or anticipated failures. State-anxiety is defined as a transitory emotional state arising from threatening or dangerous situations marked by increases in the HR and/or respiration. One study on recognizing emotions in faces reported that participants experiencing state-anxiety (i.e., with elevated amygdala responses) were more likely to categorize faces as fearful (vs. neutral), regardless of attentional focus (Bishop, Duncan, and Lawrence 2004). Trait-anxiety refers to a stable tendency to recognize and report on negative emotions that are largely independent of specific situations. Trait-anxiety is related to increased arousal levels in the behavioral inhibition system (BIS), which is particularly pronounced in cases of decision-making under uncertainty. Trait-anxiety can affect cognitive outcomes by overestimating negative effects in ambiguous situations (Gray 1982).

Previous research based on the reinforcement sensitivity theory has addressed the well-defined role of the BIS; however, the behavioral activation system (BAS) is less well-defined, particularly in terms of reward versus impulsivity (Taubitz, Pedersen, and Larson 2015). In one study on the neural correlates of BIS and BAS, it was reported that BIS was uniquely related to the N2 ERP component on NoGo trials of a Go/NoGo task, linking BIS to conflict monitoring as well as sensitivity to NoGo cues (Amodio et al. 2008). In that study, it was reported that higher BAS scores were uniquely associated with pronounced left-sided baseline frontal cortical asymmetry associated with approach orientation. However, it remains unclear how BIS/BAS is related to resting-state HRV. Several HRV indices have consistently indicated reduced vagal activity and elevated sympathetic activity under anxiety-provoking situations, suggesting that there is a negative relationship between cardiac vagal control and trait-anxiety (Friedman 2007). Anxiety disorders are generally associated with a decrease in HRV (Chalmers et al. 2014) by showing a shift from autonomic balance toward increased sympathetic activity, as characterized by the high LF power. It is important to investigate in young adults the link between resting-state HRV and their anxiety as well as BIS/BAS traits.

Short-term HRV can be analyzed in the time-domain and frequency-domain using linear or non-linear indices. As mentioned, resting states have been operationally defined as relaxing quietly under eyes-closed or eyes-open conditions. Variations in HRV indices and the definitions of resting-state conditions have led to an inconsistency among studies linking resting-state HRV to cognitive control. This study was intended to assess the latent structures underlying short-term HRV indices under either eyes-closed or eyes-open conditions. We analyzed ECGs from 96 young adults (43 women; average age 25.69 ± 4.32) whose data were recorded previously in two separate experimental studies. One study involved tasks on ambiguous sentence detection while the other investigated emotional inhibition.

In both studies ECG recordings were obtained while the participants were resting quietly under 4-min eyes-closed followed by 4-min eyes-open conditions. The State-Trait Anxiety Inventory (STAI) (Spielberger and Gorsuch 1983) was administered prior to the ECG recording. After the ECG recording, 57 participants from the first study were assessed using the Self-Referential Thought Questionnaire (STQ), whereas 39 participants from the second study were assessed using the BIS/BAS scale. As in previous reports (Young and Benton 2015), we expected that adding non-linear indices to linear HRV indices would aid in predicting behavior responses on these psychological scales. We also examined the effects of gender, age, and resting-state condition on HRV indices. Finally, we sought to determine the appropriate use of HRV latent dimensions under eyes-closed and eyes-open conditions for scientific or clinical inquiry.

METHODS

Participants

A total of 96 right-handed, neurologically normal adults were recruited in the EEG experiment as a part of two separate cohorts. The first cohort was formed of a sample of 57 participants in a language study while the second one was formed of a sample of 39 participants in an emotional inhibition study. All participants were undergraduate or postgraduate students without a history of psychiatric and neurological disorders. Specifically, the sample included 43 women aged 19–35 (average age 24.07 ± 3.863) and 53 men aged 20–39 (average age 27 ± 4.256). All participants provided informed written consent before enrollment in the study. The experiment was approved by the Human Subject Research Ethics Committee/Institutional Review Board at Academia Sinica, Taiwan, in accordance with the Declaration of Helsinki.

State-Trait Anxiety Inventory

The Chinese version of the State-Trait Anxiety Inventory (cSTAI) was used to assess the explicit anxiety levels of participants (Spielberger and Gorsuch 1983; Shek 1993). In the inventory, the 20-item STAI-Trait scale targets how participants generally feel, whereas the 20-item STAI-State scale assesses how participants feel at the time they took the inventory. State and trait anxiety scores were both considered in regression analysis, and a larger score indicated a higher anxiety level. On the cSTAI, participants were asked to rate themselves on each item based on a 4-point Likert scale, ranging from rarely to almost always. The STAI has been clinically validated in several studies (Grös et al. 2007; Kvaal et al. 2005). The STAI is socially and culturally dependent, that is, different ethnic groups present different norms. The 96 participants in this study were from the same cultural group; therefore, we used the cSTAI to evaluate relative differences among participants in terms of anxiety levels.

Self-Referential Thought Questionnaire

The Self-Referential Thought Questionnaire (STQ) was designed to measure various aspects pertaining to one's thoughts and feelings while undergoing spontaneous EEG/ECG registration under resting-state conditions (Knyazev 2013; Knyazev et al. 2012). All items were measured using a five-point Likert scale. The results of factor analysis of all questionnaire items (principal factor analysis with varimax rotation) conducted in a large sample (N = 160) revealed that a four-factor solution best fitted the data (Knyazev and Slobodskaya 2003). From the original 37 items in the questionnaire, we selected 29 items that had high loadings on a single factor. The subscale "emotions" includes 10 items used to measure the emotional response of participants during the ECG recording. Examples of typical responses are "I experienced negative emotions during the recording" and "I was calm and relaxed during the recording." A higher score indicates that the emotion(s) experienced by the participant tended to be positive. The subscale "self-referential thought (SRT)" includes 8 items used to measure intrinsic processes. Examples of typical responses are "I occasionally tried to recall things in front of me during the recording" and "I thought about employment or university problems during the recording." A higher score indicates that the participant was less able to recall events or things encountered in his/her daily life. The subscale "attention (ATT)" contains 6 items used to measure attentiveness to the recording procedure. Examples of typical responses are "During the recording, I paid attention to external odors most of the time" and "I felt hot during most of the recording." A higher score indicates that the participant paid less attention to the recording procedure. The subscale "drowsiness" contains 5 items used to reveal the physiological state of the participants. Examples of typical responses are "During the recording, I was very aroused" and "I was dozy during most of the recording." A higher score indicates that the participant was more aroused.

Behavioral Inhibition System and Behavioral Activation System (BIS/BAS) Scale

The behavioral activation system is believed to regulate appetitive motives, wherein the goal is to move toward something desired. The behavioral inhibition system (or avoidance) is said to regulate aversive motives, wherein the goal is to move away from something unpleasant. We used the 24-item BIS/BAS scale (Carver and White 1994) to assess individual differences in the sensitivity of these systems with respect to resting-state HRV under eyes-closed or eyes-open conditions. Factor analysis conducted on a large number of college students ($N = 732$) yielded four factors (Carver and White 1994). The BIS subscale contains 7 items used to measure the degree of social withdrawal. Examples of typical responses are "I have fewer fears than do my friends" and "I worry about making mistakes." A higher score indicates that the participant would be more likely to inhibit movement toward a goal. The BAS subscale (Reward Responsiveness) contains 5 items used to measure positive responses to a reward. Two typical responses are "It would excite me to win a contest" and "When I see an opportunity to get something I want, I become excited right away." A higher score indicates that the participant was prone to adaptive impulsivity.

The subscale BAS_drive contains 4 items used to measure strong pursuit of appetitive goals. Examples of typical responses are "I go out of my way to get things I want" and "If I see a chance to get something I move toward getting it right away." A higher score indicates that the participant was prone to dysfunctional impulsivity. The subscale BAS_fun_seeking contains 4 items used to measure one's ability to seek out potentially rewarding situations and act without advance preparation or deliberation. Examples of typical responses are "I often act on the spur of the moment" and "I crave excitement and new sensations." A higher score indicates that the participant was prone to functional impulsivity.

EEG/ECG Recording

Following completion of the cSTAI, participants sat comfortably with eyes open in a chair positioned 60 cm in front of a computer screen in a sound-insulated chamber. Electroencephalograms (EEGs) and electrocardiograms (ECGs) were recorded using an EEG cap with 132 Ag/AgCl electrodes (including 122 10–10 system EEG, the bipolar VEOG, HEOG, ECG, EMG, and six facial-muscle electrodes). The EEG electrodes were placed in 122 sites according to the extended international 10–10 system and were referred to as Cz with ground at FzA. Bipolar ECG electrodes were placed on the back of both the left and right hands of participants. Electrode resistance was maintained below 5 kΩ. Signals were amplified using Neuroscan amplifiers, with 0.1–100 Hz analog bandpass filtering and then digitized at 1000 Hz. Before performing experimental tasks, the resting-state EEGs and ECGs were recorded for 4-min under the eyes-closed condition followed by 4-min under the eyes-open condition. For these conditions, participants were told to relax in a chair and they were instructed to fixate their gaze on a central cross on a 24.4 x 18.3 cm screen located in front of them under the eyes-open condition (Gusnard and Raichle 2001). After resting-state EEG/ECG registration, each participant from the first cohort self-reported her/his condition during the resting-state recording using the Chinese version 37-item STQ (Knyazev and Slobodskaya 2003) while each participant from the second cohort filled out the 24 item BIS/BAS scale (Carver and White 1994).

HRV Analysis

Resting-state ECGs were processed separately for eyes-closed and eyes-open conditions using Kubios HRV-2.2 software (Tarvainen et al. 2014) for HRV indices in the time- and frequency-domains as well as non-linear analysis. The non-linear analysis provides measures of irregularity or complexity in an ECG time series and so are named as "non-linear" while time- and frequency-domain indices provide linear measures of HRV indices. Table 1 provides an overview of the 21 HRV indices employed in this study. Artifacts and linear trends were removed using built-in filtering and detrending functions. The signals were then examined manually for quality assurance purposes. Default HRV analysis was conducted using Welch's periodogram method based on the Fast Fourier transform with a 60-sec window and 50% overlap, at a sampling rate of 1000 Hz and a smoothing parameter of 500 for smoothing priors in the detrending function.

The RR interval is defined as the interval from the peak of one QRS complex to the peak of the next QRS complex in an ECG time series. The time-domain indices included the SDNN, RMSSD, and pNN50 which were calculated on the basis of RR intervals. Two indices computed from the RR interval histogram were also considered. The HRV triangular index (tri_index) is the integral of the RR interval histogram (the number of RR intervals within a time series) divided by the height of the histogram (number of RR intervals in the modal bin). The triangular interpolation of RR interval histogram (TINN) is the baseline width of a triangle fitted to the histogram. All of the above time-domain indices were computed separately under eyes-closed and -open conditions (Chang et al. 2013).

Frequency domain HRV indices were computed using power spectral analysis in which the time series was transformed into the frequency domain. The RR interval time series was converted to equidistantly-sampled series via cubic spline interpolation. The HRV spectrum was calculated using the FFT-based Welch periodogram method, which involved dividing the RR time series into 60-sec time windows with 50% overlap. Spectrum estimates were obtained by averaging the FFT spectra of the windowed segments. The average spectral power was estimated within the VLF (0–0.04 Hz), LF (0.04–0.15 Hz), and HF (0.15–0.4) bands. These indices were extracted from power spectral density estimates of the RR interval time series in absolute units (ms^2). Relative power was computed by dividing the absolute power by the total spectral power. For each participant, the LF/HF ratio was computed separately under eyes-closed and eyes-open conditions by dividing the absolute power in HF and LF bands.

Several non-linear methods were also used to assess the RR time series data.

Poincaré Plots

The Poincaré plot is a simple scatter plot, which provides indices for short-term variability (SD_1) and long-term variability (SD_2), both of which are non-linearly connected to time-domain indices (Brennan, Palaniswami, and Kamen 2001). It is a graphical representation of the correlation between successive RR intervals; that is, RR_{j+1} is expressed as a function of RR_j, where RR_j denotes the R-peak at the jth QRS complex. The interpretation of the plot is done by parameterizing the shape so as to fit an ellipse oriented to the line of identity where $RR_{j+1} = RR_j$. The standard deviation of points perpendicular to the line of identity is denoted as SD_1. Note that this is caused primarily by respiratory sinus arrhythmia. The standard deviation of the points along the line of identity is denoted as SD_2.

Entropy

Sample entropy (SampEn) and approximate entropy (ApEn) (Richman and Moorman 2000) have been used to measure the degree of irregularity or complexity of a time series. ApEn is commonly used to quantify the entropy of a system. The derivation of ApEn involves examining a time series for similar segments and measuring the likelihood that close patterns remain close in subsequent incremental comparisons. The close patterns are defined by dividing the RR time series into a set of length m vectors. Here, m was set to a default value at 2. Note that ApEn is sensitive to the data length, which means that ApEn estimates for short time series tend to be low. SampEn is similar to ApEn; however, it does not count self-matches and is less sensitive to the data length. SampEn has been defined as the negative natural logarithm of the conditional probability that data of length N, having repeated itself within tolerance r for m points, will repeat itself for m+1 points. Here, m was set at 2 and r was set at 0.2×SDNN by default.

Detrended Fluctuation Analysis

DFA measures correlations between short-term and long-term fluctuations in an RR time series (Peng et al. 1995). The DFA algorithm proceeds through four steps: (i) removing the global mean and integrating the time series of a signal; (ii) dividing the integrated signal into non-overlapping windows of equal length n; (iii) performing least squares line fitting on each data window to obtain residuals; and (iv) detrending the integrated signal by subtracting the local trend within each segment and calculating the root-mean-square fluctuations of the integrated signal as fluctuation amplitude F(n). The same four steps are repeated for the various time scales n and plotted against window size on a log-log scale. The scaling exponent DFA α indicates the slope of the line, which relates the log of fluctuation amplitudes to the log of window sizes. Short-term fluctuations are characterized by the slope α_1 obtained from the (log (n), log F (n)) graph within the range of 4 - 12 beats, whereas long-term fluctuations are characterized by the slope α_2 obtained from the (log (n), log F (n)) graph within the range of 13 - 64 beats.

Recurrence Plot Analysis

Recurrence plot analysis (RPA) is used to visualize the recurrence behavior of a phase space trajectory in dynamic systems (Marwan et al. 2007). A phase space trajectory is first reconstructed from a time series using time delay embedding m. Close states in the phase space can then be plotted as a recurrence plot in accordance with threshold r. A recurrence plot is a symmetrical matrix of zeros and ones with order [N − (m − 1) τ] by [N − (m − 1) τ], where m is the embedding dimension and τ is the embedding lag. In the current study, we used the following settings: m = 10, τ = 1, and r = $\sqrt{m}$ × SDNN. Recurrence quantification analysis was used to define measures for diagonal segments in a recurrence plot, which includes the following: (i) the recurrence rate (RPA_REC) indicating the recurrence probability measured as the percent of the plot filled with recurrent points, (ii) determinism (RPA_DET) indicating the degree of predictability measured by the percent of recurrent points forming diagonal lines with a minimum of two adjacent points, (iii) the Shannon entropy of line length distribution (RPA_ShanEn), and (iv) the maximum line length (l_{max}) which is inversely related to the largest positive Lyapunov exponent as a measure of system divergence (RPA_DIV).

Other Information Measures

The correlation dimension (CorDim) index (Grassberger and Procaccia 1983) is another measure of signal complexity, which provides information pertaining to the minimum number of dynamic variables required to model the underlying system.

Table 1. Overview of the HRV indices considered in this study

Indices	Units	Definitions
SDNN	[sec]	The standard deviation of RR intervals.
RMSSD	[sec]	The square root of the mean squared differences between successive RR intervals.
pNN50	[%]	The number of successive RR interval pairs that differ more than 50 ms divided by the total number of RR intervals.
HRV_tri_index		The integral of the RR interval histogram divided by the height of the histogram.
TINN		Baseline width of the RR interval histogram.
HF_power_prc	[%]	HF[%] = HF[ms^2] / total power[ms^2] × 100%
LF_power_prc	[%]	LF[%] = LF[ms^2] / total power[ms^2] × 100%
VLF_power_prc	[%]	VLF[%] = VLF[ms^2] / total power[ms^2] × 100%
LF/HF		The ratio between LF and HF powers.
Poincare_SD$_1$	[ms]	Poincare plot for short term variability.
Poincare_SD$_2$	[ms]	Poincare plot for long term variability.
ApEn		Approximate entropy.
SampEn		Sample entropy.
CorDim		Correlation dimension.
DFA_α_1		Detrended fluctuation analysis: Short term fluctuation slope.
DFA_α_2		Detrended fluctuation analysis: Long term fluctuation slope.
RPA_Lmean	[beats]	Recurrence plot analysis: Mean line length.
RPA_DIV		Recurrence plot analysis: Divergence.
RPA_REC	[%]	Recurrence plot analysis: Recurrence rate.
RPA_DET	[%]	Recurrence plot analysis: Determinism.
RPA_ShanEn		Recurrence plot analysis: Shannon entropy.

Principal Component Analysis

Principal component analysis (PCA) is a multivariate statistical procedure with which random observations are transformed into a smaller set of uncorrelated variables referred to as principal components (PCs) (Jolliffe 2014). In other words, the original variables are presented as a weighted sum of orthogonal basis vectors, where the basis vectors are the eigenvectors of the data correlation (or covariance) matrix and the weights are the PCs. Typical applications of PCA include dimension reduction, feature extraction, and visualization of multidimensional data. In this chapter, PCA was used to analyze the correlation matrix among HRV indices in order to interpret multidimensional HRV data in reduced dimensions. The PCA results for 42 HRV indices (under eyes-closed and eyes-open conditions with 21 indices each) generated 9 components following PCA feature extraction (Tabachnick, Fidell, and Ullman 2019). After orthogonal varimax rotation of the 9 PCs, the time-domain HRV indices and Poincare plot analysis indices were neatly loaded on the same dimension, whereas the frequency-domain, non-linear, and VLF indices were loaded on separate dimensions depending on the resting-state conditions, that is, eyes-closed (EC) or eyes-open (EO) conditions. The 9 factors explained 87% of the overall data variance. The $ApEn^{EO}$ and RPA_Lmean^{EC} indices in Table 1 measured two PCs, which were uncorrelated with other HRV indices. $ApEn^{EC}$ had a higher loading on the dimension represented by the VLF power and DFA_α_2 while RPA_Lmean^{EO} had higher loading on the non-linear HRV dimension under the eyes-open condition. For ease of interpretation, we eliminated those 4 indices (i.e., $ApEn^{EC}$, $ApEn^{EO}$, RPA_Lmean^{EC}, and RPA_Lmean^{EO}), and re-conducted PCA on the remaining indices. The time-domain indices were robust to eyes-closed and eyes-open conditions; therefore, the 8-min time-domain HRV indices were estimated again by combining the ECGs obtained under the two resting-state conditions. The resulting PCA suggested 7 components, which accounted for 85.34% of the variation among the 31 indices. The component scores were estimated for individual participants using the regression method (Tabachnick, Fidell, and Ullman

2019). PCA, varimax rotation, and estimation of component scores were conducted using IBM SPSS Statistics 20.

Statistical Analysis

To establish a link between latent HRV dimensions and STQ, cSTAI, and BIS/BAS behavioral scores, we ran a series of stepwise regressions to facilitate the selection of variables using the SPSS package.

RESULTS

Among the 31 selected HRV indices as listed in Table 2, those in the frequency-domain differed significantly in terms of gender, wherein the average HF index of women was higher than that of men (p < .001 under both resting-state conditions), and women had the lower average LF index (p < .001 under both resting-state conditions) and lower average LF/HF ratio (p < .001 under the eyes-closed condition and p = .003 under the eyes-open condition) (Koenig and Thayer 2016). It is widely known that DFA_α_1 can be estimated by LF/(LF+HF) (Francis et al. 2002); therefore, it is not surprising that this HRV index also revealed significant gender differences, wherein the α_1 values of men were higher than those of women under both resting-state conditions (Voss et al. 2015). The pNN50 index was the only time-domain index that presented significant differences between genders (Voss et al. 2015). Generally, the time-domain HRV indices were higher in women than in men. Men and women presented comparable mean values on non-linear indices under eyes-closed as well as eyes-open conditions, a case which indicates that non-linear HRV indices may be insensitive to gender differences. Under the eyes-open condition, the VLF and DFA_α_2 indices of men and women were comparable.

However, the VLF and DFA_α_2 indices of men tended to be higher under the eyes-closed condition. Also, the CorDim indices of women were slightly higher than those of men under both resting-state conditions. After controlling for gender differences, all time-domain indices were significantly correlated with ages, wherein the time-domain indices of older participants tended to be lower (e.g., Poincare_SD$_1$ and Poincare_SD$_2$). After controlling for the gender differences, the other HRV indices appeared to be uncorrelated with ages. In summary, the HRV levels of women tended to be higher than those of men (particularly under the resting-state eyes-closed condition), and time-domain indices were sensitive to age differences. Non-linear HRV indices were relatively unaffected by age and gender differences; therefore, we explored their use as covariates in predicting cognitive outcomes.

Table 2. Statistical t-test for gender and age effects

PCs	HRV indices	Men	Women	Age[a]
Time	SDNN [8-min]	.058 (.023)[b]	.060 (.026)	-.292**
	pNN50 [8-min]	25.559 (17.747)	33.419* (17.624)	-.252*
	TINN [8-min]	.394 (.165)	.450 (.251)	-.311**
	RMSSD [8-min]	.059 (.030)	.070 (.038)	-.328**
	HRV_tri_index [8-min]	12.703 (4.184)	13.143 (4.197)	-.308**
	Poincare_SD$_1$ [8-min]	.042 (.021)	.050 (.027)	-.328**
	Poincare_SD$_2$ [8-min]	.070 (.026)	.067 (.027)	-.255*
Freq[EC]	HF_power_prc[EC]	42.501 (19.160)	62.403** (15.719)	-.071
	LF_power_prc[EC]	51.112 (17.754)	33.355** (14.462)	.070
	LF/HF_power[EC]	1.747 (1.406)	.629** (.401)	.055
	DFA_α_1[EC]	1.020 (.282)	.773** (.229)	.089

Table 2. (Continued)

PCs	HRV indices	Men	Women	Age[a]
Freq^{EO}	HF_power_prc^{EO}	40.087 (17.351)	54.237** (17.559)	-.106
	LF_power_prc^{EO}	53.134 (15.804)	39.905** (16.123)	.122
	LF/HF_power^{EO}	1.932 (1.857)	.992** (.888)	.169
	DFA_α_1^{EO}	1.065 (.275)	.874** (.244)	.209
Nonlin^{EC}	SampEn^{EC}	1.592 (.324)	1.550 (.302)	.038
	RPA_DET^{EC}	.972 (.016)	.969 (.016)	-.097
	RPA_DIV^{EC}	.014 (.007)	.015 (.007)	.027
	RPA_REC^{EC}	.297 (.136)	.294 (.155)	-.078
	RPA_ShanEn^{EC}	3.014 (.431)	3.033 (.358)	-.081
Nonlin^{EO}	SampEn^{EO}	1.526 (.340)	1.551 (.269)	-.043
	RPA_DET^{EO}	.974 (.017)	.976 (.014)	-.034
	RPA_DIV^{EO}	.012 (.007)	.013 (.006)	-.091
	RPA_REC^{EO}	.331 (.171)	.342 (.159)	.005
	RPA_ShanEn^{EO}	3.048 (.401)	3.111 (.343)	-.008
VLF	VLF_power_prc^{EC}	6.290 (5.088)	4.140* (3.017)	.027
	VLF_power_prc^{EO}	6.677 (4.253)	5.753 (3.494)	-.020
	DFA_α_2^{EC}	.305 (.135)	.291 (.121)	.024
	DFA_α_2^{EO}	.347 (.142)	.351 (.108)	-.178
CorDim	CorDim^{EC}	2.893 (1.208)	3.087 (1.101)	-.124
	CorDim^{EO}	2.916 (1.155)	3.144 (.940)	-.090

[a] The partial correlations between age and HRV indices conditional on the gender effect. [b] The standard deviation of each HRV index listed in parentheses. The symbol "*" indicates that the two-sample t-test or partial correlation is significant at $p < .05$, and the symbol "**" indicates that the test is significant at $p < .01$.

As shown in Table 3, the latent dimension referred to as *Time* had positive loadings on all 8-min time-domain indices. The two latent dimensions, so-called $Freq^{EC}$ and $Freq^{EO}$ respectively, had high loadings on indices in the frequency-domain; however, HF indices had negative loadings on these dimensions and the other indices had positive loadings. As mentioned, DFA_α_1 can be approximated by LF/(LF+HF) (Francis et al. 2002). Thus, the only difference between LF/HF and LF/(LF+HF) is the denominator. We may interpret $Freq^{EC}$ and $Freq^{EO}$ as HRV dimensions reflecting a balance between sympathetic and parasympathetic activity. The two non-linear dimensions referred to as $Nonlin^{EC}$ and $Nonlin^{EO}$ respectively had high loadings on non-linear indices; however, SampEn and RPA_DET had negative loadings and the other indices had positive loadings on these dimensions. One study reported that the SampEn index had a negative loading on the non-linear HRV dimension (Young and Benton 2015), whereas the RPA_DET index had a positive loading on the non-linear HRV dimension. The ECG recordings in Young and Benton's study were obtained while the participants were relaxing and listening to calming music for 5-min. In the current study, ECG recordings were obtained with the participants in a resting state under eyes-closed or eyes-open conditions. It is possible that the difference between the findings in the two studies can be attributed to the presence/absence of calming music (Young and Benton 2015). It has previously been demonstrated that DFA_α_2 is mathematically associated with the VLF index, which means that it can be approximated by VLF/(VLF+LF) (Francis et al. 2002). The so-called *VLF* dimension is primarily a reflection of the long-memory component in DFA. The two correlation dimension indices measured a single dimension, *CorDim*. We did not combine the two indices into a single 8-min CorDim index because the correlation between the two indices was deemed insufficient (despite reaching statistical significance) ($r = 0.68$; $p < .001$).

Among the 7 HRV dimensions listed in Table 4, $Freq^{EC}$ and $Freq^{EO}$ showed significant gender-related differences; that is, the component scores of women on these dimensions were significantly lower than those of men. There were insignificant correlations between age and all component scores except for *Time*, a case which suggested that the component scores gained by younger participants during the ECG recording were higher than those of their older counterparts. The statistical test results pertaining to component scores were consistent with the indices in Table 2. In other words, the 7 latent dimensions preserved the important gender-related and age-related information in the original raw indices. In summary, the two latent dimensions related to HRV indices in the frequency-domain were sensitive to gender differences, whereas the dimension related to the time-domain indices was sensitive to age differences. Other latent dimensions were relatively independent of gender and age effects. Nonetheless, none of the subscale scores on the STQ (drowsiness, emotion, ATT, or SRT) presented significant differences between genders, and when the gender effect was eliminated, none of the correlations between ages and subscale scores reached the level of significance. Furthermore, none of the BIS scores or subscale scores on the BAS scale (drive, fun-seeking, or reward responsiveness) presented significant gender differences, and none of the partial correlations between ages and those BIS/BAS scores reached the level of significance. The state- and trait-anxiety scores of women were slightly higher than those of men, but none of those differences reached the level of statistical significance.

Table 3. Latent dimensions of 31 HRV indices after the varimax rotation

HRV	Time	Freq^{EO}	Nonlin^{EC}	Nonlin^{EO}	Freq^{EC}	VLF	CorDim
SDNN (8-min)	**.970**	-.007	.112	.140	-.006	-.019	.088
HRV_tri_index (8-min)	**.681**	-.257	-.226	-.308	-.287	-.169	.190
pNN50 (8-min)	**.758**	-.149	.146	.482	.058	.055	.021
TINN (8-min)	**.914**	-.269	.076	.093	-.128	-.064	-.007
RMSSD (8-min)	**.858**	.071	-.044	-.230	-.078	-.160	.163
Poincare_SD$_1$ (8-min)	**.914**	-.269	.076	.093	-.128	-.064	-.007
Poincare_SD$_2$ (8-min)	**.928**	.148	.119	.160	.064	.015	.146
HF_power^{EC} (4-min)	.078	-.330	-.119	-.161	**-.885**	-.178	.010
LF_power^{EC} (4-min)	-.063	.362	.130	.177	**.870**	.001	-.032

Table 3. (Continued)

HRV	Time	Freq^{EO}	Nonlin^{EC}	Nonlin^{EO}	Freq^{EC}	VLF	CorDim
LF/HF_ratio^{EC} (4-min)	-.032	.385	.197	.053	**.798**	.030	-.045
DFA_α_1^{EC} (4-min)	-.190	.463	.116	.212	**.703**	.174	-.090
HF_power^{EO} (4-min)	.050	**-.877**	.102	-.081	-.290	-.205	.060
LF_power^{EO} (4-min)	-.057	**.861**	-.114	.079	.328	.055	-.024
LF/HF_ratio^{EO} (4-min)	-.079	**.837**	.081	.041	.253	-.078	-.021
DFA_α_1^{EO} (4-min)	-.238	**.853**	.015	.132	.291	.114	-.011
SampEn^{EC} (4-min)	-.077	-.008	**-.858**	-.228	.049	.215	.015
RPA_DIV^{EC} (4-min)	.115	.042	**.895**	.242	.154	.096	-.031
RPA_DET^{EC} (4-min)	.161	-.070	**-.816**	-.045	-.185	-.089	.240
RPA_ShanEn^{EC} (4-min)	.190	-.114	**.731**	.392	.155	.222	.045
RPA_REC^{EC} (4-min)	.080	-.134	**.817**	.295	.066	.150	-.037
SampEn^{EO} (4-min)	-.245	-.236	-.511	**-.638**	-.125	-.001	.132
RPA_DIV^{EO} (4-min)	.123	.217	.322	**.827**	.128	.050	-.089
RPA_DET^{EO} (4-min)	.178	-.393	-.134	**-.664**	-.153	-.030	.062
RPA_ShanEn^{EO} (4-min)	.169	-.039	.205	**.889**	.115	.161	-.104
RPA_REC^{EO} (4-min)	.038	-.038	.327	**.855**	.086	.086	-.071
VLF_power^{EC} (4-min)	-.099	-.004	-.010	-.007	.403	**.810**	.087
VLF_power^{EO} (4-min)	.006	.424	.013	.035	-.056	**.730**	-.182
DFA_α_2^{EC} (4-min)	-.248	-.143	.126	.108	.192	**.736**	.044
DFA_α_2^{EO} (4-min)	.045	.204	.125	.224	-.197	**.741**	-.283
CorDim^{EC} (4-min)	.355	-.083	-.165	-.142	.011	-.184	**.772**
CorDim^{EO} (4-min)	.096	-.024	-.076	-.124	-.099	-.027	**.916**

Table 4. Statistical t-test for gender and age effects on the the 7 HRV component scores

PCs	Men	Women	Age[a]
Time	-.022	.027	-.328**
	(.889)	(1.132)	
Freq^{EC}	.422	-.520**	.041
	(.947)	(.807)	
Freq^{EO}	.226	-.278**	.098
	(1.056)	(.859)	
Nonlin^{EC}	<.001	<-.001	-.059
	(.954)	(1.065)	
Nonlin^{EO}	-.123	.152	.052
	(1.009)	(.980)	
VLF	.048	-.059	-.102
	(1.154)	(.778)	
CorDim	-.067	.082	-.016
	(1.080)	(.897)	

[a] The partial correlations between age and component scores conditional on the gender effect. The symbol "*" indicates that the two sample t-test or partial correlation is significant at p < .05, and the symbol "**" indicates that the test is significant at p < .01. The means and standard deviations of component scores are listed in the table according to genders and HRV dimensions.

Table 5. Stepwise regression analysis on the HRV component scores and psychological scale scores

Scale scores	Age	Gender	Time	Freq^{EC}	Freq^{EO}	Nonlin^{EC}	Nonlin^{EO}	VLF	CorDim
Self-Referential Thought (N = 57)									
Emotions							$t_{54}=$ -2.498; $p=.016$		$t_{54}=$ 2.857; $p=.006$
SRT			$t_{54}=$ 2.103; $p=.040$		$t_{54}=$ 3.316; $p=.002$				
ATT						$t_{54}=$ -2.071; $p=.043$	$t_{54}=$ 2.332; $p=.023$		
Drowsiness			$t_{53}=$ -3.341; $p=.002$			$t_{53}=$ -1.776; $p=.081$	$t_{53}=$ 2.167; $p=.035$		
BIS/BAS Scales (N = 39)									
BIS		$t_{36}=$ 1.777; $p=.084$				$t_{36}=$ -3.162; $p=.003$			
BAS_Drive									
BAS_FunSeeking									
BAS_reward									
State-Trait Anxiety (N = 96)									
Trait Anxiety						$t_{94}=$ -1.876; $p=.064$			
State Anxiety	$t_{92}=$ -2.674; $p=.009$					$t_{92}=$ -2.356; $p=.021$	$t_{92}=$ -1.912; $p=.059$		

Table 5 lists the HRV dimensions that had significant effects in predicting the scores on different psychological scales under stepwise regression analysis. To compensate for the small sample sizes, we opted for the inclusion of predictors in the stepwise procedure using the critical value α = 0.09 (rather than 0.05). For example, *Nonlin^{EO}* and *CorDim* appeared to have significant effects when used to predict emotion scores in the STQ following the inclusion of age, gender, and all 7 of the HRV dimensions within the regression model. The *Nonlin^{EO}* dimension was negatively correlated with pNN50 (r = -.308; p = .002) and HRV_tri_index (r = -.230; p = .024); however, it was positively correlated with TINN (r

= .482; p < .001) and DFA_α_1 (r = .212; p = .038). Our regression results suggest that participants presenting signs of positive emotions during the ECG recording tended to achieve lower $Nonlin^{EO}$ scores (r = -.310, p = .019). Nonetheless, emotion scores were uncorrelated with $Nonlin^{EC}$ scores (r = .002, p = .987). It is interesting to note that *CorDim* was not correlated with any of the HRV indices in the time- or frequency-domain. Furthermore, participants presenting signs of positive emotions during the ECG recording tended to achieve higher *CorDim* scores (r = .352, p = .007), which could conceivably be interpreted as a positive emotion index. The regression results also suggest that gender and $Freq^{EC}$ were significant predictors of SRT scores. The $Freq^{EC}$ dimension was negatively correlated with pNN50 (r = -.287; p = .005) given that this component had a negative correlation with the HF power and a positive correlation with the LF power. Thus, $Freq^{EC}$ scores could be considered an indicator of sympathetic activity. As mentioned, a lower SRT score is an indication that the participant was more able to recall events in his or her daily life. Our regression results suggest that men under parasympathetic control would tend to recall daily life events during the ECG recording.

The $Nonlin^{EC}$ dimension was negatively correlated with pNN50 (r = -.226; p = .027) and uncorrelated with other indices in the time- and frequency-domains. This dimension was strongly associated with the degree of attention paid by participants to odors, sounds, and skin sensations during the recordings. Participants with lower $Nonlin^{EO}$ scores (positive emotions) and higher $Nonlin^{EC}$ scores tended to pay attention to the recording procedure. It is interesting to note that higher $Nonlin^{EC}$ scores were also associated with less pronounced social withdrawal on the BIS (r = -.465; p = .003). It would be reasonable to hypothesize that the $Nonlin^{EC}$ dimension could be used as a social withdrawal index, reflecting the degree of attention paid to the recording procedure, where a higher $Nonlin^{EC}$ score was associated with more attention and less pronounced social withdrawal. Drowsiness (based on arousal scores) had significantly negative correlations with all indices in the time domain. In other words, the level of arousal in participants was proportional to the degree to which they were under sympathetic control and the level of attention they paid to ECG recording procedures (i.e., odors, sounds, and skin sensations). Note that the function of $Freq^{EO}$ scores was similar to that of *Time* scores. The results in Table 5 suggest that the BIS scores were strongly associated with gender and $Nonlin^{EC}$. Women had higher BIS scores and paid less attention to ECG recording procedures, compared with men. Younger participants also had higher state-anxiety scores and appeared to pay more attention to the ECG recording procedures. The *VLF* dimension was not strongly predictive of scale scores in the current study; however, it may be a predictor of other behavioral outcomes.

DISCUSSION

In this chapter, our analysis revealed an association between various psychological scales and the latent structures of short-term HRV indices under two resting-state conditions. We also explored the effects of gender, age, and resting-state condition on these latent structures. Frequency-domain and non-linear HRV indices could be used to differentiate eyes-closed and eyes-open conditions, as evidenced by our PCA results. Thus, we strongly recommend that indices in the time-domain be used to index short-term resting-state ECGs in cases where resting-state conditions are not an issue of primary concern. The indices in the time- and frequency-domains revealed that parasympathetic activity is more pronounced in women than in men. The time-domain indices also revealed that older participants were more profoundly affected by sympathetic activity than were their younger counterparts. This is the first study to characterize physiological and affective status during the resting-state ECG recording based on latent HRV dimensions. Our stepwise regression analysis suggested the following: (i) the latent dimension *Time* was a good indicator of drowsiness in participants; (ii) $Freq^{EC}$ was strongly associated with SRT scores and a reliable indicator of sympathetic activity; (iii) $Nonlin^{EC}$ was strongly associated with anxiety and social withdrawal and was a reliable predictor of drowsiness and the degree of attention paid to the ECG recording procedure; (iv) $Nonlin^{EO}$ was strongly associated with the emotional experience of participants during the recording process as well as the degree of attention to the ECG recording procedure; (v) *CorDim* was significantly correlated with positive emotions during the ECG recording.

Our analysis results suggested that $Nonlin^{EC}$ and $Nonlin^{EO}$ were relatively robust to gender and age differences in young adults. Previous studies have recommended using non-linear HRV indices to predict gender-by-behavior interactions in terms of attention, memory, reaction times, emotional responses, and cortisol levels (Young and Benton 2015). It was reported that the use of non-linear HRV indices could significantly increase the percentage of variation explained in regression analysis for the prediction of behavioral outcomes. For example, frequency-domain indices alone were unable to predict treatment outcomes in patients who were afraid of flying, but the predictive power was increased by 18% after adding the SampEn index to the regression model (Bornas et al. 2006). It was also reported that non-linear HRV indices were significantly related to ratings of depression and salivary cortisol levels, whereas frequency- and time-domain indices were associated with perceived stress and anxiety (Young and Benton 2015). Those researchers suggested that non-linear HRV indices capture additional information on top of those obtained based on traditional HRV indices. They also indicated that in some instances, the contribution of non-linear HRV indices was essential to predictive performance (e.g., *CorDim* and $Nonlin^{EC}$). It is interesting to note that $Nonlin^{EC}$ and $Nonlin^{EO}$ predicted ATT scores well as indicated in the results in Table 5. However, if we considered the 10 raw non-linear indices in the stepwise regression, none of these indices would have a significant effect in predicting the ATT scores at α = 0.09. This finding has demonstrated that latent dimensions of HRV indices are more predictive of psychological traits than are the original non-linear indices.

The psychophysiological underpinnings of non-linear HRV have yet to be investigated; however, there is rich evidence indicating that these indices could be used to quantify heart rate dynamics and have a strong association with the functioning of the central nervous system. Previous studies used pharmacological intervention to clarify the contribution of activity in the autonomic nervous system (ANS) to measures of complexity in characterizing HRs. For example, one study measured linear (SDNN, RMSSD, LF power, and HF power) and non-linear (short-term DFA_α_1 and ApEn) HRV indices for a 5-min period before and after the intravenous injection of 0.6 mg of atropine (a parasympathetic antagonist). The results in that study revealed a significant increase in DFA_α_1 after atropine injection (Perkiomaki et al. 2002). In addition, DFA_α_1 showed significant negative correlations with several linear HRV indices (SDNN, RMSSD, and HF power) and a positive correlation with HRs at the baseline level while this effect vanished after atropine injection. Interestingly, ApEn failed to show significant correlation with any of the linear HRV indices or HR either before or after the atropine treatment. This suggests that vagal activity has a significant contribution to the fractal nature of HR time series, but it is not a major determinant of ApEn. Our study has partially supported this notion. Specifically, PCA revealed that DFA_α_1 was loaded heavily on the same dimensions as were indices in the frequency domain; however, SampEn and the recurrent plot indices co-loaded onto a separate dimension (Young and Benton 2015) under the eyes-closed condition or eyes-open condition, respectively. We recommend measuring HR entropy and performing RP analyses since they are both able to capture information that is not attributable to ANS activity as reflected by linear HRV indices in time- and frequency-domains.

To the best of our knowledge, this is the first study to use resting-state HRV indices for the prediction of STQ scores. Previous research linked the DFA_α_1 index with anxiety scores and affective problems (Fiskum et al. 2018). By contrast, our findings indicated that SRT scores could be predicted based on *Freq^{EC}* (including DFA_α_1). Drowsiness has traditionally been associated with the parasympathetic nervous system. Research showed that the HR decreased with sleepiness in drivers, leading to increases in HRV based on the SDNN, TINN, and Poincare SD$_1$, SD$_2$ indices (Buendia et al. 2019). By contrast, we found that *Time* was a significant predictor of "drowsiness." One previous study reported that non-linear HRV indices could increase the predictive power of a regression model used to account for reaction times obtained from focused attention tasks (Young and Benton 2015). This suggests that *Nonlin^{EO}* may play a general role in attention status. In line with this finding, we demonstrated that $Nonlin^{EO}$ was positively predictive of ATT scores and negatively predictive of emotion scores.

In the current study, BIS scores were negatively correlated with $Nonlin^{EC}$ component scores (r = -.465, p = .003) and positively correlated with trait-anxiety scores (r = .781, p < .001). These findings are consistent with recent reports characterizing the relationship between anxiety and non-linear HRV. The BIS is a complex system involving the inhibition of ongoing behaviors, increasing vigilance, and promoting arousal in reaction to stimuli associated with pain, punishment, failure, loss of reward, novelty, or uncertainty (Gray 1982). Trait-anxiety is closely related to sensitivity toward BIS activation (Corr and Cooper 2016). Thus, individuals with high trait-anxiety tend to receive higher scores on the BIS scale. It was previously demonstrated that BIS scores were associated with alpha power under resting-state conditions (Knyazev, Savostyanov, and Levin 2004; Knyazev and Slobodskaya 2003), and that the BIS and anxiety scores of women were higher than those of men. One recent study reported a significant correlation between state anxiety and SampEn (Dimitriev, Saperova, and Dimitriev 2016) during rest and exam sessions as well as a significant correlation between state anxiety and DFA_α_2 during exam sessions. Another study using RMSSD as an indicator of parasympathetic control found no correlation between HRV and BIS scores (Scholten et al. 2006). Despite a small sample size, our study showed that BIS could be predicted by $Nonlin^{EC}$, suggesting that non-linear HRV indices revealed information beyond the ANS. Previous study showed strong correlations between BIS scores and scores on negative affectivity scales and neuroticism (Jorm et al. 1998). In contrast, weak correlations were reported between BIS scores and symptoms of anxiety and depression. This can be explained by the fact that BIS scores have been designed to measure one's predisposition to anxiety rather than the experience of anxiety. The fact that gender (t_{36} = 2.286; p = .028) and trait-anxiety scores (t_{36} = 4.882; p < .001) were strongly predictive of BIS scores (Table 5) means that trait-anxiety remains the best predictor of BIS, which is also strongly associated with $Nonlin^{EC}$.

Broadly speaking, our results are indicative of two separate dimensions within the sympathetic domain. Specifically, HRV indices classified to $Freq^{EC}$, $Freq^{EO}$, $Nonlin^{EC}$, and $Nonlin^{EC}$ were negatively correlated with HF, RMSSD, SDNN and pNN50. We could argue that *Time* was a measure of parasympathetic activity owing to positive loadings of RMSSD, SDNN and pNN50 on this dimension. Since $Freq^{EC}$, $Freq^{EO}$, $Nonlin^{EC}$, and $Nonlin^{EC}$ were negatively correlated with the above mentioned indices measuring parasympathetic activity, we could further argue that they might be measuring activity in the sympathetic domain. This distinction is most notable in $Nonlin^{EC}$, and $Nonlin^{EO}$, wherein eyes-closed and eyes-open conditions differed (positive and negative *t* values in Table 5) in their predictions of "attention to the ECG recording procedure." Note that state-anxiety scores were negatively predicted by both $Nonlin^{EC}$ and $Nonlin^{EO}$; that is, lower state anxiety scores were associated with higher $Nonlin^{EC}$ and $Nonlin^{EO}$ component scores. This means that state anxiety could not be used to differentiate between eyes-closed and eyes-open conditions in non-linear HRV dimensions. This distinction is yet to be accounted for in future studies on individual differences and personality traits. We were unable to find well-documented instances of gender differences pertaining to the BIS/BAS scales. Note that a relatively small sample in this study might have prevented our detection of more significant gender differences in BIS/BAS. Age had a significant effect on state-anxiety, but not on any STQ subscale. Future studies would no doubt benefit from a larger sample size with a greater age range.

In conclusion, the non-linearity of many biological processes (e.g., HRV and brain functioning) (Mattei 2014) means that linear indices must be combined with non-linear indices for the prediction of complex behaviors. The present study found that non-linear HRV indices were independently predictive of several physiological and affective states under resting-state conditions. In such cases, conventional HRV indices in the time- and frequency-domains lacked any predictive ability. In the future, researchers should consider the influence of the HPA axis on the modulation of HRV indices, and particularly on indices pertaining to heart rate entropy and recurrence quantification analysis. We recommend collecting data pertaining to cortisol levels and sex-hormones when replicating our experiment using other stress-related tasks.

ACKNOWLEDGMENT

This research was supported by grants MOST-106-2410-H-001-026 and MOST-106-2420-H-001-006-MY2 from the Ministry of Science and Technology, Taiwan.

REFERENCES

Acharya, U Rajendra, K Paul Joseph, Natarajan Kannathal, Choo Min Lim, and Jasjit S Suri. 2006. "Heart rate variability: a review." *Med. Biol. Eng. Comput.* 44 (12): 1031-1051.

Alvares, Gail A, Daniel S Quintana, Andrew H Kemp, Anita Van Zwieten, Bernard W Balleine, Ian B Hickie, and Adam J Guastella. 2013. "Reduced heart rate variability in social anxiety disorder: associations with gender and symptom severity." *PLOS ONE* 8 (7): e70468.

Amin, Hafeez Ullah, Aamir Saeed Malik, Ahmad Rauf Subhani, Nasreen Badruddin, and Weng-Tink Chooi. 2013. "Dynamics of Scalp Potential and Autonomic Nerve Activity during Intelligence Test." In: Lee M., Hirose A., Hou ZG, Kil RM. (eds.) Neural Information Processing. ICONIP 2013. Lecture Notes in Computer Science, vol 8226. Springer, Berlin, Heidelberg.

Amodio, David M, Sarah L Master, Cindy M Yee, and Shelley E Taylor. 2008. "Neurocognitive components of the behavioral inhibition and activation systems: Implications for theories of self-regulation." *Psychophysiology* 45 (1): 11-19.

Antelmi, Ivana, Rogério Silva De Paula, Alexandre R Shinzato, Clóvis Araújo Peres, Alfredo José Mansur, and Cesar José Grupi. 2004. "Influence of age, gender, body mass index, and functional capacity on heart rate variability in a cohort of subjects without heart disease." *Am. J. Cardiol.* 93 (3): 381-385.

Beauchaine, Theodore P, and Julian F Thayer. 2015. "Heart rate variability as a transdiagnostic biomarker of psychopathology." *Int. J. Psychophysiol.* 98 (2): 338-350.

Berry, Jarett D, Alan Dyer, Xuan Cai, Daniel B Garside, Hongyan Ning, Avis Thomas, Philip Greenland, Linda Van Horn, Russell P Tracy, and Donald M Lloyd-Jones. 2012. "Lifetime risks of cardiovascular disease." *N. Engl. J. Med.* 366 (4): 321-329.

Bishop, Sonia J, John Duncan, and Andrew D Lawrence. 2004. "State anxiety modulation of the amygdala response to unattended threat-related stimuli." *J. Neurosci.* 24 (46): 10364-10368.

Bluhm, Robyn L, Elizabeth A Osuch, Ruth A Lanius, Kristine Boksman, Richard WJ Neufeld, Jean Théberge, and Peter Williamson. 2008. "Default mode network connectivity: effects of age, sex, and analytic approach." *Neuroreport* 19 (8): 887-891.

Bocharov, Andrey V, Gennady G Knyazev, Alexander N Savostyanov, Tatiana N Astakhova, and Sergey S Tamozhnikov. 2019. "EEG dynamics of spontaneous stimulus-independent thoughts." *Cog. Neurosci.* 10 (2): 77-87.

Bornas, Xavier, Jordi Llabrés, Miquel Noguera, Ana Ma López, Joan Miquel Gelabert, and Irene Vila. 2006. "Fear induced complexity loss in the electrocardiogram of flight phobics: a multiscale entropy analysis." *Biol. Psychol.* 73 (3): 272-279.

Brennan, Michael, Marimuthu Palaniswami, and Peter Kamen. 2001. "Do existing measures of Poincare plot geometry reflect nonlinear features of heart rate variability?" *IEEE Trans. Biomed. Eng.* 48 (11): 1342-1347.

Buendia, Ruben, Fabio Forcolin, Johan Karlsson, Bengt Arne Sjöqvist, Anna Anund, and Stefan Candefjord. 2019. "Deriving heart rate variability indices from cardiac monitoring—An indicator of driver sleepiness." *Traffic Inj. Prev.* 20 (3): 249-254.

Camm, A John, Marek Malik, J Thomas Bigger, Günter Breithardt, Sergio Cerutti, Richard J Cohen, Philippe Coumel, Ernest L Fallen, Harold L

Kennedy, and RE Kleiger. 1996. "Heart rate variability: standards of measurement, physiological interpretation and clinical use. Task Force of the European Society of Cardiology and the North American Society of Pacing and Electrophysiology." *Circulation* 93(5): 1043-1065.

Carver, Charles S, and Teri L White. 1994. "Behavioral inhibition, behavioral activation, and affective responses to impending reward and punishment: the BIS/BAS scales." *J. Pers. Soc. Psychol.* 67 (2): 319.

Chalmers, John A, Daniel S Quintana, Maree J Abbott, and Andrew H Kemp. 2014. "Anxiety disorders are associated with reduced heart rate variability: a meta-analysis." *Front. Psychol.* 5: 80.

Chang, Catie, Coraline D Metzger, Gary H Glover, Jeff H Duyn, Hans-Jochen Heinze, and Martin Walter. 2013. "Association between heart rate variability and fluctuations in resting-state functional connectivity." *Neuroimage* 68: 93-104.

Clamor, Annika, Tania M Lincoln, Julian F Thayer, and Julian Koenig. 2016. "Resting vagal activity in schizophrenia: meta-analysis of heart rate variability as a potential endophenotype." *Br. J. Psychiatry* 208 (1): 9-16.

Colzato, Lorenza S, Bryant J Jongkees, Matthijs de Wit, Melle JW van der Molen, and Laura Steenbergen. 2018. "Variable heart rate and a flexible mind: Higher resting-state heart rate variability predicts better task-switching." *Cogn. Affect. Behav. Neurosci.* 18 (4): 730-738.

Cordero, A, and E Alegria. 2006. "Sex differences and cardiovascular risk." *Heart* 92 (2): 145.

Corr, Philip J, and Andrew J Cooper. 2016. "The Reinforcement Sensitivity Theory of Personality Questionnaire (RST-PQ): Development and validation." *Psychol. Assess.* 28 (11): 1427.

Dimitriev, Dimitriy A, Elena V Saperova, and Aleksey D Dimitriev. 2016. "State anxiety and nonlinear dynamics of heart rate variability in students." *PLOS ONE* 11 (1): e0146131.

Fiskum, Charlotte, Tonje G Andersen, Xavier Bornas, Per M Aslaksen, Magne A Flaten, and Karl Jacobsen. 2018. "Non-linear heart rate variability as a discriminator of internalizing psychopathology and negative affect in children with internalizing problems and healthy controls." *Front. Physiol.* 9: 561.

Francis, Darrel P, Keith Willson, Panagiota Georgiadou, Roland Wensel, L Ceri Davies, Andrew Coats, and Massimo Piepoli. 2002. "Physiological basis of fractal complexity properties of heart rate variability in man." *J. Physiol.* 542 (2): 619-629.

Friedman, Bruce H. 2007. "An autonomic flexibility–neurovisceral integration model of anxiety and cardiac vagal tone." *Biol. Psychol.* 74 (2): 185-199.

Grassberger, Peter, and Itamar Procaccia. 1983. "Characterization of strange attractors." *Phys. Rev. Lett.* 50 (5): 346.

Gray, Jeffrey A. 1982. "Précis of The neuropsychology of anxiety: An enquiry into the functions of the septo-hippocampal system." *Behav. Brain Sci.* 5 (3): 469-484.

Grös, Daniel F, Martin M Antony, Leonard J Simms, and Randi E McCabe. 2007. "Psychometric properties of the State-Trait Inventory for Cognitive and Somatic Anxiety (STICSA): comparison to the State-Trait Anxiety Inventory (STAI)." *Psychol. Assess.* 19 (4): 369.

Gusnard, Debra A, and Marcus E Raichle. 2001. "Searching for a baseline: functional imaging and the resting human brain." *Nat. Rev. Neurosci.* 2 (10): 685.

Hansen, Anita Lill, Bjørn Helge Johnsen, John J Sollers, Kjetil Stenvik, and Julian F Thayer. 2004. "Heart rate variability and its relation to prefrontal cognitive function: the effects of training and detraining." *Eur. J. Appl. Physiol.* 93 (3): 263-272.

Hori, Kiyokazu, Masanobu Yamakawa, Nobuo Tanaka, Hiromi Murakami, Mitsuharu Kaya, and Seiki Hori. 2005. "Influence of sound and light on heart rate variability." *J Hum Ergol* 34 (1-2): 25-34.

Hovland, Anders, Ståle Pallesen, Åsa Hammar, Anita Lill Hansen, Julian F Thayer, Mika P Tarvainen, and Inger Hilde Nordhus. 2012. "The relationships among heart rate variability, executive functions, and clinical variables in patients with panic disorder." *Int. J. Psychophysiol.* 86 (3): 269-275.

Jarczok, Marc N, Marcus E Kleber, Julian Koenig, Adrian Loerbroks, Raphael M Herr, Kristina Hoffmann, Joachim E Fischer, Yael Benyamini, and Julian F Thayer. 2015. "Investigating the associations of self-rated health: heart rate variability is more strongly associated than inflammatory and other frequently used biomarkers in a cross sectional occupational sample." *PLOS ONE* 10 (2): e0117196.

Jolliffe, Ian (2014) Principal component analysis. In Wiley StatsRef: Statistics Reference Online (Balakrishnan, N, Colton, T, Everitt, B, Piegorsch, W, Ruggeri, F. and Teugels, JL. eds.).

Jorm, Anthony F, Helen Christensen, A Scott Henderson, Patricia A Jacomb, Alisa E Korten, and Byan Rodgers. 1998. "Using the BIS/BAS scales to measure behavioural inhibition and behavioural activation: Factor structure, validity and norms in a large community sample." *Pers. Individ. Differ.* 26 (1): 49-58.

Kemp, Andrew H, Daniel S Quintana, Marcus A Gray, Kim L Felmingham, Kerri Brown, and Justine M Gatt. 2010. "Impact of depression and antidepressant treatment on heart rate variability: a review and meta-analysis." *Biol. Psychiatry* 67 (11): 1067-1074.

Kemp, Andrew H, Daniel S Quintana, Rebecca-Lee Kuhnert, Kristi Griffiths, Ian B Hickie, and Adam J Guastella. 2012. "Oxytocin increases heart rate variability in humans at rest: implications for social approach-related motivation and capacity for social engagement." *PLOS ONE* 7 (8): e44014.

Knyazev, G G, 2013. "EEG correlates of self-referential processing." *Front. Hum. Neurosci.* 7: 264.

Knyazev, G G, Alexander N Savostyanov, and Evgenij A Levin. 2004. "Alpha oscillations as a correlate of trait anxiety." *Int. J. Psychophysiol.* 53 (2): 147-160.

Knyazev, G G, Alexander N Savostyanov, Nina V Volf, Michelle Liou, and Andrey V Bocharov. 2012. "EEG correlates of spontaneous self-referential thoughts: a cross-cultural study." *Int. J. Psychophysiol.* 86 (2): 173-181.

Knyazev, G G, and Helena R Slobodskaya. 2003. "Personality trait of behavioral inhibition is associated with oscillatory systems reciprocal relationships." *Int. J. Psychophysiol.* 48 (3): 247-261.

Koenig, Julian, Andrew H Kemp, Theodore P Beauchaine, Julian F Thayer, and Michael Kaess. 2016. "Depression and resting state heart rate variability in children and adolescents—a systematic review and meta-analysis." *Clin. Psychol. Rev.* 46: 136-150.

Koenig, Julian, Andrew H Kemp, Nicole R Feeling, Julian F Thayer, and Michael Kaess. 2016. "Resting state vagal tone in borderline personality disorder: a meta-analysis." *Prog. Neuro-Psychopharmacol. Biol. Psychiatry* 64: 18-26.

Koenig, Julian, and Julian F Thayer. 2016. "Sex differences in healthy human heart rate variability: a meta-analysis." *Neurosci. Biobehav. Rev.* 64: 288-310.

Koval, Peter, Barbara Ogrinz, Peter Kuppens, Omer Van den Bergh, Francis Tuerlinckx, and Stefan Sütterlin. 2013. "Affective instability in daily life is predicted by resting heart rate variability." *PLOS ONE* 8 (11): e81536.

Kvaal, Kari, Ingun Ulstein, Inger Hilde Nordhus, and Knut Engedal. 2005. "The Spielberger state-trait anxiety inventory (STAI): the state scale in detecting mental disorders in geriatric patients." *Int. J. Geriatr. Psychiatry* 20 (7): 629-634.

Li, Kai, Heinz Rüdiger, and Tjalf Ziemssen. 2019. "Spectral analysis of heart rate variability: time window matters." *Front. Neurol.* 10.

Liou, Michelle, Jih-Fu Hsieh, Jonathan Evans, I-wen Su, Siddharth Nayak, Juin-Der Lee, and Alexander N Savostyanov. 2018. "Resting heart rate variability in young women is a predictor of EEG reactions to linguistic ambiguity in sentences." *Brain Res.* 1701: 1-17.

Marwan, Norbert, M Carmen Romano, Marco Thiel, and Jürgen Kurths. 2007. "Recurrence plots for the analysis of complex systems." *Phys. Rep.* 438 (5-6): 237-329.

Mattei, Tobias A. 2014. "Unveiling complexity: non-linear and fractal analysis in neuroscience and cognitive psychology." *Front. Comput. Neurosci.* 8: 17.

Migliaro, ER, P Contreras, S Bech, A Etxagibel, M Castro, R Ricca, and K Vicente. 2001. "Relative influence of age, resting heart rate and sedentary life style in short-term analysis of heart rate variability." *Braz. J. Med. Biol. Res.* 34 (4): 493-500.

Mikkola, Tomi S, Mika Gissler, Marko Merikukka, Pauliina Tuomikoski, and Olavi Ylikorkala. 2013. "Sex differences in age-related cardiovascular mortality." *PLOS ONE* 8 (5): e63347.

Mizuno, Kei, Kanako Tajima, Yasuyoshi Watanabe, and Hirohiko Kuratsune. 2014. "Fatigue correlates with the decrease in parasympathetic sinus modulation induced by a cognitive challenge." *Behav. Brain Funct.* 10 (1): 25.

Mozaffarian, Dariush, Emelia J Benjamin, Alan S Go, Donna K Arnett, Michael J Blaha, Mary Cushman, Sarah De Ferranti, Jean-Pierre Després, Heather J Fullerton, and Virginia J Howard. 2015. "Executive summary: heart disease and stroke statistics—2015 update: a report from the American Heart Association." *Circulation* 131 (4): 434-441.

Park, G, and Julian F Thayer. 2014. "From the heart to the mind: cardiac vagal tone modulates top-down and bottom-up visual perception and attention to emotional stimuli." *Front. Psychol.* 5: 278.

Park, G, Jay J Van Bavel, Michael W Vasey, and Julian F Thayer. 2013. "Cardiac vagal tone predicts attentional engagement to and disengagement from fearful faces." *Emotion* 13 (4): 645.

Park, G, Michael W Vasey, Jay J Van Bavel, and Julian F Thayer. 2013. "Cardiac vagal tone is correlated with selective attention to neutral distractors under load." *Psychophysiology* 50 (4): 398-406.

Peng, CK, Shlomo Havlin, H Eugene Stanley, and Ary L Goldberger. 1995. "Quantification of scaling exponents and crossover phenomena in nonstationary heartbeat time series." *Chaos* 5 (1): 82-87.

Perkiomaki, Juha S, Wojciech Zareba, Fabio Badilini, and Arthur J Moss. 2002. "Influence of atropine on fractal and complexity measures of heart rate variability." *Ann. Noninvasive Electrocardiol.* 7 (4): 326-331.

Raichle, Marcus E, Ann Mary MacLeod, Abraham Z Snyder, William J Powers, Debra A Gusnard, and Gordon L Shulman. 2001. "A default mode of brain function." *Proc. Natl. Acad. Sci. U.S.A.* 98 (2): 676-682.

Richman, Joshua S, and J Randall Moorman. 2000. "Physiological time-series analysis using approximate entropy and sample entropy." *Am. J. Physiol. Heart Circ. Physiol.* 278 (6): H2039-H2049.

Sacha, Jerzy. 2014. "Interaction between heart rate and heart rate variability." *Ann. Noninvasive Electrocardiol.* 19 (3): 207-216.

Scholten, Marion RM, Jack van Honk, André Aleman, and René S Kahn. 2006. "Behavioral inhibition system (BIS), behavioral activation system (BAS) and schizophrenia: Relationship with psychopathology and physiology." *J. Psychiatr. Res.* 40 (7): 638-645.

Schwartz, Janice B, William J Gibb, and Ton Tran. 1991. "Aging effects on heart rate variation." *J. Gerontol.* 46 (3): M99-M106.

Shek, Daniel TL. 1993. "The Chinese version of the State-Trait Anxiety Inventory: Its relationship to different measures of psychological well-being." *J. Clin. Psychol.* 49 (3): 349-358.

Spielberger, Charles Donald, and Richard L Gorsuch. 1983. *State-trait anxiety inventory for adults: sampler set: manual, test, scoring key*. Palo Alto, CA: Mind Garden.

Tabachnick, Barbara G, Linda S Fidell, and Jodie B Ullman. 2019. *Using multivariate statistics* (7th edition). Boston, MA: Pearson.

Tarvainen, Mika P, Juha-Pekka Niskanen, Jukka A Lipponen, Perttu O Ranta-Aho, and Pasi A Karjalainen. 2014. "Kubios HRV–heart rate variability analysis software." *Comput. Methods Programs Biomed.* 113 (1): 210-220.

Taubitz, Lauren E, Walker S Pedersen, and Christine L Larson. 2015. "BAS Reward Responsiveness: A unique predictor of positive psychological functioning." *Pers. Individ. Differ.* 80: 107-112.

Thayer, Julian F, Fredrik Åhs, Mats Fredrikson, John J Sollers III, and Tor D Wager. 2012. "A meta-analysis of heart rate variability and neuroimaging studies: implications for heart rate variability as a marker of stress and health." *Neurosci. Biobehav. Rev.* 36 (2): 747-756.

Thayer, Julian F, Anita L Hansen, Evelyn Saus-Rose, and Bjorn Helge Johnsen. 2009. "Heart rate variability, prefrontal neural function, and cognitive performance: the neurovisceral integration perspective on self-regulation, adaptation, and health." *Ann. Behav. Med.* 37 (2): 141-153.

Tuomainen, Petri, Keijo Peuhkurinen, Raimo Kettunen, and Rainer Rauramaa. 2005. "Regular physical exercise, heart rate variability and turbulence in a 6-year randomized controlled trial in middle-aged men: the DNASCO study." *Life Sci.* 77 (21): 2723-2734.

Voss, A, A Heitmann, R Schroeder, A Peters, and S Perz. 2012. "Short-term heart rate variability—age dependence in healthy subjects." *Physiol. Meas.* 33 (8): 1289.

Voss, A, Rico Schroeder, Andreas Heitmann, Annette Peters, and Siegfried Perz. 2015. "Short-term heart rate variability—influence of gender and age in healthy subjects." *PLOS ONE* 10 (3): e0118308.

Williams, DeWayne P, Claudia Cash, Cameron Rankin, Anthony Bernardi, Julian Koenig, and Julian F Thayer. 2015. "Resting heart rate variability predicts self-reported difficulties in emotion regulation: a focus on different facets of emotion regulation." *Front. Psychol.* 6: 261.

Young, Hayley, and David Benton. 2015. "We should be using nonlinear indices when relating heart-rate dynamics to cognition and mood." *Sci. Rep.* 5: 16619.

Zhang, John. 2007. "Effect of age and sex on heart rate variability in healthy subjects." *J. Manip. Physiol. Ther.* 30 (5): 374-379.

In: A Closer Look at Heart Rate
Editor: André Alves Pereira

ISBN: 978-1-53616-979-9
© 2020 Nova Science Publishers, Inc.

Chapter 2

ESTIMATING AND CORRECTING THE REGRESSION TO THE MEAN IN HEART RATE VARIABILITY STUDIES

Dimitriy A. Dimitriev, Elena V. Saperova, Olga S. Indeykina and Aleksey D. Dimitriev*
Department of Biology, Chuvash State Pedagogical University, Cheboksary, Russia

ABSTRACT

Background. There is now a substantial body of evidence linking the baseline level of heart rate variability (HRV) with the magnitude of stress-induced changes in autonomic control of heart rate. However, the extent to which these interindividual differences in stress responses can be attributed to the statistical phenomenon of regression to the mean (RTM) remains unproven. We sought to test the hypothesis that the statistical artefact RTM explains part of the baseline effect.

Methods. We illustrate the RTM effect using heart rate recording was carried out on 1233 volunteers, from which 137 were randomly

---

[*] Corresponding author: E-mail: rothman68@mail.ru.

selected to obtain an estimate of the stress response. Participants were monitored on a rest day and just before an academic examination for state anxiety and HRV. Participants were monitored on a rest day and just before an academic examination to establish their state of anxiety and HRV. Participants were divided into quartiles according to baseline HRV levels, and their response to academic stress was compared. In addition, we re-analyzed the dataset of orthostatic tests following strength training (ST) and high-intensity interval training (HIIT) overload and subsequent recovery.

Results. We observed a significant academic stress-induced reduction in HRV in subjects with a high-baseline HRV (>75th percentile), while a significant increase was found in the group with a low-baseline HRV. Univariate regression analysis demonstrated that the value of baseline HRV correlated with the magnitude of stress reaction consistent with the RTM model. A baseline-adjusted analysis of covariance did not reveal any significant intergroup differences in the changes in heart rate (HR) and HRV from rest to the examination. RTM-adjusted estimates confirmed an examination effect for HR, the standard deviation of the normal-to-normal interval series, and the high-frequency power of HRV, and they also revealed a significant decrease of low-frequency component of HRV spectrum. SIT and HIIT data analysis revealed that baseline heart rate was negatively associated with orthostatic reactivity that reflects the RTM. In conclusion, our findings underline the importance of controlling for RTM when examining the effect of baseline HRV on HRV reactivity.

New & noteworthy. Studies of autonomic flexibility have demonstrated that high-baseline HRV is associated with a decline in HRV and subjects with a low-baseline HRV have an inverse reaction to stress. This suggests that baseline HRV is a marker of stress-adaptive capacity. The results of our study strongly support an alternative view: RTM is the major source of variability of stress-related changes in HRV.

Keywords: heart rate variability, regression to the mean

INTRODUCTION

Sir Francis Galton (1886) observed that taller-than-average parents tended to have shorter descendants, and denoted this phenomenon 'regression towards mediocrity'. Subsequently, Das and Mulder (1983) modified this terminology to 'regression to the mode' and Senn (1990)

later employed the term "regression to the mean." Regression to the mean (RTM) is a statistical consequence of the random variation of repeated measurements that are made on the same individual. Due to the random component of variation of observed values, extreme values within a population tend to become less extreme. Davis (1976): described RTM as the phenomenon by which 'a variable that is extreme on its first measurement will tend to be close to the centre of the distribution for later measurement.' The effects of RTM are especially pronounced when selecting a subgroup with either very low or very high values.

RTM is the consequence of random fluctuation or random measurement in repeated measurement. Random fluctuation occurs when the observed values fluctuate unpredictably around their true values, and it is due to inaccurate measurement or actual biological variability, or both. The random fluctuation of parameter ta individual level can be characterized as within-subject variability. Heart rate exhibits prominent intraindividual variability, i.e., rarely are any two observations are identical, even if taken a minute apart. Grouping individuals on the basis of their initial measurements aggravates the RTM effect: the follow up values of group with extreme initial mean values will tend to the mean of the overall group.

Several methods have been developed for detecting of RTM for normal distributed values and non-parametric data (Lin, 1997). Most of these methods deal with common situation in which only two measurements per subject are available. The baseline measurement is used to determine selection and the second, obtained during exposure, is used to assess the effect. Denote by y_1 and y_2 the measurements obtained before and during exposure and assume that, in the absence of any treatment effect, y_2 and y_1 follow a bivariate normal distribution with $E(y_1) = E(y_2) = \mu$; $Var(y_1) = Var(y_2) = \sigma^2$ and $Corr(y_1; y_2) = \rho$. That is $E(y_2 - \mu|y1) = \rho(y_1 - \mu)$ or, equivalently, $E(y_2|y_1) = (1 - \rho)\mu + \rho y_1$. Now suppose a sample is selected based on the y_1. The subject is chosen when $c_L < y_1 < c_U$ (for $c_L = -\infty$ all subjects with values of y_1 below c_U are selected; for $c_U = \infty$ all subjects with values above c_L are selected). Let $z_L = (c_L - \mu)/\sigma$, $z_U = (c_U - \mu)/\sigma$, and define

$$\eta = -\frac{\phi(z_U) - \phi_L(z_L)}{\Phi(z_U) - \Phi(z_L)} \quad (1)$$

$$\lambda = -\frac{z_U \phi(z_U) - z_L \phi(z_L)}{\Phi(z_U) - \Phi(z_L)} \quad (2)$$

where $\phi(\cdot)$ is the probability density function of the standard normal distribution and $\Phi(\cdot)$ is cumulative distribution function. It follows that expectation and variance of the distribution of y_1 are:

$$E(y_1 | c_L < y_1 < c_U) = \mu + \eta\sigma \quad (3)$$

$$Var(y_1 | c_L < y_1 < c_U) = (1 + \lambda - \eta^2)\sigma^2 \quad (4)$$

Similarly, the expectation and variance of y_2 in the absence of exposure effect are as follows:

$$E(y_2 | c_L < y_1 < c_U) = \mu + \rho\eta\sigma \quad (5)$$

$$Var(y_2 | c_L < y_1 < c_U) = [1 + \rho^2(\lambda - \eta^2)]\sigma^2 \quad (6)$$

$$Var(y_2, y_1 | c_L < y_1 < c_U) = (1 + \lambda - \eta^2)\rho\sigma^2 \quad (7)$$

The effect of regression to the mean is represented as the difference between the expectations of y_1 and y_2, as follows:

$$E(y_2 - y_1 | c_L < y_1 < c_U) = (\rho - 1)\eta\sigma \quad (8)$$

As the equation indicates, the RTM effect is equal to zero if $\rho = 1$ and the RTM effect becomes more extensive as ρ become smaller. The magnitude of the RTM effect tends to become larger as both the difference between the mean of c_L and c_U, and the population mean μ increases.

Mee and Chua (1991) suggested a modified paired t-test which provides a computationally simple approach to differentiate between the RTM effect and the additive interventions effect τ. The test involves regression of y_2 on $y_1-\mu$, as follows:

$$y_2 = \mu + \tau + \rho(y_1 - \mu) + \varepsilon \qquad (9)$$

where population mean μ is fixed and known, and ε is a normally distributed random error. The null hypothesis of no effect is stated as follows:

$$H_0 : y_2 = \mu + \rho(y_1 - \mu) \qquad (10)$$

and the alternative hypothesis is

$$H_1 : y_2 = \mu' + \rho(y_1 - \mu) \qquad (11)$$

with $\mu' > \mu$.

The null hypothesis states that the true mean change equals an expected quantum because of regression to the mean, whereas the alternative hypothesis is that the actual mean change exceeds the RTM effect. According to the linear regression model (μ + τ) is the intercept β_0, and ρ is the slope. In these terms, testing of the null hypothesis is equivalent to testing H0: β_0 = μ against H1: β_0 = μ + τ. This test can then be based on the usual t statistics.

To identify the magnitude of the RTM effect, an initial examination of the data should include a scatterplot of the differences between the follow-up measure and baseline measures.

RTM can be identified by considering the regression (Barnett et al., 2005), as follows

$$(\text{Follow-up} - \text{Baseline})_i = \beta_0 + \beta_1 \times \text{Baseline}_i + \varepsilon_i \qquad (12)$$

A negative regression coefficient β_1 implies that subjects who gave extreme unusually low results at the baseline measurement have tended to more prominent positive changes, and subjects with high baseline results have tended to negative changes between the follow-up and baseline measures. This means that a significant inverse correlation occurs between the pre-post changes and the baseline level.

Analysis of covariance (ANCOVA) can be used to adjust effects for baseline measurements. ANCOVA has high statistical power, it decreases the bias, and provides precise estimates by adjusting each participant's follow-up measurement according to their baseline level. ANCOVA is a special case of multiple regression:

$$\text{Follow-up} = b_0 + b_1(\text{Baseline} - \text{Baseline mean}) + b_2(\text{group}) + \text{error} \quad (13)$$

Linearity between outcome and covariates is an underlying assumption of ANCOVA. Another method of RTM correction is computing 'correction factor' for computing the adjusted baseline level, as follows:

$$Y_{1adj} = \overline{Y}_1 + \rho(Y_1 - \overline{Y}_1) \quad (14)$$

where ρ is the baseline-test correlation, and Y_1 is the individual's baseline level.

Notwithstanding the importance of this issue, empirical evidence for the effects of RTM on physiological measures, and evidence concerning the effects of RTM on autonomic reactivity to psychosocial stress in particular, is rather sparse. Some authors consider RTM as a source of bias; they discuss results regarding RTM. Some authors consider RTM a source of bias, and discuss results regarding RTM. Unfortunately, these authors did not test the hypothesis that RTM explains observed changes (at least in part). One exception is the research of Gotfredsen et al. (1997), who tested for the RTM effect.

To demonstrate the RTM and efficiency of the RTM correction method, we implemented it on two real physiological datasets.

EXAMPLE 1. INTERINDIVIDUAL VARIABILITY IN HRV REACTIVITY TO PSYCHOSOCIAL STRESS

Stress reactivity is a multicomponent phenomenon, encompassing cognitive, emotional, physiological and behavioural responses (Campbell and Ehlert, 2012). Although the precise nature of emotion is not yet clear, theorists and researchers agree that emotion involves changes across multiple response systems (Gross et al., 2006). According to Cohen et al. (1995), psychological stress occurs when an individual perceives that the situation taxes or exceeds their adaptive capacity to cope with stress. The model of neurovisceral integration has been widely accepted as a heuristically useful framework for the study of psychological stress (Thayer and Lane, 2000). This model conceptualizes that autonomic flexibility provides the basis for adaptation to environmental challenge. Autonomic flexibility can be described as the capacity of the autonomic nervous system (ANS) to adapt to changes in the environment by modifying arousal, respiration, heart rate (HR), and attention (Friedman and Thayer, 1998).

Respiratory sinus arrhythmia (RSA), the rhythmical fluctuation in RR intervals accompanying breathing, has been widely used as an index of cardiac vagal tone (Berntson et al., 1993). Low rest RSA and redundant RSA withdrawal in response to emotional challenges are associated with psychopathology, anxiety, and panic disorder (Beauchaine, 2001; Licht et al., 2009; Chalmers et al., 2014). These data suggest that RSA can function as a reliable indicator of emotional reactivity. Diminished autonomic flexibility refers to a decrease in variability of HR and blunted RSA (Friedman and Thayer 1998). The direct manifestation of flexibility is reactivity of HR and RSA; HR and RSA reactivity can be determined as the difference between stress and rest scores. Thus, a high level of rest RSA should be associated with high RSA reactivity and baseline RSA is a predictor of emotional performance. However, observations of stress-induced changes in anxiety and RSA are equivocal.

Kok et al. (2010) found that vagal tone and psychosocial well-being reciprocally and prospectively predict one another. A high baseline RSA is related to low trait anxiety (Miu et al., 2009) and high RSA reactivity (Rottenberg et al., 2007). In contrast, Alkozei et al., (2015) reported the absence of differences at rest or in response to stress between anxious and non-anxious children. Gerra et al. (2000) found that adolescent boys with an anxiety disorder showed a higher HR reactivity to a mixed-model stress task than controls. Thus, a higher level of autonomic flexibility was typical for anxious boys. Moreover, there are a growing number of observations that do not fit the theories of Thayer and Porges (Kossowsky et al., 2012; Gorka et al., 2013; Fortunato et al., 2013; Wang et al., 2013; Kristensen et al., 2014; Spangler et al., 2015; Couyoumdjian et al., 2016; Fung et al., 2017).

The results of these studies have indicated that autonomic flexibility (i.e., reactivity) depends on the baseline level of RSA (Friedman and Thayer, 1998; Beauchaine, 2001; Rottenberg et al., 2007; Couyoumdjian et al., 2016). A high baseline RSA is associated with a decline in RSA and subjects with low baseline RSA have an opposite reaction to stress. A plausible explanation for this phenomenon is RTM, and there is a strong theoretical rationale for this proposal. The RTM prediction is that extreme baseline levels tend to become less extreme after repeated measurements, even in the absence of real change.

This study aims to evaluate the contribution of RTM and to examine implications for interpreting findings from HRV research of psychosocial stress.

Participants

Data for this study were obtained from research conducted from 2005 to 2015. A cohort of 1,156 students from Chuvash State Pedagogical University, consisting of 286 males/870 females, aged from 19 to 24 years (mean age (mean ± SE): 20.53 ± 0.11), were recruited for the study of HRV. Each volunteer underwent a comprehensive screening procedure before the study. This included a physical examination, health history questionnaire, routine laboratory tests, lung function testing, electrocardiogram, and a chest X-ray. There was no evidence of heart or pulmonary disease in any of the subjects. On the day of the study, the volunteers were instructed to avoid alcohol and caffeinated beverages for the preceding 12 h, and to refrain from heavy physical activity throughout the previous day. Informed consent was obtained from all individual participants included in the study, and the local Ethical Committee of biomedical research in the I. N. Ulyanov Chuvash State University gave approval to conduct the research.

State Anxiety and Heart Rate Variability

All subjects were administered psychophysiological evaluation composed of baseline (rest) and stressor (just before the academic exam) phases. State anxiety (SA) was assessed using State-Trait Anxiety Inventory anxiety scales (Hanin, 1976).

Electrocardiogram (ECG) was recorded continuously throughout each experiment via a three-lead ECG at a 1000 Hz sampling rate. Time series of the interbeat intervals RR were extracted automatically from the ECG signal and analysed using the heart rate variability analysis software (HRVAS) (Ramshur, 2010).

Time-domain and frequency-domain measures were derived from RR series, including mean RR; the standard deviation of the normal-to-normal (NN) interval series (SDNN); the spectral power of low-frequency (LF: 0.04 – 0.15 Hz) and high-frequency (HF: 0.15 – 0.4 Hz) band power and LF/HF ratio. The LF/HF power ratio, although the subject of discussion as to whether it may be used as an index of the sympatho-vagal interaction (Billman, 2013), has been widely used in the study of stress (Castaldo et al., 2015; Hamilton and Alloy, 2016).

Stress due to University Examination

A study of stress reactivity (defined as the difference between exam and rest values) was conducted on a sample of students randomly selected from the original cohort of 1,156 subjects. Measures of HRV were natural-log transformed (ln) to meet assumptions of parametric statistics. The sample size was calculated using MedCalc Statistical Software version 17.6 (MedCalc Software bvba, Ostend, Belgium; http://www.medcalc.org; 2017). An admission was made that the study should detect a minimal effect size at a significance level of 0.05 and 80% power (Machin et al., 2011). The minimum sample size was estimated to be N = 148.

For each variable, the students were divided into three groups, according to the values of the first measurement. The first group of was selected using a baseline measurement of less than the population 25th percentile; the second group represents the middle portion of the distribution (where scores ranged from the 25th percentile to the 75th percentile); and the third group consisted of subjects with baseline measurements greater than the population 75th percentile. Fifteen groups were formed on the basis of HR and HRV (three groups on the basis of HR, three groups on the basis of lnSDNN, and three groups on the basis of lnHF, etc.), and three groups were formed on the basis of SA. In this way, the same subjects could be in different groups, depending on the baseline levels of HR and HRV. We analysed the reaction to stress separately for each group, based on baseline HR and HRV.

Regression to the Mean

Ordinary linear-regression analysis was used to identify the RTM. The model was stated as (Follow-up – Baseline) = constant + b × baseline. The RTM effect manifests as a negative correlation between baseline values and stress-induced changes in HR and HRV.

Estimation of RTM assumes that pretest population means μ and variances (σ^2) are known. Accordingly, population means and variances were calculated from the general baseline data.

We applied the Mee–Chua t-test to establish whether observed changes in HR and HRV parameters might be due to RTM

Statistical Analysis

Repeated-measures analysis of variance (ANOVA) with Bonferroni multiple-comparison test was used to examine the effects of the stress on the HR and HRV measures.

Mean values of change between baseline and follow-up were tested for group differences using univariate analysis of covariance (ANCOVA) with 'condition' (< 25th percentile, 25th–75th percentiles, > 75th percentile) as between-subject factors and values of the rest period as covariates.

Means of within-subject distributions were tested against the rest values using a t-test for a single sample. All data are presented as mean ± SE. Significance was accepted at $p < 0.05$.

Stress due to Academic Examination

The population means of HR, lnSDNN, lnLF, lnHF, and lnLF/HF were 73.11 ± 0.13 bpm, 3.99 ± 0.012 ms, 6.70 ± 0.03 ms2, 6.81 ± 0.03ms2, and –0.11 ± 0.02, respectively. Table 1 presents the effect of academic stress on HRV measures in three groups.

The HF component of HRV was significantly reduced in the examination session compared with the rest session ($p < 0.001$), and the HR ratio was significantly higher in the examination session compared with the rest session ($p < 0.001$) (see Table 1). There was no difference in the LF component of HRV between the examination session and the rest session. lnSDNN reduced significantly from baseline during the examination session ($p < 0.001$).

Table 1. Comparison of HRV measures and SA between rest and exam stages

Variable	All subjects		P
	Rest	Exam	
HR [bpm]	73.15 ± 0.89	83.49 ± 0.98	< 0.01
lnSDNN [ms]	3.93 ± 0.03	3.78 ± 0.03	< 0.01
lnLF [ms^2]	6.37 ± 0.07	6.21 ± 0.07	> 0.05
lnHF [ms^2]	6.68 ± 0.09	6.03 ± 0.10	< 0.01
lnLF/HF	- 0.31 ± 0.06	0.19 ± 0.06	< 0.01
SA	25.28 ± 0.82	41.29 ± 0.83	< 0.01

Values are means ± SE.

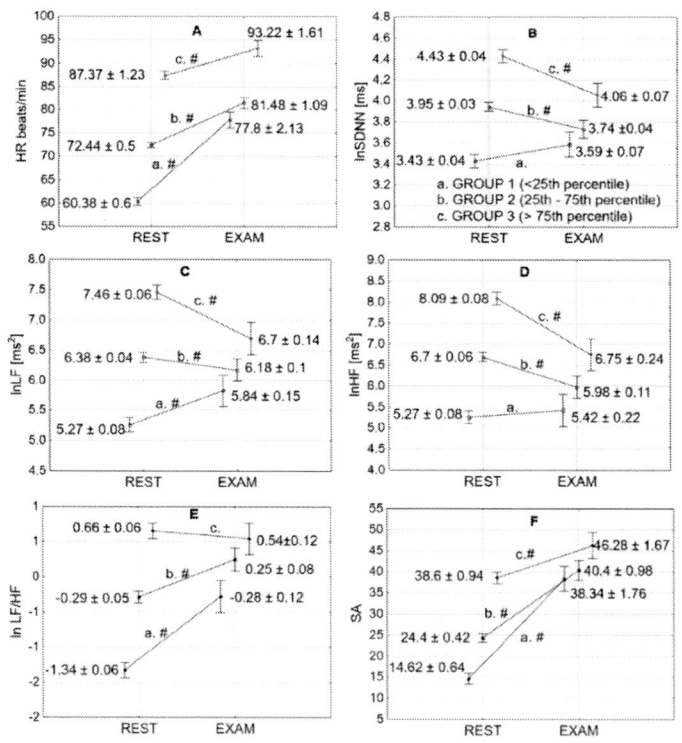

Figure 1. Effects of academic stress on HR (A), HRV (lnSDNN – B, lnLF – C, lnHF – D, lnLF/HF - E) and state anxiety SA (F). # $p < 0.01$.

Academic stress resulted in a significant increase in HR in all three groups (Figure 1).

The lnSDNN decreased significantly in the second and third groups before the examination, but not in the group with a low baseline level (p > 0.05). The transition from the rest session to the examination evoked a significant increase of lnLF in the first group (p < 0.01), whereas lnLF in the other two groups decreased significantly (F = 23.46, p < 0.01).

Statistical analysis of lnHF revealed a significant decrease in this parameter in the second and third groups and insignificant changes of LnHF were observed in the first group (F = 15.39, p < 0.01). Analysis of changes in SA during the examination session demonstrated an overall increase in SA. It is clear from Figure 1 that the first group presented a different pattern of HRV changes.

There were no significant gender differences in HRV reactivity to stress (p > 0.05).

Regression to the Mean

To reveal potentially significant associations between baseline values and stress effect, we examined scatter plots of change (examination minus rest measurements) against rest measurement (Barnett et al. 2005), as shown in Figure 2.

Figure 2 shows the changes in HRV measures plotted against baseline levels. The amount of HRV reduction for participants increased significantly as baseline lnSDNN, lnLF, and lnHF increased (p < 0.001 for linear trend for all measures). RTM is evident on the plot, as subjects from the first group tended to increase HRV, and subjects with very high baseline HRV tended to decrease lnSDNN, lnLF, and lnHF. The results for baseline and change ln LF/HF display a similar regression tendency (r = - 0.56, b = - 0.58, p < 0.001).

We applied the Mee–Chua t-test to determine whether the HRV changes were due to RTM. These tests (for HR, lnSDNN, and lnHF) confirmed an examination effect (t = 12.11, p < 0.001; t = 6.40, p < 0.001; and t = 7.88, p < 0.001, respectively). We found a significant difference in lnLF between the examination and rest sessions after adjusting for RTM (t = 6.4, p < 0.001).

For HR and HRV, the rest level was used as a covariate in an ANCOVA model to estimate the effect of RTM. Table 2 presents the descriptive statistics of change between sessions and the results of the ANCOVA.

When ANCOVA was performed to evaluate the effects of group on changes in HR and HRV, no significant effects were found regarding the changes of HR, lnSDNN, lnLF, and lnHF scores from rest to examination (HR: F = 2.03, p = 0.13; lnSDNN: F = 2.26, p = 0.11; lnLF: F = 1.14, p = 0.32; lnHF: F = 0.49, p = 0.61, lnLF/HF: F = 0.98, p = 0.37) after adjusting for the baseline level (Table 2).

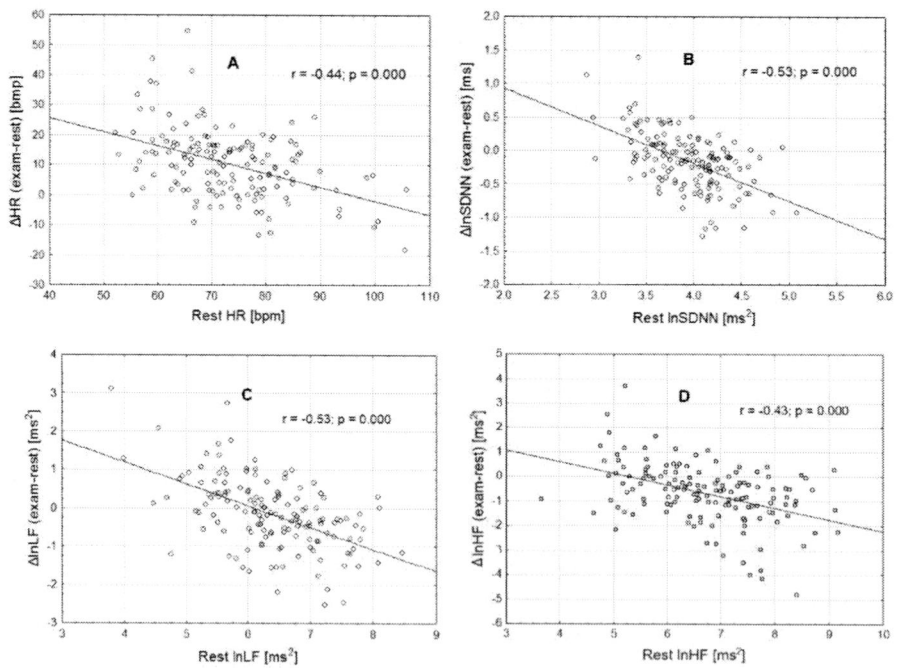

Figure 2. Change (exam – rest) is highly correlated to the baseline level. Scatter plots of baseline HR (A), lnSDNN (B), lnLF (C), and lnHF (D) vs. change. Linear-regression analysis produced significant negative r values for each metric.

Table 2. HRV changes between rest and examination (examination – rest) using the ANOVA and ANCOVA

Variable	Group	ANOVA		ANCOVA	
		Mean changes (±SE)	p*	Mean changes (±SE)	p*
HR [bpm]	1st group (< 25th percentile)	17.41 ± 2.06	< 0.001	9.44 ± 2.73	> 0.05
	2nd group (25th–75th percentile)	9.04 ± 1.16		8.60 ± 1.20	
	3rd group (> 75th percentile)	5.85 ± 1.71		14.73 ± 2.92	
lnSDNN [ms]	1st group (< 25th percentile)	0.16 ± 0.07	< 0.001	− 0.19 ± 0.10	> 0.05
	2nd group (25th–75th percentile)	− 0.21 ± 0.04		− 0.21 ± 0.04	
	3rd group (> 75th percentile)	− 0.37 ± 0.06		− 0.04 ± 0.11	
lnLF [ms^2]	1st group (< 25th percentile)	0.57 ± 0.15	< 0.001	0.14 ± 0.23	> 0.05
	2nd group (25th – 75th percentile)	− 0.21 ± 0.09		− 0.20 ± 0.09	
	3rd group (> 75th percentile)	− 0.77 ± 0.12		− 0.34 ± 0.23	
lnHF [ms^2]	1st group (< 25th percentile)	0.15 ± 0.19	< 0.001	− 0.11 ± 0.33	> 0.05
	2nd group (25th–75th percentile)	− 0.72 ± 0.11		− 0.72 ± 0.13	
	3rd group (> 75th percentile)	− 1.33 ± 0.21		− 1.07 ± 0.33	
lnLF/HF	1st group (< 25th percentile)	1.05 ± 0.11	< 0.001	0.46 ± 0.20	> 0.05
	2nd group (25th–75th percentile)	0.53 ± 0.08		0.54 ± 0.08	
	3rd group (> 75th percentile)	− 0.12 ± 0.12		0.44 ± 0.20	

Values are means ± SE.
*effect of group.

The intraindividual distributions of lnHF (Figure 3) are given below to illustrate the nature of RTM (data from our previous study (Dimitriev DA et al., 2007)). The subjects from this previous study took part in research to determine the relationships between phases of the menstrual cycle and HRV. RR intervals were recorded daily throughout one month (excluding weekends). The same subjects were examined for acute stress reaction.

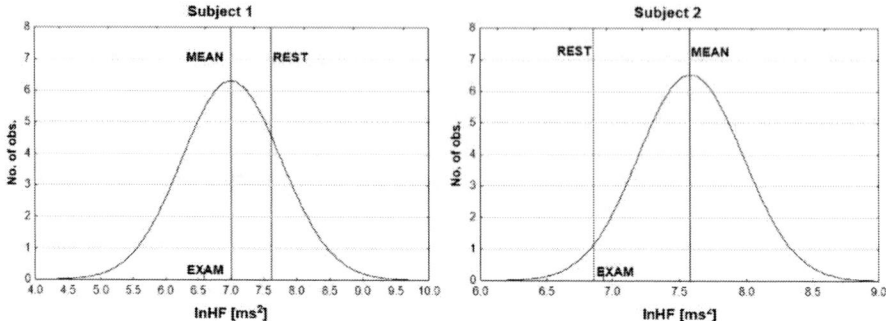

Figure 3. Within-subject distributions and RTM. A mean was calculated from daily lnHF values.

Subject 1's lnHF at rest (7.62 ms2) was significantly higher than the true mean (7.01 ms2; t = 7.18, p < 0.001). The difference between rest and examination was 1.03 ms2, and between mean and examination it was 0.42 ms2. This suggests the stress reaction was overestimated by 0.61 ms2. For the second subject, lnHF at rest (6.86 ms2) was significantly lower than the true mean (7.58 ms2; t = 10.51, p < 0.001) and was approximately equal to the lnHF before the examination (6.93 ms2). It could be considered that the subject's lnHF at the commencement of the examination had slightly increased when in fact the rest measurement was just unusually low, and the subject's true response was negative (lnHFexam – lnHFmean = − 0.65 ms2; t = 9.49, p < 0.01). SA was increased in both subjects (Subject 1: from 28 to 42, Subject 2: from 30 to 38).

EXAMPLE 2. ASSESSMENT OF THE EFFECTS OF STRENGTH TRAINING (ST) AND HIGH-INTENSITY INTERVAL TRAINING (HIIT) OVERLOAD ON CHANGES IN HR AND HRV MEASURES DURING ACTIVE ORTHOSTATIC TESTS

Our second example relates to a recent study (Schneider et al., 2019) on the effect of ST and HIIT overload on HR and HRV. The main finding of Schneider et al. was that active orthostatic tests could reveal differences in autonomic tone as a function of training. However, these orthostatic changes in cardiac autonomic regulation were not consistently different between ST and HIIT. We hypothesised that absence of differences in autonomic responses to orthostatic maneuvres can be explained by regression to the mean. Simple correlation analysis indicated that active HR response to the orthostatic test correlated negatively with the baseline (supine) level (Table 3).

In Table 4, we note a negative correlation between HR (supine), and changes in that value between supine and standing. These are the manifestations of regression to the mean.

The difference between the subgroup means of baseline HR was significant on day 8 (second day of recovery), with 63.61 ± 2.06 bpm for the ST group, and 57.37 ± 2.07 bpm for the ST group (ANOVA: F = 57.37; $p < 0.05$). We conducted regression analysis with baseline HR as the independent variable, and orthostatic change as the dependent variable for day 8. Figure 4 illustrates individual measurements of orthostatic-induced change in HR plotted against baseline HR for both groups. The gradient is -1.22 ($p < 0.001$), meaning that the estimated increase in HR change from baseline (in both treatment groups) decreases by 12.2 bpm for every 10 bpm increase in baseline HR.

A crude comparison of mean orthostatic-induced change in HR yielded a nonsignificant difference between the ST and HIIT groups ($p > 0.05$). There was a significant baseline imbalance in supine HR, with the mean baseline lower in the HIIT group. Because supine HR and HR response to orthostatic tests are negatively correlated, the crude mean orthostatic change in HR is biased toward an exaggerated effect in the HIIT group, and understated in the ST group. ANCOVA removes the effect of this correlation by producing an unbiased baseline-adjusted mean orthostatic difference. Therefore, ANCOVA was performed to test the null hypothesis that orthostatic-induced change in HR is equal across the groups (Table 4).

Table 4 shows that utilization of ANCOVA, adjusting for baseline heart rate values, reveals the significant difference between ST and HIIT in orthostatic change in heart rate.

Table 3. Relationship between baseline HR level and magnitude of HR response to orthostatic test (HR stand – HR supine) by means of simple correlation analysis

Day of baseline	r	Significance
1	− 0.5968	**
2	− 0.4839	*
3	− 0.5744	**
Day of microcycle		
1	− 0.6541	**
2	− 0.7034	**
3	− 0.5809	**
4	− 0.6412	**
5	− 0,6855	**
6	− 0.7585	**
Day of recovery		
1	− 0.7616	**
2	− 0.7103	**
3	− 0.7341	**
4	− 0.6398	**

* $P < 0.05$; ** $P < 0.01$; n.s. (not significant); + (positive relation); − (negative relation).

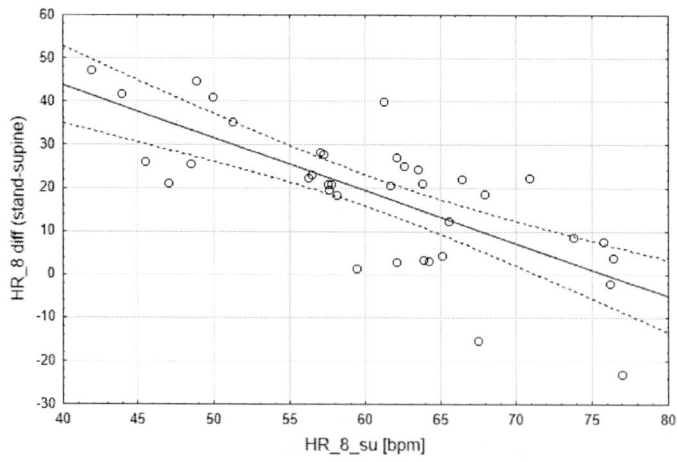

Figure 4. Scatter plot of individual orthostatic change in HR based on baseline supine HR. The negative indicates that higher baseline HR was associated with a lower increase in supine HR.

Table 4. Postural difference (ST vs. HIIT) in heart rate estimated 2 alternative methods

Test	Group	Stand − supine, mean ± SE	P
Student *t* test	ST	18.96 ± 2.31	0.9366
	HIIT	18.53 ± 2.37	
ANCOVA	ST	23.19 ± 2,38	0.014
	HIIT	14.07 ± 2.45	

DISCUSSION

A common study design in physiological research is to apply an intervention and then observe the response. For example, HRV could be measured twice: once at rest and once during stress. Despite its evident simplicity, the analysis of this form of study may produce biased results due to RTM, although this is not widely appreciated in the literature and has not been quantified. Stress studies in humans have reported that stressful life events are associated with a more prominent supression of RSA in individuals with a higher baseline HRV. However, to the best of our knowledge, none of these analyses have included correction for the RTM effect.

A linear regression analysis was used to assess the relation between stress response and baseline HRV value. The results of this analysis indicate that the difference between rest and examination states is influenced by the baseline level of HRV: subjects with unusually high baseline levels have a more prominent stress response than subjects with very low initial values of HRV variables. These findings indicate a strong RTM effect.

Mee–Chua tests for HRV variables confirmed a marked decrease in SDNN and HF. The crude difference in LF between rest and examination almost reached a significance level ($p = 0.05$) and p-value drawn from the Mee–Chua test, which was below 0.025. The authors attribute the observed difference to the RTM effect, leading to LF increasing in the first group, which includes subjects with low baseline levels of LF.

Two analytical strategies have emerged to examine changes between baseline and follow-up measurements of HRV. The first strategy is a one-way repeated measure analysis of variance (repeated-measures ANOVA), and the second is adjusting for baseline HRV data (ANCOVA). ANCOVA enables removal of the RTM effect, and permits estimation of adjusted group means. In this study of HRV reactivity, these two approaches lead to different conclusions: the results of the ANOVA suggest a greater decline of HRV in the third group (very high baseline level), and an increase of HRV variables in the first group (very low baseline level). In contrast, those results obtained using ANCOVA with a correction to baseline level suggest the similarity of reactions in all three groups. A source of difference between these two approaches is that ANOVA results are biased by RTM.

RTM is omnipresent in human studies (Gavish et al., 2011; Guenancia et al., 2013; McCambridge et al., 2014; Margaritelis et al., 2016; Forstmeier et al., 2016; Perry and Karpova, 2017), and the RTM effect can lead the researcher astray. It most commonly occurs in studies where subjects are selected because they exhibited very high or very low baseline values. Thus, participants are only eligible for inclusion in the study group if they have unusually extreme values of RSA or some other variable thought to be related to the stress response. Our results reveal that subjects with an extremely high level of baseline HRV have a more prominent stress response, regardless of the severity of the SA. In this case, individual autonomic flexibility is simply owing to a shift in RSA on the second occasion to the individual mean.

Mee and Chua (1991) presented a modified paired t-test that ensures a computationally simple approach to hypothesis testing, which accounts for the effect of RTM. The main drawback of this method is that it requires knowledge of the true mean μ and variance $\sigma 2$ in the target population. In our research population, mean and variance were estimated from HRV measurements of 1,153 students, and our number of subjects was comparable to those used in other cohort studies of HRV (Kawachi et al., 1995; Tsuji et al., 1996; Sinnreich et al., 1998; Antelmi et al., 2004). However, such data may not always be available, and it is not common to have population data as a basis for stress research protocols. To overcome this problem, Ostermann et al. (2008) developed a straightforward method based on the Mee–Chua modified t-test for the situation, where the population μ is unknown.

RTM is caused by random fluctuations in physiological parameters. Random variation is the substantial feature in HR behaviour (Laitio 2007; Castiglioni et al. 2009). The HRV can be affected by various factors, such as physical activity, caffeine beverages, menstrual cycle, mood, alertness, mental activity, and respiratory rate and depth. It is easy to control for recreational activity, natural cycles, caffeine consumption, and respiration, but we cannot completely rule out that the person's emotional and mental state may bias the results of HRV measurements.

The RTM effect can be corrected by adequate study design and/or appropriate adjustment. It has been recognised that multiple baseline measurements could significantly reduce the RTM effect (Barnett et al., 2005). Because of the study design, we could not implement an RTM correction through multiple baseline measurements, which could be regarded as a limitation of our study. We found it to be evident from a wide variety of research papers that the discussion of RTM affects many fields of physiology. Unfortunately, methods to adjust for RTM are rarely used in the analysis of physiological data. Therefore, we believe that the lack of adjustment for RTM in most of the studies probably leads to a significant bias in the results.

Conclusion

Studies of autonomic reactivity demonstrated that high baseline HRV was associated with a decline in HRV, and subjects with low baseline HRV had an inverse reaction to stress. This suggests that baseline HRV is a marker of stress adaptive capacity. However, the results of our study strongly support an alternative view: RTM is the major source of variability of stress-related changes in HRV, and the effect of baseline HRV level disappears after adjustment for RTM.

ACKNOWLEDGMENTS

The study is externally funded by the Ministry of education and science of the Russian Federation (project 19.9737.2017/BCh, http://www.goszadanie.ru). The funder had no role in study design, data collection and analysis, decision to publish, or preparation of the manuscript.

REFERENCES

Alkozei, A., Creswell, C., Cooper, P. J. & Allen, J. J. (2015). Autonomic arousal in childhood anxiety disorders: associations with state anxiety and social anxiety disorder. *Journal of Affective Disorders*, *175*, 25-33. doi: 10.1016/j.jad.2014.11.056.

Antelmi, I., De Paula, R. S., Shinzato, A. R., Peres, C. A., Mansur, A. J. & Grupi, C. J. (2004). Influence of age, gender, body mass index, and functional capacity on heart rate variability in a cohort of subjects without heart disease. *American Journal of Cardiology*, *93*, 381-385. doi: 10.1016/j.amjcard.2003.09.065.

Barnett, A. G., Van Der Pols, J. C. & Dobson, A. J. (2004). Regression to the mean: what it is and how to deal with it. *International Journal of Epidemiology*, *33*, 215-220.

Beauchaine T. (2001). Vagal tone, development, and Gray's motivational theory: Toward an integrated model of autonomic nervous system functioning in psychopathology. *Development and psychopathology*, *13*, 183-214.

Berntson, G. G. & Cacioppo, J. T. (2004). Heart rate variability: Stress and psychiatric conditions. In: Malik M, Camm AJ (Eds.), *Dynamic electrocardiography*, (pp 57-64). New York, NY: Futura.

Berntson, G. G., Cacioppo, J. T. & Quigley, K. S. (1993). Respiratory sinus arrhythmia: autonomic origins, physiological mechanisms, and psychophysiological implications. *Psychophysiology*, *30*, 183-196.

Billman, G. E. (2013). The LF/HF ratio does not accurately measure cardiac sympatho-vagal balance. *Frontiers in physiology*, *4*, 26. doi: 10.3389/fphys.2013.00026.

Billman, G. E., Huikuri, H. V., Sacha, J. & Trimmel, K. (2015). An introduction to heart rate variability: methodological considerations and clinical applications. *Frontiers in physiology*, *6*, 55. doi: 10.3389/fphys.2015.00055.

Campbell, J. & Ehlert, U. (2012). Acute psychosocial stress: does the emotional stress response correspond with physiological responses? *Psychoneuroendocrinology*, *37*, 1111-1134. doi: /10.1016/j.psyneuen.2011.12.010.

Castaldo, R., Melillo, P., Bracale, U., Caserta, M., Triassi, M. & Pecchia, L. (2015). Acute mental stress assessment via short term HRV analysis in healthy adults: A systematic review with meta-analysis. *Biomedical Signal Processing and Control*, *18*, 370-377. doi: 10.1016/j.bspc.2015.02.012.

Castiglioni, P., Parati, G., Civijian, A., Quintin, L. & Di Rienzo, M. (2009). Local scale exponents of blood pressure and heart rate variability by detrended fluctuation analysis: effects of posture, exercise, and aging. *IEEE Transactions on Biomedical Engineering*, *56*, 675-684. doi: 10.1109/TBME.2008.2005949.

Chalmers, J. A., Quintana, D. S., Maree, J., Abbott, A. & Kemp, A. H. (2014). Anxiety disorders are associated with reduced heart rate variability: a meta-analysis. *Frontiers in psychiatry*, *5*, 80. doi: 10.3389/fpsyt.2014.00080.

Cohen, S., Kessler, R. C. & Gordon, L. U. (1995). Strategies for measuring stress in studies of psychiatric and physical disorders. In: Kessler RC, Gordon UL, Cohen S (Eds.), *Measuring stress: A guide for health and social scientists*, (pp 3-26). New York, NY: Oxford University Press.

Couyoumdjian, A., Ottaviani, C., Petrocchi, N., Trincas, R., Tenore, K., Buonanno, C. & Mancini, F. (2016). Reducing the meta-emotional problem decreases physiological fear response during exposure in phobics. *Frontiers in psychology*, *7*, 1105. doi: 10.3389/ fpsyg.2016.01105.

Das, P. & Mulder, P. G. H. (1983). Regression to the mode. *Statistica Neerlandica*, *37*(1), 15-20.

Davis, C. E. (1976). The effect of regression to the mean in epidemiologic and clinical studies. *American journal of epidemiology*, *104*(5), 493-498.

Davis, C. E. (1976). The effect of regression to the mean in epidemiologic and clinical studies. *American journal of epidemiology*, *104*(5), pp. 493-498.

Dimitriev, D. A., Dimitriev, A. D., Karpenko, Y. D. & Saperova, E. V. (2008). Influence of examination stress and psychoemotional characteristics on the blood pressure and heart rate regulation in female students. *Human Physiology*, *34*, 617-624.

Dimitriev, D. A., Saperova, E. V. & Dimitriev, A. D. (2016). State anxiety and nonlinear dynamics of heart rate variability in students. *PloS one*, *11*, e0146131. doi: 10.1371/journal.pone.0146131.

Dimitriev, D. A., Saperova, E. V., Dimitriev, A. D. & Karpenko, I. (2007). Features of cardiovascular functioning during different phases of the menstrual cycle. *Rossiiskii fiziologicheskii zhurnal imeni IM Sechenova*, *93*, pp.300-305.

Forstmeier, W., Wagenmakers, E. J. & Parker, T. H. (2016). Detecting and avoiding likely false-positive findings—a practical guide. *Biological reviews*, *92*, 1941-1968. doi:10.1111/brv.12315.

Fortunato, C. K., Gatzke-Kopp, L. M. & Ram, N. (2013). Associations between respiratory sinus arrhythmia reactivity and internalizing and externalizing symptoms are emotion specific. *Cognitive, Affective, & Behavioral Neuroscience*, *13*, 238-251. doi: 10.3758/s13415-012-0136-4.

Friedman, B. H. & Thayer, J. F. (1998). Anxiety and autonomic flexibility: a cardiovascular approach. *Biological psychology*, *47*, 243-263.

Fung, B. J., Crone, D. L., Bode, S. & Murawski, C. (2017). Cardiac signals are independently associated with temporal discounting and time perception. *Frontiers in behavioral neuroscience*, *11*, 1. doi: 10.3389/fnbeh.2017.00001.

Galton, F. (1886). Regression towards mediocrity in hereditary stature. *The Journal of the Anthropological Institute of Great Britain and Ireland, 15*, 246-263.

Gavish, B., Alter, A., Barkai, Y., Rachima-Maoz, C., Peleg, E. & Rosenthal, T. (2011). Effect of non-drug interventions on arterial properties determined from 24-h ambulatory blood pressure measurements. *Hypertension Research, 34*, 1233-1238. doi: 10.1038/hr.2011.125.

Gerra, G., Zaimovic, A., Zambelli, U., Timpano, M., Reali, N., Bernasconi, S. & Brambilla, F. (2000). Neuroendocrine responses to psychological stress in adolescents with anxiety disorder. *Neuropsychobiology, 42*, 82-92.

Gorka, S. M., Nelson, B. D., Sarapas, C., Campbell, M., Lewis, G. F., Bishop, J. R. & Shankman, S. A. (2013). Relation between respiratory sinus arrythymia and startle response during predictable and unpredictable threat. *Journal of psychophysiology, 27*, 95-104. doi: 10.1027/0269-8803/a000091.

Gotfredsen, A., Bæksgaard, L. & Hilsted, J. (1997). Body composition analysis by DEXA by using dynamically changing samarium filtration. *Journal of Applied Physiology, 82*, 1200-1209.

Gross, J. J., Richards, J. M. & John, O. P. (2006). Emotion regulation in everyday life. In: Snyder DK, Simpson JE, Hughes JN (Eds) Emotion regulation in couples and families: Pathways to dysfunction and health, (pp. 13-35). Washington, DC: American Psychological Association.

Guenancia, C., Cochet, A., Humbert, O., Dygai-Cochet, I., Lorgis, L., Zeller, M. & Cottin, Y. (2013). Predictors of post-stress LVEF drop 6 months after reperfused myocardial infarction: a gated myocardial perfusion SPECT study. *Annals of nuclear medicine, 27*, 112-122., doi: 10.1007/s12149-012-0661-9.

Hamilton, J. L. & Alloy, L. B. (2016). Atypical reactivity of heart rate variability to stress and depression across development: Systematic review of the literature and directions for future research. *Clinical psychology review, 50*, 67-79. doi: 10.1016/j.cpr.2016.09.003.

Hanin, Y. L. (1976). Quick Guide to the application of the scale of reactive and personal anxiety BH Spielberger. Leningrad, LO: LNIIFK,

Kawachi, I., Sparrow, D., Vokonas, P. S. & Weiss, S. T. (1995). Decreased heart rate variability in men with phobic anxiety (data from the Normative Aging Study). *The American journal of cardiology, 75,* 882-885.

Kok, B. E. & Fredrickson, B. L. (2010). Upward spirals of the heart: Autonomic flexibility, as indexed by vagal tone, reciprocally and prospectively predicts positive emotions and social connectedness. *Biological psychology, 85,* 432-436. doi: 10.1016/ j.biopsycho. 2010.09.005.

Kossowsky, J., Wilhelm, F. H., Roth, W. T. & Schneider, S. (2012). Separation anxiety disorder in children: disorder-specific responses to experimental separation from the mother. *Journal of Child Psychology and Psychiatry, 53,* 178-187. doi: 10.1111/j.1469-7610.2011.02465.x.

Kristensen, H., Oerbeck, B., Torgersen, H. S., Hansen, B. H. & Wyller, V. B. (2014). Somatic symptoms in children with anxiety disorders: an exploratory cross-sectional study of the relationship between subjective and objective measures. *European child & adolescent psychiatry, 23,* 795-803. doi: 10.1007/s00787-013-0512-9.

Laitio, T., Jalonen, J., Kuusela, T. & Scheinin, H. (2007). The role of heart rate variability in risk stratification for adverse postoperative cardiac events. *Anesthesia & Analgesia, 105,* 1548-1560. doi: 10.1213/ 01.ane.0000287654.49358.3a

Licht, C. M., De Geus, E. J., Van Dyck, R. & Penninx, B. W. (2009). Association between anxiety disorders and heart rate variability in The Netherlands Study of Depression and Anxiety (NESDA). *Psychosomatic medicine, 71,* 508-518. doi: 10.1097/ PSY.0b013e3181 a292a6.

Lin, H. M. & Hughes, M. D. (1997). Adjusting for regression toward the mean when variables are normally distributed. *Statistical Methods in Medical Research, 6,* 129-146.

Machin, D., Campbell, M. J., Tan, S. B. & Tan, S. H. (2018). Sample Sizes for Clinical, Laboratory and Epidemiology Studies. Oxford, OX: John Wiley & Sons.

Margaritelis, N. V., Theodorou, A. A., Paschalis, V., Veskoukis, A. S., Dipla, K., Zafeiridis, A. & Nikolaidis, M. G. (2016). Experimental verification of regression to the mean in redox biology: differential responses to exercise. *Free radical research*, *50*, 1237-1244. doi: 10.1080/10715762.2016.1233330.

McCambridge, J., Kypri, K. & McElduff, P. (2014). Regression to the mean and alcohol con-sumption: a cohort study exploring implications for the interpretation of change in control groups in brief intervention trials. *Drug and alcohol dependence*, *135*, pp. 156-159. doi: 10.1016/j.drugalcdep.2013.11.017.

Mee, R. W. & Chua, T. C. (1991). Regression toward the mean and the paired sample t test. *The American Statistician*, *45*, 39-42.

Miu, A. C., Heilman, R. M. & Miclea, M. (2009). Reduced heart rate variability and vagal tone in anxiety: trait versus state, and the effects of autogenic training. *Autonomic Neuroscience*, *145*, 99-103. doi: 10.1016/j.autneu.2008.11.010.

Ostermann, T., Willich, S. N. & Lüdtke, R. (2008). Regression toward the mean—a detection method for unknown population mean based on Mee and Chua's algorithm. *BMC medical research methodology*, *8*(1), p.52. doi:10.1186/1471-2288-8-52.

Perry, A. & Karpova, E. (2017). Efficacy of teaching creative thinking skills: A comparison of multiple creativity assessments. *Thinking Skills and Creativity*, *24*, 118-126.

Ramshur, J. T. (2010). Design, evaluation, and application of heart rate variability analysis software (HRVAS) (Doctoral dissertation, University of Memphis).

Rottenberg, J., Clift, A., Bolden, S. & Salomon, K. (2007). RSA fluctuation in major depressive disorder. *Psychophysiology*, *44*, 450-458. doi: 10.1111/j.1469-8986.2007.00509.x.

Schneider, C., Wiewelhove, T., Raeder, C., Flatt, A. A., Hoos, O., Hottenrott, L. & Ferrauti, A. (2019). Heart Rate Variability Monitoring During Strength and High-Intensity Interval Training Overload Microcycles. *Frontiers in physiology*, *10*, 582.

Senn, S. (1990). Regression: a new mode for an old meaning? *The American Statistician*, *44*(2), 181-183.

Spangler, D. P., Bell, M. A. & Deater-Deckard, K. (2015). Emotion suppression moderates the quadratic association between RSA and executive function. *Psychophysiology*, *52*, 1175-1185. doi: 10.1111/psyp.12451.

Thayer, J. F. & Lane, R. D. (2000). A model of neurovisceral integration in emotion regulation and dysregulation. *Journal of affective disorders*, *61*, 201-216.

Tsuji, H., Larson, M. G., Venditti, F. J., Manders, E. S., Evans, J. C., Feldman, C. L. & Levy, D. (1996). Impact of reduced heart rate variability on risk for cardiac events. *Circulation*, *94*(11), 2850-2855.

Wang, Z., Lü, W. & Qin, R. (2013). Respiratory sinus arrhythmia is associated with trait positive affect and positive emotional expressivity. *Biological psychology*, *93*, 190-196. doi:10.1016/j.biopsycho.2012.12.006.

BIOGRAPHICAL SKETCH

Name: Dimitriy Dimitriev

Affiliation: Department of Biology, Chuvash State Pedagogical University named I Ya Yakovlev, Cheboksary, Russia

Education: I.M. Sechenov First Moscow State Medical University (Sechenov University)

Business Address: st. K. Marx, 38, Cheboksary, Chuvash Republic, 428000.

Research and Professional Experience: Head of physiology laboratory

Professional Appointments:
Honors:
Publications from the Last 3 Years:
https://scholar.google.com/citations?hl=en&user=caDDA3UAAAAJ&view_op=list_works&sortby=pubdate

In: A Closer Look at Heart Rate
Editor: André Alves Pereira

ISBN: 978-1-53616-979-9
© 2020 Nova Science Publishers, Inc.

Chapter 3

PREVIOUSLY UNRECOGNIZED FETAL BEHAVIOR WITH PRE- AND POSTNATAL CARDIORESPIRATORY IMPLICATIONS

Patrick A. Zemb[1,*], Tarik El Aarbaoui[2], Jean-Yves Bellec[3], Pauline Lelièvre[4], Marie-Laure Mille[5] and Fabrice Joulia[6]

[1]Private obstetrical practice Bove, Lorient, France
Mother-Child unit, Groupe hospitalier Bretagne Sud, Lorient, France
[2]National Center for Scientific Research, Maurice Halbwachs Center, Paris, France
[3]Private obstetrical practice Bove, Lorient, France
[4]French state registered midwife, qualified ultrasonography operator, Private obstetrical practice Bove, Lorient, France
[5]Institute of Movement Sciences, Aix-Marseille University, France
Physical therapy & Human movement Sciences, Northwestern University, Chicago, US
[6]Cardiovascular and Nutritional Research Center, Aix-Marseille University, France

---

[*] Corresponding author: E-mail: patrick.zemb@orange.fr.

Abstract

After 30 weeks, fetal behavior progressively changes and differentiates into three main states: active sleep, quiet sleep, and active wakefulness. Each state is associated with a characteristic fetal heart rate (FHR) pattern, mainly in a physiological context. Quiet sleep has been linked with parasympathetic dominance and gives rise to a specific heart-rate pattern named "Pattern A" (PA), defined by the seven following diagnostic criteria: ± 20-minute duration, reduced episodic accelerations, reduced maternal perception of fetal mobility, lower long- and short-term variability (STV) than in adjacent sequences, narrow oscillation bandwidth, and homogeneous aspect. Two homogeneous PA variants have already been identified: the "High-STV" variant and the "Oscillatory baseline" variant. Each differs in its own way from PA with respect to criteria 5 and 6.

We analyzed 14,000 antepartum FHR tracings obtained during 2,000 pregnancies (>30 weeks; high-risk cases included). This analysis led us to identify a heterogeneous PA variant called "Meta-Pattern A" (Meta-PA) in which criterion 7 differed from conventional quiet-sleep patterns. The Meta-PA was characterized by a "saltatory variability and baseline" pattern (SVBP), defined by a saltatory succession of short FHR sequences presenting with high- and low-STV (saltation> 50 centiles identified by computerized analysis over one-minute windows), and with saltatory FHR baseline (> 4 beats/minute). Typically, Meta-PA covers 4 to 6 saltatory sequences, lasting 2 to 10 minutes each. In our database, the Meta-PA/typical PA ratio is around 1/20 and 1/10 for the attenuated Meta-PA (smaller saltations).

Meta-PA could reflect a specific fetal oxygen-conserving mechanism during quiet sleep. This mechanism could trigger a major conflict between the parasympathetic inhibition required by the oxygen-conserving mechanism and the physiologically high parasympathetic activation during quiet sleep, specifically when the underlying cortisol level is high. The two high- and low-STV components of Meta-PA could be respectively related to an alternate sympathovagal antagonism and sympathovagal inhibition.

We have named "Meta-quiet sleep" (Meta-QS) the specific fetal behavior linked with Meta-PA. Recognizing Meta-QS could help assess fetal and placental status. Moreover, an inappropriate postnatal resurgence of Meta-QS could well be the cause of sudden infant death syndrome. This article reviews the place of Meta-PA among other quiet-sleep patterns and describes the main fetal pathways interfering with our understanding of Meta-QS.

INTRODUCTION

Given the respective sizes of the female pelvis and the fetal head, surviving the delivery process is a major challenge for the human fetus, all the more since the uterine contractions induce a transient weakening of maternal-fetal exchanges [1].

Compared to other species, the human newborn has an extremely low degree of autonomy [2]; instruments and surgical procedures are often required during delivery. To face this epic challenge, the human fetus has to make the most of any adaptative pathway available, thus inducing major interferences between the metabolism, growth, oxygen-conserving mechanisms, and each fetal behavioral state.

Behavioral states were identified in the infant some time ago when electro-encephalography (EEG) became increasingly popular [3]. A few years later, Junge *et al.* were the first to suspect that these behavioral states could be pre-existent in the fetus [4], a hypothesis which has since been confirmed [5]. Among the five postnatal behavioral states identified, three have been consensually recognized in the fetus during the last weeks of pregnancy: quiet sleep (QS), active sleep, and active wakefulness. Robust ultrasound identification criteria became rapidly available for fetal behavioral states: simultaneous recordings of the fetal heart rate and fetal movements at the level of the eyes, body, limbs and chest wall. This procedure is however rather fastidious, particularly the prolonged monitoring of fetal eye movements, hence the lack of robust recent data concerning the antepartum observation of each fetal behavioral state. Most studies have been conducted in antepartum physiological situations [5-13] and only few address pathological situations (fetal growth retardation [14], maternal diabetes mellitus [15], cocaine interference [16]). Some were undertaken intrapartum [17]. One outcome of this "gold standard" methodology was to determine coincidence rates, with full coincidence between fetal heart rate and fetal movements corresponding to a given behavioral state [14]. Phases of coincidence and non-coincidence have been extensively studied in the neonate using simultaneous EEG [18].

In an attempt to simplify simultaneous fetal investigations, ultrasonic "actocardiography" was introduced 2 decades ago [19], but it does not allow the detection of eyes movements. Regarding the accuracy of fetal beat-to-beat R-R measurements, ultrasonography has been supplanted by magnetocardiography [20] and electrocardiography [21]. However, neither technique provides a proper screening of fetal eyes movements, which remains difficult for practical reasons [22]. These techniques are therefore liable of introducing biases, as we will see in the QS discussion. Indeed, these biaises mean that certain fetal behavioral strategies may have been overlooked, notably those reflected by unclassified patterns.

1. Quiet-Sleep Patterns

As far as we know, the only specific study of QS patterns in "gold-standard" conditions to have been undertaken until now was that of Van Woerden *et al.* in 1988 [9]. Four types of QS patterns were identified, none of them involving the observation of rapid-eye movements.

1.1. Typical Quiet-Sleep Pattern A (Van Woerden Type 1)

Most often, quiet sleep gives rise to a specific heart-rate pattern named "Pattern A", and defined by the seven following diagnostic criteria: ± 20-minute duration; non-existent, weaker or shorter episodic accelerations; lesser maternal perception of fetal mobility; relatively low long- and short-term variability (STV); narrow oscillation bandwidth; and what could be called a homogeneous aspect [23, 24]. This corresponds to the type 1 observed by Van Woerden in 1988. Although STV was not one of the data computed by Van Woerden, one can still verify on the relevant tracings that Pattern-A STV (as calculated by the SisPorto software, 2011 version) is constantly lower than in adjacent segments. A typical Pattern A can be seen in the first Figure-1 tracing.

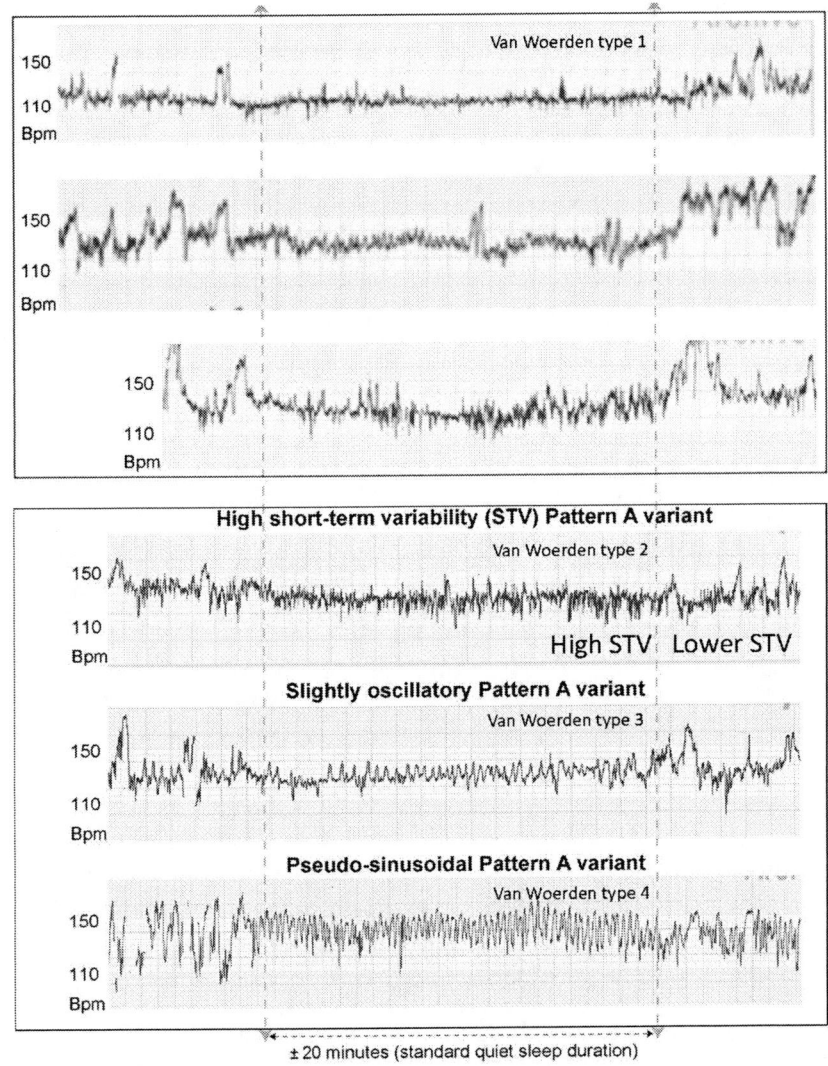

Figure 1. Homogeneous Pattern A variants (increasing deviation from typical Pattern A).

In physiological conditions, Pattern A is consensually considered as being under parasympathetic dominance, although sympathovagal balance indexes vary with the authors: Goncalves *et al.*, for instance, use the ratio of high-frequency/middle- and low-frequency power [23] whereas

Schneider *et al.* prefer the standard deviation of NN intervals (SDNN)/root mean square of successive differences, RMSSD [25].

We have shown [26] that an entropy peak (Sample Entropy 2,0.15) can be observed in the center of typical Patterns A. Furthermore, we believe that there might be a chronological and physiological correlation between the entropy peak we observed and the middle cerebral artery (MCA) resistance index peak observed during typical QS [27].

1.2. High-STV Pattern-A Variant (Van Woerden Type 2)

This pattern diverges from conventional Pattern-A by its visibly increased STV, as described in Van Woerden's publication (Type-2 QS pattern). Specific breathing movements associated to this pattern have been observed. Computing STV in similar tracings confirms this remarkable STV increase, to the point of becoming higher than in adjacent sequences. This leads to a specific inversion of the QS/AS STV ratio. In Figure 1, the fourth tracing displays a typical High-STV Pattern-A variant.

We suspect a connection between Type-2 QS patterns and a certain mild fetal metabolic syndrome. The high STV observed could reflect an accentuated norepinephrine release and a greater parasympathetic stimulation during QS, contrasting with the lesser expression of norepinephrine during active sleep. Our interpretation is supported by the observation that fetal breathing movements are usually less frequent during QS than active sleep. However, this ratio is inversed in those few fetuses with the most frequent breathing movements (aimed at raising fetal energy expenditure) [28].

Postnatal studies exploring STV during QS are rare [29]. It has been suggested that the high-frequency spectral power of heart rate variability was clinically similar to time-domain STV. Compared to the STV observed during AS, the QS STV was found to be either equivalent, or increased. This would mean that neonatal QS patterns were nearer to type-2 than type-1 Van Woerden QS patterns.

1.3. "Oscillatory-Baseline" Pattern-A Variant (Van Woerden Type 3 and 4)

Extensive studies of this pseudo-sinusoidal pattern have led us to distinguish it from the pre-agony sinusoidal pattern, which has a lower oscillatory frequency and lasts longer. Observed pseudo-sinusoidal patterns were associated with mouthing (Van Woerden type-3) or sucking (Van Woerden type-4) movements. The fifth and sixth tracings of Figure 1 display both typical oscillatory-baseline Pattern-A variants. In our experience, these patterns also occur with another type of mild fetal or maternal metabolic syndrome. Interestingly, this Pattern-A variant differs fundamentally from the "Meta-Pattern A" presented below. Note that pacifiers, which stimulate non-nutritional sucking, have a recognized protective effect against SIDS [30].

1.4. "Meta-Pattern A" A Specific Variant of Heterogeneous Pattern A

We analyzed 14,000 antepartum FHR tracings obtained during 2,000 pregnancies (>30 weeks; high-risk cases included). This analysis led us to identify an unrecognized pattern that we propose to call "Meta-Pattern A" (Meta-PA). This differed frankly from the highly homogeneous conventional QS patterns: clearly heterogeneous, Meta-PA was also characterized by its saltatory variability and baseline. Indeed, one notes a succession of short saltatory FHR sequences presenting with high- and low-STV (saltation> 50 centiles identified by computed analysis over one-minute windows) as well as the presence of a saltatory FHR baseline (> 4 beats/minute). Typically, the Meta-PA variant covers 4 to 6 saltatory sequences, lasting 2 to 10 minutes each. In our database, the Meta-PA/typical PA ratio is approximately 1/20. The last three tracings in Figure 2 show typical Meta-Patterns A.

Attenuated Meta-PAs are visible on the first three tracings in Figure 2. These correspond to a mild form of heterogeneous Pattern-A variant, the

STV-saltation and baseline-saltation staying below the proposed threshold. In our database, the attenuated-meta-PA/typical PA ratio is approximately 1/10. The extensive range of attenuated-meta-PA intermediates, ranging from typical Pattern-A to Meta-PA, is a strong argument to consider them all as reflecting behavioral quiet sleep. Attenuated Meta-PA could be the prenatal equivalent of the specific neonatal QS behavioral state characterized by periodic breathing [31].

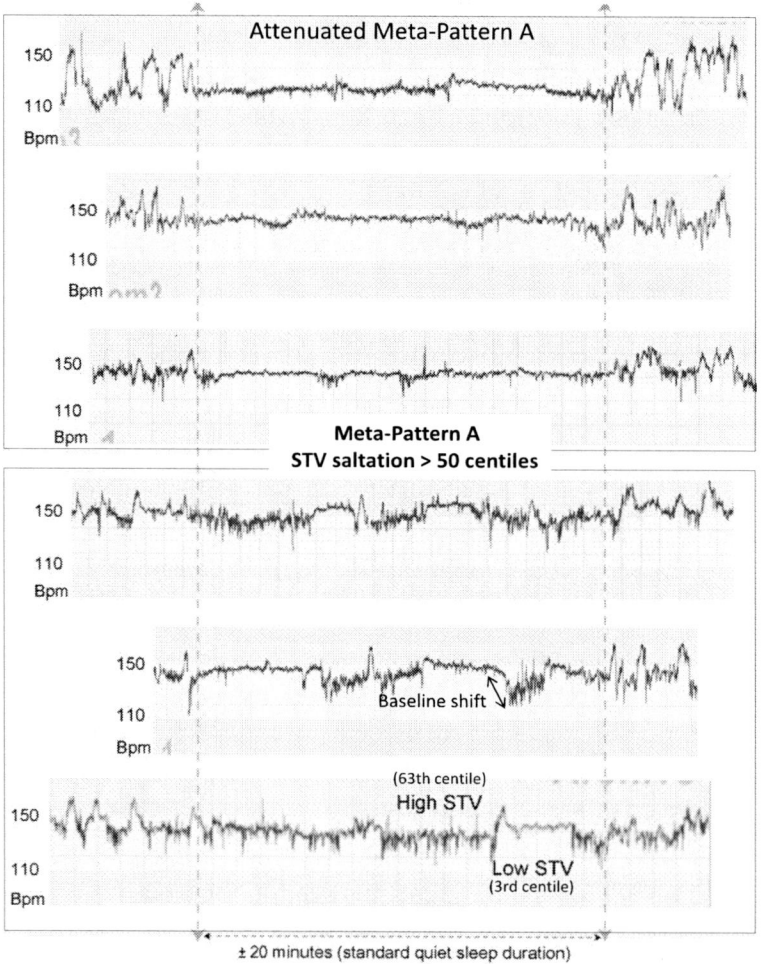

Figure 2. Heterogeneous Pattern A variants (increasing deviation from typical Pattern A).

Historically, we first observed Meta-PA in 2007 whilst searching for a pattern reflecting the unusual mix of a reduced energy consumption (a well-known feature in the end-stage of pregnancy) and the stress-induced cortisol release which signs the progression towards labor (as discussed below). Our attention was attracted by the low-STV component of the Meta-PA variant – probably reflecting fetal "lethargy" – and the upward baseline shift of the corresponding FHR sequence. We were particularly interested by the crenellated aspect of the upshift which probably reflected a transient parasympathetic collapse [32]. In 2013, we detected the high-STV component of Meta-PA and noticed that the entire pattern (both components included) always lasted as long as conventional Pattern A. We then performed an entropic analysis comparing typical Patterns A and Meta-PA. In 2015, we realized that the high-STV component was most probably due to a norepinephrine-parasympathetic co-activation. In 2018, we carried out an identification of Pattern A and all its variants in blinded conditions [33]. In the first semester of 2019, we conducted a wavelet transform spectral analysis of our selected patterns (Figure 3).

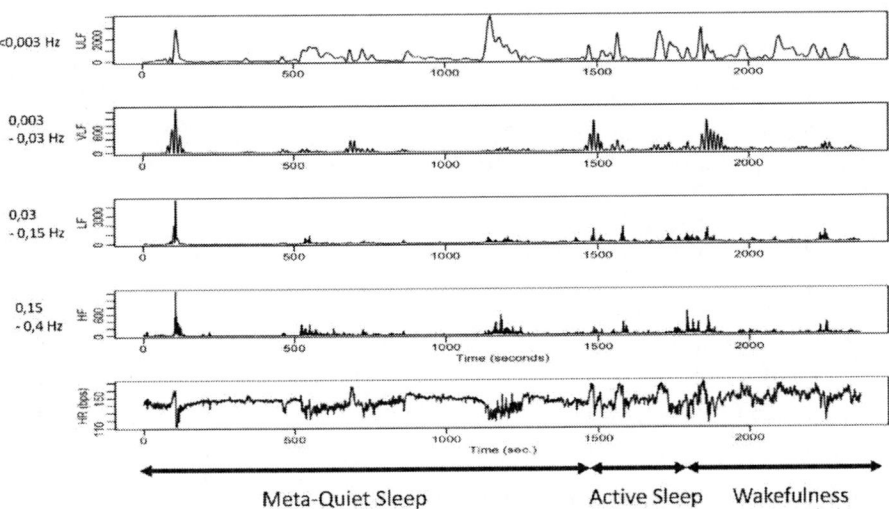

Algorithm written by Tarik El Aarbaoui (R-HRV software)

Figure 3. Wavelet-transform spectral analysis of Meta-Pattern A.

It is suspected that Meta-PA could reflect a specific fetal oxygen-conserving mechanism during quiet sleep. This mechanism would then trigger a major conflict between the parasympathetic inhibition required by the fetal oxygen-conserving mechanism and the physiologically high parasympathetic activation characteristic of quiet sleep, particularly when cortisol levels are high. The two high- and low-STV components of Meta-PA could be related to alternate norepinephrine-parasympathetic respective antagonism and inhibition.

The evolution of approximate and sample entropy during Meta-PA has been demonstrated as unstable, with minimum values tending to coincide with the STV saltations [26]. Interestingly, entropy tends to increase in the middle of each Meta-PA component, reproducing on a smaller scale what is observed in typical Patterns A.

We suspect several situations of encouraging the emergence of Meta-PA, notably in case of a relatively high overall STV, hypoxic stimulation or high cortisol levels. Cortisol is suspected of enhancing fetal oxygen-conserving mechanisms, notably by potentiating parasympathetic inhibition. Also, the enhanced cortisol/epinephrine sequence could explain why a transient, if attenuated, acceleration of cardiac frequency is visible in Meta-PA during QS (as observed in the last three Figure-2 tracings).

We propose to name "Meta Quiet Sleep" (Meta-QS) the behavioral sequence underlying MetaPattern A, despite our lack of EEG and non-REM references. We suspect that, during Meta-QS, cerebral activity diverges considerably from that observed in usual QS behavior. Nevertheless, Meta-QS undoubtedly has more connections with Quiet Sleep than with any other state, as demonstrated by the seven following arguments: (1) same duration; (2) existence of intermediary forms; (3) rarity of transient cardiac frequency accelerations; (4) similarity between Meta-PA high-STV component and Van Woerden's type-2 QS pattern; (5) even lower STV in Meta-PA low-STV component than in Van Woerden type-1 QS pattern; (6) similar entropic evolution between each Meta-QS component and typical Patterns A; and (7) absence of fetal movements perceived by the mother.

Since our 2013 publication, our postulate is that Sudden Infant Death Syndrome (SIDS) could be due to a postnatal resurgence of an underlying Meta-QS mechanism. Extensive argumentation goes beyond the goal of this chapter. However, the following notions pertaining to SIDS may suggest a few links with our Meta-QS interpretation: (1) SIDS is suspected of occurring during QS [34]; (2) Hypoxia is thought to play a part in SIDS [35]; (3) The entropic evolution of QS in future SIDS infants compared to the controls is similar to that observed in Meta-PA with respect to typical Patterns A [36, 26]; (4) The frequency peak of SIDS at 3 months of postnatal life could be related to the onset of fairly unbroken sleep and its inherent late-night cortisol peak, similar to the fetal cortisol peak observed at the end of pregnancy.

Note that, in rare cases, saltatory-STV without a saltatory baseline can be observed during an otherwise typical Pattern A. This is illustrated in Figure 4. In this case, one pregnant woman chose an excessively supine position at the beginning of the recording and suffered from the well-known malaise induced by inferior vena cava compression around the middle part of Pattern-A, before changing position. During this maternal malaise, although the fetus must have faced acute hypoxic stimulation, it did not respond by the classical diving reflex. Instead, it responded by a paroxysmal high-STV without baseline shift, thus creating a saltatory-STV mini-pattern that will be explained below. This observation supports our postulate that the heterogeneity of Meta-PA is more a reflection of a specific central cycle than a response to acute extemporaneous events.

2. OVERVIEW OF FACTORS INTERFERING WITH THE INTERPRETATION OF META-QS

2.1. Saltatory STV Observed in Other Behavioral States

Aside the saltatory-baseline and saltatory STV observed during Meta-QS, saltatory STV "mini-patterns" (without saltatory-STV) are not uncommon on FHR tracings.

The main high-STV component of the saltatory-STV mini-pattern is underlined by (*).

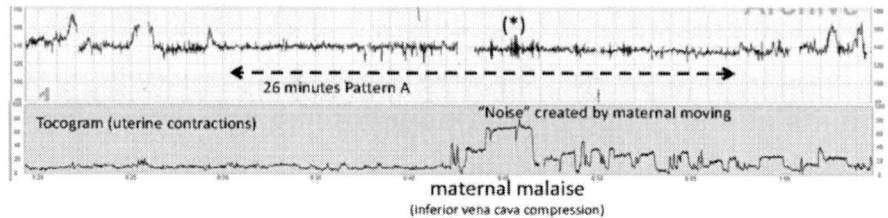

Zoom (x 8) centered on (*)
showing that the spectral power peak is situated in the Very-High Frequency Band (± 0,8 Hz)

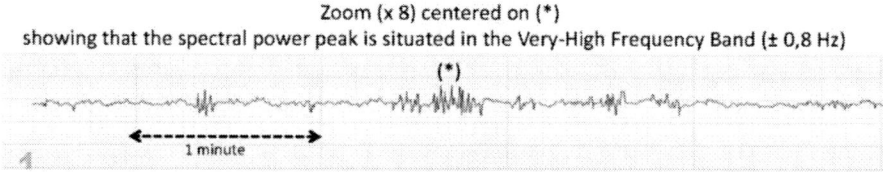

Note there is no baseline shift (a fundamental difference with Meta-Pattern A)

Figure 4. Hypoxia-induced Saltatory-STV mini-pattern within Pattern A (quiet sleep).

In our database, we also analyzed any tracing with a potential saltatory STV evolution. This led us to note that, in all tracings, the highest and lowest paroxysmal STV sequences were quite often unexpectedly adjacent which, in turn, led us to postulate that this could well be an oxygen-conserving pathway. We have not yet carried out an objective assessment of this postulate, but we have collected typical examples of such "saltatory-STV mini-patterns" which we have classified according to the suspected underlying fetal behavior.

2.1.1. Saltatory STV during Active-Sleep Patterns

Active sleep (or behavioral state 2F) conventionally gives rise to "Pattern B" which is characterized by a relative baseline stability and transient heart rate accelerations. A paroxysmal high-STV sequence can be observed during Pattern-B sequences.

The peak visible to the naked eye on enlarged tracings was confirmed by wavelet-transform spectral analysis which evidenced a very-high-frequency peak of approximately 1 Hz.

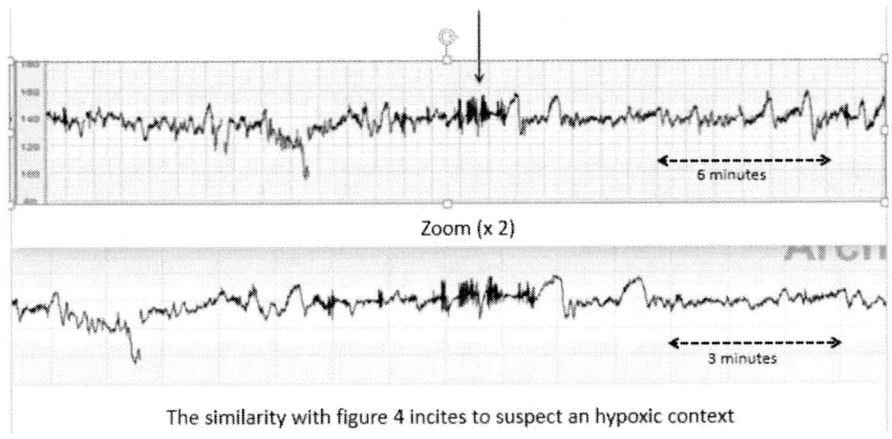

Figure 5. Spontaneous Saltatory-STV mini-pattern within Pattern B (active sleep).

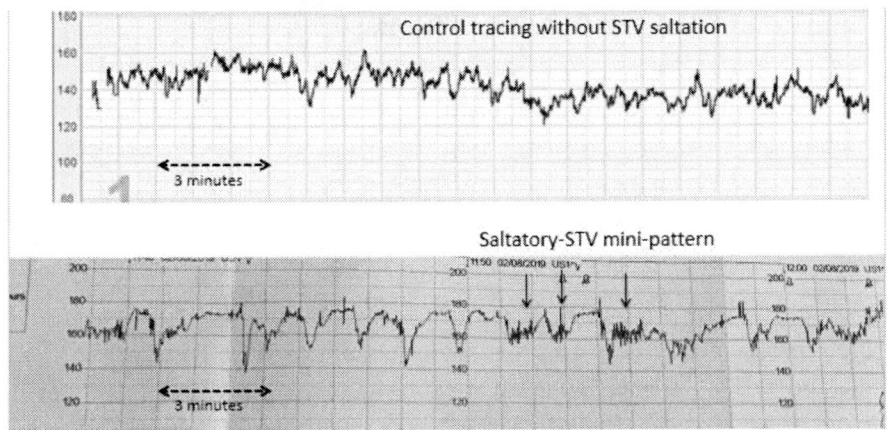

Figure 6. Identifiable Saltatory-STV mini-pattern within Pattern D (wakefulness).

2.1.2. Saltatory STV during Wakefulness Patterns

The rarest in the overall population [23], this behavioral state (or behavioral state 4F) gives rise to "pattern D", characterized by ultra-low frequency baseline fluctuations.

It is thought that these fluctuations could result from a thyroid-dependent thermoregulation process [37]. In our experience, the occurrence of Pattern D tracings is increased in case of maternal or fetal metabolic syndrome. The pathophysiology of this suspected association could be related to the disrupted thyroid profile observed in adults with uncomplicated cases of excess weight [38]. In adults, the energy expenditure is greater during wakefulness than in sleep. It is thought that, those fetuses showing numerous wakefulness episodes on their recordings tend to use the most energy possible to avoid hyperglycemia and excessive weight gain.

It seems that the cerebral cycle of these fetuses is essentially orientated towards wakefulness, and that they are thus unable to sufficiently increase their periods of active sleep and quiet sleep to avoid hypoxia. Indeed, they have no other option than to implement oxygen-conserving mechanisms during wakefulness states. This pathway could be reflected by the emergence of a saltatory-STV which is slightly difficult to evidence due to baseline fluctuations. Luckily, computed analysis could allow the detection of this type of saltatory STV patterns (Figure 6).

Also, in the last stages of pregnancy and even more so during labor, these fetuses can maintain the typical wakefulness oscillatory baseline, but with a lesser bandwidth. The corresponding visual aspect may be confused with pre-terminal sinusoidal tracings [39].

2.1.3. Saltatory STV during Unclassified Behavioral States

Figure 8 presents typical examples of saltatory-STV patterns extracted from our database. Interestingly, a similar case has been documented using quasi-simultaneous fetal electrocardiography to confirm not only that the high-STV sequences are not artifact-related, but also that they are extreme examples of sinus arrhythmia with P-wave polymorphism [40]. Note that the corresponding pregnancy was not concluded by intrapartum fetal hypoxia, a conclusion which does not mean that the fetal response was not partially due to hypoxic stimulation. Detectable both visually and by wavelet-transform spectral analysis, the spectral power is situated in the very-high frequency band (around 1 Hz).

Another kind of saltatory-STV tracing provides an interesting comparison with the above tracings: this antepartum recording was made on an obese woman who smoked, suffered from severe diabetes mellitus and was not followed medically. Paroxysmal deviant-STV sequences were here represented by low-STV sequences instead of high ones. This kind of tracing could help answer the issue of the false negatives found when using conventional FHR-analysis methodology. In these cases, despite the fact that the overall STV remains high, hypoxia is most likely to be present, even in the absence of all the usual FHR signs of hypoxia (no decelerations notably)

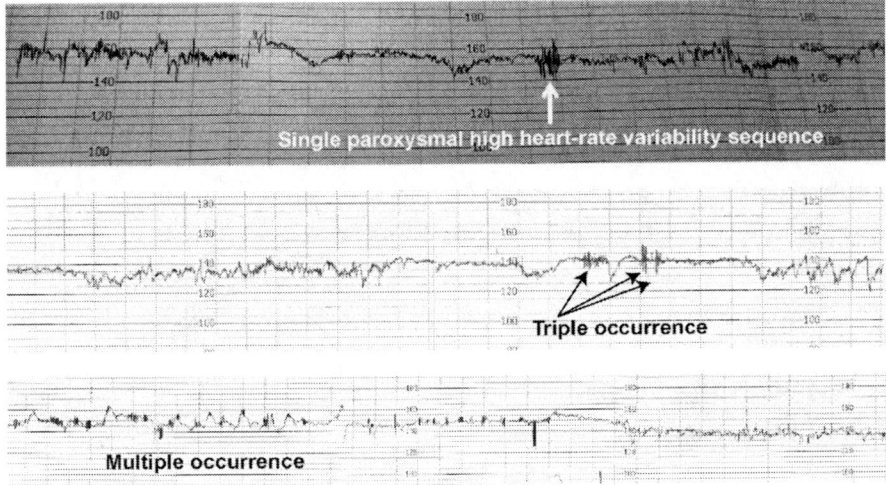

Figure 7. Accentuated forms of Saltatory-STV mini-patterns (unclassified behavioral state context).

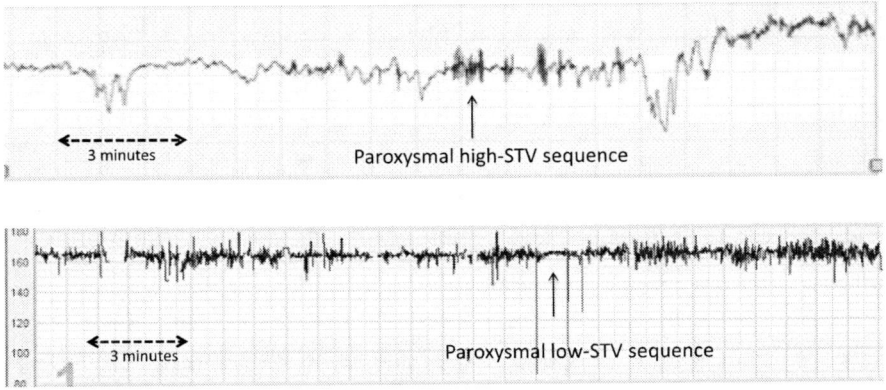

Figure 8. Predominance of low- or high-variability sequences in saltatory variability mini-patterns.

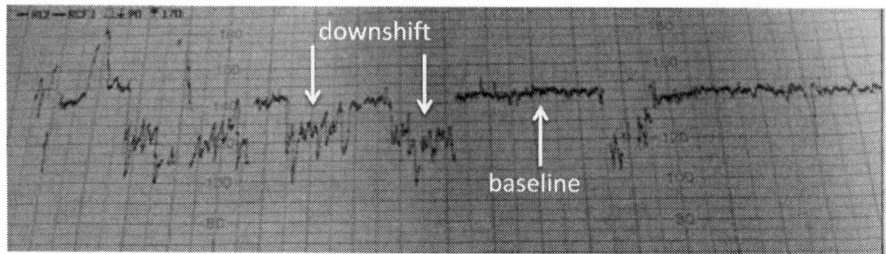

Figure 9. A saltatory-baseline shift and saltatory STV outside Meta-Pattern A.

In our database, the only occurrence of a combined STV- and baseline-saltation, outside Meta-PA, is visible in Figure 8. It was observed at 35 weeks during an unclassified fetal behavioral state in a woman with a highly pathological pregnancy. Note that the high-STV component differs here from that observed in Meta-PA. Moreover, it is similar to the diving reflex shown in Figure 10.

2.2. Meta-Quiet Sleep and Fetal Oxygen-Conserving Mechanisms

The interpretation of Meta-QS needs to take into account the effects of hypoxic stimulation on the fetal heart rate.

2.2.1. Mediators Involved in Fetal Oxygen Conserving Mechanisms

The fetal response to hypoxia is mediated by local responses at tissue level, and by the activation of carotid chemoreceptors, which, in turn, trigger both a sympathetic and a parasympathetic afferent input [41]. After central processing, efferent fetal signaling combines with local hypoxia-induced changes to produce a multiple and complex purinergic co-transmission [42] which has different expressions, depending on the part of the body. At cardiac level, an interference of the intrinsic cardiac neural network is suspected, independently of any sympathetic innervation [43].

2.2.2. The Dual Fetal STV-Response to Hypoxia

The dual FHR response to hypoxia has been studied extensively in animals, notably in sheep. It involves an initial STV increase in response to the acute hypoxia, and a secondary STV decrease in response to the chronic hypoxia [44, 45]. However, data concerning the human fetus are sparse. Furthermore, the fetal responses of humans and sheep are different and the meaning of this difference between species is unclear [46]. It is therefore difficult to predict whether fetal intrapartum hypoxia or acidosis will be associated to an STV-increase or reduction [47-49].

2.2.3. Understanding the Acute Hypoxia-Induced High-STV Phase

As detailed below, both the release of norepinephrine and the parasympathetic inhibition are fundamental components of chronic oxygen-conserving mechanisms. However, any release of norepinephrine is likely to induce a reflex rise in parasympathetic activity by stimulation of the baroreceptors [50]. The norepinephrine/parasympathetic co-activation tends to create an "autonomic conflict", leading to a paroxysmal instability of the fetal heart rate, namely a considerable STV [51, 52]. This paradoxical sympathovagal co-activation became a topic of interest several decades ago [53, 54]. To our knowledge, Mikko P. Tulppo *et al.* were the first to observe and analyze extensively the effects of a norepinephrine infusion on healthy subjects [51] and we owe them the expression "sympathoval antagonism". This antagonism has even been suspected of inducing cardiac arrhythmia [55]. Other situations of sympathovagal co-activation have since been recognized, notably cold-face stress [56, 57], trigeminocardiac reflex [58], oculocardiac reflex [52], onset of sleep apnea [59], immediate recovery from physical exercise [60], and paradoxical response to low-dose atropine [61] or low-dose epinephrine [62]. Note that sympathovagal antagonism can produce inspiratory gasping and involuntary hyperventilation [57].

2.2.4. Understanding the Acute Hypoxia-Induced Low-STV Phase

Such a violent fetal sympathovagal co-activation will most likely be followed by a drastic parasympathetic inhibition, particularly since the latter is essential for survival. Given the short half-life of acetylcholine, this parasympathetic inhibition is likely to occur extremely rapidly. The STV drop was observed by Tulppo in 1998 but, unfortunately, the tachogram was left out. Note that the parasympathetic inhibition contributes to fetal oxygen-conserving mechanisms in other ways. For instance, it also inhibits digestive activity.

2.2.5. Combination of High- and Low-STV Segments in One Saltatory Pattern

Closer examination of published tachograms recorded in presumed hypoxic conditions in the human fetus shows a saltatory evolution of STV in response to the following events: uterine contractions [64], non-lethal hypoxia [65], lethal hypoxia [66]. In animals, this saltatory evolution has also been observed in response to marked hypoxia, either prenatally [67, 43] or postnatally [68]. A similar saltatory-STV pattern has been observed following the stimulation of the hypothalamus by a microelectrode [54]. In the latter case, the long half-life of the sympathetic factor suspected of triggering high-STV phases is demonstrated.

In our experience of the human fetus, the short segments of high- or low-STV tracings tend to be adjacent, a novel feature. Furthermore, we believe we have observed such patterns in pathological or semi-pathological situations such as delayed intrauterine growth, maternal smoking, threatened premature birth, pre-eclampsia, cholestasis, gestational diabetes mellitus, or, interestingly, within four days of entering into physiological labor, even in uneventful pregnancies.

Other studies are useful to understand fetal oxygen-conserving mechanisms, notably in breath-holding divers where a combined adenosine and norepinephrine release has been suspected. The release of adenosine has been evidenced in breath-holding divers by Joulia *et al.* [69] and the release of norepinephrine has been demonstrated by Eichhorn *et al.* [70] as contributing to the increase of arterial pressure in dry breath-holders.

For instance, the high maternal pressures observed in pre-eclampsia could be partly beneficial when they balance raised fetal arterial pressures which, in turn, increases fetal resistance to hypoxia.

A striking similarity between fetal oxygen-conserving and the breath-holding reflex of divers is visible in Figure 10. These recordings compare a fetus coping with a hypertonic uterine contraction with a trained dry-breath-holder. Note that in both cases, the reaction is biphasic, with an initial increase followed by a secondary decrease of heart rate variability. In trained breath-holders, a tertiary re-increase of STV can be observed, as in certain of the fetal tracings presented above.

The high arterial pressure (related to the high-STV) which improves the performance of breath-holders lead us to suspect a similar mechanism in fetuses coping with acute hypoxia. Regarding the low fetal STV component, the corresponding energy saving is even more evident, as seen in case of intrauterine growth retardation [71].

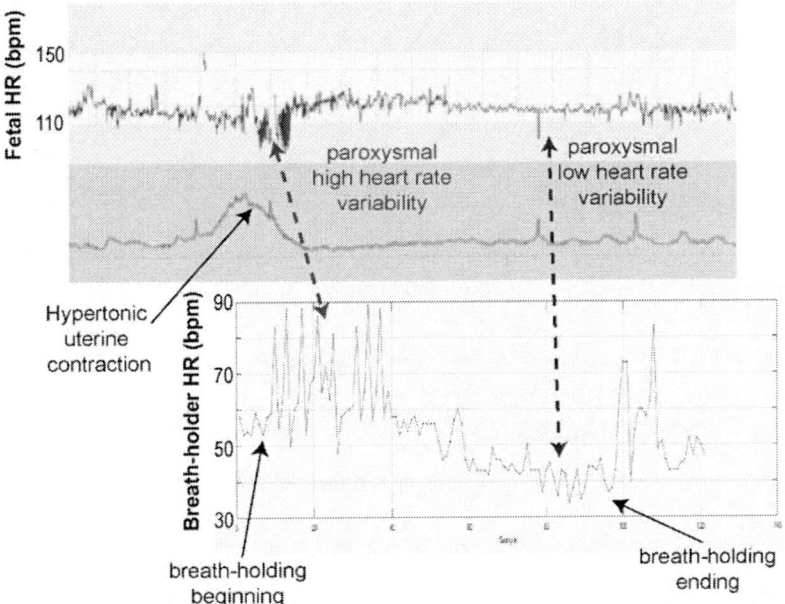

Figure 10. Similarities between the oxygen-conserving mechanisms of the fetus and the breath-holder.

The following figure illustrates a case where an extreme hypertonic uterine contraction produced a striking saltatory-STV mini-pattern, in a pregnancy bordering on the pathological (Figure 11).

Taken together, the above observations support our postulate that fetal oxygen-conserving mechanisms tend to be reflected by a saltatory-STV pattern. The high-STV component corresponds to a release of norepinephrine and the low-STV component to a release of adenosine. In case of active sleep, or wakefulness, there is no baseline shift associated with the STV saltation (saltatory STV mini-pattern). During quiet sleep, however, the inherent neurotransmitter release combines with the oxygen-conserving mechanism to generate a Meta-Pattern A, which involves a baseline shift.

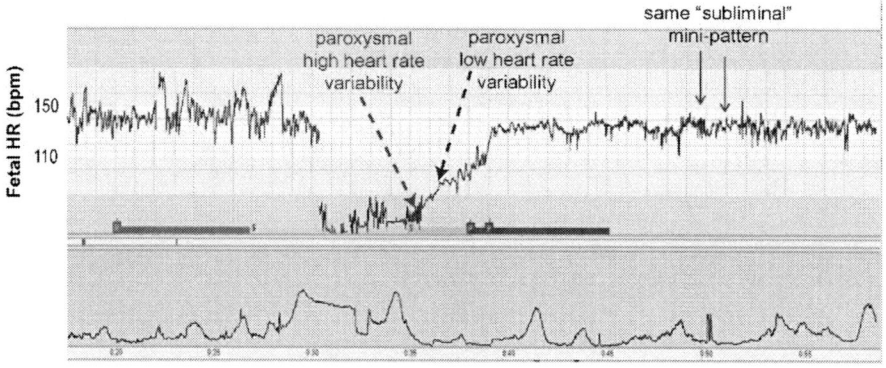

Figure 11. Saltatory-STV mini-pattern induced by a major hypertonic contraction.

2.3. Interference between Meta-QS and Fetal Metabolic/Nutritional Status

In adults, it has been demonstrated that the response to hypoxia is highly dependent on insulin levels [72], which are positively related to norepinephrine levels [73] and the nutritional status [38]. An insight into antenatal nutritional and metabolic status is therefore required to discuss Meta-QS.

The challenge faced by the fetus involves complex interactions between homeostatic constraints and growth constraints. For instance, the increased fetal breathing after maternal meals [74] enables the fetus to avoid hyperglycemia and the resulting hyperinsulinism. It also helps avoid excessive growth, given that insulin-like growth factors 1 and 2 are key elements that interfere with fetal growth [75]. The human fetus also displays a remarkable capacity for lactate consumption, a typical anaerobic substrate possibly produced by the placenta [76].

Furthermore, it seems that the human fetus anticipates potential ante- or intrapartum risks of asphyxia by reducing its growth, and therefore its energy expenditure. Accordingly, a reduction of the fetal abdominal circumference precedes cerebral Doppler alterations in cases of small for gestational age (SGA) fetuses [77].

Our poor understanding of inter-fetal variability with respect to certain criteria, notably birth weight, fetal heart rate variability, and circulatory status, is a major obstacle to our knowledge of fetal adaptive behavior, particularly concerning the fetal response to hypoxic stimulation.

2.3.1. Inter-Fetal Growth Variability

According to common sense, birth weight should follow a "physiological" distribution approaching a 1/2 ratio (2250-4500 g birth weight), but converging studies have led us to reconsider several physiology criteria. For instance, low birth weight is predictive of ulterior obesity and diabetes [78]. Another fact is interesting: a notable proportion of gestational diabetes mellitus pregnancies are associated with SGA fetuses [79]. Taken together, these observations could in fact highlight a specific series of events connecting maternal type-2 diabetes with fetoplacental type-1 diabetes and postnatal type-2 diabetes.

2.3.2. Inter-Fetal Variability of the Fetal Heart Rate (FHR)

We should now consider the third fundamental criterion: FHR variability. Here again, inter-fetal variability has already been accurately evaluated [80], notably using a longitudinal methodology. Our own observations have led us to establish that, in certain contexts, for instance, in case of maternal or fetal metabolic syndrome, the antepartum fetal short-term variability (STV) of FHR is increased, and the occurrence of transient

FHR accelerations is reduced, particularly at a distance from delivery [81]. The corresponding pattern is visible on the lower tracing in Figure 12.

One of the key points of this correlation is that the underlying mechanism is explainable. In adults, the high norepinephrine levels observed in uncomplicated cases of excess weight are not associated with high epinephrine levels if insulin release is not high [38]. The high norepinephrine level following the activation of a baroreflex probably explains the high STV of the FHR, with the instantaneously high cardiac frequency being due to the norepinephrine release and the low STV being triggered by the parasympathetic activation. The rarity of transient accelerations could be related to a low epinephrine level, as seen in the beginning of insulin resistance. Furthermore, in our study we observed that such tracings were rather related to deviant maternal post-load blood sugar levels (upwards or downwards) than to raised blood sugar levels alone. Post-load maternal hypoglycemia is thought to be due to diet-induced hyperinsulinism which is why we suspect high antepartum STV with rare transient accelerations of being related to a high middle-cerebral-artery pulsatility index (MCA-IP) as discussed further down.

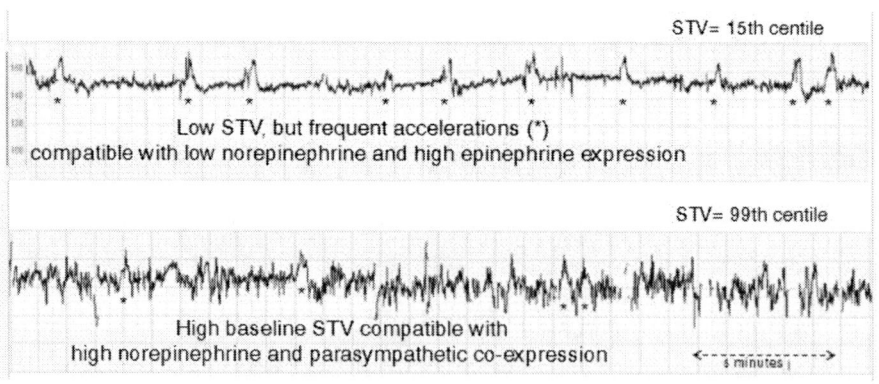

Figure 12. Why can "normal" tracings be so different?

The existence of high antepartum STV on FHR tracings a long time before labor raises a fundamental question: given that the most recognized criterion for a compromised fetal status is low STV [82], is the conventional FHR analysis at fault in these cases? If so, could the presence of saltatory STV patterns be the appropriate semiology for diagnosing a compromised fetal status?

To date, the perception of reduced fetal movements by the mother is sometimes considered as a sufficient criterion of compromised fetal status to induce labor pharmacologically. During active sleep, the most vigorous movements generally coincide with a transient increase in FHR. It would be interesting to know whether these accelerations coincide with the release of epinephrine. As mentioned previously, epinephrine and norepinephrine, which share the same beta-receptors in the sinoatrial node, have neither the same kinetics nor the same degree of activity in terms of baroreflex triggering via the alpha receptors. This is why they do not have the same degree of parasympathetic co-activation. However, most heart-rate studies using spectral analysis investigate the overall sympathetic activity without distinguishing epinephrine from norepinephrine [83, 84]. Transient FHR increases have recently become a feature of interest (under the name of R-R U-shaped accelerations) during nocturnal recordings, particularly during paradoxical sleep (the postnatal equivalent of fetal active sleep) [85]. These studies found the same very-low-frequency band as we did in the fetus.

Taken together, these elements support the postulate that the specific form of oxygen-conserving mechanism which transforms quiet sleep into meta-quiet sleep is conditioned by the fetal metabolic status, and more precisely by specific levels of norepinephrine, epinephrine, and insulin.

2.4. Interference between Cortisol Levels and the Interpretation of Meta-QS

Modern obstetrics started around 1974, when Liggins [86] established that what could be called "the door to parturition" in sheep was opened by cortisol, and that the role of cortisol was partially lost in human parturition. Presumably, Liggins was inspired by a phylogenetic reasoning: it is the dual cortisol/epinephrine release ("fight or flight") which opens the "door to hatching" in the egg-laying species which preceded mammals on our planet [87]. This pathway could be called "fight AND flight". The raised cortisol levels and fetal energy consumption near the onset of labor seem pointless in mammals (such as sheep) and even become a potential handicap in human parturition. A recent synthesis [88] suggests that the vestigial role of cortisol in human parturition could be called "the key to the door". Two notions are required to approach this vestigial role accurately:

(a) The fetal epinephrine crescendo connected with cortisol is rather restricted by the smallness of the "definitive zone" responsible for epinephrine secretions in the fetus [89], and by the placental participation to antepartum cortisol peaks, which could have essentially paracrine effects on the placenta itself [88].
(b) Nevertheless, the residual increase of fetal energy expenditure related to the antepartum cortisol peaks is likely to trigger transient hypoxic stimulation. This could help transform the human fetus into an "apnea champion" during the late antepartum, a necessary condition to survive labor.

Taken together, the above notions support our hypothesis that high cortisol levels tend induce a shift from typical Pattern-A to Meta-PA. During QS, cortisol might disrupt the physiological parasympathetic dominance and increase the release of epinephrine, thus explaining the persistence of transient FHR accelerations during Meta-QS. The corresponding increase of fetal energy consumption could explain the need for an extremely negative fetal feedback, as illustrated by the very low STV components of Meta-PA.

2.5. Interference between Meta-Quiet Sleep and Fetal Circulatory Strategies

Meta-QS is thought to be one of the fetal oxygen-conserving mechanisms of the fetus. This means that a specific circulatory strategy is involved and the circulatory status underlying Meta-QS should therefore be discussed, even without the help of simultaneous Doppler documentation.

The fetal circulatory status is known for its inter-fetal variability, notably concerning the middle cerebral artery (MCA) and the umbilical artery (UA) flow velocity indexes [90], as assessed by non-invasive Doppler ultrasound. The lower MCA pulsatility index (MCA-PI) reflects the "brain sparing" effect of the fetal response to hypoxic stimulation, and the raised UA pulsatility index (UA-PI) indicates a decreased placental efficiency.

Daily measurements lead us to postulate that the MCA-PI (and, to a lesser extent, the UA-PI) tend to be elevated in case of fetal metabolic syndrome (macrosomia, gestational diabetes mellitus or amniotic fluid excess, notably) (see Figure 12). Converging observations have been published, concerning either pre-gestational diabetes [91] or gestational diabetes mellitus [92].

Despite a raised pulsatility index, the absolute MCA flow only showed a mild reduction in the physiological slope of these contexts, possibly because the raised systolic velocity might compensate the diastolic velocity drop. Unfortunately, the absolute flow is difficult to calculate based on the blood-flow spectrum [93].

The main neurotransmitters involved in MCA vasoconstriction are norepinephrine, and the neuropeptide Y [94, 95]. In adults, it has been established that uncomplicated overweight is correlated to high norepinephrine [38] and neuropeptide Y levels [96]. Both contribute to the high arterial pressure tendency observed in metabolic syndromes. Their combined prenatal increase could therefore explain most of the MCA- and UA-PI increases described above, thus accounting for a substantial part of inter-fetal variability.

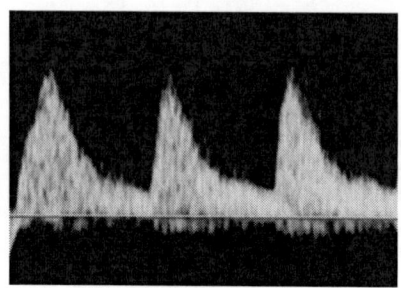
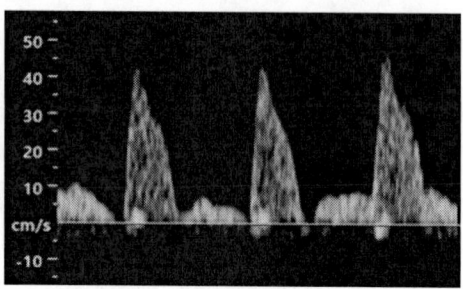

Control spectrum

Notch and low telediastolic flow

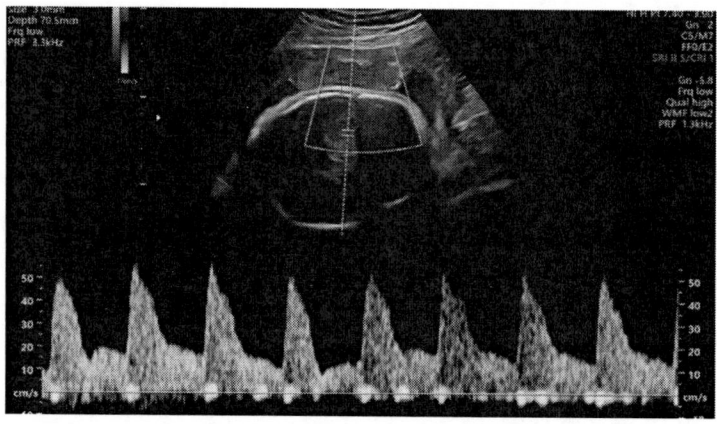

Constant systolic peak, but variable diastolic flow.
Same pregnant women as fig.12 lower tracing

(All observations around 32 weeks)

Figure 13. Interfetal variability of MCA Doppler spectra.

In a similar fetal situation (possible metabolic syndrome), we have observed a protodiastolic notch in the MCA spectrum (see Figure 13). However, it has also been observed in certain post-traumatic adult cases [97]. We believe that similar neurotransmitters may be involved in both situations.

There is also a positive relationship between FHR beat-to-beat variability and MCA spectrum beat-to-beat variability, as illustrated by the

MCA variable spectrum of the third example in Figure 13 which was obtained in the same pregnant woman, shortly after the lower tracing in Figure 12.

The main neurotransmitters involved in MCA vasodilatation are adenosine and nitric oxide. It is well known that one of the main physiological responses of the fetus to hypoxia consists in increasing adenosine levels [98]. The decreased antepartum MCA-PI/UA-PI ratio (typically < 1) is predictive of a compromised fetal issue of the pregnancy, regardless of fetal size or clinical context [99]. This association confirms that, in terms of vasodilatation, the MCA is more sensitive to hypoxia than the UA. Maintaining a degree of vasoconstriction in the UA is probably useful to make the most of an increasingly defective placenta. The MCA-PI/UA-PI ratio was initially introduced for "mathematical" reasons pertaining to the cumulative predictive value of these two major Doppler indexes. However, taking into account the above arguments explains why the clinical use of the ratio rapidly spread worldwide when it was introduced: it minimizes the bias due to inter-fetal variability of both the MCA-PI and the UA-PI. However, in case of small-for-gestational age fetuses and gestational diabetes, this procedure may be restricted by the impossibility of lowering the MCA-PI despite substantial hypoxic stimulation. Such rationale could help understand why the MCA-PI/UPI is considered less useful in case of gestational diabetes mellitus [100].

Note that the vasodilatory effect of adenosine and nitric oxide on cerebral arteries seems to be less effective than in adults [101]. Given that the main hypoxic threat to the fetus before labor is rather chronic than acute, the main homeostatic MCA response appears to be locally related to the increased cerebral arteries, via trophic effects on the endothelium and corresponding smooth vessels.

The fetal brain-sparing strategy is associated with other major circulatory adaptations. The response of the coronary artery to hypoxic stimulation is comparable to that of the MCA [102, 103]. In the fetus, the overall circulatory distribution combines both brain-sparing mechanisms: the oxygenated blood from the umbilical vein preferentially reaches the coronary arteries and the MCA via the ductus venosus and the foramen ovale.

In the fetus, the ventricles are parallel, and after birth they are disposed in series. The main fetal oxygen-conserving shunts are the ductus venosus and the foramen ovale. The aortic isthmus can also be considered as a potential shunt, but the ductus arteriosus has to be regarded as a pseudo-shunt [104]. The intra-pulmonary shunt could be part of the oxygen-conserving mechanism as it avoids the energy expenditure required by the pulmonary capillary circulation. The fetus appears able to increase salutary fetal shunting in case of life-threatening hypoxia whilst preserving the same overall distribution. There is notably a rise of the ductus-venosus/umbilical-vein flow ratio [105, 106], of the foramen-ovale/pulmonary-arterial flow ratio [107, 108], and probably of the intra-pulmonary shunt [109]. There are however potential postnatal drawbacks to this exacerbated prenatal shunting. These include the persistence or resurgence of a patent ductus venosus and/or foramen ovale, the onset of primitive pulmonary hypertension, bronchopulmonary dysplasia, and/or intra-pulmonary shunting [110].

All these elements led us to consider the underlying circulatory status during Meta-QS as an exacerbated oxygen-conserving shunt, probably associated to a specific MCA-IP and UA-IP evolution.

2.6. Meta-Quiet Sleep and Fetal Breathing Movements (FBM)

It has been observed in human fetuses that episodic fetal breathing movements do exist in utero. These are essential for satisfactory pulmonary development. If we recall the analogy with sheep fetuses, FBM could well represent one third of the fetal oxygen consumption [111]. Thus, increased FBM substantially help avoid hyperglycemia and hyperoxia, and their subsequent decrease is a major component of fetal oxygen-conserving mechanisms. Despite the fact that the carotid chemoreceptors to hypoxia are functional near term, hypoxia inhibits FBM [41]. This inhibition is of central origin and involves the activation of numerous neurotransmitters, including adenosine and opioids [112, 113], as well as the activation of Kölliker-Fuse brainstem inhibiting nucleus [114]. In parallel, FBM inhibition requires the central release of gamma aminobutyric acid (GABA), as well as the inhibition of extracellular serotonin (5-HT) [115, 116] and that of extracellular substance P [117]. Taken together, both elements could inhibit the parasympathetic component of the FBM stimulation [118]. Note that, from a phylogenetic point of view, parasympathetic motor activity is a key driver for respiration in aquatic contexts [119].

It has been assessed that in the human fetus, FBM can be triggered by isolated central hypercapnia chemoreflexes [120]. However, even if isolated hypercapnia of placental origin could exist in "real life" conditions, the FBM increase triggered by such a pathway would be likely to induce hypoxia, thus generating enough long-life central mediators to inhibit FBM.

The need for FBM inhibition to avoid stillbirths may trigger a drastic inhibition of the respiratory commands in the brainstem, to the point of inducing histologic lesions [107]. Furthermore, the efferent cardiac and respiratory networks being closely connected, the fetus may have no other choice than encouraging hypertrophy in part of the above-described structures that predominantly target the heart. This occurs, for instance, in the 5-HT neurons and astrocytes in case of brainstem hyperplasia, and with the increase of intracardiac muscarinic receptors. Note that all these alterations have noxious postnatal consequences [121-123].

CONCLUSION

Understanding previously unrecognized fetal "Meta Quiet Sleep" involves a great diversity of arguments because of the strong interconnection between nutritional status (especially the norepinephrine/epinephrine ratio), resistance to hypoxia and changes inherent to the imminence of labor (notably the cortisol crescendo). However, all these elements are required for an accurate approach of the fetal antepartum status, particularly in case of a high baseline STV where the conventional FHR criterion of low STV could be inappropriate.

The recent notion that systematic fetal Doppler screening could prove useful, regardless of clinical context and conventional FHR analysis results, supports this novel conception of antepartum care. The resulting knowledge increase in fetal pathophysiology is bound to improve our understanding of postnatal pathologies. Indeed, sleep apnea, sudden unexpected death in epilepsy (SUDEP), and Cushing's reflex could well be due to a partial or total resurgence of fetal respiratory physiology and Sudden Infant Death Syndrome (SIDS) to a resurgence of Meta-QS.

REFERENCES

[1] Muhammad, S. "Role of Uterine Contractions and Intrapartum Reoxygenation Ratio." In *Handbook of CTG Interpretation: From Patterns to Physiology*, 2017.

[2] Wong, K. "Why Humans Give Birth to Helpless Babies." *Scientific American*, 2012.

[3] Prechtl, HFR. "The Behavioural States of the Newborn Infant (a Review)." *Brain Research*, 76, no. 2, (1974), 185–212.

[4] Junge, HD. "Behavioral States and State Related Heart Rate and Motor Activity Patterns in the Newborn Infant and the Fetus Ante Partum. II. Computer Analysis of State Related Heart Rate Baseline and Macrofluctuation Patterns." *Journal of Perinatal Medicine-Official Journal of the WAPM*, 7, no. 3, (1979), 134–148.

[5] Nijhuis, JG; Prechtl, HFR; Martin, Jr. CB; Bots, RSGM. "Are There Behavioural States in the Human Fetus?" *Early Human Development*, 6, no. 2, (1982), 177–195.

[6] Arduini, D; Rizzo, G; Giorlandino, C; Vizzone, A; Nava, S; Dell'Acqua, S; Valensise, H; Romanini, C. "The Fetal Behavioural States: An Ultrasonic Study." *Prenatal Diagnosis*, 5, no. 4, (1985), 269–76.

[7] Arduini, D; Rizzo, G; Giorlandino, C; Valensise, H; Dell'Acqua, S; Romanini, C. "The Development of Fetal Behavioural States: A Longitudinal Study." *Prenatal Diagnosis*, 6, no. 2, (1986), 117–24.

[8] Swartjes, JM; Van Geijn, HP; Mantel, R; Van Woerden, E; Schoemaker, HC. "Coincidence of Behavioural State Parameters in the Human Fetus at Three Gestational Ages." *Early Human Development*, 23, no. 2, (1990), 75–83.

[9] Van Woerden, EE; Van Geijn, HP; Swartjes, JM; Caron, FJM; Brons, JTJ; Arts, NFT. "Fetal Heart Rhythms during Behavioural State 1F; "*European Journal of Obstetrics & Gynecology and Reproductive Biology*, 28, no. 1, (1988), 29–38.

[10] Arabin, B; Riedewald, S; Zacharias, C; Saling, E. "Quantitative Analysis of Fetal Behavioural Patterns with Real-Time Sonography and the Actocardiograph." *Gynecologic and Obstetric Investigation*, 26, no. 3, (1988), 211–218.

[11] Arabin, B; Riedewald, S. "An Attempt to Quantify Characteristics of Behavioral States." *American Journal of Perinatology*, 9, no. 02, (1992), 115–119.

[12] Groome, LJ; Mooney, DM; Bentz, LS; Singh, KP. "Spectral Analysis of Heart Rate Variability during Quiet Sleep in Normal Human Fetuses between 36 and 40 Weeks of Gestation." *Early Human Development*, 38, no. 1, (1994), 1–9.

[13] Groome, LJ; Singh, KP; Bentz, LS; Holland, B; Atterbury, JL; Swiber, MJ; Trimm, III. RF. "Temporal Stability in the Distribution of Behavioral States for Individual Human Fetuses." *Early Human Development*, 1997, 11.

[14] Arduini, D; Rizzo, G; Caforio, L; Boccolini, MR; Romanini, C; Mancuso, S. "Behavioural State Transitions in Healthy and Growth Retarded Fetuses." *Early Human Development*, 19, no. 3, (1989), 155–165.

[15] Mulder, EJH; Vissera, GHA; Bekedam, DJ; Prechtl, HFR. "Emergence of Behavioural States in Fetuses of Type- 1-Diabetic Women," 1987, 21.

[16] Hume, RF; O'Donnell, KJ; Stanger, CL; Killam, AP; Gingras, JL. "In Utero Cocaine Exposure: Observations of Fetal Behavioral State May Predict Neonatal Outcome." *American Journal of Obstetrics and Gynecology*, 161, no. 3, (1989), 685–90.

[17] Griffin, RL; Caron, FJM; Van Geijn, HP. "Behavioral States in the Human Fetus during Labor." *American Journal of Obstetrics and Gynecology*, 152, no. 7, (1985), 828–833.

[18] Barbeau, DY; Weiss, MD. "Sleep Disturbances in Newborns." *Children*, 4, no. 10, (October 20, 2017), 90.

[19] Maeda, K; Tatsumura, M; Utsu, M. "Analysis of Fetal Movements by Doppler Actocardiogram and Fetal B-Mode Imaging." *Clinics in Perinatology*, 26, no. 4, (1999), 829–851.

[20] Stinstra, J; Golbach, E; Leeuwen, P; Lange, S; Menendez, T; Moshage, W; Schleussner, E; et al. "Multicentre Study of Fetal Cardiac Time Intervals Using Magnetocardiography." *BJOG: An International Journal of Obstetrics and Gynaecology*, 109, no. 11, (2002), 1235–43.

[21] Panigrahy, D; Rakshit, M; Sahu, PK. "An Efficient Method for Fetal ECG Extraction from Single Channel Abdominal ECG." In *2015 International Conference on Industrial Instrumentation and Control (ICIC)*, 1083–88. Pune, India: IEEE, 2015.

[22] Zhao, H; Strasburger, JF; Cuneo, BF; Wakai, RT. "Fetal Cardiac Repolarization Abnormalities." *The American Journal of Cardiology*, 98, no. 4, (2006), 491–96.

[23] Gonçalves, H; Bernardes, J; Rocha, AP; Ayres-de-Campos, D. "Linear and Nonlinear Analysis of Heart Rate Patterns Associated with Fetal Behavioral States in the Antepartum Period." *Early Human Development*, 83, no. 9, (2007), 585–91.

[24] Mulder, EJH; Visser, GHA. "Fetal Behavior: Clinical and Experimental Research in the Human." In *Fetal Development*, edited by Nadja Reissland and Barbara S. Kisilevsky, 87–105. Cham: Springer International Publishing, 2016.

[25] Schneider, U; Frank, B; Fiedler, A; Kaehler, C; Hoyer, D; Liehr, M; Haueisen, J; Schleussner, E. "Human Fetal Heart Rate Variability-

Characteristics of Autonomic Regulation in the Third Trimester of Gestation." *Journal of Perinatal Medicine*, 36, no. 5, (2008), 433–441.

[26] Zemb, PA; Gonçalves, H; Bellec, JY; Bernardes, J. "Prenatal Observation of Heart Rate Sequences Presenting Entropic Analogies with Sudden Infant Death Syndrome: Preliminary Report." In *Computer-Based Medical Systems (CBMS), 2013 IEEE 26th International Symposium On*, 421–424, IEEE, 2013.

[27] Shono, M; Shono, H; Sugimori, H. "Dynamic Changes in the Middle Cerebral Artery Perfusion in Normal Full-Term Human Fetuses in Relation to the Timing of Behavioral State." *Early Human Development*, 58, no. 1, (2000), 57–67.

[28] Mulder, EJH; Leiblum, DM; Visser, GHA. "Fetal Breathing Movements in Late Diabetic Pregnancy: Relationship to Fetal Heart Rate Patterns and Braxton Hicks' Contractions," 1995, 8.

[29] Rosenstock, EG; Cassuto, Y; Zmora, E. "Heart Rate Variability in the Neonate and Infant: Analytical Methods, Physiological and Clinical Observations." *Acta Paediatrica*, 88, no. 5, (1999), 477–482.

[30] Moon, RY; Tanabe, KO; Choi Yang, D; Young, HA; Hauck, FR. "Pacifier Use and Sids: Evidence for a Consistently Reduced Risk." *Maternal and Child Health Journal*, 16, no. 3, (2012), 609–14.

[31] Thoman, EB. "Early Development of Sleeping Behaviors in Infants." In *Aberrant Development in Infancy: Human and Animal Studies*, 122–138, 1975.

[32] Zemb, PA; Bellec, JY. "672: The Paradoxical Adrenergic Signature of Quiet Sleep Compatible with Fetal Heart-Rate Sequences." *American Journal of Obstetrics & Gynecology*, 199, no. 6, (2008), S192.

[33] Zemb, PA; *et al.* abstract accepted: "Previously unrecognized fetal behavior, compatible with specific oxygen-conserving during quiet sleep", (2019).

[34] Watanabe, K; Inokuma, K; Negoro, T. "REM Sleep Prevents Sudden Infant Death Syndrome." *European Journal of Pediatrics*, 140, no. 4, (1983), 289–92.

[35] Sperhake, J; Jorch, G; Bajanowski, T. "The Prone Sleeping Position and SIDS. Historical Aspects and Possible Pathomechanisms." *International Journal of Legal Medicine*, 132, no. 1, (January 2018), 181–85.

[36] Pincus, SM; Cummins, TR; Haddad, GG. "Heart Rate Control in Normal and Aborted-SIDS Infants." *The American Journal of Physiology*, 264, no. 3, Pt 2, (1993), R638-646.

[37] Fleisher, LA; Frank, SM; Sessler, DI; Cheng, C; Matsukawa, T; Vannier, CA. "Thermoregulation and Heart Rate Variability." *Clinical Science*, 90, no. 2, (1996), 97–103.

[38] De Pergola, G; Giorgino, F; Benigno, R; Guida, P; Giorgino, R. "Independent Influence of Insulin, Catecholamines, and Thyroid Hormones on Metabolic Syndrome." *Obesity*, 16, no. 11, (2008), 2405–2411.

[39] Ghosh, M; Chandraharan, E. "Unusual Fetal Heart Rate Patterns." In *Handbook of CTG Interpretation: From Patterns to Physiology*, 109, 2017.

[40] Freeman, RK; Nageotte, MP; Garite, TJ. *Fetal Heart Rate Monitoring*. Philadelphia PA: Lippincot, 2013.

[41] Giussani, DA. "The Fetal Brain Sparing Response to Hypoxia: Physiological Mechanisms: Fetal Brain Sparing." *The Journal of Physiology*, 594, no. 5, (2016), 1215–30.

[42] Burnstock, G. "Hypoxia, Endothelium, and Purines." *Drug Development Research*, 28, no. 3, (1993), 301–305.

[43] Lear, CA; Galinsky, R; Wassink, G; Mitchell, CJ; Davidson, JO. Westgate, JA; Bennet, L; Gunn, AJ. "Sympathetic Neural Activation Does Not Mediate Heart Rate Variability during Repeated Brief Umbilical Cord Occlusions in Near-Term Fetal Sheep: Sympathetic Activation and Fetal Heart Rate Variability." *The Journal of Physiology*, 594, no. 5, (2016), 1265–77.

[44] Martin, Jr. CB. "Physiology and Clinical Use of Fetal Heart Rate Variability." *Clinics in Perinatology*, 9, no. 2, (1982), 339–352.

[45] Murotsuki, J; Bocking, AD; Gagnon, R. "Fetal Heart Rate Patterns in Growth-Restricted Fetal Sheep Induced by Chronic Fetal Placental Embolization." *American Journal of Obstetrics and Gynecology*, 176, no. 2, (1997), 282–90.

[46] Bocking, AD. "The Relationship between Heart Rate and Asphyxia in the Animal Fetus." *Clinical and Investigative Medicine. Medecine Clinique et Experimentale*, 16, no. 2, (1993), 166–175.

[47] Agrawal, S. "Intrapartum Computerized Fetal Heart Rate Parameters and Metabolic Acidosis at Birth." *Obstetrics & Gynecology*, 102, no. 4, (2003), 731–38.

[48] Siira, SM; Ojala, TH; Vahlberg, TJ; Rosén, KG; Ekholm, EM. "Do Spectral Bands of Fetal Heart Rate Variability Associate with Concomitant Fetal Scalp PH?" *Early Human Development*, 89, no. 9, (2013), 739–42.

[49] Lu, K; Holzmann, M; Abtahi, F; Lindecrantz, K; Lindqvist, PG; Nordstrom, L. "Fetal Heart Rate Short Term Variation during Labor in Relation to Scalp Blood Lactate Concentration." *Acta Obstetricia et Gynecologica Scandinavica*, 97, no. 10, (2018), 1274–80.

[50] Clark, M; Finkel, R; Cubeddu, LX. *Pharmacology*. Lippincott Williams & Wilkins, 2009.

[51] Tulppo, MP; Mäkikallio, TH; Seppänen, T; Juhani KE; Airaksinen, JKE; Heikki, V; Huikuri, HV. "Heart Rate Dynamics during Accentuated Sympathovagal Interaction." *American Journal of Physiology-Heart and Circulatory Physiology*, 274, no. 3, (1998), H810–16.

[52] Paton, JFR; Boscan, P; Pickering, AE; Nalivaiko, E. "The Yin and Yang of Cardiac Autonomic Control: Vago-Sympathetic Interactions Revisited." *Brain Research Reviews*, 49, no. 3, (2005), 555–65.

[53] Levy, MN. "Sympathetlc-Parasympathetic Interactions in the Heart (Brief Reviews)," 1971, 10.

[54] Koizumi, K; Terui, N; Kollai, M. "Neural Control of the Heart: Significance of Double Innervation Re-Examined." *Journal of the Autonomic Nervous System*, 7, no. 3–4, (1983), 279–94.
[55] Olsen, CR; Fanestil, DD; Scholander, PF. "Some Effects of Breath Holding and Apneic Underwater Diving on Cardiac Rhythm in Man." *Journal of Applied Physiology*, 17, no. 3, (1962), 461–66.
[56] Khurana, RK. "Cold Face Test: Adrenergic Phase." *Clinical Autonomic Research*, 17, no. 4, (2007), 211–16.
[57] Shattock, MJ; Tipton, MJ. "'Autonomic Conflict': A Different Way to Die during Cold Water Immersion?: Autonomic Conflict and Cardiac Arrhythmias." *The Journal of Physiology*, 590, no. 14, (2012), 3219–30.
[58] Schaller, BJ; Filis, A; Buchfelder, M. "Cardiac Autonomic Control in Neurosurgery the Example of Trigemino-Cardiac Reflex." *Arch Med Sci*, 2007, 6.
[59] Shouldice, R; Ward, S; O'Brien, LM; O'Brien, C; Redmond, S; Gozal, D; Heneghan, C. "PR and PP ECG Interval Variation during Obstructive Apnea and Hypopnea." In *IEEE 30th Annual Northeast Bioengineering Conference, 2004. Proceedings of The*, 100–101. Springfield, MA: IEEE, 2004.
[60] Hautala, AJ; Makikallio, TH; Kiviniemi, A; Laukkanen, RT; Nissil, S; Huikuri, HV; Tulppo, MP. "Heart Rate Dynamics after Controlled Training Followed by a Home-Based Exercise Program." *European Journal of Applied Physiology*, 92, no. 3, (2004).
[61] Picard, G; Tan, CO; Zafonte, R; Taylor, JA. "Incongruous Changes in Heart Period and Heart Rate Variability with Vagotonic Atropine: Implications for Rehabilitation Medicine." *PM&R*, 1, no. 9, (2009), 820–26.
[62] Jones, CT; Ritchie, JW. "The Cardiovascular Effects of Circulating Catecholamines in Fetal Sheep." *The Journal of Physiology*, 285, no. 1, (1978), 381–93.
[63] Tipton, MJ; Collier, N; Massey, H; Corbett, J; Harper, M. "Cold Water Immersion: Kill or Cure?" *Experimental Physiology*, 102, no. 11, (2017), 1335–55.

[64] Cesarelli, M; Romano, M; Bifulco, P. "Comparison of Short-Term Variability Indexes in Cardiotocographic Foetal Monitoring." *Computers in Biology and Medicine*, 39, no. 2, (2009), 106–118.

[65] Thaler, I; Timor-Tritsch, IE; Blumenfeld, Z. "Effect of Acute Hypoxia on Human Fetal Heart Rate: The Significance of Increased Heart Rate Variability." *Acta Obstetricia et Gynecologica Scandinavica*, 64, no. 1, (1985), 47–50.

[66] Cetrulo, CL; Schifrin, BS. "Fetal Heart Rate Patterns Preceding Death in Utero." *Obstetrics and Gynecology*, 48, no. 5, (1976), 521–527.

[67] Stånge, L; Rosén, KG; Hökegård, KH; Karlsson, K; Rochlitzer, F; Kjellmer, I; Joelsson, I. "Quantification of Fetal Heart Rate Variability in Relation to Oxygenation in the Sheep Fetus." *Acta Obstetricia et Gynecologica Scandinavica*, 56, no. 3, (1977), 205–9.

[68] Gonçalves, H; Henriques-Coelho, T; Bernardes, J; Rocha, AP; Nogueira, A; Leite-Moreira, A. "Linear and Nonlinear Heart-Rate Analysis in a Rat Model of Acute Anoxia." *Physiological Measurement*, 29, no. 9, (2008), 1133–43.

[69] Joulia, F; Coulange, M; Lemaitre, F; Costalat, G; Franceschi, F; Gariboldi, V; Nee, L; et al. "Plasma Adenosine Release Is Associated with Bradycardia and Transient Loss of Consciousness during Experimental Breath-Hold Diving." *International Journal of Cardiology*, 168, no. 5, (2013), e138-141.

[70] Eichhorn, L; Erdfelder, F; Kessler, F; Dolscheid-Pommerich, R; Zur, B; Hoffmann, U; Ellerkmann, R; Meyer, R. "Influence of Apnea-Induced Hypoxia on Catecholamine Release and Cardiovascular Dynamics." *International Journal of Sports Medicine*, 38, no. 02, (July 25, 2016), 85–91.

[71] Kouskouti, C; Regner, K; Knabl, J; Kainer, F. "Cardiotocography and the Evolution into Computerised Cardiotocography in the Management of Intrauterine Growth Restriction." *Archives of Gynecology and Obstetrics*, 295, no. 4, (2017), 811–816.

[72] Dangmann, R. "An Insulin Based Model to Explain Changes and Interactions in Human Breath-Holding." *Medical Hypotheses*, 84, no. 6, (June 2015), 532–38.

[73] Jarczok, MN; Koenig, J; Schuster, AK; Thayer, JF; Fischer, JE. "Nighttime Heart Rate Variability, Overnight Urinary Norepinephrine, and Glycemic Status in Apparently Healthy Human Adults." *International Journal of Cardiology*, 168, no. 3, (2013), 3025–3026.

[74] Rurak, D. "Fetal Sleep and Spontaneous Behavior In Utero: Animal and Clinical Studies." In *Prenatal and Postnatal Determinants of Development*, edited by David W. Walker, 109, 89–146. New York, NY: Springer New York, 2016.

[75] Nawathe, AR; Christian, M; Kim, SH; Johnson, M; Savvidou, MD; Terzidou, V. "Insulin-like Growth Factor Axis in Pregnancies Affected by Fetal Growth Disorders." *Clinical Epigenetics*, 8, no. 1, (December 2016), 11.

[76] Nicolaides, KH. "Doppler Studies in Fetal Hypoxemic Hypoxia." *Doppler in Obstetrics*, 2002, on line https://fetalmedicine.org/var/uploads/Doppler-in-Obstetrics.pdf.

[77] Harrington, K; Thompson, MO; Carpenter, RG; Nguyen, M; Campbell, S. "Doppler Fetal Circulation in Pregnancies Complicated by Pre-Eclampsia or Delivery of a Small for Gestational Age Baby: 2. Longitudinal Analysis." *BJOG: An International Journal of Obstetrics & Gynaecology*, 106, no. 5, (1999), 453–466.

[78] Jornayvaz, FR; Vollenweider, P; Bochud, M; Mooser, V; Waeber, G; Marques-Vidal, P. "Low Birth Weight Leads to Obesity, Diabetes and Increased Leptin Levels in Adults: The CoLaus Study." *Cardiovascular Diabetology*, 15, no. 1, (December 2016), 73.

[79] Esakoff, TF; Guillet, A; Caughey, AB. "Does Small for Gestational Age Worsen Outcomes in Gestational Diabetics?" *The Journal of Maternal-Fetal & Neonatal Medicine*, 30, no. 8, (April 18, 2017), 890–93.

[80] Amorim-Costa, C; Costa-Santos, C; Ayres-de-Campos, D; Bernardes, J. "Longitudinal Evaluation of Computerized

Cardiotocographic Parameters throughout Pregnancy in Normal Fetuses: A Prospective Cohort Study." *Acta Obstetricia et Gynecologica Scandinavica*, 95, no. 10, (2016), 1143–1152.

[81] Zemb, PA; et al. "Relationships between shirt-term variability of fetal heart-rate and maternal or fetal metabolic syndrome" (submitted abstract), 2019.

[82] Dawes, GS; Moulden, M; Redman, CW. "Short-Term Fetal Heart Rate Variation, Decelerations, and Umbilical Flow Velocity Waveforms before Labor." *Obstetrics and Gynecology*, 80, no. 4, (1992), 673–78.

[83] Malik, M. "Heart Rate Variability: Standards of Measurement, Physiological Interpretation, and Clinical Use." *Circulation*, 93, no. 5, (1996), 1043–1065.

[84] Vigo, DE; Siri, LN; Cardinali, DP. "Heart Rate Variability: A Tool to Explore Autonomic Nervous System Activity in Health and Disease." In *Psychiatry and Neuroscience Update*, edited by Pascual Ángel Gargiulo and Humberto Luis Mesones Arroyo, 113–26. Cham: Springer International Publishing, 2019.

[85] Solinski, M; Gieraltowski, J; Zebrowski, J; Kuklik, P. "Influence of U-Shape Accelerations of Heart Rate on Very Low Frequency Band and Heart Rate Multifractality," 2017.

[86] Liggins, GC. "Parturition in the Sheep and the Human." In *Physiology and Genetics of Reproduction*, 423–443. Springer, 1974.

[87] Tong, Q; Romanini, CE; Exadaktylos, V; Bahr, C; Berckmans, D; Bergoug, H; Eterradossi, N; et al. "Embryonic Development and the Physiological Factors That Coordinate Hatching in Domestic Chickens." *Poultry Science* 92, no. 3 (2013), 620–28.

[88] Li, XQ; Zhu, P; Myatt, L; Sun, K. "Roles of Glucocorticoids in Human Parturition: A Controversial Fact?" *Placenta*, 35, no. 5, (2014), 291–96.

[89] Ishimoto, H; Jaffe, RB. "Development and Function of the Human Fetal Adrenal Cortex: A Key Component in the Feto-Placental Unit." *Endocrine Reviews*, 32, no. 3, (2011), 317–55.

[90] Kurmanavicius, J; Florio, I; Wisser, J; Hebisch, G; Zimmermann, R; Müller, R; Huch, R; Huch, A. "Reference Resistance Indices of the Umbilical, Fetal Middle Cerebral and Uterine Arteries at 24–42 Weeks of Gestation." *Ultrasound in Obstetrics and Gynecology: The Official Journal of the International Society of Ultrasound in Obstetrics and Gynecology*, 10, no. 2, (1997), 112–120.

[91] Higgins, M; Russell, N; Foley, ME; Firth, R; Coffey, M; McAuliffe, F. "360: The Role of Middle Cerebral Artery Doppler in Diabetic Pregnancy." *American Journal of Obstetrics & Gynecology*, 197, no. 6, (2007), S110.

[92] Shabani-Zanjani, M; Nasirzadeh, R; Fereshtehnejad, SM; Asl, LY; Pooya Alemzadeh, SA; Askari, S. "Fetal Cerebral Hemodynamic in Gestational Diabetic versus Normal Pregnancies: A Doppler Velocimetry of Middle Cerebral and Umbilical Arteries." *Acta Neurologica Belgica*, 114, no. 1, (2014), 15–23.

[93] Deane, C. "Doppler Ultrasound: Principles and Practice." *Doppler in Obstetrics*, 2002, on line https://fetalmedicine.org/var/uploads/Doppler-in-Obstetrics.pdf.

[94] Adeoye, OO; Silpanisong, J; Williams, JM; Pearce, WJ. "Role of the Sympathetic Autonomic Nervous System in Hypoxic Remodeling of the Fetal Cerebral Vasculature." *Journal of Cardiovascular Pharmacology*, 65, no. 4, (2015), 308–16.

[95] Burnstock, G; Ralevic, V. "Purinergic Signaling and Blood Vessels in Health and Disease." *Pharmacological Reviews*, 66, no. 1, (2014), 102–92.

[96] McMillen, IC; Robinson, JS. "Developmental Origins of the Metabolic Syndrome: Prediction, Plasticity, and Programming." *Physiological Reviews*, 85, no. 2, (2005), 571–633.

[97] Chan, Kwan-Hon; Dearden, NM; Miller, JD; Midgley, S; Ian, R; Piper, IR. "Transcranial Doppler Waveform Differences in Hyperemic and Nonhyperemic Patients after Severe Head Injury." *Surgical Neurology*, 38, no. 6, (1992), 433–436.

[98] Koos, BJ. "Adenosine A2a Receptors and O2 Sensing in Development." *American Journal of Physiology-Regulatory*,

Integrative and Comparative Physiology, 301, no. 3, (2011), R601–R622.

[99] Dunn, L; Sherrell, H; Kumar, S. "Systematic Review of the Utility of the Fetal Cerebroplacental Ratio Measured at Term for the Prediction of Adverse Perinatal Outcome." *Placenta*, 54, (2017), 68–75.

[100] Nicolaides, KH. "Doppler Studies in Pregnancies with Maternal Diabetes Mellitus." *Doppler in Obstetrics*, 2002, on line https://fetalmedicine.org/var/uploads/Doppler-in-Obstetrics.pdf.

[101] Pearce, WJ; Butler, SM; Abrassart, JM; Williams, JM. "Fetal Cerebral Oxygenation: The Homeostatic Role of Vascular Adaptations to Hypoxic Stress." In *Oxygen Transport to Tissue XXXII*, edited by Joseph C. LaManna, Michelle A. Puchowicz, Kui Xu, David K Harrison, and Duane F. Bruley, 701:225–32. Boston, MA: Springer US, 2011.

[102] Baschat, AA; Harman, CR; Alger, LS; Weiner, CP. "Fetal Coronary and Cerebral Blood Flow in Acute Fetomaternal Hemorrhage." *Ultrasound in Obstetrics and Gynecology*, 12, no. 2, (1998), 128–131.

[103] Garcia-Canadilla, P; De Vries, T; Gonzalez-Tendero, A; Bonnin, A; Gratacos, E; Crispi, F; Bijnens, B; Zhang, C. "Structural Coronary Artery Remodelling in the Rabbit Fetus as a Result of Intrauterine Growth Restriction." Edited by Rogelio Cruz-Martinez. *PLOS ONE*, 14, no. 6, (June 21, 2019), e0218192.

[104] Fouron, JC. "The Unrecognized Physiological and Clinical Significance of the Fetal Aortic Isthmus: Editorial." *Ultrasound in Obstetrics and Gynecology*, 22, no. 5, (November 2003), 441–47.

[105] Ferrazzi, E; Lees, C; Acharya, G. "The Controversial Role of the Ductus Venosus in Hypoxic Human Fetuses." *Acta Obstetricia et Gynecologica Scandinavica*, 2019.

[106] Lund, A; Ebbing, C; Rasmussen, S; Kiserud, T; Kessler, J. "Maternal Diabetes Alters the Development of Ductus Venosus Shunting in the Fetus." *Acta Obstetricia et Gynecologica Scandinavica*, 97, no. 8, (August 2018), 1032–40.

[107] Morton, SU; Brodsky, D. "Fetal Physiology and the Transition to Extrauterine Life." *Clinics in Perinatology*, 43, no. 3, (2016), 395–407.

[108] Stenmark, KR; Fagan, KA; Frid, MG. "Hypoxia-Induced Pulmonary Vascular Remodeling: Cellular and Molecular Mechanisms." *Circulation Research*, 99, no. 7, (September 29, 2006), 675–91. https://doi.org/10.1161/01.RES.0000243584.45145.3f.

[109] Roberton, NRC. "Persistent Fetal Circulation Complicating Other Neonatal Lung Disorders—Definition and Diagnosis." In *Perinatal Medicine*, 181–187. Springer, 1985.

[110] Vali, P; Lakshminrusimha, S. "The Fetus Can Teach Us: Oxygen and the Pulmonary Vasculature." *Children*, 4, no. 8, (2017), 67.

[111] Rurak, DW; Gruber, NC. "Increased Oxygen Consumption Associated with Breathing Activity in Fetal Lambs." *Journal of Applied Physiology*, 54, no. 3, (1983), 701–7.

[112] Koos, BJ; Doany, W. "Role of Plasma Adenosine in Breathing Responses to Hypoxia in Fetal Sheep," 1991, 5.

[113] Teppema, LJ; Dahan, A. "The Ventilatory Response to Hypoxia in Mammals: Mechanisms, Measurement, and Analysis." *Physiological Reviews*, 90, no. 2, (2010), 675–754.

[114] Matturri, L; Lavezzi, AM. "Unexplained Stillbirth versus SIDS: Common Congenital Diseases of the Autonomic Nervous System–Pathology and Nosology." *Early Human Development*, 87, no. 3, (2011), 209–15.

[115] Cummings, KJ; Hewitt, JC; Li, A; Daubenspeck, JA; Nattie, EE. "Postnatal Loss of Brainstem Serotonin Neurones Compromises the Ability of Neonatal Rats to Survive Episodic Severe Hypoxia: 5-HT and Autoresuscitation in Neonatal Rats." *The Journal of Physiology*, 589, no. 21, (2011), 5247–56.

[116] Beltrán-Castillo, S; Morgado-Valle, C; Eugenín, J. "The Onset of the Fetal Respiratory Rhythm: An Emergent Property Triggered by Chemosensory Drive?" In *The Plastic Brain*, 163–192. Springer, 2017.

[117] Bright, FM; Vink, R; Byard, RW. "The Potential Role of Substance P in Brainstem Homeostatic Control in the Pathogenesis of Sudden Infant Death Syndrome (SIDS)." *Neuropeptides*, 70, (August 2018), 1–8.

[118] Groome, LJ; Mooney, DM; Bentz, LS; Wilson, JD. "Vagal Tone during Quiet Sleep in Normal Human Term Fetuses." *Developmental Psychobiology*, 27, no. 7, (1994), 453–66.

[119] Leite, CAC; Taylor, EW; Guerra, CDR; Florindo, LH; Belão, T; Rantin, FT. "The Role of the Vagus Nerve in the Generation of Cardiorespiratory Interactions in a Neotropical Fish, the Pacu, Piaractus Mesopotamicus." *Journal of Comparative Physiology A*, 195, no. 8, (2009), 721–731.

[120] Connors, G; Hunse, C; Carmichael, L; Natale, R; Richardson, B. "The Role of Carbon Dioxide in the Generation of Human Fetal Breathing Movements." *American Journal of Obstetrics and Gynecology*, 158, no. 2, (1988), 322–27.

[121] Kinney, HC; Haynes, RL. "The Serotonin Brainstem Hypothesis for the Sudden Infant Death Syndrome." *Journal of Neuropathology & Experimental Neurology*, 78, no. 9, (2019), 765–779.

[122] Haynes, RL. "Biomarkers of Sudden Infant Death Syndrome (SIDS) Risk and SIDS Death." In *SIDS Sudden Infant and Early Childhood Death: The Past, the Present and the Future*. University of Adelaide Press, 2018.

[123] Livolsi, A; Niederhoffer, N; Dali-Youcef, N; Rambaud, C; Olexa, C; Mokni, W; Gies, JP; Bousquet, P. "Cardiac Muscarinic Receptor Overexpression in Sudden Infant Death Syndrome." Edited by Rory Edward Morty. *PLoS ONE*, 5, no. 3, (2010), e9464.

In: A Closer Look at Heart Rate
Editor: André Alves Pereira

ISBN: 978-1-53616-979-9
© 2020 Nova Science Publishers, Inc.

Chapter 4

MEDITATION: A SIMPLE INEXPENSIVE TECHNIQUE FOR VOLUNTARY CONTROL OF HEART RATE

Satish G. Patil[1], Ishwar V. Basavaraddi[2] and Mallanagoud S. Biradar[3]

[1]Department of Physiology, Shri B. M. Patil Medical College,
Hospital and Research Centre, BLDE (Deemed to be University),
Vijayapura, Karnataka, India
[2]Morarji Desai National Institute of Yoga, Delhi, India
[3]Department of Medicine, Shri B. M. Patil Medical College,
Hospital and Research Centre, BLDE (Deemed to be University),
Vijayapura, Karnataka, India

ABSTRACT

High resting heart rate (HR) is an independent cardiovascular risk factor and predictor of all-cause mortality in individuals with or without cardiovascular disease. Studies have demonstrated that drugs that increase the heart rate worsen the prognosis, while those that reduce the heart rate such as beta-blockers have a beneficial effect after acute myocardial infarction and in chronic cardiac failure. Available data suggest that a strategy which reduces the heart rate and improves heart-rate variability prevents cardiovascular morbidity, increase longevity and also has a favorable effect on the prognosis of cardiovascular disease. Meditation is a practice where an individual focuses their mind on a particular object, thought or activity for self-realization and inner awareness. Meditative practices are aimed at training the mind for an achievement of a state of increased consciousness. It allows the mind to calm down and relax mentally, increases attention and concentration, reduces stress and anxiety, and enhances inner peace and happiness. In this chapter, the role of meditation in cardiovascular risk reduction through beneficial modulation in heart rate and heart-rate variability will be reviewed and discussed.

Keywords: meditation, heart rate, heart-rate variability, cardiovascular risk

1. INTRODUCTION

High resting heart rate (HR) is an independent cardiovascular risk factor and predictor of all-cause mortality in individuals with or without cardiovascular disease [1-3]. Heart rate is closely related to body temperature, oxygen consumption and metabolic demand, thus it is associated with metabolic disturbances that lead to cardiovascular morbidity and mortality [4]. Increase in heart rate increases myocardial oxygen demand and its workload. Studies have demonstrated that an increase in heart rate of 10 beats per minute increases the risk of cardiac death by about 20% [5]. The lower the oxygen consumption and energy utilized, the longer the lifespan. This shows that there is an inverse relationship between the heart rate and longevity [6, 7]. High heart rate has a detrimental effect on the artery by increasing the arterial wall stress leading to atherosclerosis [8, 9]. Reduction in heart-rate variability (HRV) due to loss of control of heart rate and rhythm by the central autonomic nervous system is a strong predictor of cardiovascular morbidity and mortality [10-12].

Clinical studies have demonstrated that drugs that increase the heart rate worsen the prognosis, while those that reduce the heart rate such as beta-blockers have beneficial effect after acute myocardial infarction and in chronic cardiac failure. Studies have demonstrated that drugs that increase the heart rate worsen the prognosis, while those that reduce the heart rate such as beta-blockers have a beneficial effect after acute myocardial infarction and in chronic cardiac failure [13]. Available data suggest that a strategy which reduces the heart rate and improves heart-rate variability prevents cardiovascular morbidity, increase longevity and also has a favorable effect on the prognosis of cardiovascular disease [6, 14, 15]. Growing evidences suggest that heart rate and rhythm can be controlled voluntarily by the simple, inexpensive holistic traditional method of "meditation" [16]. Meditation relaxes mind, reduces stress, improves concentration and achieve a state of increased consciousness. It reduces the metabolic demand and heart rate. Studies have reported the beneficial effect of several forms of meditation on cardiovascular health [16-19]. In this chapter, the role of meditation in cardiovascular risk reduction through beneficial modulation in heart rate and heart rate variability will be reviewed and discussed.

2. MEDITATION

Meditation is a practice where an individual focuses their mind on a particular object, thought or activity for self-realization and inner awareness. It is practiced to (a) increase attention and concentration, (b) calm-down mind and relax mentally (c) reduce stress and anxiety (d) increase consciousness and (e) find inner peace and happiness [16]. Since antiquity, meditation has been practiced in many religious traditions as a path for enlightenment. Its origin is thought to be from Hinduism and Buddhism and the history of the practice of meditation dates as far back as 5000 BC. The references of meditative process can also be found in Christianity, Judaism, and Islam. The meaning of meditation is "to think, to contemplate, to ponder." The word 'Dhyana' derived from a Sanskrit root 'dhyai' in Hinduism means contemplation and meditation. An uninterrupted flow of the mind towards the chosen particular object of concentration is Dhyana or meditation. Dhyana is the penultimate step of eight limb yoga (Ashtanga yoga) prescribed to reach an ultimate stage of emancipation [20].

2.1. Types of Meditation

Several styles of meditation are in practice such as, to name a few are yoga meditation, OM meditation, Transcendental meditation, Cyclic-meditation, Vipassana meditation, Zen meditation, Mindfulness meditation, Loving kindness meditation (Metta meditation), Taoists meditation. Even within the same tradition, there are variations in the method of practice of meditation. It has been observed that schools and individual teachers belonging to the same faith, teach distinct types of meditation with permutation and combination of traditional methods (which are modified based on their observations and experience) [21]. The focus of object in meditation includes awareness on breath, awareness of internal sensations, attention on chanting powerful words and sounds, and fixing the gaze (with open eyes) on the object of meditation or dhyana. In this chapter, we enumerate those meditations which are widely practiced and researched to understand its health benefits, particularly on heart.

2.2. Classification of Meditation

I. Based on the origin of meditative practices, they can be broadly classified in to two groups.
   i) Hindu meditation: origin is from ancient Vedic tradition of India.
      a) Yoga meditations
      b) OM meditation
      c) Cyclic meditation
      d) Transcendental meditation.

ii) Buddhist meditation: origin is from Buddhist teachings
   a) Vipassana meditation
   b) Samatha meditation
   c) Zen meditation (Zazen)
   d) Mindful meditation
   e) Metta meditation or loving kindness meditation

II. Based on traditional texts and modern neuroscientific conceptions, some meditative practices are broadly classified into two groups [22]:
   (1) Focused attention: include meditative practices that entail voluntary focusing of attention on a chosen object, breathing, image, words (mantra) or phrases. Yoga meditation, OM meditation, Cyclic meditation, chanting (mantra) meditation, transcendental meditation, loving kindness meditation etc.
   (2) Open monitoring meditation: include meditative practices that involve non-reactive monitoring of the content of experience from moment to moment. Instead of focusing on one object like in focused attention, here an individual strives to be in the present moment with open monitoring on all aspects of our experience, this may be an internal (thoughts, feelings, memory) or external (smell, sound etc) without becoming engrossed in or distracted by them. Vipassana meditation, mindful meditations are the examples of open monitoring meditation.

3. INFLUENCE OF MEDITATION ON HEART RATE

3.1. Yoga Meditation

Yoga is an ancient Indian science comprising psycho-somatic-spiritual discipline that helps to achieve a harmony between mind, body and soul [23]. Yoga is derived from a Sanskrit word 'Yuj' that means joining. It is joining of the individual self with the universal self. Yoga is a conscious process of gaining mastery over mind. Yogasanas or asanas (physical stretching exercise with controlled breathing), pranayama (breathing techniques), and concentration and dhyana (meditation) are the major parts of yoga practices. Yogasanas mainly aim at the achievement of positive, flexible bodily health, while meditation aims at influencing the mind and consciousness. In fact, yogasanas and pranayama also indirectly aim at influencing the mind. It is essential to first purify, vitalize and relax the joints and muscles of the body before undertaking meditation [24]. If the body is completely relaxed, and breathing becomes slow and stable then only one can focus on one point and meditate. Control of diet is a primary concern in yoga practices, so yoga meditators should adopt Sattvik (a pure vegetarian food, seasonal fruits) diet. Therefore, in yoga, asanas, kriyas (cleansing techniques), and pranayama are practiced in sequence before starting meditative practice. So, meditation is the penultimate step (eight steps of Ashtanga yoga) of yoga prescribed to reach an ultimate stage of emancipation. There are several forms of yoga based meditative practices: focusing on the breath or glabella (middle of the eyebrow) or on a particular object, chanting syllable 'OM' or mantra, silently chanting mantra in mind, guided cyclic combination of 'awakening' and 'calming practices' (Cyclic meditation). Few forms of yoga based meditative practices such as OM meditation and cyclic meditation are widely practiced individually and researched. These practices are discussed separately below.

It is believed that involuntary functions of the body (visceral and glandular functions) can be brought under voluntary control by yoga practice or meditation. So, yoga is a conscious process of gaining a voluntary control over involuntary functions through influencing the mind. Yogi, a master in yoga practice can control or reduce heart rate voluntarily. They even claim to stop the heart at will. Few classical experiments were conducted by scientists from India and other countries to investigate the yogic control on visceral functions, in particular on heart activities [25-29].

Among these, two studies have observed that yoga masters can reduce the heart rate at will [25, 26]. Anand BK et al., studied the ability of the yogi (subject who is master in yoga) to control the heart rate at will in an air-tight sealed box for 8-10 hours, where they found that the subject can reduce the heart rate voluntarily from 85 beats per minute (bpm) at baseline to about 60 bpm. They also observed a reduction in the average utilization of oxygen from 19.5 liters/hour at baseline to 13.3 liters/hour during the period of study, without any increase in respiratory rate [26]. Another study published in the American Heart Journal, investigated a Yoga Master (Yogi) who claim to control the heart voluntarily. In this study, the subject (Yogi) was examined continuously, when he remained confined in a small underground pit for eight days in a state of deep meditation (called as 'Samadhi' in yoga) in sitting posture with little garments and a bottle of 5 liters of water (may not be for drinking but to keep the air fully humid inside the pit). An ECG was continuously monitored during the entire 8 days.

Heart rate was normal at baseline (before entering into the underground pit) which suddenly started rising progressively soon after closing the pit which reached to 250 bpm on the second day. This was followed by sudden straight line in the ECG tracing indicating that the subject has completely stopped his heart or decreased the electrical activity below a recordable level, which persisted till eighth day morning. Then to a surprise of researchers electrical activity returned (heart started beating) half an hour before the scheduled opening of the pit on eight day (as per instructions of the subject), exactly in the same way as claimed by the subject/Yogi that he will begin to come out from the deep trance or suspended animation meditation (Samadhi) after about seven days. The subject was on total starvation, sensory deprivation and present in a dark and closed humid atmosphere for 8 days, during which he lost about 4.5 Kg of weight.

Although the researchers could not explain the precise mechanism, but they speculated that the subject may be was in a hypometabolic wakeful state of meditation [30]. Other studies have also shown that yoga meditation can reduce heart rate by about 10 beats per minute in healthy and patients with asthma [31-33]. Yoga training for three months reduced the heart rate significantly in elderly individuals with hypertension [34]. A significant beneficial modulation in autonomic function through a reduction in sympathetic activity and shift in sympathovagal balance towards normal parasympathetic dominance was reported in healthy athletes [35] and elderly individuals with hypertension [36].

3.2. Cyclic Meditation (CM)

This is a guided meditation technique. Cyclic meditation is designed for those who either would be restless and cannot concentrate or fall asleep during an attempt to practice meditation. This technique is derived from an ancient Indian text (Manudkya Upanishad), stating that 'awaken the mind during a state of mental inactivity, calm it when it is agitated and once the mind reaches the perfect equilibrium then do not disturb it again.' Hence, CM includes a cyclic combination of 'awakening' by yogasanasa (stretching exercises with awareness and controlled breathing) and 'calming practices' (awareness on breath, body and chanting words or sounds). The duration of each of session of cyclic meditation is 23 minutes [37].

Activities during the day are known to influence the sleep on the following night. A practice of cyclic meditation two times a day showed a decrease in heart rate, improvement in heart rate variability (HRV) with reduced sympathetic tone and enhanced parasympathetic activity during sleep on the following night in young healthy adults [38]. A decrease in heart rate, an improvement in HRV and shift of sympatho-vagal balance towards a normal parasympathetic dominance after a practice of CM has been reported in healthy individuals [39-41].

Few studies have shown a decreased consumption of oxygen during CM when compared to supine rest for the same duration [42-44]. In comparison to supine rest, energy expenditure was lesser during the practice of CM [39].

3.3. Transcendental Meditation (TM)

It is a form of silent mantra meditation developed by Maharishi Mahesh Yogi, an Indian scholar of Vedic tradition. This practice involves the use a specific mantra for different individuals. It is practiced with closed eyes for 20 minutes twice in a day. It is an effortless procedure without involving concentration, contemplation and mind control. This practice allows the mind to settle down to a state of calmness during which the person is aware of his or her consciousness. This state of consciousness is called transcendental consciousness, which is different from usual waking, dreaming and sleep state [45, 46].

Transcendental meditation is the most extensively studied style of meditation. Several studies have demonstrated that TM practice can reduce heart rate in healthy [47-49] and in adolescents with high normal blood pressure (at risk for hypertension development) [51]. However, there are few studies that did not find any influence of TM on heart rate [52, 53]. Many studies have also shown a beneficial influence of TM on cardiovascular haemodynamics. A reduction of systolic blood pressure by about 4 mmHg and diastolic blood pressure by about 3 mmHg has been reported by the practice of TM [54, 55]. There are slight discrepancies among the studies, regarding the effect of TM on heart rate and blood pressure. Few studies have reported a beneficial influence on HR but not on the BP [47] while others found a reduction in BP with no change in the heart rate [53]. Transcendental meditation was shown to have a better beneficial impact upon cardiovascular functioning than other relaxation techniques [51, 53]. It can also reduce the total peripheral resistance, which is responsible for the development of hypertension [51].

3.4. OM Meditation

'OM' or 'AUM' is the sacred syllable in Indian culture. OM is one of the most spiritual syllable or sound in Hinduism. This syllable is either chanted independently or before a mantra during meditative practices. It may be chanted loudly or silently in mind. It is usually practiced in a comfortable sitting posture with closed eyes and there is no fixed duration of practice. Vibrations created by 'OM' or 'AUM' chanting have a smoothening effect on the whole body and mind. Mental repetition of 'OM' results in mental alertness with physiological rest and increased sensitivity to sensory transmission [56, 57]. Studies have shown a significant reduction in HR by the practice of OM meditation in healthy individuals. These studies have also reported a beneficial modulation in autonomic regulation by OM meditation [58-60]. One study has demonstrated a decreased consumption of oxygen during OM meditation [58].

3.5. Buddhist Meditation

Samatha meditation, Vipassana meditation, Mindfulness meditation, Metta (loving kindness) meditation, Zen meditation are the meditative practices originated from Buddhist teachings. Samatha means "calm" and samatha meditation is often referred to as 'calm meditation.' It is a method of calming the mind by focusing on a single object, breath or image [16]. Vipassana is also known as 'insight meditation' which means 'to see into the true nature of reality' or 'to see things as they really are.' It is a method of training the mind through focused attention on emotions, internal bodily sensations and thoughts without mental reactivity to the experience. It is a technique for self transformation through self observation. The ultimate aim of this technique is an achievement of emotional stability and happiness [61]. Mindfulness meditation is mainly based on Vipassana meditation. It is a method of training the mind by observing and accepting all that arises without judgment. 'Metta' means kindness and benevolence. In Metta meditation or Loving kindness meditation, the meditator sits in a comfortable position with closed eyes and generates a feeling of kindness and benevolence in his mind. First generate loving kindness to oneself and then progressively to a good friend, to a neutral person, to a difficult person, to all the four equally (oneself, friend, neutral person, difficult person) and then gradually to the entire Universe. Zazen is the Buddhist meditation from Japan. Zazen means a 'seated meditation.' It is a means of insight into the nature of existence. It is practiced in two ways: (a) focusing attention on one's breath and (b) observing present moment, thoughts and experiences that pass through their minds and around them [16].

Studies have shown an increased cardiac autonomic regulation during meditation [61-65]. A significant difference in the HRV in Zen-meditation practitioners and non-meditators was reported. They found a significant decrease in sympathetic activity and increase in parasympathetic tone in Zen-meditation practitioners (with a mean meditation experience of 6.0 ± 3.2 years) when compared with non-meditators [64]. Another study investigated the difference in HRV between experienced and novice Zen-meditation practitioners. This study did not find any significant difference in heart rate between experienced and novice Zen-meditators. Further, they found an increased cardiac autonomic nervous system activity in the experienced meditators than novice Zen-meditators [65].

CONCLUSION

A strategy which reduces the heart rate and improves heart-rate variability prevents cardiovascular morbidity, increase longevity and also has a favorable effect on the prognosis of cardiovascular disease. Although, several types of meditative practices are in existence, they are all aimed at training the mind and calming down the mind for an achievement of a state of increased consciousness. The heart is regulated and controlled by mainly the autonomic nervous system and local hormones through the inputs from central and peripheral regions. All meditative practices, irrespective of its origin and teaching methods, appear to induce beneficial modulation in the cardiac autonomic nervous system and improve its regulatory control of heart rate, increase heart-rate-variability, reduce metabolic demand and heart rate. Meditation helps in maintaining sympathovagal balance through a reduction in sympathetic activation and restoring the normal parasympathetic dominance.

Meditation is an effective, safe and inexpensive life-style modality that can be recommended for cardiovascular risk reduction and management of cardiovascular disease.

REFERENCES

[1] Cooney MT, Vartiainen E, Laatikainen T, Juolevi A, Dudina A, Graham IM. Elevated resting heart rate is an independent risk factor for cardiovascular disease in healthy men and women. *Am Heart J.* 2010;159(4):612-619.

[2] Zhang D, Shen X, Qi X. Resting heart rate and all-cause and cardiovascular mortality in the general population: a meta-analysis. *CMAJ.* 2016;188(3):E53-E63.

[3] Aune D, Sen A, ó'Hartaigh B, Janszky I, Romundstad PR, Tonstad S, Vatten LJ. Resting heart rate and the risk of cardiovascular disease, total cancer, and all-cause mortality - A systematic review and dose-response meta-analysis of prospective studies. *Nutr Metab Cardiovasc Dis.* 2017;27(6):504-517.

[4] Rogowski O, Steinvil A, Berliner S, Cohen M, Saar N, Ben-Bassat OK, Shapira I. Elevated resting heart rate is associated with the metabolic syndrome. *Cardiovasc Diabetol.* 2009 Oct 14;8:55.

[5] Perret-Guillaume C1, Joly L, Benetos A. Heart rate as a risk factor for cardiovascular disease. *Prog Cardiovasc Dis.* 2009;52(1):6-10.

[6] Boudoulas KD, Borer JS, Boudoulas H. Heart Rate, Life Expectancy and the Cardiovascular System: Therapeutic Considerations. *Cardiology.* 2015;132(4):199-212.

[7] Zhang GQ1, Zhang W. Heart rate, lifespan, and mortality risk. *Ageing Res Rev.* 2009;8(1):52-60.

[8] Giannoglou GD, Chatzizisis YS, Zamboulis C, Parcharidis GE, Mikhailidis DP, Louridas GE. Elevated heart rate and atherosclerosis: an overview of the pathogenetic mechanisms. *Int J Cardiol.* 2008; 126(3):302-12.

[9] Custodis F, Schirmer SH, Baumhäkel M, Heusch G, Böhm M, Laufs U. Vascular pathophysiology in response to increased heart rate. *J Am Coll Cardiol*. 2010;56(24):1973-83.

[10] Thayer JF, Yamamoto SS, Brosschot JF. The relationship of autonomic imbalance, heart rate variability and cardiovascular disease risk factors. *Int J Cardiol*. 2010;141(2):122-31.

[11] Rodrigues TC, Ehrlich J, Hunter CM, Kinney GL, Rewers M, Snell-Bergeon JK. Reduced heart rate variability predicts progression of coronary artery calcification in adults with type 1 diabetes and controls without diabetes. *Diabetes Technol Ther*. 2010;12(12):963-9.

[12] Sessa F, Anna V, Messina G, Cibelli G, Monda V, Marsala G, Ruberto M, Biondi A, Cascio O, Bertozzi G, Pisanelli D, Maglietta F, Messina A, Mollica MP, Salerno M. Heart rate variability as predictive factor for sudden cardiac death. *Aging* (Albany NY). 2018;10(2):166-177.

[13] Custodis F, Reil JC, Laufs U, Böhm M. Heart rate: a global target for cardiovascular disease and therapy along the cardiovascular disease continuum. *J Cardiol*. 2013;62(3):183-7.

[14] Cucherat M. Quantitative relationship between resting heart rate reduction and magnitude of clinical benefits in post-myocardial infarction: a meta-regression of randomized clinical trials. *Eur Heart J*. 2007;28(24):3012-9.

[15] Tardif JC. Heart rate as a treatable cardiovascular risk factor. *Br Med Bull*. 2009;90:71-84.

[16] Levine GN, Lange RA, Bairey-Merz CN, Davidson RJ, Jamerson K, Mehta PK, Michos ED, Norris K, Ray IB, Saban KL, Shah T, Stein R, Smith SC Jr; American Heart Association Council on Clinical Cardiology; Council on Cardiovascular and Stroke Nursing; and Council on Hypertension. Meditation and Cardiovascular Risk Reduction: A Scientific Statement From the American Heart Association. *J Am Heart Assoc*. 2017;6(10). pii: e002218.

[17] Guddeti RR1, Dang G, Williams MA, Alla VM. Role of Yoga in Cardiac Disease and Rehabilitation. *J Cardiopulm Rehabil Prev.* 2018;27. doi: 10.1097/HCR.0000000000000372.

[18] Manchanda SC. Yoga--a promising technique to control cardiovascular disease. *Indian Heart J.* 2014 Sep-Oct;66(5):487-9.

[19] Jayasinghe SR. Yoga in cardiac health (a review). *Eur J Cardiovasc Prev Rehabil.* 2004 Oct;11(5):369-75.

[20] Taimini IK. *The science of yoga.* Madras, India: The Theosophical Publishing House; 1986.

[21] Eugene Taylor (1999). Michael Murphy; Steven Donovan; Eugene Taylor (eds.). "Introduction." *The Physical and Psychological Effects of Meditation: A Review of Contemporary Research with a Comprehensive Bibliography* 1931–1996: 1–32.

[22] Lutz A, Slagter HA, Dunne JD, Davidson RJ. Attention regulation and monitoring in meditation. *Trends Cogn Sci.* 2008 Apr;12(4):163-9.

[23] Patil SG, Mullur L, Khodnapur J, Dhanakshirur GB, Aithala MR. Effect of yoga on short-term heart rate variability measure as an index of stress in subjunior cyclists: A pilot study. *Indian J Physiol Pharmacol* 2013;57:81-86.

[24] Anand BK. Yoga and medical sciences. *Indian J Physiol Pharmacol.* 1991;35(2):84-87.

[25] Wenger MA, Bagchi BK, Anand BK. Experiments in India on 'voluntary' control of the heart and pulse. *Circulation.* 1961;24: 1319–25.

[26] Anand BK. Chhina GS, Singh B. Studies on Shri Ramanand. Yogi during his stay in an air-tight box. *Ind J Med Res.* 1961;49: 82-89.

[27] Anand BK. Chhina GS. Investigations on yogis claiming to stop their heart beats. *Ind J Med Res* 1961; 49: 90-94.

[28] Anand BK, Chhina GS, Singh B. Some aspects of electroencephalographic studies in yogis. electroenceph *Clin Neurophysiol.* 1961;13:452-56.

[29] Kothari LK, Bardia A, Gupta OP. The yogic claim of voluntary control over the heart beat: an unusual demonstration. *Am Heart J.* 1973;86(2):282-4.

[30] Wallace RK, Benson H, Wilson AF. A wakeful hypometabolic physiologic state. *Am J Physiol.* 1971;221(3):795-9.

[31] Khanam AA, Sachdeva U, Guleria R, Deepak KK. Study of pulmonary and autonomic functions of asthma patients after yoga training. *Indian J Physiol Pharmacol.* 1996;40(4):318-24.

[32] Raghavendra B, Telles S, Manjunath N, Deepak K, Naveen K, Subramanya P. Voluntary heart rate reduction following yoga using different strategies. *Int J Yoga.* 2013;6(1):26-30.

[33] Telles S, Joshi M, Dash M, Raghuraj P, Naveen KV, Nagendra HR. An evaluation of the ability to voluntarily reduce the heart rate after a month of yoga practice. *Integr Physiol Behav Sci.* 2004;39:119–25.

[34] Patil SG, Patil SS, Aithala MR, Das KK. Comparison of yoga and walking-exercise on cardiac time intervals as a measure of cardiac function in elderly with increased pulse pressure. *Indian Heart Journal.* 2017;4:485-490.

[35] Patil SG, Mullur L, Khodnapur J, Dhanakshirur GB, Aithala MR. Effect of yoga on short-term heart rate variability measure as an index of stress in subjunior cyclists: A pilot study. *Indian J Physiol Pharmacol* 2013;57:81-86.

[36] Patil SG, Aithala MR, Das KK. Effect of yoga on arterial stiffness in elderly with increased pulse pressure: A randomized controlled study. *Complement Ther Med* 2015;23:562-9.

[37] Subramanya P, Telles S. A review of the scientific studies on cyclic meditation. *Int J Yoga.* 2009 Jul;2(2):46-8.

[38] Patra S, Telles S. Heart rate variability during sleep following the practice of cyclic meditation and supine rest. *Appl Psychophysiol Biofeedback.* 2010;35(2):135-40.

[39] Sarang, SP, Telles S. Cyclic meditation: A moving meditation-reduces energy expenditure more than supine rest. *J Indian Psychol.* 2006;24:17–25.

[40] Vempati RP, Telles S. Yoga-based guided relaxation reduces sympathetic activity judged from baseline levels. *Psychol Rep.* 2002;90(2):487-94.
[41] Sarang P, Telles S. Effects of two yoga based relaxation techniques on heart rate variability. *Int J Stress Manag.* 2006;13:460–75.
[42] Vempati RP, Telles S. Yoga based relaxation versus supine rest: A study of oxygen consumption, breath rate and volume and autonomic measures. *J Indian Psychol.* 1999;17:46–52.
[43] Telles S, Reddy SK, Nagendra HR. Oxygen consumption and respiration following two yoga relaxation techniques. *Appl Psychophysiol Biofeedback.* 2000;25:221–7.
[44] Sarang PS, Telles S. Oxygen consumption and respiration during and after two yoga relaxation techniques. *Appl Psychophysiol Biofeedback.* 2006;31:143–53.
[45] Walton KG, Schneider RH, Nidich S. Review of controlled research on the transcendental meditation program and cardiovascular disease. Risk factors, morbidity, and mortality. *Cardiol Rev.* 2004;12(5):262-6.
[46] Travis F, Wallace RK. Autonomic patterns during respiration suspensions: possible markers of transcendental consciousness. *Psychophysiology.* 1997;34:39-46.
[47] Mendhurwar SS and Gadakari JG. Effect of transcendental meditation on pulse rate and blood pressure. *International Journal of Medical and Clinical Research.* 2012;3(1): 107-109.
[48] Wallace RK. Physiological effects of transcendental meditation. *Science* 1970; 167: 1751-1754.
[49] Wallace RK, Benson H, Wilson AF. A wakeful hypometabolic physiologic state. *Am J Physiol* 1971; 21: 795-799.
[50] Barnes VA, Treiber FA, Turner JR, Davis H, Strong WB. Acute effects of transcendental meditation on hemodynamic functioning in middle-aged adults. *Psychosom Med.* 1999;61(4):525-31.
[51] Barnes VA, Treiber FA, Davis H. Impact of Transcendental Meditation on cardiovascular function at rest and during acute stress

in adolescents with high normal blood pressure. *J Psychosom Res.* 2001 Oct;51(4):597-605.

[52] Michaels RR, Parra J, McCann DS, Vander AJ. Renin, cortisol, and aldosterone during transcendental meditation. *Psychosom Med.* 1979;41(1):50-4.

[53] Schneider RH., Staggers F, Alxander CN, Sheppard W, Rainforth M, Kondwani K, Smith S, King CG. A randomised controlled trial of stress reduction for hypertension in older African Americans. *Hypertension.* 1995;26(5):820-7.

[54] Ooi SL, Giovino M, Pak SC. Transcendental meditation for lowering blood pressure: An overview of systematic reviews and meta-analyses. *Complement Ther Med.* 2017;34:26-34.

[55] Anderson JW1, Liu C, Kryscio RJ. Blood pressure response to transcendental meditation: a meta-analysis. *Am J Hypertens.* 2008;21(3):310-6.

[56] Kumar S1, Nagendra H, Manjunath N, Naveen K, Telles S. Meditation on OM: Relevance from ancient texts and contemporary science. *Int J Yoga.* 2010;3(1):2-5.

[57] Telles S, Nagarathna R, Nagendra HR, Desiraju T. Alterations in auditory middle latency evoked potentials during meditation on a meaningful syllable - 'OM.' *Intern J Neurosci* 1994; 76: 87-93.

[58] Telles S, Nagarathna R, Nagendra HR. Autonomic changes during 'OM' meditation. *Indian J Physiol Pharmacol* 1995; 39 (4): 418-420.

[59] Telles S, Nagarathna R, Nagendra HR. Autonomic changes while mentally repeating two syllables--one meaningful and the other neutral. *Indian J Physiol Pharmacol.* 1998;42(1):57-63.

[60] Berad A, Lakshmi ANR, Sneha P. Effect of OM meditation on autonomic functions in healthy young individuals *Indian Journal of Clinical Anatomy and Physiology.*, 2017;4(2):263-265.

[61] Delgado-Pastor LC, Perakakis P, Subramanya P, Telles S, Vila J. Mindfulness (Vipassana) meditation: effects on P3b event-related potential and heart rate variability. *Int J Psychophysiol.* 2013;90(2):207-14.

[62] Amihai I, Kozhevnikov M. The Influence of Buddhist Meditation Traditions on the Autonomic System and Attention. *Biomed Res Int.* 2015;2015:731579.

[63] Krygier JR1, Heathers JA, Shahrestani S, Abbott M, Gross JJ, Kemp AH. Mindfulness meditation, well-being, and heart rate variability: a preliminary investigation into the impact of intensive Vipassana meditation. *Int J Psychophysiol.* 2013;89(3):305-13.

[64] Wu SD, Lo PC. Inward-attention meditation increases parasympathetic activity: a study based on heart rate variability. *Biomed Res.* 2008;29(5):245-50.

[65] Hoshiyama M, Hoshiyama A. Heart rate variability associated with experienced Zen-meditation. *Computers in cardiology.* 2008;569-572.

INDEX

A

Abraham, 38
accounting, 95
acetylcholine, 88
acidosis, 87
active sleep, vii, x, 72, 73, 76, 82, 83, 84, 90, 93
acute stress, 55, 130
adaptation, 39, 47
adenosine, 88, 90, 97, 99
adjustment, 61
adolescent boys, 48
adolescents, 36, 65, 123, 131
adults, 9, 38, 63, 84, 90, 92, 95, 97, 122, 127, 130
affective disorder, 68
age, viii, 2, 5, 8, 9, 19, 20, 21, 23, 24, 26, 27, 30, 31, 32, 37, 39, 48, 62
alcohol dependence, 67
aldosterone, 131
alternative hypothesis, 45
American Heart Association, 37, 127
American Psychological Association, 65
amniotic fluid, 95
amplitude, 15

amygdala, 7, 32
antagonism, xi, 72, 80, 87
antidepressant, 35
anxiety, ix, xi, 7, 9, 22, 26, 27, 28, 29, 30, 32, 33, 34, 42, 47, 48, 49, 52, 62, 64, 65, 66, 67, 116, 117
anxiety disorder, 48, 62, 65, 66
apnea, 94
arousal, 7, 25, 29, 47, 62
arteries, 97
artery, 76, 92, 95, 97, 116, 127
asphyxia, 91
assessment, 63, 82
asthma, 122, 129
astrocytes, 99
atherosclerosis, 116, 126
athletes, 122
atmosphere, 121
autogenic training, 67
autonomic activity, 2
autonomic nervous system, 27, 47, 62, 116, 125
awareness, xi, 116, 117, 118, 122

B

bandwidth, x, 72, 74, 84
behavioral inhibition system, 2, 7, 11, 38
behaviors, 29
beneficial effect, xi, 115, 117
benefits, 118, 127
beverages, 49, 61
biological processes, 30
biomarkers, 35
blood, 63, 64, 65, 92, 95, 97, 123, 130, 131
blood pressure, 63, 64, 65, 123, 130, 131
borderline personality disorder, 36
brain, 6, 30, 38, 95, 97
brain functioning, 30
breathing, 47, 76, 78, 90, 98, 119, 120, 122
bronchopulmonary dysplasia, 98

C

caffeine, 61
calcification, 127
cardiac arrhythmia, 87
cardiovascular disease, xi, 5, 32, 115, 116, 117, 125, 126, 127, 128, 130
cardiovascular function, 64, 123, 130
cardiovascular morbidity, xi, 116, 117, 125
cardiovascular risk, vii, xi, 33, 115, 116, 117, 126, 127
central nervous system, 27
cerebral arteries, 97
chemoreceptors, 86, 98
childhood, 6, 62
children, 34, 36, 48, 66
cholestasis, 88
Christianity, 117
chronic hypoxia, 87
clinical application, 63
clinical trials, 127
cognitive function, 34
cognitive performance, 39
cognitive psychology, 36
college students, 11
complex behaviors, 30
complex interactions, 90
complexity, 12, 14, 16, 27, 32, 34, 36, 37
conflict, xi, 7, 72, 80, 87
consciousness, viii, xi, 116, 117, 120, 123, 125, 130
conserving, xi, 72, 73, 80, 82, 84, 87, 88, 89, 90, 93, 94, 98, 103
consumption, 61, 91, 116, 122, 124, 130
coronary arteries, 98
correlation, 14, 16, 17, 20, 21, 23, 25, 28, 29, 46, 50, 57, 58, 76, 92
correlation analysis, 57, 58
correlation dimension, 16, 21
correlations, 15, 20, 21, 23, 25, 28, 29
cortisol, xi, 27, 31, 72, 79, 80, 81, 93, 94, 99, 131
creative thinking, 67
cumulative distribution function, 44
cycles, 61

D

data processing, 3
database, x, 72, 77, 78, 82, 84, 86
dependent variable, 57
depression, 27, 29, 35, 65
deprivation, 121
detection, 8, 30, 67, 74, 84
deviation, 14, 75, 78
diabetes, 73, 84, 91, 95, 97, 127
diagnostic criteria, x, 72, 74
diastolic blood pressure, 123
distribution, 16, 43, 44, 50, 91, 97, 98
dominance, x, 4, 72, 75, 94, 122, 125
ductus arteriosus, 98
dynamic systems, 15

E

education, 62
egg, 93
electrocardiogram, 2, 32, 49
emotion, 3, 10, 22, 24, 29, 39, 47, 64, 68
emotion regulation, 3, 39, 68
emotional experience, 27
emotional responses, 27
energy, 76, 79, 84, 89, 91, 94, 98, 116, 122, 129
energy consumption, 79, 94
energy expenditure, 76, 84, 91, 94, 98, 122, 129
entropy, 14, 15, 16, 28, 30, 32, 38, 76, 80
epidemiology, 64
epinephrine, 80, 87, 92, 93, 94, 99
event-related potential, 131
everyday life, 65
evidence, ix, 4, 27, 41, 46, 49, 84
evolution, 80, 81, 82, 88, 98
executive function, 34, 68
executive functions, 34
exercise, 63, 67, 120, 129
exposure, 43, 44, 63
eye movement, 73, 74

F

factor analysis, 10
false negative, 85
fear response, 63
feelings, 10, 119
Fetal Breathing Movements, 98, 103, 113
fetal growth, 73, 91
fetal growth retardation, 73
fetal oxygen -conserving shunts, 98
fetus, 73, 81, 87, 88, 89, 90, 91, 93, 94, 97, 98, 99
flexibility, x, 3, 34, 42, 47, 48, 60, 64, 66
flight, 32, 93

fluctuations, 4, 15, 33, 61, 83, 84
fMRI, 6
foramen ovale, 98
fractal analysis, 36
functional imaging, 34

G

gender differences, 5, 6, 18, 22, 30, 53
geometry, 32
gestational age, 91, 97
gestational diabetes, 88, 91, 95, 97
Great Britain, 65
growth, 73, 88, 90, 91
growth factor, 91

H

happiness, xi, 116, 117, 124
harmony, 119
health, 3, 5, 35, 38, 39, 49, 63, 65, 117, 118, 120, 128
heart disease, 32, 37, 62
heart rate (HR), vii, viii, ix, x, xi, 1, 2, 4, 5, 27, 30, 31, 32, 33, 34, 35, 36, 37, 38, 39, 41, 42, 43, 47, 49, 57, 59, 62, 63, 64, 65, 66, 67, 68, 72, 73, 76, 82, 86, 87, 89, 91, 115, 116, 117, 120, 121, 122, 123, 125, 126, 127, 128, 129, 130, 131, 132
heart rate variability, vii, viii, ix, 1, 2, 31, 32, 33, 34, 35, 36, 37, 38, 39, 41, 42, 49, 62, 63, 64, 65, 66, 67, 68, 76, 89, 91, 117, 122, 127, 128, 129, 130, 131, 132
height, 13, 16
heterogeneity, 81
histogram, 13, 16
history, 9, 49, 117
holistic tradition, 117
homeostasis, 4
hormones, 31, 125
HPA axis, 30

HR reactivity, 48
hub, 6
human, viii, 2, 34, 36, 60, 73, 87, 88, 91, 93, 94, 98, 99
human brain, 34
hyperglycemia, 84, 91, 98
hyperinsulinism, 91, 92
hyperplasia, 99
hypertension, 122, 123, 131
hypertrophy, 99
hyperventilation, 87
hypoglycemia, 92
hypothalamus, 88
hypothesis, vii, ix, 41, 45, 46, 57, 60, 73, 94
hypothesis test, 60
hypoxia, 84, 85, 86, 87, 88, 89, 90, 97, 98, 99

I

identification, 73, 79
identity, 14
image, 119, 124
impulsivity, 7, 11
in utero, 98
independent variable, 57
individual differences, 11, 30
individuals, xi, 29, 43, 59, 115, 116, 122, 123, 124, 131
infants, 81
infarction, 117
inferior vena cava, 81
inhibition, viii, xi, 2, 8, 9, 29, 31, 33, 35, 36, 38, 72, 80, 87, 98, 99
insulin, 90, 91, 92, 93
insulin resistance, 92
integration, 34, 39, 47, 68
interference, 73, 86
internalizing, 33, 64
intervention, 27, 59, 67
intrauterine growth retardation, 89

inversion, 76
Ireland, 65
Islam, 117

J

Japan, 125
joints, 120

K

kinetics, 93

L

laboratory tests, 49
latency, 131
lead, 49, 60, 89, 95, 116
lesions, 99
lethargy, 79
life experiences, 6
light, 34
Likert scale, 9, 10
longevity, xi, 116, 117, 125
lung function, 49

M

macrosomia, 95
magnitude, ix, 41, 42, 44, 45, 58, 127
major depressive disorder, 67
malaise, 81
mammals, 93
management, 126
maternal smoking, 88
matrix, 15, 17
measurement, 33, 43, 46, 50, 53, 56
measurements, viii, 2, 4, 43, 46, 48, 50, 53, 57, 60, 61, 65, 74, 95
medical, 67, 128

Index

medical science, 128
meditation, v, vii, xi, 115, 116, 117, 118, 119, 120, 121, 122, 123, 124, 125, 127, 128, 129, 130, 131, 132
mellitus, 73, 84, 88, 91, 95, 97
memory, 21, 27, 119
mental activity, 61
mental disorder, 36
mental fatigue, 4
mental state, 3, 61
Meta Quiet Sleep, 80, 99
meta-analysis, 5, 33, 35, 36, 38, 63, 126, 131
metabolic disturbances, 116
metabolic syndrome, 76, 77, 83, 91, 95, 96, 109, 126
metabolism, 73
Meta-Pattern A, x, 72, 77, 79, 86, 90
methodology, 67, 73, 85, 91
middle cerebral artery, 76, 95
moderates, 68
morbidity, 5, 116, 130
mortality, xi, 5, 37, 115, 116, 126, 130
mortality risk, 126
multidimensional, 17
multiple regression, 46
multivariate statistics, 38
muscarinic receptor, 99
myocardial infarction, xi, 65, 116, 117, 127

N

negative affectivity, 29
negative effects, 7
negative emotions, 7, 10
negative relation, 8, 58
nervous system, 125
neural function, 39
neural network, 86
neuropsychology, 34
neuroscience, 36, 64
neurotransmitter, 90
neurotransmitters, 95, 96, 97, 99
neutral, 7, 37, 124, 131
nitric oxide, 97
nonlinear dynamics, 33, 64
norepinephrine, 76, 79, 80, 87, 88, 90, 92, 93, 95, 99, 108
normal distribution, 43, 44
null, 45, 57
null hypothesis, 45, 57
nutritional status, 90, 99

O

obesity, 91
opioids, 99
oscillation, x, 72, 74
overlap, 6, 13
overweight, 95
oxygen, xi, 72, 73, 80, 82, 84, 87, 88, 89, 90, 93, 94, 98, 103, 116, 121, 122, 124, 130
oxygen consumption, 98, 116, 130

P

panic disorder, 34, 47
paradoxical sleep, 93
parallel, 98, 99
parasympathetic, x, xi, 4, 5, 21, 25, 26, 28, 29, 30, 37, 72, 75, 76, 79, 80, 86, 87, 92, 93, 94, 99, 105, 122, 125, 132
parasympathetic activity, 4, 5, 21, 26, 30, 87, 122, 132
parasympathetic nervous system, 28
participants, viii, 2, 3, 6, 7, 8, 9, 10, 12, 17, 19, 21, 22, 25, 26, 49, 53, 60
pathophysiology, 83, 100, 127
pathway, 73, 82, 84, 94, 99
Pattern A, x, 72, 74, 75, 77, 78, 79, 81, 82
peace, xi, 116, 117

percentile, ix, 42, 50, 51, 55
perfusion, 65
personality, 30
Philadelphia, 104
physiological mechanisms, 62
physiology, 38, 61, 63, 68, 91, 100
pilot study, 128, 129
population, 43, 44, 45, 50, 51, 60, 67, 83, 126
positive correlation, 25, 28
post-load blood sugar levels, 92
predictability, 15
prefrontal cortex, 6
pregnancy, 73, 79, 81, 84, 86, 89, 97
preparation, iv, 11, 62
principal component analysis, vii, viii, 2
probability, 14, 15, 44
probability density function, 44
psychological states, viii, 2
psychology, 63, 64, 65, 66, 68
psychopathology, 3, 32, 33, 38, 47, 62
psychosocial stress, 46, 48, 63

Q

QRS complex, 13, 14
quality assurance, 13
quantification, 15, 30
questionnaire, 10, 49
Quiet-Sleep, 74

R

reaction time, 27, 28
reactivity, ix, 42, 46, 47, 48, 50, 53, 60, 61, 64, 65, 124
reality, 124
recall, 10, 25, 98
reciprocal relationships, 36
recommendations, iv
recovery, ix, 42, 57, 58, 87

recreational, 61
recurrence, 15, 30
regression, vii, ix, 9, 17, 24, 26, 27, 28, 41, 42, 43, 44, 45, 46, 50, 53, 54, 57, 59, 62, 64, 66, 67, 127
regression analysis, ix, 9, 24, 26, 27, 42, 50, 54, 57, 59
regression method, 17
regression model, 24, 27, 28, 45
regression to the mean, vii, ix, 41, 42, 43, 44, 45, 57, 62, 64, 67
regulations, 3
relaxation, 123, 130
religious traditions, 117
researchers, 27, 30, 47, 121
residuals, 15
resistance, 12, 76, 88, 99, 123
respiration, 7, 47, 61, 99, 130
respiratory rate, 61, 121
response, ix, 10, 32, 42, 47, 48, 56, 57, 58, 59, 60, 65, 81, 84, 86, 87, 88, 90, 91, 95, 97, 126, 127, 131
responsiveness, 22
resting-state conditions, vii, viii, 2, 6, 8, 10, 17, 18, 19, 26, 29, 30
rhythm, 116, 117
risk, x, xi, 3, 5, 66, 68, 72, 77, 116, 123, 126, 127
risk factors, 127
root, 5, 15, 16, 76, 117
root-mean-square, 15

S

saltatory STV mini-pattern, 90
samarium, 65
scaling, 15, 37
scatter, 14, 53
scatter plot, 14, 53
schizophrenia, 33, 38
school, 118

science, 62, 119, 128, 131
selective attention, 3, 37
self-referential thoughts, viii, 2, 35
self-regulation, 39
sensations, 11, 25, 118, 124
sensitivity, 7, 11, 29, 124
serotonin, 99
sex, 31, 32, 39
sheep, 87, 93, 98
SIDS, 77, 81, 100, 104, 112, 113
signals, 13, 64
significance level, 50, 59
signs, 25, 79, 85
sinus arrhythmia, 14, 47, 62, 64, 68, 84
sleep apnea, 87, 100
social anxiety, 31, 62
social withdrawal, 11, 25, 26
software, 12, 38, 49, 67, 74
standard deviation, ix, 5, 14, 16, 20, 23, 42, 49, 76
state, vii, viii, ix, x, xi, 1, 2, 3, 4, 6, 7, 8, 10, 11, 12, 17, 18, 19, 21, 22, 26, 28, 29, 30, 33, 36, 42, 52, 62, 67, 71, 72, 73, 78, 80, 82, 83, 85, 86, 116, 117, 121, 122, 123, 125, 129, 130
statistics, 37, 45, 50, 54
stimulation, 76, 80, 81, 84, 86, 87, 88, 91, 94, 95, 97, 99
stress, vii, ix, x, xi, 27, 31, 38, 41, 42, 47, 48, 49, 50, 51, 52, 53, 56, 59, 60, 61, 63, 64, 65, 79, 87, 116, 117, 128, 129, 131
stress response, vii, ix, 41, 42, 59, 60, 63
stressful life events, 59
stretching, 120, 122
style, 37, 123, 126
Sudden Infant Death Syndrome, 81, 100, 103, 104, 113
sudden unexpected death in epilepsy, 100
suppression, 68
symptoms, 29, 64, 66
systolic blood pressure, 123

T

Taiwan, 1, 9, 31
target, 60, 99, 127
target population, 60
techniques, 74, 120, 123, 130
temperature, 116
thoughts, viii, 2, 10, 32, 35, 119, 124
time series, 2, 12, 13, 14, 15, 28, 37
top-down, 37
training, viii, ix, xi, 34, 42, 57, 116, 122, 124, 125, 129
trait anxiety, viii, 2, 9, 35, 36, 38, 48
transformation, 124
transmission, 86, 124
treatment, 27, 28, 35, 43, 57
trial, 39, 131
two sample t-test, 23
type 1 diabetes, 127

U

ultrasonography, 71, 74
umbilical artery, 95
Unclassified Behavioral States, 84

V

validation, 33
variables, 16, 17, 18, 34, 59, 60, 66
variations, 2, 3, 4, 118
varimax rotation, 10, 17, 22
vasoconstriction, 95, 97
vein, 97, 98
velocity, 95
vessels, 97
visualization, 17

W

wakefulness, vii, x, 72, 73, 83, 84, 90
waking, 123
water, 121
wavelet, 79, 82, 84
well-being, 3, 48, 132
windows, x, 13, 15, 72, 77
working memory, viii, 1, 3

workload, 116
worldwide, 5, 97
worry, 11

Y

young adults, vii, viii, 2, 6, 8, 27
young women, 36

Related Nova Publications

THE REDISCOVERED TRICUSPID VALVE: STRUCTURE, FUNCTION AND CLINICAL SIGNIFICANCE IN HEALTH AND DISEASE

EDITOR: Giacomo Bianchi, MD, PhD

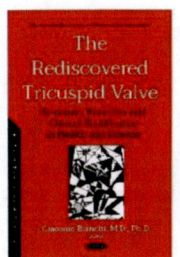

SERIES: Cardiology Research and Clinical Developments

BOOK DESCRIPTION: In order to better define the therapeutic path of a patient suffering from tricuspid valve disease, we have tried to offer a comprehensive overview to the reader, starting from historical considerations about the vision of the circulatory system and from the evidence accumulated over the centuries until the recognition of the continuum between signs and symptoms related to the valve.

HARDCOVER ISBN: 978-1-53616-098-7
RETAIL PRICE: $195

CONCEPTS, MATHEMATICAL MODELLING AND APPLICATIONS IN HEART FAILURE

AUTHORS: Massimo Capoccia, MD, MSc Eng and Claudio De Lazzari, MSc Eng

SERIES: Cardiology Research and Clinical Developments

BOOK DESCRIPTION: Although there are probably enough publications about mechanical circulatory support, they do not seem to address the theoretical aspects with sufficient details. A more detailed knowledge of the interaction between ventricular assist devices (VADs) and the cardiovascular system may help with their clinical management with a view to improve patients' outcomes.

HARDCOVER ISBN: 978-1-53614-771-1
RETAIL PRICE: $230

To see a complete list of Nova publications, please visit our website at www.novapublishers.com

Related Nova Publications

A Closer Look at Cardiovascular Diseases and Risk Factors

Editor: Faris van Kilsdonk

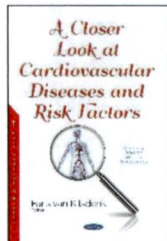

Series: Cardiology Research and Clinical Developments

Book Description: In this compilation, the authors examine treatment options for this type of population. Bariatric surgery has proven to be an effective method, generating large weight reductions and improving cardiovascular risk factors, thus increasing the life expectancy of patients who undergo it.

Softcover ISBN: 978-1-53613-939-6
Retail Price: $95

Everything You Need to Know: Out of the Operating Room and Minimally Invasive Cardiothoracic Procedures

Editors: Dalia Banks, M.D. and Ahmed Zaky, M.D.

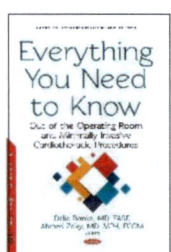

Series: Cardiology Research and Clinical Developments

Book Description: Being the first of its kind, this book is geared to meet and adapt to the rapidly expanding changes in the field of cardiothoracic surgery and anesthesia.

Hardcover ISBN: 978-1-53612-917-5
Retail Price: $230

To see a complete list of Nova publications, please visit our website at www.novapublishers.com